THE
ZURICH LETTERS.
A.D. 1558—1579.

The Parker Society.

Instituted A.D. M.DCCC.XL.

For the Publication of the Works of the Fathers and Early Writers of the Reformed English Church.

THE
ZURICH LETTERS,

COMPRISING

THE CORRESPONDENCE OF SEVERAL ENGLISH BISHOPS
AND OTHERS,

WITH SOME OF

THE HELVETIAN REFORMERS,

DURING THE EARLY PART OF

THE REIGN OF QUEEN ELIZABETH.

TRANSLATED FROM AUTHENTICATED COPIES OF THE AUTOGRAPHS
PRESERVED IN THE ARCHIVES OF ZURICH,

AND EDITED FOR

The Parker Society,

BY THE
REV. HASTINGS ROBINSON, D.D. F.A.S.

RECTOR OF GREAT WARLEY, ESSEX;
AND FORMERLY FELLOW OF ST JOHN'S COLLEGE, CAMBRIDGE.

Wipf & Stock
PUBLISHERS
Eugene, Oregon

Wipf and Stock Publishers
199 West 8th Avenue, Suite 3
Eugene, Oregon 97401

The Zurich Letters, 1558 - 1579
Comprising the correspondence of several English Bishops and others, with some of the Helvetian Reformers during the early part of the Reign of Queen Elizabeth
By Robinson, Hastings
ISBN: 1-59244-554-3
Publication date 2/13/2004
Previously published by Cambridge, 1842

INTRODUCTION.

On the accession of Queen Mary to the throne of England, A.D. 1553, she proceeded with much severity against the favourers of the Reformation; of whom upwards of a thousand persons, according to bishop Burnet[1], sought refuge among the protestant churches on the continent. Many of them settled at Zurich, where "they were entertained both by the magistrates[2] and the ministers, Bullinger, Gualter, Weidner, Simler, Lavater, Gesner, and all the rest of that body, with a tenderness and affection that engaged them to the end of their lives to make the greatest acknowledgments possible for it." After their return home, upon queen Elizabeth's coming to the crown, A. D. 1558, they maintained a close correspondence with their late hosts; and their letters, together with those of Bullinger, have long been regarded among the principal objects of interest in the Zurich archives.

Copies of these letters, or at least of a portion of them, were obtained by Bishop Burnet and Strype; both of whom have made frequent reference to them in their respective works. A few of the letters, chiefly those of Jewel, are printed, though very inaccurately, in the Historical Records appended to Burnet, who has also introduced occasional abstracts into the body of his history. The like may be said of Strype,

---

[1] Hist. of Reformation, vol. II. p. 388. The names of five bishops, five deans, four archdeacons, and fifty-seven doctors in divinity and preachers, are given by Strype, Life of Cranmer, I. 449.

[2] Burnet, as above, III. 408. Strype adds, that the magistrates offered, by Bullinger, to supply the exiles with such a quantity of bread-corn and wine, as should serve to sustain thirteen or fourteen people; but they with thanks refused it. Cranmer, I. 509.

though to a far less extent; so that the collection, as a whole, may be considered as being now for the first time presented to the public.

An account of the original autographs is given by Burnet[1], who saw them as he passed through Zurich, A.D. 1685. He says, "Among the archives of the dean and chapter there is a vast collection of letters written either to Bullinger or by him: they are bound up, and make a great many volumes in folio; and out of these no doubt but one might discover a great many particulars relating to the history of the Reformation. For as Bullinger lived long, so he was much esteemed. He procured a very kind reception to be given to some of our English exiles in queen Mary's reign; in particular to Sandys, afterwards archbishop of York, to Horn, afterwards bishop of Winchester, and to Jewel, bishop of Salisbury. He gave them lodgings in the close, and used them with all possible kindness: and as they presented some silver cups[2] to the college with an inscription acknowledging the kind reception they had found there, which I saw; so they continued to keep a constant correspondence with Bullinger after the happy establishment of the Reformation under queen Elizabeth; of which I read almost a whole volume while I was there."

A large portion of the letters here referred to are now before the reader, namely, those written during a period of about twenty-one years from the accession of queen Elizabeth. To them is added a letter of later date, written in 1590, by that monarch to the thirteen Swiss Cantons; as are also a few letters from Peter Martyr, Bullinger, and Gualter, in reply to some of those of our own reformers above mentioned.

---

[1] See, Some Letters, containing an account of what seemed most remarkable in travelling through Switzerland, &c., by G. Burnet, D.D. to the Hon. R[obert] B[oyle]. 8vo. Lond. 1724. p. 53.

[2] See p. 135.

These last contain the sentiments of these eminent divines upon the questions by which the Church of England was agitated at that period.

The copies from which the present collection is printed and the translation made, were procured from Zurich, for his own use, by the Rev. John Hunter, of Bath; who, on hearing of the formation of the Parker Society, with unsolicited kindness and liberality immediately placed them at its disposal. The accuracy of their collation with the original autographs is attested by M. de Meyer de Knonau, the keeper of the archives, to whose courtesy the Editor is considerably indebted for much valuable information respecting the letters in question. In a letter, written Nov. 28, 1841, he thus describes their present condition: "You have expressed a desire to know in what volumes the letters of your countrymen are to be found. The greater portion of them is in the archives of the state of Zurich, and the remainder in the library of that city[1]. The volumes in the archives which contain these letters are all bound in parchment, the margin not at all cut off, the leaves being filled throughout. On this account it is necessary to handle them with the greatest delicacy. They are numbered as follows, Class V. i. Nos. 108, 109, 113, 114, 164. The last number has for its title, "English Letters from the Reformation to the 17th century." The letters in the city library are dispersed through nine volumes, numbered, 38, 39, 42, 46, 56, 57, 60, 61, 62, and are in the manuscript class F. They are also bound in parchment, as the volumes in the archives, to which they bear a great resemblance. Almost all these letters are original, and with the exception of those of Richard Cox, F. Bedford, and the duke of Norfolk, who have only added their

---

[3] M. de Meyer de Knonau here refers to the whole of the Letters, including those written before the accession of Queen Elizabeth, as well as those contained in the present volume.

signatures, are in the handwriting of their respective authors. That of queen Elizabeth is only a copy[1]."

M. de Meyer de Knonau has kindly favoured the Society with accurate fac-similes of the signatures, copies of which will be found in a subsequent part of this volume, and are presented to the reader, not only as being interesting in themselves, but also as affording additional evidence, if any were needful, of the authenticity of the documents from whence they have been taken. These fac-similes include some names which are not found among the letters of the present series; but as many of them are common to these letters and to another series, which will also form a volume of the publications of the Parker Society, it has appeared desirable to present the whole at one view.

With respect to the translation, it has been the object of the Editor to make it as plain and literal as the difference of idiom will admit, and thereby to convey to the mind of the reader the very thoughts and modes of expression intended by the respective writers. How far he has succeeded in this endeavour, the classical reader will be enabled to judge for himself; and he may be encouraged to make the

---

[1] Vous avez exprimé le désir de savoir dans quels volumes se trouvent les lettres de vos compatriotes. La plus grande partie en est dans les Archives de l'état de Zurich, et les autres à la bibliothèque de la ville. Aux archives les volumes qui les contiennent sont tous reliés en parchemin, et la marge n'en est point du tout rognée, les feuilles étant remplies jusqu'an bout. Par cette même raison, il faut les traiter avec la plus grande delicatesse. Ils sont numérotés de la manière suivante. Repositoire, V. i. N. 108, 109, 113, 114, 164. Le dernier numéros a pour titre, *Anglicanæ epistolæ, a reformatione usque ad seculum decimum septimum.* Les lettres à la Bibliothèque de la ville sont dispersées en neuf volumes, portant les numéros, 38, 39, 42, 46, 56, 57, 60, 61, 62, et se trouvent dans le repositoire des manuscrits F. Ils sont reliés en parchemin comme les volumes aux Archives, auxquels ils ressemblent principalement. Presque toutes ces lettres sont originaux, et écrits des auteurs eux-mêmes, sauf celles de Richard Cox, F. Bedford, et du duc de Suffolk, qui n'ont fait que les signer. La lettre de la reine Elizabeth n'est qu'une copie.

trial, by the assurance, that the elegance of the Latinity will for the most part amply reward him for the labour of comparison[2]. The letters are printed in the order of their dates, which obviously appeared to be the most desirable arrangement for such documents, written as they are, almost exclusively, upon the public affairs of the period.

The notes, it should be observed, are added, not with the design of entering into any lengthened details of the circumstances referred to in the text, but simply by way of illustration and confirmation of the facts there recorded. To have aimed at less than this would have left the book unintelligible to a large portion of its readers; and to have endeavoured more, would have been inconsistent with the simple plan and objects of the Society under whose auspices it is published.

The edition of Strype, referred to in the notes, is that of Oxford, 1822, &c. That of Burnet, is the edition of Dr Nares, London, 1839.

H. R.

---

[2] For the inelegancies and inaccuracies in the letters of Richard Hilles, which form the chief exception to this remark, his own apology must be accepted, as given at the beginning of Letter LXXIV.

CORRIGENDA.

The reader is requested to correct the following passages in the translation, which will be found to vary from the original Latin, owing to some difficulty which arose as to a few words of the manuscript copy, which could not be finally cleared till these pages had been printed off.

Page 119, line 4, *for* "He sent me, &c." *read* "He has come over to us from France, because he perceived that his studies there were interrupted by those disturbances to which he had heretofore been unaccustomed."
    122, 15, *after* "the forger," *insert* "but not the subduer."
    133, 12, *after* "rushes down," *insert* "from the Aar."
    147, 5, *for* "to say nothing of," *read* "shall I call them? or."
    156, 12, 14, *for* "Camocensis," *read* "Camotensis."
    157, 5, from the bottom, *after* "we deny that," *add* "our propriety is to be borrowed from the enemies, &c."
    190, 18, *after* "but," *insert* "if not, I."
    231, 29, *for* "so to speak," *read* "to speak astronomically."

In a few places the precise meaning is left uncertain by the want of regular punctuation in the originals, and the autographs shew that the writing is not always easily decyphered.

CONTENTS.

LET.		PAGE
I.	Thomas Sampson to Peter Martyr...Strasburgh, Dec. 17, 1558.......	1
II.	Edwin Sandys to Henry Bullinger...Strasburgh, Dec. 20, 1558.......	3
III.	John Jewel to Peter Martyr ....Strasburgh, Jan. 26, 1559	6
IV.	The same to the same...................London, March 20, 1559.........	9
V.	The same to the same. ....London, April 6, 1559............	13
VI.	The same to the same...................London, April, 14, 1559	17
VII.	The same to the same...................London, April 28, 1559	19
VIII.	John Foxe to Henry Bullinger ....Basle, May 6, 1559	22
IX.	John Jewel to Peter Martyr...........London, no date	23
X.	John Foxe to Henry Bullinger ....Basle, May 13, 1559	25
XI.	Rich. Cox to Wolfgang Weidner ....London, May 20, 1559............	26
XII.	John Parkhurst to Henry Bullinger. London, May 21, 1559	29
XIII.	John Parkhurst to Conrad Gesner ...London, May 21, 1559	31
XIV.	John Jewel to Henry Bullinger ......London, May 22, 1559	32
XV.	John Foxe to Henry Bullinger ....Basle, June 17, 1559...............	35
*XV.	John Foxe to Henry Frensham.......Basle, June 17, 1559...............	37
XVI.	John Jewel to Peter Martyr ....London, Aug. 1, 1559............	38
XVII.	John Foxe to Henry Bullinger ....Basle, Aug. 2, 1559...............	41
XVIII.	The same to the same...................Basle, Sept. 26, 1559	42
XIX.	John Jewel to Peter Martyr ....London, Nov. 2, 1559	44
XX.	John Jewel to Rodolph Gualter ......London, Nov. 2, 1559	48
XXI.	John Parkhurst to John Wolfius ....Without date	49
XXII.	John Jewel to Josiah Simler ....London, Nov. 2, 1559	50
XXIII.	John Jewel to Peter Martyr ....London, Nov. 5, 1559	52
XXIV.	The same to the same ....London, Nov. 16, 1559	54
XXV.	The same to the same ....London, Dec. 1, 1559	59
XXVI.	John Parkhurst to Josiah Simler .....Bishop's Cleeve, Dec. 20, 1559.	61
XXVII.	Thomas Sampson to Peter Martyr .... Jan 6, [1560]...	62
XXVIII.	Bp Cox to Peter Martyr ....London, no date....................	65
XXIX.	Bp Jewel to Peter Martyr ....London, Feb. 4, 1560	67
XXX.	The same to the same ....London, March 5, 1560	70
XXXI.	Bp Sandys to Peter Martyr............London, April 1, 1560............	72
XXXII.	Thomas Sampson to Peter Martyr...London, May 13, 1560	75

xiv   CONTENTS.

LET.		PAGE
XXXIII.	Bp Jewel to Peter Martyr ....London, May 22, 1560	77
XXXIV.	The same to the same ....Salisbury, June 1, 1560	80
XXXV.	Thomas Lever to Henry Bullinger...Coventry, July 10, 1560	84
XXXVI.	Bp Jewel to Peter Martyr ....Salisbury, July 17, 1560.........	88
XXXVII.	John Parkhurst to Henry Bullinger..London, Aug. 23, 1560..........	90
XXXVIII.	Bp Jewel to Peter Martyr ....Salisbury, Nov. 6, 1560	91
XXXIX.	Bp Parkhurst to John Wolfius, &c.. Norwich, March 9, 1561	94
XL.	Bp Jewel to Josiah Simler ....London, May 4, 1561	96
XLI.	Bp Parkhurst to Henry Bullinger ...Thetford, May 23, 1561	97
XLII.	The same to the same ....Ludham, Sept. 1, 1561	98
XLIII.	Bp Jewel to Peter Martyr ....Salisbury, Feb. 7, 1562	99
XLIV.	Bp Jewel to Henry Bullinger.........Salisbury, Feb. 9, 1562	104
XLV.	Bp Jewel to Josiah Simler.............Salisbury, Feb. 10, 1562.........	106
XLVI.	Bp Parkhurst to Henry Bullinger ....Ludham, April 28, 1562.........	107
XLVII.	Bp Parkhurst to Josiah Simler, &c...Ludham, April 29, 1562	109
XLVIII.	Bp Parkhurst to Henry Bullinger ....Ludham, May 31, 1562	110
XLIX.	Bp Cox to Peter Martyr ....London, Aug. 5, 1562............	112
L.	Bp Jewel to Henry Bullinger ....Salisbury, Aug. 14, 1562	114
LI.	Bp Jewel to Peter Martyr ....Salisbury, Aug. 14, 1562	117
LII.	Bp Jewel to Josiah Simler.............Salisbury, Aug. 18, 1562.........	120
LIII.	Bp Parkhurst to Henry Bullinger ...Ludham, Aug. 20, 1562	121
LIV.	Bp Jewel to Henry Bullinger.........London, March 5, 1563	123
LV.	Bp Jewel to Josiah Simler ....London, March 7, 1563	125
LVI.	The same to the same ....London, March 23, 1563.........	126
LVII.	Bp Parkhurst to Henry Bullinger ...Ludham, April 26, 1563..........	128
LVIII.	T. Sampson to Henry Bullinger......Oxford, July 26, 1563............	130
LIX.	Bp Parkhurst to Henry Bullinger ...Ludham, Aug. 13, 1563	131
LX.	L. Humphrey to Henry Bullinger...Oxford, Aug. 16, 1563	133
LXI.	Bp Horn to Henry Bullinger..........Winchester, Dec. 13, 1563	134
LXII.	Bp Parkhurst to Josiah Simler ....Ludham, Feb. 17, 1564	136
LXIII.	Bp Jewel to Henry Bullinger ....Salisbury, March 1, 1565........	138
LXIV.	Bp Horn to Rodolph Gualter ....Farnham Castle, July 17, 1565.	141
LXV.	Bp Parkhurst to Henry Bullinger ...Ludham, Aug. 18, 1565	143
LXVI.	Bp Sandys to Henry Bullinger ....Worcester, Jan. 3, 1566..........	145
LXVII.	Bp Jewel to Henry Bullinger, &c....Salisbury, Feb. 8, 1566	146
LXVIII.	L. Humphrey to Henry Bullinger ...Oxford, Feb. 9, 1566	151
LXIX.	T. Sampson to Henry Bullinger......London, Feb. 16, 1566	153
LXX.	Bp Jewel to Henry Bullinger.........Salisbury, March 10, 1566	155
LXXI.	L. Humphrey, &c. to H. Bullinger................. July, 1566	157
LXXII.	Bp Parkhurst to Henry Bullinger ...Ludham, Aug. 21, 1566..........	165
LXXIII.	Bp Grindal to Henry Bullinger.......London, Aug. 27, 1566...........	168

CONTENTS.

LET.		PAGE
LXXIV.	R. Hilles to Henry Bullinger.........Antwerp, Dec. 20, 1566	171
LXXV.	Bp Grindal, &c. to H. Bullinger, &c..London, Feb. 6, 1567............	175
LXXVI.	Bp Grindal to Henry Bullinger ......London, Feb. 8, 1567............	182
LXXVII.	Bp Jewel to Henry Bullinger.........Salisbury, Feb. 24, 1567	184
LXXVIII.	Perceval Wiburn to Hen. Bullinger. London, Feb. 25, 1567............	187
LXXIX.	Bp Grindal to Henry Bullinger ......London, June 21, 1567	191
LXXX.	Bp Parkhurst to Henry Bullinger....Ludham, July 31, 1567..........	194
LXXXI.	Bp Grindal to Henry Bullinger.......London, Aug. 29, 1567	196
LXXXII.	The same to the same ....London, June 11, 1568	201
LXXXIII.	Bp Parkhurst to Rod. Gualter, &c. . Ludham, Aug. 4, 1568	205
LXXXIV.	Bp Cox to Henry Bullinger .... [1568]................	207
LXXXV.	Bp Grindal to Henry Bullinger.......Fulham, Aug. 13, 1569	208
LXXXVI.	Richard Hilles to Henry Bullinger...London, Feb. 6, 1570	211
LXXXVII.	Bp Grindal to Henry Bullinger.......London, Feb. 18, 1570	215
LXXXVIII.	Bp Cox to Henry Bullinger ....Ely, July 10, 1570	220
LXXXIX.	Bp Pilkington to Henry Bullinger.... July 17, 1570	222
XC.	Archbp Grindal to Henry Bullinger.. London, July 31, 1570	224
XCI.	Bp Jewel to Henry Bullinger .... Aug. 7, 1570	226
XCII.	James Leith to Henry Bullinger ...Geneva, Nov. 18, 1570	230
XCIII.	Bp Parkhurst to Henry Bullinger, Norwich, Jan. 16, 1571	232
XCIV.	Bp Cox to Rodolph Gualter ....Ely, Feb. 12, 1571	234
XCV.	Bp Jewel to Henry Bullinger ......Salisbury, March 2, 1571	238
XCVI.	Richard Hilles to Henry Bullinger...London, July 27, 1571	241
XCVII.	Bp Cox to Henry Bullinger ....[After July 27, 1751]............	243
XCVIII.	Bp Horn to Henry Bullinger ......London, Aug. 8, 1571............	245
XCIX.	Bp. Parkhurst to Henry Bullinger, Ludham, Aug. 10, 1571	255
C.	Archbp Grindal to Henry Bullinger, Bishopsthorpe, Jan. 25, 1572...	258
CI.	Bp Sandys to Henry Bullinger ......London, Feb. 17, 1572	264
CII.	Bp Parkhurst to Henry Bullinger ...Ludham, March 10, 1572	266
CIII.	Bp Cox to Henry Bullinger ....London, Ely-house, June 6, 1572.	268
CIV.	Richard Hilles to Henry Bullinger...London, July 10, 1572	270
CV.	Bp Horn to Henry Bullinger ....Farnham Castle, Jan. 10, 1573...	276
CVI.	Bp Parkhurst to Henry Bullinger ...Ludham, Jan. 20, 1573	277
CVII.	Bp Cox to Rodolph Gualter ....Ely, Feb. 4, 1573................	279
CVIII.	Bp Cox to Henry Bullinger ....Without date........................	282
CIX.	Bp Cox to Rodolph Gualter ....Ely, June 12, 1573	284
CX.	Bp Pilkington to Rodolph Gualter ... July 20, 1573	286
CXI.	Lau. Humphrey to Rodolph Gualter, Oxford, July 28, 1573............	289
CXII.	Archbp Grindal to Henry Bullinger, York, July 31, 1573................	291
CXIII.	Archbp Grindal to Rodolph Gualter, York, July 31, 1573................	293
CXIV.	Bp Sandys to Henry Bullinger ......London, Aug. 15, 1573	294

CONTENTS.

LET.		PAGE
CXV.	Bp Cox to Rodolph Gualter .... Ely, Feb. 3, 1574...............	297
CXVI.	Bp Parkhurst to Henry Bullinger ...Ludham, Feb. 6, 1574............	300
CXVII.	Bp Parkhurst to Josiah Simler ...... Ludham, Feb. 7, 1574............	302
CXVIII.	Bp Parkhurst to Henry Bullinger ...Ludham, June 29, 1574	303
CXIX.	Bp Parkhurst to Josiah Simler ...... Ludham, June 30, 1574	304
CXX.	Bp Cox to Rodolph Gualter .... Ely, July 12, 1574	306
CXXI.	Bp Cox to Henry Bullinger .... Ely, July 20, 1574	307
CXXII.	Lau. Humphrey to Rodolph Gualter, Oxford, Aug. 2, 1574	310
CXXIII.	Bp Sandys to Henry Bullinger ...... Fulham, Aug. 9, 1574............	311
CXXIV.	Bp Sandys to Rodolph Gualter....... Fulham, Aug. 9,1 574............	312
CXXV.	Bp Cox to Henry Bullinger .... Ely, Jan. 25, 1575	314
CXXVI.	Bp Cox to Rodolph Gualter .... Ely, [1575]	315
CXXVII.	The same to the same ....Ely, July 31, 1575	316
CXXVIII.	The same to the same ....Ely, [1576]	318
CXXIX.	Bp Horn to Rodolph Gualter .... Waltham, Aug. 10, 1576	320
CXXX.	Bp Horn to certain brethren .... Waltham, Jan. 15, 1577.........	321
CXXXI.	L. Humphrey to Rodolph Gualter....Oxford, Aug. 11, 1578............	324
CXXXII.	The same to the same ....Oxford, Dec. 17, 1578............	326
CXXXIII.	Bp Cox to Rodolph Gualter .... Feb. 28, 1579............	328
CXXXIV.	Archbp Sandys to Rodolph Gualter, London, Dec. 9, 1579	331
CXXXV.	Queen Elizabeth to the Swiss Cantons, Greenwich, July 18, 1590	333

FAC-SIMILES of the AUTOGRAPHS of the WRITERS.

APPENDIX.

I.	Peter Martyr to Bishop Jewel .... Zurich, Aug. 24, 1562	339
II.	Henry Bullinger to Bishop Horn...... Zurich, Nov. 3, 1565	341
III.	The same to L. Humphrey, &c....... Zurich, May 1, 1566	345
IV.	The same to Bishop Horn, &c.......... Zurich, May 3, 1566	356
V.	H. Bullinger, &c. to Bp Grindal, &c..Zurich, Sept. 6, 1566............	357
VI.	H. Bullinger, &c. to L. Humphrey, &c.Zurich, Sept. 10, 1566	360
VII.	Rodolph Gualter to Bishop Cox ......Zurich, June 9, 1572............	362

INDEX.. 367

EPISTOLÆ TIGURINÆ. (The Original Latin Letters) 1*

LETTER I.

THOMAS SAMPSON TO PETER MARTYR.

Dated at STRASBURGH, *December* 17, [1558.][1]

I ENTREAT you for Christ's sake, my excellent father, not to refuse me an answer to these few inquiries, as soon as possible.

I. How ought we to act with respect to allowing or disallowing the title of " after Christ supreme head of the Church of England," &c. ? All scripture seems to assign the title of head of the church to Christ alone.

II. In case the queen should invite me to any ecclesiastical office, such, I mean, as the government of a church, can I accept such appointment with a safe conscience, seeing that these things appear to me a sufficient excuse for non-compliance ? 1. Because, through the want of church discipline, the bishop, or pastor, is unable properly to discharge his office. 2. Because there are so many civil burdens imposed upon the bishop, or pastor; those, for instance, of *first fruits*, as we call them, that is to say, the receipts of the first year, besides tenths; in addition to which, at least in the case of bishops, so much expence must always be incurred for their equipages, retainers, and attendance at court: so that, as you well know, a very small portion of their revenue is left for the discharge of the necessary duties of a bishop, namely, for the support of learned men, the relief of the poor, and other occasions of making his ministry more acceptable. 3. I am now writing with reference to the bishops more especially; and such is the degeneracy from the primitive institution, as regards their election, (for there is required neither the consent of the clergy, nor of the people;) such too is the vanity, not to say the unseemliness of their superstitious dresses, that I scarcely think it endurable, even if we are to act in all things according to the law of expediency.

[[1] The letters are arranged in chronological order, according to their dates, or the time at which they appear to have been written.]

As far as I am personally concerned, I am not writing as if I were expecting any thing of the kind; so far from it, that I pray God from my heart that no such burden may ever be imposed upon me: but I ask your advice, as that of a most faithful father, that in case of any such event taking place, I may be the better prepared how to act. I should reply somewhat in this way, that I am quite ready to undertake the office of a preacher, in whatever place she [the queen] may choose; but that I cannot take upon myself the government of the church, until, after having made an entire reformation in all ecclesiastical functions, she will concede to the clergy the right of ordering all things according to the word of God, both as regards doctrine and discipline, and the property of the church. And if it be demanded what kind of a reformation I wish for, you can easily conjecture, from the three articles above stated, what, in my opinion, ought to be required.

I deposit, my father, with all simplicity, with yourself alone, the secrets of my heart; and I entreat you, for Christ's sake, to keep my secret to yourself, and return me an answer as soon as possible, as to what you think I ought to do in this case. Tell me also, what you would urge in addition for the furtherance of the reformation, and something too upon the reformation itself.

Send your letter to Eaton[1], who will take care it shall be forwarded to me. But I implore you, for Christ's sake, to write to me with what haste you can. I shall shortly move towards England. We have papists, anabaptists, and very many gospellers, who are enemies both to learning and a godly reformation. Who is sufficient to defend the glory of Christ, and raise the banner of Christ against such adversaries?

Oh! my father, pray God for me without ceasing.

Wholly yours,

T. SAMPSON.

[1 Or Heton. See p. 9.]

LETTER II.

EDWIN SANDYS TO HENRY BULLINGER.

Dated at STRASBURGH, *December* 20, 1558.

MUCH health in Christ. I am rather dilatory in writing to you, most esteemed sir; but it is only just now that I have any thing certain to communicate.

We yesterday received a letter from England, in which the death of Mary[2], the accession of Elizabeth, and the decease of cardinal Pole is confirmed. That good cardinal, that he might not raise any disturbance, or impede the progress of the gospel, departed this life the day[3] after his friend [queen] Mary. Such was the love and harmony between them, that not even death itself could separate them. We have nothing therefore to fear from Pole, for *dead men do not bite*.

Mary, not long before her death, sent two members of her council to her sister Elizabeth, and commanded them to let her know in the first place, that it was her intention to bequeath to her the royal crown, together with all the dignity that she was then in possession of by right of inheritance. In return however for this great favour conferred upon her, she required of her these three things: first, that she would not change her privy council; secondly, that she would make no alteration in religion; and thirdly, that she would discharge her debts, and satisfy her creditors. Elizabeth replied in these terms: "I am very sorry to hear of the queen's illness; but there is no reason why I should thank her for her intention to give me the crown of this kingdom. For she has neither the power of

[2 Queen Mary died on the morning of Friday, Nov. 17, 1558. Strype, Memor. III. ii. 118.]

[3 i.e. Nov. 18, 1558, about sixteen hours after the death of queen Mary, according to Hume's account; to which Strype adds, that his death took place at Lambeth between five and six o'clock in the morning. Memor. III. ii. 118. He states however, in another place, Annals, I. i. 52, that he died on the 17th.]

bestowing it upon me, nor can I lawfully be deprived of it, since it is my peculiar and hereditary right. With respect to the council, I think myself," she said, "as much at liberty to choose my counsellors, as she was to choose her own. As to religion, I promise thus much, that I will not change it, provided only it can be proved by the word of God, which shall be the only foundation and rule of my religion. And when, lastly, she requires the payment of her debts, she seems to me to require nothing more than what is just, and I will take care that they shall be paid, as far as may lie in my power." The messengers were dismissed with this answer.

Queen Elizabeth, on the Sunday[1] after her accession, caused the gospel to be preached at the celebrated Paul's Cross, which took place to the great delight of the people. But on the following Sunday the bishop of Chichester, by name Christopherson, (the same who some time ago called at your house on his way to Italy,) and a notorious papist[2], occupied the same place, and in his sermon, with great vehemence and freedom, (for the papists are always bold enough,) refuted every thing that had been said on the Sunday preceding; loudly exclaiming, "Believe not this new doctrine; it is not the gospel, but a new invention of new men and heretics, &c." In this way the good papist strove to confirm his own opinions, and to take away the truth of the gospel. As soon as this came to the ears of the queen, she caused this good bishop to be summoned into her presence; and after he had been examined respecting his sermon, commanded him to be sent to prison.

The queen has changed almost all her counsellors[3], and has taken good Christians into her service in the room of pa-

[1 Viz. on the 20th of November. The preacher was Dr Bill, her chaplain and almoner, a prudent and learned man. Strype, Memor. III. ii. 118. Annals, I. i. 50. He was afterwards dean of Westminster, and provost of Eton.]

[2 He was an examiner of heretics in the late reign, and in a commission for burning the bodies of Bucer and Fagius at Cambridge, where he was master of Trinity College. He died within a month after this sermon was preached, and was buried on Dec. 28, at Christ-church, London, with all the popish ceremonies. See Strype, Annals, I. i. 46.]

[3 The queen's [Mary's] counsellors towards the latter end of her reign were those that follow; whereof, says Strype, Memor. III. ii. 160, those that have asterisks were laid aside the next reign, as I took them

pists[4]; and there is great hope of her promoting the gospel, and advancing the kingdom of Christ to the utmost of her power. That she may do this, God must be entreated by all religious persons. Philip[5] has sent over to her a splendid and magnificent embassy; but we know not what he means by it. If, however, he is thinking about what your prudent fears anticipated, he will lose his labour, and get nothing by it.

[Sir Thomas] Wroth, [Sir Antony] Cook, and other persons of distinction, have begun their journey this day; I, with God's blessing, shall follow them to-morrow. As soon as I arrive in England, I will take care to let you know the state of

out of a journal of the Lord Burleigh's; the rest continued privy counsellors to queen Elizabeth, viz.

- * Reginald, Cardinal Pole.
- * Nicholas, Archbishop of York, Lord Chancellor.
- Powlet, Marquis of Winchester, Lord Treasurer.
- Fitzallen, Earl of Arundel.
- Talbot, Earl of Shrewsbury.
- * Henry, Earl of Bath.
- Stanley, Earl of Derby.
- Herbert, Earl of Pembroke.
- Edward, Lord Clinton, Lord Admiral.
- Lord Howard of Effingham.
- * Brown, Viscount Montague.
- * Thirlby, Bishop of Ely.
- * William, Lord Paget.
- * Lord Wentworth.
- * Richard, Lord Ryche.
- * Edward, Lord Hastings of Loughborough.

- * Sir Thomas Cornwalleys.
- * Sir Francis Englefield.
- * Sir Edward Waldgrave.
- * Sir John Mordaunt.
- Sir Thomas Cheyney.
- Sir William Petre.
- Sir John Mason.
- Sir Richard Sackvil.
- * Sir Thomas Warton.
- * Sir John Brown.
- * Dr Wotton, Dean of Canterbury.
- * Dr Boxal.
- * Sir Henry Jernegam.
- * Sir Henry Beddingfield.
- * Sir Edmund Peckham.
- * Sir Robert Peckham.
- * Sir William Cordell.
- * Sir Clement Higham.
- * Sir Richard Southwel.

[4 Hume states that the queen [Elizabeth], not to alarm the partisans of the Roman Catholic religion, had retained eleven of her sister's counsellors; but in order to balance their authority, she added eight more, who were known to be inclined to the Protestant Communion; the Marquis of Northampton, the Earl of Bedford, Sir Thomas Parry, Sir Edward Rogers, Sir Ambrose Cave, Sir Francis Knolles, Sir Nicholas Bacon, whom she created Lord Keeper, and Sir William Cecil, Secretary of State.]

[5 Philip, who had long foreseen this event, [the queen's accession], and who still hoped, by means of Elizabeth, to obtain that dominion over England, of which he had failed in espousing Mary, immediately dispatched orders to the Duke of Feria, his ambassador at London, to make proposals of marriage to the queen. Hume.]

affairs there. In the mean time, entreat God in behalf of the Church of England, and of us, miserable ministers of the word, upon whom a heavy and difficult burden is imposed. We in our turn will earnestly pray to God in behalf both of your church and yourselves. It is now midnight, and I am to quit this place early to-morrow morning; wherefore, most esteemed sir, I bid you farewell. In haste. Strasburgh, Dec. 20th, or if you choose, the 21st, 1558.

Your most devoted,

EDWIN SANDYS, *Anglus*.

LETTER III.

JOHN JEWEL TO PETER MARTYR.

Dated at STRASBURGH, *January* 26, [1559.]

RESPECTING my first setting out, and all the news which was then circulated at Basle, I wrote to you by our friend Simler. So wretchedly were we delayed by the badness of the roads, that it was with some difficulty that, on the fifth day after, we arrived at Strasburgh. Here we found all our friends in good health, and very anxious for your company. We have not yet heard what Sandys, Horn, and our other friends have been doing in England. Nor indeed is it to be wondered at; for, having left[1] Strasburgh on the 21st of December, they would hardly be able to reach Antwerp in twenty days after, because the Rhine being frozen over would prevent their travelling by water. All we hear is, that their return was very acceptable to the queen, and that she has openly declared her satisfaction.

If the bishops go on as they have begun, bishopricks will shortly become very cheap. For Christopherson[2], that brawling bishop of Chichester, is certainly dead; the same is also re-

[1 See the preceding letter.]
[2 See above, p. 4.]

ported of Watson[3], bishop of Lincoln; which if it be true, there are at this time no less than fourteen sees vacant. Your *friend* White, as I wrote to you when I was at Basle, delivered a most furious and turbulent[4] discourse at the funeral of [queen] Mary, in which he declared, that every thing was to be attempted, rather than that any alteration should be made in religion; and that it would be a meritorious act for any one to kill the exiles on their return. He was charged with sedition by the Marquis of Winchester, Lord Treasurer, and Heath, archbishop of York.

The bishop of London has been ordered to restore to Ridley's[5] executors the property which he had forcibly and injuriously taken possession of. He will shortly be called upon for his defence; and is in the mean time ordered to confine himself to his own house as a prisoner.

The queen has forbidden any person, whether papist or gospeller, to preach[6] to the people. Some think the reason of this to be, that there was at that time only one minister of the word in London, namely, Bentham[7], whereas the number of papists was very considerable; others think that it is owing to

[3 He had the ague, but recovered, and was afterwards deprived. Strype, Annals, I. i. 139. 210.]

[4 This sermon was preached Dec. 13, and the preacher was confined to his own house till Jan. 19, when being summoned before the Lords of the Council, "after a good admonition given to him," he was set at liberty. Strype, Memor. III. ii. 140, 536, where the whole sermon is preserved. The text was from Eccles. iv. 2.]

[5 December ult., the council wrote to Sir John Mason and Sir Clement Throgmorton, to examine diligently a complaint made to the queen's highness by certain near kinsmen of Dr Ridley, late bishop of London, for divers parcels of his goods, that came into the hands of the bishop of London that now is, [viz. Bonner,] and to signify to them what they should find out therein. Strype, Annals, I. i. 47.]

[6 The proclamation was sent to the Lord Mayor for the inhibition of preaching, Dec. 28. Strype, Annals, I. i. 59, who gives it at length in the appendix.]

[7 It is not to be passed over without remark, that there was a congregation of godly men at London, in the very mouth of danger, who met together for religious worship all the queen's [Mary's] reign. Among their ministers were Edmund Scambler, afterwards bishop of Peterborough, and Thomas Bentham, afterwards bishop of Coventry and Lichfield. Strype, Memor. III. ii. 147.]

the circumstance that, having heard only one public discourse of Bentham's, the people began to dispute among themselves about ceremonies, some declaring for Geneva, and some for Frankfort[1]. Whatever it be, I only wish that our party may not act with too much worldly prudence and policy in the cause of God.

Many persons are of opinion that [Sir Antony] Cook will be the Lord Chancellor: he is, as you know, a worthy and pious man, but I think hardly qualified for that office. The bishop of Ely [Thirlby] is still remaining with Philip, while some arrangement is making, if it please God, about this famous peace[2], which, of what nature, or how firm or lasting it may be, God only can determine.

The lady Isabella will, I hope, be invited into England. For I perceive others also of our party seriously thinking upon that matter. Zanchius[3] too will write to the queen: he was on the point of writing to the whole parliament, if I had not dissuaded him; for it seemed to me quite out of place. The boy Cranmer was left with Abel at Strasburgh, to be delivered into my care. I borrowed from Abel some crowns in the youth's name. I wish Julius would forward to him at Strasburgh the portmanteau, and the money which I left in your keeping. He will give you a receipt for it, which he will either deposit with Zanchius, or, if you choose, send onwards to yourself. Farewell, my most beloved father, and my soul's better half. I will not write *all* the news to you; for I had occasion to write somewhat to master Bullinger, a man to whom I owe

[1] For an account of the disputes among the English exiles at Frankfort, see Strype, Memor. III. i. 404, &c. and Annals, I. i. 151, &c.

[2] Thirlby, bishop of Ely, and Dr Wotton, dean of Canterbury, were queen Mary's commissioners to treat with France about the restoration of Calais, and for making peace. To them queen Elizabeth sent a new commission, and in January 1558 [1559], by her council, writ to them to proceed according to that commission. The peace was concluded in the beginning of April between the queen, and the French, and Scots. Strype, Annals, I. i. 37.]

[3] He was public professor at Strasburgh, and afterwards at Heidelberg, whence, in 1571, he wrote a letter to the queen on behalf of the puritan ministers, and, as he said, by command of the most noble prince, one of her majesty's most special friends, the prince elector Palatine. Strype, Annals, II. i. 142.]

every thing for his exceeding kindness to me. But this, whatever it was, he will, I doubt not, communicate to you.

Masters Heton, Abel, Springham, and Parkhurst, salute you very much; and though they desire for you all possible good, they desire for you at present nothing more than England. Salute in my name Muralt, Herman, Julius, his wife, and all our mutual friends. Master Fr. Beti and Acontius are now at Strasburgh. They both salute you much. I have returned to Beti the letter of the lady Isabella. I pray you let her know this.

Strasburgh, 26.
Januar.

JOHN JEWEL,

Yours from my heart,

And for ever.

LETTER IV.

JOHN JEWEL TO PETER MARTYR.

Dated at LONDON, *March* 20, 1559.

MUCH health. We have at length arrived in England, that is to say, on the fifty seventh day after our leaving Zurich. But why should I enter into a long preamble, to you especially, who rather wish for facts, and set but little value upon these tedious narrations? It was, however, a wearisome life, when both water, and earth, and the very heavens themselves seemed angry with us, and in every possible way opposed our progress. What else? Every thing turned out most disagreeable and adverse to us, throughout the whole time. But I informed both you and Bullinger of these things more fully in a former letter, while I was delayed at Antwerp. You shall now hear the sequel; although, to say the truth, there is need of some art and flowers of rhetoric; not so much for adorning and embellishing any new intelligence, (which I know not whether

I have at this time any to communicate,) as for the purpose of retouching my old narrative over again. For almost every thing that I wrote to you about when on my journey, was at that time very different, and far more pleasant in the hearing, than I afterwards found it to be in reality on my return home. For the Roman pontiff was not yet cast out; no part of religion was yet restored; the country was still every where desecrated with the mass; the pomp and insolence of the bishops was unabated. All these things, however, are at length beginning to shake, and almost to fall.

The bishops[1] are a great hindrance to us; for being, as you know, among the nobility and leading men in the upper house, and having none there on our side to expose their artifices and confute their falsehoods, they reign as sole monarchs in the midst of ignorant and weak men, and easily overreach our little party, either by their numbers, or their reputation for learning. The queen, meanwhile, though she openly favours our cause, yet is wonderfully afraid of allowing any innovations: this is owing partly to her own friends, by whose advice every thing is carried on, and partly to the influence of Count Feria[2], a Spaniard, and Philip's ambassador. She is however prudently, and firmly, and piously following up her purpose, though somewhat more slowly than we could wish. And though the beginnings have hitherto seemed somewhat unfavourable, there is nevertheless reason to hope that all will be well at last. In the mean time, that our bishops may have no ground of complaint that they are put down only by power and authority of law, a disputation is determined upon, wherein nine[3] on our side,

[[1] These were Heath, archbishop of York; Bonner, bishop of London; White, of Winchester; Pate, of Worcester; Kitchin, of Llandaff; Baine, of Coventry and Lichfield; Turbervile, of Exeter; Scot, of Chester; and Oglethorp, of Carlisle; with Feckenham, Lord Abbot of Westminster. Strype, Annals, I. i. 82.]

[[2] He hated Elizabeth from the beginning of her reign, and stirred up pope Pius IV. to excommunicate her, and the king of Spain to be her enemy. Strype, Annals, I. ii. 53.]

[[3] Dr Cox in his letter to Weidner (Letter IX. below) mentions but *eight* disputants; as does also the account kept in the Paper office. The bishop of Carlisle on the papists' side, and Sandys on that of the protestants, are misadded, says Strype, to the aforesaid disputants, though probably they were present at the conference. Annals, I. i. 129.]

namely, Scory[4], Cox, Whitehead[5], Sandys, Grindal, Horn, Aylmer, a Cambridge man of the name of Gheast[6], and myself, are to confer upon these matters before the council with five[7] bishops, the abbot of Westminster, Cole, Chedsey, and Harpsfield. Our first proposition is, that it is contrary to the word of God, and the practice of the primitive church, to use in the public prayers and administration of the sacraments any other language than what is understood by the people. The second is, that every provincial church, even without the bidding of a general council, has power either to establish, or change, or abrogate ceremonies and ecclesiastical rites, whereever it may seem to make for edification. The third is, that the propitiatory sacrifice, which the papists pretend to be in the mass, cannot be proved by the holy scriptures.

The first discussion is to take place on the 31st of March. The bishops in the mean time have been long mightily exulting, as though the victory were already achieved. When Froschover[8] comes over to this country, I will write you a more particular account of these matters. The queen regards you most highly: she made so much of your letter, that she read it over with the greatest eagerness a second and third time. I doubt not but that your book, when it arrives, will be yet more acceptable.

Two famous virtues, namely, ignorance and obstinacy, have wonderfully increased at Oxford since you left it: religion, and all hope of good learning and talent is altogether abandoned.

[4] He had been chaplain to Cranmer and Ridley, and was bishop of Chichester in king Edward's reign. He afterwards became bishop of Hereford. Strype, Memor. II. ii. 171.]

[5] An exile for religion in queen Mary's time. He had been recommended by Cranmer for the see of Armagh. Strype, Memor. III. i. 231.]

[6] Edmund Gheast, or Guest, was consecrated bishop of Rochester, and afterwards translated to Salisbury. Strype, Parker, II. 80.]

[7] The *four* bishops, (see Note 3.) were White, Watson, Baine, and Scot, bishops of Winchester, Lincoln, Coventry and Lichfield, and Chester; and the Doctors Cole, dean of St Paul's; *Langdale*, Harpsfield, and Chedsey, archdeacons of Lewes, Canterbury, and Middlesex. Strype, Annals, I. i. 129. The abbot of Westminster, Feckenham, appears hence to have taken no part in the conference.]

[8] He was a printer at Zurich, and boarded twelve of the exiles in the reign of queen Mary. Among them were Laurence Humphrey, afterwards king's Professor of Divinity at Oxford, and bishop Parkhurst. Strype, Memor. III. i. 232.]

Brooks[1], bishop of Gloucester, a beast of most impure life, and yet more impure conscience, a short time before his death exclaimed in a most woeful manner, that he was now condemned by his own judgment. Your renowned [antagonist] Smith[2], the patron of chastity, has been taken in adultery, and on that account is ordered to retire from the theological chair, by a new practice, and without a precedent, as the like was never done in Mary's time. Bruerne[3] too has been compelled, for a similar offence, only far more flagitious, to relinquish his professorship of Hebrew. I write nothing about Marshal[4], for fear of defiling my paper. You have before heard respecting Weston[5]. But why, say you, do you make mention of such persons? Simply, that you may learn by what judges it was thought fit that Cranmer, Ridley, and Latimer should be condemned.

I have no news to tell respecting the Scotch, whether about peace or war. I wrote you three letters during my journey, but know not whether they have reached you. But since we are so far distant, much farther indeed and for a much longer time than I could wish, our letters must sometimes be committed to the winds and to fortune.

Farewell, my father, and most esteemed master in Christ. Salute masters Bullinger, Gualter, Simler, Gesner, Lavater,

[[1] He had been the pope's subdelegate under cardinal Puteo in Cranmer's trial; and assisted also at that of Hoper. Strype, Cranmer, 532. &c. Memor. III. i. 286.]

[[2] Richard Smith, Regius Professor of Divinity at Oxford, had been deprived of his professorship before in 1547, and was succeeded by Peter Martyr, against whom he printed his book for the *Celibacy of Priests* and *Monastic Vows*. Strype, Memor. II. i. 63, &c.]

[[3] He was chosen provost of Eton without the queen's consent, and by her forced to resign in 1561. Strype, Parker, I. 205.]

[[4] Richard Marshal, dean of Christchurch, was a violent papist under queen Mary, and an enemy both to Jewel and Peter Martyr. He watched narrowly to have caught Jewel, when he fled from Oxford; and digged up the body of Peter Martyr's wife out of her grave in Christ's Church, where she had been some years buried, and cast it into his dunghill. Strype, Annals, I. ii. 48, and Parker, I. 199. He was mentioned in a list of certain evil-disposed persons of whom complaint hath been made; which lurk so secretly, that process cannot be served upon them. Annals, I. i. 416.]

[[5] Hugh Weston, dean of Windsor, was deprived of his deanery by cardinal Pole for his scandalous life in adultery. Strype, Memor. III. i. 174.]

Julius, his wife, your little Martyr, [Martyrillus,] Herman, and your associates of Treves. All our friends salute you. London, 20 March, 1559.

Yours,
JOHN JEWEL.

This is the *first* letter I have written to you since my return to England. I will thus number all of them in future, that you may know whether any have been lost.

LETTER V.

JOHN JEWEL TO PETER MARTYR.

Dated at LONDON, *April* 6, 1559.

MUCH health. Accept a brief account of the disputation[6] between us and the bishops, which I informed you in my last letter was appointed for the 31st of March; for it seems best thus to continue my narrative without any further preamble.

In the first place, then, to remove all ground of contention and idle debate, the council ordained that every thing, on either side, should be read from written papers, and that the time should be so marked out, that on the first day nothing should be proposed by either party beyond bare affirmations; and that at the next meeting we were to answer them, and they, in their turn, to reply to us. Accordingly, we assembled at Westminster on the 31st of March. Great were the expectations of the people, and the crowd[7], I believe, still greater. The bishops, (such was their good faith,) produced not a single line either in writing or print; alleging that they had not had suffi-

[6 For a full account of this disputation see Strype, Annals, I. i. 128, &c. Burnet, Hist. Reform. II. 600, &c. and Soames, Hist. Reform. IV. 642, &c.]

[7 The houses of parliament adjourned from March 24, till April 3, as Sir Simon D'Ewes thinks, by reason of this disputation. Strype, Annals, I. i. 98.]

cient time for the consideration of matters of such importance; notwithstanding that they had been allowed ten days, more or less, and had in the mean time assembled their auxiliary troops both from Oxford and Cambridge, and every other corner. However, that so great a number might not seem to have come together to no purpose, Dr Cole, being suborned by the others, stepped forth in the midst, to harangue, in the name of them all, respecting the first point of discussion, namely, the use of a foreign language [in public worship.] After having assailed us most unworthily with all manner of contumely and invective, and stigmatized us as the authors and firebrands of every kind of sedition; and having turned himself towards all quarters, and into every possible attitude, stamping with his feet, throwing about his arms, bending his sides, snapping his fingers, alternately elevating and depressing his eye-brows, (you know the look and modesty of the man,) he came at last to this, that England had now for thirteen hundred years received the gospel. And by what literary remains, he asked, by what annals, what monuments can it be made to appear, that the public prayers then in use in England were in the English tongue? When he had sufficiently careered within that circle, he added seriously, and with a solemn countenance and admonitory tone, that all should especially attend to and mark this, as a most precious saying, that the apostles from the beginning so divided their labours among themselves, that some of them established the eastern, and others the western churches; and that therefore Peter and Paul, in the church of Rome, which at that time comprehended nearly all Europe, gave all their instructions in the language of Rome, that is, in Latin; and that the rest of the apostles in the east never employed any other language but the Greek. You will perhaps laugh at this; yet I never heard any one rave after a more solemn and dictatorial manner. Had my friend Julius been present, he would have exclaimed a hundred times over, *Poh! whoreson knave!*[1] The speaker, however, made no scruple of betraying, among other things, the very mysteries, and secrets, and inmost recesses of his own religion. For he did not hesitate gravely and solemn-

[1] It is thus in the original manuscript, but it is suggested in a note by the transcriber that Jewel intended to have written *Poz! hosenknopf*, a vulgar exclamation of that period.]

ly to affirm, that even were all other things to agree, it would nevertheless be inexpedient for the people to know what was going on in religious worship. For ignorance, said he, is the mother of true piety, which he called devotion. Oh! sacred mysteries, and secret rites of the Bona Dea! What do you imagine I thought all the while about the pontiff Cotta[2]? This truly it is to worship in spirit and in truth! But to proceed. When he had thus taken up a great part of the time allotted to us for disputation, in calumny, abuse, and falsehood, we[3] at last recited our arguments from written papers, with so much moderation as only to treat upon the matter in dispute, without wounding our opponents. The debate was at length concluded in such a manner, that there was hardly any one in the whole assembly, not even the Earl of Shrewsbury,[4] who did not adjudge that day's victory to be on our side. It was afterwards arranged, that we should speak in the same manner respecting the second question on the Monday following, and that on the Wednesday we should reply to their first day's arguments, and they in turn to ours. On the Monday, when a vast multitude of the nobility had assembled, exceedingly desirous of hearing the debate, the bishops, I know not whether from shame at [the defeat of] the preceding day, or from despair of victory, first began to shuffle,—that they had yet much to say upon the first question, and that the matter must not go off in that way. The council replied, that if they had any thing further to say, they might be heard on the third day following, as it had been originally agreed upon; but that they were now to confine themselves to the question before them, and not disturb the order of the disputation. Being driven from this position they nevertheless still evaded the question by saying, that if they must needs speak at all, they would not speak first;—that they were in possession of the ground, and that

[2 See Cicero de Nat. Deor.]
[3 Robert Horn, formerly dean of Durham, and soon afterwards bishop of Winchester, immediately rose, and produced the written argument of his party upon the question under discussion. Soames, Hist. Ref. IV. 648.]
[4 Francis, 5th Earl. He had been distinguished in the Scottish military expeditions in the reigns of kings Henry and Edward, and by that prudence and fidelity to queen Mary, which induced Elizabeth to call him, although a Romanist, to her privy council. He died Sept 25, 1560.]

we, if we wished it, might try our strength in the first place; for that they would be doing great injury to their cause, if they should allow us to depart last, with the applause of the people, and leave the stings of our discourse fresh in the minds of the audience. The council[1] replied on the other hand, that it was originally settled that they, as being first in dignity, should be first to speak; and that this arrangement could not now be altered; they were surprised, however, at there being all this mystery, since one party must of necessity begin the discussion, or else nothing could be said by either; and it was the more extraordinary, because on the first day's disputation Cole sprung forth to speak first, even without being called upon. At last, when a great part of the time had been taken up in altercation, and the bishops would on no account consent to yield the [privilege of speaking in the] second place, the assembly broke up without any disputation at all. It is altogether incredible, how much this conduct has lessened the opinion that the people entertained of the bishops; for they all begin to suspect that they refused to say any thing only because they had not any thing to say.

On the day after your friend White[2], bishop of Winchester, and Watson, bishop of Lincoln, were committed to the tower for open contempt and contumacy. There they are now employed in *castrametation*, and[3] from weak premises draw bold conclusions. The rest are bound in recognizances to appear at court from day to day, and await the determination of the council respecting them.

Thus you have the account of an useless conference, and one which indeed can hardly be considered as such. I have, however, described it more copiously than there was any occasion for, that you might better understand the whole proceeding.

Farewell, my father, my pride, and even the half of my soul. Should there be at this time any farther news, I had rather it should be the subject of my next letter. Salute much,

[1 The Lord Keeper, Bacon, who acted as president, or moderator, in conjunction with archbishop Heath. Soames.]

[2 White had formerly attacked Peter Martyr in a book in verse, called *Diacosia Martyrion*, prefaced by an abusive epistle. Strype, Memor. II. i. 423. See above, p. 7.]

[3 A word is here illegible in the original MS.]

in my name, that reverend person, and my much esteemed master in Christ, master Bullinger, masters Gualter, Simler, Lavater, Wolfius, Gesner, Haller, Frisius, Herman, and Julius, your friend and mine. All our friends salute you, and wish you every happiness. London, April 6, 1559.

Your

JOHN JEWEL.

This is the *second* letter I have written to you since my return to England.

LETTER VI.

JOHN JEWEL TO PETER MARTYR.

Dated at LONDON, *April* 14, 1559.

MUCH health. Our friend Sandys has done me much wrong; for, notwithstanding I had already written to you, though I earnestly besought him not to do so, he sent you his own letter unaccompanied by mine. However, except that I feel this duty of mine has long been owing to you, nothing has hitherto occurred which it would give you much pleasure to hear. O [queen] Mary and the Marian times! With how much greater tenderness and moderation is truth now contended for, than falsehood was defended some time since! Our adversaries acted always with precipitancy, without precedent, without authority, without law; while we manage every thing with so much deliberation, and prudence, and wariness, and circumspection, as if God himself could scarce retain his authority without our ordinances and precautions; so that it is idly and scurrilously said, by way of joke, that as heretofore Christ was *cast out* by his enemies, so he is now *kept out* by his friends. This dilatoriness has grievously damped the spirits of our brethren, while it has wonderfully encouraged the rage and fury of our opponents. Indeed, you would hardly believe with how much greater boldness they now conduct themselves than they ever did before; yet the people every where, and especially the whole of the nobility, are both disgusted with their insolent exultation, and exceedingly thirsting for the gospel. Hence it has happened that the mass in many places has of itself fallen to the ground, without any laws for its discontinuance. If the queen herself would but banish it from her private chapel, the whole thing might easily be got rid of. Of such importance among us are the examples of princes. For whatever is done after the example of the sovereign, the people, as you well know, suppose to be done rightly. She has, however, so regulated this mass of hers, (which she has hitherto retained only from the circumstances of the times,) that although many things are done therein, which are scarcely to be endured, it may yet be heard without any great danger. But this woman, excellent as she is, and earnest in the cause of true religion, notwithstanding she desires a thorough change as early as possible, cannot however be induced to effect such change without the sanction of law; lest the matter should seem to have been accomplished, not so much by the judgment of discreet men, as in compliance with the impulse of a furious multitude. Meanwhile, many alterations in religion are effected in parliament, in spite of the opposition and gainsaying and disturbance of the bishops. These however I will not mention, as they are not yet publicly known, and are often brought on the anvil to be hammered over again.

Sandys, Grindal, Sampson, Scory, (and why should I particularize these?) all of us remain still in London, all in good health, in the same condition, the same circumstances, the same favour. Many persons make most honourable inquiry after you, where you are, how you live, what you are teaching, and whether, in case you should be recalled, you would feel disposed to return to England.

Sidall[1] lately desired me by letter, not to give credit to any injurious reports respecting him. I remember, when you were lecturing at Strasburgh respecting the power that sovereigns have over bishops, you stated that Sylverius[2] and Vigilius

[1 Sidall was canon of Christ Church, and vicar of Walthamstow. Strype, Parker, 154. See p. 45.]

[2 Sylverius, patriarch of Rome, was deposed and banished A.D. 537, through the machinations of the empress Theodora, and Vigilius was elected into the patriarchate by command of Belisarius. He was after-

were removed from their office [of patriarch] by the emperor Justinian. When you next write, I will thank you briefly to point out the place where this circumstance is recorded.

We have as yet heard nothing respecting the queen's marriage, an event which we all desire most earnestly. Farewell, my father, and much esteemed master in Christ. London, April 14, 1559.

Yours wholly,

JOHN JEWEL.

This is my *third* letter. I mention the number, that you may know whether, as may possibly be the case[3], any of them have been lost on the road.

LETTER VII.

JOHN JEWEL TO PETER MARTYR.

Dated at LONDON, *April* 28, 1559.

MUCH health. I have received three letters from you, and all of them nearly at the same time. Though they were, as they certainly ought to be, most gratifying to me on many accounts, both as coming from you, and letting me know the state of your affairs, and your affection for myself; yet for no other reason did they seem more acceptable to me, than because they expressed a desire that I should write to you, and gently though silently charged me with either forgetfulness or dilatoriness; of which the former is as much forbidden by the extent of your kindness towards me, as the latter is by the magnitude of my engagements. I have indeed written to you *three* letters since my return to England; which I perceive, however, had not reached you at the time you wrote. And it may be, as is often the case, that they are either loitering

wards thrown into prison by Justinian for opposing the decrees of the second council of Constantinople (the fifth general council), in 553, and died at Syracuse on his return to Rome two years after.]

[3 *Ut sit:* but most probably it should be *ut fit*. So also at the bottom of this page the original is printed, *ut sæpe sit*.]

somewhere or other, and are, like religion among ourselves, reposing in listless inactivity, or else have been lost on the road. But however it be, there can be no great loss in that respect; inasmuch as they were almost empty, because there was not then much that either you would like to hear, or I to write. The cause of the pope is now agitated, and with much vehemence on both sides. For the bishops are labouring that they may not seem to have been in error; and this delays and hinders the progress of religion: but it is indeed no easy matter to accelerate its course, as the poet says, with such slow-paced horses. Feckenham, the abbot of Westminster, in order, I suppose, to exalt the authority of his own profession, in a speech that he made in the House of Lords, placed the Nazarites, the prophets, nay, even Christ himself and his apostles, in the monastic orders! No one more keenly opposes our cause than the bishop of Ely [Thirlby], who still retains his seat in parliament, and his disposition along with it. The lands[1] of the bishops are to be made over to the exchequer, and the rectories which heretofore belonged to the monasteries will be given them in exchange. In the mean time there is everywhere a profound silence respecting schools and the encouragement of learning. This indeed is driving out one devil, as they say, by another.

The queen both speaks and thinks most honourably of you: she lately told lord Russel that she was desirous of inviting[2] you to England, a measure which is urged both by himself and others, as far as they are able. But unless you should be seriously and earnestly and honourably recalled, I, for my part, will never advise your coming. For myself, indeed, there is nothing that I desire more, or with greater impatience, than to behold you, and enjoy your most delightful conversations, (which I heartily wish may one day be the case), either in England or at Zurich. But, as far as I can perceive, that inauspicious arrival[3] will present an obstacle to my wishes. For

[1 For an account of this proceeding, see Strype, Annals, I. i. 142, &c. The bill passed the House of Lords on the 6th of April, 1559.]

[2 Martyr was invited to return, in 1561, it is supposed, by the influence of the Duke of Norfolk, but excused himself, from his obligations to the city of Zurich. Strype, Annals, I. i. 382.]

[3] Inauspicata illa et saxis et Saxonibus damnata $\pi\alpha\rho o\nu\sigma\acute{\iota}\alpha$.

our [queen] is now thinking of [joining] the league of Smalcald[4]; but there is one who writes to her from Germany, that this can by no means be brought about, if you should return to us. Who this person is,—if I tell you that he was once a bishop, that he is now an exile, an Italian,—a crafty knave,—a courtier,—either Peter or Paul,—you will perhaps know him better than I do. But however this may be, we have exhibited to the queen all our articles of religion and doctrine, and have not departed in the slightest degree from the confession of Zurich; although your friend Ἀρχιμάγειρος, [Sir Antony Cook] defends some scheme of his own, I know not what, most obstinately, and is mightily angry with us all. As yet not the slightest provision has been made for any of us; so that I have not yet abandoned the device which I designed for myself at Zurich, a book and a cross. I hear that Goodman[5] is in this country, but so that he dare not shew his face, and appear in public. How much better would it have been to have been wise in time! If he will but acknowledge his error[6], there will be no danger. But as he is a man of irritable temper, and too pertinacious in any thing that he has once undertaken, I am rather afraid that he will not yield. Your books have not yet arrived, which I am the more surprised at, as so many of the English have long since returned from Frankfort. When your present arrives, it will, I doubt not, be most acceptable to the queen; and since you wish it, although it is in itself most excellent, yet, should I have an opportunity, I will set forth its value in my own words. As to the book which you sent to me individually, I know not in what words to express my thanks. I choose, therefore, to sink under the weight of your present kindness, and the magnitude of all your former good offices towards me. And though I should most certainly never have dismissed you from my remembrance, yet excited as I am by this additional memorial, I shall entertain a more ardent and

[4 For an account of this, see Burnet, Hist. Ref. III. 170.]
[5 For an account of him, see Strype, Annals, I. i. 181, &c.]
[6 Jewel probably alludes to a tract written by Goodman in queen Mary's time, entitled, *How superior powers ought to be obeyed of their subjects, &c.* in which he spoke against the government of women, but was obliged to retract his opinions before the lords of the council. Strype, Annals, I. i. 184.]

reverential affection for your name, as long as I live. Your other books have long since been brought over by the booksellers, and are purchased with the greatest eagerness; for every one is most anxious to see by what hunting spears the beast has been pierced.

Farewell, my father and much esteemed master in Christ. Salute masters Bullinger, Bernardine, Gualter, Simler. I would add Frensham, did I not suppose that he was now at the bath, or on a journey; for at this season of the year, when one hears the cuckoo, he is rarely at home. London, April 28, 1559.

Your very affectionate
and most devoted,
JOHN JEWEL.

This is my *fourth* letter.

LETTER VIII.

JOHN FOXE TO HENRY BULLINGER.

Dated at BASLE, *May* 6, 1559.

HEALTH in Christ. I send you an English [messenger] with some beer; and intend also to come myself, if I hear that [Frensham] is yet alive. I have thought fit therefore to send this express before hand with a hired horse, for I was unable to procure another, that I might know the sooner; and I pray you to order him, if Frensham is living, to hasten his return to me as soon as possible. Should there be any occasion for a further supply, the beer will be more easily procurable at Arau[1], and at a less distance.

May the Lord Jesus, the fountain of all health, preserve us to his glory. May 6, 1559, the day after your letter was brought hither. Basle.

Yours in Christ,
J. FOXE.

[[1] Arau is twenty-seven miles from Zurich, where Frensham was now confined by illness.]

LETTER IX.

JOHN JEWEL TO PETER MARTYR.

London, [No date.]

Much health. And what, after all, can I write to you? For we are all of us hitherto as strangers at home. Return then, you will say, to Zurich. Most earnestly do I wish, my father, that this may some time be possible: for, so far as I can see, there is no hope of your ever coming to England. O Zurich! Zurich! how much oftener do I now think of thee than ever I thought of England when I was at Zurich! But though, as I observed, we are yet strangers in our own country, we hear sometimes ineffable and inexplicable things. Mischief, however, is often better kept at home [2].

As to religion, it has been effected, I hope, under good auspices, that it shall be restored to the same state as it was during your latest residence among us, under Edward. But, as far as I can perceive at present, there is not the same alacrity among our friends, as there lately was among the papists. So miserably is it ordered, that falsehood is armed, while truth is not only unarmed, but also frequently offensive. The scenic apparatus of divine worship is now under agitation; and those very things which you and I have so often laughed at, are now seriously and solemnly entertained by certain persons, (for *we* are not consulted,) as if the christian religion could not exist without something tawdry. Our minds indeed are not sufficiently disengaged to make these fooleries of much importance. Others are seeking after a *golden*, or as it rather seems to me, a *leaden* mediocrity; and are crying out, that the half is better than the whole.

Some of our friends are marked out for bishops: Parker for Canterbury, Cox for Norwich, Barlow for Chichester, Scory for Hereford, and Grindal for London; for Bonner is ordered to vacate his see. When they will take possession, I know not.

---

[2] Πολλάκι γὰρ τὸ κακὸν κατακείμενον ἔνδον ἄμεινον. Theognis.

From this flowering I can easily guess beforehand, as you do of wine, what kind of a vintage it will be. Our enemies in the mean time are watching their opportunity, and promise themselves that these things cannot last.

In Scotland we hear that there have been some disturbances, I know not of what kind, respecting matters of religion; that the nobles have driven out the monks, and taken possession of the monasteries; that some French soldiers of the garrison have been slain in a riot; and that the queen was so incensed as to proclaim the banishment of the preacher Knox by sound of horn, according to the usual custom in Scotland, when they mean to send any one into exile. What has become of him, I know not.

A commission is now appointed for the whole of England, with a view to the establishment of religion. Sandys will go into Lancashire, I into Devonshire, others into other parts. The queen declines being styled the head of the church, at which I certainly am not much displeased. Meanwhile, what *the hangman*[1] *of the church* [cavezzo della Chiesa] may think, or murmur, or what trouble he may give us, you who are less distant can hear more easily than ourselves. Our papists oppose us most spitefully, and none more obstinately than those who have abandoned us. This it is to have once tasted of the mass! He who drinks of it is mad. Depart from it, all ye who value a sound mind; who drinks of it is mad[2]. They perceive that when that palladium is removed, every thing else will be endangered.

A peace has been concluded between us and the French, on condition that Calais shall be restored, after eight years, into the possession of the English. It will need a marvellously strong faith to make my friend Julius believe this. However it be, we are expecting sureties from France to that effect. Nothing is yet talked of about the queen's marriage; yet there are now courting her the king of Sweden, the Saxon[3], and Charles the son of [the emperor] Ferdinand, to say nothing of the Englishman, [Sir William] Pickering. I know however,

[[1] The pope is probably intended by this expression.]

[2] Qui bibit inde furit; procul hinc discedite, queis est
  Mentis cura bonæ: qui bibit inde furit.

[[3] The son of John Frederic, Duke of Saxony.]

what I should prefer; but matters of this kind, as you are aware, are rather mysterious; and we have a common proverb that *marriages are made in heaven.*

Farewell, my father and much esteemed master in Christ. Salute, I pray you, in my name, the excellent old man master Bernardine, with masters Muralt and Wolf. The book which you sent as a present[4] to the queen, was delivered to her by Cecil. By some accident or other, it never came into my hands: as often, however, as I go to court, I inquire very particularly whether she has any thing to say about it; but as yet I hear nothing. Whatever it be, I will take care to let you know. London.

JOHN JEWEL.

This is my *fifth* letter: you will find out whether any have been lost.

LETTER X.

JOHN FOXE TO HENRY BULLINGER.

Dated at BASLE, *May* 13, 1559.

MUCH health, most learned and very dear [friend] in Christ our Lord. Master Abel, an English merchant, has within these few days written to me from Strasburgh, in which letter of his were inclosed some from England, written to yourself and masters Simler, Gualter, and Gesner. Should they reach you, I wish my letter, in which they were inclosed, to be forwarded to me at this place. Should they not reach you, I would not have you ignorant of the fact of their existence; for I have been informed of it by another letter of Abel written to myself. These letters, as far as I can learn, were dispatched to you from England in the month of March, and sent here in April; and now, in the month of May, I understand they have not yet been delivered. I had moreover written to Frensham, who is with you, on the 23rd of

[4 See p. 21.]

April, and do not yet know whether my letter has been received. I am exceedingly anxious to learn the state of his health. Your excellence will condescend to advise him in this respect, and at the same time to afford him, in case of necessity, any assistance in your power.

I am here harassed to the utmost of my strength, and almost beyond my strength, in collecting the histories of the Martyrs. Should you be in any way able to help me in this matter, I shall be glad of your assistance. And this you may do, if you will obtain from master Bernardine, and the other Italians resident in your city, a short statement of such occurrences of this kind as may have taken place in Italy; and also, if you will put down in a few words, whatever your memory may retain respecting events which have happened in your own neighbourhood, noting at least the names of the individuals and the places. For although I am more immediately concerned with British history, yet I shall not pass over the sacred history of other nations, should it come in my way.

May the Lord Jesus direct your health, studies, and labours for his glory! Basle. The day before the feast of Pentecost, 1559.

Yours in Christ,

JOHN FOXE.

LETTER XI.

RICHARD COX TO WOLFGANG WEIDNER.

Dated at LONDON, *May* 20, 1559.

WHENEVER I should leave Worms, my venerable friend, and much esteemed brother in Christ, I always determined with myself to write to you, and give you information some time or other respecting the state and condition of our affairs; which I considered it would not be disagreeable to you to hear, by reason of that ardent and sincere zeal with which you are always affected towards the gospel of Christ Jesus. I must confess that I have hitherto been constrained unwillingly to be silent, lest I should have to relate matters which would afford you no pleasure. Under the cruel reign of Mary, though but for the space of five years, popery so much increased both in numbers and strength, that it was hardly to be imagined how much the minds of the papists were hardened; so that it was not without great difficulty that our pious queen, with those about her who stood forth with alacrity on the side of truth, could obtain room for the sincere religion of Christ. The bishops, the *scribes* and *Pharisees*, opposed it in our great council, which from a French word we call the parliament; and because they had in that place but few who durst even open their mouths against them, they always appeared to gain the victory. Meanwhile we, that little flock, who for these last five years, by the blessing of God, have been hidden among you in Germany, are thundering forth in our pulpits, and especially before our queen Elizabeth, that the Roman pontiff is truly antichrist, and that traditions are for the most part mere blasphemies. At length many of the nobility, and vast numbers of the people, began by degrees to return to their senses; but of the clergy none at all. For the whole body remain unmoved,

"Tanquam dura silex, aut stet Marpesia cautes,"

as the poet sings. The matter at last came to this, that[1] eight of their leaders, either bishops, or the most select from among their men of learning, were to dispute concerning some heads of religion with eight of our abject and exiled party. And, to avoid a war of words, it was agreed to manage the debate in writing. The day was fixed: we are all present. The queen's council are present, and almost all the nobility. It was decided that the opposite party should first deliver their sentiments about the matters in dispute. One of them[2], in the name of the rest, like Goliath against David, comes vauntingly forward with his own statement, defends, and as it would seem, confirms it by irrefragable arguments, and congratulates himself as having already obtained the victory. [3]One of our party replied, relying on the truth, and not upon high-flown language; in the fear of the Lord, and not with the boasted affectation of learning. When the reply was concluded, an incre-

[1 See above p. 10, and Strype, Annals, I. i. 128, &c.]
[2 Dr Cole. See above p. 14.]   [3 Dr Horn. See above p. 15.]

dible applause of the audience was excited, to the great perturbation and confusion of our opponents. The other day arrives, appointed for a similar disputation. The opposite party is requested by the president[1] to proceed in the order before agreed upon, namely, that they should first declare their opinion respecting the next point in dispute, and that we should follow them. This however they refuse to do, being alarmed at the ill success of the preceding day's contest; and cry out that it is unjust for them to begin the dispute, who had so many years continued in possession of the catholic church; and that if we had any thing to say against them, we should bring it forward, that they might refute us by their authority, and silence us as degenerate sons, who had long since departed from the unity of the church. Thanks to Christ our Lord, they are very properly checked in their resistance to the order of the president, and lose their cause. The sincere religion of Christ is therefore established among us in all parts of the kingdom, just in the same manner as it was formerly promulgated under our Edward, of most blessed memory.

I have thought fit to write this brief but certain intelligence to one, who will, I know, truly rejoice in our joy; that you may together with us return thanks to the Lord our God, who of his truly fatherly compassion has regarded and comforted us in our low estate of humiliation and distress. May he grant that these his so great and inestimable benefits may never be forgotten by us! Your kindness will do me a great favour, if you will be pleased to communicate the above intelligence to my excellent friends master James Cornicius, the physician, and Vespasian Fittich. We are already endeavouring to break down and destroy the popish fences, and to repair under happy auspices the vineyard of the Lord. We are now at work; but the harvest is plenteous, and the labourers few: let us ask the Lord to send labourers into his harvest. These few things I had to communicate to you, as my regard dictates. May the Lord Jesus preserve you, and increase your piety even unto your last breath! London in England, May 20, 1559.

Your most devoted,
RICHARD COX.

[1 The Lord Keeper Bacon.]

LETTER XII.

JOHN PARKHURST TO HENRY BULLINGER.

Dated at LONDON, *May* 21, 1559.

JEWEL and I received your very courteous letter at the beginning of April, by which I perceived your intention of sending your son Rodolph, at some appointed time, to improve his education at the university of Oxford. This, however, as things now are, I would not advise you to do; for it is as yet a den of thieves, and of those who hate the light. There are but few gospellers there, and many papists. But when it shall have been reformed, which we both hope and desire may ere long be the case, let your Rodolph at length come over. I will not now tell you how much I shall be gratified by his arrival in England; for I would express my regard towards him by deeds rather than words.

The Book[2] of Common Prayer, set forth in the time of king Edward, is now again in general use throughout England, and will be every where, in spite of the struggles and opposition of the pseudo-bishops. The queen is not willing to be called the *head* of the church of England, although this title has been offered her; but she willingly accepts the title of *governor*, which amounts to the same thing. The pope is again driven from England, to the great regret of the bishops and the whole tribe of shavelings. The mass is abolished. The parliament broke up on the eighth[3] of May. The earl of Bedford has made a present of three crowns to our friend Wolfgang, who in this respect is more fortunate than many others.

The bishops are in future to have no palaces, estates, or country seats. The present owners are to enjoy for life those

[2 By the act for the uniformity of Common Prayer passed this parliament. For a note of the differences between the two books, see Strype, Annals, I. i. 122.]

[3 For the Lord Keeper's speech at the dissolution of parliament, see Strype, Annals, I. i. 99.]

they are now in possession of. They are worthy of being suspended, not only from their office, but from a halter; for they are as so many Davuses, throwing every thing into confusion. The monasteries will be dissolved in a short time.

I cannot now write more, for within four days I have to contend in my native[1] place, both from the pulpit and in mutual conference, with those horrid monsters of Arianism; for which end I have read with much attention your very learned treatise on both natures in Christ. I hope to come sufficiently prepared to the contest, and so to overcome the enemies of Christ. Christ lives, he reigns, and will reign, in spite of Arians, Anabaptists, and papists.

Farewell! most excellent and very dear sir. Overwhelm, so to speak, with salutations in my name your good wife, sons[2] and daughters, and most honourable sons-in-law. The good Lavater has done me a very great kindness in sending me so excellent a book, and one too which is *Zurich all over*. Salute for me masters Bibliander, Collin, Haller, Wolfius, Wickius, Frisius, Bernardine, Ammian, Meyer, Sebastian, Coler, Funckius, Pellican, Froschover, and all friends. My wife salutes you, your wife, sons and daughters, and all friends. She very frequently falls into tears when any mention is made of the ladies of Zurich.

To your honourable magistrates, to the city and all the territory of Zurich, I wish every happiness. City[3] of Zurich, farewell. Woe betide those who wish thee not all prosperity. City of Zurich, farewell. In haste. London, May 21, 1559.

Most entirely yours,

JOHN PARKHURST.

[1 Viz. Guildford in Surrey.]

[2 Bullinger had six sons and five daughters. Of the former, three died young; two were ministers, and another died in France, in the troops of the prince of Orange, in 1569. Three of the daughters were married to ministers of Zurich: namely, to Hulric Zuinglius, son of the Reformer, to Lewis Lavater; and to Josiah Simler.]

[3] Urbs Tigurina, vale: valeant male, prospera cuncta
     Qui tibi non optant: urbs Tigurina, vale.

LETTER XIII.

JOHN PARKHURST TO CONRAD GESNER.

Dated at LONDON, *May* 21, 1559.

HAIL! again and again, most illustrious and very dear Gesner. As soon as I came to London, I sought out your friend Caius[4], that I might give him your letter; and, as he was from home, I delivered it to his maid servant; for he has no wife, nor ever had one. Not a week passes in which I do not go to his house two or three times. I knock at the door; a girl answers the knock, but without opening the door, and, peeping through a crevice, asks me what I want. I ask in reply, where is her master? whether he is ever at home, or means to be? She always denies him to be in the house. He seems to be every where and no where, and is now abroad, so that I do not know what to write about him. I shall certainly tell him something to his face, whenever I have the chance to meet him; and he shall know what kind of a man he has to deal with.

The pope is again cast out of England. This sadly annoys the mass-mongers. The pseudo-bishops opposed with all their might the pious designs of the queen; and, to be brief, brought upon themselves a consummation much desired by all good men. They are now abhorred both by God and man, and never creep out into public unless they are compelled to do so, lest perchance a tumult should arise among the people. Many call them *butchers* to their face. Whatever other news there may be, I have already written in my letters to our other friends. As I think the trifle I now send you will not be sufficient, I will send more; but it must be when I am richer than I am at present, (for we are all of us at this time poorer

[4 This was the celebrated co-founder of Caius College, Cambridge, and court physician in the reigns of Edward VI., queen Mary, and queen Elizabeth. Between him and Gesner an intimate friendship existed, and the latter, who was so eminent a scholar, philosopher and naturalist, as to have acquired the name of the Pliny of Germany, speaks of Caius in terms of the highest commendation, calling him, in an epistle to queen Elizabeth, "the most learned physician of his age."]

than Irus himself,) and you shall then perceive that I am not unmindful of you.

Farewell. Salute in my name your wife, Frisius, Simler, and all my other friends. My wife salutes you all. In haste. London, May 21, 1559.

Yours,

JOHN PARKHURST.

LETTER XIV.

JOHN JEWEL TO HENRY BULLINGER.

Dated at LONDON, *May* 22, 1559.

MUCH health. Your letter, most accomplished sir, was most gratifying to my friend Parkhurst and myself, both as coming from one to whom we can never forget how greatly we are indebted, and also, as retaining the deepest traces of that courtesy and kindness of yours towards us, which we so largely experienced during the whole time of our exile. And I wish we may be able, some time or other, in some measure to requite your kindness: but however this may be, the inclination, at least, shall not be wanting. Your exhortation that we should act with firmness and resolution, was a stimulus so far from being unacceptable to us, that it was almost necessary. For we have at this time not only to contend with our adversaries, but even with those of our friends who, of late years, have fallen away from us, and gone over to the opposite party; and who are now opposing us with a bitterness and obstinacy far exceeding that of any common enemy; and, what is most vexatious, we have to struggle with what has been left us by the Spaniards, that is, with the foulest vices, pride, luxury, and licentiousness. We are doing, however, and have done, all that is in our power: may God prosper our exertions, and give them a happy issue! But at present we are so living, as scarcely to seem like persons returned from exile; for to say nothing else, not one of us has yet had even his own property restored to him[1]. Yet, although this long waiting is very tiresome to us, we doubt not but that in a short time all will be well. For we have a wise and religious queen, and one too who is favourably and propitiously disposed towards us. Religion[2] is again placed on the same footing on which it stood in king Edward's time; to which event, I doubt not, but that your own letters and exhortations, and those of your republic, have powerfully contributed. The queen is unwilling to be addressed, either by word of mouth, or in writing, as the head[3] of the church of England. For she seriously maintains that this honour is due to Christ alone, and cannot belong to any human being soever; besides which, these titles have been so foully contaminated by antichrist, that they can no longer be adopted by any one without impiety.

Our universities are so depressed and ruined, that at Oxford[4] there are scarcely two individuals who think with us; and even they are so dejected and broken in spirit, that they can do nothing. That despicable friar Soto and another[5] Spanish monk, I know not who, have so torn up by the roots all that Peter Martyr had so prosperously planted, that they have reduced the vineyard of the Lord into a wilderness. You would scarcely believe so much desolation could have been effected in so short a time. So that, although it would give me the greatest pleasure, under other circumstances, to see even a dog from Zurich in England, yet I cannot at this time recommend you to send your young men to us, either for a learned or religious education, unless you would have them sent back to you wicked and barbarous.

[1 A bill for this purpose passed the commons May 2, and was read a third time in the upper house. Yet, says Strype, I do not find it was enacted and passed into a law. Annals, I. i. 99.]

[2 See p. 28. The 24th day of June was the day appointed by the late parliament, from which the new service book was to be only used in the churches throughout England. Strype, Annals, I. i. 200. He says, p. 199, that the new morning prayer began in September at St Antholin's, London, the bell beginning to ring at five; when a psalm was sung after the Geneva fashion, all the congregation, men, women, and boys, singing together.]

[3 See pp. 24, 29.]   [4 See pp. 11, 29.]

[5 John de Villa Garsya. Strype, Mem. III. ii. 29.]

The Lord Russel lately asked me in what way he could most oblige both yourself and your other brethren and fellow ministers. He felt, in truth, an inclination to send you some acknowledgment of your kindness and hospitality, which he is continually commending. I told him, that nothing could be more acceptable to yourself and your friends, than for him studiously and boldly to promote the religion of Christ, and repress the insolence of the papists. This he promised that he would do, and he certainly does, as far as lies in his power.

The ambassadors[1] of the French king arrived to-day in London, to offer their congratulations about the peace. The head of the embassy is the young duke de Montmorenci. Nothing is yet said respecting the queen's marriage. The son of John Frederick [duke of Saxony,] and the second brother of [the emperor] Maximilian, are her suitors[2]. The public opinion, however, inclines towards [Sir William] Pickering, an Englishman, a wise and religious man, and highly gifted as to personal qualities. May God prosper the event, whatever it be!

This is the *first* letter that I have written separately to yourself since my return to England. But as I know that Peter Martyr, from the great intimacy that subsists between you, has communicated to you my letter to him, so I have no hesitation in regarding what I have written to him just the same as if it had been addressed to yourself.

Farewell, my father, and much esteemed master in Christ. Salute that excellent lady your wife, masters Gualter, Simler, Zuinglius and Lavater. Should there be any thing in which I can conduce either to the comfort or advantage of yourself or your friends, I promise you not only my labour, zeal, and diligence, but also every effort both of mind and body. London, May 22, 1559.

Your much attached,

JOHN JEWEL.

[1 For the account of their arrival, see Strype, Annals, I. i. 285.]
[2 The queen was courted almost at the same time by Charles, Duke of Austria; James, Earl of Arran; Erick, King of Sweden; Adolph, Duke of Holstein; Sir William Pickering, a brave, wise, comely English gentleman; the Earl of Arundel, of very ancient nobility; and the Lord Robert Dudley, the late Duke of Northumberland's son, and the queen's especial favourite. Strype, Parker, I. 164.]

LETTER XV.

JOHN FOXE TO HENRY BULLINGER.

Dated at BASLE, *June* 17, 1559.

HEALTH in the Lord. There was no need of your using any entreaty, my dearest Bullinger, whenever you might perceive any occasion for the employment of my services. Respecting the letters you mention, I have again called upon Peter Maclaine, a bookseller of this place, to whom those letters were directed by Abel, as he writes me word. My friend Lawrence was also with me, to whom Abel had directed (as he wrote me word) the entire packet of my letters. Peter replied to us in this way; that some one came to him with letters, who was not a carrier himself, but either hired by a carrier, or else one who had bought the letters from the carrier, that he might afterwards resell them with greater profit [upon the carriage]. Peter, being displeased at the unreasonableness of his demand, and seeing that the matter was no business of his, but of the English, for the sake of sparing his money sent the man to the neighbouring public-house, [the sign of] the Wild Man, telling him that he would there meet with some Englishmen who would take the letters off his hands. And yet I know that, besides ourselves, there were at that time no Englishmen in the town; and I cannot sufficiently wonder how it could come into Peter's mind to send the person to the Wild Man, when he knew well enough whereabouts in the town we ourselves dwelt, to whom he might much more properly have sent the man. But when I expostulated with Peter on this point, he replied, that he thought, and had heard, that there were some English at that time living at the Wild Man, &c. The case is this: because this Peter was unwilling to lay out his money on this covetous fellow, we have lost our letters. At which, however, I am not so much concerned on my own account, and that of my letters, which I have lost, (for they were inclosed in the same packet,) as for the sake of your letter, my best and dearest master

Bullinger, which, as I learn from you, was written to you by an old friend. And I wish, as I then told Peter, that I had given him three times the money, if he had but satisfied the letter-carrier, or rather, I should say, the letter-stealer. And to confess to you ingenuously and sincerely, in proportion as I perceive you to be anxious about the letter, this same thing occasions greater uneasiness to myself; nor do I know what I can do more, or where I can make any farther inquiry on the subject.

Although your letter gives me but little hope respecting Frensham, yet, as he is still alive, and as long as he continues so, we must not cease to have some hopes of him. There was an English youth here of sixteen years old, who was in this present year not only on the borders of death through a similar cough and consumption, but even looked like death itself; and yet, to the astonishment of our physicians, he recovered, and is gone with his parents into England. To Christ the Lord be the praise! And I wish that our friend Frensham may sometime have to laugh at your physicians in the same way, should it seem good to the Lord Christ, the chief Physician. But may his holy will be done.

If you have any thing concerning master Grinæus, whom you mention in your letter, I pray you to forward it hither, and let me know as soon as possible. I wish to know whether Hoper married a wife[1] from among you yonder, or here at Basle.

While I am collecting accounts of the other German martyrs, I would not have Zuinglius alone to be passed over. If you have, or if you choose, to communicate any thing respecting him, I will take care, God willing, that it shall be printed in England, if it cannot be done so conveniently by the printers in Germany.

I am desirous, if the Lord shall spare my life, of visiting and saluting you yonder, most kind and learned Bullinger, before my return home. Exhort Frensham, I pray you, if he is yet living, not to be so desponding in his mind as to cast

[[1] Strype Mem. II. i. 399, says that Hoper's wife was an *Helvetian* woman; but in another place he calls her "a discreet woman of the *Low Countries.*" Mem. II. i. 170. Other accounts make her a native of Burgundy.]

away all hope of recovery; and not to let his mental anxiety seem greater than his bodily disease. Salute, I pray you, master Peter Martyr very much in my name. May the Lord Jesus advance your labours together with your safety, to the advantage of his church! Amen. Basle, June 17, 1559.

Yours in Christ,

JOHN FOXE.

P. S. Give, I pray you, this second letter to Frensham, if he is yet alive.

LETTER XV*2.

JOHN FOXE TO —— FRENSHAM.

Dated at BASLE, *June* 17, [1559].

D. Frenshamo, animi et corporis salutem in Christo.

MASTER FRENSHAM. As you in your letters have oft comforted me, so I would I should likewise comfort you: but where my comfort is small, the Lord infuse the Comforter of all, and work in you sure consolation which may comfort both your body and soul! In whom I desire you to be strong and valiant, so much as the weakness of your disease can bear. Be nothing discouraged, nor be out of hope in yourself. I have seen some of our countrymen in the like disease of utter weakness return full well.

I desire you in your contemplation of Christ, let your spirit be so noble and high in him, that you may tread under your feet all other things, seem they never so strong, mighty,

[2 This letter is transcribed from the original *English*, which was inclosed in the preceding one to Bullinger, and did not probably reach Zurich till after the death of the person to whom it was addressed. (See Letter XIX.) It is numbered as above, to preserve the continuity of the series translated from the *Latin* originals.]

terrible, or great in this world; for he that hath overcome the world, what hath he not overcome in this world? Life or death, sickness or health, things present or to come, height or low, are nothing in Christ. Only, my brother, master Frensham, a hearty faith in Jesus Christ is altogether whereby alone we miserable and contemptible nothings are saved, do stand, do triumph, yea, in death, yea, over death, in sin, yea, over sin, and finally have victory over all evils, sin, death, hell, Satan, and all. For so it hath pleased the Father, to save us by this faith only in his Son, to the end that we seeing his justice should not otherwise be satisfied but by his Son, we might the more fear him for his great righteousness, and love him for his great mercy, being saved by this faith in his Son. To this all the scripture beareth witness. The Lord Jesus shew us the quickening and sealing of this faith in our dull senses! To will you this is my prayer; as I do not cease, so I do not despair of your recovery altogether: the mighty Lord Jesus, if it be his pleasure, put to his helping hand in restoring you again! His good will be done. The bottle ye sent is not yet come to me. Basileæ, June 27, [1559].

Truly in Christ,

JOHN FOXE.

LETTER XVI.

JOHN JEWEL TO PETER MARTYR.

Dated at LONDON, *Aug.* 1, 1559.

I HAVE hitherto, my father, written to you less frequently, because many engagements, both of a public and private nature, have prevented my correspondence. I now write, not because I have more leisure than heretofore, but because I shall have much less in future than I have at present. For I have now one foot on the ground, and the other almost on my horse's back. I am on the point of setting out upon a long and troublesome commission[1] for the establishment of religion, through Reading, Abingdon, Gloucester, Bristol, Bath, Wells, Exeter, Cornwall, Dorset, and Salisbury. The extent of my journey will be about seven hundred miles, so that I imagine we shall hardly be able to return in less than four months. Wherefore, lest you should in the mean time suppose me dead, notwithstanding I wrote to you twelve days since upon our common affairs, I think it not unmeet to send you this short greeting at the very moment of my setting out. Our affairs are now in a favourable condition. The queen is exceedingly well disposed; and the people everywhere thirsting after religion. The bishops, rather than abandon the pope, whom they have so often abjured before, are willing to submit to every thing. Not, however, that they do so for the sake of religion, of which they have none; but for the sake of *consistency*, which the miserable knaves now choose to call their *conscience*. Now that religion is everywhere changed, the mass-priests absent themselves altogether from public worship, as if it were the greatest impiety to have any thing in common with the people of God. But the fury of these wretches is so great that nothing can exceed it. They are altogether full of hopes and anticipations, (for, as you know, they are a most *anticipative* race, and mightily addicted to *futuritions*,) that these things cannot last long. But, whatever may happen in future, we render thanks to Almighty God that our affairs are as they are.

Every thing is in a ferment in Scotland. Knox[2], surrounded by a thousand followers, is holding assemblies throughout the whole kingdom. The old queen (dowager) has been compelled to shut herself up in garrison. The nobility with united hearts and hands are restoring religion throughout the country, in spite of all opposition. All the monasteries are every where levelled with the ground: the theatrical dresses,

[[1] This commission was dated July 19, 1559, and addressed to William, Earl of Pembroke, John Jewel, S. Th. P., Henry Parry, Licentiate in Laws, and Will. Lovelace, lawyer. Strype, Annals I. i. 248.]

[[2] Knox arrived in Edinburgh from France, May 2, 1559. Strype, Annals, I. i. 176.]

the sacrilegious chalices, the idols, the altars, are consigned to the flames; not a vestige of the ancient superstition and idolatry is left. What do you ask for? You have often heard of *drinking like a Scythian;* but this is *churching it like a Scythian.* The king of France that now is, styles himself king of Scotland, and in case of any thing happening to our queen, (which God forefend!) heir of England. You must not be surprised if our people are indignant at this; and how the matter will at length turn out, God only can determine. A common enemy perhaps, as is sometimes the case, may be the occasion of reconciling with us our neighbour Scotland; in which event, although the [queen's] marriage should also take place,—but I will not prognosticate. Master Heton salutes you, and that not less affectionately than if you were his father. Some of us are appointed to bishopricks; Cox to Ely, Scory to Hereford, Allen to Rochester, Grindal to London, Barlow to Chichester, and I, the least of the apostles, to Salisbury. But this burden I have positively determined to shake off. In the mean time there is a dismal solitude in our Universities. The young men are flying about in all directions, rather than come to an agreement in matters of religion.

But my companions are waiting for me, and calling to me to set off. Farewell, therefore, my father, and my pride. Salute that reverend man, and on so many accounts dearly-beloved in Christ, master Bullinger, to whom also, if I had time, I would send a separate letter. Salute masters Gualter, Simler, Lavater, Haller, Gesner, Frisius, Herman. I have five golden pistoles from master Bartholomew Compagni, for the venerable old man master Bernardine, with a letter to him from the same. I would write to him concerning the whole business, were I not prevented by want of time. I pray you, however, to let him know, that, except [the payment of] this money, nothing else is settled. Court affairs, as far as I can see, are so difficult of management, that I know not whether any thing can be made of it. The queen is now a long way off in Kent[1], so that nothing can be done.

[[1] July 17th. The Queen removed from Greenwich in her progress, and goes to Dartford in Kent. August 5th she was at Eltham. Strype, Annals, I. i. 289.]

Farewell my father, farewell. May you be as happy as I can wish you! Salute in my name your Julius, and Anna, and your little son, [Martyrillus.] London, Aug. 1, 1559.

Your every way most attached,

JOHN JEWEL.

LETTER XVII.

JOHN FOXE TO HENRY BULLINGER.

Dated at BASLE, *August* 2, 1559.

GRACE and health through Christ our Lord. Either all my conjectures deceive me, most courteous Henry, or I have at last discovered those letters of ours which were so long lost. In which matter I am more indebted to some sort of accident, than to any pains taken about it. The occasion was this: there came into a merchant's house by reason of some letters, I know not what, a certain honest Italian, the husband of Peter Perne's sister. The master and head manager of that house offered him some letters to read, thinking they were written in Italian. Although this Italian was unacquainted with English, yet seeing my name on the address, he forthwith came to me with the letters, and told me that the master of the house [above-mentioned] desired I would come to him immediately. I went forthwith, taking with me my friend Lawrence, and a certain under-schoolmaster of Basle to act as interpreter. The master states that this letter, long since thrown aside, had been lately discovered by a servant boy; and that there had also been found other letters written both to yourself and master Gesner, which he had already given to Peter Maclaine to forward to you. On opening mine, I find it to be the same as was sent to me from Abel at the same time and in the same packet with yours; which circumstance leads me to conjecture that they are the very same letters of ours which we were looking for. You will better ascertain this when you have opened them; and I wish that you would let me know at your leisure.

If master Frensham is still living, I pray God that he may long live. Do you bid and exhort him not to despair of himself, and much less of the divine favour, which, should it seem expedient, can easily exceed all the powers of medicine, and deceive the expectations of the physicians themselves. Yet I have not heard of any physician who openly and positively despaired of him. And if they did despair, they are better judges perhaps of German [constitutions] than of English ones.

I desire that you would inform me in time, if you have any information respecting the martyrs, either about Bartholomew Grinæus, as you seem to intimate in your letter, or about the whole affair and cause of Zuinglius. If the history of Zuinglius cannot be printed here, it can nevertheless be done in England, and no where better. Salute in Christ master Frensham among others, and master Peter Martyr. Be mindful of me in your prayers to the Lord. Basle, Aug. 2, 1559.

Yours in Christ,

JOHN FOXE.

LETTER XVIII.

JOHN FOXE TO HENRY BULLINGER.

Dated at BASLE, *Sept.* 26, 1559.

MUCH health. Though it was neither my inclination nor design, most learned Bullinger, to send forth in these times the[1] books on the Eucharist by the Archbishop of Canterbury,

[1 Foxe alludes to a Latin translation, finished by him in June 1557, of the controversy between Archbishop Cranmer and Gardiner, Bishop of Winchester, about the Eucharist. While he was preparing to publish this book, as appears from this letter, an order was set forth in those parts, forbidding printing of any books; and though, in fine, Froschover undertook the printing of it, and Foxe delivered part of the copy to him,

translated by me [into Latin], especially when I perceive a general conflict of judgments and opinions no less than of arms; yet as your friend Christopher here has of his own accord, and with so much candour, promised his aid and assistance in this matter, I have again begun to apply my mind to a subject long intermitted and almost despaired of. But I should be loth to occasion any delay, if only the thing shall appear either to him or yourself to be of such a nature, that the interests of the church demand my services; and I have already stated this in my former letters to you. Having at last consulted with Froschover, it has seemed necessary to both of us, and especially to myself, not to take any steps in this matter without your advice and approval beforehand. I request you therefore, most learned Bullinger, to undertake a diligent investigation into the subject. For I have determined to send you in a few days (Christ willing), by Froschover's advice, some portion [of my translation]; which I should have done at this time, only that it requires to be more accurately written out for your more easy perusal. For I am still so much busied in translating the Greek councils with a double commentary, and also in compiling the history of our martyrs, and other engagements, that I have hardly a spare moment for writing out any thing: so that you will be less surprised at my having written this present letter with so little attention. I wish, most learned Sir, that you may live in happiness. Basle, Sept. 26, 1559.

Yours in Christ,

JOHN FOXE.

the business still underwent delay; and Foxe himself seemed to be cooler in it, knowing how exulcerated those times were with sacramental controversies: so that only some part of the work was printed. See Strype's Grindal, p. 19, &c., and Cranmer, p. 375.]

LETTER XIX.

JOHN JEWEL TO PETER MARTYR.
Dated at LONDON Nov. 2, 1559.

I HAVE at last returned to London, with a body worn out by a most fatiguing journey. You probably supposed me dead, because I did not write: meanwhile, I was kept away three whole months by this very tedious and troublesome commission. While I was at Bristol, there was delivered to me that letter from you which our friend Randolph[1] had brought with him; written in so friendly and agreeable a manner, as altogether to remove from my mind the wearisomeness both of the journey and of my employments. For I could then fancy myself to be conversing with you just as if you had been present. Randolph had gone away into France before my return: so that poor I was deprived of a great part of those delightful communications which you had personally charged him with. My letter, I perceive, was lost on the road; for that which I had sent you as the *eighth*, was, I find, only the *fifth* that had reached you.

But what, you will say, has been done after all by this commission of yours? Receive then in one word, what it took me a long time to investigate. We found every where the people sufficiently well disposed towards religion, and even in those quarters where we expected most difficulty. It is however hardly credible what a harvest, or rather what a wilderness of superstition had sprung up in the darkness of the Marian times. We found in all places votive relics of saints, nails with which the infatuated people dreamed that Christ had been pierced, and I know not what small fragments of the sacred cross. The number of witches and sorceresses[2]

[[1] It would seem from the extract from the state papers given in pp. 56, 57, (No. 7) that Randolph, who was entrusted with the safe conveyance of the earl of Arran from France into Scotland, visited Peter Martyr at Zurich during this journey, from whom he brought the letter here referred to.]

[[2] A Bill against witchcraft and enchantments was brought into the house of Lords from the lower house April 27, 1559, and was passed in the following session. Strype, Annals, I. i. 88.]

had every where become enormous. The cathedral churches were nothing else but dens of thieves, or worse, if any thing worse or more foul can be mentioned. If inveterate obstinacy was found any where, it was altogether among the priests, those especially who had once been on our side. They are now throwing all things into confusion, in order, I suppose, that they may not seem to have changed their opinions without due consideration. But let them make what disturbance they please; we have in the mean time disturbed them from their rank and office.

That *consistent* man, Harding[3], has preferred to change his condition rather than his opinions. Sidall[4] has subscribed too, and with equal consistency, that is, sorely against his will. But your friend Smith[5], what has he done? you will ask. Can any good thing come out of Nazareth? Believe me, that he might retain his old consistency, he has now at last recanted for the fifth time! The silly man, when he saw religion change, changed his habit, and forthwith prepared to take refuge in Scotland; but while he was loitering on the borders, he was apprehended, and brought back from his travels. And now this grave personage, this prop and support of religion, has come over to us, deserted all his party, and become all of a sudden the most inveterate enemy of the papists. Go now and deny transubstantiation, if you can.

The ranks of the papists have fallen almost of their own accord. Oh! if we were not wanting in our exertions, there might yet be good hopes of religion. But it is no easy matter to drag the chariot without horses, especially up hill.

Yesterday, as soon as I returned to London, I heard from the Archbishop of Canterbury that you are invited hither, and that your old lectureship is kept open for you. I know not how true this may be; I can only affirm thus much, that

[3 T. Harding, of New College, Oxford; who under King Edward VI. had been a very zealous protestant, but under queen Mary came about, and was as hot the other way, being preferred under her to a prebend of Winchester, and the treasurership of Sarum. Strype, Annals, I. ii. 175.]

[4 Henry Sidall, a vigorous defender of the truth in king Edward's time, recanted under queen Mary, and subscribed to queen Elizabeth's supremacy. Strype, Cranmer, 285; Parker, I. 154. See p. 18.]

[5 See above, p. 12.]

no Professor of Divinity is yet appointed at Oxford. For my own part, my father, I most exceedingly long to see you, and especially in England; and how can I do otherwise than desire this, who am so perpetually desiring to see you even at Zurich? But I know your prudence; and you know the character and disposition of us islanders. I pray that what we now see the beginning of may be lasting. Nothing can be in a more desperate condition than the [Divinity] school is at present. You will think, that when you were formerly there, you had employed all your exertions to no purpose.

[1]"Thus in the garden that was once so gay,
The darnel and the barren weed bear sway."

Your book on Vows[2], like all your other works, is caught up with the greatest avidity. We are all now looking for you to publish your further commentaries on the book of Judges, and on the two books of Samuel; for all our friends are now aware that you have those books in hand, and are intending to publish them. The Swede[3], and Charles[4], the son of [the emperor] Ferdinand, are courting at a most marvellous rate. But the Swede is most in earnest, for he promises mountains[5] of silver in case of success. The lady however is probably thinking of an alliance nearer home. My friend Allen[6] has departed this life, after having been nominated bishop of Rochester. We hear at this time nothing from Scotland that can be new to you. The gospel is taught; churches are diligently brought together, and all the monuments of the old superstition demolished. The

[1] Infelix lolium et steriles dominantur avenæ.—VIRG.

[2 A refutation of Richard Smith's two books, concerning single life and monkish vows.]

[3 The prince of Sweden, whose title was duke of Finland, landed at Harwich on Sept. 27, 1559, and reached London Oct. 5. His object was to make suit to the queen on behalf of the king [Eric XIV.] his brother. Strype, Annals, I. i. 291. 368.]

[4 Archduke of Austria, and brother of the emperor Maximilian.]

[5 Aug. 30, 1561, the news was that the king of Sweden was sending a great number of waggons laden with massy bullion, and other things of value to England. He continued his courtship most eagerly till 1562. Strype, Annals, I. i. 405.]

[6 Edmund Allen, an exile for religion in the reign of queen Mary. He was buried on the 30th of August. Strype, Annals, I. i. 199.]

French however are still hoping to retain both the kingdom and their religion. Whatever may happen, I will write to you fully at another time. That sixtieth year is now approaching, concerning which you were sometimes wont to relate some wonderful predictions of a certain Italian, named Torquatus[7]. God grant us the enjoyment of real and substantial joy, that the man of perdition may at length be made manifest to the whole world, and the truth of the gospel of Jesus Christ be universally exhibited!

Farewell, my father, and salute your wife[8] in my name, a lady indeed personally unknown to me, but with whom I am nevertheless now well acquainted, both by your letter, and our friend Abel's commendation of her. I congratulate you on her account, and her on yours. Salute masters Bullinger, Gualter, Bernardine, Herman, Julius, his wife, and my little Martyr. A long farewell to my friend Frensham[9], who I imagine has now departed from you to be with Christ. All our friends salute you, and wish you every happiness. London, November 2, 1559.

Yours most heartily,

JOHN JEWEL.

Master Heton[10] urgently entreated me to salute you in his name. Could he write Latin himself, he would not make use of my pen: believe me, there is no one who speaks of you more frequently, or with greater commendation. His wife also sends her respects both to you and yours.

[[7] Torquatus was a physician and astrologer at Ferrara, in the 15th century. He wrote a "prognostic" of the ruin of Europe, dedicated to Matthias king of Hungary, in which he foretold events from 1480 to 1540.]

[[8] Catherine Merenda, Peter Martyr's second wife, was recommended to him from the Italian church at Geneva, where she lived an exile for religion.]

[[9] See Letter XV*.]

[[10] Thomas Heton, a merchant of London, who had been a liberal contributor to the relief of the Marian exiles.]

LETTER XX.

JOHN JEWEL TO RODOLPH GUALTER.

Dated at LONDON, *Nov.* 2. 1559.

MUCH health. That you so kindly congratulate, not myself so much on this accession of care and anxiety, as our church, respecting which you tell me that you no longer despair, I return you my thanks, most accomplished sir, not indeed on my own account, upon whom I feel such a heavy burden is imposed, but in the name of our church, concerning which I perceive your thoughts are so anxiously occupied. For, as it regards myself, you well know what an undertaking it is, especially for a man unskilled in business, and always brought up in inactivity and obscurity, to be raised at once to the government of the church; and though scarcely able to manage his own affairs, to take upon himself the management of those of others. Since however it is the cause of God, I will endeavour to make up by diligence what is wanting in ability; for though I am deficient in other respects, I shall not, I hope, be wanting in inclination. Do you meanwhile, since you have safely landed your vessels, and brought them ashore, pray to God that we may at length bring our vessel, hitherto tossed by the waves, and attacked on all sides by pirates and robbers, into harbour. For the rage of the papists among us at this time is scarcely credible; and rather than seem to have been in error in any respect, they most impotently precipitate and throw all things into confusion. May that God whose honour and glory alone we look to, aid our endeavours, and confound the conspiracies and wicked designs of his enemies! Parkhurst is gone to his people at Cleeve[1], where he now reigns like a king, and looks down upon all bishops. Whatever news I had to communicate, which, indeed, was neither certain nor of much importance, I have written at some length, both to masters Bullinger and

[[1] He was at this time rector of Bishop's Cleeve near Cheltenham.]

Martyr. If there is any thing in which I can contribute either to your advantage or enjoyment, bear in mind, that in whatever situation I may be, I am, and always shall be at your service.

Fare thee well, most excellent and accomplished Sir. Salute in my name the honoured lady your wife, as also masters Bullinger, Simler, Lavater, Zuinglius, Frisius, Gesner, Wolfius, and your other friends whom I so justly value. Though Parkhurst is a long way off, yet I salute you, your wife, and all your family, in his name. All our friends salute you and all yours. Again farewell. London, Nov. 2, 1559.

Yours from my heart,

JOHN JEWEL.

LETTER XXI.

JOHN PARKHURST TO JOHN WOLFIUS.
Without date.

I RECEIVED, most courteous Wolfius, on the 9th of February the letter which you sent me by our friend Burcher: the former, which you tell me you sent, never reached me. You recommend me to publish my epigrams[2]: why should I publish frivolous trifles of this sort? They are certainly contending in some corner of my study with the moths and beetles.

At the end of your letter you ask me to continue my affection towards you: you have no need, my Wolfius, to make such a request as that; for I cannot help loving you, both on account of your kind offices towards myself, which I shall never forget, and also for your rare learning, and those various endowments which I admire and reverence in you as the best gifts of God.

The books you gave me on my leaving Zurich were lost in the journey. Woe betide those thieves who robbed me of so great a treasure! As you are the great master of a great

[2 Many of them are published in Strype, Annals, II. ii. 495. &c.]

hypocaust, you shall pay me a severe penalty if my name be ever erased from your remembrance. You have a short reply to a short letter. You will hear all the news from our friend Gualter. Salute your wife and all your friends in my name. My wife salutes you. Farewell.

Yours,

JOHN PARKHURST.

LETTER XXII.

JOHN JEWEL TO JOSIAH SIMLER.

Dated at LONDON, *Nov.* 2, 1559.

You congratulate me, my dear Josiah, with your accustomed kindness, but I cannot congratulate myself. For though as yet nothing more has been imposed upon me than the name of bishop, (for upon the office[1] itself and its duties I have not yet entered,) I feel nevertheless that even this burden is far beyond my strength, and that I am already beginning to bend under an empty title. What think you will be the case, when I come to undertake the charge itself?

Your letter, however, arrived most acceptably; for I discovered therein your affectionate regard and love to me. And what indeed that is otherwise than agreeable can proceed from Josiah, who is himself most agreeable? Wherefore, although the subject of it seems exceedingly unpleasant and annoying to me, I return you my most grateful thanks both for your letter and your congratulations.

As to your expressing your hopes that our bishops will be consecrated without any superstitious and offensive ceremonies, you mean, I suppose, without oil, without the chrism, without the tonsure. And you are not mistaken; for the sink would indeed have been emptied to no purpose, if we had suffered those dregs to settle at the bottom. Those oily, shaven, portly hypocrites, we have sent back to Rome from

[1 He was consecrated bishop of Salisbury, Jan. 21, 1560.]

whence we first imported them: for we require our bishops to be pastors, labourers, and watchmen. And that this may the more readily be brought to pass, the wealth of the bishops is now diminished and reduced to a reasonable amount, to the end that, being relieved from that royal pomp and courtly bustle, they may with greater ease and diligence employ their leisure in attending to the flock of Christ.

In that you are so earnest in your recommendation of our mutual friend Julius, although you are Josiah, yet I must think that in this matter you do me injustice. For why? am I not sufficiently acquainted with my good Julius, my host, my friend, my brother? Can his baldness, remarkable as it is, ever slip from my remembrance? No, never. As often as I behold any bald, stooping, crooked old man, clumsy[2] and uneasy in his movements, my friend Julius is sure to come into my mind. Be assured, that under whatever circumstances, whether he may need advice, or assistance, or money, —or even a halter, Julius shall be always Julius as far as Jewel is concerned. But, joking apart, whenever my friend Julius shall come to me, if Jewel has ought to spare, he shall not want.

Fare thee well, my Josiah, and salute in my name that most excellent lady your wife, and that most talented and accomplished young man Herman. Parkhurst is gone into the country, to his *kingdom*[3]. He desired me, however, before he went, to salute you most dutifully in his name. Farewell, my Josiah, farewell; I wish I may some day be able face to face to say, Josiah, how do you do? London, Nov. 2, 1559.

Yours from my heart,

JOHN JEWEL.

[[2] The epithets here used will hardly admit of a *literal* translation.]
[[3] Bishop's Cleeve, of which he was rector. See p. 48.]

LETTER XXIII.

JOHN JEWEL TO PETER MARTYR.

Dated at LONDON, *Nov.* 5, 1559.

Two days after my return from a long and tiresome journey, when, wearied and exhausted with travelling, I had written to you I know not what, three letters from you reached me at the same moment; by the most delightful perusal of which I was so refreshed, as entirely to banish from my mind all the troubles of the preceding days. For though, whenever I think about you (as I certainly do every hour of my life, and should be very ungrateful if I did not,) I am delighted at the very thought and remembrance of your name; yet when I read your letters, I seem to myself to be at Zurich, and in your society, and in most delightful conversation with you, which indeed, believe me, I value more than all the wealth of the bishops.

As to what you write respecting religion, and the theatrical habits, I heartily wish it could be accomplished. We on our parts have not been wanting to so good a cause. But those persons who have taken such delight in these matters, have followed, I believe, the ignorance of the priests; whom, when they found them to be no better than mere logs of wood, without talent, or learning, or morality, they were willing at least to commend to the people by that comical dress. For in these times, alas! no care whatever is taken for the encouragement of literature and the due succession of learned men. And accordingly, since they cannot obtain influence in a proper way, they seek to occupy the eyes of the multitude with these ridiculous trifles. These are, indeed, as you very properly observe, the relics of the Amorites. For who can deny it? And I wish that sometime or other they may be taken away, and extirpated even to the lowest roots: neither my voice nor my exertions shall be wanting to effect that object.

As to your writing that there are some persons[1] who as yet have given no expression of their good will to you, I rather suspect to whom you allude. But believe me, they are neither in the rank or position you suppose them to be, and in which all [our] Israel hoped they would be. For if they had been— They have hitherto refrained from writing to you, not from any disinclination or forgetfulness of you, but because they were really ashamed to write. Both of them are now suffering most severely under an attack of ague; but Ἀρχιμάγειρος [Sir Antony Cook], as being of a more melancholy temperament, is much the worse.

With your usual affection to the common cause, you were grieved at hearing that no provision had been made for any one of us. You may now resume your grief, for nothing whatever has been done up to the present moment. We only bear about the empty titles of bishops, and have deserted the ranks of [Duns] Scotus and Thomas [Aquinas] for those of the Occamists and *Nominalists*. But as you know, state affairs move slowly. The queen herself both favours our cause, and is desirous to serve us. Wherefore, although these beginnings are painful enough, we do not lose our spirits, nor cease to hope for better things. That which easily comes to maturity, easily decays.

I wrote to you, as I remember, at some length, respecting your book, before I left London; but my letter, as is often the case, was probably lost on the road: I added also, that the queen of her own accord eagerly perused both your letter and the book itself, and wonderfully commended both your learning and character in general; and that your book was made so much of by all good men, that I know not whether any thing of the kind was ever so valued before. But alas! what must I say, when no recompence has been as yet made to you? I am ashamed, and know not what to answer. The queen however made diligent inquiry of the messenger, as to what you were doing, where you lived, in what state of health and what circumstances you were, and whether your age would allow you to undertake a journey. She was altogether desirous that you should by all means be invited to England, that as

[[1] Sir Thomas Wroth, and Sir Antony Cook. See next letter, p. 59.]

you formerly *tilled*, as it were, the university by your lectures, so you might again *water* it by the same, now it is in so disordered and wretched a condition. But since then, the deliberations about Saxony and the embassy from Smalcald[1] have put an end to those counsels. Yet, whatever be the reason, nothing is at this time more talked about, than that Peter Martyr is invited, and daily expected to arrive in England. Oh! how I wish that our affairs may sometime acquire stability and strength! For I am most anxious, my father, to see you, and to enjoy your most delightful conversation and most friendly counsels. If I should ever see that day, or rather, as I hope I may say, *when* I shall see it, where is the Amiens or Salisbury that I shall not look down upon? Farewell, my pride, and more than the half of my own soul. Salute in my name that excellent lady your wife: may God grant her a happy delivery[2], and make you the father of a beautiful offspring! Salute masters Bullinger, Gualter, Lavater, Simler, Gesner, Frisius, Julius, his wife, and my little Martyr, likewise Herman, your friend and mine. All our friends salute you. London, Nov. 5, 1559.

Yours most heartily,

JOHN JEWEL.

LETTER XXIV.

JOHN JEWEL TO PETER MARTYR.

Dated at LONDON, *Nov.* 16, 1559.

MUCH health. Although I wrote to you not many days since, and there is nothing going on here at this time which you would much desire to know, yet since I doubt not but that you wish it, I had rather write that *nothing*, than dismiss

[1] See p. 20.]
[2] Peter Martyr had two children by this wife, who both died very young, and before him; and he left her with child of a third, which proved a daughter. See note, p. 78. and Appendix.]

the courier, who, as I have just learned accidentally, is about to proceed to Cologne, without a letter from me.

Religion among us is in the same state which I have often described to you before. The doctrine is every where most pure; but as to ceremonies and maskings, there is a little too much foolery. That little silver cross, of ill-omened origin, still maintains its place in the queen's chapel. Wretched me! this thing will soon be drawn into a precedent. There was at one time some hope of its being removed; and we all of us diligently exerted ourselves, and still continue to do, that it might be so. But as far as I can perceive, it is now a hopeless case. Such is the obstinacy of some minds. There seems to be far too much prudence, too much mystery, in the management of these affairs; and God alone knows what will be the issue. The slow-paced horses retard the chariot. Cecil favours our cause most ardently. The bishops are as yet only marked out [for promotion], and their estates are in the mean time gloriously swelling the exchequer. Both our universities, and that especially which you heretofore cultivated with so much learning and success, are now lying in a most wretched state of disorder, without piety, without religion, without a teacher, without any hope of revival. Many of our leading men, and those not unknown to you, are fixing their thoughts upon yourself, and are anxious that you should be invited at the earliest opportunity, in spite of all the German leaguers[3]. But I, who most of all mankind, anxiously and above all things desire to see you, cannot but recommend you, if you should be invited, (which however I scarcely think will be the case in the existing state of affairs,) to do nothing in a hurry. I know your prudence, and you also, I hope, on your part, are aware of my regard for you. I can indeed with truth affirm thus much, that there is no man to whom your presence would be more agreeable than to myself. But yet, as our affairs are so fluctuating, uncertain, unstable, and in one word, *insular*, I had rather hear of you absent and in safety, than see you present among us and in danger.

But all this is very little to the purpose; for it is but just that learning should be silent amid the din of arms. We

[[3] See the preceding page.]

are aiding our neighbours, the Scots, both by land and sea. For you know [the old saying],

"'Tis like to prove your own concern,
When neighbouring walls begin to burn."[1]

They say that the French king is coming with all his army; and he will probably be met by no inferior numbers.

Pamphilus[2], the companion of your friend Crito, has lately

[1] Tum tua res agitur, paries cum proximus ardet."

[2] The fictitious names of *Pamphilus* and *Crito* occur not unfrequently in Jewel's correspondence with Peter Martyr. The following extracts from the state papers of the time are presented to the reader, with the view of aiding him in the detection of the persons intended by them.

1. In a letter from Sir Nicolas Throgmorton to secretary Cecil, dated Paris, June 21, 1559, is the following passage: "I praye you Sr. in case *Thomas Randal* be not dispatched before the receipt hereof, to worne him, that after his arrivall in France he take upon him to be a merchant,...... *and that his passage may be as secretly as may be.*" Forbes's Full View of the public transactions in the reign of queen Elizabeth. Vol. i. p. 136.

2. Another letter from the same to the same, dated June 28, 1559, states, "The French king hath lately sent sertayne commyssyoners to apprehend th' *erle of Arrayne*, with grete severite and extremity, to bringe hym either quicke or deade. Whereupon the sayd erle of Arrayne, to save hys lyfe, is fled, no won can tell whyther." Forbes, p. 147.

3. The queen thus writes to Sir N. Throgmorton, July 17, 1559. "Touching the *erle of Arrayne*, as theis bearers can declare unto you, we be desyroose that he shold be helped from Geneva into this realme, or into *Scotland;* and for that purpoose, our meaning shall better appeare in a memoryall, ciphred by the new last ciphre, sent from you...... whereunto we remitt you." Forbes, p. 162.

4. Extract from the above mentioned memorial. "The sauff conveying of the *earl of Arrayne* hither unto this realme, or *Scotland*, semeth here a thing both proffitable, and nedeful. The doing of it cannot be here prescribed, but is referred to your discretion; wherein ye shall observe great commendation. It must be done *secretly*, as well in respect of th' emperor's subjects and friends, and the king Catholique's as of the French's......Ye must nedes take the chardge to appoint one for the expedition of the earl of Arrayn, from Geneva."

5. The queen again writes to Sir N. Throgmorton, July 19, 1559. "Common charite, the honor of the partye, and our own experience of such lyke calamities, moveth us to have compassion; and therefore we wold, that ye shuld employe your wisedome, how he might be safely counselled to preserve hymselfe from the danger of the Frenche king and the Guises. Wherein although there maye many other wayes be devised; yet we see not presently, if he shall be forced to depart thence, (which we wold not without evident necessite,) than ether,

written to me from Scotland, as well about other matters, as that I should write to you something, I hardly know what,

persona dissimulata, to goo to Geneva, and there to remayne, untill tyme shall reveale hym furder counsell; or els to come into our ile of Jersaye, and so to come to Plimmonth or Hampton, and so to passe to his father unto *Scotland*." Forbes, p. 166.

6. It appears from a memorial dated July 21, 1559, that Henry Killigrew was sent to Sir N. Throgmorton, to "devise the most *secret* and spedy wayes to convey the erle of Arrayne from Geneva." His directions were "to provide that the said erle comme not into the possessions of th' emperor, the kings of Spayne, the bishops papists, nor others confederate with the French, *that he in no wise appeare who he is, in all his journaye, not to his most assured, but ether as a merchant, or scoller.*" Forbes, p. 171.

7. Killigrew arrived at Paris July 22, and on the 27th, Sir N. Throgmorton writes to the queen, "Of the *earle of Arrayne* I have not learned any thing certainly, since the dispatching of *Mr Randall* from hence to Chastelereu, in the company of th' erle of Arrayne's master of the horse; and whether th' erle of Arrayne be at Geneva, or *Tigure*, where order was by me taken for his arryvall, I do not yet know." Forbes, p. 172. If he visited Tigure, (Zurich), as seems probable from the above extract, it will account for Jewel's mentioning him as the friend and guest of Pet. Martyr. See letter XXIX. It appears that Randolph met the earl of Arran at Geneva, and accompanied him from thence.

8. Sir N. Throgmorton writes to Sec. Cecil, July 29. "I suppose youe shall hear of the earl of Arrayne there in England before I can now here of hym; for he departed the 6 of July from Losanna in Suyser-land in post, and sent me word he wold embark, where he cold most commodiously find passage." Forbes, p. 183.

9. By a letter of Cecil to Sir R. Sadler and Sir James Croft, of Sept. 11, 1559, it appears that the earl of Arran travelled under the feigned name of Monsr. de Beaufort. He says, "I wold be gladd to here of the sure entry of Monsr. de Beaufort, *ye knowe what erle I mean*." Sir R. Sadler's state papers. Vol. I. p. 437.

10. A letter from Sir R. Sadler to Cecil, dated Berwick, Sept. 16, 1559, states, without mentioning the earl's name, that "*he was safely delivered in Teeydale to one of his friends hands, that undertoke to convey him surelie and secretlye to his father;* so you shall understande that we have now certein advertisement, that he is *safely in the castell of Hamilton with his father;* ......and hitherto he remaineth there, so *secret*, that at the writing thereof it was *not known in Scotland, that he is arrived there*. He hath *sent hither for Randall whom we woll send unto him by the same man that conveyed him before, with as moch spede as we may covenyently*." Sadler, p. 447.

It will readily be concluded from a comparison of these extracts, that the Pamphilus and Crito in Jewel's correspondence, are the Randolph and earl of Arran above mentioned.]

(for he did not clearly express himself,) respecting our friend Frensham. He seemed, however, to wish me to make some inquiry respecting Frensham's will. What has been done about it, I do not know; but I entreat you, since there is no one else in those parts, upon whom I can take the liberty of imposing so much trouble, to undertake the management of this business, together with your friend Julius. If Frensham is still alive, I wish him well: if he is, as I suppose, and am informed by letter, no longer living, I hope it is well. I hear that a packet of your book upon vows, against Smith, has arrived in London, and that there is among them a copy sent by you expressly to myself. I have not yet seen it, for I am often absent from London, and am much taken up by my engagements in different parts of the country; but wherever it may be, I will scent it out. Meanwhile, however, I offer you, as I ought to do, and as your kindness demands, my lasting thanks. I would not that master Bernardine[1] should suppose that I have forgotten him. My influence and exertions have not been wanting; but every thing is now sought after, and retained for the support of the army. The five Italian crowns, which I received from master Barthol. Compagni in his name, I handed over to Acontius. We are now exerting ourselves about his canonry; and there is a good prospect of obtaining it.

If my friend Julius should come to us, I promise him every kindness: I advise him, however, to wait a little while, lest we should be obliged to return together to Zurich. Farewell, my father and much esteemed master in Christ. Salute the excellent lady your wife, and give a kiss for me to your little son Isaac, whom I can fancy that I hear bawling even here. Salute masters Bullinger, Bernardine, Gualter, Simler, Gesner, Lavater, Wickius, Haller, Wolfius, (that most agreeable man, and native of a most honourable city), Frisius, Herman, our friend Julius, his wife, and that most good tempered boy Martyrillus. Almost all our friends are dispersed among the Gentiles. Bishops Grindal of London, Sandys of Worcester,

[[1] Bernardine Ochinus accompanied Peter Martyr into England in 1549, and was received into the family of archbishop Cranmer. Strype, Memorials, II. i. 309. Cranmer, 279.]

Cox of Ely, together with [Sir Antony] Cook², and [Sir Thomas] Wroth, who are still suffering with ague, salute you. Again and again, my father, farewell. London, Nov. 16, 1559.

Wholly yours,

JOHN JEWEL.

LETTER XXV.

JOHN JEWEL TO PETER MARTYR.

Dated at LONDON, *Dec.* 1, 1559.

THERE was brought me yesterday from Scotland a letter from Pamphilus³, the presiding angel and companion of our friend Crito, respecting the whole state of affairs in that kingdom from the very beginning of the disturbances; all which he entreated me to communicate to you with diligence, and in the order of events. He would rather have written to you himself, if either the circumstances of time or place had allowed him to do so. As for me, since I know that you especially delight in brevity, I will write briefly.

The Scotch [congregation] at the beginning published certain declarations; first, that they only regarded the public weal, and that none of them sought any individual advantage to himself; next, that it appeared to be for the general interest, that the queen should desist from fortifying Leith, a maritime town and most convenient for the French, should there be any occasion for their services. Should she refuse to accede to this, they would then act as became men zealous for liberty, and lovers of their country. The queen however, being a haughty woman, and of French blood, rejected these terms, exclaiming that it was an indignity to her to be dictated to by her subjects. Nor were there wanting a great many Scots, who were still obedient to her authority. The result, however, was that they came to an engagement; when the

[² See p. 53.]   [³ See p. 56. note.]

bishop of St Andrews, a soldier, and worthy, forsooth, to be the slave of a weak woman, was deserted by all his own people before the battle. Only two little boys remained with him, I suppose that he might not have to return to his mistress alone and unattended.

The Scots have in their camp the preachers Knox and Goodman, and they call themselves the "congregation of Christ." Their next step was to send to the queen to retire from Leith, if she would not be driven from thence by force and violence. And from this time they began to treat about an alliance with England. The queen, a woman with a man's courage, though she was every day deserted by some of her own party, was nevertheless nowise dismayed; she kept possession of the garrison, made sallies against the enemy, planned every thing, surveyed every thing with her own eyes. The Scots are a powerful and numerous people; and had they not been unskilled in sieges and the art of war, they would have effected something long before this time. Slight skirmishes took place on both sides up to the sixth of November, after which the Scots retired into winter quarters; whereupon a rumour was spread abroad by the queen's party, that the Scots had run away with their spirits broken. But they, with their leaders, still maintain their ground, and hold councils, and increase their numbers, and levy money, and have troops in readiness, should there be any occasion for their services.

I have but briefly touched upon these matters: I will write more at length hereafter, when I shall be better informed respecting them; for great news is expected. We are raising troops, and seriously thinking about war.

Farewell, my father. Salute your wife, masters Bullinger, Bernardine, Herman, Julius and his wife.—London, the first of December, on which day I first heard of the death of (queen) Mary.

Yours,

JOHN JEWEL.

LETTER XXVI.

JOHN PARKHURST TO JOSIAH SIMLER.

Dated at BISHOP'S CLEEVE, *Dec.* 20, 1559.

I CANNOT express to you, my very kind Josiah, the pleasure it gave me to learn from your letter that you are in good health; which indeed our friend Gualter had before informed me of, but not having paid sufficient attention to his letter, I imagined you were dead. So great was my stupidity, or rather, so great my love, that on very slight grounds I suspected what was by no means the case, and which indeed grieved me most exceedingly. *Res est solliciti plena timoris amor.*

I was restored to my [rectory at] Cleeve on the second of September, that is, after harvest, when every thing had been taken away, and nothing left for me. How then, you will say, can you subsist? Not by plunder, but by borrowing. A single harvest will set every thing to rights. Let others have their bishopricks; my Cleeve is enough for me. Many of the bishops would most willingly change conditions with me; though one or two perhaps, a little ambitious, might decline doing so. And you must know, that I myself[1] also was to be enrolled among their number; but I implored some of our leading men, and my intimate friends, that my name should be erased from the list which the queen has in her possession; and though I could not effect this by my prayers and entreaties, yet I have hitherto, by their assistance, kept my neck out of that halter. When I was lately in London, one of the privy counsellors, and Parker, the archbishop of Canterbury, threatened me with I know not what bishoprick. But I hope for better things; for I cannot be ambitious of so much misery. I am king here in my parish, and for two years act as sole bishop. The bishop of Gloucester is living all this time away from hence; but every third year he has some business to transact here, as also in other places.

[1] He was consecrated bishop of Norwich, Sept. 1, 1560. Strype.]

Thus much of my affairs, respecting which you desired information. I thank you very much for your "astronomical institutes." You have, moreover, made I know not what collections from Athanasius, and others. When do you mean to publish? I was anxious to write you a very full letter, but am prevented by my various engagements.

Salute in my name your excellent wife and recent bride, your Anna. Commend me most dutifully to Wonlychius, and his very amiable Susanna. What I write to you I write to him. Salute also in my name masters Martyr, Bibliander, Bernardine, Lavater, Zuinglius, Frisius, Pellican, Liberian, Christopher Rotaker, Stumphius, Renner, Hirter, your neighbours, male and female, and all. My wife salutes you and all the rest. Farewell. Bishop's Cleeve, Gloucestershire, Dec. 20, 1559

Yours,

JOHN PARKHURST.

LETTER XXVII.

THOMAS SAMPSON TO PETER MARTYR.

Dated *Jan.* 6, [1560.]

I RECEIVED on the third of January the letter which you wrote on the fourth of November. I have now been in England one year, and that not a quiet one; but I fear that the year now coming on will bring me yet more trouble. I am not however the only one who am afraid for myself, but we are all of us in fear for ourselves; yet I dare not commit to writing the evils that seem to be hanging over us. I implore you therefore, most revered fathers, by Jesus Christ, and especially you, Peter [Martyr], my father and very dear master, to pray God most earnestly on our behalf. Contend for this, for this I say, that the truth of the gospel may be neither obscured nor overturned in England.

I thank you, my much endeared father, for your promptitude in writing to me. You have satisfied my inquiries, as has also master Bullinger: may our God reward you both! The consecration of some bishops[1] has already taken place. I mention, as being known to you by name, Dr Parker, [archbishop] of Canterbury, Cox, [bishop] of Ely, Grindal of London, Sandys of Worcester. There is one other of the name of Barlowe, also a bishop[2], but with whom you are not acquainted. Pilkington [bishop elect] of Winchester[3], Bentham of Coventry, and your friend Jewel of Salisbury, will follow shortly; for they are soon, as I hear, to be *consecrated*, as we call it. I am yet loitering on the threshold, for there is neither ingress nor egress. Oh! how glad should I be to find an egress! God himself knows how much I desire it. Let others be bishops; as to myself, I will either undertake the office of a preacher, or none at all: may the will of the Lord be done!

Oh! my father, what can I hope for, when the ministry of the word is banished from court? while the crucifix[4] is allowed, with lights burning before it? The altars indeed are removed, and images also throughout the kingdom; the crucifix and candles are retained at court alone. And the wretched multitude are not only rejoicing at this, but will imitate it of their own accord. What can I hope, when three of our lately appointed bishops are to officiate at the table of the Lord, one as priest, another as deacon, and a third as subdeacon, before the image of the crucifix, or at least not far from it, with candles, and habited in the golden vestments of the papacy; and are thus to celebrate the Lord's supper without any sermon? What hope is there of any good, when our party are disposed to look for religion in these dumb remnants of idolatry, and not from the preaching of the lively word of God? What can I hope, when injunctions are laid upon those appointed to preach, not to handle vice with too much severity; when the preachers are deemed intolerable, if they say any thing that is displeasing? But whither is my warmth

[1 Besides those here mentioned, Scory, Bishop of Hereford, and Merick of Bangor, were consecrated at or about the same time. Strype, Annals, I. i. 230.]

[2 Consecrated bishop of Chichester, Dec. 20, 1559.]

[3 He was consecrated bishop of Durham, March 2, 1560. Horn was appointed to Winchester, Feb. 16th. Strype, Annals, I. i. 230.]

[4 See Strype, Annals, I. i. 259.]

of feeling carrying me away? I must be silent, though I have scarcely touched upon the heads of the misery that is hanging over us. Eternal Lord, have mercy on us, through Jesus Christ, our God and Saviour.

I will propose this single question for your resolution; for I wish, my father, to employ you as my medium of correspondence with masters Bullinger and Bernardine. It is this: whether the image of the crucifix, placed on the table of the Lord with lighted candles, is to be regarded as a thing indifferent; and if it is not to be so considered, but as an unlawful and wicked practice, then, I ask, suppose the queen should enjoin all the bishops and clergy, either to admit this image, together with the candles, into their churches, or to retire from the ministry of the word, what should be our conduct in this case? Should we not rather quit the ministry of the word and sacraments, than that these relics of the Amorites should be admitted? Certain of our friends, indeed, appear in some measure inclined to regard these things as matters of indifference: for my own part, I am altogether of opinion, that should this be enjoined, we ought rather to suffer deprivation. I now beg of you, my father, this once to perform your part; that is, to inform me as diligently and speedily as possible, what your piety thinks of these matters, and what is the opinion of you all, I mean yourself, Bullinger, and Bernardine. His authority, I know, has very great weight with the queen. Should he at any time be disposed to write to her, to exhort her to persevere with all diligence in the cause of Christ, I can most cordially testify, what I certainly know to be the fact, and assert most confidently, that she is indeed a child of God. But she has yet great need of such advisers as himself; for what Augustine said to Boniface, is true of princes in general, namely, that they have many friends in their temporal concerns, and but few who are concerned for their souls. And what I am so anxious to obtain from him, I would also, if I dare, request from yourselves; but I submit myself in this matter to your discretion. She is acquainted, as you know, with Italian, and also well skilled in Latin and Greek. If any thing is written in these languages either by yourself, or master Bernardine, I am quite of opinion, that you will not only afford much gratification to her majesty, but perform a most useful service to the church of England. May God for ever guide you by his Spirit!

Farewell, and reply to me for this once as speedily as you can. Salute affectionately in my name master Bullinger, and your wife, and Julius. Communicate only to masters Bullinger and Bernardine what I have now written; for I should be loth to have any rumours spread abroad under my name. I should not indeed have written this even to you, were it not that I hoped some good might ensue. You will perhaps either write, as I have above mentioned, or at least give me some good advice as to the question proposed. Act according to your godly discretion. Again farewell. In haste. January 6, [1560].

Yours,
THOMAS SAMPSON.

P. S. If either yourself or masters Bernardine or Bullinger should think of writing to the queen's majesty, you are well aware that it must not seem as if you had been urged by any one to do so. My friend Chambers cordially salutes you. My wife is afflicted with the ague. Jane is well, as I believe are also Heton and his wife. I am living in the country, preaching Christ to the peasantry according to my measure. Pray God for me. Either Springham or Abel will take care that your letter is forwarded to me.

LETTER XXVIII.

BISHOP COX TO PETER MARTYR.

[LONDON.][1]

IT is a long time, my very dear friend in Christ, since I received your letter; but the book which you so courteously dedicated to me, has not yet come to hand. I happened very lately to look into a little book in the possession of some friend,

[[1] This letter has no date, but must have been written after Dec. 21, 1559, when Cox was consecrated bishop of Ely.]

which I found had been published with a dedication to myself. I acknowledge myself very much your debtor, even on this account, that some degree of notoriety has accrued by your means to such an obscure individual as I am; for it is a matter of great importance to be commended by those who are themselves distinguished both for learning and piety. And I hope that I may, some time or other, by some little act of courtesy on my part, be in a position to deserve your kindness. I will not be wanting to myself: may the Lord second my desires!

I congratulate you on your new wife, and hope also to be able to congratulate you on a new offspring. We are here diligently exerting ourselves on behalf of your friend Julius, and have already effected something. Richard Bruerne[1], an excellent Hebraist, is in possession of your prebend. If you will send me your letters of attorney for the restoration of your stall, I may possibly be able to do something for you in that respect.

As I was writing this, your book was brought to me as a present from the author. Respecting our affairs, what shall I write? By the blessing of God, all those heads of religion are restored to us which we maintained in the time of king Edward. We are only constrained, to our great distress of mind, to tolerate in our churches the image of the cross and him who was crucified: the Lord must be entreated that this stumbling-block may at length be removed[2].

The perfidy and ambition of the French [king], at the instigation of the antichrist of the church, are threatening to occasion us some trouble. The popish priests among us are daily relinquishing their ministry, lest, as they say, they should be compelled to give their sanction to heresies. Our enemies are many and mighty, but the Lord is mightier than all of them.

[1 See p. 12.]
[2 "Cox, bishop of Ely, being appointed to minister the sacrament before her there, [viz. the queen, in her chapel] made it a matter of conscience to do it in a place which he thought so dishonoured by images; and could scarce be brought to officiate there, denying it a great while; and when he did it, it was with a trembling conscience, as he said." Strype, Annals, I. i. 260, who has preserved a letter which the bishop wrote to the queen on this subject.]

Our neighbours, the Scots, have for the most part embraced the gospel, and are professing it under a heavy cross, which they are still forced to bear, through the violence of the French king, who is daily making attacks upon them, and contriving schemes for their extermination; so that, unless there should arise help from some other quarter, an end will shortly be put both to them and to the gospel among them. Meanwhile they must be aided by the prayers of the godly.

Greet your wife in my name, though unknown to me, and also Julius. May the Lord Jesus very long preserve you to us in safety!

Your most affectionate,

And very dear brother in Christ,

RICHARD COX,

Bishop of Ely.

LETTER XXIX.

BISHOP JEWEL TO PETER MARTYR.

Dated at LONDON, *Feb.* 4, 1560.

Much health. O my father! what shall I write to you? My materials are not great, but my time much less. However, as I know that you delight in brevity, I will write briefly after your example.

This controversy about the crucifix is now at its height. You would scarcely believe to what a degree of insanity some persons, who once had some shew of common sense, have been carried upon so foolish a subject. There is not one of them, however, with whom you are acquainted, excepting Cox. A disputation upon this subject will take place to-morrow. The moderators will be persons selected by the council. The disputants on the one side are the archbishop of Canterbury and Cox; and on the other, Grindal the bishop of London and myself. The decision rests with the judges. I smile however, when I think with what grave and solid reasons they will defend their little cross. Whatever be the result, I will write to you more at length when the disputation is over; for the controversy is as yet undecided; yet, as far as I can conjecture, I shall not again write to you as a bishop. For matters are come to that pass, that either the crosses of silver and tin, which we have every where broken in pieces, must be restored, or our bishopricks relinquished.

For your kind entertainment of my friend Frensham I return you, my father, the thanks I ought to do. Your letter first informed me of his death. I know not what to say respecting the money which he left at Zurich on his decease; for I have never seen his will myself, and my friend Randolph[1], who has seen it, is now in Scotland. However should there be any thing, I would by all means have provision made for my friend Julius. And I beg you to make it known to him in my name, that should there be any thing which Frensham has not bequeathed to any one by name, he may keep a portion for himself, and use his own discretion in the matter[2].

Various reports, and all of them favourable, are announced from Scotland. And it must suffice, at present, to have told you this in one word; for I have as yet nothing certain to relate as to the particulars. We have a large body of troops on the borders, and are bringing succour to the Scots, both by land and sea. Your guest Crito[3], and his friend Pamphilus, are not idle. The saucy youth came to Athens, and won the good graces of Glycerium[4]. Do you know? But what am I doing? I am in want of time, overwhelmed with business, and

[1] See p. 56. This affords further evidence of the identity of Randolph with Pamphilus.]

[2] The words, κατ''Ἀλκόξονον tuum, are added in the original MS.]

[3] See above p. 57, note.]

[4] That the queen was courted by the *earl of Arran*, appears from the note in p. 34. The following extract from a letter of Sir N. Throgmorton to the queen will throw additional light upon this subject. It is dated Paris, August 25, 1559. "I perceive by his (the king of Navarre's) discourses to me, he wolde have yowe marry none of the house of Austria, neyther the *earl of Arran*, neither any that I have heard namyd...I wolde wyshe your majestie should honorablye and very graciously receave the earl of Arran in your courte, geving hime as

unwillingly obliged to conclude. You should know, however, that your friend White, the *great* and *popular* bishop of Winchester, Oglethorpe of Carlisle, Baines of Lichfield, and Tunstall the *Saturn*[5] of Durham, all died some days since. Sampson is in the country, a long way off; Parkhurst in his kingdom[6]. You must not therefore be surprised, if they do not often write to you.

Salute, I pray you, the most reverend father, master Bullinger, Bernardine, Wolfius, Herman, and Julius, to all of whom I would gladly write at this time, had I leisure. Salute the excellent lady your wife, and Anna, and my little Martyr. Heton, Abel, and their wives, Grindal, Sandys, Scory, Falconer, Aylmer, salute you; and though they wish all good things for you, they nevertheless desire nothing more than England. However, as matters now stand, believe me, it is as well to be at Zurich. Farewell, my father, farewell. London, February 4, 1560.

Your most devoted,

JOHN JEWEL.

good hope as any other; for yf he be the same that they here report of him, he is as well worthy as any other." Forbes's Full View &c. Vol. I. p. 212. The interest manifested by the queen for the earl of Arran appears from her letter to Sir N. Throgmorton, of which an extract is given in p. 56. She added, however, "In any wise, let not hym think this our promptnesse to releve hym commeth uppon any other cause, than that in honor both for God's cause, and his parentage, we cannot permitt hym to be oppressed with this calamitee, adding hereunto the experience that we ourselves have in these and worse cases felt and yet passed, through the inestimable goodness of Almighty God." Forbes, p. 166. Agreeable to this is the instruction sent to Sir N. Throgmorton, that the earl "must be informed that this the quene's majesty's inclination to helpe hym is of hir princely nature, to releve such noble personages as be in adversite, uppon the experience of hir oune lyk trooble, and for the preservation of the sayd erle." Forbes, p. 171.]

[5 He died Nov. 18, 1559, having lived to the age of eighty-five or eighty-six years. Strype, Annals, I. i. 213.]

[6 i. e. his rectory at Cleeve, where he calls himself king, p. 61.]

LETTER XXX.

BISHOP JEWEL TO PETER MARTYR.

Dated at LONDON, *March* 5, 1560.

MUCH health in Christ. Although these engagements of mine have the effect of making me write to you less frequently, they will never make me either love you less, or have you less frequently in my thoughts. For how can I do less, especially to one whom I ought to regard as a father? I wrote to you not long since by our friend Burcher, by whom also I received your letter, though after a long interval; for notwithstanding it was written at the beginning of October, I did not, I think, receive it till the thirteenth of January; so long was he compelled to linger on the road. This, I imagine, has likewise not unfrequently been the case with respect to my letters to you; and especially since our friend Abel has left Strasburgh, where there is no Englishman now remaining, who can undertake the management of these matters.

Should the will of my friend Frensham be at this time sent to Frankfort, I have given a commission to Conrad, the servant of Arnold Birkman, an honest and trustworthy young man, to receive it from Froschover, and take it away with him, and keep it under his own care. For I shall not be in London when he returns, as I have long been anxious to go to Salisbury, but have been prevented by a thousand hindrances. In the mean time, while I am detained here, I know not what Pan is tending my sheep! But I know nothing about that will and the money; and can do nothing without Randolph. For if I did know, or were able to act, I would make over liberally, and without solicitation, a certain sum to our friend Julius. But Randolph is still absent in Scotland, a long way off; so that I still keep by me unbroken the letters written to him both by Bullinger and yourself. Indeed, I do not see by what means they can be safely forwarded to him, at so great a distance.

Religion is now somewhat more established than it was. The people are every where exceedingly inclined to the better part. The practice of joining in church music has very much conduced to this. For as soon as they had once commenced singing in public, in only one little church in London, immediately not only the churches in the neighbourhood, but even the towns far distant, began to vie with each other in the same practice. You may now sometimes see at Paul's cross, after the service, six thousand persons, old and young, of both sexes, all singing together and praising God. This sadly annoys the mass-priests, and the devil. For they perceive that by these means the sacred discourses sink more deeply into the minds of men, and that their kingdom is weakened and shaken at almost every note. There is nothing, however, of which they have any right to complain: for the mass has never been more highly prized within my memory; each being now valued, to every individual spectator, at not less than two hundred crowns. Your friend White, who so *candidly* and *kindly*[1] wrote against you, is dead, as I think, from rage; and religion, which you may be surprised at, has not suffered in the least. It sorely vexed this patient man to see both himself and his party laughed at by the very boys in the streets.

If our friend Julius should come over to me, he shall not want for either board, or clothing, or money; for I greatly esteem and wish him well, not only for your sake, to whom I owe every thing, but also for his own. However, as matters are at present, my advice is that he should wait a little, till the present confusion shall have subsided. Meanwhile, my father, do not suppose that there are none here who think of you in your absence. Your Divinity lecture at Oxford is still kept open, and, as I hope, for no one but yourself, if you are so disposed. Cecil is your friend. (Sir) William Petre speaks of you with the greatest kindness. After a while, when the work is finished, and the affairs of religion and the state thoroughly settled, should you be spontaneously and honourably recalled, in the name both of the queen, who still bears you in mind, and of the commonwealth, I entreat you not to be

[[1] The work here alluded to is, "De veritate corporis et sanguinis Christi in Sacramento altaris, contra Petrum Martyrem Hæreticum."]

unwilling to return. You will return, I hope, to men who are not ungrateful, and who still remember you with kindness.

Farewell, my father, my pride, and the better half of my own soul. Salute in my name your wife, and your dear little boy. Salute masters Bullinger, Gualter, Simler, Lavater, Gesner, Haller, Wolfius, Frisius, and especially Bernardine, (whose affairs here I could wish to see more speedily settled), the most talented young Herman, Julius, his wife, and my little Martyr. Farewell, my father, farewell. Oh! that I may sometime or other be allowed to say, "My father, how do you do?" London, March 5, 1560.

Your most attached friend,

JOHN JEWEL,

[Bishop of] Salisbury.

This, if I am not mistaken, is my 13th letter. You will perceive whether they have all reached you. Should master Lælius return to his head quarters, salute him, I pray you, in my name.

LETTER XXXI.

BISHOP SANDYS TO PETER MARTYR.

Dated at LONDON, *April* 1, 1560.

HEALTH in Christ. That I have not written to you, reverend sir, of so long a time, does not proceed from any forgetfulness of my duty to you, or from any light estimate of what your kindness deserves at my hands; but having been overwhelmed with a multitude of engagements, I unwillingly put off for a while the business of writing, which, now the opportunity of sending a letter is afforded me, I perceive can no longer be delayed. When I wrote to you at the beginning of August, I was sent by the command of the queen into the northern parts of England[1], as an inspector and visitor, as they call it, for the purpose of removing the abuses of the church, and restoring to it those rites which are consistent with true religion and godliness; and having been employed in those quarters up to the beginning of November, in a constant discharge of the duties entrusted to me, and with excessive fatigue both of body and mind, I at last returned to London. New labours here awaited me on my arrival, and an increased weight of business was laid upon my shoulders; for my services were required by the queen for the government of the see of Worcester; and the episcopal office is at length imposed upon me, though against my inclination. I wished, indeed, altogether to decline this bishoprick, as I did that of Carlisle, to which I had been nominated before; but this could not be done without drawing upon myself the displeasure of the queen, and in some measure deserting the church of Christ.

While this was going forward, Burcher delivered me your letter, full of all kindness; which, however, I delayed to reply to by him on his departure from hence, partly because our English affairs being at that time not much altered, but remaining in pretty much the same state, afforded very few materials for writing; and partly, because my new burden (for it may be more truly called so than an honour) distracted me most wonderfully with cares and engagements. And thus, my most esteemed sir, you have the reason of my long silence.

The doctrine of the Eucharist, as yet by God's blessing unimpugnéd, remains to us, and we hope will continue to remain, pure and inviolate. For both myself and my episcopal brethren will maintain it, by God's help, to the utmost of our power, as long as we live. We had not long since a controversy respecting images[2]. The queen's majesty considered it not contrary to the word of God, nay, rather for the advan-

[1 The commissioners were Francis, earl of Shrewsbury, president of the council in the north; Edward, earl of Derby; Thomas, earl of Northumberland, lord warden of the east and middle marches; Thomas, Lord Evers, Henry Percy, Thomas Gargrave, James Crofts, Henry Gates, Knts; Edwin Sandys, D.D., Henry Harvey, LL.D. Richard Bowes, George Brown, Christopher Escot, and Richard Kingsmel, Esq. The commission began at St Mary's, Nottingham, Aug. 22, 1559, *Die Martis*. Strype, Annals, I. i. 245, &c.]

[2 See p. 67.]

tage of the church, that the image of Christ crucified, together with [those of the virgin] Mary and [Saint] John, should be placed, as heretofore, in some conspicuous part of the church, where they might more readily be seen by all the people. Some of us [bishops] thought far otherwise, and more especially as all images of every kind were at our last visitation not only taken down, but also burnt, and that too by public authority; and because the ignorant and superstitious multitude are in the habit of paying adoration to this idol above all others. As to myself, because I was rather vehement in this matter, and could by no means consent that an occasion of stumbling should be afforded to the church of Christ, I was very near being deposed from my office, and incurring the displeasure of the queen. But God, in whose hand are the hearts of kings, gave us tranquillity instead of a tempest, and delivered the church of England from stumblingblocks of this kind: only the popish vestments remain in our church, I mean the copes; which, however, we hope will not last very long.

How much injury England is now receiving by your absence, as to the affairs of the church and religion, I am accustomed very frequently and earnestly to impress upon those to whom is committed the management of the state. But their minds are so much occupied with other matters of the greatest importance, that nothing, I see, has been hitherto determined with respect to inviting you back. The queen[1] I know was at one time very desirous of recalling you: you will easily comprehend, I suppose, what prevented it. The cause of Christ has always many adversaries, and the best persons are always the worst spoken of. This pretence of unity is daily giving rise to many divisions.

I congratulate you on your new marriage, and pray that it may be happy and prosperous; as I also wish for myself, who have lately entered into the same state of matrimony[2]. There is a wonderful preparation for war, partly to repel the French forces, if, in attempting to subjugate Scotland, they should invade our borders; and partly to aid the Scots against the French, if the latter at any time should violate the treaty

[1] See p. 53.]
[2] This second wife was Cecilia, daughter of Thomas Wilford, of [Hastridge, in] the county of Kent, Knight. Strype, Annals, III. ii. 65.]

of peace³ that they have made with us. God grant that all things may turn out to the glory of his name, and the advancement of the gospel.

I have thought it right to let you know these things by letter, before I set off for Worcester, where I hope to arrive shortly. But I should have written more fully, did I not know that my brother Jewel, the bishop of Salisbury, has given you frequent and diligent information about all our affairs. Should I be able to serve you in any way, believe me, my honoured Peter, you may use my services as long as I live (nay, were it possible, even after life), according to your discretion.

Salute very much in my name, I entreat you, the illustrious master Bullinger. I am a letter in his debt; indeed, I owe every thing to him, and, should opportunity arise, I will repay him as far as I am able. Salute your wife, Julius and his wife, Herman, Paul, and my little Martyr, to all of whom I wish every happiness. Farewell, most courteous, learned, and much esteemed master Peter. In haste. London, April 1, 1560.

Yours from my heart,

EDWIN WORCESTER.

LETTER XXXII.

THOMAS SAMPSON TO PETER MARTYR.

Dated at LONDON, *May* 13, 1560.

RELEASED at length, by the power of God, from the cares of episcopacy[4], I am enabled, my most esteemed father, to converse with you more freely than usual. But lest you should suppose that I am set free by any fault of my own, I would give you an account of the whole affair, did not want of time prevent me, wearisomeness dissuade me, and some other circumstances seem to forbid me. Meanwhile I entreat you

[³ April 8, [1559] peace was proclaimed between the queen and Henry the French king, the Dauphin of France, and Scotland, for ever. Strype, Annals, I. i. 283.]

[⁴ It seems that Norwich was the bishoprick that was offered to him. Burnet, Hist. Reform. III. 440.]

thus much, not to give too easy a credence to every informant. For not only many of those persons who are most inclined to speak freely about it, are quite in ignorance of the real state of the case; but others also, who are still your friends, as they formerly were mine, and who know more themselves than they wish me to know, will perhaps relate to you (if they tell you any thing at all) what is not exactly the truth. I do not write this either as lamenting my own lot, or the injury I have received from others. I feel nothing of the kind; all I desire is, that when you hear of this matter, you will suspend your judgment till you hear, if ever you do hear it, the whole state of the case. If I am not mistaken, I have received all your letters, and return you my best thanks for having given me such advice on the subject; and I had altogether determined to adopt your wholesome counsel, and that of master Bullinger; but the thing was never carried so far as to compel me to that step. My friend Parkhurst now holds the bishoprick in question, namely, of Norwich, and I wish him every success, as we all do. The danger of any improper person obtaining that see was well provided against: to God Almighty be the praise. My own unfitness too, under the circumstances, was at the same time well considered. I scarcely know how to be sufficiently thankful to the Lord God. Do you, my father, praise him, and do not cease to pray for me.

Religion is flourishing among us as heretofore, and I pray that it may flourish more and more to maturity. We are now on the point of being involved in war. May the Lord vouchsafe also to deliver us for the glory of his name! We are in fear of evil, and that to a great extent; nor will it be undeserved. But may the good Father of mercies come to our aid, and in his compassion relieve us from our troubles! In a word, I must say, that our state of affairs is such as to demand the repeated prayers of every godly person. You have therefore England most earnestly commended to your prayers.

Farewell, my excellent father, and most esteemed master. Salute most dutifully in my name master Bullinger, likewise your wife and children, Julius, and all your friends. Again farewell. London, May 13, 1560.

Yours,
THOMAS SAMPSON.

LETTER XXXIII.

BISHOP JEWEL TO PETER MARTYR.

Dated at LONDON, *May* 22, 1560.

MUCH health. If, as you tell me, eight of my ten letters have reached you, my very dear friend and father, there is much less loss than I expected; for I could never entertain the hope that even one third of the number would arrive in safety. But although they are, as usual, idly loitering on the road, or lying hid in some place or other, or even lost on the journey, I shall not on that account desist from doing my duty; nor shall I ever so act as to seem inclined to get rid of my engagement, through the treacherousness of the courier. For believe me, I am never employed more to my satisfaction than when I am either writing to you, or thinking about you. Hence, how often do I imagine myself at Zurich, and, agreeably to the delightful intimacy that exists between us, fancy that I am now hearing you, now conversing with you; to the end that, although I cannot in reality enjoy that pleasure, I may at least enjoy an ideal and shadowy gratification! But when our affairs are settled, and peace established, and the government placed on a firm footing, as I hope will shortly be the case, I shall dismiss these shadows and idealities, and, I hope, behold you face to face. For you ought to know that[1] this is anxiously endeavoured both by myself and all good men. In the mean time, our universities, and more especially Oxford, are most sadly deserted; without learning, without lectures, without any regard to religion. The blind deity will some time or other be more favourable to us. But at present you see what is the character of these times. War, destructive war, is utterly draining the very source of wealth. As soon as a calm shall return, and these disorders shall have subsided, there shall not be wanting to your Eleazar[2] of Damascus either that which you mention, or other things of more importance.

[1 Peter Martyr was invited over to England in the year following, but excused himself on account of his obligations to the city of Zurich, and also his age and infirmity. See Strype, Annals, I. i. 383, and note 1, p. 81, infra.]   [2 Julius, the attendant of Peter Martyr.]

If he should, or rather when he shall, come to me, I shall regard him as a brother.

I do not assume so much to myself as to be able to afford you any consolation concerning your Eliperius[1]. But I know your good sense, and that you are wont to anticipate by reflection that comfort which time would otherwise impart. I wish, however, that you could have had, especially in your declining years, a son to survive you, so endearing, and so like yourself; not only to have amused you with his prattling, but also to have been the inheritor of your talents and piety, of all your virtues, and of your learning. But since the great and good God has willed things to be as they are, they cannot be better than as they are.

Respecting those five Italian crowns, I have written three times to our friend Julius, and twice to master Bernardine. But I delivered them seven months since to Acontius[2], an Italian, who is now with the earl of Bedford. He promised to take care that they should be sent over to Zurich most faithfully, and at the earliest opportunity. I am surprised therefore that in all this time Bernardine has neither received his money, nor had any intelligence either from me or from Acontius.

The will of our friend Frensham has been placed in my hands. Those two hundred crowns are still at Antwerp, in the care of Arnold Birkman[3], with whom they are as safe as if I had them myself. Pamphilus[4] is in Scotland, diligently exerting himself for his friend Crito. The business therefore will not be entered upon till his return.

On the seventh of May the great spire of my cathedral at Salisbury was, not merely struck, but so shattered by lightning, that a continued fissure was made from the top for sixty feet downwards: consider whether there is any thing ominous in this circumstance. It so happened that I had not yet arrived there: had I done so, so foolish and superstitious are men's minds, that all this mischief would have been ascribed to my coming. I shall, however, go thither to-morrow, and put my hand to the plough. May God prosper his own cause!

[[1] Eliperius seems to have been the son who, Peter Martyr writes to Sampson on March 20, 1560, " was borne unto me the 2nd day of March, and died the 10th day of March."]

[[2] See p. 58.]   [[3] See p. 70.]   [[4] See note p. 56.]

Peter Alexander[5] came to me on the first of May, and after some days was completely reinstated in his prebend. He is now staying in London with your friend Heton, and preaching in the French church.

Crito[6] is in high favour. Whatever enemies he had heretofore, he has at length by his piety and discretion converted into friends. This our friend Pamphilus has made known to me by letter; but concerning all these matters I am writing more fully to master Bullinger.

Our friend Falconer is dead. Parkhurst is made bishop of Norwich. Bonner[7], the monk Feckenham[8], [Dr] Pate[9], [Dr] Story the civilian, and Watson, are sent to prison, for having obstinately refused attendance on public worship, and every where declaiming and railing against that religion which we now profess. For the queen, a most discreet and excellent woman, most manfully and courageously declared that she would not allow any of her subjects to dissent from this religion with impunity.

We are raising forces in all quarters, and making all manner of preparation for war. If the French should come, they will not, I hope, find us unprepared. Yet, as the times now are, that enemy[10] has not so much leisure at home as to allow of his interference in the concerns of others. May God at length put an end to these disorders, that when our affairs are settled, we may be able to recall you to England! For,

[5 Of Arles. He was encouraged to come over to England by archbishop Cranmer, and was made a prebendary of Canterbury, and rector of Allhallows, Lombard-street. Strype, Memor. II. i. 321.]

[6 See p. 58.]

[7 Sent to the Marshalsea April 20. He grew old in prison, and died a natural death in the year 1569. Strype, Annals, I. i. 214.]

[8 May 20th, *Feckenham*, late abbot of Westminster, *Watson*, late bishop of Lincoln, *Cole*, late dean of St Paul's, *Chedsey*, late archdeacon of Middlesex, at liberty, as it seems, before, were all sent to the Tower. And the same day, at eight o'clock at night, Dr *Story*, the civilian, was sent to the Fleet. Strype, Annals, I. i. 220.]

[9 He went away privately beyond sea, after some confinement in the Tower, where he was again a prisoner in 1563, perhaps for presuming to sit in the council of Trent. Strype, Annals, I. i. 215.]

[10 The Guises discovered a conspiracy among the French nobles at home, which made them desirous of recalling their army from Scotland for their own protection.]

believe me, there is no one living about whom our friends are wont to discourse more frequently, or with greater interest and respect. Cecil, with whom I dined yesterday at court, Knolleys, and Wroth, desired me to salute you very much in their name. And, what perhaps you would hardly expect, Sir William Petre, when he heard you mentioned, earnestly entreated me to do the same for him.

Give my kind remembrances to the excellent lady your wife, Bullinger, Gualter, Lavater, Gesner, Haller, Simler, Wolfius, Frisius, Herman, Paullus, my friend Julius, his wife, and the little Martyr; to all of whom, and to the whole church and commonwealth of Zurich, I pray and desire every blessing.

Farewell, my father, my father, farewell. Farewell, my most esteemed master in Christ. I commend our church and cause to your prayers. London, May 22, 1560.

Most cordially and sincerely yours,

JOHN JEWEL.

LETTER XXXIV.

BISHOP JEWEL TO PETER MARTYR.
Dated at SALISBURY, *June* 1, 1560.

MUCH health in Christ. I wrote to you, my father, not long since, two days before I left London; and gave my letter, as I was going away, to our friend Heton, that it might be forwarded to you by the first opportunity. Now, since I have come among my people at Salisbury, though there is no diminution in my regard for you, yea, though it is in many respects increased, and is daily increasing, by your very long, and to me most painful, absence; yet my opportunities of letter writing seem not to be what they were some time since. For I am now far distant from the crowd and bustle [of London], and am much less conversant with passing events; and when I am ever so much inclined to write, I cannot meet with a courier who is going your way. However, I will write, whatever it may be; aye, even though it be nothing at all. My letter may be lost on the road, if it should so happen; but my regard, and respect, and affection for you will never perish. The time, I hope, will at length arrive, when we may be able to salute each other in person. Should I ever see that day, and live to welcome you [in England], I shall think that I have lived long enough. This subject is one of great interest to us all; and we do not see[1] what should hinder you, unless perhaps, as I suspect, and as I have sometimes written to you, that Peter and Paul have stopped the way to your return. Woe betide such apostles! Your lectureship, however, is still vacant, and I do not know for whom it should rather be kept open than for yourself. In the mean time every thing there is falling into ruin and decay; for the colleges are now filled with mere boys, and empty of learning.

Smith is gone into Wales, where, they say, he has taken a wife, with the view, I suppose, of refuting all your arguments. However this may be, he boasts of his grey hairs and empty head. He now keeps a victualling house, and gains his livelihood by a hired tavern, despised by our friends and his own; by those who know him, and those who do not; by old and young, by himself, by every one.

Our friend Sidall[2] is a disciple of Harpocrates, and conceals his opinions; so that he is now reckoned neither among the birds nor beasts. He is, as you know, and as I also am convinced, a good sort of man, and one who esteems and loves you. And perhaps, when he sees our forces increased, he will lay aside this dissembling, and join us of his own accord, and

[1] Martyr was invited to return to England in 1561 by the earl of Bedford, to whom he thus wrote in reply: "Now as touching leave to see you again safe and sound in person, for the commodity, as you write, both of your country and my own comfort, I am very sorry that I cannot answer you in such sort as may satisfy both you and myself. Truly if I might have my own will, I would no less serve the church of England than beforetime I have done: howbeit neither mine age nor the strength of my body will any longer endure the same, being not able to endure a voyage so long, so divers, and not altogether easy. Wherefore to the intent that I become not unprofitable both unto you and also to them that be here, it seemeth better for me that I remain where I am."]

[2] See p. 45. Among some of the first subscribers [to the queen's supremacy] was Henry Syddall, a thorough-paced man, who, being a canon of Christ's church, Oxon, had complied in the beginning of king Edward's reign, and was a great zealot the other way under queen Mary, and one of those that were much about archbishop Cranmer at Oxford, when he was induced to recant. His subscription I find again as vicar of Walthamstow in Essex. Strype, Parker, I. 154.]

[ZURICH LETTERS.]

openly come forward. But in mustering an army some one must needs be hindmost.

Some of the Marian bishops are in the tower. The bishop[1] of London is in his old lodging, which he formerly occupied in king Edward's time. When he was conveyed thither, and had arrived in the interior of the prison, where (being a most courteous man, and gentlemanly both in his manners and appearance) he politely saluted the prisoners who were present, and addressed them as his friends and companions; one of them immediately disclaimed this, and cried out, "Do you take me, you brute, for a companion of yours? Go to hell, as you deserve; you will find companions there. As for me, I only slew one individual, and that not without reason; while you have causelessly murdered vast numbers of holy men, martyrs of Christ, witnesses and maintainers of the truth. Besides, I indeed am sorry for what I did, while you are so hardened, that I know not whether you can be brought to repentance." I write this, that you may know in what a state he must be, when even wicked and abandoned men reject and avoid him, and will not endure him in their society.

There is a prevailing report, which is indeed confirmed, both by the common discourse of many persons, and also by letter, that our forces have at length, after a long siege, taken Leith[2] by capitulation, and driven out the French garrison with only the clothes on their backs. There are various rumours respecting the terms, but we have not yet received any certain information. It is now of the utmost consequence that the English and Scots should be united, not only in a political, but also in a religious alliance. Should this take place, as I hope and desire, it will be all well respecting Crito and Glycerium. And I wish that those may not prevent it, who neither wish well to them nor to ourselves. But these matters are as yet only in their infancy, and, so to speak, immature; after a while we shall see all things more clearly. Pamphilus has not yet returned. He was appointed by Glycerium to accompany Crito. He sometimes writes to me when he has

[1 Bonner's first imprisonment was in September 1549, of which the reason was, because he did not publish in a sermon the king's authority during his minority, as he was commanded. Strype, Memor. II. ii. 185.]

[2 The capitulation took place July 5, 1560. For the terms, see Camden's Elizabeth, p. 42.]

an opportunity, and hopes that things will turn out as we wish. Whatever may happen, Crito will occasion no delay.

The Swede is expected with a numerous fleet; he is a powerful prince, with plenty of money, and very liberal in regard to expense. But he resides a long way off, and all the seas are frozen over in the winter, so that he can neither come to us, nor get back again if he did.

May God at length put such an end as we could wish to these disorders in France, and restrain the rage and wickedness of the Guises! By the blessing of God, all is now quiet among us, not only as regards religion, but also the state. The harvest is plenteous, labourers only are wanting. Yet, as the French are said to be arming a fleet, and threatening some mischief or other, lest any danger should arise unexpectedly, as is not improbable, we are raising levies in all quarters, and getting troops in readiness, in case we should require their services. For my own part, however, as times now are, I scarcely think they have sufficient leisure from their own affairs to attend to ours. You have now all our news.

I desist from making any promises respecting my friend Julius. Only let him come; he knows the way hither, and he shall not want any thing that I can give him. But why do I bid him come by himself? Let him rather wait a little while, and come with you. Yet why should I bid him wait, when he ought to have come long since?

Farewell, my father, farewell. I shall one day, I hope, say to you face to face, "My father, how do you do?" Salute in my name that most excellent lady your wife, masters Bullinger, Gualter, Lavater, Frisius, Simler, Gesner, Haller, Wickius, Herman, (if he is still with you,) Julius, his wife, and the little Martyr. We are all so scattered in this dispersion of the nations, that I cannot at all write for certain as to what our brethren are doing. I doubt not however, but that they are piously occupied in the furtherance of the gospel, and that they are mindful of you and of all your friends.

Again, my father, farewell, and pray God that he may make this our present light to be perpetual. Salisbury, June 1, 1560.

Your most attached,

JOHN JEWEL, *Anglus*.

LETTER XXXV.

THOMAS LEVER TO HENRY BULLINGER.

Dated at COVENTRY, *July* 10, 1560.

MUCH health in Christ Jesus. I have received two letters from your reverence, since my return to England; and I have once written to you both concerning religion, and also something about myself; which letter of mine, I learn from your first letter, came safe to hand. In your last from Zurich of the 20th of March, (which however did not reach me in England until the 22nd of June,) you state that various and uncertain reports respecting our affairs are circulating amongst you, but that you are looking for more certain intelligence from ourselves. This then is a true and certain statement which I am now writing, as were also those other things which I wrote last year, both to yourself and the people of Berne; namely, to masters John Haller, and Musculus. The true and sincere doctrine is freely preached throughout England, by those who are known to possess both ability and inclination for this work, by commendatory letters from the queen, or one of the bishops, to authorise the admission of strange preachers into the churches. No discipline is as yet established by any public authority; but the same order of public prayer, and of other ceremonies in the church, which existed under Edward the sixth, is now restored among us by the authority of the queen and parliament; for such is the name of our great council.

In the injunctions, however, published by the queen, after the parliament, there are prescribed to the clergy some ornaments, such as the mass-priests formerly had and still retain. A great number of the clergy, all of whom had heretofore laid them aside, are now resuming similar habits, and wear them, as they say, for the sake of obedience[1]. There are indeed but

[[1] The first bishops that were made, and who were but newly returned out of their exile, as Cox, Grindal, Horn, Sandys, Jewel, Parkhurst, Bentham, upon their first returns, before they entered upon their ministry, laboured all they could against receiving into the church

few of us, who hold such garments in the same abhorrence, as the soldier mentioned by Tertullian[2] did the crown. But we are not ignorant what occasion the papists will take from thence, as a cause of stumbling to the weak. For the prebendaries in the cathedrals, and the parish priests in the other churches, retaining the outward habits and inward feeling of popery, so fascinate the ears and eyes of the multitude, that they are unable to believe, but that either the popish doctrine is still retained, or at least that it will shortly be restored. Many of our parishes have no clergyman, and some dioceses are without a bishop. And out of that very small number who administer the sacraments throughout this great country, there is hardly one in a hundred who is both able and willing to preach the word of God; but all persons are obliged to read only what is prescribed in the books. Thus indeed is the Lord's harvest very abundant among us, but the labourers are very few. Those who were heretofore bishops, with the other leading papists, preferring the supremacy of the pope to the authority of the queen, are deprived of all their honours and emoluments in England. Some[3] of them also have been lately committed to custody and confinement, and it is not yet known what is to become of them.

The gospel is received in Scotland, not indeed universally and by general consent, but yet with great zeal and sincerity by the greater part. And the Scots have now for a long time been trying to drive the French out of Scotland, so that

the papistical habits, and that all the ceremonies should be clean laid aside. But they could not obtain it from the queen and parliament, and the habits were enacted. Then they consulted together what to do, being in some doubt whether to enter into their functions. But they concluded unanimously not to desert their ministry for some rites, that, as they considered, were but a few, and not evil in themselves, especially since the doctrine of the gospel remained pure and entire. Strype, Annals, I. i. 263.]

[2 In his treatise *De Coronâ militis*, (written upon occasion of a donative granted by the emperors Caracalla and Severus to the soldiers, about A.D. 209), in which he defends a soldier, who having refused to place upon his head a garland such as his fellow-soldiers wore, and being brought before the tribune, and asked the reason of his non-compliance, answered, he was a Christian, and therefore could not wear it, it being unlawful for a Christian thus to adopt a pagan custom.]

[3 See note 8, p. 79.]

we are making great preparations for war, and sending a great number of troops to their assistance. There is a harbour in Scotland, which in our language is called Leith: this, fortified with ditches, ramparts, cannon and [other] arms, is in the possession of the French; the English[1] are besieging it. Numbers are slain on both sides, and, as it is said, no quarter is allowed. I have heard, what I suspect to be the case, that such now-a-days are the conditions of a peace among the powers of the world, that if a single prisoner is kept alive by either party, they are altogether violated, but that whatever numbers may be slain on either side, they remain in all their force. And this I gather from the circumstance, that as yet no war has been publicly declared between the French and English, but rather such a peace, as that there is free liberty of trade on both sides; while in the mean time the troops of both nations are perishing in this miserable and hostile conflict in Scotland.

If you wish for any tidings respecting myself, I would have you know, that immediately after my return to England, I travelled through a great part of it, for the sake of preaching the gospel. And there is a city in the middle of England, called Coventry, in which there have always been, since the revival of the gospel, great numbers zealous for evangelical truth; so that in that last persecution under Mary, some were burnt[2] [at the stake], others went into banishment together with myself; the remainder, long tossed about in great difficulty and distress, have at last, on the restoration of pure religion, invited other preachers, and myself in particular, to proclaim the gospel to them at Coventry. After I had discovered, by the experience of some weeks, that vast numbers in this place were in the habit of frequenting the public preaching of the gospel, I consented to their request, that I should settle my wife and family among them; and thus, now for nearly a whole year, I have preached to them without any hindrance, and they have liberally maintained me and my family in this city. For

[1 Lord Grey of Wilton advanced to the attack on Leith, at the head of 6000 English foot, and 1200 horse. Camden's Elizabeth, p. 41.]

[2 Among whom were Robert Glover, and Cornelius Bungey, about Sept. 20, 1555. To these may be added John Careless, who died n prison, July 1, 1556. See Foxe.]

we are not bound to each other, neither I to the townsmen, nor they to me, by any law or engagement, but only by free kindness and love.

My wife has lately borne me a daughter, who is alive and well, together with three other little children, which she had brought me from her late husband. We therefore salute you and yours, and pray for you every happiness in Christ. For when I understood from your letter, that your wife, your children and sons-in-law with their children, were well, it afforded me the same pleasure as if I had been by nature, as I am in affection, one of those your children, whom I pray God in Christ to bless to you, and make happy for ever.

I hear with much satisfaction, that you have written against the sect of the anabaptists: and I do not wonder at your headaches becoming more painful and frequent with your advancing age; but I grieve, when I think upon your years and labours, and pray God, that he may be pleased long to preserve you safe and sound to us and to his church.

Many of us English, who lived together in the same house at Zurich, are now of necessity dispersed all over England, and at a great distance from each other. It is, however, impossible but that we shall all of us retain a grateful remembrance of that exceeding hospitality and beneficence, which Zurich exhibited to us under your patronage, with so much comfort and benevolence and friendly regard. Although therefore I am writing alone and separate from the rest, I must entreat you to offer thanks in all our names, both to the magistrates of the commonwealth, the ministers of the church, and the other good people of Zurich, for the seasonable, agreeable, and so much needed hospitality there afforded to us exiles for the cause of Christ. And I beg you will salute from us in the Lord that good woman Elizabeth, who attended upon us. I entreat you likewise to be so kind as to salute in my name those most pious and learned persons, Peter Martyr, Bernardine Ochinus, R. Gualter, Theodore Bibliander, your very dear sons-in-law[3], Lavater, Zuinglius, and Simler; and also John ab Ulmis, who formerly lived in England, and John Burcher, an Englishman, with the other pious persons among you, known to me in the Lord. It would also be doing me a kindness, if sometime in

[[3] See note 2, p. 30.]

your letters to the people of Berne[1] or Arau[2], you would make mention of me with thanks. I have written, after my poor way, to the ministers and head schoolmasters of both churches, and will shortly write again, God willing. May he grant that we may always be mindful and ready upon all occasions to repay the debts we owe you in Christ! Farewell. Coventry, July 10, 1560.

Yours faithfully in Christ,

THOMAS LEVER.

LETTER XXXVI.

BISHOP JEWEL TO PETER MARTYR.
Dated at SALISBURY, *July* 17, 1560.

MUCH health in Christ. I wrote to you, if I remember right, not long since, on the first of June, respecting the general state of our affairs, as it then was, or at least was reported to be, at the time of writing. You shall now receive the intelligence which is every where spread abroad among the people, and which has this day been sent to me from court.

Matters are all settled respecting Scotland. The French garrison, having sustained from our troops a siege so long and tedious, as if they were only in sport, were at last compelled to surrender[3]. Especial care was taken by our party, to avoid every thing that might have the appearance of undue severity, through the wantonness or rage of the soldiery; so that, with the exception of those skirmishes which occasionally, as usual, took place on both sides, and which could not be without bloodshed, as little of human life was wasted as could have been expected.

[1 In a letter from Lever to the martyr Bradford, he says, "I have seen the places, noted the doctrine and discipline, and talked with the learned men of Argentine, Basil, Zurich, Berne, Louvain, and Geneva. Strype, Memorials, III. i. 404.]

[2 He had been minister of the English congregation at Arau. Strype, Annals, I. i. 153.]

[3 See p. 82, and note 1, p. 86.]

The French[4] king, when he made overtures of peace, promised that he would in future relinquish those titles and armorial[5] bearings of the kings of England, which he had heretofore assumed, together with his own, in right of his Scottish wife, the great[6] niece of Henry the eighth; and that he would be content only with his lilies and ancestral titles. He engaged too, that the government of Scotland should be administered by twelve[7] commissioners, all Scotchmen; and that in case there should arise any dispute about matters of religion or civil polity, the decision thereof should rest with the parliament of the whole kingdom: that only a hundred and twenty French soldiers should be left in all Scotland; and this, not as hostile to the government, but as evidences of the defeat and disgrace they had sustained, should any one hereafter venture to call it in question: that he would have them obey the directions of the twelve commissioners, in whatever they should command. Both sides separated upon these conditions. The fortress of Leith was levelled to the ground by our troops; the French were sent on board the fleet, to be taken home, sorrowful and dejected, and with scarcely the clothes on their backs. I doubt not, my father, but that all this intelligence has already reached you either by messengers, or report; yet I doubt not likewise, but that my relation of these events, even now, will neither be unpleasant nor unacceptable to you.

The Duke[8] of Holstein has returned home after a magnificent reception by us, with splendid presents from the queen,

[4 Francis II. His plenipotentiaries were the bishop of Valence, and count Randau; those of Elizabeth were Secretary Cecil and Dr Wotton.]

[5 The debating of satisfaction for wrongs offered to queen Elizabeth, and about caution for the fifth article (respecting the title and arms of England and Ireland) was referred to another meeting to be holden at London; and if then it could not be agreed, it was to be committed to the catholic king. See Camden's Elizabeth, p. 43.]

[6 Mary, queen of Scots, grand-daughter of Henry's sister Margaret, by James IV. of Scotland.]

[7 The states were to name twenty four persons, of whom the queen of Scots should choose seven, and the states five. Hume.]

[8 The duke was nephew to the king of Denmark, who sent him to be a suitor to the queen, to obtain her for his wife. And this the rather to intercept the Swede, his neighbour, endeavouring the same thing. Strype, Annals, I. i. 296.]

having been elected into the order of the garter, and invested with its golden and jewelled badge.

The Swede[1] is reported to be always coming, and even now to be on his journey, and on the eve of landing; yet, as far as I can judge, he will not stir a foot. Every one here is talking about a peace, I know not upon what terms; and that a general council is expected for settling the affairs of religion. For my own part I neither think that a peace will suit these times, nor that a council will ever come together.

You have now, my father, received all the news we have at present. Farewell, and take care of yourself, that is of the half of my own soul. Salute the excellent lady your wife, masters Bullinger, Gualter, Simler, Lavater, Wolfius, Haller, Gesner, Frisius, Herman, Julius, his wife, and the little Martyr. Salisbury, July 17, 1560.

Yours from my heart,
JOHN JEWEL.

LETTER XXXVII.

JOHN PARKHURST TO HENRY BULLINGER.

Dated at LONDON, *Aug.* 23, 1560.

I AM overwhelmed, my Bullinger, by such a sea of business, that I am compelled to be more brief than I could wish. I make a brief reply, therefore, to your letter, and that in order. I will most willingly shew kindness to Burcher, both for your sake and his own. I wish his wife's character corresponded with his own; but this is for your private ear.

[[1] Eric XIV. son of Gustavus Vasa. About the beginning of September, she [the queen] came to Windsor, and was there every hour in expectation of the king of Sweden's coming; being very shortly looked for at Westminster, where certain works were in hand, and the workmen wrought day and night to finish them against his reception. His business was to court the queen for his wife. But he came not himself, being advised to the contrary, yet his brother [John] the Duke of [Finland] did; and was a passionate advocate for his brother with the queen. Strype, Annals, I. i. 368.]

Gualter has disappointed my expectation, by not having written me a single word. I was at the house of your friend Abel when the packet of letters arrived, but at that time I received none but from yourself and Julius, which I was much surprised at.

Respecting the state of this kingdom as to religion, this is the case. Many pious persons are *quite* satisfied; as for myself, a few things still remain unsatisfactory, but I hope for an improvement. The Scots have made greater progress in true religion in a few months, than we have done in many years. A peace has been agreed upon between the Scots, French, and ourselves, on the surrender of the fortified town of Leith[2]. Abel has informed you of the terms. Calais[3] is not yet recovered by us: indeed nothing of the kind has been attempted.

Salute in my name your excellent wife, sons, daughters, sons-in-law, and all my learned friends. I wish all happiness to your city, and to the whole territory of Zurich. My wife desired me to send her kind remembrances to you all. Farewell. In haste. London, Aug. 23, 1560.

Yours,

JOHN PARKHURST.

LETTER XXXVIII.

BISHOP JEWEL TO PETER MARTYR.

Dated at SALISBURY, *Nov.* 6, 1560.

Much health in Christ. What to write to you at this time, my father, I do not know. For I have very little news, and much less time for writing, as I am now preparing for the assembling my clergy, and the visitation of my diocese; which will be a work of two months. I was on the point of writing to you, I know not what, about a month since; indeed

[2 See p. 86.]

[3 It was taken by the duke of Guise, by treachery, in January, 1558. Its restitution was demanded by queen Elizabeth, by her ambassador Sir Thomas Smith in 1562. Strype, Memor. III. ii. 25; Annals, I. i. 551.]

I had already begun my letter. But when a rumour was every where circulated about you, unfavourable to yourself, painful to us all, and to myself especially most distressing; and this too, not only confirmed by common report, but also by the letters of Grindal and the archbishop of Canterbury, I was, believe me, compelled through grief and anxiety of mind to leave off, and tear up what I had begun. Now, however, since our brethren from Geneva, who have very lately returned among us, relate that all is with you as we desire, I cannot refrain from writing something to you, though in truth I have at this time nothing to write about.

Our church, by the blessing of God, is at length in peace. And no wonder; for those winds which heretofore stirred up the waves, are now admirably confined by Æolus, to prevent their doing any mischief. We are only wanting in preachers; and of these there is a great and alarming scarcity. The schools also are entirely deserted; so that, unless God look favourably upon us, we cannot hope for any supply in future. The existing preachers, who are few in number, those especially who have any ability, are listened to by the people with favour and attention. We found at the beginning of the reign of Elizabeth a large and inauspicious crop of Arians, anabaptists, and other pests, which I know not how, but as mushrooms spring up in the night and in darkness, so these sprung up in that darkness and unhappy night of the Marian times. These, I am informed, and hope it is the fact, have retreated before the light of purer doctrine, like owls at the sight of the sun, and are now no where to be found; or, at least, if any where, they are no longer troublesome to our churches.

That volatile Ubiquitarian[1] doctrine cannot by any means gain footing among us, though there have not been wanting

[[1] The Ubiquitarian controversy was another plague, which our church was likewise fortunate enough to escape. The discussion was one which, naturally enough, grew out of the sacramental dispute; for they who contended for the bodily and local presence of Christ in the eucharist,—whether Romanists or Lutherans,—must also maintain that his body might be in many places at the same instant; and this assertion seems to imply, as a necessary consequence, that his body has the attribute of omnipresence, [or ubiquity, from whence the controversy derived its name]. Le Bas, Life of Jewel, p. 127. See also Mosheim's Institutes, Ed. Soames, Vol. III. p. 379.]

from the first outset those who had the subject much at heart. In the French church, which they now have in London[2], I hear there are some unquiet and turbulent men, who are openly beginning to profess Arianism. May God at length remove these tares from us!

The queen[3], now that our affairs are settled, promises to give us a pure and undebased currency, and is therefore beginning to call in all the base coinage of the late times. There is no further news from Scotland, beyond what I acquainted you with in my last letter, respecting the surrender of the garrison, and the settlement of affairs according to agreement. What Crito is doing, I know not. Pamphilus has not yet returned. As to Glycerium, I wish—, but these things are in the hand of God. May[4], the dean of St Paul's, and intended for the archbishoprick of York, is dead. Dr Horn is to be the bishop of Winchester. Other matters are in the same state as when I last wrote. As for Parkhurst, Sandys, Sampson, Lever, and our other friends, we are so entirely scattered,—not for the dispersion, but, as I hope, for the gathering of nations,—that I now see almost as little of them as yourself. I hear that letters, and some other things have been brought over for me from Germany, but I know not whence, or from whom, though I suspect, from yourself;

[2 In Threadneedle street, which they had either borrowed or hired, belonging to the dean and chapter of Windsor, and which they have to this day; being part of St Anthony's hospital dissolved. Strype, Annals, I. i. 175. See also Strype's Life of Grindal.]

[3 Francis Alen, September 3, 1560, writes to the Earl of Shrewsbury, "There is like to be a calling downe of the base money, I understande, very shortlye; and the quene's majestie hath sworne that the daye and tyme shall be kept secrete to herselfe, and that fewe besyds shall knowe. So as the very tyme, whensoever it chaunceth, will be so shorte and sodeyne, that men are like to have small warninge of the matter." The persons who undertook and executed the gigantic task of reforming the debased coinage of England were Daniel Ulstat and Co. of Antwerp, as appears by a letter of theirs to Sir Thomas Gresham, dated at Antwerp, July 8, 1560: see Burgon's Life and Times of Sir Thomas Gresham, Vol. I. p. 354, &c, and Strype, Annals, I. i. 396, who gives a full account of this proceeding.]

[4 May died Aug. 8. He had been a counsellor to king Edward, one of his visitors, and one of those that sat in the court of requests in his reign. Strype, Annals, I. i. 306.]

so that every thing will appear tedious to me, till I come to know what it is. As for myself, excepting that you are so far distant, I am in other respects very well.

Farewell, my father, farewell, the better half of my heart. I would write at this time to that most accomplished man, Bullinger, were I not prevented by business. He must forgive me for the present: I will hereafter write to him more at length, whatever it may be. Salute him, I pray you, most dutifully in my name, as also Gualter, Simler, Gesner, Haller, Wickius, Lavater, Zuinglius, Wolfius, Frisius. I dearly love them in the Lord, and all that belong to them. I am surprised that my friend Julius has neither written to me, nor come to you. I desire his welfare just as much as if he were my own brother. If he doubts my friendship, let him put it to the proof. To him likewise, and his wife, and first and foremost, or rather before all first and foremost, whether men or women, salute the excellent lady your wife, my little Martyr, and Herman. Again, my father, farewell. Salisbury, Nov. 6, 1560.

Your most attached,

JOHN JEWEL, *Anglus.*

LETTER XXXIX.

BISHOP PARKHURST, TO JOHN WOLFIUS, JOSIAH SIMLER, AND LEWIS LAVATER.

Dated at NORWICH, *March* 9, 1561.

SINCE the same city, the same fellowship in study, and a mutual friendship equally binds you together; and since likewise the same profession and love of our common religion unites you yet more closely, you will pardon me, my most delightful companions and very dear friends, or rather impute it to the engagements by which I am now distracted, if you, whom these attractions already bind together, are combined also in one and the same letter. For if there is any truth in the old proverb, that a friend is a second self, and if there is that power in friendship, to knit together, and form as it were one man out of many, however naturally different from each other, I shall seem entirely, though writing but one letter to this united triumvirate, as if I were addressing the same individuals in separate letters.

To reply therefore at once, and as it were with one hand, to your three most copious letters to me, I must return you my thanks for your friendly congratulations; and I would not have you esteem them less, because they are not offered to each of you individually; for love is no more disturbed on this account, even if the duty of writing is somewhat contracted. Meanwhile you will with your wonted kindness divide among you this letter, common to you all, as a pledge and memorial of my grateful regard for you, just as if I had separately and expressly replied to each, as my duty required. Hereafter, when greater leisure from business shall be afforded me, I will try, God willing, if I can in any way express how much I value my Zurich friends, that is, my ancient hosts; not by any means intending, in this kind of duty which belongs to friendship, to yield to any of you, although in other things I would willingly acknowledge myself inferior. And let this suffice for me to have written to you, on account of the great pressure of my engagements; although it is painful to break off one's converse with such most agreeable companions. Take it, I pray you, in good part. I ardently wish that your christian kindness may daily increase more and more, and that you may greatly prosper in the Lord. Farewell. In haste.

Norwich, March 9, 1561.

I thank you, my Josiah, for the book of Bullinger, which you translated into Latin, and sent me. My wife salutes you all.

     Yours,

       JOHN PARKHURST,

        [Bishop] of Norwich.

LETTER XL.

BISHOP JEWEL TO JOSIAH SIMLER.

Dated at LONDON, *May* 4, 1561.

Much health. O my Josiah! what thanks shall I give you now? That little book of yours, so piously and learnedly written at first, and then so elegantly and opportunely translated by you, was on both accounts most acceptable to me. Happy you, upon whom is bestowed such ability, and talent, and leisure, for occupations of this kind. As for me, since I am unable to do this, it is right that I should do what I can. Go on, my Josiah, as you do, and long have done, to your great credit, to dedicate your mind, adorned and furnished as it is, to the service of God.

There was no occasion for your writing so seriously about our friend Julius; for I know him, and he me. I commend, however, your motives and your kindness, in so cordially interesting yourself on behalf of your friend; and I have no doubt but that he will be provided for by us.

I confess, my Josiah, that I have been longer silent than I ought, or than I wished. But the magnitude of the affairs in which I am constantly engaged, often takes the pen out of my hands. For though I enjoy all other requisites, life, health, and strength, yet I can scarcely ever find leisure for writing. And at this very time[1] Julius himself can bear witness how much I am occupied.

I am just now going from London on my way home. My horse has been waiting for me for some time; wherefore I shall leave all the news, and the history of our affairs to Julius. Whatever he may say, though he may perhaps invent something of his own, as people generally do when they return from abroad, yet your kindness must lead you to regard him as a good man; and should he conduct himself as such, you will not be wrong.

[[1] This sentence will not bear a literal translation.]

Farewell, my Josiah. Salute in my name your wife, and Herman, and Frisius, that excellent and accomplished young man, and take in good part this trifling present. Farewell. In haste. London, May 4, 1561.

Yours from my heart,
JOHN JEWEL. *Anglus.*

LETTER XLI.

BISHOP PARKHURST TO HENRY BULLINGER.

Dated at THETFORD, *May* 23, 1561.

HAD not the courier been at hand, my very dear Bullinger, I should not at this time have replied to your letter; for I have now less leisure than ever, being occupied whole days together in the discovery and extirpation of errors and irregularities. I have no certain information respecting Scotland; but what I have, Julius will communicate. He will serve instead of a packet of letters to you all. My wife salutes you. Farewell. May 23, at Thetford, on my visitation.

You tell me that you have been writing concerning councils, and that you have sent me two books, which I have not yet seen. I hope however that they will come to hand. Should your friend Christopher come to England, I will shew him all the kindness in my power. Julius has been with me, and I wrote to Oxford on his behalf. I hear that the son of your standard-bearer is with the Earl of Bedford. When I come to London, I will send for him, and treat a Zuricher after the Zurich fashion. I wish every happiness to all at Zurich. My wife salutes you all. Again farewell. I wrote to you in the month of March.

Yours,
JOHN PARKHURST,
[Bishop] of Norwich.

LETTER XLII.

BISHOP PARKHURST TO HENRY BULLINGER.
Dated at LUDHAM, *Sept.* 1, 1561.

YOUR very friendly letter, most learned Bullinger, written on the 23rd of June, I received on the last day of August. I cannot easily express how much encouragement it afforded me, how it animated me to be active in my office and strong in the Lord. Urge me on, I pray you, from time to time with incitements of this kind: spurs must be applied to a slow-paced horse. May the Lord convert or crush the five satrapies of the Philistines, who do not cease from troubling the godly! I am glad to hear that Burcher[1] is at last divorced from that shameless harlot: may he be happy and prosperous in his second marriage! I am now writing to him about himself and his affairs. You will learn the rest from himself. I wish the Ubiquitarians a better mind, if indeed they have a mind at all; being both out of their mind and without a mind; and persons over whom you[2] and Martyr will gain an easy conquest. But I well know the nature of these boasters. They will not yield even when conquered; but unless they repent, Christ will overcome them and Satan bind them. May the Lord strengthen with his Spirit and long preserve in safety the Palatine of the Rhine and the Hessian!

Julius will tell you all other matters, as he was not only an ear but an eye-witness of many of them. Salute again in my name your good wife, sons, daughters, sons-in-law, masters Martyr, Gesner, Wolfius and all. My wife salutes you all. In haste. Ludham[3], Sept. 1, 1561.

Yours,

JOHN PARKHURST,

[Bishop] of Norwich.

[1 See p. 90.]

[2 Bullinger's dispute with Brentius about the doctrine of ubiquity began this year. The contest lasted two years. See note 1, p. 92.]

[3 In Norfolk. Here was formerly a grange belonging to the abbey of St Bene't, the house connected with which, after the reign of Mary, became the residence of the diocesans.]

I have given directions to all the ministers of the word throughout Suffolk and Norfolk, to procure either in Latin or English your sermons[4] on the Apocalypse. For John Daus, a good and learned man, and schoolmaster in the town of Ipswich, has translated them into our mother tongue. Again farewell, both to yourself and the people of Zurich.

LETTER XLIII.

BISHOP JEWEL TO PETER MARTYR.

Dated at SALISBURY, *Feb.* 7, 1562.

MUCH health in Christ. Your letter, my father, was most gratifying, not only as coming from you, from whom every thing ought to be, and is, most agreeable; but also, as most lucidly describing the revival of religion in France; and because, when I read it, and perceived you were so near[5], I fancied that I heard you yet nearer to me, and that I was enjoying your conversation. For though the affairs of France were made known to us by report, as usual, and by the couriers, yet the information seemed both more certain and

[4 This year, 1561, came forth an hundred sermons upon the Apocalypse, made by Henry Bullinger, chief pastor of Zurich; translated out of Latin into English by John Daus of Ipswich, dedicated to Sir Thomas Wentworth, Lord Wentworth, lieutenant of the county of Suffolk; set forth and allowed according to the queen's order appointed in her injunctions. Strype, Annals, I. i. 383.]

[5 In a letter from Peter Martyr to bishop Parkhurst, dated August 23, 1561, he writes, "I am called into France to deal in conference as touching religion; safe conduct is brought hither in the name of the king and of the queen mother, both subscribed and sealed. And through the letters of the king of Navarre, I am called with great entreaty, so as it hardly seems that my journey can be deferred. And seeing the matter is great and full of danger, I heartily desire your lordship that you will commend the same and myself earnestly in your prayers to God." Martyr remained in France during the conferences at Poissy, between the papists and the French protestants, and returned to Zurich on Nov. 21. See his correspondence, Lett. 49—61, and also Thuanus, II. 117—126, and Spon. I. 307—309, for a full account of the proceedings of the conference above referred to.]

far more agreeable, when communicated by yourself, and more especially, as I knew you to have had much to do with them. As to what you write, that those at the head of affairs are altogether desirous of some alteration in religion, not so much from a zeal and love of godliness, as from a conviction of the ridiculous absurdities of the papists, and that the people can be kept to their duty in no other way; whatever may be the principle, and whatever the reason of the change, only let Christ be preached, *whether in pretence or in truth, and I therein do rejoice, yea, and will rejoice.* That disputation of yours, however, has of necessity much advanced the gospel, and discomfited the adversaries. But as to your statement, that a kind of *interim* and farrago of religion is aimed at by some parties, may God prevent it! I know that all changes of importance in the state are offensive and disagreeable, and that many things are often tolerated by sovereigns by reason of the times. And this at first, probably, was not attended with inconvenience; but now that the full light of the gospel has shone forth, the very vestiges of error must, as far as possible, be removed together with the rubbish, and, as the saying is, with the very dust. And I wish we could effect this in respect to that linen surplice: for as to matters of doctrine, we have pared every thing away to the very quick, and do not differ from your doctrine by a nail's breadth; for as to the Ubiquitarian[1] theory there is no danger in this country. Opinions of that kind can only gain admittance where the stones have sense. Must I tell you that I thank you for your *Orothetes?*[2] I doubt not but that the individual you mention, if he is wise, will think himself much indebted to you. He will perhaps, however, summon courage, and de-

[1 See note 1, p. 92.]

[2 Peter Martyr had composed a dialogue upon this [the Ubiquitarian] question; in which he introduced Jewel, under the name of *Palæmon*, as moderator between two disputants; the one, an Ubiquitarian, under the name of *Pantachus;* the other, an orthodox thinker, relative to the circumscription of Christ's humanity, under the name of *Orothetes*. Pantachus may signify an Ubiquitarian, from $\pi\alpha\nu\tau\alpha\chi o\hat{v}$, *every where;* Orothetes, ($\dot{o}\rho o\theta\acute{\epsilon}\tau\eta s$) in like manner, implies a *settler of boundaries;* in other words, an advocate for the doctrine that the human body of Christ is circumscribed within limits. Le Bas, Life of Jewel, pp. 127, 128. See Peter Martyr's Epistles, Lett. 49.]

fend his *Pantachus*, and prepare himself for a reply, and make his exceptions both against yourself and your *Palæmon*. I disclaim the praise which you so bountifully bestow upon me, as I am aware that it rather belongs to yourself, and to yourself alone. Yet it is sweet, my father, as the saying is, to receive praise from one who is himself commended. Your commendation was not so much an evidence of your judgment, as of your love; and, although I cannot deserve it in other respects, I certainly shall by my affection for you.

The Marian bishops[3] are still confined in the tower, and are going on in their old way. If the laws were but as rigorous now as in the time of Henry, they would submit themselves without difficulty. They are an obstinate and untamed set of men, but are nevertheless subdued by terror and the sword.

We have lately published an apology[4] for the change of religion among us, and our departure from the church of Rome. I send you the book, though it is hardly worth sending to such a distance. It is faulty in many places, as is almost every thing that is printed in this country: such is the negligence of our printers.

Our queen has fully made up her mind not to send any representative to the council, as to the existence or locality of which we are totally ignorant: certainly, if it is held any where, or has any being at all, it must be very secret and obscure. We are now thinking about publishing[5] the reasons which have induced us to decline attendance. I am fully persuaded, for my part, that no effectual progress can be made at the present time by these assemblies and discussions;

[3 See p. 79.]

[4 This was the celebrated *Apologia Ecclesiæ Anglicanæ*, a work recommended to bishop Jewel by the archbishop (Parker) and his colleagues, to vindicate the church of England before all the world, for her departure from the bishop of Rome, and for her rejection of his pretended authority, and for what was done in reforming religion. See Strype, Annals, I. i. 424, and Parker, I. 197, where is preserved a congratulatory letter from Peter Martyr to Jewel on the occasion of this work.]

[5 This design Jewel afterwards accomplished in the form of a letter to a Venetian gentleman by the name of Scipio, with whom he had become acquainted at Padua.]

and that God will not employ such means for the propagation of the gospel.

The queen, to our great sorrow, still remains unmarried, nor is it yet known what is her intention. I think however, you have long since been aware of my suspicions on the subject. The Swede[1], a most constant and assiduous suitor, has very lately been dismissed; and now he has received his refusal, threatens, as I hear, to look towards Scotland; that since he cannot settle among us, he may at least establish himself in our neighbourhood.

There is a certain noble lady, the lady Margaret[2], a niece of Henry the eighth, and one who is beyond measure hostile to religion, more violent indeed than even queen Mary herself. The crown, it is surmised, will descend to her son[3], a young man of about eighteen, should any thing unhappily happen to Elizabeth, which God forbid! The husband of this woman, the Scottish Lenox, has within these few days been committed to the tower. The son they say is either carried away by his mother, or has taken refuge in Scotland. There are, as is usually the case, various reports respecting him. The queen[4] of Scotland is, as you know, unmarried, so that a matrimonial alliance may possibly be formed between them. However this be, it is believed that the papists are planning some scheme or other, and expecting something, I know not what, no less than the Jews do their Messiah.

The pope's nuncio[5] is still loitering in Flanders; for he cannot yet obtain a safe-conduct to come over to England. The bishop of Aquila[6], Philip's ambassador, a clever and crafty old fox, and formed for intrigue, is exerting himself in his

[1 See note 1, p. 90.]

[2 Margaret Douglas, daughter of Margaret, sister of Henry the Eighth, by Douglas, Earl of Angus, her second husband.]

[3 Lord Darnley, her son by Matthew Stuart, earl of Lenox, descended from Robert Stuart, the next successor to Robert Bruce, king of Scotland. He was afterwards the unhappy husband of Mary, queen of Scots.]

[4 Mary, queen of Scots, then the widow of Francis the second, of France, who died in 1560.]

[5 The abbot of Martinengo. Strype, Annals, I. i. 166.]

[6 This bishop instigated the conspiracy of Arthur Pole and others against queen Elizabeth in 1562. Strype, Annals, I. i. 557.]

behalf as much as he can; at least, that he may have an audience, that he may not have come so far to no purpose: for he hopes that something, I know not what, may be effected at a single conference.

There is a noble young lady, the lady Catharine[7], daughter of the duke of Suffolk, of the blood royal, and as such expressly mentioned in his will by Henry the eighth, as fourth in succession in case any thing should occur. The earl of Hertford, son of the duke of Somerset, has a son by her, born, as many think, out of wedlock, but as the parties themselves declare, in lawful marriage; for that they made a private contract between themselves, and were married by a Romish priest in the presence of a few witnesses. This affair has much disturbed the minds of many persons; for if this marriage is a legal one, the son now born will be brought up with the hope of succeeding to the crown. O how wretched are we, who cannot tell under what sovereign we are to live! God will, I trust, long preserve Elizabeth to us in life and safety, and that will satisfy us. Do you, my father, pray God for the preservation of our church and state.

Farewell, my father, farewell, my pride. Salute in my name your wife, masters Bullinger, Gualter, Lavater, Zuinglius, Haller, Wickius, Gesner, Frisius, and Wolfius, together with Julius, his wife, and my little Martyr. Salisbury, Feb. 7, 1562. From England.

Your most attached,
JOHN JEWEL, *Anglus*.

[[7] Younger sister to the Lady Jane Grey, and grand-daughter of Mary, sister of Henry the eighth. She had been married to Lord Herbert, son of the earl of Pembroke; but having been divorced from that nobleman, she made a private marriage with the earl of Hertford, son of the Protector. Elizabeth committed them both to the tower, where he lay nine years, till the death of his wife, by freeing Elizabeth from all fears, procured him his liberty. Their imprisonment was probably lengthened by a book written by John Hales about this time, and which favoured the Lady Catharine's succession to the throne. Her life was apparently shortened by her imprisonment. The marriage was not established till 1566, when, the priest being produced, and other circumstances agreeing, a jury at common law found it a good marriage. See some very interesting letters on this subject in Ellis's Original letters illustrative of English History. Second series, Vol. II. p. 272—290.]

P. S. Queen Elizabeth has restored all our gold and silver coinage to its former value, and rendered it pure and unalloyed; a truly royal act, and which you will wonder could have been effected in so short a time.

LETTER XLIV.

BISHOP JEWEL TO HENRY BULLINGER.

Dated at SALISBURY, *Feb.* 9, 1562.

MUCH health. Scarcely any thing, most illustrious and esteemed master in Christ, now remains for me to write to you about. For I have carefully detailed all matters necessary to mention, and which occurred to me as I was writing, in my letter to Peter Martyr. My regard, however, and affection for yourself will not allow me to leave you unremembered, that you may at least know that I am still alive, and that I still retain a grateful recollection of the many and great favours I have received from you. As for Parkhurst, Sandys, Lever, Aylmer, and Samson, we have not seen each other these two years. I doubt not however, but that they all entertain the regard they ought to do, both towards yourself, your family, and friends.

We have no news from Scotland, except that religion is most favourably received, firmly maintained, and daily making progress in that country. They say, however, that the queen[1] of Scots still retains her mass. God will, I trust, some time

[1 When the queen attempted to celebrate mass in her own chapel of Holyrood-house, a violent mob assembled, and it was with the utmost difficulty that the Lord James Stuart and some other persons of high distinction could appease the tumult. Randolph wrote to Cecil, Sept. 12, 1561. "Her mass is terrible in all men's eyes. The erle of Cassilis said unto myself that he wolde never here any moe. I know not yet what mischief it may worke." Mary attempted to allay these ferments by promising to take the advice of the states in religious matters; and in the mean time, to punish with death any alteration of the religion which she found generally established on her arrival in Scotland, which took place on Aug. 19, 1561. Hist. of Scotland.]

open her eyes: for in other respects she is, it is said, not badly disposed. I wish she would entirely lay aside her high spirit and Lorrain feelings.

With us all things are quiet. Some few of the bishops, who were furious in the late Marian times, cannot as yet in so short a time for very shame return to their senses. They are therefore confined[2] in the tower, lest their contagion should infect others. The pope both in public and private is plotting mischief to the utmost of his power. Fourteen months since he sent a nuncio[3] to queen Elizabeth. But as he cannot yet be admitted into England, he is still loitering in Flanders. They still hope that something may be done; for that all their roots of folly are not yet plucked up, and there are still remaining some persons whom they doubt not to belong to their party. But why do I tell you of these things, which, as I said just now, I have more fully related to Peter? Since our friend Julius left England, I have not once seen that young townsman of yours, master John Schneider; nor is it to be wondered at, as we are so far distant from each other. I heard however, some months since, that he was very comfortably situated; but should he stand in need of any thing, and I become acquainted with his plans, I will take care that nothing shall be wanting to him on my part: for I owe this, both to your kindness, and to the state of Zurich; and I acknowledge the debt. I am rather surprised that our friend Burcher has not arrived here before this time; for he wrote me word that he was coming, and from his letter he appeared to be already on the road. I take a great interest in him, and thank you in his name.

May God preserve you all, and especially thee, my father, and your church and commonwealth; and should there be any who wish you evil, may he grant him a short life and little ability for mischief. I would write more, if more subjects occurred to me worthy of being recorded at such a distance.

Salute that excellent woman your wife, masters Gualter, Josiah Simler, Lavater, Zuinglius, Haller, Gesner, Wolfius, Wickius, Frisius, Henry Bullinger your son, that excellent youth. Though none of our friends are with me, yet I hesitate

[[2] See p. 79.]
[[3] See note 5, p. 102; and Camden's Elizabeth, p. 55.]

not to greet you in the name of all; for I know that they regard you with the respectful deference they ought. Farewell, my father, and most esteemed master; and if I either am any thing, or have any power, think it all your own. Salisbury, Feb. 9, 1562.

Your most devoted,
JOHN JEWEL, *Anglus.*

LETTER XLV.

BISHOP JEWEL TO JOSIAH SIMLER.

Dated at SALISBURY, *Feb.* 10, 1562.

MUCH health in Christ. What, my Josiah, shall I now write to you? For I have already detailed all the news that has occurred, and some, possibly, that has not occurred, in the letters which I wrote to Bullinger and to Peter Martyr. But a repetition of the same dish is, you know, fatal; and it would be impertinent to write about things now become antiquated and obsolete. Shall I then, (say you,) hear nothing from you? Has John then nothing to write to Josiah? Jewel to Simler? A dear friend to a dear friend? I will certainly write, were it only that you should know that I am still alive, and that I bear you and all yours constantly before my eyes; and that no intervals either of time or place can ever remove from my mind those most agreeable recollections of Josiah [*Josietatis tuæ*]. As for your thanking me with respect to our friend Julius, I must thank you, in my turn, for his own sake. I indeed desire, and wish well to my Julius, and profess myself ready to afford him any assistance, as far as my slender means will allow. And I must candidly acknowledge this to be his due, both on his own account, and more especially for the sake of Peter [Martyr]. As for yourself, my very dear Josiah, and how greatly I am indebted for all your kindness to me, I shall say nothing. This only would I have you know, that from the time I first became acquainted with you, I ever have been, am, and shall be yours.

Farewell, my very dear and best friend, farewell. Salute your wife, and her sisters, and mother, Bullinger, Gualter, Lavater, Wolfius, Zuinglius, Haller, Wickius, Frisius. Again my Josiah, farewell. Salisbury, Feb. 10, 1562.

Yours in the Lord,

JOHN JEWEL, *Anglus.*

LETTER XLVI.

BISHOP PARKHURST TO HENRY BULLINGER.

Dated at LUDHAM, *April 28, 1562.*

HEALTH to you in Christ, most renowned Bullinger. You accuse my countrymen here of ingratitude, because they never write to you. And I am afraid that you will charge me with the same neglect, for not having written to you at the last fair. My Bullinger, lay any thing to my charge rather than ingratitude. Believe me, I had rather not be at all, than be ungrateful. You must impute my not writing to illness, and that a very dangerous one; and not to myself. Can I indeed be forgetful of my Zurich friends? Indeed I cannot, *dum memor ipse mei, dum spiritus hos reget artus.* And that you might not think I had forgotten you, (since I was unable to write through illness), I sent you a small present. Whenever I shall have paid my first fruits, and extricated myself from debt, you shall know who and what kind of a man is your friend Parkhurst.

As for my brother bishops, and others whom you accuse of ingratitude, and not without reason, I shall handle them severely enough, and *authoritatively* enough, when I see them, (although they have said enough in favour of *authority*). Nor shall I cease writing to them in the mean time; for I have an amanuensis, who can write English, but not Latin. Meanwhile, my good friend, speak well of my countrymen, although they deserve to be ill spoken of.

I thank you for the book which you have sent me, and which contains, as you say, your last winter's lucubrations against Brentius[1]. But I have not yet received it, though I hope to receive it shortly. May the Lord open the eyes of Brentius and all the Lutherans, lest in so great a light they should be overwhelmed with darkness!

I have not yet seen the son of your standard-bearer, Fabricius. In three days' time I shall send for him to Norwich; for he probably declines coming to me without an invitation. He will arrive most welcome, nor shall he leave me altogether without a present. If but a Zurich dog should come over to me (though I am not acquainted with any except Gualter's Wartley) I would make the most of him, and not treat him after dog-fashion.

Thus briefly [have I replied] to your two letters. Religion is in the same state among us as heretofore; a state, I say, not altogether to be thought lightly of. But I hope for an improvement at the approaching convocation. There are in England many good and zealous men; there are many too cold, and not a few lukewarm, whom the Lord[2] *will spue out of his mouth*. But, to be plain with you, I fear many evils are hanging over our heads. For almost all are covetous, all love gifts. There is no truth, no liberality, no knowledge of God. Men have broken forth to curse and to lie, and murder, and steal, and commit adultery. And what Empedocles[3] said of his Agrigentines, I may also say of my English: The English indulge in pleasures, as if they were to die to morrow; while they build, as if they were to live always. But God grant that we may repent from our inmost soul!

Fare thee well, my most delightful Bullinger. Salute in my name your excellent wife, sons and daughters, all your

[[1] Or Brentzen, the great patron of the Ubiquitarian doctrine. Calvin thus writes to Bucer concerning him: *Non tenes quid inter alia scripserit Brentius, Christum, dum in præsepi jaceret, gloriosum in cœlo fuisse, etiam secundum corpus.* Calv. Bucero, p. 49. col. 2. Epistolæ. Op. vol. IX. It should be added, however, that on looking into the statements of Brentius, it appears hardly fair not to have given a fuller explanation of his views on this subject.]

[[2] Rev. iii. 16.]

[[3] This saying is attributed to Empedocles by Diogenes Laertius; but by Ælian to Plato. See Bayle.]

learned sons-in-law, the magistrates, and all my friends. I pour forth prayers to God night and day in behalf of your republic. Again farewell. My wife salutes you all. In haste. Ludham, April 28, 1562.

Yours from my heart,

JOHN PARKHURST.

[Bishop] of Norwich.

LETTER XLVII.

BISHOP PARKHURST TO JOSIAH SIMLER
AND LEWIS LAVATER.

Dated at LUDHAM, *April* 29, 1562.

You will learn from master Gualter the reason of my not having written to you last fair. Religion is making a favourable progress both in England and Scotland. There are very few things which I dare object to. We hope for some improvement at the approaching meeting of convocation. It is the inconsistency of the lives of the English with the gospel, that alone displeases me. The gospel was never preached among us more sincerely or with greater zeal. May the Lord give us his Spirit, that we may follow the things of the Spirit, and mortify the deeds of the flesh!

Our queen will shortly make a progress to York, whither also the queen of Scotland will repair. A sheep in Essex has lately discovered a murderer, like the crows in Switzerland. From whence comes that Tilman Hellhouse?[4] Perhaps from that infernal abode whence he appears to derive his name. I commend the people of the Grisons, for not acknowledging

[[4] The true name of the person was Tilman Heshusius, a divine of the Confession of Augsburg. He appears to have been of a morose and turbulent character, in consequence of which he was repeatedly banished from the cities where he had taken up his residence. He wrote commentaries on the Psalms, on Isaiah, and on the Epistles of St Paul. His death took place in 1588. See Bayle and Moreri.]

antichrist as their father. I will write to Froschover respecting the works of Œcolampadius. It must be your business to translate into Latin such of them as are written in German, just as you, my Josiah, did last year, when, to the great advantage of all students, you translated into Latin the books of Bullinger against the anabaptists and the articles[1] of Bavaria.

Salute in my name those most honourable ladies, your wives, Zuinglius, Wolfius, Haller, Wickius, Frisius, Pellican, Guldebeckius, all the Bullingers with all their wives, and lastly, all my Zurich friends. Farewell, most excellent friends, and continue to love me, as you do. I have not as yet sent any thing to you, Lavater; but I will next winter, God willing, if not in the course of this summer. Farewell. In haste. Ludham, April 29, 1562. The Lord preserve all the people of Zurich! My wife salutes you all.

Yours under whatever circumstances,
JOHN PARKHURST,
[Bishop] of Norwich.

LETTER XLVIII.

BISHOP PARKHURST TO HENRY BULLINGER.

Dated at LUDHAM, *May* 31, 1562.

HEALTH to you, most courteous Bullinger. I received your book against Brentius on the 16th of May, but have not yet

[[1] Melancthon also wrote "answers to the impious articles of the Bavarian inquisition," in August 1559, and in his dying moments wished to have them considered as the confession of his faith. His work is entitled "Responsiones scriptæ a Philippo Melancthone ad impios articulos Bavaricæ inquisitionis." See Melancth. Op. Omn. Vol. I. p. 360. In the dedication to the duke of Bavaria, Melancthon speaks of his desire to answer these articles, "quia insidiæ multæ sunt in illis quæstionibus, quæ sunt tanquam Sphyngis ænigmata." The articles were thirty-one, all of them searching questions; seemingly well calculated to detect the slightest trace of the principles of the Reformers.]

read it, as I gave it to my bookseller to be bound. But I will read it in a few days, as soon as my Norwich bookseller shall have sent it back; and I thank you very much for it. Send me always, I pray you, your very learned lucubrations: you can do nothing more agreeable to me. Story[2], that little man of law and most impudent papist, has been arrested, as I understand, in the west of England, in his barrister's robes. Fabricius came to me on the 15th of May, and I treat him as a Zuricher, that is, as my ownself. I am very sorry that he cannot make a longer stay with me, for I would rather keep him with me some months, aye, some years, than some days. I converse with him in Latin, English, and (what you will be surprised at) in German. He is astonished also that I can speak German so well.

The dizziness in my head has not yet left me, but is somewhat better. You will hear the news from Gualter. I wrote towards the end of April a letter to yourself, masters Martyr, Gesner, Gualter, Lavater, Simler, Julius, and Froschover, which I hope you have received. Master Walter Haddon, a learned and pious man, dined with me three days since. He desired to be kindly remembered to you, and to master Martyr and others. Salute all your friends in my name. I wish all happiness to all my Zurich friends.

Farewell, very dear Bullinger, and love me, as you do, and pray to God for me. In haste. Ludham, May 25, 1562. My wife salutes you all.

I have sealed this letter on the last day of May 1562.

Yours,

JOHN PARKHURST,

[Bishop] of Norwich.

[[2] See p. 79. He was afterwards condemned and executed as a traitor. Strype, Annals, I. i. 115.]

LETTER XLIX.

BISHOP COX TO PETER MARTYR.

Dated at LONDON, *August* 5, 1562.

Too long an interval seems to me to have elapsed, since we have mutually addressed each other by letter; though I must fain acknowledge the receipt of letters *from* you, since I have written any thing *to* you. Meanwhile, however, I derive much gratification both from yourself and others, in that you are so diligently and unweariedly labouring in the Lord's vineyard, for the advancement and edification of the church of God in this wicked age. I now and then receive most agreeable intelligence of your labours, to my great delight and advantage. I have lately been employed in your book on Judges, which you most kindly sent to me; and I am waiting for the commentaries which you promised on the books of Kings, that I may often hold intercourse with my friend Peter, as long as I am able to range at large among his writings. It is not in my power to estimate your kindness towards me: meanwhile, however, I have sent you twenty crowns by master Springham[1], as a small testimony of my gratitude. I know that you will take it in good part. If you wish for any information respecting our affairs,—when we consider the temper and fickleness of mankind, when we regard either the contempt of the word [of God] or the neglect of a religious life, we can hardly dare to expect a long continuance of the gospel in these parts. There is every where an immense number of papists, though for the most part concealed: they have been quiet hitherto, except that they are cherishing their errors in their secret assemblies, and willingly shut their ears against the hearing of the word. When however we reflect upon the infinite goodness of God, which has restored us to our native land, and given his word free course, and committed to us the ministry thereof, we take

[1 Richard Springham was a merchant of London, a contributor to the afflicted gospellers, temp. queen Mary. Strype, Memorials, III. i. 224.]

courage, and cherish a firm hope that we shall not again be forsaken by so kind a Father. Let us therefore continue to serve him with a courageous and strong mind, casting all our care and the success of our affairs upon him.

The heads[2] of our popish clergy are still kept in confinement. They are treated indeed with kindness, but relax nothing of their popery. Others are living at large, scattered about in different parts of the kingdom, but without any function, unless perhaps where they may be sowing the seeds of impiety in secret. Our neighbours the Scots, thank God! are happily furthering the gospel. The papists are wonderfully raising their spirits, since the disorders in France. May God of his accustomed goodness turn all things to the good of those who love him! may he defend his own people, and shortly break in pieces the fury of his enemies! Amen. We are anxiously desirous to learn what is going on in your parts, and especially in reference to the kingdom of Christ. May the Lord Jesus preserve you to us very long in safety! Salute in my name master Henry Bullinger, a man worthy of all possible regard. I and my wife salute you and yours. London, Aug. 5, 1562.

Your brother in Christ,

RICHARD COX,

Bishop of Ely.

No one has as yet crushed the furious Hosius[3].

[2 See p. 79.]
[3 A cardinal, sent by Pius IV. to engage the emperor Ferdinand to continue the council of Trent, where he was employed as legate, to open and preside at the council. His chief works are, 1. *Confessio catholicæ fidei*, said to have been reprinted, in various languages, thirty-four times. 2. *De communione sub utraque specie*. 3. *De sacerdotum conjugio*. 4. *De missa vulgari lingua celebranda*. He died in 1579. In a letter from Cox to Cecil, from Downham, dated Dec. 28, 1563, the bishop says, "Hosius' bokes flye abrode in all corners, *unica gloriatio omnium papistarum*, who swarme in all corners, saying and doing almost what they lyste." MS. Lansd. 6, 87.]

LETTER L.

BISHOP JEWEL TO HENRY BULLINGER.

Dated at SALISBURY, *Aug.* 14, 1562.

Your letter written at Zurich on the 5th of March has but lately been delivered to me; and though a little scolding and querulous, it was nevertheless very gratifying, not only as coming from you, all of whose writings and conversation have always been so much esteemed by me, but also, as so earnestly claiming the performance of my duty, and stirring up my negligence and remissness in writing. But, my father and much esteemed master, although, perhaps, I write to you less frequently than I could wish, yet as often as any opportunity presents itself, I never decline this duty. In proof of this, I have lately written you two letters, one to Frankfort at the March fair, and the other immediately after Easter; and if these are still delayed on the road, as may possibly be the case, they will some time or other be released, and will, I hope, reach you at last. In the mean time I never cease either to think of, or speak about you as honourably as I ought to do.

To write to you at the present time about the affairs of France would probably be impertinent; for all the news is brought you without the help of either wind or vessels. The most holy [father] will leave nothing untried:

> Flectere si nequeat superos, Acheronta movebit.

For he sees that the struggle is not about things of no importance, but a matter of life and death. I wish our friends may not suffer themselves to be overreached.

As the duke of Guise, by holding out I know not what hope of settling the affairs of religion, and receiving the confession of Augsburg, has prevented the princes of Germany from intermeddling in this war; so he has endeavoured by all possible means to persuade our queen that the present contest in France is not about matters of religion, but that there is an evident conspiracy against the government; that it is the cause of the king, whom, as being herself also invested with royal authority, she ought not to oppose. Meanwhile he has caused his niece, the queen of Scotland, to court the favour and friendship of our queen, and send her presents, and make I know not what promises;—that she purposes this summer to come upon a visit of honour into England[1], and to establish a perpetual treaty of friendship, never to be dissolved. She has sent her a diamond of great value, a most beautiful gem, set in gold, and accompanied by some beautiful and elegant verses[2]. What next? They seem to suppose that by festive interviews, and hunting matches, and flatteries, our attention will easily be diverted from the noise of war, and lulled to sleep. In the mean time our queen, when she saw through the whole affair, and perceived what was doing, (and this was not a matter of much difficulty,) changed her purpose respecting her progress, gradually withdrew her alliance with the Guises, and not obscurely intimated her determination to assist the prince of Condé[3]. [The duke of] Guise was very angry at

[1 "Whereas the queen of Scots was the first that desired an interview, it was not without suspicion that she did it to serve her turn, and to temporize, that she might either strengthen her title to England, or else give hope and courage to the papists in England, and to the Guises her kinsmen in France." See Camden's Elizabeth, p. 60. In a letter of Cecil, dated Oct. 11, 1562, he writes, "The quene's majestie was contented in June to accord upon an enterview in August with the quene of Scotts, coming to Nottingham, so as the matters in Fraunce looke good; and before the last of July, and because at that tyme the trobles grew to be more desperate, the enterview was disappointed, and so excuse was sent to the quene of Scotts by Sir Henry Sidney, with offer to mete at Yorke betwixt Midsomer and the end of August, which is lyke to succede as the planets of Fraunce shall be disposed." MS. Cotton. Vespas. c. VII. 224.]

[2 Written by Buchanan, then in her court. Burnet, III. 451.]

[3 Elizabeth made a contract with the prince of Condé, Rohan, Coligni, and others, "that she would pay them an hundred thousand angels; that she should send them over into France six thousand men, whereof three thousand should be employed for the defence of Dieppe and Rouen; and that they should deliver into her hands, for caution, Franciscopolis, a town built by king Francis the first at the mouth of the Seine, which the English call New-haven, and the French Port de Grace, or Havre de Grace, which town three thousand English soldiers should hold and defend in the French king's name, till Calais should be restored." Camden's Elizabeth, p. 61. See also the letter of Cecil, referred to in note 1.]

this interruption to his designs, and received our ambassador with reproaches; and declared by a public proclamation, that the queen of England was planning intrigues against the kingdom of France, and that she alone had occasioned those disorders. Our queen could not bear this charge with patience, nor indeed ought she to have done. She forthwith began to act with openness, as I hear, to recal her ambassador, to enlist troops[1], to dismast all vessels, both English and foreign, from whatever place, or wherever they might be, to prevent their getting away, and giving information of what she was doing. Oh! if she had acted in this manner some time since, or if the German princes would even now follow her example, the whole business would have been settled much more easily, and with much less waste of christian blood. And indeed the queen has now sent into Germany, to the princes: and there is now at court an ambassador from Guise, with new blandishments, as I suppose, to delay and hinder us. But it will not, I think, be so easy a matter to deceive people with their eyes open.

The affairs of Scotland, as to religion, are tolerably quiet. The queen[2] alone retains her mass, contrary to the general wish. There has been here, throughout the whole of this present year, an incredibly bad season both as to the weather and state of the atmosphere. Neither sun, nor moon, nor winter, nor spring, nor summer, nor autumn, have performed their appropriate offices. It has rained so abundantly, and almost without intermission, as if the heavens could hardly do any thing else. Out of this contagion monstrous births have taken place; infants with hideously deformed bodies, some being quite without heads, some with heads belonging to other creatures; some born without arms, legs, or shin-bones; some were mere skeletons, entirely without flesh, just as the image of death is generally represented. Similar births have been

[1 Strype relates, that November the 14th at night came a commandment to London, that prayers should be used there three days successively to God, to grant his help and good success to the English army now gone beyond sea, against the duke of Guise, sworn enemy to the protestants, whom the prince of Condé intended to meet in the field on Tuesday next. Strype, Annals, I. i. 545.]

[2 See note, p. 104.]

produced in abundance from swine, mares, cows, and domestic fowls. The harvest is now coming on, rather scanty indeed, but yet so as we have not much to complain of. Salisbury, Aug. 14, 1562.

Yours in Christ,

JOHN JEWEL, *Anglus*.

LETTER LI.

BISHOP JEWEL TO PETER MARTYR.

Dated at SALISBURY, *Aug.* 14, 1562.

MUCH health in Christ. I wrote to you, and also separately to Bullinger, immediately after Easter, and hope my letters have been received before now; for as to the former letters which I sent to Frankfort at the March fair, and took care should be delivered to the younger Froschover, I doubt not but they have reached both yourself and my other friends· yet Bullinger seems in his letter as if he were complaining somewhat of my neglect. Since then your letter dated Zurich, March 4th, has been brought to me; and you may easily imagine, from my love and affection towards you, how agreeable and delightful it was. For although the subjects you wrote about were already old and almost out of date, (for that letter of yours could scarcely reach me before the 27th of June, out of breath, and weary with its journey,) nevertheless I seemed therein to recognize and hear your voice, and hold most delightful intercourse with you. I rejoice greatly, as I ought to do, that you returned safe and sound from France[3], and that you retain your bodily strength and health.

What you wrote me word, when you were in France, that you saw no appearance of an approaching war, and yet that

[[3] Peter Martyr returned to Zurich from France, Nov. 21, 1561, as he writes to Beza in a letter dated on the 25th of that month.]

matters could be settled in no other way, we now too truly see to have actually occurred. May the Lord God of hosts at length arise, and overthrow and scatter his enemies; and inspire courage into our brethren, who worship him in holiness! The duke of Guise is a powerful enemy, and being wary both from age and experience, seems to aim at nothing so much as to obtain a favourable opinion of his character. Therefore, some days since, messengers and letters were passing to and fro, together with honorary presents; and favour and popularity was courted by him in every possible way.

By such pretences, forsooth, did he hope to deceive our simplicity. He did not however, gain his object with us; for we have already enlisted our troops, armed our fleet, and are quite ready to afford our assistance whenever it may be wanted. All disaffected persons of any eminence or note among us are ordered to be kept in custody to prevent their doing mischief.

I wish your rulers and commonwealth would at last rouse themselves, and consider that the case is a common one; that they also may be involved, and that they should be cautious of gazing so long and so unconcernedly upon the proceedings of others. Matters are now in that state, that delay will neither restore them nor check their progress. But what are your *Dii selecti* of Trent about? Are they suddenly struck dumb? O holy fathers, and great lights of the world! Not a single word in so long a time, even in seventeen whole months! And yet the most holy [father] has long since expected his *apotheosis*, and thinks perhaps that they have done him an injury. Master Baldwin[1] writes me word, that he is very much pleased with our moderation in the late change of religion, and that he will use his endeavours, (for he thinks he has some influence,) that a like moderation may prevail in the kingdom of France; but that your preciseness, as well as that of Geneva, is by no means agreeable to him. In this respect

[[1] Francis Baldwin was Professor of Civil Law at Paris and elsewhere. He was appointed by the king of Navarre to be his orator at the Council of Trent; and was there in 1562, when his patron was killed at the siege of Rouen. His quarrel with Calvin arose from his having introduced into France a work, published at first anonymously, by George Cassander, on the duty of a christian man with respect to differences in religion; and for which he was attacked by Calvin, as the reputed author. He died in 1572. See Moreri.]

he is, I think, rather unjust to Calvin, probably from bearing in mind their ancient quarrel. Peter[2] Alexander is in London, laid up with the gout; a good man, but somewhat weakened by age. Your friend Herman is now with me. He sent me information from France, of what he was an eye witness to respecting the late disorders, by which he had not before suffered his studies to be interrupted. Oh! as often as we talk together about yourself, and Bullinger, your wife, your whole family, and all Zurich, how sweetly and with what pleasure do we converse! His society is most agreeable to me; for he is, as you well know, an excellent and well-principled young man, and one who is very much devoted to literature.

Our affairs as to religion are going on well. The obstinacy of the papists is now greater than ever. They are depending, it seems, upon the result of events in France: we have heard nothing from that country these twenty days.

There are a few other matters to write about; but of them I write more fully to Bullinger, who, I see, reads my letters with avidity, and sadly complains to me of the interruption of them, occasioned however by no fault of mine. I send you ten French crowns, which I desire may be expended, at the discretion of yourself and Bullinger, upon a public supper in your common-hall, to which may be invited, as usual, the ministers of the churches, and young students, and any others whom you may think fit. I send my Julius the twenty French crowns, which I promised him annually, when he was in England; besides eight crowns, and I know not how many batzen[3] besides, making in all fifty English shillings, which I squeezed with difficulty from Ann's father-in-law.

Farewell, my father and much esteemed master in Christ. Salute, I pray you, in my name that excellent woman your wife, Bullinger, Gualter, Lavater, Simler, Wolfius, Zuinglius, Gesner, Wickius, Haller, Frisius, Franciscus, and the dear boy Martyrillus. Salisbury, Aug. 14, 1562.

Your most devoted,
JOHN JEWEL, *Anglus*.

[2 See p. 79.]
[3 A *batzen* is somewhere about the value of twopence.]

LETTER LII.

BISHOP JEWEL TO JOSIAH SIMLER.

Dated at SALISBURY, *Aug.* 18, 1562.

Your Herman, my Josiah, is at last become mine; yes, mine altogether, both by acquisition and possession. How so? you will exclaim. I will tell you. By the rising of the waters; for he reached Salisbury on the 8th of July, having escaped with difficulty from the tumults in France. Oh! how often do we converse with each other about the state of the republic of Zurich, and especially about our friend Josiah! I have now the entire benefit of those delightful conversations, which, to say the truth, I rather envied you the enjoyment of. And if you were now with us, nothing could be more pleasant, or more to be desired by me, provided only you would leave that gout of yours at home. Believe me, my Josiah, although your griefs are, and ought to be, a grief to me, yet when I sometimes think about you, and place you, as it were, before my eyes, I see a wrinkled old man, bowed down, with bent body, leaning on crutches, dragging one foot after the other, and delicately treading on the ground. But I am not a little surprised that the gout can lay hold upon you, as you have always been a brisk and active young man, while that old woman is so indolent and sedentary.

The queen of Scotland, niece of the duke of Guise, has within these few days, by way of courting the favour and friendship of our queen, sent her a most splendid and valuable diamond, inclosed and fixed in a plate of gold, and set off with some flattering and elegant verses[1]. I send you a copy of them, that you may know the truth of that saying, attributed, if I remember right, to Louis XI. *He who knows not how to dissemble, knows not how to govern.*

[1 See p. 115.]

Farewell, my Josiah, farewell. Salute most dutifully in my name your most excellent wife, masters Gualter, Wolfius, Zuinglius, Haller, Wickius, Frisius, Guldebeckius. Herman salutes you. Salisbury, Aug. 18, 1562.

Yours in Christ,
JOHN JEWEL, *Anglus*.

LETTER LIII.

BISHOP PARKHURST TO HENRY BULLINGER.

Dated at LUDHAM, *Aug.* 20, 1562.

I RECEIVED your letter, written June 22nd, about the beginning of August. There has been a little book published here, entitled[2] "an apology for the church of England;" in which it is shewn, why we have gone over from the pope to Christ, and why we refuse to acknowledge the council of Trent. It may be that two books have been published, but I have only seen this one. I ordered my servant to inquire in London for one or both, if there are two, and to give them in charge to Birkman, to be sent over to Froschover at the approaching fair. Our London friends seem to forget their duty, in not sending over to you books of this kind. Unless the archbishop of Canterbury had sent me a copy, I should not have seen it even now.

There is in my diocese, in Norfolk, a venerable old man, an excellent preacher, and an ancient enemy of antichrist. The opinion of Brentius[3] fell into his hands, which when he had read, he embraced with both hands, and even strenuously and obstinately defended it against some pious and learned men. When this came to my ears, I sent him the copy of your answer which you had presented me with; which when he had attentively perused, he returned to me with many thanks, first to you for having published such a work, and then to myself for having lent it to him for some days: for

[2 See p. 101.]   [3 See p. 108.]

he has now bade farewell to the opinion of Brentius, and through your instrumentality, has embraced the truth. He is, I believe, nearly ninety years old; I have never seen him, for he lives a great way off, and is quite unable to ride, and indeed scarce able to walk. He preaches constantly in the church of which he is rector. If you would reduce your discourses on Jeremiah to a single volume, you would, in my opinion, do a service.

I have written to our friend Gualter about the queen's fleet and the English troops; and also, about the letter which poor Burcher wrote to me. I received a letter from my lord of Canterbury four days ago; the substance of it is this, that I should diligently ascertain by every means in my power, though secretly, who, and how many there are in my diocese, who do not comply with the true religion. This is, I suspect, with the intention of punishing their breach of faith. I shall carefully attend to this, and shall give every intelligence, as soon as possible, concerning the enemies of Christ. This step is very gratifying to me; for I gather from it that his grace of Canterbury intends firmly to support the true religion. May the Lord grant it!

Salute in my name your excellent wife, sons, daughters, daughters-in-law, sons-in-law, and all your connections; Haller, Wolfius, Frisius, Collin, Wickius, Pellican, Meyer, the Froschovers, &c. My wife salutes you all.

After I had written this, lo! good news was brought me, namely, that the crucifix[1] and candlesticks in the queen's chapel are broken in pieces, and, as some one has brought word, reduced to ashes. A good riddance of such a cross as that! It has continued there too long already, to the great grief of the godly, and the cherishing of I know not what expectations in the papists. Moreover, the pseudo-bishops, who are in the tower of London, will very soon render an account of their breach of faith. So I hear. Farewell, my good Bullinger. In haste. Ludham, Aug. 20, 1562.

Yours,

JOHN PARKHURST.

[Bishop] of Norwich.

[1 See note 2, p. 66.]

LETTER LIV.

BISHOP JEWEL TO HENRY BULLINGER.

Dated at LONDON, *March* 5, 1563.

MUCH health. Though grief for Peter[2] Martyr is unavailing, yet there is something pleasant, I know not why, even in the very feeling of sorrow. Alas! he was one who, from the greatness of his talents, the variety of his attainments, his piety, his morals, his life, seemed worthy of never being taken away from us. But I had long before suspected this would be the case, when I first heard of a man of his age turning his thoughts to marriage[3]. May our great and good God mercifully look upon his church, and raise up for her other defenders in the room of the departed! Ye are few, my father, ye are but few, upon whom the whole matter rests; and I have always reckoned yourself among the foremost. Oh that there may always be some, to whom you may[4] be able to transfer your duties with satisfaction! But to pass over these things, I do not wonder that your Hercules[5] of Tubingen, the forger of monstrosities, is now triumphing at his ease: I wonder whether he is able to confine himself within the ample limits and regions of his Ubiquitarian kingdom. Should he make any attack upon our departed friend, and his writings come to my knowledge, unless some of you should be before hand with me, I shall think it my duty to reply to him, as far as my engagements will permit; if for no other reason, at least to let the world know, that England and Switzerland are both united against these Ubiquitarians.

[2 He died Nov. 12, 1562, in the sixty-third year of his age.]
[3 See note 2, p. 54.]
[4 *Quibus possitis hanc lampadem committere.* A metaphorical expression, borrowed from the custom of running with lighted torches at the feast of Prometheus at Athens, which they passed on from one to another till they reached the goal. See Lucret. II. 77. Pers. Sat. VI. 61.]
[5 Brentius. See note 1, p. 108.]

The death of the Guisian[1] Pharaoh, which I have to-day heard as an ascertained and undoubted fact, has, believe me, affected my inmost heart and soul. It was so sudden, so opportune, so fortunate, and so far exceeding all our hopes and expectations. What spirits must we now suppose our brethren to possess, whom that monster had already closely besieged, and whom in hope and imagination he had already almost devoured with his cruel jaws? Blessed be the name of the Lord! Châtillon[2] is now besieging the castle of Caen, and is daily gaining strength; and there is good hope that the enemy will come into our terms, and that all will end as we wish. Our queen is collecting troops from Germany, and keeps them in her pay, regardless of expence.

We are now assembling the great council of the nation, and are going on successfully both as to the affairs of religion, and of state, and also with respect to the sinews of war, namely, money[3].

We have very favourable accounts from Scotland. The queen, almost alone, retains both her Guisian obstinacy, and her mass, against the general wish. Our queen last autumn was taken ill of the small pox, and in some danger: she had almost lost her life through her impatience of the fever, and the wearisomeness [of the disease.] But we thank God, who has delivered her from danger and us from fear. We hear nothing about what your little Tridentine fathers, and the dropsical Pope, are bringing forth. Perhaps the Holy Spirit declines being present, or cannot speak. Whatever may be the reason, it is strange, that in so numerous an assembly, and so great expectation, nothing is accomplished.

[1 Francis of Lorraine, duke of Guise and Aumale, was killed by a pistol shot, Feb. 24, 1563, while preparing to besiege the city of Orleans, the strong hold of the protestants in France.]

[2 The admiral de Coligny. The castle surrendered on the 2nd of March.]

[3 This parliament made sundry laws for relief of the poor, for navigation, and husbandry, against rogues, cheaters, conjurors, perjured persons; and for translating the Bible and Common Prayer into Welch; and against advancing the pope's authority, which is made treason, and refusal of the oath of supremacy. And subsidies were granted; by the ecclesiastical men one subsidy, and by the laity another, with two fifteenths and tenths. Whitlocke's Memorials, p. 230, and Camden's Elizabeth, p. 63.]

I am at last beginning to recover my health, after the unseasonable weather of the last summer and this winter, and the spasms and cough which lasted for some days. I doubt not, you will take care that the writings of Peter Martyr be not lost: they cost their author much labour, and deserve, as you know, to be highly esteemed.

Farewell, most accomplished Sir, and much esteemed brother and master in Christ. Salute in my name that excellent lady your wife, your sons, daughters-in-law, masters Gualter, Simler, Lavater, Zuinglius, Wickius, Wolfius, Haller, Gesner, Frisius. May the Lord long preserve you to us safe and sound! London, March 5, 1563.

Your brother in Christ,

and most attached,

JOHN JEWEL.

LETTER LV.

BISHOP JEWEL TO JOSIAH SIMLER.

Dated at LONDON, *March* 7, 1563.

I would write to you also, my Josiah, did not my engagements prevent me. But, as you know, we are now assembled in parliament, and are deliberating about the affairs of the church and state, peace and war. And though in all this turmoil I can scarcely remember myself, I cannot be forgetful of my Josiah, whom, although on so many accounts I admire and reverence, and bear in mind, as either discoursing, or writing, or reading; yet when I think upon him with the stoop of old[4] age, leaning on two crutches, drawing after him one or both feet, cautiously looking about, for fear any thing should run against his toes, softly and delicately treading on the ground, and coughing just as old Chremes, painfully, and like

[[4] See p. 120. Simler was now only thirty-two years old. He died in 1576, in his 45th year.]

an old man; believe me, I can scarce refrain from laughing. For do tell me, my Josiah, what kind of old age is this? or rather, what kind of shamming is it? Can such a change have taken place in so short a time? But, however it be, you are, I believe, a worthy man, and do not let your looks belie your feet. Our mutual friend Herman is with me. I wish you were here also; you would easily get rid of your gout, and bandages, and crutches. Farewell, my Josiah.

Yours in Christ,
JOHN JEWEL.

LETTER LVI.

BISHOP JEWEL TO JOSIAH SIMLER.

Dated at LONDON, *March* 23, 1563.

I HAVE at all times, most learned Josiah, duly appreciated your kindness and courtesy and affection. For who could do otherwise than love one of such a disposition, so courteous, so learned, so mindful of an old friend, in a word, so amiable? But when my regard for you seemed incapable of increase, your deserts have nevertheless produced this effect, that I daily seem to feel that if what is now *most* great could become *more* so, I should love you yet more than I now do.

I have received from you a silver image of that excellent old man Peter Martyr, with an account of his life and death. In the figure indeed, although there is in many respects an admirable resemblance (to the original), yet there was a something, I know not what, in which I was unable to perceive the skill of the artist. And what wonder is it, that there should be some defect in producing the likeness of one, the like of whom, whenever I look around me, I can scarce believe ever to have existed? Your little book, however, I perused with the greatest eagerness and delight. For I seemed to myself to behold the same old man with whom I had formerly lived upon such affectionate terms; and to behold him too, I know not why, more nearly and thoroughly, than when we were living together.

You have refuted that obscure and insolent reviler, Stancarus[1], (whose very existence I was ignorant of,) both skilfully and learnedly, and, as I hope, with great advantage to the church. But, my Josiah, I am sparing in writing *to* you, especially when concerning yourself. For it is neither consistent with my friendship or my modesty, to utter these things in your ears. I have read this work[2] with the greatest eagerness, as I do all your writings; for they are written most copiously on barren subjects, and most clearly on obscure ones. I acknowledge and confess your kindness, and own myself, moreover, in your debt.

Our church, by the blessing of God, is free from these monsters. We have only to do with some of the popish satellites, who are giving us as much disturbance as they can in their corners and hiding places; and even at this moment are preventing me from throwing together what I had meditated against the Ubiquitarians: but on this subject I have written more fully to Bullinger. Should you publish the writings of Peter Martyr, you will both confer a benefit on the church, and satisfy the expectation of many good men who desire it. As to the Commentaries on Genesis, respecting which you seem to require my opinion, indeed, my Josiah, I have never read them. I doubt not, however, that they are such, as when published, will be acknowledged to be the work of Peter Martyr.

[[1] He was professor of Hebrew at Cracow, and afterwards at Konigsberg; and maintained that our Lord was mediator between God and man in his human nature alone. He was opposed by Osiander, Calvin, Bullinger and Melancthon. See Bayle, who says of him that "il versait des torrens d'injures dans les ecrits qu'il composait contre ses antagonistes; et il s'excusait de cela sur le droit de représailles, et sur l'importance des Hérésies qu'il croiait combattre, et même sur l'example des apôtres." He died in 1574.]

[[2] The work here referred to was a confutation of a book written by Stancarus, and entitled, "De Trinitate, et Mediatore Domino nostro Jesu Christo, adversus Henricum Bullingerum, Petrum Martyrem, et Joannem Calvinum, et reliquos Tigurinæ ac Genevensis ecclesiæ ministros, ecclesiæ Dei perturbatores, etc. Basle, 1547."]

Whatever news I had to relate, I have thrown together in my letter to master Bullinger. Were not your Rhine so much in the way, I should both write and send to you much more frequently. But the journey is long, and besides I can scarce find any one who is going thither at this next fair; added to which, I am uncertain as to the fair itself. But, whatever may become of my letter, whether I write, or am silent, I am, my Josiah, wholly yours. [London] March 23, 1563.

Salute, &c.

JOHN JEWEL.

LETTER LVII.

BISHOP PARKHURST TO HENRY BULLINGER.

Dated at LUDHAM, *April* 26, 1563.

WHEN I was in London, I rebuked those of my countrymen who had been at Zurich, for having been so unmindful of you as never to write to you. Some were ashamed of their long silence, and some likewise expressed their sorrow. But I hope they have now written, and that they will write more diligently in future. Foxe has written a large volume on the English Martyrs[1], and that too in English; it was published four days before Easter. The papists themselves are now beginning to be disgusted with the cruelty of their leaders.

Six or seven persons were convicted of treason, and condemned to death at the beginning of Lent; but the queen's mercy still suffers them to remain in the Tower of London.

[[1] Parkhurst here refers to the well known work, Foxe's Acts and Monuments, the first edition of which was published about five weeks previous to the date of this letter. It is unnecessary here to add any particulars respecting that laborious work. Strype has given some interesting information respecting it, Annals I. i. 374.]

Two of them bear the name of Pole[2], being relatives of Cardinal Pole. The Earl of Huntley, one of the principal noblemen in Scotland, and a notorious papist, influenced by the counsel of Guise, was purposing to pour forth the blood of the godly in Scotland, just as Guise did in France; and there was a great conspiracy of many seditious persons, and the same tumult and bloodshed would certainly have taken place in Scotland as in France, had not the design, by God's blessing, been discovered in time. Some were slain in battle[3], among whom was one of the sons of Huntley; the other son was condemned with some others. Huntley himself was being taken to prison; but in his way thither he fell backwards from his horse, and died of a broken neck. It is doubtful whether this was done by accident or on purpose.

I wrote you word that the cross[4], wax candles, and candlesticks had been removed from the queen's Chapel; but they were shortly after brought back again to the great grief of the godly. The candles heretofore were lighted every day, but now not at all. The lukewarmness of some persons very much retards the progress of the gospel. I wish well from my heart to all the people of Zurich, whom I beg you to salute in my name, and especially your excellent wife, sons, daughters, &c. My wife salutes you all. In haste. Ludham, April 26, 1563.

Yours,

JOHN PARKHURST,

[Bishop] of Norwich.

[2 Arthur Pole, Edmonde Pole, Anthonye Fortescue, John Prestall, Humfrey Barwycke, Edward Cosyn, and others, seven in all, were condemned on the 26th of February. Their treasons were intentions to come with a power into Wales, and to proclaim the Scottish queen. Both the ambassadors of France and Spain were concerned in the matter. Strype, Annals, I. i. 546, 555. Camden, Elizabeth, p. 58.]

[3 At Corrichie, near Aberdeen, where Huntley was defeated by the Earl of Murray. His sons, John and Adam Gordon, were made prisoners; the former was executed, the latter pardoned on account of his tender age. By their confession, it appears, that he intended high treason to the queen of Scots. See a letter from Cecil to Sir Thomas Smith, dated Nov. 17, 1562. MS. Lansdown, 102. 20.]

[4 See p. 122.]

LETTER LVIII.

THOMAS SAMPSON TO HENRY BULLINGER.

Dated at OXFORD, *July* 26, 1563.

I wish you, reverend Bullinger, eternal life in Christ our Lord. You will perhaps wonder at my freedom in troubling you with this letter. Excuse me, I will write very briefly.

There was *one*, not long since, at Zurich, into whose bosom I could pour out all my cares. His remains are now with you. Zurich therefore often comes into my mind. But to what purpose should I idly prate of my thoughts at such times? Martyr is yet alive: may Zurich live well and happy! and that the remembrance of the kindness I received at Zurich may not be buried with Peter Martyr, is the object of my now addressing you. I had once a little cottage at Zurich; and if God would now grant my wishes, I should most anxiously return to it. I am perhaps selfish in desiring this: I do not deny it. But since the glory of Christ our Lord should be the supreme object of our desire, I wave all my petitions as far as they regard myself. In this matter therefore, namely, in looking out for me a small lodging, I am loth to give you any farther trouble. Oh that we may sometime be permitted to arrive at those mansions prepared for us in heaven by Christ our Lord! Meanwhile, most reverend father, I commend both my country and myself to your prayers. The affairs of England are in a most unhappy state; I apprehend yet worse evils, not to say the worst: but we must meanwhile serve the Lord Christ. Happy is he whom our Christ adopts into his family! Consider, then, that England is most earnestly commended to your prayers, and remember me also. As a lasting token of my regard, I send you by your countryman, master Blaarer, some Oxford gloves. They indeed will grow old; but may your love of England and of myself never grow old! Farewell, and may you, my very dear father, live most happy in the Lord! Oxford, July 26, 1563.

Yours,

THO. SAMPSON.

Salute Julius Terentianus in my name and in that of my wife.

LETTER LIX.

BISHOP PARKHURST TO HENRY BULLINGER.

Dated at LUDHAM, *Aug.* 13, 1563.

HEALTH to you in Christ, most learned Bullinger. I wrote you a letter on the 26th of April, which I hope you received: yours, however, written on the 6th of March was delivered to me on the 23d of May; but I have not received the copy of your second reply to Brentius, which you write of. What do I not imprecate against those men who have robbed me of so great a treasure! If you had tied it up with the letters of Gualter, Lavater, and Simler, it would have reached me in safety. I have not yet seen any thing that Brentius has written, either against yourself or Peter Martyr; nor do I much regard any writings or trash of that kind.

Your letter written October 16, 1562, I did not receive till the 27th of June. Hyperius sent it to Luncher, and Luncher to me. I have not seen him of a long time, but I sent some money to him on the 4th of July, and I inclose you his letter to me, by which you will learn how harsh and inexorable are the heads of his college, who will not allow him any leave of absence.

Within these few days there has come to me a young Scotsman, a most excellent preacher, recommended to me by letter from Grindal, bishop of London, and Coverdale, late bishop of Exeter. He is now settled in my diocese, namely, in a sea-port called Lynn. He has brought me news from

Scotland, that the archbishop[1] of St Andrew's has been condemned to death for hearing mass; and that two or three of the nobility have been imprisoned for the same reason. They have decreed in parliament that adultery shall be punished with death.

The Queen of Scotland demanded in the house of parliament these three things: 1 That she might be allowed to hear mass; 2, that she might declare war against the English; 3, that the German, (viz. the popish) guards might be about the court, to whom should be committed the charge of her person. But none of these requests were complied with. These things he told me.

There was a violent thunder storm here about the beginning of July. The spire of the cathedral church in the city of Norwich was violently shaken, though not thrown down; but it was repaired shortly after. The plague is raging in London[2] and at Newhaven[3], and, as it is reported, in the French army. You will hear every thing else from my letter to Gualter. On the 20th of July I sent by one of my principal attendants a letter to the council. On the 26th of the same month he brought their answer, and died of the plague four days after. The Lord have mercy upon us! About the beginning of August war was publicly declared against France[4].

Salute in my name the most honourable lady your wife, also your sons and daughters, learned friends, and most courteous citizens, whom you know me to be acquainted with. In

[1 Murray cast the Archbishop of St Andrew's into prison, because he had not abstained from celebrating mass, for which he hardly obtained pardon with many tears. Camden, Elizabeth, p. 68.]

[2 Out of the city of London alone, which consisteth of a hundred and twenty-one parishes, there were carried forth to burying about 21,530 corpses. Camden, Elizabeth, p. 67.]

[3 Now Havre de Grace, till then occupied by the English, but surrendered in July by reason of the plague here mentioned, which was brought into England, and the latter end of August raged in London, about a thousand in a week dying. Strype, Annals, I. ii. 94.]

[4 Sir Nicolas Throgmorton, the queen's ambassador in France, was put under restraint; and the queen, to be even with the French for this injurious dealing with her ambassador, lodged the French ambassador at Eton in Sir Thomas Smith's old lodgings, very commodiously, but under restraint. Strype, Annals, I. ii. 94.]

haste. Ludham, August 13, 1563. My wife salutes you all, and thanks you for your letter. As no one who understands German is at hand she is unable to reply to you, which she very much regrets.

Yours,
JOHN PARKHURST,
[Bishop] of Norwich.

⁵I hear that peace is about to be made between the French and ourselves. God grant it! I know for certain that a truce has been established for some time. My wife sends you two pair of boots, which you may wear when rude Boreas rushes down, bringing cold, frost, and snow.

LETTER LX.

LAURENCE HUMPHREY TO HENRY BULLINGER.

Dated at OXFORD, *August* 16, 1563.

HEALTH in Christ, and everlasting peace! I rejoice and congratulate you again and again that the tumult of war has subsided. I lament, however, that the affairs of religion have made so little progress. Jesus will at length afford us halcyon days, when the gospel shall meet with more acceptance, and the church, I hope, will have her sons, and the gospel its course, in spite of, and with the opposition of, all the powers of hell. For the truth will prevail, and no power or cunning of man shall be able to resist the divine will and operation. But to you and yours, our fathers and brethren, do we wish a long life, lest the christian commonwealth should be deprived of her parents, and patrons, and guardians.

[⁵ This peace " was proclaymed in London the 22d [of April, 1564], and on the 23d a notable good sermon made at Pooles [St Paul's], with *Te Deum* and all incident solemnities." Cecil to Sir Thomas Smith, MS. Lansd. 102. 49. and see Strype, Annals, I. ii. 115. The articles are recorded by Camden, Elizabeth, p. 70.]

Respecting the subject of the habits, I wish you would again write me your opinion, either at length, or briefly, or in one word: first, whether that appears to you as *indifferent* which has been so long established with so much superstition, and both fascinated the minds of the simple with its splendour, and imbued them with an opinion of its religion and sanctity: secondly, whether at the command of the sovereign, (the jurisdiction of the pope having been abolished,) and for the sake of order, and not of ornament, habits of this kind may be worn in church by pious men, lawfully and with a safe conscience. I am speaking of that round cap and popish surplice, which are now enjoined us, not by the unlawful tyranny of the pope, but by the just and legitimate authority of the queen. To the pure, then, can all these things be pure, and matters of indifference? I ask your reverence to let me know very exactly what is your opinion.

Sampson had sent his letter by another hand. He salutes you and master Gualter and the rest again and again. May the Lord preserve your church and his! Oxford, August 16, 1563.

Yours,
LAURENCE HUMPHREY.

LETTER LXI.

BISHOP HORN TO HENRY BULLINGER.

Dated at WINCHESTER, *Dec.* 13, 1563.

I HAVE now received, my very dear Bullinger, your three letters; two of which, namely, the first, dated October 10, [1562], and the second, dated March 10, 1563, reached me only on the 31st of last May; the third, dated on the 29th of August, reached me in good time in October. I perceived in them the great strength of your regard, which expressed itself in such delightful terms, and could be satisfied only with my letter, or my trifling presents. They were sent by me however, to make you understand that not myself only, but my property and fortune, is ready to do you service.

As for your thanking me for the cloth, and expressing your intention of returning the obligation, I therein acknowledge your exceeding kindness in confessing yourself to be under any obligation to me, who am so deeply indebted to yourself. And when you daily refresh your remembrance of me in that silver cup, I take it thus, that as nothing can be more gratifying to me than your kindness and esteem, so it is a source of exceeding pleasure to me to be in your frequent recollection, and to be as it were constantly before your eyes. But since a cup of so moderate a price must be very small, I have sent you fourteen crowns more, together with my coat of arms, as you desire, that you may get a cup made that is larger and more suitable for a full party.

I am equally troubled with yourselves at the insidiousness and fury of the enemies, from which you are in danger: but I am, on the other hand, relieved by the consolation which you derive through him who has overcome the world, and whose people cannot be conquered or overcome by the world. And we are not so much distressed by the evils of popery, as the glory of God is illustrated, and the gospel magnified. We have throughout England the same ecclesiastical doctrine as yourselves; as to rites and ceremonies———[1] nor, as the people are led to believe, do we at all differ in our estimation of them. But we have never ceased, according to your advice, to teach, warn, and enforce what is right and necessary to be followed, from the holy scriptures; lest the flock committed to our charge should, through our fault, be scattered by those inveterate errors which are still circulated by the papists in secret.

Of the books you mention in your second letter, I have received three upon the same arguments, against the Ubiquitarianism of Brentius; which subject a certain Englishman has undertaken as you desire, and by the divine assistance will treat with zeal and eloquence, that it may be manifest to every one, that the people of England entertain on these points the same opinions as you do at Zurich. I had heard of the

[[1] The original MS. is here illegible.]

death of that illustrious man, Peter Martyr, before the arrival of your letter. I rejoice at the successor whom he appointed in his dying moments. When the Tridentine Council, framed as it is against Christ, shall have reached its utmost height, he that sitteth in the heavens, and laugheth them to scorn, will disperse it, as he has always made the vain counsels of men of no effect, and brought them to nought.

It now remains for me, my Bullinger, to salute affectionately, in my wife's name as well as my own, both yourself and the excellent ladies, your wife and Froschover's; also your sons in law, Simler, Lewis, Lavater, and Zuinglius; as well as my beloved brethren in Christ, masters Gualter, Bibliander, Wolfius, and Haller; my landlord too, and that poor widow who waited upon us when we lived together in Froschover's house, and to whom I have sent two crowns. I wish you health from the Lord. I will henceforth take care that you shall not be in want of a letter from me, and I ask you again and again to do the same on your part. Farewell. May the Lord Jesus long preserve you in safety to his church! Winchester, December 13, 1563.

Yours wholly in Christ,

ROBERT WINTON.

LETTER LXII.

BISHOP PARKHURST TO JOSIAH SIMLER.

Dated at LUDHAM, *Feb.* 17, 1564.

I SEND you, according to your request, two letters written to me by Peter Martyr: should I find any more, I will send them. I wrote to you on the 26th of April[1], and also on the 14th of August. For the silver [image of Peter] Martyr

[[1] These letters are not preserved. Those of Parkhurst to Bullinger of the same dates are given above.]

I sent a golden Elizabeth. You are right in preparing an edition of the works of Martyr; for you will thus deserve well of all pious persons, and perform a most useful service to the church of Christ. May the Lord prosper your undertaking and bring it to a happy issue! The wife[2] of the duke of Norfolk died in childbed on the 10th of January, and was buried at Norwich on the 24th of the same month. I preached her funeral sermon. There were no ceremonies at the funeral, wax candles or torches. Except the sun nothing shone, which sadly annoyed the papists. Nothing of the kind has been ever seen in England, especially at the funeral of a peer or peeress. Other news you will learn from my letters to others. Farewell, my Simler. Salute in my name all my friends, especially your excellent wife. Mine salutes you and yours and all our friends. Ludham, Feb. 17, 1564.

    Yours,

JOHN PARKHURST,

[Bishop] of Norwich.

Give this catalogue to master Gesner[3].

[2 This was Margaret, daughter and heir of Thomas Lord Dudley, of Walden, widow of Lord Henry Dudley. She was the second wife of Thomas, fourth duke of Norfolk. The duke's council appointed the dean of Christ church, Sampson, to preach at her interment. But the bishop hearing of it, for doing the greater honour to the duke, sent his letter to the council, offering his service in that behalf. For although, as he said, the other could do much better than he, yet he thought it his bounden duty to do all things that he might to God's glory, to do honour to the duke's grace. Therefore the dean buried her, and the bishop made the sermon. He wrote to Mr Fox, telling him, after his jocose way, "All things were done honourably, *sine crux, sine lux, at non sine* tinkling. There was neither torch, neither taper, candle, nor any light else, beside the light of the sun; singing there was enough." Strype, Annals, I. ii. 45. See MS. Harl. 416. 175.]

[3 Gesner was minded to publish the ancient ecclesiastical authors from good copies. For which purpose he sent to the bishop of Norwich a catalogue of books of that sort, that search might diligently be made in all our best libraries for MS. copies of them. This is the catalogue here referred to. The bishop sent one copy of it to Fox, to search the queen's library; one to Mr Sampson, or Dr Humphrey, that search might be made in Oxford; and another to Mr Beaumont, master of Trinity College, that he might do the like in Cambridge. See Strype, Annals I. ii. 45.]

LETTER LXIII.

BISHOP JEWEL TO HENRY BULLINGER.

Dated at SALISBURY, *March* 1, 1565.

WHAT shall I say to you, most learned sir, and renowned father? I am both ashamed and grieved: ashamed, in the first place, that I have not written more frequently; and also grieved, that the letters which I have written have not been able to reach you. I beseech you, however, not to entertain the thought that either the school of Zurich, or the republic, or, lastly, your exceeding kindness can so quickly have passed away from my mind. Indeed I have all of you in my eyes and in my heart, and yourself especially, my father, who are now the only light of our age.

And now, as to my correspondence, I, for my part, the last year only excepted, when all intercourse was every where prevented by the plague and pestilence, have never omitted writing to yourself, Lavater, Simler, and Julius. Had I not done so, I should scarcely seem to have retained any sense, I will not say of duty, but even of common courtesy. But what has become of my former letters, I do not know. I hear that my last was taken by the French in a sea-fight, and carried off to Calais.

But no more of this. Attend now to some affairs of ours, in which I know, from your usual kindness, you will take more interest. First then, by the blessing of our great and good God, all things are settled with us in the matters of religion. The popish exiles are disturbing us and giving us all the trouble in their power; and in their published books, I know not whether through any ill luck, (shall I say?) or desert of mine, aim at me alone; and this too, three of them have done at once, and with most outrageous clamour: as I alone have to answer them all, you must not imagine that

I have nothing to do. Among other things, the Ubiquitarian¹ question is pressed upon me, which, for the sake of our old Tubingen² friend, I have purposely treated of very copiously, to the best of my power, and as the subject required; but in our own language, as being intended for our own people. If I have leisure, I will copy a part, and send you. But as to that old man, I cannot make out what I ought to think about him; he appears to me to become more insane every day. For I have read the new "Phasma³ of Menander," which he has lately published; and I have to thank you, both for that book, and for all your letters, and all your kindness.

The state is in tranquillity, both at home and abroad, by land and sea. We are at peace with France⁴, and the disorders in Flanders are at last settled. Merchants go backwards and forwards from both countries, the Flemish to us and our merchants in turn to them. [Cardinal] Granvelle⁵, through whose knavery alone all those disturbances began, so managed matters, that by the irregularity and stoppage of the markets, (neither imports nor exports being allowed,)

[¹ "His controversy with Harding gave him an opportunity of incidentally considering the subject. The sixth article in his challenge relates to the question, whether Christ's body is, or might be, in a thousand places, or more, at one and the same time. Nothing can well be imagined more triumphant than the reasoning of Jewel, or more ridiculous than the arguments of his adversary." Le Bas, Life of Jewel, p. 128.]

[² Brentius. See note 1, p. 108.]   [³ See Ter. Eun. Prol. 9.]

[⁴ The 29th of April [1564] the two treaties of peace with France were sealed with the queen's ratification. Strype, Annals, I. ii. 116. See note 5, p. 133.]

[⁵ "The English merchants removed to Embden by means of Granvelle, the Cardinal of Arras, who, hating the English for their religion, had practised to blow the coals between the Low Countries and them, and to spoil their ancient commerce, by fomenting jealousies and complaints one against another. And the duchess of Parma, governess of the said Low Countries, being of the same disaffection towards the English nation, at length forbade all English cloths to be imported; whereat the English, partly resenting this dealing, and partly out of fear of the inquisition now brought in, departed with their effects to Embden. But an ambassador [Don Diego Gusman] sent from Spain to the queen, of a more grave and wise head, moderated their differences soon after, and set the trade on foot again between both people." See Strype, Life of Grindal, ch. ix. p. 125, &c. Also Burgon's Life of Sir T. Gresham, vol. II. p. 45, &c.]

the tradesmen all aghast, and the town's-people, who literally gain their livelihood by spinning wool, reduced to idleness and destitution, some popular commotion[1] or domestic sedition might be the consequence. For he hoped by this means our religion would be shaken at the same time. But God has rather turned these counsels upon their author: for our people remained in their duty, as it was right they should; but the people of Flanders, when our merchants took their departure, and settled their trade at Embden[2], were exceedingly indignant, and did every thing but break out into open disorders.

The Irish, as I know you have heard, are now subject to us, and adopt our laws. The pope, not very long since, sent over an unprincipled and crafty agent, with orders to raise a commotion in that island. He was an Irishman, and was to stir up that wild and savage race against us for the cause of religion. But the knave was apprehended on his first attempt, and examined, and sent prisoner to England. And thus the most holy father has determined, that since he is unable to move the powers above, he will stir up hell beneath. In Scotland[3] [affairs are] as we desire. The queen alone retains her mass, against the general wish.

[1 "Ytt ys moche to be douttyd," Sir R. Clough, who was on the spot, writes to Sir T. Gresham, "of an insourrecyon within the towne, and that, out of hande; for here ys syche mysery within thys towne, that the lyke hathe nott bene sene. Allmost every nyght, howsys [are] broken up and robbyd." See Burgon, as above, vol. II. p. 54.]

[2 The English merchants, says Stowe, made trial of Embden, in East Friesland, as a mart for their commodities, by sending their cloth fleet thither, about Easter, 1564. See Strype, Life of Grindal, p. 125, &c. Sir R. Clough, in a memorial to Sir T. Gresham, on the comparative merits of Embden and Hamburgh for purposes of trade, remarks, among the inconveniencies of the former, that "the people of the towne are rude both in worde and deede, not meete to interteyne merchants; and not *that* only, but also withowte order of beleefe, not fearing God nor the devell, maynteyners of Anabaptists, Libertines, and all other kynde of damnable sects, withowte any reverence to God; as it is well to be seen by their churches; for that in one place they preache, and in other place of the churche there lyeth feathers, netts, and barrells, with dyvers other unseemely things, not fitt to be set in those places." Burgon, as above, vol. II. p. 59.]

[3 Some words are wanting in the original MS.]

Parkhurst, Horn, Sampson, Sandys, Lever, Chambers, are well, and at their respective posts. It is now two years since I have seen any of them. Farewell, my father: may the Lord Jesus very long preserve you alive and well! Salute Gualter, Lavater, Simler, Wolfius, Haller, Gesner, Frisius, Zuinglius, Wickius, to each of whom I would write if I had leisure, or rather, if I were not quite overwhelmed with business. Salisbury, in England, March 1, 1565.

Your much attached and devoted,

JO. JEWEL.

LETTER LXIV.

BISHOP HORN TO RODOLPH GUALTER.

Dated at FARNHAM CASTLE, *July* 17, 1565.

You may easily imagine, my Gualter, with what affection and delight I received your first letter, because it informed me of the prosperity of the state of Zurich, on the good faith and liberality of which I was thrown, when an exile; and also of the good health, both of yourself and my other very dear and valued friends. To this was added your lucubration on St John's gospel; which afforded you, as you say, an opportunity of writing. This I highly approve of, as judging it will greatly contribute both to a true knowledge of scripture, and also to godliness; and I think it should be read, not only by the students, whose benefit you principally have in view, but also by the professors themselves.

In the treaty between France and Switzerland, I commend the clear-sightedness of Zurich, in having detected the artifices of the French, disguised under the pretence of religion; and I hope that your neighbours, the Bernese, will, after your example, withhold their concurrence in so dishonourable a league. As to the pestilence which has lately visited your district, I am of opinion that even the godly themselves are sometimes afflicted for the sake of the ungodly. And as father Bullinger[1], though attacked with it, has escaped danger, we ought to think that he, who has endured these harder times, is reserved by the Lord for happier ones. I ascribe it to the mercy of God, who willed not that your labours should be interrupted, that your house was free from that contagion.

Such is the state of our affairs, that as you are afraid of the treachery of your French neighbours, so we are in fear of intestine treachery from the papists. The heads of that party are in public custody; the rest, affecting to be exiles, are endeavouring, by some of their writings dispersed among the people, to bring themselves into power and us into odium, having obtained a handle of this kind, (small enough indeed,) through the controversy lately arisen among us about square caps and surplices. The papists cried out, that there is not among us that unanimity in religion which we profess to have; but that we are guided by various opinions, and unable to remain in any fixed purpose. This calumny has gained strength from the act of parliament for repressing the impiety of the papists, which passed before our return; by which, though the other habits were taken away, the wearing of square caps and surplices was yet continued to the clergy, though without any superstitious conceit, which was expressly guarded against by the terms of the act. This act cannot be repealed unless by the agreement and consent of all the estates of the kingdom, by whose concurrence it was enacted. It was enjoined us, (who had not then any authority either to make laws or repeal them,) either to wear the caps and surplices, or to give place to others. We complied with this injunction, lest our enemies should take possession of the places deserted by ourselves. But as this matter has occasioned a great strife among us, so that our little flock has divided itself into two parties, the one thinking that on account of this law the ministry ought to be abandoned, and the other, that it ought not; I beg of you, my Gualter, to write me at the earliest oppor-

[1 Two of his daughters died of the plague this year. He lost his wife and another daughter by the same disease in the year preceding.]

tunity what is your opinion of this controversy, which is the only thing that troubles us. We certainly hope to repeal this clause of the act next session; but if this cannot be effected, since the papists are forming a secret and powerful opposition, I nevertheless am of opinion that we ought to continue in the ministry, lest, if we desert and reject it upon such grounds, they insinuate themselves [into our places.] For which reason, my Gualter, I await[2] your opinion, whether we can do, what we are thus doing, with a safe conscience? I am also so anxious about your church, that, as I suspect many faithful ministers have died of the plague, I wish to know by letter from you the names of those who are yet alive. May the Lord Jesus, the great guardian of his flock, guard you and his universal church! Farewell in him. Farnham Castle, July 17, 1565.

Yours in Christ,
ROB. WINTON.

LETTER LXV.

BISHOP PARKHURST TO HENRY BULLINGER.

Dated at LUDHAM, *Aug.* 18, 1565.

I WAS grieved beyond measure at your illness[3], and I rejoice beyond measure at your recovery. You write me word that you inclosed in your letter to me one directed to [Bishop] Jewel; and you request me to cause a copy of it to be taken as far as this mark (†), and to send it to [Bishop] Horn. In truth, my Bullinger, I have not seen Jewel's letter, so that I can neither comply with your request, nor satisfy Horn's expectation; for Abel opened my letter, and gave the inclosure to Jewel in London. He

[2 For Bullinger's letter to Bishop Horn on this question, see Appendix. It is dated Nov. 3rd.]

[3 The plague: see p. 142.]

promised Abel that he would send me a copy at the earliest opportunity. [1] Any one may be rich in promises, and he promised indeed, but nothing further; and has thus defrauded both you, and myself, and Horn. But I impute this to the very numerous occupations by which he is distracted. You ask my pardon for having imposed upon me this burden. But I do not esteem it *onerous* but an *honour*, if I am able upon any occasion to be of service to Bullinger. When I read to my wife your letter in German, as soon as she heard of the [2]death of your wife and daughter, she burst into a flood of tears. I was therefore obliged for some time to discontinue reading, as she was unable to listen.

The queen of Scotland was married, on the 1st of August, to Henry, lord[3] Darnley, eldest son of the earl of Lennox. Some of the Scotch nobility[4] are by no means favourable to this new connection. We are as yet uncertain what will be the consequence. The gospel has certainly taken very deep root in that country. It was reported not long since that our queen was about to marry the duke of Austria. What will be the case, I cannot tell; but as soon as I have ascertained the truth, I will let you know. I am expecting your most learned discourses on Daniel.

Farewell, my excellent Bullinger, with all your friends, to whom I desire all happiness. May the Lord preserve all the people of Zurich from evil! Amen. In haste. Ludham, Aug. 18, 1565. My wife salutes you and your friends.

Yours from my heart,

JOHN PARKHURST,

[Bishop] of Norwich.

[1] *Pollicitis dives quilibet esse potest.*   [[2] See note, p. 142.]

[[3] He was Mary's cousin-german, by the lady Margaret Douglas, niece to Henry VIII., and daughter of the earl of Angus, by Margaret, queen of Scotland.]

[[4] Because the family of Lennox was believed to adhere to the Roman Catholic faith. Randolph, writing to the Earl of Leicester an account of the Queen of Scots' marriage, says of her husband, "I speake leaste of that which I thynk is most earnestlye intended by this Quene and her housbande, when by hym it was lately sayde that he cared more for the Papistes in Englande then he did for the Protestants in Scotlande." MS. Cott. Calig. b. IX. 218.]

LETTER LXVI.

BISHOP SANDYS TO HENRY BULLINGER.

Dated at Worcester, *Jan.* 3, 1566.

Your most courteous letter, my illustrious friend, together with your very learned commentary on the prophet Daniel, has been delivered to me within these few days by our friend Abel. By the which I both rightly perceive your regard for myself, and easily understand how much I owe you in return. That you have written to me in so affectionate and brotherly a manner, is indeed most gratifying, and I sincerely thank you for it; but by your condescension in sending me this excellent work of yours so enriched with all kinds of learning, and also, which I esteem a singular favour, in sending it forth to the public with my name, you have indeed done me a most particular kindness. This courtesy of yours, by which you are wont to attach to yourself the affections of all who know you, is remarkable towards every one, but towards myself it is peculiar and extraordinary. For you not only received me most kindly, and treated me with the greatest benevolence, when as an exile and wanderer without a home I formerly came to Zurich; but even now, when by the providence of God I am restored to my country, you not only continue your affection, but strive to shew me honour and respect by every means in your power. When I anxiously reflect with myself what return I can make to you for your exceeding kindness, I can discover nothing whatever to repay you, worthy of such great benefits. Since then your kindness to me is far greater than I can possibly repay on equal terms, inasmuch as it has been your part to bestow benefits, mine to receive them, I willingly acknowledge myself your debtor; and since I cannot repay you myself, I will intreat Him to repay you, who has fully satisfied for all our debts. In the mean time I have forwarded to our friend Abel a token, such as it is, of my affection towards you: he has undertaken that it shall be safely transmitted to you. I earnestly entreat you kindly to accept it, and in your kindness, not to regard the smallness of the gift, but the inclination of the giver.

What is doing here, and in what condition our affairs are placed, you will learn from the letters of others. I will mention however what is of the most importance. The true religion of Christ is settled among us; the gospel is not bound, but is freely and faithfully preached. As to other matters, there is not much cause for anxiety. There is some little dispute about using or not using the popish habits; but God will put an end to these things also.

Farewell, most esteemed Sir, and love me, as you do, and remember me in your prayers to God. Salute, I pray you, in my name, masters Gualter, Simler, your son Henry, and the others, my masters and very dear brethren in Christ. Worcester, Jan. 3, 1566.

Your most loving brother,

EDWIN WORCESTER.

LETTER LXVII.

BISHOP JEWEL TO HENRY BULLINGER AND LEWIS LAVATER.

Dated at SALISBURY, *Feb.* 8, 1566.

MUCH health in Christ Jesus. I write to you, reverend father, and you, my good Lewis, much less frequently than either I desire or you expect. How you will take this, I know not; yet I hope not unkindly; for the more I feel myself obliged by the kindness of you all, and have always valued your good opinion of me, the less would I desire to be accused by you of forgetfulness or neglect.

It may probably appear affected in me to ascribe my long silence to my own occupations; yet did you know me and my engagements, there would be no need of any other excuse. For in addition to my other incessant troubles, my own and other people's, domestic and public, civil and ecclesiastical, (from which no one in my office can in these times be exempt,) I am compelled, almost alone, to engage with external enemies, to say nothing of domestic ones. They are indeed our own countrymen, but enemies in heart, and enemies in the land they dwell in. For our fugitives at Louvaine began during the last year to be in violent commotion, and to write with the greatest asperity against us all. Me alone they have attacked by name. And why so? you will say. I know not, unless it be that they know me to be of all men the most averse from strife, and the most unable to resist. Yet, six years since, when I preached at court[1] before the queen's majesty, and was speaking about the antiquity of the popish religion, I remember that I said this among other things, that our enemies, when they accuse our cause of novelty, both wrong us and deceive the people; for that they approved new things as if they were old, and condemned as new things of the greatest antiquity; that their *private masses*, and their *mutilated communions*, and the *natural and real presence* and *transubstantiation*, &c., (in which things the whole of their religion is contained,) have no certain and express testimony either of holy scripture, or ancient councils, or fathers, or of any thing that could be called antiquity[2].

At all this they were in great indignation: they began to bark in their holes and corners, and to call me an impudent, bold, insolent, and frantic boaster. Four years after one Harding unexpectedly came forward; a man who, not very long since, was a hearer and admirer of Peter Martyr, and a most active preacher of the gospel, but is now a wretched apostate, and one whose character is well known to our friend Julius. This man would fain refute me out of the Amphilochiuses, Abdiases, Hippolytuses, Clements, Victors, supposititious Athanasiuses, Leontiuses, Cletuses, Anacletuses, the decretal epistles, dreams,

[[1] As bishop Jewel had preached at court this Lent, [1560,] so he had his day at the cross, which was the second Sunday before Easter. In both places he preached that famous sermon, wherein he openly challenged the papists. Strype, Annals, I. i. 300. His text was from 1 Cor. xi. 23, &c. Le Bas, p. 91.]

[[2] i.e. within 600 years from the birth of Christ.]

and fables. I replied to him last year, as well as I could. But, gracious heaven, what a life is this! Oh that strife might perish from among gods and men![1] I had scarce finished my work, when there suddenly flies abroad a *Confutation of my Apology*; an immense and elaborate work, and filled with abuse, contumely, falsehoods and flatteries. Here I am again pelted at. What would you have? He must be answered[2]. You thus perceive, reverend father, that we are far from idle, myself more especially, whose lot it is, I know not by what fatality, to be always battling with these monsters. May the Lord give me strength and courage, and beat down Satan under our feet! I have thought it right to acquaint you at length with these things, that should my letters in future arrive less frequently than either you expect or I wish, you may ascribe it to any thing rather than forgetfulness or ingratitude.

Our country is now free from war, and quiet as to matters of religion. Those countrymen of ours at Louvaine disturb us as much as they can; but our people are faithful to their duty, and I hope will continue to be. The queen is in excellent health, and averse from marriage. The last winter so injured the rising corn, that there is now much distress throughout all England from a scarcity of wheat. This year, by the blessing of God, all kinds of grain were most abundant.

I have not seen Parkhurst, bishop of Norwich, nor Sandys, bishop of Worcester, nor Pilkington, bishop of Durham, for the last three years[3]; so completely are we dispersed. We are all, however, safe and well, and with a grateful recollection of you. The only one that has died is Richard Chambers[4], who departed piously in the Lord.

The contest respecting the linen surplice, about which I doubt not but you have heard either from our friend Abel or

---

[1] Ὡς ἔρις ἔκ τε θεῶν ἔκ τ' ἀνθρώπων ἀπόλοιτο.
[Hom. Il. xviii. 107.]

[2 And this at length produced his [Bishop Jewel's] admirably useful, learned book, entitled his Defence [of the Apology]. Strype, Annals, I. ii. 178.]

[3 i.e. since the last synod.]

[4 Richard Chambers was one of the exiles at Frankfort, and with Grindal was an agent to the Strasburgh exiles to treat with those at Frankfort about the English service book in 1554. Strype, Life of Grindal, p. 14.]

Parkhurst, is not yet at rest. That matter still somewhat disturbs weak minds[5]. And I wish that all, even the slightest vestiges of popery might be removed from our churches, and above all from our minds. But the queen at this time is unable to endure the least alteration in matters of religion.

The affairs of Scotland are not yet quite settled. Some of their leading nobility are exiles among us; others have remained at home, and are preparing for resistance in case of any attempted violence; and from time to time sally forth from their castles, and drive off and carry away what they can from the lands of the papists. The queen herself, though obstinately devoted to popery, hardly knows where to turn. For with regard to religion, she has a great part both of the nobility[6] and people against her; and, as far as we can learn, the number is daily increasing. Within these few days king Philip privately sent thither a certain Italian abbot, with Spanish gold; a crafty man, and trained for intrigue. His business was to aid the king and queen with his subtle advice, and to throw every thing into confusion. The new king, who had hitherto abstained from going to mass, and had of his own accord attended the sermons, for the sake of popularity, when he first heard of the ship being expected to arrive on the morrow, became on a sudden more confident, and having taken courage,

[[5] The first bishops that were made, and who were but newly returned out of their exiles, as Cox, Grindal, Horn, Sandys, Jewel, Parkhurst, Bentham, upon their first returns, before they entered upon their ministry, laboured all they could against receiving into the church the papistical habits, and that all the ceremonies should be clean laid aside. But they could not obtain it from the queen and the parliament; and the habits were enacted. Then they consulted together what to do, being in some doubt whether to enter into their functions. But they concluded unanimously not to desert their ministry for some rites, that, as they considered, were but a few, and not evil in themselves, especially since the doctrine of the gospel remained pure and entire. Strype, Annals, I. i. 263.]

[[6] "The duke, the erles of Argile, Murray, and Rothoss, with sundry barons, are joynid together not to allow of the mariadg otherwise than to have the religion stablished by law, but the quene refuseth in this sort; she will not suffer it to have the force of law but of permission to every man to lyve according to his conscience; and herewith she hath reteyned a great nombre of protestants from associating oppenly with the other." Cecil to Sir T. Smith, Aug. 21, 1565. MS. Lansd. 102. 62. See Ellis's Original Letters.]

would no longer play the hypocrite. He went to church, and ordered mass to be said before him as usual. At that very time Knox, who is a preacher in the same town, and in the next church, was declaiming with his accustomed boldness, before a crowded congregation, against the mad idolatries, and the whole pontifical dominion. In the mean time this ship of king Philip, tossed about by the winds and tempests, shattered and broken by the waves, with its mast sprung, its timbers stove in, the pilots lost, bereft of crew and cargo, is driven, a mere wreck, and filled with water, upon the coast of England. I doubt not but that this has happened by divine providence, to teach the infatuated king what a dangerous thing it is to hear mass.

There is a report of great disorders in France. That house of Guise can never rest without some great mischief. But these things are much nearer you than ourselves.

The Dane and Swede have had some bloody battles with each other, and are reported to be still in arms[1]. Each of them has sustained much loss, nor can it be yet determined which is superior.

Your books, yours, my reverend father, on Daniel, and yours, my learned Lewis, on Joshua, have reached me in safety. I both thank our gracious and almighty God for you, and you for these labours and studies, and for all your kindness. I have sent herewith twenty crowns to our friend Julius for his yearly stipend, and the same sum to you two, that you may expend them, as is usual, either upon a public entertainment, or for any other purpose you may prefer. May God preserve in safety yourselves, the church, your state, and school! Salute in my name masters Gualter, Simler, Zuinglius, Gesner, Wickius, Haller, Henry and Rodolph Bullinger. Salisbury, Feb. 8, 1566.

Your attached and devoted in the Lord,

JOHN JEWEL, *Anglus.*

[[1] This war was occasioned by the voluntary submission of Esthonia to Sweden in 1561.]

LETTER LXVIII.

LAURENCE HUMPHREY TO HENRY BULLINGER.

Dated at Oxford, *Feb.* 9, 1566.

I CONGRATULATE you, reverend father in Christ, ourselves, and the church, that you are recovered from the long disease with which you were afflicted, and are now, by the blessing of God, raised up again and restored to health. And I pray again and again, that you may be strengthened more and more.

Your lucubrations on Daniel, together with the preface and honourable mention both of myself and my brother exiles, I saw and perused with great pleasure, and gratefully acknowledge your kindness. I am glad that you promise to comment upon Isaiah, and earnestly entreat you, with the help of the Lord, to persevere and finish the work you have begun. The book is altogether evangelical, full of mysteries, and in some parts, by reason of the concise structure of the sentences, and intermixture of history, and frequent figurative language, and some interruptions, rather obscure. Wherefore, though some excellent and learned men have thrown great light upon it, and have diligently laboured in the illustration of it, yet the addition of your own labour will be both pious and profitable. In the third chapter, where the prophet is discoursing about ornaments and female attire, should you think fit to insert any thing respecting this affair of the habits, it would in my opinion be worth your while. I am not ignorant of what you have already written; but you seem to have expressed your sentiments too briefly, and without sufficient perspicuity. Wherefore I again and again entreat your piety to reply in few words to those little questions of mine[2]; first, whether laws respecting habits may properly be prescribed to church-

[[2] These questions are given with a little variation by Strype, Annals, I. ii. 137. Bullinger's reply is given, Annals, I. ii. 505, and well deserves attention. It will be found in the Appendix.]

men, so as to distinguish them from the laity in shape, colour, &c.? Secondly, whether the ceremonial worship of the Levitical priesthood is to be reintroduced into the church of Christ? Thirdly, whether in respect of habits and external rites, it is allowable to have any thing in common with the papists, and whether Christians may borrow ceremonies from any counterfeit and hostile church? Fourthly, whether the distinguishing apparel of the priesthood is to be worn [upon all occasions] like a common dress? Whether this does not savour of monkery, popery, and Judaism? Fifthly, whether those persons who have till now enjoyed their liberty, can with a safe conscience, by the authority of a royal edict, involve in this bondage both themselves and the church? Sixthly, whether the clerical dress of the papists may be regarded as a matter of indifference? Seventhly, whether the habit is to be worn, rather than the office deserted? I had sent both to master Beza and yourself some other questions; I know not whether you received them. I entreat you to condescend to explain your judgment and opinion a little more fully as soon as possible; and also to touch upon and note the reasons upon which it is founded. You see that it is the Lernæan Hydra, or the tail of popery. You see too what the relics of the Amorites have produced. You see my importunity. Confer, I beseech you, on the whole matter with master Gualter and your colleagues, and write their opinion either to me or master Sampson. Oxford, Feb. 9, 1565, according to the English computation [1].

May Christ long preserve you to his church in health and happiness!

Your most attached,

LAURENCE HUMPHREY.

[[1] Until the introduction of the new style, A.D. 1752, the year in England commenced from the 25th of March.]

LETTER LXIX.

THOMAS SAMPSON TO HENRY BULLINGER.

Dated at LONDON, *Feb.* 16, 1566.

REVEREND father in Christ, I wrote you a letter six months since, and should have satisfied the wishes of many of my brethren, if, as I then earnestly requested, I had received an answer from your worthiness. But since either my letter was not delivered to you, or yours (if you have written any) appears to have been intercepted, I am under the necessity of repeating what I before stated.

Our church remains in the same condition as was long since reported to you. For, after the expiration of seven years in the profession of the gospel, there has now been revived that contest about habits, in which Cranmer, Ridley, and Hooper, most holy martyrs of Christ, were formerly wont to skirmish. The state of the question, however, is not in all respects the same, but the determination of those in power is more inflexible. This indeed is very gratifying to our adversaries at Louvaine, for they praise these things up to the skies.

But that you may more readily understand the matter in controversy, I have thought it best to reduce it into certain questions, which are these:

I. Whether a peculiar habit, distinct from that of the laity, were ever assigned to the ministers of the gospel in better times, and whether it ought now to be assigned to them in the reformed church?

II. Whether the prescribing habits of this kind be consistent with ecclesiastical and christian liberty?

III. Whether the nature of things indifferent admits of coercion; and whether any violence should be offered to the consciences of the many who are not yet persuaded?

IV. Whether any new ceremonies may be instituted, or superadded to what is expressly commanded in the word?

V. Whether it be lawful to revive the Jewish ceremonies respecting the habit of the priesthood, and which were abolished by Christ?

VI. Whether it be expedient to borrow rites from idolaters or heretics, and to transfer such as are especially dedicated to *their* sect and religion to the use of the reformed church?

VII. Whether conformity and general agreement must of necessity be required in ceremonies of this kind?

VIII. Whether those ceremonies may be retained which occasion evident offence?

IX. Whether any ecclesiastical constitutions may be tolerated, which, though from their nature they are free from any thing impious, do not, nevertheless, tend to edification?

X. Whether any thing of a ceremonial nature may be prescribed to the church by the sovereign, without the assent and free concurrence of churchmen?

XI. Whether a man ought thus to obey the decrees of the church; or on account of non-compliance, supposing there is no alternative, to be cast out of the ministry?

XII. Whether good pastors, of unblemished life and doctrine, may rightfully be removed from the ministry on account of their non-compliance with such ceremonies?

Here you have, most esteemed Sir, our difficulties. Here many pious men are hesitating; for the sake of whom I again ask it as a favour from you, that, having well considered the matter with master Gualter and the rest of your colleagues, with your wonted piety, you will plainly state your opinion, and send a written answer to each of the above questions. You will confer an exceeding kindness upon many, and on myself especially; and you will also confer an excellent benefit upon our church.

There is also another subject about which I desire to acquaint you. On the decease of our friend Chambers[1], there were entrusted to me some writings, which were, it seems, once much valued by master Hooper. Among others I found a copious manuscript commentary of master Theodore Bibliander[2], upon Genesis and Exodus. Since this book, as far as I am aware, was never printed, I am unwilling that the church of Christ should be any longer deprived of so great a benefit. If your worship will inform the heirs of master Bibliander that this writing is in my possession, and they are willing to publish it, let me know to whom I shall transfer it, or by what means it may be sent over to you with safety, and you will find me most ready to execute your wishes. These are the subjects on which I shall be daily expecting an answer[3]; and as to the questions especially, I humbly ask you, on behalf of many persons, to declare to us both your own opinion, and that of your brethren. May God Almighty very long preserve you to his church in life and health! London, Feb. 16, 1566.

Your worship's most devoted,
THOMAS SAMPSON.

LETTER LXX.

BISHOP JEWEL TO HENRY BULLINGER.
Dated at SALISBURY, *March* 10, 1566.

MUCH health in Christ. Although I have written to you, my reverend father, at great length within these few days, yet having met with some things in which I have great need of your judgment, I thought it would not be out of place

[1 See p. 148.]

[2 The proper name of this divine was Theodore Buchmann, which he translated into Greek, according to the usual practice of scholars in that age. He succeeded Zuingle as Professor of Theology at Zurich, where he died of the plague in 1564.]

[3 For Bullinger's answer to this letter, see the Appendix. It is in Strype, Annals, I. ii. 505, and Burnet, Hist. Ref. IV. 577.]

for me to write again. The things are of such a nature, that I doubt not, but that from your multifarious learning you will easily be able to afford me the information I require.

I wish to know, whether those Christians who are at the present time scattered throughout Greece, Asia, Syria, Armenia, &c. use *private* masses, such as are every where customary among the papists; and what kind of masses, private or public, are now in use among the Greeks at Venice? Again, a certain Camocensis[1] is sometimes quoted, as having written with asperity against the lives and insolence of the popes. Who was this Camocensis, of what order, and in what time and country did he live?

Lastly, what is your opinion respecting that German council[2], which is said to have been formerly held under Charlemagne, against the second Nicene council concerning images? For there are some persons who confidently deny such council ever to have existed. I ask it of your kindness not to think me impertinent in making these inquiries of you, especially at so great a distance; for you are almost the only remaining oracle of the churches. If you will write me an answer by the next fair, it will be sufficient.

Again and again farewell, my revered father, and much esteemed master in Christ. Salisbury, March 10, 1566.

Yours in Christ,
JOHN JEWEL, *Anglus*.

[[1] There is here a mistake in the name. "Jewel was gravely charged by Harding with naming *Johannes Camotensis* for *Johannes Carnotensis*," whom Mr Le Bas has shewn to be the celebrated John of Salisbury, who towards the close of his life was promoted to the see of Chartres, and was therefore sometimes entitled *Johannes Carnotensis*. Le Bas, Life of Jewel, p. 159. He flourished in the last half of the twelfth century.]

[[2] This council was convoked at Frankfort by Charlemagne, A.D. 794; and condemned, unanimously and strongly, the service and adoration of images. Le Bas, ut sup. p. 160. This too was in spite of a letter of pope Adrian in vindication of image-worship, and directed to Charlemagne himself. There were 300 bishops of France, Italy and Germany. The pope's legates were present, and it is considered in France as a general council. Du Pin, Bibliothéque, Tom. VI. p. 156. Paris. 1693.]

LETTER LXXI.

LAURENCE HUMPHREY AND THOMAS SAMPSON TO
HENRY BULLINGER.

Dated *July*, 1566.

As your diligence, most illustrious Sir, is proved to us by your writing, so also your incredible love towards us, and especial affection for our church, and most ardent desire for peace, are all evident from your very courteous letter[3].

We sent your reverence some questions, upon which the force, and as it were the hinge, of the whole controversy seemed to turn.

To these your reverence has accurately replied; but, if we may be permitted to say so, not entirely to our satisfaction. In the first place, your reverence replies, that such regulations respecting their habits may be prescribed to ministers, as that they may be distinguished both by colour and shape from those of the laity; for that it is merely a civil ordinance, and the apostle required the bishop to be κόσμιος, orderly[4]. But since this question is brought forward concerning churchmen, and relates to *ecclesiastical* polity, we do not see how the peculiar and clerical habit of ministers can be regarded as a mere *civil* matter. We admit, indeed, that a bishop must be κόσμιος, but this we refer with Ambrose to the ornaments of the mind, and not the decoration of the person. And as we require in dress both decency, and dignity, and gravity, so we deny that decorum is the object aimed at by the enemies of our religion.

In the second place, you answer hypothetically, that if a cap, and a habit not unseemly and without superstition, be prescribed to the clergy, Judaism is not on this account

[3 The letter of Bullinger to which this is an answer, will be found in the Appendix. See note 3, p. 155.]

[4 See 1 Tim. iii. 2, where the word is translated *of good behaviour*, or, in the marginal version, *modest*.]

brought back. But how can that habit be thought consistent with the simple ministry of Christ, which used to set off the theatrical pomp of the popish priesthood? For not only (as our people wish to persuade your reverence) are the square cap and gown required in public, but the sacred garments are used in divine service; and the surplice, or white dress of the choir, and the cope are re-introduced. Which things not only do the papists declare in their books to be copies and imitations of Judaism, but your reverence has more than once taught the same from Innocent. We most willingly subscribe to the testimony of our most revered master, Doctor Martyr: but the instances which he produces, tend to decency and order; these deform the church, disturb order, overturn all that is decent. The former [instances] are agreeable to the light of nature; the latter are unnatural and monstrous. Those, according to Tertullian's rule, had a shew of necessity and use: these are altogether frivolous, and superfluous, and useless; and neither conducive to edification nor any good end whatever, but more truly, to use the language of the same Peter Martyr, they were splendid accompaniments of that worship which all godly persons now abominate. The papists themselves are boasting that the distinction of ecclesiastical habits now adopted was a popish invention; the constitutions of Otho speak the same thing; the Roman pontifical shews it, and the eyes and lips of all prove it to be the case. The use of churches, stipends, baptism, the creed, &c. was established by divine command long before the pope was born. And, whatever we meet with in any heresy, that is of divine and legitimate authority, we do not deny that, with Augustine, we both approve and retain it. But because this matter is peculiarly one of error and disagreement, we resolutely argue and contend with it.

As to your adding, that the use of the habits was not abolished at the beginning of the Reformation, your informants have again stated what is by no means the fact. For in the time of the most serene king Edward the Sixth, the Lord's supper was celebrated in simplicity in many places without the surplice; and the cope[1], which was then abrogated by law, is

[[1] The use of this vestment, however, observes Mr Soames, must have been merely optional after the queen's injunctions were issued. It

now restored by a public ordinance. This is not to extirpate popery, but to replant it; not to advance in religion, but to recede. You say that the priestly garment is a matter of civil concern, and deny that it savours of monachism, popery, or Judaism. What the papists babble about the surplice, of how great importance the clerical dress is esteemed among them, and to what religion it is dedicated, we doubt not but that your prudence is well acquainted with from their books. In the next place, this ambitious and Pharisaical prescribing of a peculiar dress savours of monkery and popery, and those of the present age ascribe no less virtue to it than the monks of old did to their cowls. Nor in truth has this opinion of holiness and merit burst forth all at once, but has crept on insensibly by little and little. We are therefore hesitating, not without reason, and are endeavouring to check at the outset, what we fear will come to pass in this country. We do not agree with Eustathius[2], who placed religion in dress; so far from it, that we are at issue with those who superstitiously require peculiar and religious habits as badges of their priesthood. The like also may be said of the canon of the council of Gangra[3] and Laodicea[4], and of the sixth synod; and to depart from that liberty in which we have hitherto stood, we consider to be giving a kind of sanction to slavery. But neither in this are we too scrupulous; we make no vexatious opposition; we always avoid any bitterness of contention; we are ready to enter into an amicable conference; we do not voluntarily leave [our churches] to the wolves; but constrained and driven from our places, we depart with unwillingness and regret. We leave our brethren and the bishops to stand or fall to their own master; and we look most submissively, but in vain, for the like forbearance towards

is a pity, therefore, he adds, that the excellent writers mentioned it, as they were thus plainly denying a liberty to others which they insisted upon for themselves. Soames' Elizabethan Religious History, p. 31.]

[2 Eustathius was a Greek monk of the fourth century, whose errors were condemned at the council of Gangra. See next note.]

[3 Held about A.D. 365 or 370. The canon here referred to is the twelfth, "against those who fancy themselves to be more holy than others, because they wear a singular habit, and who condemn those that wear decent apparel." Du Pin, Bibliothèque, Tom. II. p. 340. Paris 1693.]

[4 Held A.D. 363.]

ourselves. In the rites nothing is discretionary; not that the queen's majesty has been excited to this by us, but she has been influenced by the persuasion of others; so that at length that is established, not which is for the interest of the church, but merely what is not unlawful; and what is not altogether impious, is accounted wholesome, and salutary, and holy, and is confirmed by law.

As ceremonies and sacerdotal habits are signs of religion and marks of profession, they are not of a civil character; and being borrowed from our adversaries, as all allow them to be, they cannot be convenient; and being marked with the divine anathema, and detested by all godly persons, and had in honour by the wicked and the weak, who think that without them we can neither be ministers, nor that the sacraments can be rightly administered, they neither can nor ought to be reckoned among things indifferent. The ancient fathers had their habits; but they were neither peculiar to bishops, nor distinguished from those of the laity. The instances of St John[1] and Cyprian[2] are peculiar. Sisinius was a heretic, and is neither to be held out for our commendation nor example. The *pallium* was a dress common to all Christians[3], as Tertullian relates in his book[4], and as your reverence has elsewhere remarked. Chrysostom makes mention of a white garment, but only incidentally; he neither commends it nor finds fault with it, and it is not yet ascertained whether it was peculiar to the priests or to the Greeks in general; linen or woollen; white or merely *clean in appearance*. In the address to the people of Antioch it is certainly opposed both by him and Jerome to a *sordid* [garment,] and in Blondus there is mention of a pallium

[1 Bullinger had quoted a passage from Eusebius, Hist. v. 24, speaking of St John as τὸ πέταλον πεφορηκώς, *wearing a plate* [of gold]. Epiphanius relates the same of James, the brother of our Lord. Hær. LXXVIII.]

[2 Pontius, the deacon, as quoted in Bullinger's letter, says of him, that at his martyrdom, *exuit se lacernam birrum,—dehinc tunicam tulit, et stans in lineâ expectabat spiculatorem.*]

[3 This was the opinion of Scaliger; Salmasius, on the contrary, maintained that it was peculiar to the priests.]

[4 *De pallio*, written about A.D. 209. It is a kind of satirical defence of Tertullian's having laid aside the Roman toga or *gown*, and assumed the pallium or *cloak*.]

[cloak] of woollen; so that in a matter of so much doubt nothing can be determined.

That the prescribing habits [to the clergy] is inconsistent with christian liberty, we have the testimony of Bucer, who was of opinion that the distinction of dress should be entirely done away with, as well on account of the present abuse of it in the English churches, as for a more decided declaration of our abhorrence of antichrist, a more full assertion of our christian liberty, and the removal of dissensions amongst brethren. These words he made use of in his letter to master à Lasco, who was altogether on our side. Whence it is evident, that great offence is occasioned, and edification impeded by it. We must indeed submit *to* the time, but only *for* a time; so that we may always be making progress, and never retreating. Far be it from us either to sow schisms in the church by a vexatious contest, or by a hostile opposition to our brethren to do an injury to ourselves[5]: far be it from us, most excellent Bullinger, to charge with impiety things which are in their nature indifferent: far be it from us either to make our own feelings the pretence of abuse, or under the name of conscience to conceal a fondness for dispute. These dregs and this leaven of popery are, believe us, the source of the whole controversy: we desire it to be taken away and buried in eternal oblivion, that no traces of antichristian superstition may remain. The assumption of preeminence and pride has always displeased us in the papacy; and can tyranny please us in a free church? A free synod among Christians hath heretofore untied the knots of controversy: why should every thing be now referred to the pleasure of one or two individuals? Where the liberty of voting and speaking prevails, the truth is vigorous and flourishing.

You will understand then, reverend father, in a few words, that these things are our principal object,—the authority of the scriptures,—the simplicity of the ministry of Christ,— the purity of the earliest and best churches, which, for the sake of brevity, we refrain from mentioning. But on the other side it has not hitherto been our lot either to hear or

[[5] The original is, *Camarinam moveamus*, a proverbial expression, derived, according to Suidas, from a lake of that name in Sicily, which being drained contrary to the advice of the oracle occasioned a pestilence.]

read of any law or general decree, either of Almighty God, or of any reformed church, or general council, (which is the rule of Augustine). We have discovered moreover, that the precedents hitherto adduced are particular ones, and do not confirm the general case.

Besides, we are of opinion, not that whatever may be in *any* way lawful, should be obtruded, but what in *every* way tends to the edification of the church should be introduced; and that what may be lawful to some, is not forthwith lawful to all. We have, (praised be God!) a doctrine pure and incorrupt: why should we go halting in regard to divine worship, which is not the least important part of religion? Why should we receive Christ rather maimed, than entire, and pure, and perfect? Why should we look for precedents from our enemies, the papists, and not from you, our brethren of the reformation? We have the same confession in our churches, the same rule of doctrine and faith; why should there be so great a dissimilarity and discrepancy in rites and ceremonies? The thing signified is the same; why do the signs so differ as to be unlike yours, and to resemble those of the papists? We have the same captain and leader, Christ; why are the banners of the enemy set up in our churches? which, if we were men of God, if we were endued with any zeal, we should long since have abominated and destroyed. We have always thought well of the bishops; we have put a candid interpretation upon their display of grandeur: why cannot they endure us who formerly bore the same cross with them, and who now preach the same Christ, and bear that most delightful yoke together with themselves? Why do they cast us into prison? Why do they persecute us on account of the habits? Why do they spoil us of our property and means of subsistence? Why do they publicly traduce us in their books? Why do they in their published writings commend a bad cause to posterity? For they have translated into our language some papers of Bucer and of Peter Martyr, and they have now sent forth to the public your private letters to us without our knowledge and consent. So that in pleading their own cause, and vindicating their honour, they neither consult the interests of our church, nor their brethren, nor your dignity, nor the succeeding generation.

But that your reverence may understand that the controversy is of no light or trifling character, but of great importance, and that we are not merely disputing about a cap or a surplice, we send you some straws and chips of the popish religion[1], from which with your wonted prudence you may imagine the rest, and with your wonted piety think upon a remedy as soon as possible. And we pray our Lord Jesus Christ to allay these tumults and disorders, to assert his glory, to send forth labourers into his vineyard, that a joyous and abundant harvest may ensue. And we implore you, that by your paternal advice, public writings, and private letters, you will exert yourself, and be active in effecting either the removal of these evils, or the toleration of those good men who are not yet convinced; lest the Roman ceremonial should disunite those whom the firm bond of doctrine hath joined together.

Give our salutations to Gualter, Simler, Lavater, Wolfius, our esteemed masters, with whom if you will confer, you will exceedingly gratify both ourselves and the church at large. May the Lord Jesus Christ bless his tabernacle and your Zurich! — July, 1566.

We have written briefly and in haste, and not so much by way of reply, as of admonishing you that there is no end to what might be said upon this subject. Do you then not decide upon what *may* or *can* be done, but upon what *ought* to be done[2].

Your reverence's most devoted,

LAURENCE HUMPHREY,
THOMAS SAMPSON.

Some blemishes which still attach to the church of England:

1. In the public prayers, although there is nothing impure, there is however a kind of popish superstition, which

[[1] See at the end of this letter.]

[[2] For Bullinger's reply to this letter in conjunction with Gualter, declining to enter further into the dispute, see Burnet, Hist. Reform. IV. 583. It will also be found in the Appendix to this volume.]

may not only be seen in the morning and evening service, but also in the Lord's supper.

2. In addition to the exquisite singing in parts, the use of organs is becoming more general in the churches.

3. In the administration of baptism the minister addresses the infant; in whose name the sponsors, in the absence of the parent, make answer concerning faith, and renouncing the world, the flesh, and the devil. The person baptized is signed with the [sign of the] cross.

4. Licence is also given to women to baptize in private houses.

5. The sacred habits, namely the cope and surplice, are used at the Lord's supper; kneeling is enjoined to those who communicate, and an unleavened cake is substituted for common bread.

6. The popish habits are ordered to be worn out of church, and by ministers in general; and the bishops wear their linen garment, which they call a *rochet*; while both parties wear the square cap, tippets, and long gowns, borrowed from the papists.

7. But what shall we say respecting discipline, the sinews of religion? There is none at all, neither has our church its rod, or any exercise of superintendence.

8. The marriage of the clergy is not allowed and sanctioned by the public laws of the kingdom, but their children are by some persons regarded as illegitimate.

9. Solemn betrothing takes place after the popish method and rites, by the [giving of a] ring.

10. Women continue to wear a veil when they come to be churched.

11. In the ecclesiastical regimen there are retained many traces of the church of antichrist. For as formerly at Rome every thing might be had for money in the court of the pope, so almost all things are saleable in the court of the metropolitan[1]; pluralities of benefices, licences of non-residence, for not entering into orders, for eating meat on days forbidden, and in Lent, at which time also it is forbidden to celebrate marriages without a dispensation and a fee.

[[1] For a list of dispensations and their prices, see Strype's Life of Grindal, p. 542.]

12. The free liberty of preaching is taken away from the ministers of Christ: those who are now willing to preach are forbidden to recommend any innovation with regard to rites; but all are obliged to give their assent to ceremonies by subscribing their hands.

13. Lastly, the article composed in the time of Edward the Sixth respecting the spiritual eating, which expressly oppugned and took away the real presence in the Eucharist[2], and contained a most clear explanation of the truth, is now set forth among us mutilated and imperfect.

LETTER LXXII.

BISHOP PARKHURST TO HENRY BULLINGER.
Dated at LUDHAM, *Aug.* 21, 1566.

MAY you be safe in Christ, my excellent Bullinger! I wrote to you on the 2nd of February, and sent with my letter twenty crowns, or else ten crowns and cloth for a gown; for I left it to Abel's discretion.

I received your letter on the 23rd of May. Shortly after the bishop of London sent me a copy of your reply to the letter of Laurence Humphrey and Thomas Sampson. It is printed here both in Latin and English. I received likewise, on the 12th of July, a most excellent little book, *The confession of the orthodox faith.*

In the month of March[3] an Italian, called Signor David

[2] The 28th of the thirty-nine Articles, which contained, in the time of Edward VI. the following paragraph: "Forasmuch as the truth of man's nature requireth, that the body of one and the self-same man cannot be at one time in divers places, but must needs be in one certain place; therefore the body of Christ cannot be present at one time in many and divers places. And because, as holy scripture doth teach, Christ was taken up into heaven, and there shall continue unto the end of the world, a faithful man ought not either to believe or openly confess the real and bodily presence, as they term it, of Christ's flesh and blood in the sacrament of the Lord's supper."]

[3 Viz. on March 9, 1566. The following circumstantial account of Rizzio's murder is given in a letter from the earl of Bedford and Ran-

[Rizzio], skilled in necromancy, and in great favour with the queen of Scots, was forcibly dragged out of her chamber in her presence, and died wretchedly pierced by many stabs. A certain abbot was wounded at the same place, and escaped with difficulty, but died of his wounds shortly after. A monk named Black, a Dominican friar, and a chief man among the papists, was killed in the court at the same time.

> Seized by black death, this blacker knave
> Descended to the gloomy grave[1].

The lords of the council, who were then assembled in one chamber, to consult about some matters of importance, when they heard of these massacres, (for they had no previous suspicion of any thing of the kind,) quickly betook themselves to flight, some one way, some another; some[2] threw themselves

dolph to the Council of England, dated Berwicke, March 27, 1566. "Upon the Saturdaye, at night, nere unto eight of the clocke, the king conveyeth himself, the Lord Ruthen, George Duglos, and two other, thorowe his own chamber, by the privie stairs up to the quene's chamber, joyning to which there is a cabinet about twelve footes square, in the same a little lowe reposing bedde, and a table, at the which there were sitting at the supper the quene, the ladie Argile, and David, with his cappe upon his heade. Into the cabinet ther cometh in the king and lord Ruthen, who willed David to come forthe, saying that ther was no place for him. The quene sayde that it was her wyll. Her husbande answerde that it was agaynste her honor. The lorde Ruthen saide that he sholde learne better his duetie, and offering to have taken hym by the arme, David tooke the quene by the blightes of her gowne, and put himselfe behinde the quene, who wolde gladly have saved hym, but the king having loosed his hands, and holding her in his armes, David was thruste oute of the cabinet thorowe the bed-chamber into the chamber of presence, where were the lord Morton and lord Lindesaye, who intending that night to have reserved him, and the next day to hang him; so manie being aboute them that bore hym evill will, one thruste hym into the bodie with a dagger, and after hym a great many other, so that he had in his bodie above sixty wounds. It is tolde for certayne that the king's owne dagger was lefte sticking in hym; whether he struck him or not, we cannot knowe for certayne. He was not slayne in the quene's presence as was saide, but going down the stayres oute of the chamber of presence." Ellis's Original Letters. MS. Cott. Calig. x. 373.]

[1] Sic niger hic nebulo, nigrâ quoque morte peremptus,
Invitus nigrum subito descendit in orcum.

[2 "In this mean tyme there rose a comber in the courte, to pacifie which there wente downe the lord Ruthen, who wente straighte to the earles Huntlye, Bothwell, and Athall, to quiet them, and to assure them

out of the windows at the risk of their lives, and thus escaped. The queen of Scots has brought forth a prince[3]; and whereas heretofore she had no great regard for her husband, I know not for what reason, she is now on the best of terms with him. She has lately received into favour the lord James[4], her brother by the father's side, whom she formerly detested; and not only him, but, as I hear, all the evangelical leaders. I wish it may be true. The gospel, which was lulled to sleep for a time, is again raising its head.

While I was writing the above, a certain Scottish refugee, a good and learned man, has informed me, that the queen was brought to bed ten weeks since, but that the child is not yet baptized. On my asking him the reason, he replied, that the queen will have her son baptized in the high church, and that many masses are to be celebrated. But the people of Edinburgh will not allow this: for they would rather die than suffer the detested mass to insinuate itself again into their churches. They are afraid however of her calling over auxiliary troops from France, that she may more easily overwhelm the gospellers. Let us entreat God for our pious brethren. She ordered some pious nobleman to turn Knox, who was residing with him, out of his house. May the Lord either convert or confound her! I am unable to write more, for I have been ill a long time, and am not yet entirely recovered. My hand is weakened by writing this. Farewell, my very dear Bullinger. Salute all your friends, and therefore all the godly, in my name. May the Lord with his right hand defend the state of Zurich! Ludham, Aug. 21, 1566.

In haste, yours,
JOHN PARKHURST, N[orwich.]

from the king, that nothing was intended against them. Theie notwithstanding taking feare when theie heard that my lord of Murraye wolde be there the nexte daye, and Argile meete them, Huntlye and Bothwell got oute of a wyndow, and so departe." Earl of Bedford to the Council, as above.]

[3 James the First, afterwards king of Great Britain. He was born June 19, 1566, and queen Elizabeth sent sir Henry Killigrew to congratulate the queen of Scots on her safe delivery.]

[4 The earl of Murray.]

LETTER LXXIII.

BISHOP GRINDAL TO HENRY BULLINGER.

Dated at LONDON, *Aug.* 27, 1566.

HEALTH in Christ, most illustrious master Bullinger, and my very dear brother in Christ. Master John Abel gave me the letter from you, addressed to the bishops of Winchester and Norwich in common with myself, together with what you had written on the controversy about the habits; copies of all which I immediately forwarded to them. As to myself, I return you my best thanks, both for manifesting so much interest for our churches, and for acquainting me, a man personally unknown to you, with what has been written to our brethren concerning the matters in dispute.

It is scarcely credible how much this controversy about things of no importance has disturbed our churches, and still, in great measure, continues to do. Many of the more learned clergy seemed to be on the point of forsaking their ministry. Many of the people also had it in contemplation to withdraw from us, and set up private meetings; but however most of them, through the mercy of the Lord, have now returned to a better mind. Your letter, replete with piety and wisdom, has greatly contributed to this result; for I have taken care that it should be printed[1], both in Latin and English. Some of the clergy, influenced by your judgment and authority, have relinquished their former intention of deserting their ministry. And many also of the laity have begun to entertain milder sentiments, now that they have understood that our ceremonies were by no means considered by you as unlawful, though you do not yourselves adopt them; but of this, before the publication of your letter, no one could have persuaded them. There are nevertheless some, among whom are masters Humphrey and Sampson, and others, who still continue in their former opinion. Nothing would be easier than to reconcile

[[1] Bullinger's letter here referred to will be found in the Appendix.]

them to the queen, if they would but be brought to change their mind; but until they do this, we are unable to effect any thing with her majesty, irritated as she is by this controversy. We, who are now bishops, on our first return, and before we entered on our ministry, contended[2] long and earnestly for the removal of those things that have occasioned the present dispute; but as we were unable to prevail, either with the queen or the parliament, we judged it best, after a consultation on the subject, not to desert our churches for the sake of a few ceremonies, and those not unlawful in themselves, especially since the pure doctrine of the gospel remained in all its integrity and freedom; in which, even to this day, (notwithstanding the attempts of many to the contrary,) we most fully agree with your churches, and with the confession[3] you have lately set forth. And we do not regret our resolution; for in the mean time, the Lord giving the increase, our churches are enlarged and established, which under other circumstances would have become a prey to the Ecebolians[4], Lutherans, and semi-papists. But these unseasonable contentions about things which, as far as I am able to judge, are matters of indifference, are so far from edifying, that they disunite the churches, and sow discord among the brethren.

But enough of our affairs. Things in Scotland are not so well established as we could wish. The churches indeed still retain the pure confession of the gospel; but the queen of Scotland seems to be doing all in her power to extirpate it. She has lately given orders that six or seven popish masses should be celebrated daily in her court, where all are admitted who choose to attend; whereas she was till now content with only one mass, and that a private one, no Scotsman being allowed to be present. Moreover, when the reformation first began, it was provided, that out of the estates of the monasteries, which were made over to the exchequer, salaries should

[2 See note 5, p. 149.]

[3 The Helvetic Confession, enlarged and improved in 1566. It extorted an unwilling eulogy from Bossuet. It has lately been reprinted by the Rev. Peter Hall, in his new edition of the Harmony of Protestant Confessions of Faith.]

[4 Ecebolus was a sophist of Constantinople in the fourth century, and teacher of rhetoric to the emperor Julian, whose apostacy he followed, but after his death sought to be reconciled to the church.]

be paid to the ministers of the gospel; whereas she has not made any payment whatever these three years. She has lately banished John Knox from her royal city of Edinburgh, where he has hitherto been chief minister, nor can she be induced to allow him to return. However, no public changes have as yet been made, except at court; and the leading men of the kingdom, the nobility and citizens, have, by a great majority, made a profession of the gospel, and manifested numerous and convincing proofs of their firmness. One of the most powerful is the lord James Stuart, earl of Murray, the queen's natural brother, a pious man, and of great influence with his party. They write me word from Scotland that the king and queen are on the worst of terms[1]. The reason is this: there was a certain Italian of the name of David [Rizzio], recommended to the queen by the cardinal of Lorraine. This man became her secretary and privy councillor, and had almost the entire administration of the government without any deference to the king, who is a young man of very trifling character. He was greatly offended at this, and having entered into a conspiracy with some of the nobility and persons about the court, he caused this Italian to be dragged out of the queen's presence, in vain imploring her protection; and, without assigning any reason, to be pierced with many daggers and murdered. The queen, although she has lately borne the king a son, cannot dismiss from her mind the memory of this atrocious act.

I have written these tidings from Scotland at greater length, as you probably hear but seldom from those parts. I entreat you to salute in my name master Gualter, and your other colleagues. May the Lord very long preserve you to us and to his church! London, Aug. 27, 1566.

Your most devoted in the Lord,
EDMUND GRINDAL, bishop of London.

[1 See the last letter.]

LETTER LXXIV.

RICHARD HILLES TO HENRY BULLINGER.

Dated at ANTWERP, *Dec.* 20, 1566.

MAY the Lord Jesus comfort you in every thing, and support you in your declining years, and above all never fail you in your old age!

I have so long abstained from writing to you, most learned Sir, chiefly on account of my harsh and barbarous and unsuitable Latinity, that I am almost ashamed and grieved to reply to your most gratifying letter to me, written from Zurich on the 28th of last August. Together with it I received from my very dear brother, master Abel, the united confession[2] of the Helvetian churches, written in German. You desire by your book to renew our ancient friendship, as indeed you will do, and I thank you very much for it. The Latin edition I already had in my possession at London, by means of the same master Abel; and this, if I remember right, on its being received from you at the last Lent fair at Frankfort. The book itself pleases me greatly, as it ought to do; for it every where prescribes godly and sincere doctrine.

Master Abel also informed me that your three married daughters had died of the plague[3]. I doubt not but that they died in the Lord, and are therefore blessed, not only because they rest from their labours, but also because they without doubt enjoy everlasting life with Christ our Saviour; as does also their excellent mother, your pious wife[4]. Since you are now, by divine providence, left a widower, and no longer a

[2 See note 3, p. 169.]

[3 Three of Bullinger's daughters were married to clergymen of Zurich; namely, to Hulric Zuinglius, (son of the reformer of that name,) Lewis Lavater, and Josiah Simler. They all died of the plague, the second in 1564, the two others in 1565. Bayle, Dict. Hist. See note 2, p. 30.]

[4 Bullinger's wife also died of the plague in 1564.]

young man[1], I doubt not but that you will follow the counsel of the apostle St Paul, where he says, "*For I would that all men were even as I myself. But every man hath his proper gift of God, one after this manner, and another after that. I say therefore to the unmarried and widows, it is good for them if they abide even as I.*" And again, "*Art thou bound unto a wife? seek not to be loosed. Art thou loosed from a wife? seek not a wife.*"

God be praised that you have finished the hundred and ninety homilies on the prophet Isaiah! When they are printed, I will, God willing, if I live, procure a copy; for I doubt not but that their publication will be attended with much advantage. I am sorry that you feel your strength is gradually failing; yet I hope for certain that our good and gracious God will not desert you in your old age, and I will pray to him on your behalf, as you desire me to do. God grant that he may hear my prayer, who hath said, "*Whatsoever ye shall ask of the Father in my name, he shall give it you.*"

I will salute my wife in your name. I know she will rejoice greatly, as soon as she hears of your good wishes; for she has a great regard for you. It will give her much pleasure when she hears from me that you are still, as you say, by the blessing of God, in tolerable health. She is every now and then greatly afflicted with the stone; sometimes indeed almost to death. Entreat, I pray you, the Lord in her behalf. I fear this disease will at length prove fatal. Since master Abel has had a large stone extracted, he has not been so well as before, and I am greatly afraid that he will not long remain with us. He is a pious man, a faithful friend, and an Israelite indeed. He has, as you have doubtless heard, or know to be the case, a pious and excellent wife. She is in good health, but has been lame in her feet ever since she left Strasburgh; as indeed she was for two years at that place before she left it. "*Whom the Lord loveth he chasteneth, and scourgeth every son whom he receiveth.*" And, "*Many are the afflictions of the righteous, but the Lord delivereth him out of them all.*"

I am anxious to explain to my wife some portion of the confession of the Helvetic churches. She occasionally reads

[1 Bullinger was at this time sixty years old.]

in the book, and sometimes makes it the subject of her meditation, as she is tolerably conversant with your language.

I have at home the other two letters which you sent me soon after the death of queen Mary, but I have quite forgotten the day and year when they were dated from Zurich. I thank you very much for them, as they abound in pious exhortation and most excellent comfort. May our Lord Jesus Christ repay you in turn abundant consolation in that day when your body shall be separated from your soul, and also when it shall again be united and restored!

My strength has been so declining for nearly the last three years, and my mind so weak, that I often wonder that I have lived so long. May the will of the Lord evermore be done! But I desire to be dissolved and be with Christ. In the mean time, while I remain here, I am often so tormented by innumerable cares and vain anxieties, (those namely arising from my calling as a merchant,) that I would far rather, if the Lord had so willed, be destitute of the trifling pleasures and empty joys of this world, so mingled, or rather altogether imbued, as they are with anxieties and disturbances of mind, than be in the enjoyment of such things. But the will of the Lord be done!

I have been here at Antwerp for nearly fourteen weeks, during which interval I have made our common friend, Christopher Mont[2], from time to time acquainted by letter with the state of affairs in Brabant, and especially at Antwerp, as far as relates to the change of religion and the toleration of evangelical preaching. And I doubt not but that you have received abundant intelligence respecting these matters, either from the Strasburgh ministers or the letters of other of our brethren; wherefore I do not think it necessary to repeat them.

Those who are in the habit of receiving letters from Spain, Italy, France and England, are now every where affirming that king Philip will come over in the course of the next spring on a visit to Brabant and the whole of lower Germany,

[[2] Dr Christopher Mount or Mundt, was an agent of queen Elizabeth, and resided chiefly at Frankfort or Augsburg. Many of his letters are still extant among the state-papers. He had been employed also in a diplomatic capacity both by Henry VIII. and Edward VI.]

either for the purpose of holding the general assembly of the nation, (by the authority of which all matters in dispute respecting religion may be reformed or altered,) or else to restore and establish the popish superstition, idolatry, and cruelty. But may God, in whose hand are the hearts of all princes, take away from this king and the rulers of this country their hearts of stone, and give them hearts of flesh, that being truly from the heart converted to Christ, they may be greatly grieved for their past sins and wickedness, and repent them of them; that they may obtain forgiveness and mercy from the Lord, and henceforth with all their might promote his glory!

It is to be lamented, that certain Lutherans, as you write, though they offer peace, yet do not desist from their annoyance of you. But here the Martinists, (as the Lutherans in general choose to be called, rather than Lutherans,) cease not openly to censure and reprove their orthodox fellow-ministers, (whom also they denominate Calvinists,) in their public discourses, and with the utmost boldness. The Martinists, however, have fewer churches than the orthodox; for they have only two, (one of which they assemble in a large barn,) while those whom they call Calvinists have three or four. Hitherto however both parties, except the minister who preaches in the barn above-mentioned, have preached in the open air, and not under cover: but now within these two months they have begun to erect churches, and proceed with great expedition in building them. As yet however the walls only (which are of brick and stone) shew themselves, and the buildings still remain uncovered.

Farewell in Christ Jesus, most reverend Sir, and may he evermore preserve you! Amen. Antwerp, Dec. 20, 1566.

Yours,
RICHARD HILLES.

LETTER LXXV.

BISHOPS GRINDAL AND HORN TO HENRY BULLINGER AND RODOLPH GUALTER.

Dated at LONDON, *Feb.* 6, 1567.

YOUR erudite letter to Humphrey and Sampson, so well adapted for allaying both our diversities of opinion respecting the habits, and our verbal altercations and disputes, we have received with the greatest satisfaction. We have also undertaken, not however without due consideration, and with the omission of the names of our brethren, to have it printed and published, from which step we have derived the good effect we expected. For it has been of much use to sound and sensible men, who look to the general design and object of the gospel; and has certainly persuaded some of the clergy, who were thinking of withdrawing from the ministry on account of the affair of the habits, (which was the only occasion of controversy and cause of contention among us,) not to suffer the churches to be deprived of their services on so slight a ground; and it has established and brought them over to your opinion. The laity too, who were excited by the importunate clamour of certain persons, and divided into various parties, and loud in their abuse of godly ministers, your letter has quieted, as it were, by a semblance of agreement with them, and soothed by its moderation. As to the morose, and those who cannot endure any thing but what they have themselves determined upon, although your letter has not satisfied them, it has been so far of use, that they are either less disposed or less able to load the godly with their invectives; and they do not deform with so much effrontery the wholesome peace of the church by their foolish discourses. We confess and lament that some of these have been dismissed from their office, although it is occasioned by their own fault, not to use a harsher term. But we think that we can bear this more easily, inasmuch as they are not many, but few in number; and though pious, yet certainly not very learned. For among those who have been deprived, Sampson alone can be regarded as a man whose learning is equal to his piety. Humphrey however, and all the more learned, still remain in their places. If your letter had been printed and published with a view to vindicate those who deprived them; or if those who have been deprived had been removed on account of any other points of controversy among us, and not solely on account of the habits; or if, lastly, that letter which handles the vestiarian controversy alone in such exquisite and perspicuous language, that it cannot be perverted to any thing else, had been dragged forwards in support of your approbation of other points upon which we are ignorant, and which, by the blessing of God, are not yet agitated among us, (for no differences of opinion except in this affair of the habits have hitherto arisen among our brethren,) it would in truth have been a manifest injustice to you whom we love, and reverence, and honour in the Lord; just as a manifest calumny is brought against us by those who are the authors of a most groundless report, whereby it has been stated that it is required of the ministers of the church either to subscribe to some new articles, or to be deprived of their office.

The sum of our controversy is this. We hold that the ministers of the church of England may adopt without impiety the distinction of habits now prescribed by public authority, both in the administration of divine worship, and for common use; especially when it is proposed to them as a matter of indifference, and when the use of the habits is enjoined only for the sake of order and due obedience to the laws. And all feeling of superstitious worship, and of the necessity [of these habits] as far as making it a matter of conscience, may be removed, rejected and utterly condemned, both by the terms of the laws themselves, and the diligent preaching of purer doctrine. They contend on the other hand, that these habits are not on any account now to be reckoned among things indifferent, but that they are impious, papistical, and idolatrous; and therefore that all pious persons ought rather with one consent to retire from the ministry, than to serve the church with these rags of popery, as they call them; even though we have the most entire liberty of preaching the most pure doctrine, and likewise of exposing, laying open, and condemning, by means of sound instruction, errors and abuses of every kind, whether as to ceremonies, or doctrine, or the sacraments, or moral duties. We cannot accept this crude advice of theirs, as neither ought we to be passive under the violent appeals by which they are unceasingly in the pulpit disturbing the peace of the church, and bringing the whole of our religion into danger. For by their outcries of this kind, we have, alas! too severely experienced that the mind of the queen, otherwise inclined to favour religion, has been much irritated; and we know for a certain fact, that the minds of some of the nobility, to say nothing of others, diseased, weak, and vacillating, have been wounded, debilitated, and alienated by them. And who will venture to doubt, but that the papists will lay hold of this opportunity to send forth and vomit their most pestilent poison against the gospel of Jesus Christ and all who profess it, encouraged by the hope that an opportunity is now afforded them of recovering the Helen that has been stolen from them? But if we were to acquiesce in the inconsiderate advice of our brethren, and all unite our strength illegally to attack the habits by law established, to destroy and abolish them altogether, or else all lay down our offices at once; verily we should have a papistical, or at least a Lutherano-papistical ministry, or none at all. But, honoured brethren in Christ, we call Almighty God to witness, that this dissension has not been occasioned by any fault of ours, nor is it owing to us that vestments of this kind have not been altogether done away with: so far from it, that we most solemnly make oath that we[1] have hitherto laboured with all earnestness, fidelity, and diligence, to effect what our brethren require, and what we ourselves wish. But now we are brought into such straits, what is to be done, (we leave you to conjecture, who are prudent, and sagacious in foreseeing the impending dangers of the churches,) but that since we cannot do what we would, we should do in the Lord what we can?

We have hitherto then explained the matter in dispute, and which occasions so much disagreement among us, according to the real state of the case. Hear now what we have yet further to communicate. That report[2], if indeed it may be

[1 See note 5, p. 149.]

[2 Bullinger's letter containing the report here referred to is given by

called such, (for we know and commend your prudence and moderation,) respecting the acceptance, subscription, and approbation of these new articles which you enumerate, is altogether a falsehood. Nor are those parties more to be depended upon, who either in their written letters, or verbally[1] in your presence, have under this pretext endeavoured to blind your eyes, and to brand us with a calumnious accusation. For almost all these articles are falsely imputed to us; very few indeed are acknowledged by us; and not one of them is obtruded upon the brethren for their subscription. We do not assert that the chanting in churches, together with the organ, is to be retained; but we disapprove of it, as we ought to do. The church of England, too, has entirely given up the use of [prayers in] a foreign tongue, breathings, exorcisms[2], oil, spittle, clay, lighted tapers, and other things of that kind, which, by the act of parliament, are never to be restored. We entirely agree that women neither can nor ought to baptize infants, upon any account whatever. In the receiving of the Lord's supper, the laws require, custom sanctions, and our Anglo-Louvaine calumniators in their reckless writings bear us witness, that we break the bread in common to every communicant, not putting it into his mouth, but placing it in the hand[3]: they testify also to our expla-

Burnet, Hist. Ref. IV. 584. It will be found in the Appendix. See also Soames, Elizabethan Religious History, p. 67.]

[1 Perceval Wiburn seems to be especially referred to. See below, Letter LXXVIII.]

[2 "In the first book of Edward VI. the priest, looking upon the children, was required to say, 'I command thee, unclean spirit, in the name of the Father, of the Son, and of the Holy Ghost, that thou come out, and depart from these infants, &c.' which form, says Mr L'Estrange, was agreeable to the usage of the first church, who applied it not only to the energumeni, or persons possessed by evil spirits, but also to infants, whom they accounted under the dominion of Satan, until he was by such increpation expelled. *Si Diabolus non dominatur infantibus, quid respondebunt Pelagiani quod illi exorcisantur?* saith Augustine. Of this custom there is very frequent mention in Cyprian, Tertullian, and other ancients." Hamon L'Estrange, Alliance of Divine Offices, p. 243.]

[3 So was the celebration observed by Christ himself, and so the primitive custom. One, mentioned in Eusebius, is said χεῖρα εἰς ὑποδοχὴν τῆς ἁγίας τροφῆς προτείνειν, to stretch out his hands for the receiving of the sacred food. In tract of time some indiscreet persons,

nation of the manner of the spiritual feeding and presence of the body of Christ in the holy supper. The wives of the clergy are not separated from their husbands; they live together, and their marriage is esteemed honourable by all (the papists always excepted). Lastly, that railing accusation of theirs is equally false, that the whole management of church government is in the hands of the bishops; although we do not deny but that a precedence is allowed them. For ecclesiastical matters of this sort are usually deliberated upon in the convocation, which is called together by royal edict, at the same time as the parliament, as they call it, of the whole kingdom is held. The bishops are present, and also certain of the more learned of the clergy of the whole province, whose number is three times as great as that of the bishops. These deliberate by themselves upon ecclesiastical affairs apart from the bishops, and nothing is determined or decided in convocation without the common consent and approbation of both parties, or at least of a majority. So far are we from not allowing the clergy to give their opinion in ecclesiastical matters of this kind. We receive, it is true, or rather tolerate, until the Lord shall give us better times, the interrogations to infants, and the sign of the cross in baptism, and kneeling at the Lord's supper; also the royal court of faculties, or, as they call it, of the metropolitan. We publicly profess, and diligently teach, that questions of this kind are not very suitable to be proposed to infants, notwithstanding they seem to be borrowed from Augustine[4].

We do not defend the signing with the sign of the

pretending greater reverence to the mysteries, as if they were defiled with their hands, were at the cost to provide certain saucers, or little plates of gold, to receive it, until they were forbidden by the sixth council in Trullo, (held at Constantinople under Justinian II. A.D. 692) the 101st canon of which enjoins, "that those that will receive the eucharist must hold their hands across and so receive it; and forbids using vessels of gold, or of any other matter, to receive it in." Another abuse the church of Rome brought in, where the priest puts it into the people's mouth, lest a crumb should fall beside; which, favouring transubstantiation, is by our church discontinued. See L'Estrange, ut sup. p. 218, and Bishop Mant on the Common Prayer, 4to. edition, p. 366.]

[4 For the practice of the ancient church on this subject, see Suicer, v. ἀποτάσσομαι. The passage referred to in Augustine seems to be taken from his tenth sermon, de verbis Apost. where he says, speaking

cross the forehead of the infant already baptized, although the minister declares in set terms that the child is signed with the [sign of] the cross, only "in token that hereafter he shall not be ashamed of the faith of Christ crucified;" and though it seems to have been borrowed from the primitive church[1]. We allow of kneeling at the receiving of the Lord's supper, because it is so appointed by law; the same explanation however, or rather caution, that the very authors of the kneeling, most holy men and constant martyrs of Jesus Christ, adopted, being most diligently declared, published and impressed upon the people. It is in these terms: "[2] Whereas it is ordained in the book of prayers, that the communicants should receive the holy communion kneeling; yet we declare, that this ought not so to be understood, as if any adoration is or ought to be done, either unto the sacramental bread and wine, or to any real[3] and essential presence of Christ's natural flesh and blood there existing. For the sacramental bread and wine remain still in their very natural substances, and therefore may not be adored, for that were horrible idolatry, to be abhorred of all Christians; and as to the natural body and blood of our Saviour Christ, they are in heaven, and not here; it being against the truth of the true natural body of Christ, to be at one and the same time in more places than one."

The court of faculties[4], from whencesoever it has been introduced, is the court of the sovereign, and not of the metropolitan. For that prudent father, learned as he is, and

of children, "accommodat illis mater ecclesia aliorum pedes, ut veniant, aliorum cor ut credant, aliorum linguam ut fateantur." Serm. CLXXVI. Tom. v. col. 1214. Paris. 1837.]

[1 See Suic. Thes. v. σταυρός. II. 1009, and Mant on the Common Prayer, p. 400.]

[2 A protestation, in effect, though not in words, the same as that cited above, was inserted in the liturgy of King Edward, in 1552, but on queen Elizabeth's accession was laid aside, and was again added at the last review [in 1561]. See Wheatly in loc.]

[3 The words *real and essential* presence were thought proper at the last review of the liturgy to be changed for *corporal* presence. Wheatly.]

[4 Archbishop Parker had much trouble with the court of faculties, and wished it were wholly suppressed, or else committed to some others. The rules he made for the better regulation of this court are given by Strype, Life of Parker, II. 15.]

exceedingly well disposed towards the propagation of the most pure religion, is exceedingly anxious, and earnest, and active, in entirely washing away the Romish dregs of every kind. And although we are unable to remove all the abuses of this fiscal court, as also some others, yet we do not cease to find fault with and censure them, and send them back to that hell from whence they proceeded. Believe us, reverend brethren, every minister is at liberty to speak against all matters of this kind, [so as it is done] with modesty and sobriety; and we by no means deprive of their office those ministers who refuse to receive or approve of those articles falsely ascribed to us.

Continue therefore to love, to advise, and to assist us, that the flame which has been stirred up amongst us solely on account of this affair of the habits, may be extinguished; and we will endeavour, to the utmost of our power, as we did at the last convocation, even although we could obtain nothing, that all errors and abuses may be corrected, amended and purified, according to the rule of the word of God. We commend you, brethren, to the grace of our Lord Jesus Christ, whom we pray to preserve you in safety, and your churches in peace, as long as possible. Salute your brethren and all your fellow-ministers at Zurich in our name. London, Feb. 6, 1567.

Your most loving

EDM. LONDON.
ROBERT WINTON.

P.S. And I also entreat you, my much-esteemed brethren, to pardon me that I have not yet replied to your letter written privately to myself; and that I have not as yet returned you my thanks for your most learned commentaries which you sent over to me. Neither let Wolfius and Lavater blame me for the like neglect. I entreat you to salute them most respectfully in my name, and to make my apology to them, for I know that my duty requires this; and I doubt not but that both you and they were in expectation of a letter from me. I will henceforth endeavour to satisfy you all by writing, and will not be wanting in my duty. Salute also, I pray you, from me, Simler, Zuinglius, and Haller. Live all of you, and farewell in Christ.

Wholly yours,

ROBERT WINTON.

LETTER LXXVI.

BISHOP GRINDAL TO HENRY BULLINGER.

Dated at LONDON, *Feb.* 8, 1567.

HEALTH in Christ, most renowned Bullinger, and very dear brother in Christ. I thank you that, in addition to your general letter, you have written separately to myself. But there is no reason why you should so studiously thank me, for having so frequently, and with so much satisfaction, made honourable mention of you. For I do this on account of your merit, as well knowing how much you have benefited the church, as you still continue to do, both by your ministry and your writings. Besides, I owe this to you as an individual, that by the perusal of your Treatise on the "Origin of Error[1]," about twenty years since, I was first led to entertain a correct opinion respecting the Lord's supper; whereas before that time I had adopted the sentiments of Luther on that subject. It is but just therefore that I should respect him from whom I have received so much benefit.

I have thus briefly replied to your letter, which was most acceptable to me. The churches in Scotland are in a some-

[1] Zanchius, in a letter to Bullinger, mentions with high commendation his book *De Origine Erroris*, and relates an anecdote of Montallinus, a monk, who was burnt at Rome for the cause of the truth, that the said good man, before Zanchius had seen the tract, persuaded him earnestly to peruse it; adding, that if it could not be had upon other terms, he might esteem it a good bargain, to pluck out his right eye for the purchase, and read it with his left. I soon bought the book, says Zanchius, without losing my eyes, and found it the delight of my soul. Zanchii Epist. Tom. II. p. 26. Hanov. 1609.]

what better condition than when I last wrote to you; but the queen herself remains unchanged. Her eldest[2] son was baptized in December last, after the popish manner, by some mitred pseudo-bishop; but two[3] only could be found out of the whole nobility of that kingdom, who thought proper to be present at the christening. The rest only accompanied the infant, both in going and returning, as far as the door of the chapel. You are, I suppose, not ignorant of what is going on in Brabant and Flanders. They will not, I hope, be without the divine assistance, since they appear to be in a great measure destitute of all human aid; and especially if, as I fear, the king of Spain should come with an army to overwhelm them. Greet, I pray you, master Gualter, and your other colleagues, in my name. May the Lord preserve you! London, Feb. 8, 1567.

Your most devoted in the Lord,

EDMUND GRINDAL,

Bishop of London.

[2 The ceremony was performed at Stirling on the 17th of December, 1566. Queen Elizabeth, being requested to be godmother, sent the earl of Bedford with a font of gold for a present. The prince was held up at the font by the Countess of Argyll, in the name and by the special appointment of the Queen of England. She was afterwards summoned for this before the general assembly of the reformed church, and professing her sorrow, was appointed to do penance for what was considered an offence to the religious profession. After the baptismal rites were performed, the name and titles of the prince were three times proclaimed by the heralds to the sound of trumpets. He was called and designed, Charles James, James Charles, prince and steward of Scotland, Duke of Rothesay, Earl of Carrich, Lord of the Isles, and Baron of Renfrew.]

[3 Bedford, the English ambassador, and all the Scottish Protestant nobility stood outside of the door while the ceremony was performed. Bedford afterwards observed to Elizabeth, that of twelve earls present only two had countenanced the rites. See Spottiswood, and Melville's Memoirs.]

LETTER LXXVII.

BISHOP JEWEL TO HENRY BULLINGER.

Dated at SALISBURY, *Feb.* 24, 1567.

Much health in Christ. As my last letter, most accomplished sir, arrived in London rather too late, so that it could not be forwarded in time for the fair at Frankfort, it returned to me without the accomplishment of its object; and I am rather afraid of the same thing happening to the one now before me.

For your late long and very learned letter to me I return you many thanks, and most gladly acknowledge myself to be completely satisfied respecting that synod at Frankfort, as a matter of doubt and controversy. Our ecclesiastical affairs, public and private, are in the same state as heretofore. Our Louvaine friends are making as much noise and disturbance as they can; and they have some auxiliaries, who, though not very numerous, are yet much more so than I could wish. And though they are many, and write against every one in general, yet I know not by what fatality they are all carried out against me alone; so that while I am replying to them, you must not think me idle.

We have assembled within these few months the parliament[1] of the whole kingdom, at which, however, owing to ill health, I have been unable to be present. Laws have been enacted concerning religion[2], by which the obstinate malice and insolence of the papists are kept within due bounds. The question respecting the succession was likewise brought forward; that is, to what family belongs the right of sovereignty, in case any thing, which we should much regret, should happen to Queen Elizabeth. This question occupied the minds of all

[1 The first day of the sitting of this parliament was Wednesday, Oct. 2.]
[2 The chief of these was a bill for confirming the consecration of archbishops and bishops. Strype, Annals, I. ii. 229.]

parties for a month or two[3]; for the queen was unwilling that any discussion should take place upon the subject, while every one else was exceedingly anxious about it; and the contest was carried on with great earnestness and ability on both sides. What next? after all nothing could be done; for the queen[4], who is a wise and cautious woman, suspects, that when her successor is once determined upon, there may hence arise some danger to herself[5]. For you know the saying, that there are more worshippers of the rising than of the setting sun.

As to religion, the affair of the habits has at this time occasioned much disturbance. For it is quite certain that the queen will not be turned from her opinion; and some of our brethren are contending about this matter, as if the whole of our religion were contained in this single point; so that they choose rather to lay down their functions, and leave their churches empty, than to depart one tittle from their own views of the subject. They will neither be persuaded by the very learned writings either of yourself and Gualter, or by the counsels of other pious men. However, we thank God that he does not suffer us at this time to be disquieted among ourselves by questions of more importance. One alone of our number, the bishop of Gloucester[6], hath openly and boldly

[[3] Namely, from Oct. 18 to Nov. 25. For a particular account of this discussion, see Strype, Annals, i. ii. 232, &c.]

[[4] The question respecting a successor had been moved in the session of 1562, when Sir John Mason, in a letter to Sir Thomas Chaloner, thus expressed his opinion of the queen's prudent conduct: "Bothe our howses have byn earnestly in hand with the queene to appointe her successor, but she wyll not byte at that bayte; wherein in myne opinion she hathe a better judgment than manye have of them that be so earnest in the matter." MS. Cotton. Galba. c. i. 87. This, and other letters referred to in several of these notes, may be found in Wright's Queen Elizabeth and her Times, London, 1838.]

[[5] Nov. 6th. Rogers and Cecil read in writing notes of the queen's sayings before the lords and committees of the commons; importing that her grace had signified to both houses, by the word of a prince, that she, by God's grace, would marry, and would have it therefore believed. And touching limitation for succession, the perils were so great to her person, and whereof she had felt part in her sister's time, that the time would not yet suffer to treat of it. Strype, Annals, i. ii. 235.]

[[6] Richard Cheney, consecrated Bishop of Gloucester, Apr. 19, 1562. He had also the bishoprick of Bristol *in commendam*. A character of

declared in parliament his approval of Luther's opinion respecting the eucharist; but this crop will not, I hope, be of long continuance.

There is some little disturbance now in Ireland. One John O'Neale[1], a bastard, has lately been levying troops, and insolently defying our soldiery. But this is a matter of more tediousness than danger; for he conceals himself afar off in the bogs and wastes, where our forces cannot easily overtake him.

From Scotland, however, (what shall I tell you, or what will you believe?) horrible and atrocious reports are announced. And though they are of such a nature as that I can hardly believe them possible, yet they are written to me from court, and are every where noised about, and believed by all. The young king, they say, has within the last few days[2], together with an attendant whom he has had from his cradle, been murdered in his house, and carried out of doors, and left in the open air. Believe me, my mind shudders to relate such things, whether they are true or not; yet if they should be true, I will hereafter give you entire information as to the motives, or to what treachery he has fallen a victim, as soon as I shall have become acquainted with all the circumstances

him is given by Strype, Annals, I. i. 418, who confirms the statement in the text, by saying, "We may conclude him not a papist, but a Lutheran rather, in his opinion of the eucharist." Annals, I. ii. 285.]

[1 Shane, or John, O'Neale, the son of Con O'Neale, who had been created Earl of Tyrone, usurped the sovereignty of his clan in opposition to the will of his father, who had appointed his illegitimate son Matthew for his successor. Shane had rebelled in queen Mary's days, and again in 1561, when he was induced, by the persuasions of the Earl of Kildare, to make his submission to queen Elizabeth, and accordingly went to London for that purpose in Jan. 1562. See a letter from Cecil to the Earl of Sussex. MS. Cotton. Titus. b. XIII. 69. He rebelled a third time in 1566, and was reduced by the Lord President to such extremity, that he was on the point of submitting, but was persuaded, by one of his attendants, to make a last attempt upon the Scots. They pretended to embrace his advances, and at a feast treacherously murdered both him and his companions, and sent his head to Dublin. For an account of his last rebellion see the Sidney Papers, Vol. I. p. 15, and a letter from the Archbishop of Armagh [Loftus] to the Earl of Sussex, MS. Cott. Titus, b. XIII. 159.]

[2 Namely, on Feb. 10th. For a detail of the circumstances attending this murder, see Lett. LXXIX, and Camden's Elizabeth, p. 88.]

of the case. At present, I can neither be wholly silent upon a subject which is so universally spoken of, nor can I affirm too confidently what I do not yet know to be the fact.

I hear that my friend Julius is dead at Zurich. I send him, however, twenty French crowns, for his own use, if he is still living; but if, which I hope is not the case, he is dead, let them be expended upon a scholastic entertainment. Had I leisure, I would write to masters Lavater, Simler, Wolfius, Haller, and others; and especially to Gualter, to whom, ungrateful that I am, I have never yet written. Salute all of them, I pray you, affectionately in my name, and especially your [sons] Rodolph and Henry.

Farewell, my father, and most esteemed master in Christ. Salisbury in England, Feb. 24, 1567.

Yours in Christ,

JOHN JEWEL, *Anglus*.

LETTER LXXVIII.

PERCEVAL WIBURN[3] TO HENRY BULLINGER.

Dated at LONDON, *Feb.* 25, 1567.

HEALTH. When I was with you, reverend sir, at Zurich last summer, your having so kindly received me, an obscure individual, and uncommended to you by any public testimony, as to entertain me at your table, was a singular proof of your courtesy and hospitality; for which I acknowledge myself most deeply indebted to you. But that I was prevented by your illness from conversing with you as freely and fully as I wished respecting our affairs, and the state and condition of the church in this country, this indeed was very mortifying to me during my stay in your city, inasmuch as through

[[3] For some account of Perceval Wiburn see the Index.]

this circumstance I was deprived of the greatest advantage of my visit: afterwards, however, I perceived that this turned out most happily, and not without the direction and providence of God.

You remember, excellent sir, if I am not mistaken, that on the day on which you sent for me, by your son, from my lodgings, and desired me to declare the object of my visit, master Gualter being also present, I did not complain at any length concerning the calamity and distress of this our church; partly because you considered yourself as possessing clearly a more than sufficient acquaintance with our affairs; and partly too because you had been so well informed of all these things by the letters of some of our brethren, and especially of master Beza, that there was no occasion to add any thing to that intelligence. Having therefore placed in your hands two schedules, of which mention was made in master Beza's letter to you, I was dismissed by you to my lodgings, so that in the mean time I did not utter a single word upon any given point of religion. And afterwards too, during the two days in which I was waiting for your letter, it is quite evident that I had no conversation either with yourself or others, excepting only that I proposed some questions respecting habits and ceremonies in general to one or two of your congregation. But lo! most learned father, on my return home to my friends, I am charged with detraction and calumny, as if I had gone to you expressly to defame and detract from others, which would have been very unbecoming, or as if I had purposely studied to give a false and feigned report respecting our church. And upon anxiously inquiring the cause and origin of this charge, I find all the mischief to have arisen from your letter to the bishops, which, as I received it sealed, and evidently ignorant of its contents, I had some time before taken care should be delivered into their hands. Why should I prolong my statement? Being fully conscious of my innocence in this matter, I forthwith waited upon the bishop of Winchester, who was then in London, and conversed with him seriously, (as it was right I should do,) upon this business: at length a letter was produced in your handwriting, stating that reports had reached you respecting a strange language, clay, spittle, candles, and I know not what else, here made use of in the public service; for I was only permitted at that time to look over one or two sentences. They will have it that I am the author of this report[1]. But, though this is so very trifling in the relation, and the very supposition falls to the ground by its own absurdity, yet since it has acquired so much strength, either by the instigation of the devil himself, or by the hatred and malice of some individuals, and the too great credulity of others, that I am meanwhile labouring under a heavy suspicion with those persons whom I have now for some years embraced as friends and brethren in Christ, and with whom also I desire to live henceforth upon friendly terms, as far as lies in my power; I am therefore compelled to have recourse at this time to your friendship, that, known as you are for piety and integrity, you may by your testimony vindicate my innocence from being thus slandered. You cannot easily forget, reverend sir, what were the heads I complained of in the articles; so that there was not the slightest occasion to scrape together the strange language, clay, spittle, candles, and other superfluities, to increase this mischief. I would that this church were as free from other burdens and blemishes, as by the grace of God she is free from these evils: the complaint of the godly would not certainly in that case be so well founded, as it now is, alas! too much so.

You will take in good part my freedom in making this request, when you consider, first, that my own testimony respecting myself in this matter, however simple and true, cannot easily be confirmed; and next, that the affair has come to that pass, by the rashness and inconsiderateness of some parties, that it is made known to some of the highest authorities in this kingdom; lastly, that the cause of the ministers, otherwise good and holy, has under this pretext come into bad odour with many persons, whence it happens, that abuses are now sticking closer and retained more pertinaciously, and all hope of reformation is almost entirely abandoned. For, (besides that the ancient superstitions and relics of popery are too agreeable to many parties, and there are also found among ourselves patrons of those things, who distort the writings of learned men, and your own especially

[1 See above p. 178.]

into that direction,) if the rest of the ministers should once be convicted of circulating false reports, it is easy to conjecture how little their diligence and exertions will avail them in future even in the best of causes; so that not only my own danger as an individual, but the common cause, which is certainly not that of man, but of Jesus Christ, especially demands your aid and support. I do not therefore entertain any doubt but that you will promptly and with alacrity put forth your hand in so honourable and necessary a cause. For my own part, I by no means desire you to glance at or censure others, (though this indeed might be done according to the general practice, yet unless it were done in general terms, and with much discretion, it would not be very safe for myself;) but I only ask this, that you will defend and vindicate me, now in danger, upon just grounds; and this, if it please you, in a private letter to myself, lest greater disquiet should arise, in case it should be known to some parties; but if they will be at peace, I wish for nothing else, but desire only to have something which it is in your power to grant, and which may serve them for an answer. And though this, whatever it be, might, and perhaps should, have been sought for by me at an earlier period, yet I have hitherto abstained from writing that I might spare you, who are both old and infirm, and already more than enough troubled by this matter. And I wish that I could still and altogether spare you any trouble; but when the first counsellor of this kingdom has lately sent for me in a private and friendly way to advise me about this business, and recommended me to obtain two or three words from you, to be ready if necessary, I have at last, most excellent sir, as you see, thrown myself with confidence upon your justice, in which I earnestly implore and entreat you not to reject me, and thereby at the same time provoke those persons yet more against me, whom I find sufficiently harsh and hostile already. And if you will be kind enough to send to Geneva what you may think proper to write, either to master Beza, or master Raymond, by whom it may be afterwards forwarded to the minister of the French church in London, (a thing they do very frequently,) your letter will by this means safely reach me, if it is directed to me by name.

You may readily infer, my father, from this, that I do not so ardently and seriously request an answer from you, as I expect it with anxiety and solicitude. I shall, in the mean time, comfort and support myself as well as I can, by the testimony of my conscience. May the Lord Jesus long preserve you in safety to his church, and daily visit you with his increasing power!

Salute, I pray you, from me, that most excellent servant of Jesus Christ, master Rodolph Gualter and his wife, whom if you will thank for my sake, or rather in my name, you will gratify me exceedingly. Salute also, I pray you, your other fellow-ministers with whom I am acquainted, masters Simler, Wolfius, both your sons, and especially the younger, to whom I am greatly indebted for the kindness which he shewed me at Zurich.

Farewell, most reverend father in Christ, and remember, I pray you, this tottering church in your prayers to God. Again farewell. London, Feb. 25, 1567.

Your reverence's most devoted,

PERCEVAL WIBURN.

LETTER LXXIX.

BISHOP GRINDAL TO HENRY BULLINGER.

Dated at LONDON, *June* 21, 1567.

HEALTH in Christ, master Bullinger, and very dear brother in the Lord. I heartily thank you for having received my letter with such acceptance, and likewise for your Homilies on Isaiah, which I received through master John Abel. The bishop of Winchester and myself replied at the last Frankfort fair to your letter of September, sent by Wiburn[1], but delivered to us by some one else; and I hope you have long since received our answer.

[1 See p. 188.]

With respect to the publication of your letter on the vestiarian controversy, I knew indeed that you did not write it with that view; but as I foresaw for certain that great advantage would arise to our churches from its publication, I persuaded myself that you would take it in good part.

Our affairs are pretty much in the same state as heretofore. We have now with us count Stolberg[1], a German ambassador from the emperor Maximilian. He demands, as I hear, an annual subsidy of money for the war with the Turks. But he does not seem likely to get any thing here, unless other kingdoms and states will unite in making a common contribution. There is also some talk respecting a marriage between our queen and Charles of Austria[2]; but religion is duly provided for throughout the whole business; so that unless Charles chooses to renounce popery, he has nothing to hope for in this quarter. Henry, who was lately king of Scotland, as I suppose you know, was found[3] dead on the tenth of last February, in a garden adjacent to a seat he had at some distance from the court. Persons are not yet agreed as to the manner of his death. Some say that the house was blown up by means of some barrels of gunpowder placed on purpose under the chamber in which he slept, and that he was carried by the explosion into the adjoining garden[4]. Others however affirm, that he was violently dragged from his chamber in the dead of night, and afterwards strangled, and that the house was last of all blown up with gunpowder. A certain lord named Bothwell is universally suspected of this murder. The queen of Scotland[5] married him on the fifteenth of May, after he had di-

[1 Count Stolberg was sent over to treat for a marriage between the archduke Charles and the queen of England.]

[2 For the conditions offered see Strype, Annals, I. ii. 240. After various proposals, the article of religion was found to be an insurmountable difficulty, and the match was broken off.]

[3 See p. 186.]

[4 This supposition is contradicted, according to Hume's account, by the confession of the criminals.]

[5 The ceremony was performed in a private manner, after the rules of the popish church; but to gratify the people, it was likewise solemnized publicly, according to the Protestant rites, by Adam Bothwell, bishop of Orkney, an ecclesiastic, who was afterwards, Hume states, deposed by the church for this scandalous compliance.]

vorced his lawful wife[6] by the authority of the archbishop of St Andrews, and raised him to be duke of Orkney. A short time before this marriage almost all the nobles of the kingdom[7], perceiving that no inquiry was made concerning the murder of the king, retired from the court, and held a separate assembly at the town of Stirling. In this assembly it was discovered by indisputable evidence, that this abominable murder had been perpetrated by Bothwell. Wherefore they collect troops, and endeavour to seize upon him; he betakes himself to flight, but whither he is gone, as yet no one knows. Some say that the queen[8] is besieged in a certain fortress; but others assert that she is detained prisoner in Edinburgh Castle, as being privy to the murder of her husband. Whatever be the fact, it is impossible but that this infamous marriage must end in some dreadful tragedy. But we are in

[[6] Sister to the earl of Huntley, to whom he had been married two years before.]

[[7] The leaders of this confederacy were the earls of Argyle, Athol, Morton, Mar, and Glencairn; the lords Hume, Sempil, and Lindsay; the barons Kirkaldy of Grange, Murray of Tullibardin, and Maitland of Lethington.]

[[8] "On June 4th, 1567, Morton, Mar, Hume, and Lindsay, with other inferior barons, and attended by 900 or 1000 horse, on a sudden surrounded the castle of Borthwick, where Bothwell was in company with the queen. Bothwell had such early intelligence of their enterprise, that he had time to ride off with a few attendants; and the insurgent nobles, when they became aware of his escape, rode to Dalkeith, and from thence to Edinburgh, where they had friends who declared for them in spite of the efforts of Mary's partisans. The latter, finding themselves the weaker party, retreated to the castle of Edinburgh, while the provost and armed citizens, to whom the defence of the town was committed, did not indeed open their gates to the insurgent lords, but saw them forced without offering opposition. These sad tidings were carried to Mary by Beaton, archbishop of Glasgow, who gives the above statement in a letter to his brother, dated June 17th. He found the queen still at Borthwick, 'so quiet, that there were not with her passing six or seven persons.' She had probably calculated on the citizens of Edinburgh defending the capital against the insurgents; but when this hope failed, she resolved on flight. Her majesty, says the letter, in men's clothes, booted and spurred, departed that same night from Borthwick to Dunbar; whereof no man knew save my lord duke [Bothwell] and some of his servants, who met her about a mile from Borthwick, and conveyed her to Dunbar." Mackie's Castles of Mary Queen of Scots, p. 162.]

daily expectation of more certain intelligence of all these things, of which I will shortly take care to let you know.

I write nothing concerning the persecutions in Flanders, because I think you are not ignorant of them. There are many rumours here about Geneva being besieged, but I hope they are not true. May the Lord Jesus preserve your piety in safety to us and to the church! Your most devoted in the Lord,

EDMUND GRINDAL,
Bishop of London.

LETTER LXXX.

BISHOP PARKHURST TO HENRY BULLINGER.

Dated at LUDHAM, *July* 31, 1567.

I RECEIVED a letter from you on the 17th of October, and also on the 16th of May; for both of which, and for your very learned discourses on Isaiah, I return you my warmest thanks. Nicolas Carvil[1] died last summer, and at the beginning of this month Robert Beaumont, master of Trinity College in the University of Cambridge. They have gone before us: we shall follow them when the Lord shall think fit.

John O'Neale[2], a chieftain and possessed of great authority among the wild and uncivilized Irish, has, notwithstanding his

[1 Nicolas Carvil had been one of the exiles at Zurich in queen Mary's time, as had also Rob. Beaumont. Strype, Memorials, III. i. 233.]

[2 See note 1, p. 186. Cecil writes, in a letter to the earl of Sussex, dated Jan. 7. 1561. "On Saturday he (O'Neale) cam to the lord keeper's house, where wer with the lord keeper, the lord Marquis of Northampton, the earle of Pembrook, the vice-chamberlayn, and poore I. There he humbly requyred that we wold be meanes for hym to come to her majesty's presence to acknowledg his obedience. After some sharp rehersall to hym of his generall faults, we promised him our meanes. We wold not suffer him to reply for his defence, meaning to leave that untill your lordshipp come. So I thought mete that his submission shuld be both in Irish and English, which he made uppon his knees, and first prostrat upon his face." MS. Cotton. Titus. b. XIII. 69.]

oath, excited a rebellion against our queen. During this whole year he has been in arms, and was lately killed in an affray. There is now some hope that this rude and savage people, living only upon plunder, will become more humane and civilized.

After the murder of Henry [Darnley,] king of Scotland, the queen married the earl of[3] Bothwell, who has lately been created duke of Orkney. His wife[4] is yet living, and is, as I am told, a most noble and excellent lady. The nobility[5] have humbled the queen; but they notwithstanding treat her with great kindness, remembering, as it is right they should, the allegiance due to her. The duke[6] has fled, I know not whither, detested by almost every one on account of this cruel murder of his sovereign. With whose concurrence he did this, I will not say; but fame circulates some wonderful and horrible rumours:

"Fama, malum quo non aliud velocius ullum,
Tam ficti pravique tenax quam nuntia veri."

The nobles of Scotland have at their command some regiments, and in all their colours or standards they bear this painted representation. There is depicted a green and beau-

[3] See p. 192.   [4] See note 6, p. 193.]
[5] After a conference with Kirkaldy of Grange, the queen put herself, upon some general promises, in the hands of the confederates, and was conducted to Edinburgh amidst the insults of the populace. Hume.]
[6] His end is thus told by Sir James Melvil: "Now the laird of Grange, his two ships being in readinesse, he made sail towards Orkney, and no man was so frank to accompany him as the laird of Tullibardin, and Adam Bothwell, Bishop of Orkney. But the earl [Bothwell] was fled from Orkney to Sheatland, whither also they followed him, and came in sight of Bothwell's ship; which moved the laird of Grange to cause the skippers to hoise up all the sails, which they were loath to do, because they knew the shallow water thereabout. But Grange, fearing to miss him, compelled the marriners, so that for too great haste the ship wherein Grange was did break upon a bed of sand, without loss of a man; but Bothwell had leisure in the mean time to save himself in a little boat, leaving his ship behind him, which Grange took, and therein the laird of Tallow, John Hepburn of Bantoun, Dalgleesh, and divers others of the earl's servants. Himself fled to Denmark, where he was taken, and kept in strait prison, wherein he became mad and dyed miserably." Wright's Life and Times of queen Elizabeth, Vol. I. p. 257.]

tiful tree, under which is lying a tall man, naked, and strangled with a rope: near him is a young man, also naked, and pierced with many wounds: next is painted a little boy with a crown of gold upon his head, with bended knees and uplifted hands, and these words written as proceeding from his mouth, " Lord, have mercy on me, and avenge my father's blood." Hereby are represented the king, his attendant, and his son. I cannot write more. Business presses. The courier is in haste. Rodolph Gualter will tell you every thing else.

I would have written to Wolfius, Lavater, Simler, Wonlychius, Froschover, and Julius: but I can not; I wish I could. They must take it in good part. I will write to them at another time. Farewell. Salute all my friends. In haste. Ludham, July, 31, 1567.

Yours,

JOHN PARKHURST,

[Bishop] of Norwich.

LETTER LXXXI.

BISHOP GRINDAL TO HENRY BULLINGER.

Dated at LONDON, *Aug.* 29, 1567.

HEALTH in Christ our Saviour. The affairs of Scotland, respecting which I promised in my last letter to write more fully, are now, in this condition. The nobility[1] of the kingdom, having taken offence at the marriage[2] of the queen of Scots with the regicide Bothwell, about the end of June last collected together a numerous body of troops. When Bothwell, who had also assembled some forces, discovered his inferiority, he fled with four or five ships to the Orkney[3] islands. The queen surrendered herself to her nobles, who conveyed her to a strongly fortified castle in the middle of the lake called Lochleven, where she is still in custody. After some days the

[[1] See note 7, p. 193.] [[2] See note 5, p. 192.] [[3] See note 6, p. 195.]

queen, by a solemn public instrument[4] resigned her royal dignity to the prince her son, who was crowned king of Scotland towards the end[5] of the July following. Not long after was held a convention[6] of the estates, in which were decreed these five things: first, they declared the Lord James Stuart, earl of Murray, or Moray, of whose piety I think I have before written to you, the king's guardian and regent of the kingdom. Next, they prohibited, under a heavy penalty, all exercise of the popish religion. Thirdly, an universal reformation of the churches was determined upon. Fourthly, the stipends of the clergy were confirmed and augmented. Fifthly, and lastly, they decreed that the advisers and perpetrators of the king's murder should be sought out and punished. The queen is still kept in the closest confinement, and there are those who think it will be perpetual. It is reported that there were found in Bothwell's writing desk some letters written in the queen's[7] own hand, in which she exhorted Bothwell to

[4 The confederate lords, by putting the queen in fear of death, compelled her, unheard, to set her hand to three writings: by the first whereof she resigned the kingdom to her son, who was scarce thirteen months old; by another, she constituted Murray to be vice-roy or regent in the minority of her son; and by the third, she named, in case Murray should refuse the charge, these governors over her son, James, duke of Chatelherault, Matthew, earl of Lennox, Gillespie, earl of Argyle, John, earl of Athol, James, earl of Morton, Alexander, earl of Glencairn, and John, earl of Mar. Camden's Elizabeth, p. 96. "She was urged to the resignation of the crown by the implacable Lindsay, who with his mailed hand seized the delicate arm of the queen, and swore that unless she subscribed the deeds without delay, he would sign them himself with her blood, and seal them on her heart." Mackie, Castles of Q. Mary, p. 202.]

[5 He was proclaimed July 29, by the name of James VI., and soon after crowned at Stirling. Hume.]

[6 Sir Nicholas Throgmorton writes to the earl of Bedford, in a letter dated Edenborowghe, July 20, 1567, and preserved in the state paper office, "The assembly contynueth the 20th day of thys moneth: where I thynke lytle wyl be done to the quene of Scotlande's advantage."

[7 This subject has long been involved in great uncertainty. On the one side, Camden states that some servants of Bothwell's, who were put to death by Murray for being present at the murdering of the king, protested at the gallows that they understood from Bothwell, that Murray and Morton were the authors of the king's death. The queen they cleared from all suspicion; as Bothwell also himself, being prisoner in Denmark, many times witnessed, both living and dying, with

accelerate the death of the king, her husband. How true this may be, I know not. A certain baron (Grange[1] by name) was lately dispatched with four armed vessels in pursuit of Bothwell. For it is now generally agreed that he strangled the king with his own hands, and then blew up the house with gunpowder, that it might appear accidental. From this you may easily imagine what great and terrible commotions have lately taken place in Scotland. In the mean time we entertain the most lively hopes, that all these things will turn out to the further advancement of evangelical doctrine. John Knox has lately returned, amidst the great rejoicing of the people, to his church in Edinburgh, from which he had heretofore been altogether banished[2].

Thus much of the affairs of Scotland. Our own are pretty much in the same state as when the bishop of Winchester and myself last wrote to you. All men's minds are not yet settled, but we are daily hoping for an improvement. We were exceedingly glad that no attack was made last summer upon the people of Berne or Geneva; for we were much afraid that the duke of Savoy, with the aid of Spain, would have done them some great mischief. You will salute from me master Gualter and your other colleagues. May the Lord bless you and your labours, and preserve your piety in safety as long as possible to his church! London, Aug. 29, 1567.

Your most devoted in the Lord,

EDMUND GRINDAL,

Bishop of London.

With respect to the acts passed in the general assembly of the kingdom, I will briefly write you a summary of those by which the true religion of Christ is established, and the

a religious asseveration, that the queen was not privy thereto: as did also Morton, fourteen years after. See Camden's Eliz. p. 97. On the other side, however, Soames, in his Elizabethan history, p. 87, observes, "Her guilt is unquestionable, if certain letters and sonnets, produced as evidence against her, be genuine; and that they are, is more than probable." Robertson's dissertation, he adds, at the close of his history, fully and accurately discusses the genuineness of these conclusive documents.]

[1 Kirkaldy of Grange. See note 5, p. 195.]   [2 See p. 24.]

impious superstition of the papists abolished. I shall however omit such as relate to the civil government of the kingdom, as it would be a work of infinite labour to record them; and besides most unnecessary, to yourself especially, whom I fully believe to be sufficiently acquainted with them all.

1. First, then, not only are all the impious traditions and ceremonies of the papists taken away, but also that tyranny which the pope himself has for so many ages exercised over the church, is altogether abolished; and it is provided that all persons shall in future acknowledge him to be the very antichrist, and son of perdition, of whom Paul speaks.

2. The mass is abolished, as being an accursed abomination and a diabolical profanation of the Lord's supper; and it is forbidden to all persons in the whole kingdom of Scotland either to celebrate or hear it: should any one do otherwise, on the first offence all his goods, whether moveable, as they say, or immoveable are forfeited to the exchequer, and the offenders themselves are to be punished at the discretion of the magistrate in whose jurisdiction they shall have been apprehended. For the second offence they are to be punished with banishment; the third is capital.

3. All those acts of parliament are repealed, by which the pope's authority in the bygone times of darkness had been either declared or confirmed.

4. The king's coronation is confirmed, because the queen, his mother, voluntarily laid down the royal authority, and appointed him by her letters to be proclaimed king.

5. The lord James, earl of Moray, is elected regent, as they call it, of the kingdom; and authority is given to him to administer the government in the king's name; and this, until the king himself shall have attained his seventeenth year. This too was done at the command of the queen, who also fixed the time of his majority.

6. A form of oath is prescribed, which all future sovereigns are to take at the time they are proclaimed. They must solemnly promise and swear that they will endeavour, to the utmost of their power, that the christian religion which is now preached throughout the whole kingdom shall be faithfully retained, without being contaminated by any traditions of papists and other heretics, which oppose its purity.

7. In the seventh is prescribed the mode of presenting benefices to those who shall undertake the office of the ministry. Those to whom belongs the hereditary right of patronage are to present some one to the church, whom if the church shall upon diligent examination find to be duly qualified, she shall admit [to the living]; if otherwise, she must reject him, and appoint to that office a more worthy candidate.

8. None are to be appointed judges, scribes, notaries, public apparitors, and beadles, until they have made a profession of the christian religion.

9. The third only of the tithes is to be paid to the ministers of God's word, so long as until, after the decease of the old incumbents, they may enjoy the entire benefice.

10. None shall be admitted to the instruction of youth in learning and morals, until he shall have made an open profession of religion.

11. Authority is given to ministers that they may sincerely preach the word of God, lawfully administer the sacraments, and sharply reprove the vices and corrupt manners of the people.

12. The patrons of those preferments which the mass-priests heretofore enjoyed in the colleges, may now convert them to the support of those whom we commonly call bursars[1], into the number of whom are generally chosen such young men as, being without friends or means of support, would otherwise be unable to procure a learned education.

13. A punishment is decreed against fornicators. For on the first offence they are to pay eighty[2] pounds, or to be committed to prison for eight days, and there fed only upon bread and the smallest beer: they are afterwards, on the next market day, to be placed in some conspicuous situation whence they may easily be seen by every one, there to remain from ten o'clock till twelve, with their heads uncovered, and bound with rings of iron. For a second offence the penalty is one hundred and thirty pounds[3], or sixteen days' imprisonment upon bread and water: then, as before, they are to be exposed to the people in the public market, with the

[1 Or exhibitioners.]
[2 Pounds Scotch, i.e. of 20d. each, in all £6. 13s. 4d.]
[3 i.e. £10. 16s. 8d.]

addition of having their heads shaved. For the third offence the penalty is two hundred pounds[4], or imprisonment for thrice the former number of days; and at the expiration of that time, after having been dipped three times in deep water, they are to be for ever banished from the city or parish. Both the man and woman, as often as they shall offend, are liable to these punishments.

14. Incest is made a capital offence. Nothing however was determined upon in the assembly with regard to adultery; but the consideration of that crime was deferred till the next session.

15. Marriages contracted between persons related in the second degree, such as those between brothers' and sisters' [children], are declared lawful.

LETTER LXXXII.

BISHOP GRINDAL TO HENRY BULLINGER.

Dated at LONDON, *June* 11, 1568.

HEALTH in Christ. Your affectionate letters, I believe, have all reached me, for which I return you my best thanks. I did not reply to them at the time of the last Frankfort fair, because at the beginning of Lent I was suffering with a tertian ague, which was succeeded by a disease in my eyes; but by the mercy of the Lord I am now recovered.

I congratulate you and the people of Geneva on the quiet posture of affairs, which indeed is almost miraculous; for you have on every side the most bitter adversaries.

Our controversy concerning the habits, about which you write, had cooled down for a time, but broke out again last winter; and this by the means of some who are more zealous than they are either learned or gifted with pious discretion. Some London citizens[5] of the lowest order, together with four or five ministers, remarkable neither for their judgment nor learning, have openly separated from us; and sometimes

[4] i.e. £16. 13s. 4d.]
[5] See Strype, Life of Grindal, p. 168, &c.]

in private houses, sometimes in the fields, and occasionally even in ships, they have held their meetings and administered the sacraments. Besides this, they have ordained ministers, elders, and deacons, after their own way, and have even excommunicated some who had seceded from their church. And because masters Laurence Humphrey, Sampson, Lever, and others, who have suffered so much to obtain liberty in respect of things indifferent, will not unite with them, they now regard them as semi-papists, and will not allow their followers to attend their preaching[1]. The number of this sect is about two hundred, but consisting of more women than men. The privy council have lately committed the heads of this faction to prison, and are using every means to put a timely stop to this sect.

You are, I suppose, well acquainted with the state of affairs in France and the Netherlands. New commotions have lately arisen in Scotland. On the second of May last the queen, who was kept a prisoner in the castle of Lochleven[2], having bribed her keepers, escaped from confinement,

[1 When Bishop Grindal reproved some of this party for not going to church, one of them replied, that he had as lief go to mass, as to some churches; on which the Bishop said, that they ought not to find fault with all for a few, and that they might go to other places; and particularly mentioned Laurence, and Sampson, and Lever, who preached in London, being dispensed with, though they wore not the habits, besides Coverdale. See Strype, Grindal, p. 171.]

[2 George Douglas, brother to the laird of Lochleven, conveyed her in disguise into a small boat, and himself rowed her on shore. Hume. See Camden, Eliz. p. 108. She had previously attempted an escape on the 25th of March, the manner of which is thus related in a letter of Sir William Drury to Cecil, dated Berwick, April 2, 1568. "There cometh into her the landresse early as other tymes before she was wonted, and the quene (according to such a secret practice) putteth on the weede (clothes) of her landresse, and so, with the fardell of clothes and her muffler upon her face, passeth out and entreth the bote to passe the Loughe, which, after some space, one of them that rowed said merrily, ' Lett us see what manner of dame this is!' and therewith offered to pull downe her muffler; which to defend she put upp her hands; which they espyed to be very fayre and white, wherewith they entered into suspition whom she was, beginning to wonder at her enterprise. Whereat she was litle dismayed, but chardged them uppon danger of their lives to rowe her over to the shore, which they nothing regarded, but eftesones rowed her back agayne, promising her that it shud be secreted, and in especiall from the lord of the house under whose gard she lieth. MS. Cotton. Calig. c. I. 53.]

and fled to Castle Hamilton³, where she collected troops⁴. On the 13th of May the lieutenant of the kingdom, (called the regent,) assembled his forces and engaged in a skirmish with the queen's party⁵. Her army was put to flight: about a hundred escaped; the rest, who could have been destroyed to a man, were allowed quarter; but she herself, with a few attendants, fled to the sea⁶, and going on board a small vessel, crossed the narrow frith at the mouth of the river Solway, and arrived at the city of Carlisle, which is in this kingdom. She still remains, but however in honourable custody, in the castle⁷ of that city. The queen⁸ of Scotland seeks aid from

[³ "The Quene would willingly have gone for her more suerty to Dumbarton castle; but the Ambletons wyll not therunto condescend, alledging that there she should be in lyttell better estate then in Loghleven, consydering the practice that the Lord of Ledington would use to the Lord Fleming. But as that may be one cause, so they thynk by having her in theyr possession they shol be the stronger, and bryng theyr purpose the better to passe." Sir Wm. Drury to Cecil, May 12, 1568. MS. Cott. Calig. b. ix. 365.]

[⁴ Within a day or two so great a multitude flocked unto her from all parts, that she levied an army of six thousand warriors. Camden, Elizabeth, p. 108. The following letter is given verbatim as it was written by her on this occasion to the laird of Nether Polloc, and which is still preserved in the family: "Traist freind, We greit zow weill. We dowt not bot ze knaw that God of his gudenes has put us at libertie, quhome we thank maist hartlie, qwharefore desyres zow w̄t all possible diligence fail not to be heir at us in Hamylton, w̄t all zō̄r folks, freinds and serwands bodin in feir of weir as ze will do us acceptable service and plessrs. Becaws we knaw zor q̄utance [constancy] we neid not at ȳis pnt (present) to mak langar l̄ie (letter) bot will byd zow fair weill. Off Hamylton ye 5 of Maii 1568. (Signed) Marie R." See Mackie, Castles of Q. Mary, p. 126, who gives a fac-simile of the original letter.]

[⁵ Namely, at Langside, near Glasgow, on May 14, as Sir William Drury writes to Cecil from Berwick on the following day. He says, "the Earle did his best to stay bloud to be shed, yea, by his contraryes [enemies] the same is affirmed." MS. Cott. Calig. c. I. 67.]

[⁶ She embarked on board a fishing boat in Galloway, and landed the same day at Workington in Cumberland, about thirty miles from Carlisle.]

[⁷ Sir Francis Knollys, who was sent to Carlisle to receive the queen of Scots, writes to Cecil, from Richmond, Thursday, May 27th. "The quene of Scotts is staied still at Carlile by the Deputie warder's good behaviour and discretion toward her Highnes' service." MS. Cott. Calig. b. ix. 290.]

[⁸ Queen Mary's letter to Elizabeth is given by Camden, Eliz. p. 109.]

us, that she may be restored to her kingdom, which under the influence of fear (as she says) she resigned to her son; or at least, that she may have a safe conduct to France[1], where she may make trial of the fidelity of her friends. The Scottish nobles, on the other hand, by their ambassadors, require her to be again delivered into their custody, alleging it to be unfit for her to resume the crown, who not only procured the death of her husband, but afterwards united herself in an adulterous marriage with his very murderer, and one too, who had a wife yet living. What decision will be come to as to these matters, I am yet ignorant. May the Lord overrule them all for good! Whatever it may be, should the Lord spare my life, I will endeavour to inform you. Salute, I pray you, master Gualter and the rest of the brethren in my name. May the Lord preserve you, my very reverend friend and dear brother in the Lord! London, June 11, 1568.

Your most devoted in the Lord,

EDMUND GRINDAL,

Bishop of London.

Just as I was about to seal this letter, news was brought me, that the duke of Alva, at Brussels, on the fifth of this month, had inflicted capital punishment on the Counts Egmont[2] and Horn[3], and about twenty other noblemen. The

[1 " Well, sayd she (queen Mary), " I woll not detayne this Frenche ambassador untyll Master Mydelmore's comyng, neither woll I be any longer delayed; for I woll require the quene, my good sister, that either she will lett me go into France, or that she woll put me into Dunbritone, unlesse she woll hold me as a prysoner." Sir F. Knollys to Cecil, from Carlisle, June 21. MS. Cott. Calig. c. i. 107.]

[2 Lamoral, Count Egmont, had been ambassador in 1553 from Charles 5th to queen Mary respecting her marriage with his son Philip. He was afterwards governor in the provinces of Flanders and Artois, and was of so popular a character, that when the Duchess of Parma was made Regent of the Low Countries, the public voice had already nominated Egmont to fill that exalted station. See Burgon's Life and Times of Sir Thomas Gresham, Vol. II. p. 126, where, in p. 233, is a curious letter from Sir Richard Clough describing the arrest of the Counts Egmont and Horn.]

[3 Philip de Montmorenci, Count Horn, had been governor of the province of Gueldres, which was taken from him and given to Count

man, it seems, is cruel enough by nature, and has descended to this degree of ferocity through irritation at the unfortunate result of the battle near Groningen, with Louis of Nassau. For the duke of Alva, it is reported, lost there two thousand Spaniards and three thousand Walloons, as they call them. There fell also the Count von Orenberg, and some Spanish generals of consequence. Egmont admitted a monk as his confessor, and adored the cross at the very place of execution. The Count Horn rejected all such things, and died in the confession of the truth.

LETTER LXXXIII.

BISHOP PARKHURST TO RODOLPH GUALTER AND HENRY BULLINGER.

Dated at LUDHAM, *Aug.* 4, 1568.

I WROTE a letter to you at the end of February, and hope it came safe to hand. I received letters from Bullinger and Lavater on the 11th of May, and from you, Gualter, on the 18th of the same month. The queen of Scotland made her escape from prison about the same time. A bloody fight[1] immediately took place between the papists, the friends[2] of

Meghem. His trial, with that of Count Horn, is thus noticed in a letter from Sir R. Clough to Sir Thomas Gresham, dated Sept. 15, 1567. "We have news from Brussells, that there are 12 appointed to sit upon the County of Egmont and the County of Horne; 2 of them to be of the Lords of the order [of the golden Fleece], and all the rest presidents of the counsell of these Low Countries; who are all papists (saving one, who is the president of Gawntt, who is takyn for a man of good judgment,) so that by them both they and all the rest shall be tried." Burgon, as above, p. 236.]

[1 At Langside near Glasgow, May 14th. See note 5, p. 203.]

[2 A bond of association for her defence was signed by the Earls of Argyle, Huntley, Eglinton, Crawford, Cassilis, Rothes, Montrose, Sutherland, Errol, nine bishops and nine barons, besides many of the most considerable gentry. And in a few days an army, to the number of six thousand men, was assembled under her standard. Hume.]

the queen, and the protestants, who were on the king's side. She was on an eminence[1], mounted on a swift horse, when the battle was at its height, and had a view of the whole engagement. But when she perceived at length that the victory lay with the regent James and his party, she fled with a few of her attendants into England; for she had rather trust herself to the English than her own subjects, and I believe it was more safe for her to do so. She is now at Carlisle[2], a town well fortified, but is shortly, as I am told, about to reside in the middle of England.

On the 13th of July[3] Dr William Turner, a good physician and an excellent man, died at London. Lever preached at his funeral. I have written this single letter, short as it is, to you both; for I am in doubt whether, in the present confused state of affairs, it will ever reach you. I am therefore unwilling now to write more.

Salute in my name all my friends, especially masters Simler, Lavater, Wolfius, Haller, Wickius, Wonlichius, Zuinglius, &c. Farewell. In haste. Ludham, August 4, 1568.

Yours entirely,
JOHN PARKHURST,
[Bishop] of Norwich.

[1 "The quene [was] a reasonable distance of, and gave the looking on, till she saw howe it [the battle] proceded." Sir W. Drury to Cecil, MS. Cott. Calig. c. I. 67. "On a hill opposite to Langside queen Mary stood during the battle, and witnessed the discomfiture of her friends and the annihilation of her hopes: a hawthorn bush, commonly known by the name of Queen Mary's thorn, long marked out the place, till it decayed through age; when another was reverentially planted on the same spot to preserve the memory of the scene." Mackie, Castles of Queen Mary, p. 127.

[2 See p. 203.]

[3 William Turner, Doctor of Physic, and a zealous divine, who under King Edward VI. had been Dean of Wells, but outed in the next reign, and became an exile. He was restored to his deanery by Archbishop Parker in 1559. He was buried in Crutched Friars' Church, London, where he hath a monument yet remaining. Strype Parker, I. 93. The Bishop of Bath and Wells [Gilbert Berkley] thus complained of him to Cecil, in a letter dated March 23, 1564. "I am much encombered with master Dr Turner, Deane of Welles, for his undiscrete behaviour in the pulpitt; where he medleth with all matters, and unsemelie speaketh of all estates, more then is standing with discretion." MS. Lansd. 8. 3.]

LETTER LXXXIV.

BISHOP COX TO HENRY BULLINGER.

[1568.]

HEALTH in Christ Jesus, my Bullinger, my very dear brother, and a most shining light in the church of God. I have by me three letters of yours, written last year, the first of which is dated January 6, 1568; the second, March 20th, 1568; the third, August 24th, 1568. I have, in addition to these, your books[4] on the "Origin of Error," presented by yourself. For my not having yet replied to your most gratifying and pious letters, I had rather assign no reason at all than a light and futile one. Passing over, then, all excuses, I return sincere thanks to my friend Henry, both because he has so frequently vouchsafed to converse with me by letter, and also for his continuing to oblige me with such pious presents. I do indeed thank God from my heart, that he has set you up as a most solid pillar for the propagation of his truth. I pray that the Lord our God may prolong your life to his glory and the good of his church; which is now confined and oppressed on every side, and over which the adversaries are meditating and most eagerly anticipating a triumph. But "why do the heathen rage? &c."—(Ps. ii. 1.) We may hope most confidently that God will not desert his people for ever. May the Lord confound the counsels of those Swiss, who with so much animosity deserted you for the French! The Assyrians raged terribly against Jerusalem, but it was to their great discomfort. If God be for us, who can be against us? Our affairs, thank God, are hitherto tolerably quiet, except that the Canaanites are wonderfully thickening among us, daily looking for the time when the ass will speak.

Our excellent friend Abel is still alive, but most grievously tormented with the stone. There is an abundant crop of pious

[4 See note 1, p. 182.]

young men in our universities. The Lord, we hope, will increase the number of the labourers who may be sent into his harvest; and this ought to be a singular comfort to myself, who must soon expect my own dismission, when my spirit shall return to heaven, and my body be consigned to the earth.

Farewell, my very dear brother, and let us aid each other by our mutual prayers to God. Salute my friend Julius; he is not quite a stranger to me. 1568.

Your most attached,

RICHARD COX,

[Bishop] of Ely.

LETTER LXXXV.

BISHOP GRINDAL TO HENRY BULLINGER.

Dated at FULHAM, *Aug.* 13, 1569.

HEALTH in Christ. That I seldom write to your reverence, my very dear master Bullinger, you must impute to our late wars and interrupted commerce with the Netherlands. I received last year your books "on the Origin of Error," and "on Councils," for which also I return you my best thanks.

The dissensions[1] in our Dutch church at London, about which you wrote to me, are, by the grace of God, at length composed. The judgment of your churches was of very great advantage to us.

The duke of Alva[2] is clearly acting the part of Phalaris

[1 For an account of these disputes, see Strype, Grindal, 189, &c.]

[2 The duke of Alva's first act, after he found himself sole governor of the provinces, in 1568, was to erect a tribunal, so arbitrary in its objects, so inhuman in its proceedings, that the common people designated it by the epithet *bloody;* and that tribunal might well be called

among our Low-Country neighbours. All persons of wealth, of whatever religion, are living in the greatest danger. For men, the rich especially, are daily dragged to execution, without regard to any form of law. As to the affairs of France, you know them all better than we do. Through the mercy of God we are in great tranquillity, notwithstanding Alva's threatenings. Our commerce with the Netherlands has been interrupted on this account. Last winter the Spanish[3] vessels, which through the medium of the Genoese merchants conveyed money to Alva from the pope, were driven by a tempest into our harbours, which are both numerous and safe. The sum, I believe, was 300,000 crowns. This sum, sent as it were from heaven, as all the neighbouring nations are raging with war, our queen, that she might have money ready against every emergency, determined to borrow from the merchants themselves, giving sufficient security for the repayment, at a given time, both of the principal and interest; a plan which has often been adopted by other sovereigns. When Alva[4]

so, which enabled the duke to boast on his return to Spain, that he had caused the death of upwards of 18,000 persons by the hands of the executioner. He might have added, that he had been the ruin of 300,000 besides. Burgon, Vol. II. p. 259.]

[3 These ships were chased by some of the prince of Condé's ships of war, and took refuge in England. It was thought proper, for better security, to land the money, which was all in Spanish reals, and amounted to 400,000 ducats. The queen was informed by the cardinal de Châtillon, that the money did not belong to the king of Spain, but to some Genoese and Italian merchants, who were afraid the duke (of Alva) would seize it for his own use, as he indeed intended; and the queen, knowing it would be employed against the protestants, and the merchants being willing to lend it her, she borrowed it of them, and gave security for its repayment. Alva, incensed at a disappointment which put him under difficulties in the measure he was taking, caused all the English merchants at Antwerp to be arrested; and took an inventory of their ships and effects, which he sold afterwards to his own profit. Carte's Hist. of England. See also Burgon's Life of Sir Thomas Gresham, Vol. II. p. 277, &c. and Camden, Eliz. p. 120, &c., who states, p. 191, that the money was faithfully repaid in 1573.]

[4 The earl of Leicester writes to Randolph, May 1, 1569: "The duke of Alva hath ruffled with us ever since Christmas, and not only emprisoned our merchants, but also stayed their goods and shippes, whereupon the quene's majestie hathe done the lyke here, and stayed certayne treasure which by force of weather was dryven uppon the

heard this, he caused all our merchants now in the Netherlands to be arrested, together with their vessels and their freight. Our government did the same both to the Spaniards and Netherlanders. Our merchants therefore are now compelled to exercise their trade at Hamburgh, a place far less convenient, and this to the great detriment of the whole of the Netherlands.

In Scotland, our next neighbour, all affairs are still carried on, as heretofore, under the authority of the youthful king. The administration (of the government) is in the hands of an excellent man, the Lord James Stuart[1], earl of Murray, the king's uncle, to whom the rest of the nobility, who formerly opposed his authority, have at length submitted. Their disagreement was not respecting matters of religion; for each party, even when the dispute was at the highest, professed, as they still continue to do, the doctrine of the gospel. The queen of Scotland, who is still detained here in sufficiently honourable and free custody[2], will not confirm this regency of Scotland, and thinks herself wronged by it. She is therefore urging [the assistance of] her friends as much as she can; but unless she is supported by foreign aid, she will not easily recover her kingdom.

Thus much have I thought fit to write to you at this time concerning our own affairs and those of our neighbours. Bishops Horn, Parkhurst, Jewel, Cox, Sandys, Pilkington, are all well, and entreated me, whenever I should write to you, to salute your reverence in their name. Greet, I pray you, from me master Rodolph Gualter, and your other brethren in the ministry. Commend us to the Lord in your prayers. May the Lord Jesus long preserve you in safety to us and to

west coast. She hathe likewise armed forthe certayne of her shippes to keepe the narrow seas, which have taken dyvers of their hulks and therein greate substance and treasure, all which is surely kept uppon a reckoning till we may see howe matters will fall out betwixt us and them." MS. Lansd. II. 36.]

[1 See p. 197.]

[2 The queen of Scots was removed from Bolton to Tutbury Castle in the January of this year, and placed under the care of George Talbot, sixth earl of Shrewsbury. In the month of August she was again removed to Sheffield Castle.]

his church, my very reverend and dear brother in the Lord!
Fulham, on the banks of the Thames, 13th August, 1569.

Your most devoted in the Lord,

EDM. GRINDAL,

bishop of London.

Our brother John Abel, after having been long afflicted with the stone, exchanged this life for a better some months since.

LETTER LXXXVI.

RICHARD HILLES TO HENRY BULLINGER.

Dated at LONDON, *Feb.* 6, 1570.

THIS, most learned sir, is my letter, whereby you will understand, that on the death of our friend, John Abel, your letter of the 14th of March last, together with one from master Rodolph Gualter of the 17th of the same month, both of them being addressed to me in the absence of the aforesaid John Abel, were delivered into my hands. I therefore opened [the packet] and read the letters, and forwarded them, together with the books which you mention therein, to the persons to whom you had directed them. I received also a letter from Julius, of the 16th March, 1569, and some works tied up in separate parcels, addressed to the bishops of Salisbury, Ely, and Worcester, and Sir Antony Cook, together with some little books for each of them; and which I forwarded with the parcels to the individuals above mentioned. I wish you to be informed of all this; for your letter dated August 24th has also reached me, and as you seem therein to desire that, both as to the forwarding letters from yourself to others, and also conveying them from others to you, I will supply the place of our friend Abel, (who has died in the Lord, and therefore is now, I doubt not, blessed and delivered from those pains which he endured when alive in this world,) I will most readily do this as far as I can. As to the writings which you state to have been inclosed with the aforesaid letter, as soon as they came into my hands, I sent them to the reverend the bishops and other learned persons to whom you had directed them. But it pained me much to perceive, from the letter which you sent to John Abel, that although you were not tormented, as he was, with the stone in the bladder, you have nevertheless been afflicted with the same disease in the reins, so that from Martinmass up to the 14th of March you parted with sixty calculi, some of which were of a considerable size. I am glad, however, that although you have been suffering so severely under that kind of disorder, so much patience has been bestowed upon you by divine providence; and I pray God it may abide with you to the end.

Two years since I sent you a letter, of which I derived the chief materials verbatim from one written by a certain individual to master Christopher Mont[1] of Strasburgh, informing him of the state of lower Germany, and especially of Antwerp, a little before the arrival of the duke of Alva. I sent a duplicate [copy] of this letter to the Lent fair at Frankfort in 1568, inclosed in my letter to you, that it might be given in charge to one of the Zurich booksellers, who would deliver it to you. But as you make no mention whatever of this letter to Christopher Mont in yours of the 24th of August 1569, I rather suspect that it has been lost than that it has reached you, and therefore I inclose a duplicate in this present letter. But when you state that if a letter to you from hence can by my means be conveyed to master Christopher Mont, it will doubtless reach you, [and] that the reverend bishop of London, Edmund Grindal, if I avail myself of his assistance, can be of great use in forwarding it to the aforesaid Christopher Mont, I am but seldom able to be of much use in matters of this kind. For I was generally accustomed, as long as that route was permitted, to be of use in sending letters, as well to Christopher Mont as

[1 Mont was a German, who had been employed in embassies by Henry VIII.; and was the queen's agent at Strasburgh. Strype, Memorials, I. 355; Annals, II. i. 63.]

to yourself, by way of lower Germany. But now for a whole year I have not sent a single letter to any learned men, either in upper Germany or Switzerland, by way of lower Germany, lest it should be opened in that quarter; so that I have been necessarily obliged to send my letters to Hamburgh. Wherefore, until this long-pending dispute[2] between our most serene queen and the king of Spain shall be settled, I am of opinion that both yourself and the aforenamed Christopher Mont will receive very few letters from hence, except at the Frankfort fair.

I thank you for acquainting me with the news relating both to yourselves in Switzerland, and on the borders of France on the Swiss side. There is no news in this country which I can relate for certain, except that two earls, those namely of Northumberland and Westmoreland (as I fancy you have heard from hence some days since), whom the queen's majesty ordered, in the month of December last, to appear before her honourable council, (to clear themselves from a suspicion of a conspiracy premeditated by them against the religion and doctrine proved by the holy scriptures, and established by the authority of our most serene queen, at least ten years since,) have raised a rebellion; and together[3] with some of the queen's subjects, inhabitants of the bishoprick of Durham, (over which bishop Pilkington presides,) whom they had jointly stirred up to battle, they most impiously took up arms. The rest of the people, however, in

[2 See note 4, p. 209.]
[3 In a letter from Sir George Bowes to the earl of Sussex, dated Bernard Castle, Nov. 10, 1569, the writer states that "Yesterday at four of the clock in the afternoone, the sayd Erles.........wythe others to the nomber of *three hundred* horsemen, armed in corsetts, ... with speres, harquebusses, and daggers, came to Durham." MS. Cott. Calig. b. ix. 331. Stowe says they marched to Durham on the 14th of November, and on Tuesday the 22nd, (which Camden and Whitlocke call the 12th day of their rebellion) they mustered on Clifford Moor to the number of *sixteen hundred horsemen*, (or *six hundred* according to Camden and Whitlocke) and *four thousand* footmen. A letter from Thomas Stanhope, dated Newark, Dec. 1, (MS. Lansd. Calig. b. ix. 351,) states, on the report of Sir William Bellewes, at York, "that they were not above four thousande footmen at the moste; the moste part whereof, rude, unarmed, and ill appointed; and are eight hundred horsemen, or under a thousand."]

other parts of the country, by the great mercy of God, continued in their allegiance, preserved the peace, and lived godly therein under the authority of God and the queen. Those too who dwelt in the neighbourhood of the bishoprick of Durham, rendered their assistance towards the suppression of the rebellion to those noble personages whom the queen had sent for that purpose[1]; and thus they so pursued those two earls and their whole army, that they themselves, with some cavalry who accompanied them, took refuge in Scotland, where they were forcibly seized[2] by lord James the regent, and a nobleman of the family of Hume. So that I hope they will shortly be brought to England, where I doubt not they will receive the condign punishment that their crimes demand. While the aforesaid persons were in arms prosecuting their impious attempt, they not only threw down the communion tables[3], tore in pieces the holy bible and godly books, and trod under foot the printed homilies, but also again set up the blasphemous mass as a sacrifice for the living and the dead. And as a farther cloke to their pretended piety, they caused some

[1 Namely, the earl of Sussex, who marched against them with seven thousand men, accompanied with Edward, Earl of Rutland, the Lords Hunsdon, Evers, and Willoughby of Parham. The rebels fled to Hexham, and shortly after to Naworth castle; where, hearing that the earl of Warwick and Clinton, Lord Admiral, pursued them in haste with twelve thousand men from the south parts of England, the two earls with a small company, unknown to the rest, presently withdrew themselves into the neighbouring country of Scotland. See Camden's Elizabeth, p. 135.]

[2 Northumberland was delivered by the Grahams into Murray's hands, by whom he was confined in the castle of Lochleven. Westmoreland found a lurkingplace with Kerr of Fernihurst, and Buccleugh, and at length escaped into the Netherlands, where he led a very poor life, even to his old age, living upon a very slender pension [of £200. a year] from the Spaniard. See Camden as above, and Strype, Annals, I. ii. 344.]

[3 The rebels went first to Durham, an episcopal see hard by, where they went and trampled under feet the English Bibles and books of Common Prayer, which they found in the churches. From thence they went small journeys, celebrating mass in all places where they came, trouping together under their colours, (wherein were painted, in some the five wounds of Christ, in others the chalice); Richard Norton, an old gentleman, with a reverend gray head, bearing a cross with a streamer before them, as far as Clifford Moor, not far from Wetherby. Camden's Elizabeth, p. 134.]

crosses, and some banners of certain saints, whom they either believed to be their patrons and defenders, or pretended they would be, to be carried in procession among their arms.

Whereas our friend Rodolph Gualter inquired of John Abel to tell him the price of a piece of cloth in England, and how many German ells it contains, you may learn from me that our pieces are of different prices and lengths; but that the common and coarser ones contain about 28 or 30 Frankfort or Strasburgh ells, and are each worth from eight to ten French crowns; and the cost of dying or tinging with woad will be about two and a half or three French crowns each.

Before I had sealed this letter, certain intelligence is brought me that the above-mentioned lord James, regent of Scotland, has been wounded by a gun-shot and killed[4] by a certain nobleman of the Hamilton family.

Farewell in Christ Jesus, my very reverend sir, and may he evermore preserve you! Amen. London, Feb. 6, 1569, according to the computation of the church of England.

Yours,

R. H.

LETTER LXXXVII.

BISHOP GRINDAL TO HENRY BULLINGER.

Dated at LONDON, *Feb.* 18, 1570.

My very dear and honoured brother, master Bullinger, I have received your letter, dated August 24th. I had received also in the course of last year your book on the "Origin of Error," and "on Councils," as I wrote to you more fully in my letter sent to the autumn fair at Frankfort, and which I hope you received some months since. We cannot now send our letters except by way of Hamburgh, to one or other of the Frankfort fairs, by reason of

[4 In the streets of Linlithgow, (Jan. 23.) See p. 218.]

the road being closed against us by the duke of Alva. Had not this been the case, nothing would have been more delightful to me than to have conversed with you by letter more frequently.

I most sincerely congratulate you on your recovery from your sickness of last summer, and greatly desire to hear that your health is entirely re-established. Should you be able to regain a tolerable degree of strength in the summer succeeding the disorder, we shall, it seems, have reason to hope for a yet longer enjoyment of you: for the disease itself very often acts as a medicine, or rather as a cure.

Our affairs, through the mercy of God, are now tolerably quiet, though they have of late been very unsettled. An attempt[1] was made, last summer, to marry the queen of Scotland to Thomas Howard, duke of Norfolk; but our queen, offended at the proposal, committed the above-named nobleman, on the 11th of September, to the tower of London, where he now remains a prisoner. At the beginning

[[1] The queen of Scots gave her consent to the marriage, but first desired that queen Elizabeth's consent might be obtained: the latter, it appears, first heard of the proposition through some ladies of the court, on which she took the duke to her board at Farnham, and pleasantly gave him warning to "beware on what pillow he leaned his head." Leicester afterwards more fully revealed the matter to the queen, on her coming to visit him, when he either fell sick, or counterfeited himself so, at Titchfield. The queen sharply reproved Norfolk, and commanded him to desist; and shortly afterwards, on the representation of Murray, (who first moved this match to the duke, but who wrote to the queen that the duke had propounded it to him,) committed him to the tower. See Camden's Elizabeth, p. 126, &c. and Whitlocke's Memorials, p. 237, &c. There is a very interesting letter from John Foxe the martyrologist to the duke of Norfolk, to dissuade him from the above-mentioned marriage, in which the writer says: "There is a great rumour with us here in London, and so far spread that it is in every man's mouth almost, of your marriage with the Scottish quene; which rumour as I trust to be false, so would I be sorry that it should be true, for two respects: the one, for the good will I beare to you; the other for the love I beare to the commonwealthe, for that I see no other, (and many besides me do so no lesse,) but the day of that marriage, whensoever it beginneth, will end with such a catastrophe as will be either ruinous to yourself, or dangerous to the tranquillity of the realme, the peace whereof standing so long amongst us through the great mercy of God, God forbid it should now begin to break by you!" MS. Harl. 416, 154.]

of November two earls, namely those of Northumberland and Westmoreland, collected troops and raised a rebellion in the counties of York and Durham, for the purpose of restoring the catholic religion, falsely so called[2]. Their army consisted of twelve hundred cavalry and four thousand infantry. They supposed that at the name of Mass vast multitudes would come over to them; besides which they expected assistance from the duke of Alva; for they had determined upon releasing the queen of Scotland from her confinement: but their expectations were altogether disappointed. For the queen of Scotland, on the discovery of the plot, was transferred to the city of Coventry[3], in the very heart of the kingdom: her friends at home were prevented from acting, partly by the severity of the winter, and partly by the passes being pre-occupied: armed vessels were also sent out to prevent any foreign aid. The queen then collected an army of twenty-four thousand men, consisting both of cavalry and infantry, and which the rebel army had not the courage to resist. So that on the 16th of December the rebels disbanded their infantry; the cavalry, however, fled to the borders of Scotland, where the greater part surrendered, and the remainder consulted their safety by flight. The two earls themselves fled into Scotland with a hundred chosen troops. But Northumberland[4] was taken prisoner by the regent of Scotland, where he still remains in confinement. Westmoreland[5],

[2 See note 3, p. 213, and below note 1, p. 247, for a summary account of this rebellion.]

[3 The queen returned to Tutbury Castle in January, 1570. Haynes, p. 526.]

[4 The earl of Northumberland was delivered by Morton for a sum of money to the English, and conveyed to York, where he was condemned of high treason, and executed on Aug. 22, 1572. Sir Thomas Gargrave, who was president of the council of the North, writes to lord Burghley from York, on the day after his execution, that "he contynued obstynate in religion, and declared he would die a catholicke of the pope's churche. He accompted his offences nothing, and especially after he heard he should die; but before he seemed to confesse he had offended, and would greve lyke it, saying, he dyd that he dyd by compulsion and for fear of his lyfe." MS. Cott. Calig. c. III. 381. Saunders says that the earl "suffered martyrdom."]

[5 He afterwards escaped into Flanders, where he got a pension of £200. a year from the king of Spain. See note 2, p. 214.]

however, who is a young man, and with the spirit of a Catiline, is living among freebooters in the wilds of Scotland. Thus was this rebellion suppressed within forty days, and without bloodshed, except that five hundred of the rebels were afterwards executed, and many are still kept in prison awaiting a like punishment[1]. The rebel army had on their colours the five wounds, as they are called, and the representation of a cross with this inscription, *In hoc signo vinces.* They performed their masses in every church; the bibles moreover, translated into our language, which are found in all our churches, they either tore in pieces, or committed to the flames. They ransacked the property of the bishop of Durham, and that of all the pastors and ministers; but they put no one to death. Pilkington, the bishop of Durham, (God having so ordered it) was at that time staying in London for the recovery[2] of his health: he would otherwise have been without doubt in great danger of his life. As soon as our disturbances were suppressed, we received most sad news from Scotland respecting the death of the most excellent and pious prince, James Stuart, regent of Scotland; who was shot through the lower part of the belly by a musket-ball on the 23rd of January, and died two days after. As the regent was riding on that day, (for thus the murder was committed,) in a street of the town of Linlithgow, surrounded by his nobles, as usual, a certain traitor, of the Hamilton[3]

[1 See p. 214.]

[2 Pilkington thus wrote to Cecil on the 4th of January: "According to your honor's appointment I have sent my man to know by your gudd meanes the quene's majestie's pleasure for my repairing homeways." After describing the state of the country, he adds, "but God is present ever with his people, and his vocation is not rashly to be forsaken, nor his assistance to be dowted on. His gudd will be done!" MS. Lansd. xii. 29. Another interesting letter from the bishop to Cecil in 1573 is given by Strype, wherein he desires the queen's leave to come up to London that winter, being by reason of his age very much pinched by the winter's cold in that northern part of the nation. "There is," he said, "a highway to heaven out of all countries; of which free passage, I praise God, I doubt not." Strype, Annals, ii. i. 437.]

[3 James Hamilton of Bothwellhaugh, who had been taken at Langside, and condemned to death, had made his escape out of prison, and his estate was forfeited. His wife, heiress of Woodhouslie,

family, aimed a gun at him from a window, and shot him. The assassin mounted a fleet⁴ horse, which he had ready saddled at the back door of the house, and took refuge in a certain castle⁴. It is to be feared that great changes will take place in consequence of the death of this illustrious personage: we hear, however, that the nobility and council of Scotland, who have embraced the gospel, have unanimously and resolutely determined to take upon themselves the defence of religion and the commonwealth. We are in daily expectation of more certain intelligence. We have lately had news from Spain, that the Moors, or Moriscoes, have defeated the royal army with great slaughter, and taken the camp. Alva has a fleet in readiness, but its destination is unknown. Some think that he is about to send aid to Spain; others suspect that he will land an army in Scotland; nor are there wanting those who imagine that he is meditating some attempt against ourselves. We are therefore sending out a fleet thoroughly prepared for any thing that may happen, to observe his movements.

I am writing this account both of ourselves and our neighbours more fully, that I may in some measure make amends for my long silence. The bishops of Winchester,

still expected she might enjoy her own in quiet; but Murray, giving it away to one of his favourites, sent officers to take possession of her house, who turned her out into the fields, and treated her with such inhumanity, that she became raving mad. From that moment her husband resolved to revenge himself by the murder of the regent. See Carte's History of England, and Robertson's History of Scotland, who says that Hamilton owed his life to the Regent's clemency.]

[⁴ In a letter from lord Hunsdon to lord Burghley, dated Berwick, Aug. 24, 1575, the writer says, "The regent's dealings in many thyngs are greatly mislyked withall by the most part of the nobylytie of his owne faction, but chiefly for one matter, whych is, for that he hathe of late, (as it is credibly reported, and I thynk is very trew,) taken a secret submission of the lorde of Arbrothe, by delivering to the regent hys sworde with the hylt forwarde, the poynt in his hande, being knowne to be the pryncipall procurer of the kylling of th' erle of Murrey; for the harquebuss that kyld him was hys, the horse the murderer fled upon was hys, and he receivyd hym into Hambelton, and sent hym into France." MS. Cott. Calig. c. v. 37. This enterprise thus appears to have been connected with the same plots as had produced the rebellion of the two northern earls. See Wright's Queen Elizabeth and her Times. Vol. I. p. 358. Note.]

Norwich, Durham, and Salisbury, are all in good health, as are also Humphrey, Sampson, and Foxe. I communicated your letter yesterday to Sampson and Foxe, who respectfully salute you in return. Salute your colleagues in my name. Commend, I entreat you, me and my ministry to the Lord in your prayers. I pray our heavenly Father to give his choicest blessing to you all, and to your labours which you daily undergo. May the Lord Jesus long preserve your piety safe both to us and to his church! London, Feb. 18, 1569.

Your most devoted in the Lord,
EDM. LONDON.

LETTER LXXXVIII.

BISHOP COX TO HENRY BULLINGER.

Dated at ELY, July 10, 1570.

I RETURN your salutation from my heart, my beloved brother in Christ. Your letter dated on the 2nd of March last did not reach me till the 22nd of June. This is usually the case, either from the great distance between us, or from the carelessness of the couriers. I read it however, when it came, with attention and pleasure, because it announced to me that you were in the enjoyment of tolerable health, notwithstanding you are so advanced in years[1], and worn out by numerous labours, and weakened by [former] illness. I willingly took up your books both upon Daniel and on Isaiah, (in which I occupy myself from time to time, and not without a holy delight,) and return you many thanks for them; and all who have any regard for religion acknowledge themselves much indebted to you for the same. Your German discourses, as soon as they reach me, I will endeavour to make out either by myself or with the assistance of others.

[1 Bullinger was now in the sixty-sixth year of his age.]

But now, my Henry, since the Lord has for so many years past employed you as his instrument to the great advantage of his church, you must persevere in the defence of the church of Christ, as far as your age will allow you, even to the end of your life. Many of the heads of antichrist yet remain to be cut off, which from time to time occasion us much trouble. I wish you would in earnest use your endeavours for their extirpation. Antichrist, relying on the authority of his church and councils, contends that faith is not to be kept with heretics, that is, with those whom he judges to be such. Then he arrogates to himself the authority of recalling, and withdrawing, and absolving subjects from their fidelity and obedience to their princes and magistrates, and commands foreign powers to invade, desolate, and destroy godly magistrates, and deprive them of every right of government. This has been fully confirmed during the last month by a popish[2] bull introduced by stealth into this country. Lastly, there are among us some papists, and those not of the lowest rank, who strain every nerve that they may be permitted to live according to their consciences, and that no account of his religion be demanded from any one. Meanwhile many iniquitous practices take place in secret, and by the bad example they afford are a stumblingblock to the godly. If you will turn your attention to these three points, you will do a very acceptable service to Christ and his church. The schism about the habits of the clergy is still increasing, I grieve to say, among men of a purer character. May God at length grant that we may all of us think the same things!

The Lord Jesus preserve you and yours, with your illustrious state! Let us rejoice in the Lord, and aid each other by our mutual prayers.

From my Tusculum at Ely, 10 July, 1570.

Your brother in Christ,

RICH. COX, [bishop] of Ely.

[[2] This year Pius V. caused a bull to be publicly set up in London against the queen; which was daringly done by one Felton, upon the bishop of London's palace. Strype, Annals, i. ii. 354. The bull is given at length by Camden, Eliz. p. 146, and was printed with observations and animadversions upon it in English.]

LETTER LXXXIX.

BISHOP PILKINGTON TO HENRY BULLINGER.
Dated *July* 17, 1570.

Your letter, my reverend father in Christ Jesus, dated on the 2nd of March, and rebuking me for not having written to you of so long a time, I received on the 29th of June. Go on then as you have begun; instigate me, rouse me up, and at length you will at least extort something. " Better are the wounds of a friend, &c." [Prov. xxvii. 6.] I am a dilatory and unfrequent correspondent; but I have not cast off all shame, nor has my remembrance of you become so cold, but that I can truly say of your happy Zurich what the psalmist speaks concerning Jerusalem : " If I do not remember thee, Jerusalem, above my chief joy, let my right hand forget her cunning." [Psal. cxxxvii. 6, &c.]

Your prudence has heard, although but lately, as you tell me, concerning those disturbances which have so sharply and suddenly burst upon us; and likewise, how happily they have been quelled,—I wish I could say entirely extinguished.

I informed you in my last letter that the Queen of Scots had fled over to us, and I compared our situation with that of the people of Lais[1]. I feared lest that should happen to us which occurred to them; and my fears have been realized[2]. The earls of Northumberland and Westmoreland, between whom I reside, having planned a rebellion, roused us from our slumbers, and as long as they could, persecuted us with the greatest harshness. They offered all manner of violence to religion and all its ministers. But the Lord has delivered us all from the mouths of the lions, uninjured indeed in our persons, although stripped of all our fortunes and plundered of our property. You perhaps wonder how this has happened. The world cannot bear two suns; much less can the kingdom endure two queens or two religions. Our Lou-

[1 Judg. xviii.]   [2 See p. 213.]

vaine friends obtained bulls from the pope, that they might absolve the people from the allegiance due to the queen's majesty; those who would no longer attend our church and liturgy were to be reconciled to their synagogue, and those who would submit themselves to them were to obtain pardon of all their sins, without even purgatory. These impieties are so deeply settled in the minds of many, that I am in doubt whether they will ever be eradicated. Some persons are detained in prison for these things; many have absconded; but the greater number are lying in concealment, eagerly expecting an occasion of fresh disturbances. Some of the nobility joined themselves to them: but our good Lord disappointed all of them of their hope, and hath preserved our Elizabeth to us, and long will preserve her, as all good men both hope and desire. Northumberland, having fled into Scotland, is there kept in prison, with some others of the same faction; Westmoreland[3] is wandering about in exile in the same country with a few others like himself. Others, convicted by their own consciences, have sought refuge in Flanders, with a view of obtaining assistance. But the Lord will not be wanting to his people. James, the guardian of the king of Scotland, and regent of the kingdom, has been murdered[4] by the treachery of a certain Scotsman whom he had saved from execution. This is a great grief to many good persons; for he was a good man towards all, and one who feared God. The better part of the Scots side with our queen; the rest we are pursuing with fire and sword.

I am, by the blessing of God, restored to my flock[5]; and though the minds of all are not so settled as I could wish, there is, notwithstanding, both here and in Scotland quite liberty enough both for the administration of the laws and for religion. The Lord will give [us] yet better things [in answer] to your prayers. The bishop of London is now

[3 "The lord regent had lyked to have gotten betrayed the earle of Westmoreland, at a place called Blood-lanes; it is the lord of Fernyhurst's; but he got knowledge, and so escaped that end." Allayn King to Sir Henry Percy. MS. Cott. Calig. b. ix. 400.]

[4 See p. 218.]

[5 The bishop, it seems, had been required by the queen to return to his diocese, from which he had been absent in London during the rebellion. See above, note 2, p. 218.]

made archbishop of York, and my neighbour; at which I rejoice exceedingly.

Thomas Lever, as soon as he comes to London, will make a collection in behalf of our good landlady, and will send it over. I should now send it myself, if I knew in what way it could be forwarded; but since our good friend Abel, who was our general messenger, has been so long dead, I do not even know how this letter will reach you. Farewell, my master, with all your fellow-ministers. Prosperity to Zurich! July 17, 1570.

Yours in Christ,

JAMES PILKINGTON.

LETTER XC.

ARCHBISHOP GRINDAL TO HENRY BULLINGER.

Dated at LONDON, *July* 31, 1570.

HEALTH in Christ. I have received your discourses written in German, for which I thank you. I am still sufficiently conversant with German writing; for I laboured hard to learn your language; but I have lost the habit of conversing in it.

I transmitted the pension of Julius Santerentianus to Richard Hilles a month ago, that he might take care it should be paid to Froschover at the next Frankfort fair. I hope you received the letter which I sent at the last spring fair. Since then it has seemed good to our most gracious queen to translate[1] me from this city to the see of York, where things are not yet properly settled[2]. In

[1 He was translated May 1st, 1570, and installed by proxy June the 9th. Strype, Grindal, 239.]

[2 Archbishop Parker told Secretary Cecil, that my lord of London would be very fit for York, "who were, as he styled them, *a heady and stout people:* witty, but yet able to be dealt with by good governance, as long as laws could be executed, and men backed." Strype, Grindal, 234.]

the counties of York and Durham there arose, as I lately wrote you word, last winter a rebellion of the nobles and the peasantry for the purpose of restoring the papacy. Notwithstanding many executions[3] took place, I am informed that the feelings of the people are much exasperated, and panting for renewed disturbances. What therefore may await me there, I cannot tell. But if new tumults should arise in that quarter, it is impossible but that both myself and my very dear brother Pilkington, the bishop of Durham, must be in the greatest danger. But these things do not move me; the will of the Lord be done! However, I tell you of them, that you may commend both us and our ministry more earnestly to the Lord in your prayers.

When I was writing the above, I was almost on the point of setting off on my journey to York, so that I could not at this time write to you more at length. Our affairs, through the mercy of God, are tolerably quiet. Our army[4] entered Scotland at the beginning of last May, under the command of the Earl of Sussex, with the view of reducing the rebels and those who harboured them in Scotland. Our troops destroyed within a few days fifty castles in Scotland by means of gunpowder, and burned three hundred villages without any resistance. Scotland is now sufficiently tranquil. But this is probably owing to our queen, who is keeping an army on the borders; for otherwise the party of the queen of Scotland, who is still in our custody, seem as if they would

[3 Three-score and six petty constables and others were hanged for a terrour at Durham, among whom the man of most note was one Plumtree, a priest. At York were executed Simon Digby, J. Fulthorp, Thomas Bishop, Robert Peneman; and at London, some few months after, Christopher and Thomas Norton; and some others elsewhere. Camden's Elizabeth, p. 135.]

[4 In the midst of April, Sussex, with the lord Hunsdon, Drury marshal of Berwick, and an English army, entered into Scotland, fired the towns and villages of Buccleugh and the Kerrs all over Teviotdale, spoiled their fields, and demolished Fernihurst and Craling, two castles of Thomas Kerr's. On the other side, Henry lord Scroop entered at the very same time into the west March of Scotland, and wasted far and wide all over Annandale the territories of Johnston and others which had harboured the English rebels. At this time were burnt 300 villages, and about 50 castles razed. Camden. Eliz. p. 141. See also Strype, Annals, I. ii. 358.]

[ZURICH LETTERS.]

be plotting some new disturbance. The king's party now prevail, and have chosen the Earl of Lenox, grandfather of the young king, to be regent. He has taken upon himself the defence of religion and of the king. York is 160 of our miles distant from this city. I shall not, therefore, be able to send letters to you so conveniently as I have been used to do. I will write, however, from time to time, even though you should be longer in receiving them; and I shall anxiously expect to hear from you. May the Lord Jesus preserve your piety in safety to me and to his church, my very reverend and dear brother in the Lord! London, July 31, 1570.

Yours in Christ,

EDMUND EBOR.

Greet, I pray you, your colleagues in my name, and especially master Rodolph Gualter.

LETTER XCI.

BISHOP JOHN JEWEL TO HENRY BULLINGER.

Dated *Aug.* 7, 1570.

MUCH health in Christ. Your letter, my much esteemed father and master in Christ, was most gratifying to me, both as coming from you to whom alone I owe every thing, and also as seeming somewhat angry and complaining, and claiming from me the performance of my duty [of writing.] I confess my fault, and beg for pardon; for it is much better to do this, than to stand upon one's defence, though I doubt not of my being able to defend myself, even before the most severe judge. For in the first place, I am at a great distance from London: in the next place, John Abel, the mutual agent of our correspondence, has departed this life: lastly, the disorders in the Low Countries have for some years thrown so many obstacles in the way of travelling, that neither our merchants can pass over to Antwerp, nor the Antwerp merchants to us. And then, our letters are often left on the road, often carried to other places, often come back, and are often lost. And what is to become of the one I am now writing, it is impossible to tell. This reason certainly makes me write to you both less frequently, and more sparingly and cautiously, than I could wish.

I rejoice, however, that your affairs are in the condition you mention. May God send you help from his holy place, and aid you out of Sion! For there are enemies gaping upon you at this time, not less numerous or ferocious than upon ourselves. For antichrist seems now to have ventured his last cast, and to have thrown the world into confusion by seditions, tumults, wars, fury, fire and flame. He perceives that it is now all over with him, and that destruction and death are impending over him and his party; so that his wretched object now is, not to perish ignobly or obscurely. Let the remembrance of them perish then with a noise.

That vague rumour which was generally reported among you, respecting a change in our circumstances, was altogether unfounded. For both our queen, by the blessing of our good and gracious God, still holds the government, and religion is in the same state as heretofore, and as we wish it to be. Our papists, however, by the persuasion and influence of pope Pius, have endeavoured to regain their power. But blessed be our God, the Father of our Lord Jesus Christ, that while they seek to destroy others, they perish themselves. Two of our nobility[1] indeed, young and foolish and dissolute, who cared more for dice than for religion, raised, towards the end of last autumn, some thousands of peasantry in the remotest parts of England. And relying on their numbers, these silly men were bold enough to publish a proclamation[2],

[1 The earls of Northumberland and Westmoreland, see p. 213. and note 1, p. 247. This rising gave occasion to the homily against wilful rebellion. Strype, Annals, I. ii. 322.]

[2 The two earls set forth a writing, wherein they declared, that they had not taken arms with any other intent, than that the religion of their forefathers might be restored, corrupt counsellors removed from the queen; the duke, and other faithful lords, that were put from their rank and degree, restored to liberty and grace; and that they attempted

to the effect that they intended to remove some persons, I
know not whom, (for they mentioned no names,) from the
sacred council of the queen, and to restore the old religion.
What more? Without delay altars are erected in their camp;
the holy bibles are committed to the flames[1], and masses are
performed. After some weeks the earl of Sussex, a good and
active man, and of great discretion, was sent against them
at the head of a handful of troops. They began gradually
to disperse and retreat, while Sussex was skilfully and resolutely pursuing them, and pressing upon their rear. At last
the wretches, when they perceived the enemy hanging over
them, being utterly unskilled in action, and men who had
never seen an enemy before, were afraid of trying the fortune
of war; and struck with the consciousness of their crime, mad
and blind, they leave the army without a leader, and quitting
the camp secretly by night, with only a few adherents, take
refuge in Scotland. Here then you have the history of our
affairs, which I cannot even call to mind without a blush;
for I am ashamed that men of such ignorance and folly should
have been found in England. Our queen demands through
her ambassador the rebels from Scotland, where there are
at this time two parties; one of which cherish the pure religion
and the gospel, and depend upon us; the other are enemies
to godliness, and friendly to popery, and are inclined towards
the French. The leader of these is the duke of Hamilton,
a man, they say, much more influential in name than in
counsel. The states are assembled, the deliberation is begun,
our party are of opinion that the rebels should be given up;
the Hamilton party maintain the contrary, and at length are
successful. Our people, impatient of the offence, arm troops
and march into the very midst of Scotland without any opposition, and lay waste, after an enemy's fashion, the castles and
towns belonging to the duke of Hamilton. But those notable
enemies of ours above mentioned, when they could no longer
keep themselves in Scotland, fled over into Flanders, where

nothing against the queen, to whom they owned themselves now and
ever to be dutiful and faithful subjects. Camden's Eliz. p. 134. See
also a letter from Sir G. Bowes to the earl of Sussex, in Wright's Elizabeth and her Times, vol. I. p. 333, from the MS. Cott. Calig. b. IX. 351.]

[1 See p. 214.]

they are now remaining with the duke of Alva, and are making all the disturbance in their power.

The most holy father has occasioned us all these disorders. For in his holiness and wisdom he secretly sent to his friends in England a bull (shall I call it a golden or a leaden one?) of great importance. It was for some months carried about in obscurity and confined to a few. The good father declared that Elizabeth was not queen of England, for that her institutions did not please him; and he therefore ordered that none should acknowledge her as queen, or obey her in that character. Whosoever should act otherwise, he devoted to all the furies, and delivered to destruction. O holy see! Thus it was, forsooth, that Peter used to act of old! There were some, however, to whom on other accounts these decrees seemed holy; others were not so flexible to every nod of the pope, and had not so learned the gospel. I send you a copy of this most offensive and empty bull, that you may understand with what solemn impudence the beast is now raging. Within these few days new disorders have arisen in Norfolk[2]. But their authors were forthwith apprehended at the very outset, and thrown into prison.

The queen of Scots, an exile from her country, is, as you know, here in custody; with sufficient honour indeed, yet so as that she cannot raise any disturbances. This is she to whom pope Pius not only freely promises Scotland, but England likewise; for he hopes that a woman, a catholic, a murderer of her husband, and an adulteress, will have great influence in the restoration of popery! We are preparing a fleet, and have troops in readiness. Our church in other respects, by the blessing of God, is quiet. Dr Grindal is made archbishop of York, and Dr Sandys, who was heretofore bishop of Worcester, is now translated to London. Parkhurst, [bishop] of Norwich, is alive and well; but I have not seen

[[2] The object of this rebellion was, to set the queen of Scots at liberty; to rescue the duke of Norfolk, who was a prisoner for listening to a match with that queen; likewise to seize the persons of the lord keeper, the earl of Leicester, and secretary Cecil, persons near about the queen, and to make insults upon the poor protestant strangers, and drive them out of the land; and finally to bring in the duke of Alva from Flanders to invade England. Four were condemned for high treason, and two more to perpetual imprisonment. Strype, Annals, I. ii. 364.]

him these six years. May God preserve you very long for the advancement of his gospel and of his church!

Salute in my name masters Gualter, Simler, Lavater, Zuinglius, Wickius, Haller, and your Bullingers, whom I love in the Lord. On my journey: for I am now visiting my diocese. Aug. 7, 1570.

Yours in Christ,

JO. JEWEL,

bishop of Salisbury.

LETTER XCII.

JAMES LEITH TO HENRY BULLINGER.

Dated at GENEVA, *Nov.* 18, [1570].

SINCE, most learned sir, my master [Sir] Henry Denny has not yet written to you, although on the 19th of May, while he was enjoying your most agreeable society at Zurich, he promised you of his own accord, that in case he should learn any news when at Geneva which might seem worthy of being related, he would communicate it to you; you must know that he has been prevented from performing his promise by his sudden departure from this place. For when he went from Geneva to Lyons about three months since, being obliged by some private business of his own, and not in the least expecting but that he should return, lo! he heard there of some unforeseen occurrences, which required his immediate presence in England. But when, making all the haste he could, he had almost reached Calais, and was at most within half a day's journey of that port, he opportunely met on the road, as if dropped from heaven, that most accomplished man Sir Francis Walsingham, his cousin-german, who was then sent[1] ambassador from her most se-

[1 In Aug. 1570. See Strype, Annals II. i. 19. who says, "the chief and main of his business was for the sake of the reformed religion, and for an accord between that king and the protestant princes, viz. the prince of Navarre, the prince of Condé, and the admiral."]

rene highness queen Elizabeth to king Charles, with congratulations upon the recent peace; and being now appointed successor to Sir Henry Norris, he is discharging the duties of a resident ambassador at the court of France. Having ascertained from him the whole state of affairs both at home and abroad, and being thus relieved from great anxiety and distress of mind, he returned with him to Paris, where he intended, by God's blessing, to pass the winter with him in the same house. He has therefore written to me from Paris, within these few days, desiring me, among other things, to make you acquainted with these circumstances as soon as I possibly could, by letter in his name, that he might thus acquit himself of his promise; and also, that I should declare the continuance of his affectionate regard for you, which inclines him to do any thing for your sake that may lie in his power, and that you may wish for, and this in deeds rather than in words; and especially, that I should return you equal, that is, the greatest possible thanks for that exceeding courtesy which you exhibited towards him. He adds moreover, that if my assistance can in any way be of use to you, (and I am lodging in the college of Geneva, with master Portus, the professor of Greek,) I must both offer it by letter, and am to bestow the same attention and care upon any affairs of yours, which you may commit to my management, as I should upon his own. And this I do most willingly, not only, as I ought, for the sake of my master, who, I perceive, desires this, but also for your own sake, whom I so much admire and reverence for those noble gifts of God and excellent qualities with which, so to speak, you shine as a star of the first magnitude in the church of God. Bid me therefore, command me, order me: you will find me ready in every thing to obey your wishes; and, in case I should be unable to effect any thing by prudence, industry and exertion, I will not at least be wanting to its accomplishment by my activity, diligence, and fidelity. Nothing therefore now remains, but that I await your commands, although I may not perhaps satisfy your expectation.

But I had almost forgotten to salute you in my master's name, as he especially commanded me; but I dare not tell you in what terms. For if I should say that he ordered me *diligently* to salute you, that word *diligently* might occasion a prejudice against me, inasmuch as you might well doubt of my diligence in the management of your affairs, who have shewn such want of diligence in sending you this message of salutation, by throwing it into the end of my letter, wherein it should have occupied an early place. Wherefore you are the more to be entreated by me, to salute from myself master Julius the Martyritian[1] (for I know not what other name he has), who is employing himself in correcting Froschover's press. You see how one degree of impudence leads on to another, in that I, a poor mean fellow as I am, am so acting towards a man of your quality, as to presume to impose any burden upon you; and this too, before I have received any commission to execute for you, who have the right of prescribing to and commanding me. But I know the kindness of master Bullinger, to whom I commend myself, and him to Christ.

Farewell, most reverend sir. Geneva, Nov. 18, [1570.]

Yours truly from my heart,

JAMES LEITH, *Anglus.*

LETTER XCIII.

BISHOP PARKHURST TO HENRY BULLINGER.

Dated at NORWICH, *Jan.* 16, 1571.

HAIL, my Bullinger. The death of Abel, to whom alone I was accustomed to entrust my letters, and whatever other things I had to send, has been the reason of my writing to you less frequently. For he was a most faithful friend, and I cannot tell where I shall be able to find such another. But the Lord, I trust, will raise me up one like him, and who may

[[1] This name given to Julius Santerentianus, from his having been the attendant of Peter Martyr, affords an incidental proof of the estimation in which the latter was held by his contemporaries.]

in future supply his place. Norwich is nearly a hundred miles from London, which I am not in the habit of visiting, unless when summoned to parliament, which will be the case this winter. I must there seek out some trustworthy person, who will undertake that my letters shall be safely delivered to you. Our merchants are not over fond of going either to Flanders or Spain. For they fear the Spanish inquisition more than that of the devil, which neither spares its own subjects nor strangers.

Grindal, late bishop of London, is made archbishop of York. Sandys, bishop of Worcester, is translated to London. About the beginning of November great inundations of the sea occasioned extensive mischief in many parts of England; nor did my diocese escape with impunity in Norfolk and Suffolk. Flanders was injured more than any other country. The ground here has been for some weeks buried in deep snow, such as I never saw before, and still continues to be so. There is not a spot of green any where. A murrain is apprehended among the cattle through want of food.

My wife has been ill from the beginning of November to the present time, and is not yet recovered. Should I be able to ascertain that these my letters have reached you in safety, I will endeavour to write more frequently. But the death of Abel, the disturbances in Belgium, and spies in every quarter, have hitherto retarded in great measure every attempt.

I wish all happiness to your chief magistrates, the council, the ministers of the word, the citizens, and the whole state of Zurich. Farewell all of you in the Lord. And I bid you again farewell, most agreeable Bullinger. My invalid salutes you all. In haste. Norwich, Jan. 16, 1571.

Yours from my heart,

JOHN PARKHURST, N.

LETTER XCIV.

BISHOP COX TO RODOLPH GUALTER.

Dated at ELY, *Feb.* 12, 1571.

THE copy of the letter, most learned Gualter, and very dear brother in Christ, which you wrote to the Bishop of Norwich, was forwarded to me very late, namely in September, 1570. It treats in a cursory manner of some ceremonies of religion in England, and of some of our brethren who disapprove of them. We are persuaded that you are one who entertain a pious and sincere regard for us, and for that pure religion of Christ which we profess. I wish indeed you had not lent so ready an ear to a few of our somewhat factious brethren. And it were to be desired that a man of your piety had not so freely given an opinion, before you had fully understood the rise and progress of our restoration of religion in England. There was formerly published by command of King Edward of pious memory, and with the advice and opinion of those excellent men, master Bucer[1], and master Peter Martyr, then residing in England, a book of common prayer[2] and sacraments

[1 After Bucer's perusal of the book, he gave this judgment in general: "that in the description of the communion and daily prayers, he saw nothing enjoined in the book but what was agreeable to the word of God, either in word, as in the Psalms and lessons; or in sense, as the collects. Also, that the manner of their lessons and prayers, and the times of using them, were constituted very agreeable both with God's word, and the observation of the ancient churches; and therefore that that book ought to be retained and vindicated with the greatest strictness." Strype, Life of Cranmer, 300. Peter Martyr's opinions upon the Liturgy coincided in all respects with those of his friend Bucer. The particular animadversions they both made upon it may be found in Soames's Hist. of the Reformation, Vol. III. chap. 6. See also Bucer, Scripta Anglicana.]

[2 A committee of bishops and other learned divines, of whom Dr Cox, then dean of Christ Church, was one, was appointed in 1547, the first of King Edward VI. to compose "an uniform order of communion, according to the rules of Scripture, and the use of the primitive church." And the same persons, in the following year, being empowered by a new commission, in a few months' time finished the whole Liturgy, for the use of the church of England. But now, as soon as our illustrious queen Elizabeth had succeeded to the kingdom, she restored this holy little book[3] to the church of England, with the highest sanction of the whole kingdom. At that time no office or function of religion was committed to us who now preside over the churches; but when we were called to the ministry of the churches, we embraced that book with open arms, and not without thanks to God who had preserved for us such a treasure, and restored it to us in safety. For we know that this book ordains nothing contrary to the word of God.

It will not be foreign to the subject to state what master Peter Martyr of pious memory wrote to us when exiles at Frankfort. "I find nothing," he says, speaking of this book, "in that book contrary to godliness. We know that some contentious men have cavilled at and calumniated it. Such persons ought rather to have remembered that our Lord is not a God of contention, but of peace." Had you been aware of these circumstances, master Gualter, you would not have been so alarmed, as you say you are, lest after the imposition of the habits some greater evil might ensue. The statements indeed, which are whispered in your ears by the contentious, are most absurd: for instance, that besides the habits many other things are to be obtruded on the church; and that there are some who make an improper use of the name of the queen; and moreover, that the ministers who refuse to subscribe to the injunctions of certain individuals, are to be turned out of the

which was then set forth "by the common agreement and full assent both of the Parliament and convocations provincial," and is frequently called the first book of Edward VI. But about the beginning of 1551, some exceptions were taken at some things in this book, whereupon Archbishop Cranmer proposed to review it; and to this end called in the assistance of Martin Bucer and Peter Martyr, who had Latin versions prepared for them, and the book thus revised and altered was again confirmed in Parliament in 1551. It is frequently called the second book of Edward VI. and is very nearly the same with that which we now use. See Bp. Mant's Introduction to his edition of the Book of Common Prayer. Strype, Mem. II. i. 133 &c. Life of Cranmer, 381.]

[3 The differences between the Book of Prayers of King Edward and queen Elizabeth are few and unimportant. They are stated by Soames, Hist. of Reformation, IV. 674, and Strype, Annals, I. i. 123. See also Bp. Mant's Introduction as above, p. iii. and Keeling, *Liturgiæ Britannicæ*.]

churches: just as if there were any persons in England who would dare to frame laws by their private authority, and propound them for the obedience of their brethren. But this is not only false, but injurious both to the queen and the ministers of the word, to wit, that we humour her royal highness, and make her more decided in ordering every thing according to her own pleasure. But far be any one from suspecting any thing of the kind in so godly and religious a personage, who has always been so exceedingly scrupulous in deviating even in the slightest degree from the laws prescribed. Moreover, she is in the habit of listening with the greatest patience to bitter and sufficiently cutting discourses. Again, far be it that the ministers of the word should be said to have foully degenerated into base flattery. We indeed do not as yet know of any one who has abused either your authority, Gualter, or that of any godly fathers, in approval of the popish dress, which we seriously reject and condemn equally with themselves. Nor is it true that we have obtruded any thing upon our brethren out of the pope's kitchen. The surplice was used in the church of Christ long before the introduction of popery. But these things are proposed by us as having been sanctioned by the laws, not as the papists abused them to superstition, but only for distinction, that order and decency may be preserved in the ministry of the word and sacraments. And neither good pastors nor pious laymen are offended at these things.

You seem to take it ill that the bishops were appointed to the management of these matters. Nay, you seem to insinuate, from the parable of Christ, (Matt. xxiv. 49,) that we are perfidious, drunken, and smiters of our fellow-servants; as if we approved the figments of the superstitious courtiers, and treated the godly ministers with severity, and exhibited ourselves as the ministers of intemperate rashness. You thought that we should defend the cause of such ministers.

These imputations are very hard, and very far from the truth. Has not the management and conservation of ecclesiastical rites, from the very origin of a well-constituted church, been at all times under the especial controul of bishops? Have not the despisers and violators of such rites been rebuked and brought into order by the bishops? Let the practice of the holy church be referred to, and it will be evident that this is the truth. And it would certainly be most unjust to number those who now discharge the episcopal office, among the perfidious or the drunken. You candidly and truly confess, master Gualter, that there are some among those brethren who are a little morose; and you might add too, obstreperous, contentious, rending asunder the unity of a well-constituted church, and everywhere handing up and down among the people a form of divine worship concocted out of their own heads; that book, in the mean time, composed by godly fathers, and set forth by lawful authority, being altogether despised and trodden under foot. In addition to this, they inveigh in their sermons, which are of too popular a character, against the popish filth and the monstrous habits, which, they exclaim, are the ministers of impiety and eternal damnation. Nothing moves them, neither the authority of the state, nor of our church, nor of her most serene majesty, nor of brotherly warning, nor of pious exhortation. Neither have they any regard to our weaker brethren, who are hitherto smoking like flax, but endeavour dangerously to inflame their minds. These our brethren will not allow us to imitate the prudence of Paul, who became all things to all men, that he might gain some. Your advice, and that especially of the reverend fathers Martin Bucer, Peter Martyr, and Henry Bullinger, can have no weight with these men. We are undeservedly branded with the accusation of not having performed our duty, because we do not defend the cause of those whom we regard as disturbers of peace and religion; and who by the vehemence of their harangues have so maddened the wretched multitude, and driven some of them to that pitch of frenzy, that they now obstinately refuse to enter our churches, either to baptize their children, or to partake of the Lord's supper, or to hear sermons. They are entirely separated both from us and from those good brethren of ours; they seek bye paths; they establish a private religion, and assemble in private houses, and there perform their sacred rites, as the Donatists of old, and the Anabaptists now; and as also our papists, who run up and down the cities, that they may somewhere or other hear mass in private. This indeed is too disgusting, to connect our queen with the pope. Let the pope be sent where he deserves. We must render an account of our function to the queen, as chief magistrate, who does not require any thing that is unreasonable, and also before God.

These few things I had, my beloved brother, to notice in your letter, that henceforth you may not believe every spirit; and that, since God has endowed you with so much learning and piety, you may have regard to your own reputation. These remarks, proceeding from a candid mind, I do not doubt but that you will take with kindness and in good' part. Farewell in Christ.

From the Isle of Ely in England, Feb. 12, 1571.

Your brother in Christ,

RICHARD COX,

bishop of Ely.

LETTER XCV.

BISHOP JEWEL TO HENRY BULLINGER.

Dated at SALISBURY, *March* 2, 1571.

MUCH health in Christ. I wrote to you, most accomplished sir, and much esteemed father in Christ, towards the beginning of September, and at some length, concerning the general posture of our affairs. I know not what has become of that letter; for it often happens in these turbulent times that our poor innocent letters are either destroyed or lost on the road. Should I hear that it has reached you in safety, I shall be more encouraged to write in future.

Our churches are now, by the blessing of God, in peace. The most holy father has endeavoured to create confusion by every means in his power. He sent over to us by stealth his most senseless bull[1], by which he would deprive queen

[1 See p. 229.]

Elizabeth of the government of the state, and Christ of his kingdom. I sent a copy of it to you at the last fair, that you might know with what solemnity that old and foolish man is raving. All his secret counsels have been so ably detected, and skilfully and opportunely counteracted by those who hold the helm of government, that they are now perceived even by children. Those wretched and infatuated rebels, who, eighteen months since, began to raise disorders in the county of Durham[2], are now utterly defeated, and exiles in Flanders. Our *friends* at Louvaine have not written any thing for two years. The queen of Scotland is still kept here, as you are aware, in a free custody, honourably, and with almost a royal attendance; but still she is in custody, which she bears with impatience and indignation, and complains that she is unjustly dealt with. You well know the spirit and disposition of the Guises. They say that the brother of the king of France is courting her for his wife. The affairs of Scotland, meanwhile, are under the direction of those who profess the gospel. That intercourse, which formerly existed between us and the people of Antwerp, having been violated some years since by their injustice and breach of faith, cannot as yet be renewed. In Spain the Moors are increasing in number, strength, and victories; Philip is growing weaker every day. But what can I tell you about the affairs of Cyprus[3] and Venice? The Turk, they say, is now hovering upon Italy. He will at least bridle the ferocity of antichrist; for the sovereigns of christendom, though so often warned, pay no attention. Our queen Elizabeth hath summoned the peers, and proclaimed a par-

[2 See p. 213.]

[3 In a letter to the countess of Shrewsbury, dated London, Aug. 31, 1570, the unknown writer says: "It is written, by letters of the 28th of the last, from Venice, that the Turke hath landed in Ciprus a hundred thousand men or moo; and hathe besieged the two great cities within that kingdome, Nicosia and Famagosta .... The Turke hath sent another army by land against the Venetians, into Dallmatia, and are besieging of Zora with 20,000 footmen and 20,000 horsemen; .... and it is written that the Turke's severall armies be above 200,000 men against the Venetians .... A man may see what accompte is to be made of these worldly thinges, as to see in a small tyme the thirde state of Christendome in security, power, and welthe, to be in danger of utter overthrowe in one yere." Shrewsbury Papers, Lodge.]

liament¹ for the 2nd of April, which I hope will be for the prosperity and welfare both of church and state. There, at length, I hope to see our friend Parkhurst, whom I have not seen of seven whole years.

Walter Haddon², a pious and eloquent man, has departed this life. Grindal [archbishop] of York, Sandys [bishop] of London, Horn of Winchester, are a great way from me, each on his watch-tower. All of them, however, desire your welfare, and send their respects.

I owe my friend Julius forty French crowns, being his pension for the two past years. I have desired him by letter once or twice to let me know to whom he wishes me to pay them. The money is forthcoming, as soon as there is any one to receive it. If he does not choose to write, he must not accuse me of not keeping my promise, for it is altogether his own fault.

Farewell, my father, and much-esteemed master in Christ. May the Lord Jesus very long preserve you in safety to his church! Salisbury, March 2, 1571.

Yours in Christ,

JOHN JEWEL,

bishop of Salisbury.

[¹ For the proceedings of this Parliament, see Strype, Annals, II. i. 90.]
[² Walter Haddon was esteemed one of the most learned and religious men of these times. He was master of requests to queen Elizabeth, and employed by her in many foreign embassies. Of him it was that, when asked whether she preferred him or Buchanan for learning, she replied, *Buchananum omnibus antepono, Haddonum nemini postpono.* See Strype, Parker, II. 145. Burgon's Life of Sir Thomas Gresham, II. 67.]

LETTER XCVI.

RICHARD HILLES TO HENRY BULLINGER.
Dated at LONDON, *July* 27, 1571.

MUCH health in the Lord. I wrote a letter to you, very reverend Sir, on the 8th of March, which my son Barnabas, as he afterwards informed me, transmitted to you by Christopher Froschover, at the last Frankfort fair. You have received it, I hope, before this time; and would learn from it that your last copious letter of the month of August in the past year has long since reached me. I have only, however, received this day your most gratifying letter from Zurich, of the 25th of February in this present year, together with your three letters addressed to the reverend the bishops of York, Ely, and Salisbury; and also the three copies in manuscript, of which you write in the letter above mentioned; all of which I will take care shall be faithfully delivered to the bishops to whom you have directed them. I certainly much wonder where they have been so long delayed in their journey: but I am very glad to have received them even now; and I have to thank you also for your present of a book printed in German, entitled, A promised Answer to the Testament of John Brentius, &c. Of this I have received two copies, besides five books printed in Latin, and three letters, viz. one to the bishop of London, another to the bishop of Durham, and the third to Henry Butler, together with the three manuscript copies above-mentioned; which letters, as well as all the aforesaid seven printed books, I will take care shall be delivered as soon as possible, to the persons to whom in your letter you desired them to be sent[3]........ This cloth I make you a present of; and I pray God that you may long enjoy it, though it is not very likely that you will: for Jerome says most truly, quoting some philosopher or poet, The young *may* die soon, but the old *cannot* live long.

[[3] A paragraph respecting some cloth that Bullinger had bespoken, is here omitted. It is given in the original letter at the end of this volume.]

That labour of yours, of which you inform me, in replying to the whole of that impudent popish bull which the Roman antichrist has vomited forth against our most serene queen, will be, without doubt, very greatly approved by the three bishops afore-mentioned, to whom you have sent those three copies; and if they think it for the good of the kingdom, and that it will be agreeable to her most serene highness, they will publish it. I am much grieved at your so humbly entreating me to take in good part your writing to me, and that you ask my pardon for so freely employing my services; for you may always employ them most freely as long as I live.

By the blessing of God, before the dissolution or ending of the Parliament held at Westminster, the above-mentioned Henry Butler was here with his master, Parkhurst, bishop of Norwich, and was anxiously expecting a letter from his mother; for, as he then told me, he had not heard from her since his arrival in England. Master doctor Mont, however, informed him in my house, that a packet of letters had been left at his house in Strasburgh, in which he thought there were some addressed to this Henry Butler.

In the month of June now last past, the very learned divine David Whitehead, who was an exile in queen Mary's time for the profession of orthodox doctrine, departed happily in the Lord. He also lived about seven years a widower, as you write me word is now your own case; but very lately, before the middle of this year, he married a young widow when he was himself about eighty. Master Cole too, who was also at that period an exile in Germany for preaching the gospel, died about the same time of the quinsey, on the day after he was taken ill. The archdeacon of Essex, in the diocese of London, who was preferred a month or two before his death to the deanery of Salisbury, died here at London, on the same day, as is reported, or on the day preceding that on which he had determined to go from London to Salisbury to receive induction, attended by many friends and domestics.

Thus from a slight and slender thread all human things depend,
And those which seem the strongest now may soonest have an end[1].

[1] "Omnia sunt hominum tenui pendentia filo,
 Et subito casu quæ valuere ruunt."

I have taken care, previous to my finishing this letter, that all the manuscript copies aforesaid, and all the other printed books, have been delivered to the right reverend bishops to whom they were addressed; and I hope that they will shortly acknowledge the receipt of them to your worship. Farewell, my very reverend master in Christ our Saviour. London, July 27, 1571.

Yours heartily, as you know,
RICHARD HILLES, *Anglus*.

P.S. July 31. Since my letter was sealed, I have seen and read your letter to the three right reverend bishops, viz. York, Ely, and Salisbury, already in print; and the first part also of your work above-mentioned, (from the manuscript copy, I understand, which you sent to the lord bishop of Ely,) also printed. And I am informed that some more pages of the same work are also printed; so that the whole of that manuscript copy of yours will be printed and published as soon as possible.

LETTER XCVII.

BISHOP COX TO HENRY BULLINGER.

After *July* 27, 1571.

Your letter, my very dear brother in Christ, which however I did not receive till almost the end of June, was most gratifying to me. I received at the same time two little books, the one against the Testament[2] of John Brentius, a man who is gone crazy through a variety of error. To this error of his, creeping on as it was by degrees, you have seasonably closed the way. The other book is a most power-

[2 This Testament was published at Wittenberg, for the purpose of forewarning all states not to allow the Zuinglians a toleration.]

ful defence against that terrific bull, which however is lighter than any bubble; in which you have so mauled the author, that he has no more breath remaining in him. We are all much in your debt for having so zealously taken up the common cause. I wrote to you on this subject very weakly and vapidly; but one of my brethren[1] has treated it more fully and copiously, and has also made for you a copy of the bull itself. It was your regard for us, and your indignation at the thing, and the most ardent zeal for the truth, that extorted from your piety this attack upon it. You have hitherto lived in the most holy and devout study of the divine word, so as to cherish and promote its progress by every possible means. You were called to this from your earliest life; you have sedulously adorned this your calling; and God will enable you to persevere in it even to the end of life, to the peace of your own conscience, and the most eager expectation of all good men. Hence it is that you always take occasion to deserve well of the christian religion, and to attack with severity the enemies of godliness. Hence it is, that you both seasonably interpose a remedy for the disorder occasioned by Brentius, and restrain the fury of the [papal] bull. I will most diligently take care that our queen, who is well skilled both in Latin and Greek, may be made acquainted with your respect and courtesy towards herself, and I will make her to have a most agreeable taste of your little book[2]. But since you refer to us the best manner of dealing with your book, we are of opinion that it should be printed, and published in the name of Henry Bullinger, as soon as possible; and I will send you some copies by the earliest opportunity.

That Henry Butler, of whom you write, has not yet called upon me. I will do my best, that when he comes, he shall have no occasion to require my assistance. May the good

[1 Bishop Jewel. See p. 229.]

[2 In the month of September the Archbishop caused it to be fairly bound and sent to her, and further procured the printing of it in Latin, not without the advice of the Lord Treasurer, and had it translated and printed in English too. The Latin, printed by John Day, had this title, *Bullæ Papisticæ ante biennium contra sereniss. Angliæ, Franciæ et Hiberniæ Reginam Elizabetham, et contra inclytum Angliæ regnum promulgatæ, Refutatio, orthodoxæque Reginæ et universi regni Angliæ Defensio Henrychi Bullingeri.* Strype, Parker, II. 78.]

and great God preserve you, my most beloved brother in Christ, and that for many years, to the advantage of the church; and I pray you to commend us to God in your prayers, those of us especially who are labouring in his vineyard. I write no news to you; for my brother Horn has promised to take that office upon himself.

Your very dear brother in the Lord,

RICHARD,

bishop of Ely.

LETTER XCVIII.

BISHOP HORN TO HENRY BULLINGER.

Dated at LONDON, *Aug.* 8, 1571.

THOUGH, my dearest Bullinger, neither love will admit of a suspicion of ingratitude, nor will prudence permit rashness of judgment, yet delay both weakens the ardent expectation of a duty that is owing, and negligence requires a serious apology for the omission of it. But the present case will not admit of any accusation, inasmuch as I am neither conscious of an offence, nor does your disposition, far from being suspicious or angry, require any apology to be made. Since however, you may be in doubt as to the reason [of my not writing,] you shall be acquainted with it, lest your opinion of me should be shaken; or since, perhaps, you may desire to know it, I will satisfy your wish, lest that opinion should be wounded. Do not however suppose that my not having replied to your letter sent so long since arises from a rash disregard of my duty, or a negligent forgetfulness of it; or in any way from unkindness. The reason is, that we are somewhat in confusion at home, and there is a vehement commotion on all sides of us abroad, so that the very seas, even unto the coast nearest to yourselves, have been lighted up with the daily flames of war; whereby there has neither been afforded me any certain opportunity of writing, nor since the death of our friend Abel has any method presented itself of forwarding a letter; nor, if I had chosen to write, and been able to send my letter, could I have ascertained with certainty whether it had been delivered. Now however, having met with both an opportunity and a courier, no inducement ought to be wanting to one who has been so long invited by your most affectionate letter, and also incited by your most friendly salutations lately offered in the epistle prefixed to the pope's bull; neither could inclination be wanting to me who have so long and earnestly desired [to write]. But I am acting as those are wont to do, who when they are so encumbered with debt as to owe much to many persons, and have not wherewith to discharge the whole, surrender their property to one or other of their creditors, to make an equal distribution among the rest; and thus they satisfy each according to their means. In the same way, being greatly in debt not only to you, but also to my friends Gualter, Simler, Zuinglius, Lavater, Wolfius, and my other beloved brethren in Christ at Zurich, I pay all that I have into your hands, that you may therewith satisfy both yourself and my other creditors in those quarters. You must therefore equally distribute and share with them, whatever new wares I have to dispose of, from England, Scotland, France, and Flanders. I do not offer you any commodities from Rome; for I am aware that such are becoming cheap among you, as is apparent in many ways, and especially by that most learned refutation of the pope's bull, which you sent over some time since, and which is now being printed also for general circulation.

Our government has been for almost the last three years in a dangerous and dreadful state of agitation; being not only shaken abroad by the perfidious attacks of our enemies, but troubled and disturbed at home by internal commotions. Both these kinds of pestilence, as is always the case, are the brood and offspring of popery, that pernicious and accursed fury of the whole world. But our noble and excellent virgin [queen], reposing in security at home, has broken both their forces at the same time, and destroyed the one without difficulty, and the other without bloodshed. Every thing turned out so unexpectedly as it were from above, that it seemed as though the Lord of hosts and of might had undertaken from his heaven the cause of his gospel, and had fought, as it were, with his own hands. The winds from heaven brought us in, as if with spontaneous gales, the arms, treasures, and ships of the one; while the report that the royal army was advancing, dismayed and scattered the soldiers, baggage, and military stores of the other. Thus the one party were unconquered till they were completely routed; the others were manifestly conquered before they had made any progress. There were only two noblemen[1], and those of no influence or reputation; men, to say the least of them, of the most worthless character, and of the old

[1 The earls of Northumberland and Westmoreland. See p. 213. In addition to the account there given, the following summary will be acceptable, taken from the preface to Memorials of the Rebellion of 1569. London 1840, p. xvi. xix. "The earls, after refusing to obey the queen's commands to repair to her presence, committed themselves irrevocably, by entering Durham in arms on the 14th November. For a short period they acted with vigour, and proceeded rapidly to Ripon, Wetherby, and Tadcaster, and finally they assembled on Clifford Moor. The queen of Scots was suddenly removed from Tutbury to Coventry, and the earls hesitated what course to pursue. The earl of Sussex, with Sadler and Hunsdon, felt insecure in York, which however they durst not leave on account of their inferiority in cavalry. They could not act on the offensive, as their levies came slowly in; and they were reduced to the mortifying alternative of keeping a watchful eye on the movements of the rebels. The earl of Sussex, (now lieutenant general of the army in the north,) directed Sir George Bowes, in the event of their proceeding southwards, to join him immediately with the northern horsemen.

"From whatever cause—whether from 'mistrusting themselves', according to Hollinshed; from 'disagreement amongst themselves', according to lady Northumberland; or, more probably, from perceiving that no response was made to their movements by the great body of the [Roman] Catholics of England,—the rebels suddenly retreated and returned to the county of Durham; where, instead of pursuing vigorous measures to restore their 'moral force', and increase their numbers, they wasted their time and strength in laying siege to Barnard castle; during whose prolonged and gallant resistance, the army of the south, commanded by the lords Warwick and Clinton, arrived at Doncaster; when Sussex, thus powerfully supported, advanced rapidly toward the county of Durham; and on his approach the earls, without waiting for an attack, suddenly dismissed their infantry, and flying with their cavalry towards Hexham, afterwards took refuge in Scotland.

"Thus

leaven, or, as they choose to call it, the old religion; their reputation was certainly somewhat out of date. These men, having secretly crossed the channel after these events, still lie hid in the parts beyond sea, and are, as is reported, miserable vagabonds, as though they were accursed and fugitive Cains. This torch afterwards kindled some sparks of sedition in other parts of the kingdom[1]; but by the prudence of the government, or rather by divine providence, it was put out and extinguished without any difficulty; so that now, thanks to immortal God! all England is at rest, and in the enjoyment of halcyon days.

And I wish, if it had so pleased God, that I could say the same really, or nearly at least, (verè aut ferè) of the church. For our church has not yet got free from those *vestiarian* rocks of offence, on which she at first struck. Our excellent queen, as you know, holds the helm, and directs it hitherto according to her pleasure. But we are awaiting the guidance of the divine Spirit, which is all we can do; and we all daily implore him with earnestness and importunity to turn at length our sails to another quarter. Meanwhile, however, we who stand in a more elevated situation do not act in compliance with the importunate clamours of the multitude; for it would be very dangerous to drag her on, against her will, to a point she does not yet choose to come to, as if we were wresting the helm out of her hands. But we aim at this, that although *badly habited*, we may yet be *strong hearted* in doing the Lord's work; and we are not so much concerned about the fitness[2] of our apparel, as about rightly dividing the bread of the Lord; nor, in fine, do we deem it of so much consequence if our own coat appears unbefitting, as it is to take care that the seamless coat of the Lord be not rent asunder. There are not however wanting some men of inferior rank and standing, deficient indeed both

"Thus terminated an enterprise, begun without foresight, conducted without energy, and ending in dastardly and inglorious flight; entailing on the families of those concerned lasting misery; and inflicting on the leaders, attainder, proscription, and death."]

[1 Namely in Norfolk. See p. 229.]

[2 There is a play upon the words *pannus* and *panis*, which cannot be preserved in the English translation.]

in sagacity and sense, and entirely ignorant and unknown, who, since they do not yet perceive the church to square with their wishes, or rather vanities, and that so far from agreeing with their follies, the wind is rather directly contrary, for this cause some of them desert their posts, and hide themselves in idleness and obscurity; others, shaping out for themselves their own barks, call together conventicles, elect their own bishops, and holding synods one with another, frame and devise their own laws for themselves. They reject preaching, despise communion, would have all churches destroyed, as having been formerly dedicated to popery; nor are they content with merely deriding our ministers, but regard the office itself as not worth a straw. And thus, as far as lieth in them, they are too rashly and precipitately accessory to the wretched shipwreck of our church, and are doubtless retarding not a little the free progress of the gospel. They themselves, in the mean time, wonderfully tossed about by I know not what waves of error, and miserably borne along, I know not whither, on the various gales of vanity, are reduced to the most absurd ravings of opinion. They therefore cut themselves off, as they say, from us; or rather, like Theudas, they depart with their own party, and act just like persons who, perceiving the wind somewhat against them, so that they cannot directly reach the point they aim at, refuse to reserve themselves for a more favourable breeze, but leaping out of the ship, rush headlong into the sea and are drowned. But here it is wonderful how fit an instrument, as they think, the adversaries of our religion have laid hold of for dishonouring the gospel. They whisper in the queen's ears, that this is the fruit of our gospel now coming to maturity; that this is the only harvest of our doctrine to be expected; so that, unless her pious heart had been altogether inflamed with the love of the truth, it would long since have been cooled by their aspersions. You see I have endeavoured, my excellent Bullinger, as briefly as I could, to make you perceive, as it were at one glance, the whole state of our affairs, and the aspect of the government, and the entire condition of the church.

France, long since disabled by her own wounds, and as if wearied with wars, has at length allowed herself a little breathing time[1]. She admits the gospel indeed, but as if it were a pestilence; so that it visits no cities[2], save a few, and those of no importance, or, if any of larger size, in such a manner as to abide without the walls. Very great precaution is taken for the court, lest Christ should sometimes be admitted even as a guest; and he is therefore ordered to be banished, under a heavy penalty, to some miles distance[3]. A cardinal[4], a man of rank and piety, and an exile here among us for the sake of religion, while he was sojourning some days at Canterbury, waiting for a wind for his prosperous and safe return, was taken off, (as they report, and it is indeed credible,) by the deadly poison of the papists, and wasted away, destroyed by wickedness and crime. But why am I exporting any news from France to Zurich? for nothing can be conveyed from France which is not well known to the people of Zurich, and which you have not in abundance. I think however that you have not heard this one circumstance, or at least that it is but little known among you. The duke of Anjou[5], brother to the

[1 A treaty of peace with the Huguenots was concluded at St Germain on Aug. 15th, 1570; and early in the following spring the 7th synod of the Reformed Church of France assembled at Rochelle, being the first which received the sanction of royal authority, and it commenced its sittings under the direct protection of the king's letters patent. Smedley's Hist. of the Reformed Religion in France. Vol. I. p. 346.]

[2 As an especial gratification to his "dear and most beloved aunt," the queen of Navarre, the king empowered her to have divine service performed, in the presence of as many persons as chose to assist, in one house in each of her fiefs, even during her absence from it. Smedley, ut supra, I. 344.]

[3 The suburbs of certain provincial towns, expressly named, were set apart for the exercise of general worship, provided such towns were neither the actual residence of the court for the time being, nor within two leagues of that residence. In Paris and within ten leagues it was altogether prohibited. Smedley, ut supra.]

[4 Odet de Coligny, archbishop of Toulouse, and Cardinal de Châtillon, was condemned by the council of Trent for embracing the protestant faith. He fled hither out of France, in 1568, after the battle of Saint Denis, and on his return, in 1570, was poisoned by one of his servants. He was honourably buried among the metropolitans, in the cathedral at Canterbury. See Strype, Annals, II. i. 353.]

[5 For a full account of all particulars relating to the proposed marriage, see Strype, Annals, II. i. 48. &c. and Camden, Eliz. p. 160. &c.]

king of France, has become an ardent suitor of our queen. What will be the event of this, is not yet known. As I do not hear that it is altogether approved of, so neither do I understand that it is altogether disliked. If you ask what I myself think, it is a difficult thing to be a judge in the affairs of princes. I shall merely say, that in my opinion this expected marriage will never take place. There are many reasons which make me fear it, and not a few which lead me to wish for it. But I leave these matters, like all others which concern us, to be well and happily disposed of by the wisdom and goodness of God. And should he make it tend as much to the propagation of the gospel, and the setting forth of the glory of the name of Christ, as it seems at first sight likely to conduce both to the private advantage of individuals, and the public good, both my life and my wishes will be abundantly satisfied.

And now to interweave a few observations respecting our neighbour Scotland. Having been lately almost ruined by the most foul homicides, and stained with the blood of her first nobility, both of her king[6], a most illustrious youth from England, and after him of the excellent regent James[7], both of whom they took off by horrible and lamentable murders, she is still in a flame through the mutual abhorrence of these events in both parties. The queen, being suspected of the murder of her husband, and required by the nobles of her kingdom either to prove her innocence, or suffer for her guilt, as I mentioned in my last letter, has secretly taken refuge here in England, where she is still detained captive. She has often meditated an escape, and others have contrived plans for her rescue, but hitherto to no purpose, for she is very diligently and carefully guarded: with what design, few can tell; with what result, does not yet appear; with what hope, or rather what fear, I grieve to say. He who has forced her to this step, both easily can, (for he is powerful,) should it seem good to him, and he readily will, (for he is merciful,) if he is entreated, order all things according to his will, and also according to our own. But in this country how wonderfully and beyond all expectation the God of all goodness and the Lord of glory has preserved every thing safe

[6 See note 2 p. 186.]   [7 See p. 218.]

and sound, as it is certain from experience, so it is true in the relation of it; yet as being of rare occurrence, will almost be incredible in the hearing. For both in the commotions in France, and the contests in Scotland, and moreover with the secret hatred of Spain, none of which could ever be overcome by any slight means or ordinary exertions, our Elizabeth, the sole nurse (as it were) of these affairs, and solely for the sake of the gospel, has preserved the friends of godliness, who would otherwise doubtless have been destroyed long since, free from harm. But observe that ancient and most convenient, and in a manner the leading stratagem of the papists, which is now both rendered familiar to us by daily experience, and peculiar to themselves by long use and possession. They besiege the tender frame of the most noble virgin Elizabeth with almost endless attacks, and most studiously endeavour to compass her death, both by poison, and violence, and witchcraft, and treason, and all other means of that kind which could ever be imagined, and which it is horrible even to relate. Hitherto however, as God has had for his gospel a faithful and active Deborah, so truly has he made her a triumphant Judith; and we implore him also to make her an aged Anna.

These Scottish wares which I have given you, are not only sordid and unsound, but really black. Now then accept of some from Flanders, few indeed in number, but which however you will without doubt call elegant. A certain person was here not long since, a doctor of laws, of some learning, such an one, I imagine, as those among the Jews who menaced Christ with death: his name is Story, a man, as it were, born for cruelty, a most raging persecutor[1] in the Marian times, to whom it was

[[1] Dr Story was one of the examiners of the martyr Philpot. His character may be judged of from the following language, addressed to Philpot, and recorded by Foxe: "Well, Sir, you are like to go after your fathers, Latimer the sophister, and Ridley, who had nothing to allege for himself but that he had learned his heresy of Cranmer. When I came to him with a poor bachelor of arts, he trembled as though he had had the palsy; as these heretics have always some token of fear whereby a man may know them, as you may see this man's eyes do tremble in his head. But I despatched them; *and I tell thee that there hath never been yet any one burnt, but I have spoken with him, and been a cause of his despatch.*" Acts and Monuments, vii. 628. See also Strype, Annals, i. ii. 297.]

gain to kill the saints, and sport to shed blood. This man then, after the happy day had shone upon us in which God raised our Elizabeth to the head of the English government, was apprehended and thrown into prison on an evident charge of treason. A short time afterwards, when the gaoler was not so careful as he should have been, he broke out of prison and escaped into Flanders, where he entered into the service[2] of the duke of Alva, the capital enemy of our kingdom, who is resident in that country. Here, like a fury fresh from hell, or more truly, like a wicked Davus, it is wonderful how he is continually making mischief. Having obtained licence from the duke, he plunders, annoys, and imprisons the merchants arriving in those parts; he entices the people of England to rebellion, is strenuously and solicitously urgent with Alva to afford a liberal supply both of men and means for so holy an object; lastly, he is endeavouring hand and foot, with all his might, to procure by some unheard-of cruelty[3] the premature and lamentable destruction of the most noble queen his sovereign, and that of the government of his honoured country. Here however the merchants, who being daily scourged by the most cruel stripes of this Davus, had a fuller perception of them to their greater sorrow, and without any hope of relief, take common counsel among themselves, and cry out as it were with one voice, that he must be carried off, which they thus effected with consummate artifice. There comes to him one of his friends[4] whose fidelity he least suspected, but who had been suborned by the merchants: this man privately whispers in his ear that a ship[5] has just arrived from England, laden with I know not what golden mountains of treasure. Fired with the love of plunder, he straightway sallies forth, promising the money to himself, and certain death to the

[[2] He was appointed searcher of all ships at Antwerp for English goods and heretical books, (Strype, Parker, II. 366,) and was allowed a moiety of the confiscation. Carte's Hist. of England.]

[[3] Story was arraigned, and was to be charged with treason, for having consulted with one Prestall, a man much addicted to magical illusions, against his prince's life. Camden's Elizabeth, p. 168.]

[[4] One Parker, who was afterwards cast into prison, by the craft and malice of Story's private friends. Strype, Parker, II. 367.]

[[5] He was decoyed on board the ship of Cornelius de Eycke, at Bergen op Zoom. Carte's Hist. of England.]

merchants. After he had entered the ship, and was prying about in every corner, and had just gone down into the interior of the vessel, they suddenly closed the hatches, and with their sails set are carried by a prosperous and safe breeze into England. And here, if in addition to all the ships of the Turkish empire laden with treasure even the whole Venetian fleet with all its wealth had met them, and been offered to them on their way, I well know that they would not have exchanged this merchandize and worthless lading of their little vessel for all those treasures. And so at length he was brought to London, amidst the great congratulations of the people, awaiting him on his return; and shortly after being convicted of treason, hung[1] and quartered, was made an ill-savoured martyr of the Roman church, and enrolled in the popish catalogue of saints, next to Felton, who affixed the pope's bull to the palace-gates of the bishop of London.

I have moreover transmitted to you, my Bullinger, by this carrier ten crowns, not so much by way of an honourable, or at least an honorary present, as a token, such as it is, of my regard towards you. The whole of this sum I desire to be expended upon a public entertainment in your common hall, devoted to the remembrance of me, though without a sacrifice.

Farewell all of you, and live happy. I desire you would so think of me, just as you are accustomed to regard one who for your sake would willingly plan any thing by his advice, or accomplish it by his assistance, or embrace it in his thoughts, or lastly, promote it by his influence. May Christ Jesus preserve the church which he has redeemed by his precious blood, disappoint the designs of all her adversaries, frustrate their attempts, and break their power! Farewell, most loving Bullinger, and live in him who is the author of life. London, Aug. 8, 1571.

Wholly yours,

ROBERT WINTON.

[1 Story suffered at Tyburn in June 1571, and was made a saint at Rome, and his martyrdom printed, and set up in the English college there. Strype, Annals, I. ii. 297.]

LETTER XCIX.

BISHOP PARKHURST TO HENRY BULLINGER.

Dated at LUDHAM, *Aug.* 10, 1571.

HEALTH to you, most agreeable Bullinger. On the 4th of March Boxall[2], a notorious papist, and secretary to queen Mary, died at Lambeth[3]; where also Thirlby, one of her counsellors and bishop of Ely, died before him. About the end of June David Whitehead[4], an octogenarian, and a man adorned with all kinds of learning, departed this life at London. Thomas Spencer[5], a doctor in divinity and archdeacon of Chichester, died on the 8th of July. He was a most diligent preacher in the Suffolk part of my diocese. He was with us at Zurich. Master Cole, not the one who

[2 John Boxall was removed from office by Elizabeth on her accession, to make way for Cecil, and his behaviour on the occasion sets his character in a favourable light; for instead of interposing obstacles to his successor in office, it is clear, from a few of his letters to Cecil dated about this period, that he cherished no sentiment but that of anxiety to afford him all the assistance in his power. See Burgon's Life and Times of Sir T. Gresham. Vol. I. p. 214.]

[3 In 1563, the Council removed Boxall and Thirlby from the tower, on account of the plague having appeared in London; and on Sept. 15, wrote to the archbishop to receive them, "and to give them convenient lodging, each of them one man allowed them, and to use them as was requisite for men of their sort; and that they would satisfy his lordship for the charges of their commons." Boxall was doctor of divinity of Oxford, and had been dean of Peterborough, Norwich, and Windsor. Strype, Parker, I. 279, &c.]

[4 Whitehead had been recommended by archbishop Cranmer to be archbishop of Armagh, and was afterwards an exile for religion, and pastor of an English congregation at Frankfort. Strype, Memor. III. i. 231.]

[5 Spencer subscribed, as a member of convocation, the Articles of 1562. Strype, Annals, I. i. 488.]

was at Zurich[1], but whom master Wolfgang Weidner was so fond of, the archdeacon of Essex[2], departed this life about the same time. Both of them were remarkable for their eloquence in the pulpit.

Almost two years since there was an implacable quarrel here at Norwich among the foreigners; nor are they even yet reconciled, though there is some hope that things will be on a better footing and more peaceable in future. You would scarce believe what labour I have undergone, to say nothing of expence, during the whole time; and yet these refractory people will not give up a single point. I have always treated them with the greatest mildness and consideration, though of late a little harshly, contrary to my nature. But what could you do? If we cannot succeed in one way, we must try another. Three[3] of their preachers, ambitious and aspiring men, occasioned and continued all this disturbance. The whole congregation was very near being broken up. Their number was about four thousand. The English, I allow, were somewhat troublesome in Germany; but, if you compare them with these, they were quietness itself. I do not in the least exaggerate. There have been great dissensions among their countrymen, both at Sandwich in Kent, and likewise in London, which, as I hear, are not yet composed. In the French church here every thing is very quiet. They are in number about four hundred.

The true religion is flourishing in Scotland. But the

[[1] This was William Cole, fellow, and afterwards president, of Corpus Christi College, Oxford, and concerned in the translation of the Geneva Bible. Strype, Memor. III. i. 232. Annals, I. i. 343. Parker, i. 528.]

[[2] Thomas Cole, an exile at Frankfort, and afterwards Rector of High Ongar, and one of the subscribers to the Articles of 1562. Strype, Memor, III. i. 404. Cranmer, 52. Annals, I. i. 488.]

[[3] There was a church allowed in the city of Norwich for strangers that fled thither for religion from the parts of Flanders; which church was supplied with three ministers named Anthonius, Theophilus and Isbrandus. These, falling in their sermons upon particular doctrines controverted among themselves, preached so earnestly in answers and confutations one of another, that the congregation was all in confusion, and the peace of the church broken. Whereupon the bishop interposed, and enjoined them to forbear that manner of preaching one against another. Strype, Annals, II. i. 174. Parker, II. 82.]

nobles are sometimes quarrelling with each other, not on account of religion, to which all parties are favourable, but for the custody of the king, which is their chief object. The queen of Scotland is still detained in England. The archbishop of St Andrew's[4], the author of many disturbances in Scotland, was hung on a gibbet last May.

The marquis of Northampton[5] (the brother of queen Catharine, the last wife of Henry the eighth, and my most gentle mistress, whom I attended as chaplain twenty-three years since,) died about the beginning of August. When I was in London, he married a very beautiful German girl, who remained in the queen's court after the departure of the margrave of Baden and Cecilia[6] his wife from England. Our

[[4] James Hamilton, the natural son of James, first Earl of Arran. He was one of the Queen of Scots' privy council, and performed the ceremony of christening her son. He was in the castle of Dumbarton when that fortress was taken by surprise, from whence he was carried to Stirling, where on April 1st, 1570, he was hanged on a live tree, which gave occasion to the following lines:
"Vive diu, felix arbor, semperque vireto
Frondibus, ut nobis talia poma feras."
He was put to death because he was strongly suspected of being concerned in the death of the regent Murray, by whom he had been declared a traitor. Beatson's Political Index. Carte however says (in his History of England) that he was condemned, not for Darnley's or Murray's murder, with which they endeavoured to blacken him, though innocent, but for rebellion against the prince of Scotland in adhering to his mother; and that the sentence was the effect of Lenox's personal enmity to the house of Hamilton.]

[[5] William Parr, first baron Parr of Kendal, created marquis of Northampton 1547; attainted 1554, when his honours became forfeited; again created marquis Northampton 1559; ob. 1571. s. p. Nicolas's Synopsis of the Peerage.]

[[6] She was sister to the king of Sweden, and arrived in England with her husband Sept. 7, 1565. The margrave returned to Germany in November, but "hathe lefte here behynd him in the courte the lady Cecilie his wyfe, with whose companye and conversation the quene is so muche delighted, as she doothe not onely allowe her very honourable bouge of courte, three measse of meat twyse a daye for her mayds and the rest of her familye, but also her majestie hathe delte so liberally with her husbande, that he hathe a yearly pension of 2000 crownes, which he is to enjoye so longe as he suffereth the ladye his wife to resyde here in Englande." Lodge's Illustrations, Vol. I. p. 358. Strype, Annals, I. ii. 198, 210.]

marquis was sixty years old, and I believe much more. Your young friend, Henry Butler, is in good health. I wish every happiness to your chief magistrates, council, preachers, citizens, and the whole estate of Zurich.

Salute in my name your sons Henry, Rodolph, and the third, whose name I have forgotten, your daughters Truth and Dorothy, Simler, Lavater, Zuinglius, your sons-in-law; Wolfius, Haller, Wickius, Froschover, Julius, John Henry Fabricius, and all the rest. My invalid salutes you and yours, sons, daughters, and all. In haste, Ludham. Aug. 10, 1571. You will learn all the other news from the letter to Gualter.

Yours,

J. PARKHURST, N.

LETTER C.

ARCHBISHOP GRINDAL TO HENRY BULLINGER.

Dated at BISHOPSTHORPE, *Jan* 25, 1572.

HEALTH in Christ. Your letter dated 25 Feb. 1571, I did not receive till the 25th of last August. I received also at the same time the MS. refutation of the pope's bull, and a Reply to the "Testament of Brentius[1]." I wonder that Brentius would leave so virulent a will behind him. Your reply is moderate and pious. The refutation of the bull is printed both in English and Latin, and you have, I believe, received some copies of the impression before this time.

I thank you for your pious anxiety with respect to our churches. You shall learn, in a few words, the state of my affairs after my translation to this diocese. On the 1st of August, 1570, I left London; two days after I was seized on my journey with a tertian ague arising from fatigue, (for

[1 See note 2, p. 243.]

during my residence in London, I had not been accustomed to riding on horseback;) on which account I was forced to rest ten days in the midst of my journey. At length on the 17th of August I arrived at Cawood[2] (where I have a palace on the banks of the Ouse, about seven miles from the city,) my fever, as the event proved, not being sufficiently cured; for I was seized on the second of September following with another very severe and acute fever, which weakened me to such an excess, that not only my physicians and friends despaired of my recovery, but I myself also received the sentence of death in myself. But the Lord, who killeth and maketh alive, restored me at length after six months to my former health, the violence of the disorder gradually decreasing, yet so as I was not able to leave my chamber the whole winter. Since then I have laboured to the utmost of my power, and still continue to do, in the visitation of my province and diocese, and in getting rid of those remaining superstitions[3] which have maintained their place more firmly in this part of the country, suffering as it does

[[2] This place was the residence of the archbishops of York, having been given by king Athelstan to Wulstan, the fifteenth archbishop; and where they had a magnificent palace, or castle, in which several of the prelates lived and died, and in which cardinal Wolsey was arrested by the earl of Northumberland on a charge of treason, in the reign of Henry VIII. This castle was dismantled, and in part demolished, at the conclusion of the parliamentary war; since which time, being abandoned by the archbishops, it has remained in a state of gradual dilapidation, and has nearly fallen into ruin. Lewis's Topogr. Dict.]

[[3] In his letter wrote to the secretary, August 29 [1570], he says, "they keep holidays and fasts abrogated; they offer money, eggs, &c. at the burial of their dead; they pray beads, &c. so as this seems to be as it were another church, rather than a member of the rest." Strype, Grindal, 243. Other popish customs then prevalent in the north were, the frequent use and veneration of crosses, month's minds, obits and anniversaries, the chief intent whereof was praying for the dead; the superstitions used in going the bounds of the parishes; morris-dancers and minstrels coming into the church in service-time, to the disturbance of God's worship; putting the consecrated bread into the receiver's mouth, as among the papists the priest did the wafer; crossing and breathing upon the elements in the celebration of the Lord's supper and elevation; oil, tapers, and spittle in the other sacrament of baptism; pauses and intermissions in reading the services of the church; praying Ave Marias and Pater-nosters upon beads; setting up candles in the churches to the Virgin Mary on Candlemas-day, and the like. Strype, Grindal, 251.]

under a dearth of learned and pious ministers. After the suppression of the late rebellion I find the people more complying than I expected, as far as external conformity is concerned: the reason is, that they have been sufficiently distressed, and therefore humbled, by those calamities which are always the concomitants of civil war. I wish I had found them as well instructed in the true religion, as I left my flock in London and Essex to my successor. But yet I hope that, with the Lord giving the increase, much may be effected in time even here. The Lord [Bishop] of Durham, who is in constant ill health, has lately been dangerously ill, but through the mercy of the Lord is now recovered.

The excellent Bishop Jewel, of Salisbury, (the jewel and singular ornament of the Church, as his name implies,) we lost, or rather I should say, sent before us, about the beginning of October[1] last.

It is not, as I am well aware, from a feeling of curiosity, but, as you say, from other most important reasons, that you are anxious for information concerning our affairs; just as we are desirous of hearing about yours, whatever they may be: for we are members of the same body. I hope therefore that, as our affairs are now settled, I shall in future write to your reverence twice at least in every year, and as usual at each of the Frankfort fairs. Matters here are at present, through the great mercy of God, tolerably quiet: however, at the end of last summer, no one suspecting anything of the kind, we were in the greatest danger, as you may probably conjecture from a document inclosed in this letter, and both published in our language in the form of a letter, and translated into Latin. The daughter of the Guises, who calls herself the queen of Scotland, is now consigned to closer custody[2]. Thomas duke of Norfolk was brought

[1 He died Sept. 23, 1571.]
[2 She was removed from Tutbury to Sheffield castle in August 1569. The following document, copied from the original in the Cottonian Library, will shew the nature of the restrictions under which she was placed.

ORDERS FOR THE QUEEN'S HOUSEHOLD.

"To the Mr. of the Scottis queene's household. First, that all your people wch. appertayneth to the queene shall depart from the queene's chamber, or chambers, to their own lodging at ix of the clock

to trial[3] on the 16th of this month, and condemned to death for high treason: but whether the sentence will shortly be put into execution, my distance from court prevents me from knowing[4]. Other accomplices in the same conspiracy are now in custody, and will undergo a like sentence.

at night, winter and summer, whatever he or she, either to their lodging within the house, or without in the towne, and there to remain till the next day at vi of the clock.

"Item, that none of the queene's people shall at no time weare his sword, neither within the house nor when her grace rydeth or goeth abroade, unless the master of the household himself to weare a sword, and no more, without my special licence.

"Item, that there shall none of the queene's people carry any bow or shaftes at no tyme, neither to the field nor to the butts, unless it be foure or fyve, and no more, being in the queene's company.

"Item, that none of the queene's people shall ryde or go at no tyme abroad out of the house, or towne, without my special licence; and if he or they so doth, they or he shall come no more in at the gates: neither in the towne, whatsoever he, she, or they may be.

"Item, that you, or some of the queene's chamber, when her grace will walk abroad, shall advertise the officier of my warde, who shall declare the messuage to me one houer before she goeth forth.

"Item, that none of the queene's people, whatsoever he or they be, not one at no time, to come forth of their chamber or lodging when any alarum is given by night or daie, whether they be in the queene's chambers within the house, or without in the towne; and giff he or they keep not their chambers or lodging wheresoever, that he or they shall stand at their perill for death.

At Shefeild, the 26 daie of April, 1571, per me,

SHREWSBURIE.]

[3 In Westminster Hall upon the judgment-seat, sate George Talbot, earl of Shrewsbury, constituted Lord High Steward of England for that day. There were besides 25 peers present, by whom the duke was unanimously found guilty of the high treasons wherewith he stood arraigned. See below, note 3, p. 267, and Camden's Eliz. p. 170, &c. where is given a full account of the proceedings.]

[4 The queen was very reluctant to order the duke of Norfolk's execution. Randolph writes on March 21st, to the bishop of Durham, "I feare that the bishop of Lincoln's words in his sermone before her majestie will prove true, alleged out of Augustine, that there was *misericordia puniens, crudelitas parcens*, in consyderation whereof great evil dyd ensue." MS. Lansd. 13. 22. He was, however, at length executed on the 2nd of June, on a scaffold erected on Tower-hill. See Camden, Elizabeth, p. 177.]

Scotland has been sorely distressed the whole of this year with intestine commotions. For after the death of the regent James, the grandfather[1] of the young king was elected in his room. About a year ago he made an unexpected attempt upon the well fortified castle of Dumbarton at the mouth of the Clyde, which he took in the night-time by means of scaling ladders, having first killed the sentinels; and he compelled the archbishop of St Andrew's, whom he found there, and who was a natural brother of the duke of Hamilton, to put an end to his life by hanging[2]. In revenge for this, about the beginning of last May, the Hamiltons with three hundred horse entered by night the town of Stirling, and there put to death on the spot the new regent[3], whom they seized in his chamber. The earl of Mar[4] was chosen by the king's party in his room; a good man, but not possessing much influence. The Scots therefore, divided into many factions as well public as private, are attacking each other with mutual violence. The queen's party have seized upon the town and castle of Edinburgh. The king's adherents have fortified the neighbouring harbour of Leith, and strengthened it with a garrison. The regent James had given the command of the castle of Edinburgh to one Kirkaldy[5], as

[1 Matthew Stuart, earl of Lenox, and father of lord Darnley.]

[2 See note 8, p. 257.]

[3 Lord Burghley gives, in a letter to Thomas Smith, dated Sept. 8th, 1574, the following account of his death: "On monday last, two hundred and forty horsemen, a hundred footemen, all of the castle of Edenborough, stole to Sterling towne, which they entered quietly, and tooke the regente and all the lords of his present, in their beds, and when they were carrying them away, their soldyers fell to spoyle, and a power of the castle of Styrling issuing out rescued them all, and slew their takers; but in this fight the regent was hurt, and by some advertisements I hear that he is dead." MS. Cott. Calig. c. III. 227. In another letter from Burghley to the earl of Shrewsbury, dated Sept. 13, he writes, "It is true that the erle of Lenox, late regent, was slain after that he was taken, by commandment of Claud Hamilton, and he that killed hym named Calder, who hath confessed it."]

[4 "The erle of Marr is confirmed regent by parlement at Sterling, whereto the erles of Argile, Eglinton, Cassels, and Crawford, with the lords Boyd and St. Colme, have sworne and subscribed." Burghley to lord Shrewsbury, Sept. 13, as above.]

[5 Sir William Kirkaldy of Grange. See note 7, p. 193. He was afterwards executed.]

being most faithful to himself and most hostile to the queen: this man, not long after, during the regent's lifetime, bribed probably with French gold, went over to the queen. This defection was the cause of all the mischief; for the queen's party would otherwise have found no safe position whence to carry on the war. However, we hope that our queen will shortly put an end to these calamities. For if matters cannot be settled by the conference and treaty of peace which is now in progress, there is no doubt but that our queen will become the enemy of that party which shall refuse to accept of such fair terms as shall be offered; in which case the other party will of necessity be forced to submit.

I wrote to Richard Hilles to send some crowns to Julius. I will bear Butler in my favourable recollection. If he will learn our language, he may some time or other become a minister in our church. I send you together with this letter a history lately published by George Buchanan, a Scotsman, respecting the virtues of the queen of Scotland[6]. May the Lord Jesus very long preserve your reverence! Bishopsthorpe, near York, 25 Jan. 1572.

Your most devoted in the Lord,
EDMUND YORK.

I was just about to seal this, when I received your letter and that of Gualter, in which you recommend to me your nephew, and he his son. I am far distant from our universities; I will write however to my friends that they may recommend them. I hear that the lord bishop of London has sent them to Cambridge, and supplied them with means: I too will sometimes assist them with money, which is all I can do. Salute, I pray you, master Gualter in my name, to whom I have not now leisure to reply. I suspect that the anonymous little book you sent me was written by our bishop of Salisbury of pious memory; but I have no reason for this conjecture except from the style and manner of writing. Once more farewell, my very dear and reverend brother in Christ.

EDMUND YORK.

[6 The book referred to is entitled "De Mariâ reginâ Scotorum, totâque ejus contra regem conjuratione," &c. It was dedicated to queen Elizabeth.]

LETTER CI.

BISHOP SANDYS TO HENRY BULLINGER.

Dated at LONDON, *Feb.* 17, 1572.

HEALTH in Christ. That I have not replied, my very dear brother, and most reverend master, to your frequent letters, I would have you ascribe, not so much to my want of gratitude, as to most troublesome hinderances of various kinds. For to pass over many other things which have prevented this intercourse of regard and accustomed correspondence, the first and most afflictive is this, the extreme violence and extent of my late attack of illness, by which the Lord exercised me so painfully and for so long a time, that I had altogether given up thinking upon these matters. To this must be added a constant accession of business, which the station in which I am now placed daily occasions me, and by which I am almost so overwhelmed, that I have no opportunity either for personal relaxation or correspondence with others. In fine, even if sufficient time and leisure were afforded, such is the present unsettled state of affairs, that nothing can be transmitted from us to you; especially since there is so close a blockade both by land and sea, that it is not safe to send letters.

I received your last letter at the end of December, and when I had read it, endeavoured, as diligently as I could, to comply with your request. In recommending your grandson[1] and those other friends of yours to the bishop of Norwich,

[[1] Rodolph Zuinglius, whose father married Bullinger's daughter. He came over to England with a son of Rodolph Gualter, by whom they were recommended to bishop Parkhurst. With him they were in the beginning of December at Ludham, where, says Strype, he treated them with oysters, which the young men wondered to see him eat. But however young Gualter *ventured at last upon them*; for so the bishop merrily wrote to his father: but as for Zuinglius, as the bishop went on, he dared not *cum vivis animalibus congredi.* Strype, Annals, II. i. 336.]

you lighted upon the very man who, while he had the greatest desire to serve you, yet possessed at the same time no means whatever of doing so. For[2] having lately entrusted with too great confidence the management of his affairs to men of dishonest character, it has come to pass by their means that he is so overwhelmed with debt, as to be unable to extricate himself from these misfortunes, much less to afford any assistance to others. As to me, however, moved partly by the remembrance of your kindness, and partly because I considered I should be acting acceptably to God, and especially to yourself, I took upon myself the charge of assisting them[3]. I speedily therefore took care to send them to the university of Cambridge; and that they might have a better opportunity of learning both our language and others, I thought it best to place them in different colleges, lest their frequent intercourse should prevent their application in learning a foreign language. Though indeed I am much distressed by difficulties concerning my income and expenditure, I have nevertheless presented each of them with twenty crowns out of my own purse, to diminish the unpleasantness of living in a strange place. In all other respects, as far as my means will permit, I promise that I will not be wanting to them, that they may engage with greater freedom in those studies which may some time or other be of advantage to the church of Christ. For I have always thought it a most excellent thing to *sow* a benefit which the flock of Christ may *reap* in due season. I have sent you their own letters in testimony, not indeed of

[2 The bishop had the misfortune to entrust one [George Thymelthorp] with the collection of the tenths of his diocese, who took the sums that he had received of the clergy, and converted them to his own use, instead of paying them into the exchequer. So that at length a heavy debt fell on the poor bishop, for two or three years' arrears of the tenths, that almost broke his back, and drove him to great necessity. For the revenues of his bishopric were obliged to make good his debt to the queen. Which was the reason he was fain to absent from Norwich, and live more privately at Ludham, a country seat belonging to the see. Strype, Annals, II. i. 330.]

[3 From the bishop [of Norwich] they took their journey to London with their letters, and waited upon bishop Sandys there, who received them very obligingly, for their relations' and country's sake; and assigned each of them £5 against their going to Cambridge. Strype, Annals, II. i. 336.]

very great liberality on my part, yet of my good inclination and regard, that you may learn what I have done more fully from their letters than from my own. I entreat you again and again to salute my friend and very dear brother in Christ, master Rodolph Gualter. May the Lord Jesus Christ prosper you, and the labours which you undergo for the furtherance of the gospel of Christ! Dated London in England, 17 Feb. 1572.

Your very dear brother in Christ,

EDWIN SANDYS,

bishop of London.

LETTER CII.

BISHOP PARKHURST TO HENRY BULLINGER.

Dated at LUDHAM, *March* 10, 1572.

YOUR most learned refutation of the pope's bull is in the hands of every one; for it is translated into English, and is printed at London. You have done well in replying with so much diligence to the stupid and furious Testament of Brentius.

Those three[1] troublesome preachers in the Dutch Church [at Norwich] have been silenced, and two others appointed in their stead. Seventeen members of the same church were banished from our city on the first of November, for the disgraceful vice of drunkenness. About the middle of December the Spanish ambassador[2] was ordered to depart from England

[1 Their names were Antonius, Theophilus, and Isbrand Balkius. The last was soon afterwards appointed minister of the strangers' church at Stamford. Strype, Parker, II. 84, 149.]

[2 This proceeding was occasioned by the discovery of some letters of the queen of Scots, importing that "she gave herself, and her son, now king of Scotland, into the hands of the king of Spain, to be governed and ruled only by him; and to assure him, that if he would send any power, the young king should be delivered into his hands." She added, that "the king of Spain, in setting her up, would not only govern both these realms, but should also set up, within three days, on pain of losing his head. This intelligence some friend wrote to me from London; but I know not whether it is correct. At all events he has left the kingdom; *abiit, excessit, evasit.*

The duke of Norfolk pleaded his own cause in Westminster Hall, on the 16th January, from seven in the morning till night. There are many charges of treason against him, which he refuted as well as he could. The entire cognizance and jurisdiction in this cause is referred to nine earls, one viscount, and fifteen barons[3]. All these unanimously declared him guilty, and so he is at last condemned to death. He is still living however, between hope and fear, in the tower of London[4].

The snow last year melted towards the beginning of February. This year it only began to fall at that time, and did not leave us till about the beginning of March.

We are on good terms with the French, but the Spaniards are knitting their brows. I thank you very much for the very elegant little book on the Authority of Scripture and of the Church. Whoever wrote it is certainly a learned and pious man. If your Zuinglius[5] require my assistance, he shall not be disappointed of it: I wish both you and himself to be fully

in both, the catholic religion again." See Strype, Annals, II. i. 74, 177; in which latter passage he mistakenly confounds the date of this letter of Parkhurst's with that of the banishment of the ambassador.]

[3 These were, George Talbot, earl of Shrewsbury, Reginald Grey, earl of Kent, Thomas Radcliffe, earl of Sussex, Henry Hastings, earl of Huntingdon, Francis Russell, earl of Bedford, Henry Herbert, earl of Pembroke, Edward Seymour, earl of Hertford, Ambrose Dudley, earl of Warwick, Robert Dudley, earl of Leicester, Walter Devereux, viscount Hereford, Edward lord Clinton, William lord Howard of Effingham, William Cecil, lord Burghley, Arthur lord Grey of Wilton, James Blount, lord Mountjoy, William lord Sands, Thomas lord Wentworth, William lord Burroughs, Lewis lord Mordaunt, John Powlet, lord Saint-John of Basing, Robert lord Rich, Roger lord North, Edmund Bruges lord Chandos, Oliver lord Saint-John of Bletnesbro, Thomas Sackvill lord Buckhurst, William West lord Delaware. See Camden's Elizabeth, p. 170. Strype, however, adds William earl of Worcester to the number of peers present, according, as he says, to a MS. in the Cottonian Library.]

[4 See note 4, p. 261.]

[5 Bullinger's grandson. See note 1, p. 264.]

persuaded of this; for I shall certainly never falsify your good opinion of me. I cannot write more, for I am overwhelmed by numerous and important engagements. Farewell, my Bullinger. Salute all my friends. My wife salutes you all. In haste. Ludham, 10th March, 1572.

Your

JOHN PARKHURST,
[bishop] of Norwich.

LETTER CIII.

BISHOP COX TO HENRY BULLINGER.

Dated at LONDON, ELY HOUSE, *June* 6, 1572.

MUCH health in Christ, my brother. Your letter, which was on many accounts most gratifying to me, and which you state to have been written on the 12th of March, came to hand about the end of May; from which I understand that you have not yet received those books printed in this country, which you most learnedly and piously composed against the pope's bull. I sent, however, to the autumn fair at Frankfort both a letter and four books, together with a little money for the use of yourself and our friend Julius. The money I hear arrived safe; but I am told that the letter and books are still loitering on the road. I therefore again send you a few copies for you to make use of, in case you should not receive the others.

As to the news about which you write, may the great and good God turn all things to our good and the glory of his name! It is a great satisfaction to us that your churches are at peace, and not without an accession of other churches to the sincere profession of the christian religion. When I have an opportunity of obtaining an audience from the queen's majesty, I will not forget to acquaint her with how great zeal and good will you espouse her cause. She was exceedingly delighted with your book against that *bulled* nonsense[1], and read it with the greatest eagerness, as I informed you in my last letter, which you have not yet received.

Respecting the Turkish war I shall only say thus much, that
> When the next house begins to burn,
> 'Tis like to prove your own concern[2].

Hitherto the *pope* has been antichrist. Should it please God to raise up another, even the *Turk*, it is only what our sins deserve. Our own affairs are in this condition. The duke of Norfolk[3], who most wickedly contrived a plot against our queen, has met with the punishment he deserved. Mary, the late queen of Scots, is publicly declared the enemy of our kingdom and queen, and is strictly kept in custody. She was meditating indeed both the destruction of our kingdom, the death of our queen, and the overthrow of our religion, by all possible means.

Respecting your grandson Zuinglius[4] I had rather say little, than much with grief. The affairs of mankind are not governed by our will, but by divine providence. His condition, however, is most blessed, although our earthly affections would foolishly have it otherwise. In fine, we must endure, and not find fault with that which cannot be avoided. May the Lord Jesus Christ, my esteemed brother, long, very long preserve you to us in safety! London. From my house in Holborn, June 6, 1572.

Your most attached

RICHARD COX,

bishop of Ely.

I intended to send you the books; but this messenger of mine will only take charge of a letter, and not of a parcel. The books must be sent, if possible, by another conveyance to the next Frankfort fair.

[1 *Bullatas nugas*, the pope's bull against queen Elizabeth. See note 2, p. 244.]

2 "Tua res agitur, paries cum proximus ardet."

[3 He was executed on Tower-hill, June 2nd. See note 4, p. 261, and Camden, Eliz. p. 177, who gives a full account of the proceedings.]

[4 He died in the beginning of this present month. See the next letter.]

LETTER CIV.

RICHARD HILLES TO HENRY BULLINGER.

Dated at LONDON, *July* 10, 1572.

MUCH health. In March last I sent my letter, dated on the 18th of the preceding February, to my son Barnabas, that it might be delivered to the care of Christopher Froschover at the Frankfort spring fair; and I hope you have received it from him. At the same time I received two very long and friendly letters from you, the first written on the 20th of December, and the other on the 12th of last March, together with a slip of paper inclosed in them, in which you write me word what you have heard from Venice respecting the defeat[1] of the Turks, and what you can learn respecting the state of Germany and the cessation of the persecution, &c. For these letters and this intelligence I sincerely thank you.

At the time of the same fair I received from you some other letters to certain of our bishops, which I gave in charge with all diligence to Rodolph Gualter and Henry Butler, who had other matters of their own to transact with the bishops, (who are now engaged at the public assembly, which we call the [2]Parliament,) that they might deliver them to each, as they write me word they have done, except the one which you wrote to Jewel, bishop of Salisbury, which, as he is dead, I handed over, according to your desire, to Parkhurst, bishop of Norwich. But what do you think? How it has happened, I know not; but neither then, nor at any time since, have I received the books you mention, written concerning Exhortation, neither in Latin, nor in German; so that I know not what answer to make respecting them. I have however to thank you in the mean time for those

[[1] Namely, at the battle of Lepanto, gained by Don John of Austria in 1571.]

[[2] This parliament began May the 8th. Strype, Annals, II. i. 183.]

two copies in German, and one in Latin, which you ordered to be sent to me here. Moreover, the above-named Rodolph and Henry have no certain intelligence respecting those books. I have received, however, the books published in Latin by Rodolph's father, together with those which the said persons have distributed to those to whom Rodolph's father wished them to be sent: thank him, I pray you, in my name, for the book which he sent me, and the very friendly letter which he wrote to me on the 10th of March last.

As for the thirty-two pieces of gold about which you write, my son Gerson paid sixteen of them at the last winter fair at Frankfort to Christopher Froschover, for those ten crowns of the right reverend the bishop of Winchester which you mention. The other sixteen were for those other ten crowns which the bishop of Ely paid here to the aforesaid Gerson, to repay to you. My son added, moreover, that he paid over to the said Froschover at the same time ten pieces of gold for Julius Sancterentianus, which the right reverend the bishop of Ely had before placed here to be paid to the said Julius. As to your writing me word to this effect, "that it was without doubt through a mistake at the spring fair, that the twenty-seven dollars," &c.[3] I know not how to set you at ease, because you do not mention whether my son Barnabas, who was present at that Frankfort fair, paid over those twenty-seven dollars to Froschover.

Your grandson[4] Zuinglius departed from this most corrupt generation to God, here at London, in June last, and is added to the assembly of the saints, among whom he sings praises to God his Redeemer. But Rodolph Gualter[5], together with Henry Butler, are now returned to Cambridge, whence they came hither at the opening of parliament with the bishop of Norwich, whom I hear to be the especial patron of Henry Butler; to whose mother or friends I will thank you to write, to say that he has received no remittances from them since he

[3 The MS. is here unintelligible.]

[4 See p. 269.]

[5 Bishop Parkhurst maintained him, first at Cambridge, and then at Oxford, (in fellows' commons at Magdalen college,) and gave him a *viaticum* to bear his charges when he returned home. Strype, Annals, II. i. 508.]

came to England. Wherefore, when he was ill at Cambridge, and also a short time before, I lent him two pounds ten shillings of English money, worth in German money thirteen florins and five batzen[1]; which I will beg of you to receive from her, and retain for yourself out of them twelve florins and twelve batzen for the eight French crowns which the reverend the bishop of Norwich sent me, with the paper which I have inclosed in this letter. The remaining eight batzen I would have you present to some poor student. It is but just (as I told you before) that those who send their sons to England, should rather deposit their money at Frankfort beforehand, than require others to advance it for them here in England, and then to have to demand payment at Frankfort. Henry Butler's mother, as he informed me, is living at Lindau.

On the second of this[2] month the duke of Norfolk was beheaded, having been long since condemned for high treason. I am glad to hear from you that you are by the blessing of God in tolerable health and peace; but grieve much to hear that you are distressed by the dearth of provisions and all other things. I hope however, that after the supplication appointed by public authority, God will in mercy look upon you, and again remove that fatherly correction with which he is wont for the most part to punish those whom he loves. I am also very sorry that you had been so ill with a severe cough for three weeks before you wrote. But you well know that God often visits those whom he loves. I pray that he may grant you patience, and, as you express yourself, deal with you in mercy according to his good pleasure. My wife salutes you very much, and entreats you to commend her to God in your prayers, as she is greatly afflicted with a contraction of the muscles and nerves, which we call spasms, and also with the gravel.

A treaty[3] has been entered upon this year between our

[1 A batzen is here considered equivalent to three pence of our money; a florin to three shillings and ninepence; and a French crown to six shillings.]

[2 The duke was beheaded on Monday the second of June, having been condemned five months before. Strype, Annals, II. i. 191, and Camden's Elizabeth, p. 177.]

[3 In this league the French obliged themselves not to assist the Scottish queen; being content to make no mention of her, or of being

most serene queen of England, France, and Ireland, and the king of France, a solemn engagement having been entered into by both parties on Sunday the 15th of June[4] last in the cathedral church of St Peter in Westminster.

On the 25th of June I first received your letter, dated Zurich, October 1st, 1571, and sent by Frederick Conders, a gentleman whom you commended to me. And if I can serve him in any thing, without inconvenience or trouble to myself, I will, as you request, most willingly do so. I add this moreover, to let you know the news that I have received from the Netherlands, which are now under the authority of king Philip; namely, that towards the end of last March, a Dutch[5] gentleman, named Mons. Lumell [Lumey] attacked a certain seaport in Holland, called the Brill, and took it by force from the dominion of king Philip. I have heard too, that afterwards a thousand Spaniards and Walloons, subjects, I mean, of king Philip who speak the French language, entered the town of Middleberg, and in their progress laid waste a certain village of Zeeland called Armuyden. There is also a large body of troops collected in Flushing from France and England and other neighbouring countries; but I hear that nothing of any consequence has been done by the Spaniards against those who are at the Brill, or in Flushing above mentioned, except what I shall afterwards state. But a very short address was lately brought hither from Flanders, printed both in French and Dutch, in which the prince of Orange adopts the same titles of honour and authority as he did in the Netherlands before his exile[6]; and he exhorts the Dutch, who have already been

her friend and ally; but gave her over to the queen's majesty, whatsoever demands they had made for her before. The league was afterwards confirmed and signed by very honourable ambassadors sent over on both sides; viz. Montmorency from France, and the lord admiral from England. Strype, Annals, II. i. 211, 214. For all the articles of this treaty see Camden, Eliz. p. 185.]

[4 The treaty was confirmed on *May* 15th at Westminster. Camden, as above.]

[5 William Vandermarke, lord of Lumey. See Camden, Eliz. p. 184.]

[6 William, prince of Orange, had opposed, by all regular and dutiful means, the progress of the Spanish usurpations; and when Alva conducted his army into the Netherlands, and assumed the government, this prince, well acquainted with the violent character of the man, and the tyrannical spirit of the court of Madrid, wisely fled from the danger

resisting the Spaniards, either now or never to shew themselves men against the tyranny and unjust exactions of that people, and against the bishops of those parts, and the clergy their companions; and he assures them, that if they will but shew themselves men, they can easily shake off the heavy yoke of bondage, which the duke of Alva with the Spaniards and bishops aforesaid has most iniquitously imposed upon them, not only against the common weal or public good of that country, but also against the honour and good faith of king Philip. Moreover, in the month of March last, part of the city of Valenciennes, in the province of Hainault, in French Flanders, revolted from the government of the aforesaid duke of Alva, and drove out the Spaniards and leading authorities of the place; and allowed the Count Lewis, brother of the prince of Orange, with eight hundred or a thousand armed soldiers (of whom the greater part are French,) to enter and garrison the city for the service of king Philip, as they pretended, though they reject the authority of the duke of Alva and his party. But from that time, because the said troops neglected to occupy the fortress of Valenciennes, they were forced again to retreat, and leave the city to the duke and his soldiers, who very lately arrived there in great numbers.

We have next heard for a fact that a city called Venlo, the least city in Guelderland, has also sent back his messenger to the duke of Alva; and that, like Brill and Flushing, many other cities in the Netherlands have revolted and fallen away from the duke of Alva, on account of the tyranny which he has of late years exercised among them. Besides this, it is related to me as a certain fact, that two small vessels coming from Flushing have arrived in the Thames, in which letters are brought conveying the intelligence to some Dutch residents in this country, that a great sea-fight took place last week on the sea-coast of Flanders, not far from Sluys. The citizens of Flushing, whose strength and power seems now to be composed of foreigners, took at the same time, midway between Flanders and Flushing, fifteen or sixteen vessels laden with spices and

which threatened him, and retired to his paternal estate and dominions in Germany. He was cited to appear before Alva's tribunal, was condemned in absence, was declared a rebel, and his ample possessions in the low countries were confiscated. Hume.]

rich merchandise, besides some specie; which ships had come from Spain and Portugal, and were on their way to Antwerp, together with thirty or forty ships of war and transports which conveyed the duke of Medina Celi with twelve hundred Spanish soldiers who accompanied him, and landed in the Netherlands. For king Philip has appointed this duke of Medina Celi his vice-roy in Flanders, because the said king, as it is reported, has determined that the duke of Alva shall go back to Spain.

Then again, it is stated, and this too as a certain fact, that the same citizens of Flushing drove upon the shallows two or three other of the ships which they took, and there wrecked them; besides which they set on fire and destroyed two or three more. But, as many persons here assert, these two or three ships last mentioned as being burnt, were laden with Spanish wool on their way to Bruges, and were included in the thirty or forty ships which came from Spain under the care and convoy of the said duke of Medina Celi; and not of the number of the fifteen or sixteen vessels which were going to Antwerp, and which were taken in sight of Flushing and Middleberg: but it seems to me very lamentable that the merchants of Antwerp, (who without doubt are not more favourably inclined to that impious and cruel duke of Alva than those who are now at the Brill and Flushing,) and the merchants of Spain and Portugal, should be plundered in this way of their goods and merchandise, and perhaps the greater part of their crews slain, drowned, or hung; so that there is reason to fear, that in the countries subject to king Philip there will be for some years to come as little business and traffic, as it is called, and as great and extensive civil wars as have within these few years taken place in France, unless it should please Almighty God to turn aside his indignation from the Netherlands, as we must pray him to do according to his mercy. Farewell; and may Almighty God very long preserve you to the advancement of his glory and the edification of his church! London, July 10, 1572.

Your

RICHARD HILLES.

LETTER CV.

BISHOP HORN TO HENRY BULLINGER.

Dated at FARNHAM CASTLE, *Jan.* 10, 1573.

GRACE and peace in Christ! Though you truly describe me, my Bullinger, beloved in Christ, as one who is for the most part distracted by numerous and important engagements, as well by those of a private nature as by the public affairs both of church and state; yet, however I may be occupied, I have always leisure both for reading and answering your letters. For as your conversation, when present, was always delightful to me, so now your letters in your absence are most pleasant and agreeable; by which alone, when I am *here*, I seem to myself to be listening, to my great and incredible comfort, to one whom, when I was *there*, I never beheld without great and peculiar pleasure. But to come to that part of your letter which is of the greatest importance, and wherein you make so earnest and positive a request, that you may learn from me what is the present posture of affairs both in church and state, in this and the neighbouring countries.

Respecting France first of all, you have doubtless heard long since, and not without the greatest concern, the wretched and calamitous condition of the churches in those quarters; how that unhappy country, still dripping (as it were) with a horrible and bloody slaughter[1], is foully dyed in the blood of the saints. In which we have this solitary but yet certain comfort, that, as the blood of Christians is the seed of the gospel, so, in proportion as they shall have sown the seed more abundantly, we may expect a more abundant harvest.

Respecting the Belgic affairs I have hardly any thing to communicate. The Prince [of Orange], resting the whole of this winter season in Holland, has done nothing worthy of notice that I know of. It does not yet appear what he will

[1 Namely, the massacre of St Bartholomew, Aug. 24, 1572, for the particulars of which the reader is referred to Davila's History of the civil wars, Sully's memoirs, Mezeray's History of France, Wraxall's History of the House of Valois, Thuanus, &c. See p. 291.]

do when the spring comes on. But as the alliance with France is now at an end, I am afraid lest all things should become worse.

Scotland, under her present circumstances, is quiet, and desires peace. For the majority have gone over to the king's party, who reigns by almost universal consent. But what will be the issue of this peace, in this uncertain state of affairs in general, we are unable to determine; we hope indeed, as we also wish, for the best.

Our England, having secured tranquillity at home and peace abroad, is sailing as it were with full sails and a prosperous breeze. The church, however, is vehemently agitated, and not without danger; not so much from the opposition of the papists, who are daily restrained by severe laws, as by the stumbling-blocks occasioned by false brethren, who seem to be sliding into anabaptism. May the Lord Jesus at length, by his coming down from heaven, extinguish all the flames of this tumultuous world, and so take away the sorrows of the militant church, that all tears may be wiped away from our eyes, and we may all triumph together with him for ever in the heavenly and new Jerusalem!

Farewell in Christ Jesus. From my castle at Farnham, Jan. 10, 1572. [1573.]

Yours wholly in Christ,

ROBERT WINTON.

LETTER CVI.

BISHOP PARKHURST TO HENRY BULLINGER.

Dated at LUDHAM, *Jan.* 20, 1573.

I RECEIVED on the 23rd of May your most beautiful and pious address, together with your letters to myself and Jewel. Jewel's letter I retained in my possession, as he had departed this life before its arrival[2].

[[2] See note 1, p. 260.]

The queen of Scotland still remains among us. She was in great alarm for herself last parliament[1], and not without reason; for had not the extreme clemency of our queen prevented it, it would have been all over with her. What will be done respecting her in the next parliament, I cannot tell. She has certainly very few friends in this country. And what wonder, when she has been hankering after this kingdom, and is defiled and almost overwhelmed with so many and great crimes?

Since those three quarrelsome preachers[2] have been sent away from hence, the greatest quiet and unanimity is prevailing in the Dutch church. Your reply to the Bavarian articles[3] is translated into English, and is in every one's hands. I received another letter from you on December 10th, in which you write that a great disturbance had arisen in the Grisons. The pope, who is the author of this and every thing else that is bad, is going on in his old way. But it is well that it is put an end to by the death of that most popish vagabond, who endeavoured to restore popery. On the first of April will commence our famous sittings of parliament. The frost and snow have continued these eight weeks, and almost without intermission during the whole time. But, praised be God! they have at length left us.

Farewell, my excellent Bullinger. Salute in my name all

[1 A few days after the parliament met, the lord keeper sent for the lower house, and declared to them, that it was the queen's pleasure, that a certain number of the upper house, and of the lower, should the next morning meet together in the star-chamber, to consult and debate upon the queen of Scots' matters. A committee accordingly was appointed of commoners, to meet with the lords, to consider how to proceed in that great cause. And after the conference, Mr Attorney of the court of wards made report of that conference. And at length it was resolved, for the better safety and preservation of the queen, and the present state, to proceed against the Scottish queen in the highest degree of treason. And therein to touch her, as well in life, as in title and dignity; and that of necessity, with all possible speed, by the voice of the house. The queen however, for certain respects by herself conceived, thought good for this time to defer, but not to reject, that course of proceeding. Strype, Annals, II. i. 196, 197.]

[2 See above, p. 256.]

[3 See note, p. 110.]

your family, male and female, and all my Zurich friends. My wife, who is now ill of the gout, salutes you all. In haste. Ludham, 20 Jan. 1573.

Yours most sincerely,

JOHN PARKHURST,

[bishop] of Norwich.

LETTER CVII.

BISHOP COX TO RODOLPH GUALTER.

Dated at ELY, *Feb.* 4, 1573.

YOUR two letters, Rodolph, dearly beloved in Christ, were brought to me last summer, and received not without great satisfaction. The[4] first exhibited the exceeding ingenuousness of a pious breast: for you will rarely meet with persons endowed with such sincerity of mind, as to take in good part the advice of a friend; but the grace of the Holy Spirit has enlightened and imbued you with that charity, that you hope all things, and believe all things, and interpret all things for the best. But your last letter most clearly manifested a true brotherly affection to our church, as well as towards myself and some of my episcopal brethren; since, namely, you vouchsafed to do us the honour of dedicating to us your exposition of the epistles of Saint Paul to the Corinthians[5]. This exposition indeed is so learned, pious, and perspicuous,

[4 This letter is preserved in Strype, Life of Parker, III. 193, and will be found in the appendix to this volume.]

[5 About the autumn of 1572 did Gualter publish ninety-five homilies upon the former epistle to the Corinthians, which he dedicated to bishops Grindal, Sandys, Horn, Cox, Parkhurst, and Pilkington. In his prefatory epistle to them, his argument ran chiefly of the unity of the church; wherein he shewed, that none ought rashly to depart from its society for the vices of any that lived in it. See Strype, Life of Parker, II. 113. Annals, II. i. 462.]

that it needs no commendation of mine, which indeed is but of little value. By your having subjoined an admonition to brotherly unity, you manifestly evince that you entertain the greatest affection towards our church, and desire that we should serve the Lord our God without hinderance and distraction of mind. For it is in this way that the glory of God and the gospel of our Lord Jesus Christ may be promoted with the greatest success, although there must needs be heresies in the mean time for the trying of the elect. You make use of many arguments in your preface, and those most powerful ones; but I dare not decide what weight they will have with our innovators. Meanwhile, however, I will not doubt but that the word of the Lord will bring forth its fruit in due season.

I return you my best thanks for the book you sent me. If I am unable fully to return your kindness, I will not in the mean time cease from taking care of and providing for your son of excellent promise, so long as he shall sojourn among us. And as far as he is concerned, I must desire you to shut both your ears: for you would deservedly think me most ungrateful, if I did not shew you some little kindness. When I had entirely gone over your preface, I was exceedingly sorry that it had been published before you had been fully acquainted with the absurdities of our people. For they have lately broken down, by their abusive writings, the barriers of all the order of our church. But that you may partly understand their design, I send you some heads or articles, which they have printed, and taken upon themselves to maintain. I could wish that you, together with my very dear brother in Christ, master Bullinger, would consider and decide upon them; and if it is not too much trouble, that you would send me your opinion respecting them.

Articles drawn up by certain Englishmen now disturbers of the state of the Anglican church:

I. The names and functions of archbishops, bishops, and other officials, ought to be altogether abolished.

II. The election of the ministers of the word and sacraments should be restored to the people, as not belonging to the episcopal office.

III. No one ought to be confined to set forms of prayer.

IV. No sacrament ought to be administered without being preceded by a sermon, preached, and not read.

V. The father alone ought to answer for his child in baptism, without any other sponsors.

VI. All the ministers of the church ought to be equal, not one superior to another.

VII. They condemn the order of confirmation, in which the bishops lay their hands upon the children on their repeating the catechism, and pray the Lord that he may vouchsafe to increase in them the knowledge of his word and godliness.

VIII. They cannot endure the sermons which are preached at the burial of the dead.

IX. They cannot endure the reading of the holy scriptures in the church.

There are, moreover, other things really too absurd, with which I am unwilling to take up your time, and weary you with my too troublesome importunity. Satan is envious of our prosperity. It is not enough to have the papists our enemies, without stirring up men of their opinion who are labouring to bring about a revolution in the church. One thing I had almost forgotten to mention. There came out last summer an immense volume by one Nicolas Saunders, who is, they say, a countryman of ours; the title of which is "The Monarchy of the Church[1]." He appears to have been a mercenary employed by certain cardinals, aided by the assistance of others, and decked out like Æsop's jack-daw. The tempest is violent, and would seem to demolish all our pretensions at one blast. It takes away from christian magistrates the right of deciding in matters of religion, and claims it entirely for the pope and his officers as the supreme governor of the church. Our friend Jewel is dead, and has left among us but few equal to him.

[[1] The title in Latin is, *De visibili monarchiâ*. It was answered by Dr Bartholomew Clerk, of King's College, Cambridge, (in a book entitled, *Fidelis servi subdito infideli responsio, cum examine errorum N. Sanders in libro de visibili monarchiâ,*) and also by Dr Ackworth. Strype, Life of Parker, II. 181.]

It is therefore both your concern and mine, to cut off the heads of this hydra. I have your book respecting the pope being antichrist, which this man takes much pains to refute. You will not, I hope, allow him to triumph. May the great and good God preserve you many years for the safety of his church!

From the Isle of Ely in England. Feb. 4, 1572, according to the English computation.

I send you a remembrance, though a very small one, of five English crowns.

Your most attached brother in Christ,
RICHARD ELY,
bishop in England.

LETTER CVIII.

BISHOP COX TO HENRY BULLINGER.

[Without date.]¹

Your letter, reverend brother in Christ, cannot be otherwise than agreeable to me, breathing as it does so much piety and kindness. I heartily congratulate you on the possession of those bodily powers which you mention, and which by the grace of God will enable you to perform your office. May our gracious Lord preserve them to you for many years, to the glory of his name and the edifying of the church!

I glory in the Lord together with you, that having reached through his bounty my seventy-fourth year, I am not so deprived of strength as to be unable to do credit, in some measure at least, to the situation in which I am placed; excepting only that a trembling of my hands in some degree hinders the use of my pen. I only entreat my Lord that I may never become indolent in my office, but that I may grow more and more active even unto the last act of the drama. I

[¹ This letter seems to have been sent at the same time with the preceding one, and is therefore arranged accordingly.]

am sorry that you are without a copy of your books. I gave directions to our printer to forward you some, which I hear from him that he will faithfully undertake to do, unless all the copies should be dispersed.

As to what you write respecting the Turks, and those who side with them, I must confess that we live in an evil age, and are fallen upon most perilous times. And when this circumstance comes into the minds of pious persons, they admire even to amazement the inscrutable judgments of God, as to what will become of the godly, when so many christian kingdoms are invaded and laid waste by the Turk; when he is even now hanging over our heads; when the religion of Christians is thrust into a corner, and distracted and torn in pieces by innumerable disputes and contentions; and lastly, when it is every where harassed and oppressed by the most cruel persecutions of the papists. *For three transgressions and for four the Lord will not turn.* [Amos i. 3.] I greatly fear also, what will be the consequence of these most obstinate contentions of ours, and of those principles of ungodly men so entirely opposed to christian love. I wish, indeed, they would follow the advice of that book which you lately published concerning the agreement of ministers; but this is rather to be desired than hoped for. You may obtain some information about these disputes from our excellent friend, master Gualter. Our people are still persisting in making innovations. They find fault with that prayer wherein we pray God that we may be delivered from all adversities[2]. We use in our prayers the song of the blessed Virgin, of John the Baptist[3], and of the aged Simeon. This they cannot endure. We use also to repeat at the end of each psalm, when they are said before the people, " Glory be to the Father, and to the Son, and to the Holy Ghost." This they call vain repetition. But I will desist from troubling you any farther with these vanities; we ask of God a remedy for them. Meanwhile, however, we do not cease

[2 " Exceptions were taken to prayer against tempest, when none seems at hand; to the Magnificat, and other scriptural hymns, introduced for no conceivable purpose but to honour the Virgin, the Baptist, or similar personages, therefore profanations of scripture." Soames's Elizabethan Hist. p. 167.]

[3 i. e. the Benedictus, uttered at the birth of John the Baptist. Luke i. 68, &c.]

to oppose evils of this kind, as far as the Lord may vouchsafe to afford us strength.

I have not yet received your book on the persecutions of the church. I desire, my esteemed brother in Christ, that you may live in safety many years, and that you may use your exertions for the restoration of the church of God, even to the end. I have sent six crowns of this country to my friend Julius.

Your most attached brother in Christ,
The bishop and servant of the church of Ely,
RICHARD COX,
bishop of Ely.

LETTER CIX.

BISHOP COX TO RODOLPH GUALTER.

Dated at ELY, *June* 12, 1573.

I RECEIVED your letter, Gualter, dearly beloved brother in Christ, in this present month of June, 1573. I am surprised that the letters have not yet reached you, which I wrote at the beginning of last spring both to yourself and to my reverend father and brother, master Bullinger. It would have been far more gratifying and agreeable to me for you to have learned from the letter I then wrote, with how much delight your discourses were received, together with your letter noticing with so much prudence, learning, and piety, some points now controverted among us. You would have learned moreover from that letter of mine, what confusion has been occasioned in our not ill-constituted church, by some factious and heady men, who in their writings[1] and sermons, and private

[1 The bishop seems to refer to the celebrated admonition to the parliament, for an account of which see Strype, Life of Whitgift, I. 54, &c. and Soames's Elizabethan History, p. 163, &c. The latter writer states that "its authors, ostensibly, and perhaps principally, were John Field and Thomas Wilcox, two puritanical clergymen of great

conversation, condemn and pull in pieces the whole economy of our church, and bring all the bishops and other ministers of the word into incredible disfavour with the people, and also with the magistrates and nobility. Nay, they even reject this order as being of no use to the church of Christ, and are striving by every means in their power that it may be altogether abolished. But the Lord God has imbued our most religious queen and some of her principal ministers with that discretion and piety, that these men, as I hope, will strive to no purpose. Their object is to revive the ancient presbytery of the primitive church, and to establish such an equality among all ministers, that they may be despised and rejected even by the church itself; so that it is to be feared lest Christ himself should be banished by little and little.

As to your son having sent a letter in the way you mention, he has ingenuously performed the part of a well principled young man. If he would come and see me more frequently, or address me by letter, he should not have to repent the performance of so trifling a courtesy. You must not be grieved, my Gualter, that the sectaries are shewing themselves to be mischievous and wicked interpreters of your most just opinion. For it cannot be otherwise, but that tares must grow in the Lord's field, and that in no small quantity. Of this kind are the Anabaptists, Donatists, Arians, papists, and all the good-for-nothing tribe of the sectaries. But our solid comfort is from Christ: "Blessed are ye when men shall speak evil of you falsely, for my sake." Your remarks about observing moderation in external matters, provided that the truth of Christ and faith is maintained inviolate, proceed from sincere piety and most solid judgment. With respect to their estimation of your character, they are indeed contemptible, who desist not from attacking the character of all good men: they are unable however to injure either your reputation or mine by their revilings. For it is not to them, but to the Lord, that we stand and fall.

I hope you have received before this time my former letters sent to master Bullinger and yourself. I took care that they

note among the Londoners of their party." To these "Gilbye, Sampson, Lever, are added by Abp. Bancroft, in his Survey of the pretended Holy discipline."]

should be delivered, together with twenty-five gulden[1], as they call them, by Richard Hilles, a merchant of this country, to your friend Froschover, to be forwarded to you. May the Lord Jesus very long preserve you in safety to us, for the very great advantage of his church! Salute in my name that pillar of the church of Christ, master Henry Bullinger. From my episcopal house in the isle of Ely, in England, June 12, 1573.

Your most loving friend in Christ,

RICHARD COX,

bishop of Ely.

LETTER CX.

BISHOP PILKINGTON TO RODOLPH GUALTER.

Dated *July* 20, 1573.

Jesus. Much health. If the same proportion of leisure and health were afforded me to read what you with unwearied labour have committed to the press, as there has been time and strength allotted you to write, I should indeed think myself a happy man; but since I am prevented from being able to do so by my frequent infirmities, and, besides the daily care of the churches and public business, am perpetually struggling with disease and death, I congratulate the church of God, in the defence of which you are so great and so active a labourer; (though in this old age of the world and my own declining years I grieve for myself, as one who can scarcely hope to enjoy the agreeable fruits of your exertions;) and I wish you the years of Nestor, that you may be enabled the more successfully to complete what you have so successfully begun. How many are greatly delighted with your most learned commentaries, and especially your last upon both the epistles to the Corinthians, (for which also I return you individually my warmest thanks,) I am unwilling now to tell you by recounting them; neither will I declare how highly I think of them, lest I should seem rather to be a vain flatterer than

[[1] A gulden is about half-a-crown of English money.]

one who sincerely praises you to your face. Go on as you have begun. Exalt the Lord God in your writings; edify the church by explaining her mysteries, instruct the unlearned, excite the learned to exertion; exhort, advise, rebuke each; and you will have the Lord, who is the universal inspector of all mankind, as the most ample approver and rewarder of the labours you have bestowed in the dressing of his vineyard.

But here, I pray you, pause awhile with me, and mourn over this our church at this time so miserably divided, not to say, wholly rent in pieces. Commend her to the Lord your God, and entreat him that, having compassion upon us, he may very soon provide some godly remedy for the healing of her wounds, that she may not be utterly destroyed. Your prudence has heard, I well know, and that often enough to weary you, of that unhappy dispute among some of our friends respecting the affair of the habits and the dress of the clergy, and how great a disturbance it had excited; but it has now so broken out afresh, nay more, that which heretofore lurked in dissimulation has now so openly discovered itself, that not only the habits, but our whole ecclesiastical polity, discipline, the revenues of the bishops, ceremonies or public forms of worship, liturgies, vocation of ministers, or the ministration of the sacraments,—all these things are now openly attacked from the press, and it is contended with the greatest bitterness, that they are not to be endured in the church of Christ. The doctrine alone they leave untouched: as to every thing else, by whatever name you call it, they are clamourous for its removal. The godly mourn, the papists exult, that we are now fighting against each other, who were heretofore wont to attack them with our united forces; the weak know not what or whom to believe; the godless are altogether insensible to any danger; the Romish priesthood are gaping for the prey, and are like bellows carefully blowing up the flame, that the mischief may increase. It is lamentable to behold, and dreadful to hear of such things taking place among those who profess the same religion; and yet the entire blame is laid upon the bishops, as if they alone, if they chose, were able to eradicate all these evils. We endure, I must confess, many things against our inclinations, and groan under them, which if we wished ever so much, no entreaty can remove. We are under authority, and cannot make any innovation without the sanction of the queen, or abrogate any thing without the authority of the laws; and the only alternative now allowed us is, whether we will bear with these things or disturb the peace of the church. I wish all parties would understand and follow your wholesome advice in your preface to the Epistle to the Corinthians, respecting the variety of rites and discipline in individual churches. But these men are crying out that nothing is to be endured in the rites of the church, which is later than the times of the apostles, and that all our discipline must be derived from thence, and this at the peril of the soul and our eternal salvation.

Accept, I pray you, in good part these few crowns in token of my regard for you and for your sound doctrine. I would have offered more, but we are making a collection for the poor French[1] [protestants], who, exiled and plundered of their property, have taken refuge partly at Geneva, and partly in this country.

You will learn from the accompanying verses all that has been done in Scotland. I salute in the Lord all your brethren in the ministry, and especially the reverend master Bullinger, to whom I beg my excuses for not having written to him individually; and I pray, that since you are both one, you will be satisfied with this one letter. Communicate it, if you please, to him, that he may sympathise and condole in our misfortunes. May the Lord Jesus long preserve happy Zurich in her ancient peace and the fear of God! Farewell in the Lord, my very dear brother in Christ. July 20, 1573.

The great admirer of your learning and piety,

JAMES PILKINGTON,

Dunelm.

[1] The case of the French Church in London had been before recommended by the queen to the Archbishop of Canterbury and other bishops in 1569, on the breaking out of the third civil war in France between the papists and the confederate protestants. The archbishop recommended the case to the dean and chapter of Canterbury, in whose register this order is extant: "Anno 1569, June 8, agreed, that there shall be, at the contemplation of the lord archbishop his grace's letters, given out of the church treasury to the poor [afflicted] French Church in London, towards their relief, six pounds, thirteen shillings and fourpence." Strype, Annals, I. ii. 290.]

LETTER CXI.

LAURENCE HUMPHREY TO RODOLPH GUALTER.
Dated at OXFORD, *July* 28, 1573.

IMMANUEL. Your son Gualter, together with your letter, came to me at Oxford. He is the very image of yourself, and a true Zuinglian[2]. He is living in Magdalene college, agreeable to myself, acceptable to my friends, and welcome to the university. The Earl of Bedford, and Parkhurst, your friend and our bishop, reverenced by me on many accounts, have given him letters of introduction; so that both for your sake and at the request of these distinguished men, I have admitted him to my friendship and to my college, congratulating myself that I have such an inmate[3]. Parkhurst most fully promises to supply him with every thing necessary, and I willingly offer my aid and assistance to contribute in any way to the benefit of so excellent a youth. For I both love the ingenuous manners and frank disposition of the man, and confess that I owe every thing to such a father, who has employed so many days and nights in raising up children of the gospel, and in planting a nursery of the christian church. Persevere in employing yourself in that holy work; that while time is afforded us, we may still defend the purity of religion, and illustrate that truth which has hitherto, through ignorance or malice, been hidden in the dark den of the Romanists. For it is most delightful to continue singing even unto grey hairs; and hence the voice of the aged, like the descant of the swan, is sweetest and

[2 His mother was the daughter of Zuinglius. See note 2, p. 30.]
[3 Parkhurst wrote to Gualter himself, being upon his departure to Oxford: "When you come to Oxford, you shall be provided with all things. If any thing be wanting at any time, I have written now once again to Dr Umphrey and Mr Cole, to provide the same for you. And at one of their hands you shall receive what you have need of; and I will see the same discharged." He concluded his letter with his counsel: "If you apply yourself to your studies, and do well, you shall want nothing, but shall find me, not a friend only, but another father unto you. God keep you, and give you grace to do that becometh you, to his glory, and all your friends' comfort." See Strype, Ann. II. i. 337.]

most solemn. For this it is that a talent is bestowed on you by the Lord; for this, peace and leisure and retirement are afforded you; for this, the convenience of a most excellent press, that in this abundance of every thing, and with this best of opportunities, you may be of use to us Britons, divided as we are from all the world, and standing in need of almost all these means of assistance. However, by the blessing of God, all things are now at peace among us, notwithstanding our neighbour's house is on fire. For the torch of civil war in France and Flanders is not yet put out, although a conference is being held respecting some honourable conditions of peace.

In Scotland, the virgin castle of Edinburgh[1], for so the Scots called it, albeit hitherto unconquered, is at last reduced and taken. Our queen[2] subdued it, not for herself, but for the young king. Their queen, therefore, being kept in custody in this country, and all the conspirators having either surrendered or been destroyed, not only a mutual alliance is taking place among us, but the same religion received by universal consent is prospering in that kingdom. May the Lord Jesus preserve, and load with every blessing, both yourself and your friends, masters Bullinger, Simler, Lavater, &c. and the whole church! In haste, in the midst of our Magdalene commemoration. Oxford, July 28, 1573.

Your most devoted,

LAURENCE HUMPHREY.

[1 The castle surrendered on the 28th of May, being the 33rd day of the siege; for an account of which see Camden's Elizabeth, p. 197.]

[2 Sir Thomas Smith was earnest with the queen, to send aid to reduce the rebels in Scotland, who had fortified Edinburgh Castle against the king and regent; and for that purpose he let the queen understand from Mr Killigrew, her ambassador in Scotland, how dangerously things stood there, and therefore that it was his desire that the *peace-makers* (as he phrased it) might shortly be transported thither; to whom, when the queen asked, "who be they?" "Marry," said he, "your majesty's cannons; they must do it, and make a final conclusion." "Then," said the queen, "I warrant you, and that shortly." Strype, Life of Smith, 129. See Smith's Letter to Lord Burghleigh, MS. Harl. 6991, 14.]

LETTER CXII.

ARCHBISHOP GRINDAL TO HENRY BULLINGER.

Dated at YORK, *July* 31, 1573.

HEALTH in Christ! About the end of December last, my dearest master Bullinger, I received your letter written on the 24th of August; on which day, by a savage and unheard of cruelty, the Admiral[3] with other nobility, and the greatest part of the faithful, were massacred at Paris. These are the fruits of that egregious treaty with France, from which we expected so much advantage! The Sicilian Vespers[4] indeed were infamous of old; but these French Matins, if I may so call them, leave them far behind. The Lord beholds these things, and will make inquisition. Many exiles[5] from France have sought refuge in London, and among them many ministers of the churches, who are there kindly received with hospitality, and supported by the alms of the godly.

Our affairs, after the settlement of the controversy respecting ceremonies, were for some time very quiet: when some virulent pamphlets[6] came forth, privately printed, contrary

[3] Viz. Coligni. "De Thou, perhaps, falls short rather than exceeds in his computation, when he fixes the whole number of Huguenots who perished, at little below thirty thousand; of that number at least one-third may be allotted to Paris." See Smedley's Hist. of the Reformed Religion in France, Vol. II. p. 34, and the testimonies there cited.]

[4] The massacre of the French in Sicily on Easter Monday, March 30, 1282.]

[5] See p. 288.]

[6] The admonition to the Parliament, soon after the publishing of it, was backed with three other pamphlets, sent to Dr Whitgift, as it were a challenge; which he briefly answered towards the end of his answer to the admonition. The first was a preface to the other two. The second was called, *An Exhortation to the Bishops to deal brotherly with their brethren*. The third, *An Exhortation to the Bishops and their Clergy, to answer a little Book that came forth the last Parliament; and to the other brethren, to judge of it by God's word, until they see it answered; and not be carried away with any respect of men.* See Strype, Life of Whitgift, Vol. I. p. 80, &c. who gives a full account of the above writings.]

to law, in which almost the whole external polity of our church was attacked. For they maintain that archbishops and bishops should altogether be reduced to the ranks; that the ministers of the church ought to be elected solely by the people; that they ought all to be placed upon an equality; that in every city, town, parish, or village, a consistory should be established, consisting of the minister and elders of the place, who alone are to decide upon all ecclesiastical affairs: (they state) that the church of England has scarcely the appearance of a christian church,—that no set form of prayer ought to be prescribed, but that in the holy assemblies each minister should pray as the Holy Ghost may dictate; that the infants of popish recusants, as far as the use of baptism is concerned, are unclean, (I use their own words,) but yet that they are not on that account to be excluded from the election of God. I pass over many things which it would be tedious to recount. But a royal edict was lately published, in which libels of this sort are forbidden to be circulated for the future; which circumstance, as I hope, will retard their endeavours. They are young men who disseminate these opinions, and they have their supporters, especially from among those who are gaping for ecclesiastical property: but yet I am glad to say, that Humphrey, and Sampson, and some others, who heretofore moved the question about ceremonies, are entirely opposed to this party.

The castle of Edinburgh in Scotland, about which I before wrote, having been battered for twenty successive days by our English cannon, was at length forced to surrender on the 28th of May last. The chief rebels[1] were punished; so that at this time the whole of Scotland is reduced to obedience under the young king, and is altogether alienated from the French, both on account of the difference of religion, and the cruelty which was last year exercised towards the faithful; but most devoted to our queen (who has so often defended the liberties of the Scots,) as you may easily see by the inclosed verses, printed at Edinburgh.

[1 "Grange and his brother, with eleven Scots goldsmiths, were hanged at Edinburgh." Lord Burghley to the Earl of Shrewsbury, in Lodge, Vol. II. p. 33.]

The affairs of France are sufficiently known to you. In Holland and Zealand the prince of Orange is superior in his navy, but on land the contest is always doubtful. May the Lord take compassion on his church, and at length put an end to these evils, that we may with one mouth glorify him, whom I pray very long to preserve your piety in safety to his church! York, the last day of July, 1573.

Your most devoted in the Lord,

EDMUND YORK.

P. S. It was my intention, God willing, to have sent you at the spring fair some little remembrance of me, which however was not ready at that time through the neglect of the workman.

LETTER CXIII.

ARCHBISHOP GRINDAL TO RODOLPH GUALTER.

Dated at YORK, *July* 31, 1573.

HEALTH in Christ, my very dear master Gualter! Your desire that your lately published Homilies[2] on the first Epistle to the Corinthians should appear under my name and that of some other very dear brethren and fellow-labourers, was very gratifying to me; and on that account, as far as concerns myself, (and I hope the others will do the same,) I return your piety my best thanks. Your son sent me two copies bound, one of which I forwarded to the lord bishop of Durham, to whom, as he writes me word, the present was most acceptable; the other I retain myself. There is no reason why you should be so careful to apologize for your freedom in writing to me. For although you are not personally known to me, you are well known to me by your writings, abounding as they do in singular erudition and learning; and on account of the excellent piety which they breathe, and I will add too, on account of our most close agreement in the true doctrine of Christ, you are most dear to me.

[[2] See note 5. p. 279.]

As I am myself far distant from Cambridge, I have earnestly recommended your son to Dr John Whitgift, the master of his college[1]; whom I have also requested to shew himself a sufficiently severe censor of his morals, should there be any occasion for his doing so. But I hope there will be no occasion for this; for I hear that your son is very studious and modest, and far removed from all levity of conduct.

I wrote a few lines to Bullinger respecting our affairs, which he doubtless will communicate to you. I wrote likewise to Richard Hilles, a merchant of London, that he should take care to transmit to you, at the next Frankfort fair, fifty French crowns; namely, thirty from myself, and the remaining twenty[2] from the bishop of Durham, whose letter you will receive at the same time with this. We pray you to take in good part this little present. Farewell in Christ, my very dear brother in the Lord. York, the last day of July, 1573.

Yours in Christ,
EDMUND YORK.

LETTER CXIV.

BISHOP SANDYS TO HENRY BULLINGER.

Dated at LONDON, *Aug.* 15, 1573.

On many accounts, most esteemed sir, I am greatly in your debt; both because you have always regarded me with the greatest kindness and affection, and because you have condescended to write to me so diligently and so frequently. For all which things, though I cannot make an equal return, yet I will thank you as much as I can, and shall at all times readily acknowledge myself very much indebted to you for your peculiar kindness.

You must not impute it to neglect that I so seldom write to you, but to the unfrequency of the means of communication between us, especially in these most turbulent times, when war

[1 i.e. Trinity College.] [2 See p. 288.]

and tumults and slaughter are every where rife. For there is no one to whom I should write with greater pleasure than to master Bullinger, whom, as I have always loved him exceedingly for his great courtesy, so have I also much venerated for his singular erudition, and rare piety, and other excellent qualities. For when I call to my remembrance, as I very often do, with how much favour and regard I was entertained by you, how like a brother and a friend you treated me when an exile, and the comfort in which I seemed to myself to live among you, I wish for nothing more than that, relieved from those cases and anxieties with which I am now overwhelmed, I might pass the remainder of my life at Zurich as a sojourner and private person. Thoughts of this kind are continually occurring to me; nor is there any thing that I should wish for more. But I perceive that this cannot be. I am not born for myself: our church, which is most sadly tossed about in these evil times, and is in a most wretched state of confusion, vehemently demands all my exertions; I dare not desert the spouse of Christ in her danger; for conscience would cry out against me, and convict me of having betrayed her. New orators are rising up from among us, foolish young men, who while they despise authority, and admit of no superior, are seeking the complete overthrow and rooting up of our whole ecclesiastical polity, so piously constituted and confirmed, and established by the entire consent of most excellent men; and are striving to shape out for us, I know not what new platform of a church. And you would not imagine with what approbation this new face of things is regarded, as well by the people as the nobility. The people are fond of change, and seek after liberty; the nobility [seek for] what is useful. These good folks promise both, and that in abundance. But that you may be better acquainted with the whole matter, accept this summary of the question at issue reduced under certain heads:

1. The civil magistrate has no authority in ecclesiastical matters. He is only a member of the church, the government of which ought to be committed to the clergy.

2. The church of Christ admits of no other government than that by presbyteries; viz. by the minister, elders, and deacon.

3. The names and authority of archbishops, archdeacons,

deans, chancellors, commissaries, and other titles and dignities of the like kind, should be altogether removed from the church of Christ.

4. Each parish should have its own presbytery.

5. The choice of ministers of necessity belongs to the people.

6. The goods, possessions, lands, revenues, titles, honours, authorities, and all other things relating either to bishops or cathedrals, and which now of right belong to them, should be taken away forthwith and for ever.

7. No one should be allowed to preach who is not a pastor of some congregation; and he ought to preach to his own flock exclusively, and no where else.

8. The infants of papists are not to be baptized.

9. The judicial laws of Moses are binding upon christian princes, and they ought not in the slightest degree to depart from them.

There are many other things of the same kind, not less absurd, and which I shall not mention; none of which, as far as I can judge, will make for the advantage and peace of the church, but for her ruin and confusion. Take away authority, and the people will rush headlong into every thing that is bad. Take away the patrimony of the church, and you will by the same means take away not only sound learning, but religion itself. But I seem perhaps to prejudge the matter. I anxiously desire, most learned sir, to hear your opinion, and those of masters Gualter, Simler, and the rest of the brethren, respecting these things; which for my own part I shall willingly follow, as being sound and agreeable to the word of God. For if the whole matter in controversy were left to your arbitration, it would doubtless much contribute to the peace of our church. These good men are crying out that they have all the reformed churches on their side.

I say nothing of the state of our commonwealth: every thing is quiet hitherto, but it is to be feared that these intestine dissensions may tend at length to the ruin of the country.

I send your reverence as much English cloth as will make you a gown. Make use of it, I pray you, and accept it with your wonted kindness. Farewell, most esteemed sir, and com-

mend me, I pray you, to God in your prayers. In haste.
London, England, Aug. 15, 1573.

Your brother in Christ,

EDWIN SANDYS,

bishop of London.

LETTER CXV.

BISHOP COX TO RODOLPH GUALTER.

Dated at ELY, *Feb.* 3, 1574.

I RETURN you my best thanks, my dear brother in Christ, for having sent me a most courteous letter, which I received in December, and in which you clearly manifest your anxiety for the church of Christ, though at so great a distance from you. This indeed ought to be the chief solicitude of every pastor in the church, but of those more especially, who in the endowments of learning and judgment and piety are superior to the rest. When Dr Whitgift, the most vehement enemy of the schismatics, and the chief instrument against them in our church, had perceived these unruly men to have burst by their reckless attacks the barriers of law and of religion, which had been so well and so peacefully established; and that they had openly distributed infamous pamphlets[1] which had been privately committed to the press; and also that from your letter[2] to our friend Parkhurst, which they had communicated

[1 One book here referred to is called, *An admonition to the Parliament*, by Thomas Cartwright. It had been printed and reprinted privately no less than four times, notwithstanding the diligence of the bishops to suppress it. Strype, Parker, II. 110. See note 6, p. 291.]

[2 The discontented brethren, in 1565 or 1566, thought it convenient to certify the foreign churches of the transactions then against them. And for that intent they dispatched two of their party to Geneva and Helvetia; who, when they were come to Zurich, declared unto Gualter and the other ministers there the same that they had done at Geneva, (filling his ears with grievous accusations of the bishops' dealings with the ministers.) Gualter hastily composed and sent a letter to his old

to many persons, they had already obtained a handle for confirming their errors, he thought that the publication of your letter[1] to me would tend very much to the defence of the truth. Your first letter was extorted from you by those who falsely accused us; but the simple truth brought the second to light. And there is no reason why you should be disturbed about the publication of what has procured credit and reputation to yourself, inasmuch as it espouses the cause of truth, of which no one ought to be ashamed.

I acquainted you with some of the errors of our men, in the questions I proposed to you; and you have gratified me most exceedingly by the candid and sincere declaration of your sentiments: for the opinions of masters Bullinger and Gualter are of no little weight in our church. But these disputants of ours are so shuffling and so tenacious of their own opinion, that they will give way to no one who opposes their judgment; and they are striving to draw all your writings over to their side by a perverted interpretation of them. To give you an instance of their candour, they are zealously endeavouring to overthrow the entire order of our Anglican church. Night and day do they importune both the people and the nobility, and stir them up to abhorrence of those persons who, on the abolition of popery, are faithfully discharging the duties of the ministry; and they busy themselves in everywhere weakening and diminishing their credit. And that they may effect this with greater ease and plausibility, they bawl out to those harpies who are greedily hankering after plunder and spoil, that the property and revenues of the cathedral churches ought to be diverted to I know not what other uses. Nor will they allow bishops to take any other precedence than as individual pastors in their respective parishes, whose highest authority they wish to be

---

friend Bishop Parkhurst, who had sojourned four years at his house at Zurich; and therein he sharply blamed him, and the rest of the bishops, for pressing such indifferent things, and punishing so heavily those who complied not with them. Of this letter, (for bishop Cox's reply to which see Letter xciv.) several copies were taken, so that falling into the hands of the Puritans, they printed it with one of Beza's in the said book, called *The Admonition*, in justification of themselves. See Strype, Parker, II. 111.]

[1 This letter will be found in the Appendix.]

that of governing, together with their presbytery, the rest of the parishioners. And in this way they set up and establish the equality they speak of. Besides this, they will not acknowledge any government in the church. They propose moreover, that the estates and houses of the bishops should be appropriated to pious uses; but, more blind than moles, they do not perceive that they will soon be swallowed up by the devouring wolves. There are in this country twenty-three bishopricks, the endowments of some of which are little enough; others have moderate ones, and others more abundant. But all are within the bounds of moderation. None of the bishops interfere in any matters but the ministry of the word and sacraments, except when the law requires them, or at the command of the sovereign. Nor in these things, as far as I am aware, do they deal harshly with the brethren, but temper what is severe with surprising lenity. Our opponents, however, would complain most grievously, were our jurisdiction transferred to the laity, as they call them: they would soon find out that the gold had been exchanged for brass. But how true are the insinuations which they have whispered against us in the ears of the godly, time will shew. And "our rejoicing is the testimony of our conscience." I wish they would acquiesce in your wholesome and prudent counsel, namely, to put up with what cannot be amended without great danger. At first they attacked only things of little consequence; but now they turn every thing, both great and small, up and down, and throw all things into confusion; and would bring the church into very great danger, were not our most pious queen most faithful to her principles, and did she not dread and restrain the vanity and inconsistency of these frivolous men. But because we do not decline to execute the orders of the government, whenever it commands us to interfere, in bridling in these our tumultuous brethren, on this ground an undue severity, not to say cruelty, is most unjustly laid to our charge. But we have this one comfort, that the religion of Christ is ever accompanied by the cross, which he will, by his Holy Spirit, enable us willingly to bear.

Your son, a youth of excellent promise, has only this fault, that he rarely comes to see me. But I am now obliged to excuse him, because he is residing in our other university,

I mean Oxford, which is a great way off. But I hope that he will take leave of me before he goes away. You have acted prudently in so carefully providing for your son, that like Ulysses, he may see the customs and cities of many people, and like the industrious bee, extract piety from all the churches. May God bring him back to be a blessing to his father! May Christ Jesus very long preserve you to us in safety! From the Isle of Ely in England, Feb. 3, 1573, according to the English computation.

Your most loving friend in Christ, RICHARD COX,

pastor and servant of the church at Ely,

RICHARD ELY.

LETTER CXVI.

BISHOP PARKHURST TO HENRY BULLINGER.

Dated at LUDHAM, *Feb.* 6, 1574.

HAIL, most agreeable master Bullinger! Your letter of the 27th of August I received on the 21st of November, at which time[1] new and severe proclamations were set forth against those who either despise our ceremonies, or refuse to observe them. May God direct it for the best, and have compassion upon all the churches of Christ! God grant that there be not a snake in the grass! I thank you very much for your most learned treatise on the persecutions of the church, translated into Latin by our friend Simler, and which I have just now received. The German [original] never came to hand.

You write me word that you are a *septuagenarian:* I wish that you may at length become a *centenarian*, were it only for the sake of the church herself. For my own part I have almost completed my sixty-third year, namely, my

[1 Oct. 20, a proclamation was published against the despisers and breakers of the orders prescribed in the book of common prayer. See Strype, Parker, II. 320.]

climacteric. My wife is, according to her own account, sixty-seven years old and more. I rejoice that all is quiet in Switzerland. I am not sorry that the business about the hired troops turned out so unhappily. The harvest with us here in Norfolk did not begin before the feast of Bartholomew[2], and was very wet and showery. There was scarce a fine day during the whole harvest, so that no small quantity of grain was lost, though the greatest portion was saved by the unwearied diligence of the labourers. The dearth not only of wheat, but of every thing else, is very great among us. Do you ask, whence proceeds this *carity?* It is because our *charity* is growing cold among us[3]. Before the feast of the Purification[4] we had no snow in these parts, and scarcely felt the cold. We have now plenty of both.

Salute, I pray you, in my name all my friends, and Julius himself not among the last of them. Woe betide that worst of all collectors, Thymelthorp[5], who will not allow me to collect any thing for my friends! But I hope better things. May God preserve you, and all my Zurich friends! Amen. In haste. London, February 6, 1574. My wife salutes you and yours. Farewell.

Yours,

JOHN PARKHURST,

[bishop] of Norwich.

[2 Namely, the 24th of August.]

[3 This remark is borrowed from a Homily of Basil's, written on occasion of a great famine and dearth.]

[4 Namely, the 2nd of February.]

[5 See note 2. p. 265. This man was imprisoned for his defalcation, and during his imprisonment obtained leave of the council to go for a while into Norfolk, where he was twice at Ludham with the bishop, and there, holding up his hands and falling on his knees, beseeched him that he would pardon him the injury. To whom the bishop christianly answered, that he would pardon the injury done him, but the payment of money due to him and the queen he could not pardon. Strype, Annals, II. i. 336.]

LETTER CXVII.

BISHOP PARKHURST TO JOSIAH SIMLER.
Dated at LUDHAM, *Feb.* 7, 1574.

ON the 20th of August I received your letter of the 22nd of February, 1573. That youth William Barlow, to whom you gave it, was never, as far as I am aware, known to, or seen by me. That ubiquitarian James Andreas[1], who threatens to write against the divines of Wittemberg[2] and my Zurich friends, will lose his labour and betray his folly to every one. So far are we English from defending either the ubiquitarian or any other monstrous opinions, that we cannot endure them. We only dispute about ceremonies and habits, and things of no importance. O that these skirmishes and contentions may at length be laid to rest and buried in oblivion! The papists are certainly cherishing, I know not what expectations; but I hope without reason. May the Lord grant an end (*finem*) to these things, and a halter (*funem*) to the papists. I hope our friend Magdalen has many months since recovered from the ague.

May the Lord release from the gout both you and my wife. Amen. Ludham, February 7, 1574. Salute your wife and all my friends. My wife salutes you all.

Yours,

JOHN PARKHURST,

[bishop] of Norwich.

[1 Jacobus Andreas was a professor at Tubingen, and head of the Ubiquitarians in Germany. See Strype, Annals, II. ii. 104. He was now employed, under the patronage of the elector of Saxony, and others, in composing a form of doctrine, in which all the controversies that divided the church should be terminated and decided. See Mosheim.]

[2 Among whom was Peucer, son-in-law to Melancthon, and head of the university of Wittemberg. He aimed at nothing less than abolishing the doctrine of Luther concerning the eucharist and the person of Christ, with a design to substitute the sentiments of Calvin in its place. For these principles he was imprisoned from 1574, after the convocation of Thorgau, till 1585. See Mosheim, and also Casparis Peuceri Historia carcerum et liberationis divinæ. By Christopher Pezelius, Tiguri, 1605.]

LETTER CXVIII.

BISHOP PARKHURST TO HENRY BULLINGER.

Dated at LUDHAM, *June* 29, 1574.

MAY you be safe in Christ, my very dear Bullinger!

In my former letter, which I sent you on the 6th of February, I expressed my warmest thanks for that very learned little treatise which you sent me respecting the persecutions of the church; and I now repeat them. The Latin edition I have received; that in German I have not yet seen. Your letter of March 10th came to hand on the 26th of June, in which you state that you have now forwarded to me a certain reply to the Brentian party, and also two homilies on the 130th and 133rd Psalms. Neither of these have I received. Woe betide those persons by whom so great a treasure has been taken from me!

A certain young Dutch[3] woman about seventeen or eighteen years of age, a servant of the preacher of the church at Norwich, was during a whole year miserably vexed by Satan. In all her temptations, however, and dilacerations, she continued stedfast in the faith, and withstood the adversary with more than manly fortitude. At last, by God's help, the devil being overcome left her, and almost at the same instant attacked the son of a certain senator, whom he also tormented in a most incredible manner for some weeks together. Public prayers were offered in the city by my direction, and a fast proclaimed until evening. The Lord had mercy also on the boy, and overcame the enemy. The boy was thirteen or at most fourteen years old, and, for his age, well versed in the scriptures, which, stedfast in faith, he boldly launched forth against the enemy. The Lord liveth, by whom this boy and girl, of a weak constitution in other respects, were enabled to overcome so great and terrible an adversary. To God be the praise!

[3 See Strype, Annals, II. i. 484, and Soames's Elizabethan History, p. 203, where are related other stories of the same kind.]

That confession[1] of true religion which you published in 1566, is now read in English, and in the hands of every one. The scarcity of all things still continues among us. Rodolph, the son of our friend Gualter, is coming back to you: he is a youth well learned, of good talents, and pious conduct. His father is displeased with him for not living more economically[2]. If he has acted improperly in this respect, we must make allowance for his youth. Do you earnestly entreat his father not to receive his returning son less favourably than that excellent parent in Luke xv.

Salute, I pray you, in my name all my friends, your sons and daughters, Dorothy especially, whom I wish it would please God to unite in marriage to my friend Rodolph. Indeed I earnestly desire this, and should rejoice most exceedingly were it to take place with your consent, and that of my friend Gualter; and you also, as I hope, will rejoice, and the Lord will bless their union. Farewell, my Bullinger, and continue to love me. My wife salutes you all. In haste. Ludham, June 22, 1574.

Yours,

JOHN PARKHURST, N[orwich.]

LETTER CXIX.

BISHOP PARKHURST TO JOSIAH SIMLER.

Dated at LUDHAM, *June* 30, 1574.

HAIL, my Simler. You have no occasion to thank me so heartily on account of our friend Rodolph[3]. He is one

[1] The latter confession of Helvetia was written by the pastors of Zurich in 1566, and approved and subscribed, not only by the Tigurines themselves, and their confederates of Berne, Schaffhausen, St Gall, Grisons, Mulhausen, and Bienne; but by the churches of Geneva, Savoy, Poland, and likewise of Hungary and of Scotland.]

[2] He was somewhat a prodigal youth. Strype, Annals, II. 1. 508.]

[3 Viz. Gualter's son, whom the bishop had maintained first at Cambridge, and then at Oxford, and in other places, while he was in England, at his sole expense, though he were somewhat a prodigal youth; and gave

upon whom far greater benefits might worthily be bestowed. Being summoned by his father in a letter sent to me, and persuaded by your advice, he is now hastening home. I had intended to have kept him longer in England, and supported him at the University of Oxford, and that without any expense to his father; but since it is your wish, he shall depart, not only without any opposition on my part, but with my entire consent. I will advance his interests even in his absence.

It is a marvellous occurrence that a cow should have brought forth a fawn! But the wonder is diminished, when the circumstance took place in the neighbourhood of these portentous monks.

I have neither received your little book against the Brentians, nor the Bibliotheca [of Conrad Gesner] enlarged by you[4]. Froschover has probably forgotten it; but, however it be, I thank you for your kindness. I wish you would look out for a wife for Rodolph. If you are inclined to take my advice, Dorothea, Bullinger's daughter, shall be the person: for she is pious, and, like our friend, the offspring of pious parents: so that you will do well if they should, by your means, be joined together in holy matrimony.

Fare thee well, my dearest Josiah. Greet in my name our friends Magdalen, Anna, Nobilitatula, together with their husbands. Heartily salute Haller, Lavater, Wonlichius, Wickius, Julius, Froschover, John Henry Fabricius, Michaelis, (if he is yet alive;) the Meyers, Cellarii, Thaddeus Betta, and all the rest. My wife salutes you all. Again farewell. In haste. Ludham, June 30, 1574.

Yours,
JOHN PARKHURST, N.

him a *viaticum*, to bear his charges when he returned home. Strype, Annals II. i. 508.]

[4 Josiah Simler published at Zurich, in 1574, an abridgement of the Bibliotheca, or Universal Dictionary of Conrad Gesner. Conrad Lycosthenes [Wolfhart], minister at Basle, had previously undertaken a compendium of this great work; but the abridgement of Simler was a much more able performance, wherein he not only avoided the defects of Wolfhart, but enriched the work with many valuable additions, which he marked with an asterisk to distinguish them from the original work. Frisius published a second edition of Simler's abridgement in 1583.]

LETTER CXX.

BISHOP COX TO RODOLPH GUALTER.

Dated at ELY, *July* 12, 1574.

YOUR letter, written March 16th, 1574, my very dear brother in Christ, I received in the June following: it was indeed most gratifying to me, both as proceeding from so dear a friend, and as warning us that all the enemies of the truth are now every where plotting together, and preparing for the destruction of all who profess the religion of Christ. It is indeed very important that all godly persons should know this, that they may arm themselves in time with the whole armour of God. And though we may for the present seem to be safe, we see nevertheless the dangerous machinations of the papists surrounding us on every side. Nay more, even from ourselves, from time to time, venomous serpents come forth, as from their dens, brandishing their poisonous stings, which by the grace of God we have hitherto escaped. But when I reflect upon the wickedness which every where overflows, and upon not only the neglect but the contempt of the word of God, I am struck with horror, and think with trembling what God is about to decree concerning us. If the psalm, *The fool hath said in his heart, &c.*, or that *Let God arise, and let his enemies be scattered, &c.*, was ever applicable, it is at this time.

You rightly judge, most learned Gualter, concerning the presbyterian system of our people, and the sounder portion of the clergy of the church of England agree with you; and these noisy disturbers now give us scarcely any trouble, except that they continue to carp at our rites, like ghosts in the dark: they have for some time past been restrained by a rather severe correction, and are now vanquished by a most learned confutation[1]. When we have so many san-

[[1] Namely, Dr Whitgift's reply to Cartwright's "Admonition to the Parliament," for an account of which see Strype, Life of Whitgift, I. 66, &c.]

guinary enemies on all sides, (besides the Turks,) namely the papists, it is indeed to be lamented that so many dissensions exist in the reformed churches, as that they seem to be destroying themselves with their own weapons. May the Lord Jesus Christ, our only physician, at length afford a remedy for these evils! I doubt not but that the force of truth is so powerful in yourself, that should she want an advocate either with us or with you, or indeed in any place whatever, you will shew yourself a soldier of Christ. We retain in some measure the moral discipline of which you make mention in your letter; but should any one seek to compel our great men to submit their necks to it, it would be much the same as shaving a lion's beard.

The absurdities of the ubiquitarians have been long since most learnedly and courageously repressed by Peter Martyr, and very lately by your countryman Josiah Simler. *But he that shall come, will come, and will not tarry,* [Heb. x. 37,] who shall bruise with his hammer and break in pieces all those who are obstinate.

Your son, a youth of excellent disposition, courteously took leave of me upon his quitting this country. I pray God that he may return to you in safety, and that as an aged parent you may have the enjoyment of a pious son. Farewell. From the Isle of Ely in England. July 12, 1574.

Your most loving brother in Christ,

RICHARD COX.

LETTER CXXI.

BISHOP COX TO HENRY BULLINGER.

Dated at ELY, *July* 20, 1574.

I UNDERSTAND from your letter, which, written last spring, I received in the month of June, that the letter which I wrote to you in the year 1573 had not been delivered. This circumstance might afford you reason to suspect that I had neglected writing. Such neglect, my dearly beloved brother in Christ, would certainly have been criminal, had I suffered myself so to be branded with the mark of ingratitude as to be inattentive to the letters of my friends, so pious and learned and full of kindness, and neglected to return a courteous answer. I wrote a letter to you, I hope not an ungrateful one, in the year 1573, which, with a little present[1], (trifling as it was,) I gave in charge to one Richard Hilles, by whose means it was to be delivered to you. If this has not been done, I will endeavour to ascertain without loss of time, by whose fault the failure of it has been occasioned.

I understand from your letter, that you are not labouring under such a decay of old age as to be unable to discharge without inconvenience the trust committed to you. This [blessing] you have, in my opinion, obtained, partly by habit, the teacher of all things, and partly by the pious feeling with which you have ever been actuated, so as never to have ceased to promote without intermission the interests of the gospel and of godliness; but, most of all, because, inflamed by the Spirit of Christ, you have always obeyed its motions. However it be, I heartily congratulate both yourself and the church of Christ, that after so many labours accomplished for the glory of God, you have at length arrived at a vigorous old age, and which still retains its interest in behalf of all the churches: and this indeed is evident from your writings, in which you instruct, advise, comfort, not only the church of Zurich, but the truly universal church of Christ. Your little book on persecutions is especially useful in these latter times, wicked and dangerous as they are, to confirm the godly in the patience of Christ and in the purity of religion.

You are mistaken if you suppose that I understand German. It is now about fifteen years since I had a very slight knowledge of that language; but I will take care that your Swiss sermons shall be translated into Latin, that I may peruse them with greater delight and profit. I grieve that your churches are disturbed by these unhappy controversies: how truly did Christ say that the enemy soweth tares! Oh, may we, all of us, at length be made good ground! Our puritan brethren are now lying in concealment, partly terrified by the

[1 Six crowns. See p. 284.]

authority of our queen, and partly silenced by a most able treatise written by a most learned man[2]. Meanwhile, we know not what monstrosities they are hatching in secret.

Certain of our nobility[3], pupils of the Roman pontiff, either weary of their happiness or impatient of the long continued progress of the gospel, have taken flight, some into France, some into Spain, others into different places, with the view of plotting some mischief against the professors of godliness. So difficult is it to keep the church of Christ in a state of defence against the ministers of Satan. But the strength of the Lord and his strong tower have hitherto defended us; and the Lord will defend his own even to the end, in spite of the chafing and assaults of those two antichrists. In the mean time we must entreat the Lord night and day to arise and let his enemies be scattered.

May the Lord Jesus make your old age of long continuance to his church! As to myself, though in my 75th year, by the blessing of God I am in good health, except that the trembling of my hands makes it difficult for me to write. Farewell, my very dear brother in Christ. From the isle of Ely, in England, July 20, 1574.

Your most attached brother in Christ,

RICHARD,

First minister of the church at Ely.

[2 Namely, Dr Whitgift. See note 1, p. 306.]
[3 Among whom were Lord Edward Seymour, Lord Morley, the Archbishop of Cassel, and the Bishop of Meath. A complete list is given by Strype, Annals II. i. 495; II. ii. 551.]

LETTER CXXII.

LAURENCE HUMPHREY TO RODOLPH GUALTER.
Dated at OXFORD, *Aug.* 2, 1574.

IMMANUEL. Health in Christ Jesus, most esteemed Gualter. Your son returns to you, not, as you state[1], a prodigal, but improved both in learning and manners. For my own opinion respecting him, as well as that of the whole university, will easily be seen from their very copious testimonials. He so lived amongst us, that all are unanimous in praise of his modesty, his frankness, his many and great virtues; and consider you most fortunate, that the Lord hath given you such a Gualter as the inheritor of your name and piety. The bishop of Norwich will address you by letter, of whom I shall say nothing; for he is sufficiently known to you, and your son can bear ample testimony that he has never found his munificence straitened towards himself. But since he will explain by letter both the cause of your son's return, and other matters of the like kind, there is no occasion for me to repeat them to no purpose.

Dr Parkhurst has informed me that it is your desire, and I have also learned by other letters from Zurich that his friends are desirous, that at his present age he should think both about a matrimonial connection, and also about entering upon the ministry. That all things may turn out for him most happily and auspiciously, is my most earnest prayer.

I have received the copy of your treatise on Christ's presence on earth, but have nothing to send you in return, unless you wish to see my, or rather your[2] Jewel, whom I now send by my friend Gualter, and beg you both to correct and take in good part this trifling present.

[1 See p. 304.]
[2 The Archbishop [Parker] and the Bishop of London [Sandys], knowing the eloquence of Dr Laurence Humphrey's Latin pen, sent to him to Oxon commending the writing of Jewel's life to him; who finished and published it anno 1573, and dedicated his work to those two venerable prelates. Strype, Life of Parker, II. 50.]

We are here, by the blessing of God, in the possession of peace, and the pearl of the gospel, and pray that we may long enjoy them. Our neighbour's wall is on fire, and we are greatly afraid lest some spark of that fire should set us in a flame. So heedless are we, and unconcerned, that we seem to be daily kindling the flames of divine wrath. May the Lord Jesus, remembering, not our merits, but his mercy, avert every evil, preserve your church, our fathers and brethren, Bullinger, Simler, Lavater and the rest, together with yourself and family! In haste, at Oxford, Aug. 2, 1574.

Yours,

LAURENCE HUMPHREY.

LETTER CXXIII.

BISHOP SANDYS TO HENRY BULLINGER.

Dated at FULHAM, *Aug.* 9, 1574.

Much health in Christ, most esteemed sir and reverend father.

I thank you most sincerely for your very ready and affectionate inclination to write to me; for indeed nothing could have been more gratifying to me than to ascertain your opinion respecting the matters in dispute. You write most fully your own judgment concerning the whole affair: I see and embrace it. But I hope that this new fabric of new discipline will shortly fall in pieces by its own weight, since it appears that many of our countrymen who formerly admired it, are now grown weary of it; and those who seemed most zealous in the establishment of this new platform, have now begun to grow wonderfully cool, as it were, through a change of opinion. May the Lord grant that, all our dissensions and strife being removed, we may all of us speak and think the same thing according to Jesus Christ, and that we may with one mind and mouth glorify God, even the Father of our Lord Jesus Christ!

I will not write to you about the affairs of England, since the pious and learned[1] young man, who will bring you this letter, will give you certain information respecting them. The pirates of Flushing have intercepted the first[2] piece of cloth that I sent you: I ordered a second piece to be sent you, which I hear has come safe to hand. Farewell, most esteemed sir. I earnestly entreat you to commend me to God in your prayers. In haste.

Fulham in England, Aug. 9, 1574.

Your brother in Christ, and most affectionate,

EDWIN SANDYS,

bishop of London.

LETTER CXXIV.

BISHOP SANDYS TO RODOLPH GUALTER.

Dated at FULHAM, *Aug.* 9, 1574.

HEALTH to you, most learned sir, and very dear brother! There is no need for me to write to you. Lo! receive your son. He will be to you in the place of a letter from me, as one who will be able fully to acquaint you with the present state of our affairs in England. Our innovators, who have been striving to strike out for us a new form of a church, are not doing us much harm; nor is this new fabric of theirs making such progress as they expected. Our nobility are at last sensible of the object to which this novel fabrication is tending. The author of these novelties, and after Beza the first inventor, is a young Englishman, by name Thomas Cartwright[3], who, they say, is now sojourning at Heidelberg. He

[1 Rodolph Gualter. See p. 307.]
[2 See p. 296.]
[3 Thomas Cartwright was sometime fellow of St John's, and afterwards of Trinity, Cambridge: he was deprived of his fellowship for not taking orders according to the statutes. His controversy with Whitgift has before been alluded to. See note 1, p. 297, and Soames's Elizabethan

has lately written from thence⁴ a treatise in Latin, in defence of this new discipline which he wishes to obtrude upon us. I have not yet seen the book, but I hear that it is printed, and has been brought over to us. As soon as it shall come into my hands, I will take care it shall be sent you. Respecting other matters which are agitated here, your son will give you information. He is preparing for his journey, and I for the public affairs of the church, with which I am overwhelmed.

The first piece of cloth that I sent you was taken by pirates: I sent you another, which the merchant tells me that you have received. It is well if it is so. Farewell, most esteemed sir, and continue to love me as you do. In haste. Fulham in England, Aug. 9, 1574.

Your brother and friend in Christ,

EDWIN SANDYS,

bishop of London.

History, p. 141, where his character is drawn at length. Beza, in a letter to one of his English correspondents, thus expressed himself concerning Cartwright: "Here is now with us your countryman, Thomas Cartwright, than whom I think the sun does not see a more learned man."]

[⁴ Soames gives the following extract from a letter from Wilcox to Gilby, dated Feb. 2, 1574. "Our brother Cartwright is escaped, (God be praised!) and departed this land, since my coming up to London, and I hope, is by this time at Heidelberg." A warrant had been issued for his apprehension, to be attributed probably, Mr Soames thinks, to the fear of assassination engendered in Elizabeth and her advisers, by the fatal ebullition of insanity then lately manifested by Peter Birchet, in the murder of a man whom he mistook for Sir Christopher Hatton. Among the signatures to this warrant, besides that of Sandys, are those of Nowell and Goodman, and nine others of the High Commission. See Soames's Elizabethan History, p. 198.]

LETTER CXXV.

BISHOP COX TO HENRY BULLINGER.
Dated at ELY, *Jan.* 25, 1575.

HEALTH in Christ. I confess myself, my very dear brother, greatly in your debt, for having so courteously addressed me by letter, although it was a short one. Your occasional illness is not to be wondered at, seeing old age itself is a kind of disease. Should you discontinue your literary exertions, I shall in the mean time content myself with what you have by the blessing of God written heretofore, to his glory and the edifying of his church. But may God bestow upon you sufficient strength for the performance of what you are piously proposing to accomplish! I rejoice exceedingly that harmony is restored among you. With ourselves, the faction is become in some measure less active through fear of punishment; for our government is apprehensive that danger may arise from frivolous and unnecessary innovations. And by the same fear do they keep within bounds the fury of the papists. We hear however, that in France the adherents of the pope are bringing matters to the last extremities. May the Lord Jesus vouchsafe to be present with his people! Oh that the Lord would bow the heavens and come down, and bridle the mouths of the papists, Turks, and schismatics! But our sins will not suffer him. God grant that we may all strive together for that unity to which, by numerous and solid arguments, you beautifully exhort all the clergy.

Salute my brethren in my name, as opportunity presents itself. I send a small testimony of my regard to be divided between yourself and Julius, and I commend myself to your prayers. May the great and good God preserve you and your most religious city!

From the Isle of Ely in England, Jan. 25, 1574, according to our computation.

Your most attached and very dear brother in Christ,

RICHARD,

bishop of Ely.

LETTER CXXVI.

BISHOP COX TO RODOLPH GUALTER.

Dated at ELY, [1575.]

HEALTH in Christ. On November 7th, A.D. 1574, I received your letter dated on the 26th of August of the same year, by which I learn your most correct judgment respecting those who are so tenacious of their own opinion as that they know not how to yield to truth, and are loth to depart from their preconceived notions. They complain that we treat them with severity, while in the mean time they attack us with the most bitter abuse, both in public and private; and every where calumniate us in their sermons and printed writings. They are replied to by our friends with sufficient moderation; and in the mean time our excellent queen, a sincere lover of truth and peace, attacks them with the authority of the law; by which they are somewhat terrified, and are gradually slipping away: except that from time to time they vomit forth the venom of strife in secret. I cannot but admit that we have been aided by your pious and learned writings, although our adversaries did not consider them of so much importance. I hope also that the treatise of that venerable old man, master Henry Bullinger, in which he invites and persuades the ministers of the churches to unity, will be of great benefit to this kingdom: I wish it might be so throughout all Germany. I am exceedingly grieved at the persecutions that have lately taken place in Saxony[1]: that Lutheran party is very cruel. May the Lord vouchsafe to aid those who are sincerely pleading his cause! Oh, the enemy of mankind, who, wherever the good seed is sown, ceases not to sow tares

[[1] This refers to the famous convocation of Thorgau summoned in 1574 by Augustus, Elector of Saxony; where, after a strict inquiry into the doctrines of those who, from their secret attachment to the sentiments of the Swiss divines, were called Crypto-Calvinists, he committed some of them to prison, sent others into banishment, and engaged a certain number, by the force of the secular arm, to change their sentiments. See Mosheim.]

among them! Meanwhile by the grace of God we must do our best, and leave the issue to the Lord our God. The Lord hitherto by his favour preserves us at peace. The papists are grumbling, and nursing I know not what monstrosity. But may God himself destroy the wicked, and long preserve you in safety to his church!

Commend me to God in your prayers. From the Isle of Ely in England.

Your very dear brother in Christ,

RICHARD COX,

bishop of Ely.

LETTER CXXVII.

BISHOP COX TO RODOLPH GUALTER.

Dated at ELY, *July* 31, 1575.

YOUR letter, most learned Gualter, and very dear brother in the Lord, dated March 8th, 1575, was delivered to me in the May of the same year, and read by me with much pleasure. For it is full of grateful acknowledgement, and speaks much more highly of me than I can admit with truth. I cannot think without admiration of divine providence, who at one time tries his people in the fire of affliction, at another affords them breathing time, and allows them the enjoyment of a most delightful calm. Although our sins deserve the severest punishment, we trust notwithstanding that our Lord Jesus Christ has his little flock, by whose piety and prayers the most righteous vengeance of God is wont to be turned aside and stopped. But most wretched is the condition of the hypocrites, whom the Lord in his most righteous judgment, on account of their overflowing wickedness, is wont to deliver into the hands of the destroyer; such as are at this time the Turk, the pope, and the furious band of schismatics. And this band indeed among us by their plausible doctrine easily allure the nobility into their net; while by their great noise and clamour they subvert the credulous minds of wretched persons, and especially those who are gaping, like hungry wolves and ravens, after the revenues of the cathedral churches, colleges, and bishops. Thus Satan employs every engine to overthrow the gospel. I am much grieved that that Saxon[1] is so much incensed against the godly. Nor do I less grieve for that afflicting intelligence which is brought us, that the most solid pillar of the church, master Henry Bullinger, is labouring under a most severe disease. May our gracious Lord have compassion on his church, and restore his Henry to his former health! But should it seem good to the divine mercy to place him in his heavenly tabernacle, the Father of our Lord Jesus Christ must be entreated to pour down the spirit of this second Elijah upon the many Elishas, who by the singular grace of God may now be sojourning in the most pious city of Zurich.

There have been lately removed from us by death, having obtained a better condition with Christ, Parkhurst[2], the bishop of Norwich, and Matthew Parker[3], archbishop of Canterbury and primate of all England, a man of an even and firm character, and a zealous defender of true religion. We must entreat the Lord that he may vouchsafe to send labourers not less suitable into his harvest, which is very abundant. May the Lord Jesus very long preserve you in safety to his church!

From the Isle of Ely in England. July 31, 1575.

Your very dear brother in Christ,

RICHARD,

bishop of Ely.

[1 See note 1, p. 315.]

[2 Parkhurst died about the 2nd of February, 1575. See Strype, Parker, II. 362. Like the other writers of these letters, he kept up his correspondence with the divines of Zurich to the end of his life.]

[3 Parker died May 17, 1575, having "closed a difficult, upright life, with all the foresight, firmness, and complacency, that marked a vigourous, equable and religious mind." See Soames's Elizabethan Hist. p. 205, where his character is given at length, and also as described by Hallam, Neal, Fuller, and others.]

LETTER CXXVIII.

BISHOP COX TO RODOLPH GUALTER.
[1576.]

Your last letter, most learned Rodolph, I received on the 13th of February. The preceding one however affected me much more forcibly, both with exceeding sorrow, and also with no common delight. My sorrow was excessive for the death of Henry Bullinger[1], whom, by his letters, and learned and pious writings, I had been acquainted with, and I may say, known intimately for many years, although he was never personally known to me. Who would not be made sorrowful by the loss of such and so great a man, and excellent a friend? not to mention that the whole christian church is disquieted with exceeding regret, that so bright a star is forbidden any longer to shine upon earth. John writes, that inauspicious stars fell down from heaven[2]; but we are persuaded that *our* star has ascended up into heaven, and is fixed in heaven, and as it shone on earth, so it now shines more brightly in heaven. As to what he was on earth, his pious reputation is not silent, his pious life proclaims, his most learned writings abundantly testify: and what he now is in heaven, God knows, the angels rejoice, and the souls of the godly exult. And this is no small consolation to those who regret the loss of such a man. Add also another circumstance, from which I have, with good reason, received comfort, namely, that the church of Zurich, on Bullinger's bidding it farewell, is nevertheless not without a pastor. For the most gracious Lord, who never forsakes his flock, has set in the place of Bullinger yourself, who possess no less zeal in feeding the flock, and no less courage in keeping off its enemies. Blessed are you, who have of your own inclination taken upon yourself this burden, that you may subserve the glory of God, and faithfully advance his religion.

[1 Bullinger departed this life on the 17th Sept. 1575.]
[2 Revel. viii. 10, 12.]

With respect to the disturbances and heresies of the churches, we know that there must needs be heresies that the elect may be proved; and that through much tribulation we must enter into the kingdom of God, and in patience possess our souls. It is certainly much to be lamented that the Saxon[3] is so furiously hostile. May God grant, some time or other, a holy reconciliation! We see no hope of peace in France. All things there are carried on in a tyrannical manner. The king has decreed, with his brother and his mother, to send all the protestants into banishment, or else to put them to death. It is not yet fully known what is doing in Flanders, except that our queen is busy in settling the disputes. Our *men of singularity* are quiet through fear of punishment, except that they are hatching I know not what mischief in secret. And those too, who pursue the cares and things of this world, give us much trouble; for they are striving by I know not what arts and stratagems, to take away from us our property[4], and reduce us to beggary, that they may bring us back to the condition of the primitive church and the poverty of the apostles. May God have mercy upon his afflicted church, and defend it from the wickedness of the world; and may he bless you all, who profess Jesus Christ!

I have sent you a small token of my regard, a part of which I wish you to bestow upon Julius Terentianus.

Your brother in Christ Jesus,
RICHARD COX,
[bishop] of Ely.

[3 The Elector of Saxony. See note 1, p. 315.]
[4 The bishop had been required not long before to alienate Ely House in Holborn to Christopher Hatton, the queen's vice-chamberlain; and Lord North also obtained letters from the queen to the bishop, dated in May, 1575, to part with the manor and lands of Somersham. For an account of these proceedings, and the bishop's behaviour in consequence, see Strype, Annals, II. i. 533, &c.]

LETTER CXXIX.

BISHOP HORN TO RODOLPH GUALTER.

Dated at WALTHAM, *Aug.* 10, 1576.

GRACE and peace in Christ! Although the frequent and almost daily conversation, my very dear friend in Christ, which I have with my friend Barlow respecting our brethren at Zurich, is exceedingly delightful to me and full of interest; yet my mind is not satisfied with that intercourse, gratifying as it is, nor can it rest without my conversing, at least by letter, with my friend Gualter, whom I dearly love, and through him with the other ministers of Zurich, who are so much esteemed by me. But my letter must be somewhat brief, because more abundant materials for writing do not at present occur to me.

We have here scarcely any news to write about. All things, (praised be God!) remain satisfactorily enough in the same state. But those contentious, or, if you choose, vainglorious, and certainly mischievous men, who by their ungovernable zeal for discord were retarding the free progress of the gospel among us, and drawing away the people, maddened by their follies, through every vain variety of opinion, or rather madness of error, into what they call *purity*, are now silenced, sculk about, and are become of no importance. But how much you, Gualter, and the rest of our brethren yonder, who did not agree with them, are yet indebted to them, you may easily perceive if you will turn to the forty-sixth page of a book which one of them wrote "Concerning the departure of the church of England from true discipline."

Other matters indeed now continue among us as they were at first established, and especially peace and godliness. The gospel is flourishing, and has very free course. The church is sound in other respects, except that she is yet struggling with that old disease, under which she has laboured even from her infancy: for she will not entirely recover from popery before the last coming of that great physician, Jesus Christ. The government is at peace. The queen is alive and in good health; and I pray God that she may continue to be so for many years, and that she may live for ever. The supreme assembly of all the states, which we call a parliament, was held at London at the beginning of spring; but our queen, after your Swiss fashion[1], will allow of no change, but is solely intent upon this object, to advance the truth of the gospel with full sails both at home and abroad. As she has always abominated popery from her infancy, so also will she never admit Lutheranism, which is a great disturber of christianity.

Scotland under her auspices continues stedfast in the pure profession of the gospel. The king is imbued with the best precepts of true piety. His mother is detained in safe custody with us, as heretofore. You know the posture of affairs in France: we expect a happy issue in those of Flanders; but we are in much doubt respecting both. Our friend Pilkington[2], the most vigilant bishop of Durham, died lately, and shortly before him my other half, my wife.

Salute, I pray you, from me all my Zurich brethren beloved in Christ, and especially masters Simler, Lavater, Haller, Rodolph Gualter the younger, and Henry Bullinger, now the elder. May the Lord Jesus Christ very long preserve you all safe for the edification of his church! Farewell. From my house at [Bishop's] Waltham, Aug. 10, 1576.

Your loving friend, and that of all the people of Zurich,

ROBERT WINTON.

LETTER CXXX[3].

BISHOP HORN TO [CERTAIN BRETHREN.]
Dated at [BISHOP'S] WALTHAM, *Jan.* 16, 1577.

GRACE and peace in Christ. I am truly sorry, my very dear brethren in Christ, that such unprofitable folly can be

[1 The bishop probably alludes to the rejection by the Swiss divines of Jacob Andreæ's Form of Concord.]

[2 Bishop Pilkington died Jan. 23, 1575-6.]

[3 There is a mystery about this letter, and it is difficult to conjecture how it came to be at Zurich. It seems evidently to allude to circumstances which came under the bishop's immediate cognizance.]

found in any person, as that when the enjoyment of a holy peace is within his power, he unhappily prefers to procure his individual quiet, as it would seem, by the discomfort of many; when in fact, while he is labouring to satisfy his own blind, rash, and impious cupidity, he does not so much inconvenience others, as he rushes headlong into the greatest danger himself. But we are not ignorant of Satan's devices: and how prompt is his wicked inclination to disturb the tranquillity of the church, how adapted is his wicked counsel to the most flagitious actions, how he has his ministers ready prepared to do his bidding with carefulness and cunning, there is no occasion for me to tell you; for who is such a novice in embracing the wholesome gospel of Christ as not to know it? You, my brethren, I am assured for certain, have learned from experience, I will not say by your own ill doing, but by the greatest inconvenience both of yourselves and the church, how many and what fearful deceivers Satan has heretofore raised up, and daily continues to do, that they may throw all things into confusion, and especially destroy the peace of the church. That outrageous beast is attacking the fold of Christ with all the ferocity in his power; that most malicious wolf is meditating the dispersion, yea, even the destruction, of the Lord's flock. The wretched sheep is dragged away by the cruel violence of the raging lion. What can you do? We must resist the beast with unflinching faith, by imploring in our continual prayers succour from the chief Shepherd, Jesus Christ; and when the machinations of the wolf are laid open and detected, he must be driven away by the staff of the shepherds and the barking of the dogs; the stupid herd must be snatched away from the claws of the lion, before they are torn in pieces by his teeth, and, if possible, brought back into the fold. In this respect, however, (as far as I can understand from your letter,) you have left nothing untried: you have exerted all your care and diligence in preserving that mischievous Bonamy[1]; and, which is the duty of

[[1] *Haud bonum Bonamy.* He was probably one who was falling into popery. In the county of Southampton, (says Strype, Ann. II. ii. 344,) washed on one side by the sea, (and so conveniently situate to let in priests from abroad,) were many of these papists, and so multiplied by revolting from religion, that the Bishop of Winchester, in whose diocese

the most faithful pastors, you have used your active endeavours in softening, restraining, repressing his insolence, pride, and obstinacy, by every means in your power. And as you cannot accomplish what you desire, you require me to help you. Doubt not, my brethren, but that you will have many helpers; and as for me, I profess myself most ready to afford my assistance in this matter, as far as I am able. I hope to bestow upon it such consideration as to make that false brother (if indeed he may be called a brother) feel what it is to provoke the chief Shepherd of souls, Jesus Christ, to despise the church of God, and to make a mockery of, yea, even to tread under foot, all godly discipline.

I have explained the nature of what I propose to our common friend and brother in Christ, and one greatly beloved by me, master Leighton[2], governor of the Isle. In fine, brethren, I entreat you to strive earnestly with me in your prayers to God for me. And for my part, I will not be unmindful of you, unless I am forgetful of myself. Salute, I pray you, from me all your fellow-labourers and the whole church. Farewell. From my house at [Bishop's] Waltham, Jan. 16, 1576 [1577].

Your very affectionate brother in Christ,

and fellow-minister,

ROBERT HORN, Winton.

it lies, near about this year [1580] sent intelligence thereof to the lord-treasurer and other lords of the council, in order to repress the boldness and waywardness of the recusants in that county. Even last Easter, (he said,) upon some secret pact purposely wrought, five hundred persons have refused to communicate, more than before did [refuse to do it.] In consequence of great clerical irregularities in the Isle of Wight, and *some other portions of Winchester diocese*, [of which the Isle of Guernsey also forms a part,] Archbishop Parker undertook, by the bishop's desire, in 1575, a metropolitical visitation, which was followed by general preparations for conformity. Soames's Elizabethan History, p. 203.]

[2 Sir Thomas Leighton appears to have been Governor of the island of Guernsey, from whence letters are dated from him to the earl of Leicester. See MSS. Cotton, Galba, D. I. 148, and II. 69.]

LETTER CXXXI.

LAURENCE HUMPHREY TO RODOLPH GUALTER.
Dated at Oxford, *Aug.* 11, 1573.

IMMANUEL. I recognise in your letter, most learned Gualter, express manifestations of your wonted kindness and discretion. For I regard it as a proof of the greatest kindness, united to peculiar condescension, that you were inclined to address one who had been so long silent, and almost ungrateful. But though I have written too seldom, you must not attribute it either to ingratitude or forgetfulness in me, who am frequently recalling to mind, and who, God permitting, will cherish in my memory as long as I live, the favours which you so often and so largely conferred on myself and on my brother exiles. But now that I am challenged to write, I will seize upon every occasion and opportunity [of doing so], and will never allow a messenger to go from hence to you without a little note from myself. For in truth I had rather seem unpolished and extemporaneous, than regardless and neglectful.

Your great anxiety respecting the progress of your Swiss friends, Ulmius[1] and his companion[2], is a mark of your prudence; for it is always better to cherish a prudent fear than a too sanguine hope: this however I can truly affirm, that each of them is both studying hard with us, and conducting himself with propriety; which assertion I have no doubt but that they will fully make good both to you and the senate. Since therefore I feel assured that the result will make this manifest to you, I cannot but recommend to you these young men of such excellent hope. I wrote to the bishop of Winchester, who has already contributed somewhat, and promises also that he will take charge of them from this time. Your intelligence of the death of P. M. and our other fathers, and of your son[3], formerly my pupil, is indeed most painful and

[1 He was the son of John ab Ulmis, who had been fellow of St John's, Oxford.]
[2 John Huldrich.] [3 See note 3, p. 289.]

distressing; on my own account, individually, who deservedly regarded and loved them; publickly, for the church's sake, for whom it is so grievous and lamentable to be continually losing everywhere so many of her brightest ornaments. You, however, most reverend father, are a host in yourself, and I therefore entreat you to continue to benefit the christian commonwealth by your learned and pious lucubrations; so that the meditations of your old age, like the song of the swan, may delight us again and again. How severe is this loss of our most excellent men, England has long known to her cost; nor can she, I think, ever forget, and certainly ought not to remember without grief, so many funeral piles of martyrs yet recent; so many deaths of our most excellent men, Jewel[4], Parkhurst[5], Pilkington[6], and others. But these are the signs preceding the end of the world, and the latest and most awful on which this our age has fallen. Satan is roaring like a lion, the world is going mad, antichrist is resorting to every extreme, that he may with wolf-like ferocity devour the sheep of Christ: the sea is full of pirates, the soil of Flanders is wet with the blood of Christians; in France, Guise is reported to rage in his new slaughter-house against the protestants. England, by the favour of God, is yet safe; but how can she be secure from human malignity? For it is greatly to be feared that the flames of our neighbour's house may reach us; the Tridentine fathers enforcing that bloody decree of theirs, and our daily sins deserving the execution of it.

The news is now reported in Flanders, that [duke] Casimir[7] is lingering still in Guelderland, and is laying siege to Deventer, and that he shortly intends to unite his forces with our troops; that the Austrian [Don John] is fortifying himself within the city, with ditches and trenches and walls; that on the first of August he sent forth his light troops against the English, French, and Scots; that there was sharp fighting on both sides from eight o'clock till five in the evening; that two hundred and fifty of our troops were slain, and eight hundred of

[4 See p. 260.]   [5 See p. 317.]
[6 Pilkington died Jan. 23, 1575-6.]
[7 Duke Casimir was the son of the Elector Palatine. He brought down an army of German horse and foot into the Netherlands, at the charge of Elizabeth. Camden's Eliz. p. 226.]

the enemy's; that our side bore away the victory; that Norris[1], an Englishman, had four horses killed under him, and then escaped, not without honour to himself and destruction to the Spaniards, whom they either routed or cut down. What will be the end of this war, God Almighty knows, to whom I commend again and again the universal church, as well as yours and mine in particular, and your studies, and all our fathers and brethren, namely, masters Lavater and Ulmius, and Christopher Froschover, and all Zurich, formerly the hospitable retreat of Englishmen. Farewell, my most illustrious friend. Master Cole is well, and is now in the country. Oxford, Aug. 11, 1578.

Your most respectful

LAURENCE HUMPHREY.

LETTER CXXXII.

LAURENCE HUMPHREY TO RODOLPH GUALTER.

Dated at OXFORD, *Dec.* 17, 1578.

HEALTH in Christ Jesus. It is partly from my private regard and kind feeling towards them, and partly from their merit and necessity, that I am induced to write somewhat to you at this time about the private affairs and situation of Rodolph Ulmius and John Huldrich. For I must candidly confess that there is not here for them that provision which you ask, and which I desire myself; because those very members of the university who ought to assist others, are themselves in want, and dependent upon the liberality of their friends. I wrote to the bishop of Winchester, who gave something to Rodolph; and likewise to the earl of Bedford, who has always paid that regard to my letters, and especially

[1 "John Norris, the lord Norris his second son, the general of the English, fighting stoutly, had three horses slain under him, and got great commendations in this battle for his martial valour." Camden's Eliz. p. 226.]

to yours, which it was right and proper he should do. He [Rodolph] has lately returned to us from Devonshire, where the earl is now residing, not indeed overburdened with money, but yet in some measure provided with it, and presented with a salary. I have placed both the young men in Broadgate Hall[2], as we call it, not far from Christchurch, where John's father was most liberally and kindly entertained in king Edward's time. Should I be able to afford any money, I will most willingly bestow it. But since charity is getting cold in this declining age of the world, and many of the French [protestants] are continually coming over to us with their families; and as our people imagine that the Swiss are travelling for their own pleasure out of mere curiosity, rather than that they are necessarily banished on account of religion; for this reason they have been supplied more sparingly and grudgingly than others. I therefore entreat you to aid them by your patronage, and earnestly to undertake their cause, so that care may be taken for the payment of their promised stipend as soon as possible. They appear amiable and studious; and though they are at present unknown to our people, on account of the absence of Rodolph, who has been staying with the earl, yet when they shall have become known, they will more and more recommend themselves, and conciliate the regard and good will of all.

We, as the saying is, are doing as we can. All things are settled at home: the pope attacks us, not with open hostility, but intrigue; with bulls, abusive pamphlets, and secret machinations. The French are quiet, nor is a single spark of war bursting forth: besides, in Flanders they are all extinguished, since John of Austria is at rest, or rather removed by the pestilence[3]. There is danger, however, of their

[2 Broadgate Hall is now merged in Pembroke College.]

[3 According to the most common opinion, says Moreri, he died of poison in his camp near Namur, Oct. 1, 1578. But Lord Burghley thus wrote to the earl of Shrewsbury, from Theobald's, October 8th. " By letters which I have received within this three hours at London, I am certainly advertised that Don John de Austria is dead of the plague." Strype, Annals, ii. ii. 159. Camden adds, that he died, " as some say, out of very grief, because he found himself neglected by the king his brother, after he had gaped first after the kingdom of Tunis, whereby Guleta or Goletta in Africa was lost, [being taken from the Spaniards in

quarrelling amongst themselves, and that, distracted by war or internal dissensions, they will run headlong against their own vitals; for what will not the dregs of faction effect? May the Lord Jesus restrain in his goodness the malignity of these latter times!

Garland Holland, an Oxford bookseller, salutes both you and master Christopher Froschover. Master Cole is now absent: master Westphaling[1] desires me to send his regards to Julius, as I do also for myself, wishing all of you every happiness. Master Lavater is, I hope, in good health. Continue to promote by your pious labours the cause of learning and religion, to the end that in this benighted age men, becoming by your means more and more enlightened, may behold the light of divine truth by the blessing of God, whom I pray again and again to preserve your piety, together with all your friends, and the church at Zurich, (formerly the hospitable abode of the English,) both to you and to ourselves. In haste. Oxford, December 17, 1578. Farewell, most learned sir.

Your most respectful

LAURENCE HUMPHREY.

LETTER CXXXIII.

BISHOP COX TO RODOLPH GUALTER.

Dated *Feb.* 28, 1579.

As I was delighted by your letter, and the book which was sent me after the last Frankfort fair, so I am much distressed, my Gualter, that some part of Germany is disturbed

1574 by Selim II.] and then after the kingdom of England; and had secretly entered into a confederacy with the Guises, without the privity of the French king and the Spaniard, for the defence of both crowns. Camden's Elizabeth, p. 227.]

[1 Herbert Westphaling was a canon of Christ Church, and afterwards Bishop of Hereford, Strype, Parker, II. 6; Whitgift, I. 466.]

by those mischievous dissensions, of which God is not the author, but that wicked one, who daringly employs his agents in involving great men in error, in disturbing the church, and instigating unto iniquity the enemies of godliness.

We have good hopes of [the archbishop of] Canterbury. Our queen, who is in general most benign, was somewhat[2] offended with him. She is herself chastising the papists and contentious in good earnest. She will have all things done with order and decency. She possesses learned, and prudent, and pious counsellors. The ministers of the word, however, are not yet admitted into that reverend assembly.

As to what you write concerning Ireland (in which country the Roman antichrist is so wont to make mischief,) should any disturbance arise, it will easily be repressed, either by our soldiers, who are always quartered there, or, should occasion require it, by a regular army. A short time since, however, the Earl of Essex, a man of the highest rank, and devotedly attached to our holy religion[3], and the most severe scourge of the Irish, was taken off by disease[4], to the great sorrow of many persons.

[2 Grindal was confined and sequestered in June, 1577, for his non-compliance with the queen's command with respect to the putting down the religious exercises and conferences of ministers, called prophesyings. See Strype, Grindal, 343. "The period expired without affecting his virtuous constancy, and subsequent severities kept him in disgrace and inactivity nearly to the end of his life." Soames's Elizabethan Hist. p. 227.]

[3 Sir Nicholas White gives the particulars of the death of the Earl of Essex in a letter to Lord Burghley, dated Sept. 30, 1576. He writes, among other things, that at the last yielding up of his breath, he cried, *Couradge, couradge, I am a soldier that must fight under the banner of my Saviour Christ.* See Strype, Annals, II. ii. 84.]

[4 The earl of Essex died Sept. 22, 1576, not without suspicion of being poisoned by means of the earl of Leicester. See Strype, Annals, II. i. 576, and ii. 83. "A very excellent man certainly he was, in whom honesty of carriage vied with the nobility of birth; both which notwithstanding could not prevail against envy. For after he was constrained to give over his laudable enterprise in Ireland, he returned into England, having much wasted his estate; where openly threatening Leicester, whom he suspected to have done him injuries, he was by his cunning court tricks, who stood in fear of him, and by a peculiar court mystery of wounding and overthrowing men by honours, sent back into Ireland with the insignificant title of Earl Marshal of Ireland, where pining

I am filled with joy, that God by his wonderful providence has delivered the people of Geneva from their enemies sent by Satan. This it is to trust in the Lord as a most strong tower; this it is to be anxiously concerned for the glory of God, and to lay down one's life for it. This faith and godly unity vanquishes and puts to flight even the most bitter enemies. "Behold, how good and how pleasant it is for brethren to dwell together in unity." Duke Casimir[1], a man of great fortitude and faith, is now with us, and he is here too not without a great hope of good. May the Lord Jesus protect you with your most pious flocks, both from popish enemies, and from those who went out from us, when yet they were not of us!

But I must not be altogether unmindful of my friend Julius. I send you five pounds of our money: take three parts for yourself, and let Julius have two from you. Feb. 28, 1579.

The attached friend of your piety, and most holy function,

RICHARD COX,

bishop of Ely.

---

away with grief and sorrow, he piously rendered his soul to Christ, dying of a bloody flux in the midst of grievous torments." Camden's Elizabeth, p. 217.]

[1 Duke Casimir was the son of Frederick, Elector Palatine of the Rhine, and came into England in the month of January, in a sharp and snowy winter, to excuse himself about the miscarriage of his expedition, laying the whole blame upon the French. He was most honourably received, and conducted with great pomp into London, with torches lighted, by the Lord Mayor, the aldermen and citizens, and to the court by the chief of the nobility; where he was entertained with tilting, barriers, and costly banquets, and honoured with the order of St George, the queen herself buckling on the garter about his leg. Camden's Elizabeth, p. 232. See also Strype, Annals, II. i. 160.]

LETTER CXXXIV.

ARCHBISHOP SANDYS TO RODOLPH GUALTER.

Dated at London, *Dec.* 9, 1579.

At one and almost the same moment, most learned and, on so many accounts, most honoured sir, I received two letters from you; and almost two years after they were sent, through a mistake, I suppose, in the address. For they were directed to the bishop of London, though three years have elapsed since my translation to the archbishoprick of York; so that your letters, seeking me in London, were later in reaching these northern parts of the kingdom. Now, however, as I am desirous of replying to your letters, these are the points more especially on which I wish you to be satisfied; that I keep in remembrance your regard for me, and that I still firmly remain your friend and faithful brother.

It does not escape my observation, that we are arrived at such a state of the times as is daily bringing forth some novelty or other: I should commit to paper such as are most fitting for you to be acquainted with, were it not that through the unhappiness of this age I have seen many things soberly written and piously conceived, partly from being lost, and partly from being intercepted, occasion very great danger to those who wrote them. That I may not, however, decline all information, accept the following. A treaty of marriage[2]

[2 The articles propounded on the part of the duke of Anjou, when he was here, in order to his marriage, to be granted by the queen and the lords of her council, with their answers to each article, are preserved in Strype, Annals II. ii. 631. See also p. 317, &c. for an account of the duke's departure, from which it appears that "such was her majesty's presence of mind, and care of her subjects' welfare, that she subdued her private affection for the public good." This is farther evident from her letter to Sir Edward Strafford in the following year, whom she had sent away to France, to observe the behaviour of the French towards the Low Countries, of which the sovereignty had been offered to the duke of Anjou, and which she wished him to decline. She writes therein, "My mortal foe can no ways wish me a greater

is now on foot between the queen's majesty and the brother of the king of France. What, however, will be the result, and what bearing it will have upon our affairs, scarce any one can tell. We pray God that he may deign to continue propitious to us. The purity of the christian religion is flourishing and prosperous among us, and can neither be overturned nor defiled by any devices of Satan. For although we are unable altogether to banish from the church, so as to prevent the appearance of a remarkable variety of names and opinions, those *new* men whom we call puritans, who tread all authority under foot; or the *veteran* papists, who celebrate their divine service in their secret corners; or the profane disputants, who deride the true worship of God; such, however, is the number and influence of the truly faithful, that both in numbers and appearance it very far takes the lead of all the separatists; and we entertain the best hope, that he who hath begun this good work in us will perfect it unto the day of the Lord Jesus. The archbishop of Canterbury, Edmund Grindal, who presided over the churches of London and York before me, not having acted altogether in compliance with the queen's wishes, is now confined[1] to his palace, from which he is not allowed to move: I hope, however, and believe that in a short time he will be fully restored to liberty. Dr Horn, the bishop of Winchester, has departed[2] this life; but no successor is yet appointed to that diocese.

Ireland[3] is in a state of disturbance, owing to the seditious tumults of the rebels. Generals however are assigned, and soldiers enlisted, to reduce them to obedience. The affairs of the protestants in Flanders are going on well; for the

losse than England's hate, neither should death be less welcome unto me than such mishap betide me." Queen Elizabeth and her Times, Vol. II. p. 151.]

[1 See note 2, p. 329.]

[2 Bishop Horn died in the month of June, 1579. His will was proved on the 27th of that month. Strype, Annals, II. ii. 378.]

[3 That land indeed was now oppressed with the popish nobility and gentry there, who had raised a rebellion against the queen, headed by the earl of Desmond, lord Baltinglas, with an invasion of Italians and Spaniards, accompanied with the pope's blessing. Strype, Annals, II. ii. 330. For a full account of this rebellion see Camden's Elizabeth, p. 256, &c.]

papist malcontents, who are plotting against both their lives and fortunes, have recently suffered a most severe loss, and are thought to be not far from the total loss of all their influence in those parts.

As a testimony and token of my regard for you, my very dear friend, I was exceedingly desirous of sending you some of our wares, if any merchant would be willing to export them. But as I could find no one bold enough to undertake the risk, (as these times are so surrounded with danger on all sides,) I hope that you will take in good part this lone and naked letter. And so, wishing you no less happiness than myself, now living in London, and waiting for the opening of parliament on the 20th of January, I desire for you and all your friends health in Christ. London, in England, December 9, 1579.

Your brother in Christ, and most loving friend,

EDWIN SANDYS, Ebor.

LETTER CXXXV.

QUEEN ELIZABETH TO THE THIRTEEN CANTONS OF SWITZERLAND[4].

Dated at GREENWICH, *July* 18, 1590.

ELIZABETH, by the grace of God, of England, France and Ireland, queen, defender of the faith, &c.; to the high and mighty lords, and right worthy masters, the consuls and proconsuls, rulers, syndics, authorities and governments of the thirteen cantons of the illustrious Swiss nation, greeting.

High and mighty lords, and right worthy sirs: As allies and neighbours, you cannot be ignorant of the aid and as-

[[4] This letter is interesting, as manifesting the desire of queen Elizabeth to cultivate a friendly relation with the Protestant churches on the continent. As for the confession of faith set forth by Bullinger and others for the churches of Helvetia, this, says Strype, our church did then heartily consent to, and own. Annals, I. ii. 229. See above, p. 169.]

sistance that is required by the distressed condition of your confederate city of Geneva, oppressed as it has now been for many years with an almost uninterrupted blockade by two most powerful enemies, the king of Spain, and the duke[1] of Savoy, his son-in-law. And we have no doubt but that your mightinesses, in accordance with the good faith of the treaties[2] mutually contracted between you, and for the honour of your nation, will have such regard to your common defence in this dispute, as not to allow that city to be abandoned and exposed to the licentiousness of upstart pretenders, as far as may be in your power to prevent it. To such a resolution, if it were necessary, we certainly should not fail to exhort you: but forasmuch as those who of their own accord are sufficiently intent upon the public welfare, have no need of any one to prompt them, we willingly abstain from that kind of address; only requesting your mightinesses, in conformity with the good-will and friendship which has so long subsisted between the kings of England our ancestors and your illustrious nation, not to be neglectful of your own individual security.

For it is meet that your mightinesses should consider, that in this beleaguerment of the Genevese, the beleaguerment of all and every of your own several states is the thing finally aimed at; and that in the fall of that city is involved the destruction of you all. You may take as a proof of this the plots and machinations which this same king has essayed against ourself and our dominions, as well as those which he is even now attempting against the very flourishing realm of France, together with his impotent lust of power, inasmuch as nothing either happens or can happen, but that it alloweth him no rest day nor night from taking up arms and forming offensive alliances throughout almost all parts of this our western world. Which alliances however he will in vain either establish amongst us or set in activity against us, if you, with souls united in conformity with the league of you aforetime mutually sworn to, will not brook the unripping and

[1 Charles Emanuel, duke of Savoy, married Catherine, daughter of Philip the Second.]

[2 In 1584, the republic of Geneva concluded a treaty with Zurich and Berne, by which it became allied to the Swiss cantons.]

undoing of your respective amities and coalitions. For in this alone consists both the most powerful safeguard of our enemies and redoubtableness of their arms, and also the strongest bulwark and impregnable fortress of every just defence. And forasmuch as this alone is the only key to so much power on either side; and as those who suffer themselves to be overcome by the lust of empire, exert their entire energies to this object; it is necessary for you to be on your guard, who have now for so many years, by the blessing of this union, been in the enjoyment of that liberty which your forefathers conquered for you by their valour, and which these haughty despots envy you beyond measure. If you would enjoy this in perpetuity, and transmit it as an inheritance to your posterity, rather than, like slaves, live in a bondage devoid of liberty, you must be on your guard against the first attack, and not think of listening for a moment to insidious and enticing promises, as bearing in mind that many more have been deceived and undone by the craftiness of the fox than have ever been conquered by force of arms. And rest assured, that the pretence of ancient treaties, the shew of long-continued friendship, the tender of good offices, may be held out as a guise; but that there are no enmities more dangerous and more destructive than those which are concealed under the pretence of friendship.

And although in all human estimation the city and territory of Geneva may be regarded as an object of not much value or importance, just as Corinth of old was by the Acheans, Chalcis by the Euboeans, and Demetrias by the Thessalians; yet as they were made the fetters of all Greece, so it is to be feared that the Genevese, when subjugated by the Spanish Savoyard, shall prove in like sort the fetters of your whole confederate nation. Compare only the nature of the country, the spirit and daring of the enemy, his very power unwieldy through its excess, with your own narrow resources; and judge whether it be credible, that he who envies the majesty of the French king, he who has for more than twenty years been fighting against the liberties of the Low-Countries, he who has a design against the sovereignty of France, and is parched up with thirsting after the crown of England, is it to be believed that he will ever rest as long as your own ancient rights, and laws, and liberty remain unsubverted? Which in proportion as it would be a more dreadful spectacle to yourselves, and a more painful one to us, we again and again advise and entreat you to be forearmed and on your guard, lest such an event should occur; so that, mutually congratulating yourselves on the preservation of your ancient dignity and independence, you may be a comfort to your friends, a protection to your neighbours, and an everlasting benefit to posterity. Ourself, though a woman, has taken the lead in this contest, preferring as we do to our own ease, dignity, kingly possessions, to whatever in short we hold or can hold most dear, the liberty of the neighbouring nations, and the preserving in their integrity the just rights and authority of others. We are placed and appointed of God for this very purpose, that as far as lieth in us we should do violence to none, but avert it from all, as being well aware, that he who, having the ability, useth it not for another's help, is as much to blame as though he were that other's destroyer.

But you of your prudence know these things right well; and of your friendly inclination, good will, and pious zeal towards each other, are sufficiently ready to succour the oppressed, as to make due provision for your own safety. Wherefore we forbear adding more, save only that, for the sake of the piety which you exhibit towards God and man, we commend to you and to your good faith the battered remnant of your severely besieged countrymen: and may the God of salvation evermore bless and prosper you!

Given at our court at Greenwich, the 18th of July, in the year of our Lord 1590, and in the thirty-second year of our reign.

ELIZABETH R.

Frater noster Ivan. Abelus, ante aliquot
menses, post tongos ex calculo cruciatus,
hanc vitam cum meliore commutavit. Edm. Grindallus
Episcop. Londinens.

Abiit regiopolis ex Arundel urg in Angliam
inniscitium et spes nos Matheor quae nos redire
jubit. E huic tamen Marsham profecti. Dr. Massa, lic
et, ius ad Glow f. tamen Glorusehig cohibent
Augusti 1551.

Ioannes Hopper
Glouestric Ecclesia Epus.

Si quid unquam erit in quo possim aut tibi
aut tuis esse voluptati, aut usui polliceor tibi non tantum
operam, studium, diligentiam, sed etiam animam, et corpus
meum Londini. 22. Maij. 1559.

F. Jacobus.

Senties me re ipsa non immemorem tui. Vale. Uxorem
tuam Frisii similiter et alios amicos tuos meo nomine salutabis.
Uxor mea vos omnes salutat. Raptim. Londini 21. Maij 1559.

Joannes Parkhurstus.

F. Bedford

R. maiestas nō aliud esse a verbo Dei, imo in
cōmodum Ecclesia fore putabat, si Imago sī Crucifixi vna cū
Maria et Joane, vt solet, in celebrioni Ecclesiæ loco ponerentur
vbi ab oib[us] populo facillimē cognoscerentur
Londini fuertātur Aprichis Ianno. 1580.

Edwinus Wigorn.
[signature]

Feci brevem Incens in Aulicos Anglie. Habemus Papistas, Anabaptistas, et Anusinos
sua gestitātes adversarios, et doctrina et pia retomor. (Otra hos et meos et
Suam et commoneasj vexillū nri quis idoneus? oh mi patre, et me rogā
prā incessantē.

Fr. Sazlon.

Rogo ut Sp̅r̅i̅m̅ Vignerij paulo fusius indicis
sua opinionem explicare; & vos, me id scitis, admoneŷe pro nos-
taro. Vides Lernua hydra est: sed caudas papulo.
Oxon. Febr. 9 a° 1505.

Laurent Humfredus.

mi chius suo accepisti ā in Anglia duxta misisti Salwan a Basilea
Ad D. Nicolas ep Anglia recepi.

Humfredus Anglus.

bonus Ihesus magnus Gregis sui custos vos et vniuersa sua Ecclesiam custodiat. In code Vale. Datū e Ferromiens castro. 16. catt. Augusti. 1565°.

Henricus. Epūs.

Henricus Suffolchig. epus

Saluta quaeso Charissimam uxorem tuā & m̃rem meam
& honestā illam matronā, quas nobis Angliā ministranit cū
eramus pariter in ōris lãdibus; et matre familiās n̄ra.
Deus et sĩn nobis ad ecclesiæ Christi ốtilitatē servet. vale
Geneuæ 17 Januarij.
                                    THOMAS LEUERUS

Sī plura ad tuam prudētiam, et pietatem, Nayopus
ĩ mea opa uti uis, parat̃ss. inuenies. Cõiugē[?] statueris
Anglutoz ad ṕidie calend. September. 1554. vale in Dn̄o plurĩm̃

                                    Jacobus Haddon

Rachel tua salutat tibi, proueratur et uxoribus Daniel adjunt(?) ex ig
Anglia gravis(?) ego uxorabs mutal gratiaug honestiss matronas
D. uxiji hacken〈〉 coniugi. Ego D. marshal meum uxoris precibus comendo.

ANNe Hoper

Ego Sigd〈...〉 nobis posui. tius vos fructuß hoc sarule itegs
in die fanm anne bale. 7. ap'lis.

Jaco. pilkitong /

Th. Leverus
Richardus Langhornus
Hub. Donnollus
Walter znob Kelley
Alb. Bardie
Thomas Crayton
Thomas a thy

David Lethedus
Joanes Halehus
Johames Wilfordus
Guihelmus Maistenus
Thomas Scotobay
Gregorius Railton
f. tournours
Edmundus Duttonus

Richardus elect̄ epus

APPENDIX.

LET.		PAGE
I.	Peter Martyr to Bishop Jewel. ....Zurich, Aug. 24, 1562	339
II.	Henry Bullinger to Bishop Horn...................Zurich, Nov. 3, 1565	341
III.	Henry Bullinger to Laurence Humphrey, &c....Zurich, May 1, 1566	345
IV.	Henry Bullinger to Bishop Horn, &c. ....Zurich, May 3, 1566	356
V.	Henry Bullinger, &c. to Bishop Grindal, &c....Zurich, Sept. 6, 1566	357
VI.	Hen. Bullinger, &c. to Laurence Humphrey, &c. Zurich, Sept. 10, 1566	360
VII.	Rodolph Gualter to Bishop Cox. ....Zurich, June 9, 1572	362

LETTER I[1].

PETER MARTYR TO BISHOP JEWEL.
Dated at ZURICH, *Aug.* 24, 1562.

By the favour of the bishop of London, most worthy prelate, and my ever honoured lord, was brought hither a copy of your Apology for the church of England, the which had not been seen before either by myself or any of our people. In your last letter indeed you rather gave an intimation of its intended appearance, than an express announcement of it. But so long was the journey hither, that it could not reach us till about the first of August; whereby you may figure to yourself how much loss we are continually sustaining on account of the distance of places. As for the Apology, it hath not only in all points and respects satisfied me, (by whom all your writings are so wonderfully well liked and approved,) but it appeared also to Bullinger, and his sons and sons-in-law, and also to Gualter and Wolfius, so wise, admirable, and eloquent, that they can make no end of commending it, and think that nothing in these days hath been set forth more perfectly. I exceedingly congratulate your talents upon this excellent fruit, the church upon this edifying of it, and England upon this honour; and beseech you to proceed in the same way you have entered. For though we have a good cause, yet in comparison of the number of our enemies there are but few who defend it; and they now seem so awakened, that by their goodness of style and crafty sophisms they much recommend themselves to the unlearned multitude. I speak of the Staphili[2], Hosii[3], and most other writers

[1 This letter was written by Peter Martyr less than three months before his death, which took place on Nov. 12, 1562. It is in reply to bishop Jewel's letter, given in p. 99, and is partly translated also in Strype, Parker, I. 197.]

[2 Frederic Staphilus was a native of Osnaburg, and professor of theology at Konigsberg. He joined the church of Rome in 1553, and was made a councillor of the empire, and of the duke of Bavaria. He died at Ingoldstadt in 1564.]

[3 Hosii. For an account of cardinal Hosius see above note 3, p. 113.]

of the same stamp, who are at this time shewing themselves strenuous patrons of the pope's lies. Wherefore, since you have excited so great expectations of yourself in your most learned and elegant Apology, know for certain, that all good and learned men are assuring themselves that, while you are alive, the truth of the gospel will not be attacked by its enemies with impunity. And I rejoice most exceedingly, that I have seen the day in which you are made the parent of so noble and elegant an offspring. May God our heavenly Father grant of his goodness, that you may often be honoured with the like fruit!

As to other things that you are doing yonder, I am as ignorant as a Parthian or Indian is of the affairs of Germany. But I persuade myself that your affairs are in a flourishing, or at least in a tolerable condition, because we know from experience, that there is no messenger more swift than he who brings tidings of the afflictions, calamities, and death of our friends; while their happiness, joy, and prosperous condition is very much and for a long time kept from us. But however it be, we ought mutually to hope the best one of another, since it is most certain that God is continually and every where present, and this too after a gracious manner, unto those that be his, of which number are we.

But as touching myself, if you desire to know more particularly how I do, understand that I am of a cheerful mind in Christ, and that I am occupied in the same labours in which I was engaged when you were here; but in body I am not so strong and lusty as I was heretofore. For the burden of old age daily becomes more heavy. Now, for the space of a year and a half, I have been altogether toothless, neither hath my stomach performed its office of exciting me to eat with an appetite. I am troubled also with rheum; in addition to which I have no small pain in my legs, by reason of two sores wherewith I am at times greatly tormented. Wherein though the body properly and by itself be afflicted, yet by reason of that connection between them which the Greeks call *sympathy*, the mind also cannot choose but be affected.

These things, which I am sure for the good will you bear me you will be sorry to hear, I would by no means have inserted in this letter, had I not very great need of your prayers, which I have persuaded myself I shall obtain to be more earnest, because of the necessity wherewith I am urged.

Respecting the French affairs I write nothing, as I feel assured that they are no less known to you than to myself. The Tridentine synod is feigning to make progress; but it advances so slowly, that in these five sessions it hath decided nothing to the purpose. Its definitions are old and mouldy, so that they seem not to act the part of fathers, but of beetles, who are always turning over the self-same ordure of traditions.

Farewell, most accomplished prelate, and more than the half of my own soul. May God very long preserve, keep, and increase you with every good, both for the church and commonwealth! All friends and learned men salute you. Zurich, August 24, 1562.

Lavater hath published his Commentary on the book of Proverbs.

LETTER II.

HENRY BULLINGER TO BISHOP HORN[1].

Dated at ZURICH, *Nov.* 3, 1565.

WHAT you write, reverend father in Christ, touching the controversy which has arisen among you concerning the vestments of the clergy, I had previously learned from the letter of our common friend, John Abel, to which I have lately replied. It grieved me exceedingly, as it still continues to do, that this occasion is afforded to our adversaries by the mutual dissensions of those among you who preach the purer doctrine of the truth. As however I am most probably unacquainted with all the circumstances, I hesitate to pronounce any opinion upon the subject. But, that I may not seem wanting in my duty, when required by yourself and other friends to declare my sentiments, I will here repeat what I have lately stated in my letter to Abel.

[1 See above, p. 143. The original Latin is printed in Burnet's Hist. of the Reformation. Records, Book VI. No. 76.]

I approve the zeal of those persons who would have the church purged from all the dregs of popery; for I am aware of that passage of the prophet, where God warns us to put away [her] whoredoms out of [her] sight, and [her adulteries] from [between her] breasts. [Hos. ii. 2.] On the other hand, I also commend your prudence, who do not think that churches are to be forsaken because of the vestments [of the clergy]. For since the great end of the ministry is the edification and preservation of the church, we have need of great circumspection, lest we should depart from this, even while we are defending a cause, which in itself is good and holy. Nor are we only to consider what is *now* the state of that church which we think of forsaking, but also what it will be when we have left it. If it be certain that it will improve, we are at liberty to depart; but if, on the contrary, it will suffer loss, we are not to give place to wicked and treacherous workmen. But, as far as I can form an opinion, your common adversaries are only aiming at this, that on your removal they may put in your places either papists, or else Lutheran doctors and presidents, who are not very much unlike them. Should this come to pass, not only will all ecclesiastical order be disturbed, and the number of most absurd ceremonies be increased, but even images (which we know are defended by the Lutherans) will be restored; the artolatry[1] in the Lord's supper will be reintroduced; private absolution, and after this, auricular confession will creep in by degrees; and an infinite number of other evils will arise, which will both occasion confusion in general, and also bring into danger many godly individuals. For I doubt not but that you have met with so much success in your ministry, as that you have very many throughout the whole kingdom, both nobility, citizens, husbandmen, men, in short, of every rank and class in society, who are most favourably disposed to religion, and who abhor all doctrine that may open the door to superstition and idolatry; and who would feel it intolerable that a tyranny should again be set up in the church, to burden the consciences of the unhappy people. These, if you depart from the helm of the church, will most assuredly be subjected to the rage of their adversaries, who will establish examinations and inquisitions against them, as

[¹ Or worshipping of the bread.]

well public as private; will accuse them of heresy and sedition, and through them will render the whole cause of religion suspected and hateful, both to her most serene majesty, and all the nobility of the realm. We must therefore carefully guard against their wicked artifices, lest we should yield to them of our own accord what they have now for many years endeavoured to obtain with much labour and diligence.

But if any one should ask me whether I approve of those who first enacted, or are now zealous maintainers of, those laws by which the dregs of popery are retained, I candidly and freely answer that I do not approve of them. For they are either acting too imprudently, if they are on our side; or else they are treacherously laying snares for the liberty of the churches. But although they have obtruded upon you these dregs, as if they were necessary for the worship of God, for a safe conscience, and the salvation of the soul, I should think that every thing ought rather to be submitted to, than that you should suffer a godly people to be led away by them from a pure profession of faith. And since it is expressly provided, as you write me word, in that proclamation, that the square caps and surplices are to be retained without any superstitious conceit, I think that sufficient consideration has, at the same time, been shewn to your consciences. For you are at liberty, if I am not mistaken, to assign a reason for what you do, to remove any opinion of superstition from every one's mind, and to make a protest that may take away all ground of offence. In the meanwhile, let the most serene queen and the illustrious nobles of the realm be instructed, urged and pressed, no longer to stain and defile a reformation, effected with so much praise and with the admiration of the whole world, with dregs and filthiness of this kind, nor to give occasion to the neighbouring churches of Scotland and France for any suspicion of disunion.

I am aware that many questions are raised by some parties respecting the authority of kings and magistrates, whether they ought to make any laws for the church, and whether the clergy are bound to obey such laws. But I do not consider these inquiries of so much consequence in the present case, since, as I have above stated, all conceit of superstition is removed by the words of the proclamation itself. And we must take care, lest, by raising questions before the people respecting the extent of magisterial authority, we should give occasion to some disorders. These things, however, ought to be lawfully discussed in the public assembly of the realm; and those, who from their situation have it in their power to remind the queen and the nobles of their duty in private, ought by no means to be wanting in their endeavours.

I have now stated, reverend father in Christ, what I had to write at this present time, because you were desirous of hearing my sentiments on the question before us. I would by no means burden any man's conscience; but nevertheless I think that we ought to beware, lest, while we are consulting our own feelings and reputation as individuals, we should bring the church at large into some grievous peril. And I do not think this opinion of mine is at variance with the mind of Paul, who was wont to *become all things to all men, that he might gain some;* and who thought good to circumcise Timothy, lest he should alienate the Jews of that place from the christian religion, and that he might exercise his ministry with greater advantage; but who, on other occasions, thought it not fit to yield in the least to those who placed any merit in circumcision itself. But as many as have made the edification of the church the scope and end of their designs and actions, have not erred in controversies of this kind.

I have nothing to write about our own affairs. The Lord so regarded us during the pestilence of the last year, that we did not lose a single minister.[1] One or two died in the country. The plague, indeed, now seems to be skirmishing in some degree in our city, but is not likely to be violent. We are in the Lord's hands; let his will be done. On the 20th of November there will be a congress of the princes electors at Worms, in which a consultation will be had concerning the restoration of peace in Germany, and some points of great importance will be discussed respecting the bishops and their reformation. May the great and good God direct by his Spirit the minds and counsels of all parties to his glory and the safety of the church! My wife desires her most respectful salutations to the honourable lady, your wife. Farewell, reverend father in Christ. Zurich, Nov. 3, 1565.

[1 See above, p. 143.]

LETTER III.

HENRY BULLINGER TO LAURENCE HUMPHREY AND THOMAS SAMPSON.

Dated at ZURICH, *May* 1, 1566.

MAY the Lord Jesus bless you, most accomplished sirs, and very dear brethren, and preserve you from all evil!

I have received your letters[2], from which I learn, Laurence, that you complain that my reply to your question appears too concise. But, my brother, I neither perceived at that time, nor do I now perceive, the necessity of writing more copiously. For you only inquired what was my opinion with respect to the vestiarian controversy now agitated in England. To this question I thought it best to give you a short answer; for I could express my sentiments in few words. Besides, I was aware that master Peter Martyr, of blessed memory, had both here and at Oxford frequently and fully handled the same question, and I had nothing to add to his remarks. But I remember, that in my letter addressed to you, my brother Sampson, I also gave a statement of my own opinion. And to repeat my sentiments in few words, I could never approve of your officiating, if so commanded, at an altar laden, rather than adorned, with the image of him that was crucified, and in the appropriate dress of the mass, that is, in the alb and cope, on the back part of which also the same image is represented. But, as far as I can understand by a letter from England, there is now no dispute concerning habits of this kind; but the question is, whether it be lawful for the ministers of the gospel to wear a round or square cap, and a white garment which they call a surplice, by the wearing of which the minister may be distinguished from the people? And, whether it be a duty rather to relinquish the ministry, or sacred office, than to wear vestments of this kind? I replied to this question at the last fair, in a letter to the reverend master doctor Robert Horn, bishop of Winchester, and briefly repeated the words of master Martyr.

[2 See above, letters LXVIII. and LXIX, to both of which Bullinger replies in this letter.]

My colleague and very dear relative, master Rodolph Gualter, had written to the same person a short time before; a copy of which letter I send to yourself and our other brethren, inclosed in this. If, therefore, you are disposed to listen to us, and desire our opinion respecting the vestiarian controversy, as you signified to me in your last letter, behold! you possess our opinion in this epistle: in which if you are unable to acquiesce, we are indeed most exceedingly grieved; and since we have no other advice to offer, we heartily and continually pray the Lord, who is under all circumstances and at all times to be looked up to, that by his grace and power he may provide a remedy for this afflictive state of things.

Some questions, my brother Laurence, have been proposed by yourself, but our brother Sampson has framed a greater number upon the same subject. But although in my homely simplicity I could never approve of the subject being divided into so many questions, and entangled in such complicated knots, which otherwise, simple in itself, might be stated with sufficient perspicuity in few words; yet I will remark somewhat upon each question, that in this matter also I may be of service to you, my honoured masters and very dear brethren, as far as my lack of utterance, and power of perception rather blunted than sharpened, will permit me. And I entreat you to receive with kindness these remarks from me, your brother, and who love you so much; and to judge respecting them with a mind calm and free from prejudice. I altogether abominate all controversy, and I implore nothing more suppliantly from the Lord, than that he may take away from the church those contentions which from the beginning, and at all times, have been most injurious to true piety, and torn the church, however peaceful and flourishing, in pieces.

1. To the question, *whether laws respecting habits ought to be prescribed to ecclesiastics, that they may be distinguished by them from the laity*, I reply, that there is an ambiguity in the word *ought*. For if it is taken as implying what is necessary and appertaining to salvation, I do not think that even the authors of the laws themselves intend such an interpretation. But if it is asserted, that for the sake of

decency, and comeliness of appearance, or dignity and order, some such regulation may be made, or some such thing be understood, as that which the apostle requires, namely, that a bishop or minister of the church should be κόσμιος, (I mean *decent* or orderly,) I do not see how he is to blame, who either adopts a habit of this sort himself, or who commands it to be worn by others.

2. *Whether the ceremonial worship of the Levitical priesthood is to be reintroduced into the church?* I reply, if a cap and habit not unbecoming a minister, and free from superstition, are commanded to be used by the clergy, no one can reasonably assert that Judaism is revived. Moreover, I will here repeat the answer that I see doctor Martyr made to this question, who, after having shewed that the sacraments of the old law had been abolished, and ought not to be reintroduced into the church of Christ, which has [those of] baptism and the Lord's supper, subjoined, "there were notwithstanding in the Levitical law some ordinances of such a character, as that they cannot properly be called sacraments; for they served unto decency and order, and a certain becomingness, which, as agreeable to the light of nature, and furthering some utility of ours, I judge, may not only be restored but retained. Who seeth not that the apostles for quietness sake, and for the better living together of believers, commanded the gentiles to abstain from things strangled and from blood? These things were beyond dispute legal and Levitical. Also, no man is ignorant that at this day tithes are instituted in many places for the support of ministers. It is most evident too, that psalms and hymns are sung in the holy assemblies, which nevertheless the Levites also practised. And, not to omit this, we have feast days in remembrance of our Lord's resurrection, and other things. Are all these things to be abolished because they are traces of the old law? You see then, that all the Levitical rites are not to be so abrogated, as that none of them may be lawfully retained." Thus far Peter Martyr[1].

[[1] The epistle from whence the above passage is quoted, is dated from Oxford, Nov. 4, 1550, and seems to have been written to Hooper, although in the author's own copy there is no name put thereto. See Martyr's Divine Epistles, at the end of his common places.]

3. *Whether is it allowable to have a habit in common with papists?* I answer, it is not yet proved that the pope introduced a distinction of habits into the church; so far from it, that it is clear that such distinction is long anterior to popery. Nor do I see why it should be unlawful to use, in common with papists, a vestment not superstitious, but pertaining to civil regulation and good order. If it were not allowable to have any thing in common with them, it would be necessary to desert all the churches, to decline the receipt of stipend, to abstain from baptism, and the reciting of the apostles' and the Nicene creed, and even to reject the Lord's prayer. But after all, you do not borrow any ceremonies from them; for the use of the habits was never set aside from the beginning of the reformation; and it is still retained, not by any popish enactment, but by virtue of the royal edict, as a matter of indifference and of civil order.

4. The use[1] therefore of a distinctive cap or habit in civil matters *savours neither of Judaism nor monachism;* for they affect to appear separated from civil life, and make a merit of their peculiar dress. Thus Eustathius, bishop of Sebastia[2], was condemned, not merely on account of his peculiar dress, but because he made religion to consist in that dress. The canons of the councils of Gangra, Laodicea, and the sixth synod are known. And if some of the people are led to believe that this savours of popery, Judaism, and monachism, let them be admonished and rightly instructed in these matters. And should any be disquieted by the importunate clamours of some individuals, lavishly poured forth upon this subject among the people, let those who act thus have a care, lest they should impose heavier burdens upon themselves, irritate the queen's majesty, and end by bringing many faithful ministers into dangers from which they will hardly escape.

5. To the question, *whether those persons who have till now enjoyed their liberty, can with a safe conscience, by the authority of a royal edict, involve in this bondage both themselves*

[1 For Humphrey's fourth question, to which this paragraph is an answer, see above, p. 152.]

[2 Du Pin states that the Eustathius whose errors were condemned at the council of Gangra, was a different person from the bishop of Sebastia. See above p. 159, note 2.]

and the church, I reply, that in my opinion great caution is to be observed lest this dispute, and clamour, and contention respecting the habits should be conducted with too much bitterness, and by this importunity a handle should be afforded to the queen's majesty to leave that no longer a matter of choice to those who have abused their liberty; but being irritated by these needless clamours, she may issue her orders, that either these habits must be adopted, or the ministry relinquished. It appears indeed most extraordinary to me, (if I may be allowed, most accomplished and very dear brethren, to speak my sentiments without offence,) that you can persuade yourselves that you cannot, with a safe conscience, subject yourselves and churches to vestiarian bondage; and that you do not rather consider, to what kind of bondage you will subject yourselves and churches, if you refuse to comply with a civil ordinance, which is a matter of indifference, and are perpetually contending in this troublesome way; because, by the relinquishment of your office, you will expose the churches to wolves, or at least to teachers who are far from competent, and who are not equally fitted with yourselves for the instruction of the people. And can you be said to have asserted the liberty of the churches, who minister occasion of oppressing the church with burdens even yet more grievous? Are you not aware of what is the object of many, in what manner they are affected towards the preaching of the gospel, of what character will be those who are to succeed you, and what is to be expected from them?

6. *Whether the dress of the clergy is a matter of indifference?* It certainly seems such, when it is a matter of *civil* ordinance, and has respect only to decency and order, in which things religious worship does not consist.

Thus, my most learned and dearly beloved brother, Laurence, have I thought fit briefly to reply to your letter. I now come also to the questions of our friend master Sampson, in the discussion of which I shall probably be yet more brief.

1. *Whether a peculiar habit, distinct from that of the laity, were ever assigned to the ministers of the church; and whether it ought now to be assigned to them in the reformed church?* I reply: that there was in the primitive church a habit peculiar to the priests, is manifest from the ecclesiastical

history of Theodoret, Book II. chap. 27, and of Socrates, Book VI. chap. 22[1]. And no one who has but cursorily considered the monuments of antiquity, can be ignorant that the ministers always wore the *pallium* upon sacred occasions; so that, as I have before intimated, the distinction of habits does not derive its origin from the pope. Eusebius truly bears witness from the most ancient writers, that the apostle John at Ephesus wore on his forehead a *petalum*[2], or pontifical plate [of gold]; and Pontius[3], the deacon, relates of the martyr Cyprian, that when he was about to present his neck to the executioner, he first gave him his *birrus*[4], and his *dalmatic*[5]

[1] The following is the story to which Bullinger refers. Sisinius, the Novatian bishop, going one day to visit Arsacius, bishop of Constantinople, one of the clergy asked him why he wore a garment which did not become a bishop? and, where it was written that a priest ought to be clothed in white? To whom he replied, You first shew me where it is written, that a bishop ought to be clothed in black? See Bingham's Antiquities, Book VI. ch. 4. §. 18.]

[2] The *petalum* was the name given to the thin plate of gold which the Jewish high priest wore on his forehead. See above, p. 160, note 1.]

[3] See above p. 160, note 2.]

[4] The *birrus*, says Mr Bingham, was not peculiar to bishops, nor yet to the clergy, and was no more than the common *tunica* or coat worn generally by Christians in Africa, as may appear from a canon of the council of Gangra, made against Eustathius the heretic and his followers, who condemned the common habit, the *birrus*, and brought in the use of a strange habit in its room. The canon runs in these words: Εἴ τις ἀνδρῶν διὰ νομιζομένην ἄσκησιν περιβολαίῳ χρῆται, καὶ ὡς ἂν ἐκ τούτου τὴν δικαιοσύνην ἔχων καταψηφίσοιτο τῶν μετ' εὐλαβείας τοὺς βήρους φορούντων, καὶ τῇ ἄλλῃ κοινῇ καὶ ἐν συνηθείᾳ οὔσῃ ἐσθῆτι κεχρημένων, ἀνάθεμα ἔστω. If any man uses the *pallium*, or cloke, upon the account of an ascetic life, and, as if there were some holiness in that, condemns those that with reverence use the *birrus* and other garments that are commonly worn, let him be anathema. Bingham, as above, §. 19. See above, p. 159, note 3.]

[5] There were two kinds of *tunica*, the dalmatica and collobium, the latter being a short coat without long sleeves; whereas the dalmatica was the *tunica manicata et talaris*, a long coat with sleeves down to the wrists. This was seldom in use among the Romans; for Lampridius notes it as a singular thing in the life of the emperor Commodus, that *dalmaticatus in publico processit*, he wore a dalmatica in public. This, Mr Bingham thinks, is a good argument to prove that the clergy of this age did not wear the dalmatica in public, since it was not then the common garment of the Romans. And he approves of the con-

to the deacon, and thus stood forth wearing only his linen garment. Besides, Chrysostom makes mention of the white garment of the clergy; and it is certain, that when Christians were converted from heathenism to the gospel and the church, they exchanged the *toga* for the *pallium*, on which account when they were ridiculed by unbelievers, Tertullian[6] composed his most learned treatise *de pallio*. I could produce many other instances of the same kind, did not these suffice. I should prefer indeed, that no difficulties had been thrown in the way of the clergy, and that they might have been at liberty to follow the practice of the apostles. But since the queen's majesty only enjoins the wearing a cap and surplice, which, as I have often repeated, she does not in any way make a matter of religion; and since the same things were in use among the ancients, when the affairs of the church were yet more prosperous than at present, and this too without superstition or any thing to find fault with; I could wish that pious ministers would not make the whole advancement of religion to depend upon this matter, as if it were all in all; but that they would yield somewhat to the present time, and not dispute offensively about a matter of indifference, but modestly conclude that these things may be endured at present, but that an improvement will take place in time. For those persons come the nearest to apostolic simplicity, who are unconscious of these distinctions, or who do not urge them, while yet they do not act without a proper regard to discipline in the mean time.

2, 3. *Whether the prescribing habits be consistent with christian liberty?* I answer, that matters of indifference admit sometimes of *prescription*, and therefore of being imposed by force, as far as their use, so to speak, though not their moral effect is concerned; so that, for instance, something which is in

jecture of bishop Fell, who thinks that in the passage from Pontius the deacon, (given above p. 160, note 2,) for the words *tunicam tulit*, some officious modern transcribers changed the word *tunicam* into *dalmaticam* (as Bullinger appears to have read it), as being more agreeable to the language and custom of their own time, when the dalmatica was reckoned among the sacred vestments of the church, though we never find it mentioned as such in any ancient author. Bingham, as above, §. 20.]

[6 See above, p. 160, note 4.]

its nature indifferent, may be obtruded upon the conscience as necessary, and thus made a matter of religion. In fact, the times and places of religious assemblies are assuredly regarded among things indifferent; and yet, if there is no *prescription* in such cases, consider, I pray, what confusion and disorder would ensue?

4. *Whether any new ceremonies may be superadded to what is expressly prescribed in the word of God?* I answer, that I by no means approve the addition of new ceremonies; but yet I am not prepared to deny that some may lawfully be instituted, provided the worship of God is not made to consist in them, and that they are appointed only for the sake of order and discipline. Christ himself observed the feast or ceremony of the dedication, though we do not read that this feast was prescribed in the law. On the whole, the greater part of the propositions or questions touching the vestiarian controversy turn upon this, whether laws concerning habits may or ought to be framed in the church? And it recalls the *general* question, namely, what regulations is it lawful to make concerning ceremonies? To these propositions I reply in few words, that though I would rather no ceremonies, excepting such as are necessary, should be obtruded upon the church, yet I must confess in the mean time that regulations respecting them, though possibly not altogether necessary, and sometimes, it may be, useless, ought not forthwith to be condemned as impious, and to excite disorder and schism in the church; seeing that they are not of a superstitious character, and also that in their very nature they are matters of indifference.

5, 6. *Whether it be lawful to revive the antiquated ceremonies of the Jews, and to transfer such as were especially dedicated to the religion of idolaters, to the use of the reformed churches?* I have before replied to this question, when I remarked touching the Levitical rites. But I should be loth that any idolatrous rites should be transferred to the reformed churches, without being purified from what is amiss in them. But it might also be demanded on the other hand, whether established ceremonies, void of superstition, may not be retained in the church without any impropriety, for the sake of discipline and order.

7. *Whether conformity must of necessity be required in ceremonies?* I reply, that conformity in ceremonies is perhaps not necessary in every church. Meantime however, if a thing is commanded, which, though not necessary, is on the other hand not sinful; the church, it seems to me, ought not on this account to be relinquished. There was not conformity in rites in all the more ancient churches; those, however, which adopted rites in conformity with each other, did not censure those who wanted such conformity[1]. And I can easily believe that wise and politic men are urgent for a conformity of rites, because they think it will tend to concord, and that there may be one and the same church throughout all England; wherein, provided nothing sinful is intermixed, I do not see why you should oppose yourselves with hostility to harmless regulations of that kind.

8. *Whether those ceremonies may be retained which occasion evident offence?* I answer, that we ought to avoid offence; but we must take care in the mean time, lest we cloke our own feelings under the pretext of offence. You are not ignorant that one thing is given, and another thing received; and that offence is readily taken. I am not now inquiring whether you can, without grievous offence, desert, for a thing in itself indifferent, those churches for which Christ died.

9. *Whether any constitutions may be tolerated in the church, which in their nature indeed are not impious, but do not, nevertheless, tend to edification?* I answer, that if those constitutions which the queen's majesty wishes to impose upon you, are free from any impiety, they are rather to be tolerated than that the churches should be deserted. For if the edifying of the church is the chief thing to be regarded in this matter, we shall do the church a greater injury by deserting it than by wearing the habits. And where there is no impiety, and the conscience is not wounded, it is proper to submit, even if some degree of bondage be imposed. In the mean time, however, it might be demanded on the other hand, whether the imposition of the habits, as far as it tends to

[[1] This statement may be compared with the 34th article of the church of England, as also with the preface to the Liturgy respecting ceremonies, why some be abolished and some retained.]

decency and order, may justly come under the denomination of bondage?

10. *Whether any thing of a ceremonial nature may be prescribed to the church by the sovereign, without the consent and free concurrence of the clergy?* I answer, if the consent of the clergy is always to be waited for by the sovereign, it is probable that those most wise and pious kings, Asa, Hezekiah, Jehoshaphat, and Josiah, and other godly princes, would never have brought into proper order the Levites and ministers of the churches. Though I would not altogether have the bishops excluded from the consultations of churchmen. But on the other hand, I would not have them assume to themselves that power, which they heretofore usurped over kings and magistrates in the time of popery. Nor again, would I have the bishops sanction by their silence the unjust ordinances of princes.

11, 12. The last two questions come more closely to the point. *Whether it is more expedient thus to obey the church, or on account of disobedience to be cast out of the ministry?* And, *whether good pastors may lawfully be removed from the ministry on account of their non-compliance with such ceremonies?* I answer, if in these ceremonies there is no superstition, no impiety, but yet they are imposed upon godly pastors, who would rather that they should not be imposed upon them; I will certainly allow, and that most fully, that a burden and bondage is imposed upon them; but I will not allow, and this for most just reasons, that their station or ministry is on that account to be deserted, and place given to wolves, as was before observed, or to ministers less qualified than themselves: especially, since there remains the liberty of preaching, and care may be taken that no greater bondage shall be imposed; with many other things of this kind, &c.

I have now stated what it seemed to me might be said upon the proposed questions, being well aware that others, in proportion to their erudition, might have discussed the subject with far greater elegance and effect; but since it was your wish that I myself should answer them, I have done what I could, leaving both a free pen and an unfettered opinion upon these matters to others. As to what remains, I wish not to force and entangle the conscience of any one by what I have written, but merely propose it for consideration; and I would have you beware, lest any one in this present controversy should conceal a contentious spirit under the name of conscience. And I also exhort you all, by Jesus Christ our Lord, the Saviour, head, and king of his church, that every one of you should duly consider with himself, whether he will not more edify the church of Christ by regarding the use of habits for the sake of order and decency, as a matter of indifference, and which hitherto has tended somewhat to the harmony and advantage of the church; than by leaving the church, on account of the vestiarian controversy, to be occupied hereafter, if not by evident wolves, at least by ill-qualified and evil ministers. May the Lord Jesus give you to see, to understand, and to follow what makes for his glory, and the peace and safety of the church!

Farewell in the Lord, together with all faithful ministers. We will earnestly pray the Lord for you, that you may both perceive and do what is holy and beneficial. Master Gualter salutes you most affectionately, and prays for you every happiness. We too, the other ministers, do the same. Zurich, May 1, 1566.

HENRY BULLINGER,

minister of the church of Zurich,

in his own name and that of GUALTER.

P. S. I would advise you, my dear Sampson, not to publish any thing of master Bibliander's; as the papers in your possession are mere collections from his hearers, and not written by Bibliander himself. For his executors are in possession of his commentaries, his manuscript notes on the Bible, or on the old Testament; and they would be very angry if any thing were to be published under his name, which he himself had not written. Meanwhile, I have to thank your kindness for acquainting me with these things. But your letter, written on the 16th of February, was only delivered to me on the 26th of April.

LETTER IV[1].

HENRY BULLINGER TO BISHOPS HORN, GRINDAL, AND PARKHURST.

Dated at ZURICH, *May* 3, 1566.

REVEREND sirs, right honourable lords, and very dear brethren. May the Lord Jesus bless you, and preserve you from all evil! We send our letter on the vestiarian controversy, written by us to the learned men, and our honoured godly brethren, N. and M. And we send it to you on this account, that ye may understand that we would not have any private communication with the brethren, without the knowledge of you, the principal ministers; and that in all things we seek the peace of your churches, according to our power. We pray also the Lord, that he may always direct your affairs, and preserve you in peace. We exhort you, reverend sirs, and very dear brethren, to have respect to faithful ministers and learned men. They have their own feelings; whence the apostle has instructed us to *bear one another's burdens.* Your authority can effect much with her most serene highness, the queen. Prevail upon her majesty to grant that these worthy brethren may be reconciled and restored.

We entreat likewise that you, master Horn, our honoured lord and very dear brother, to whom this letter will first be presented, will forthwith take care that it may be forwarded to the bishop of Norwich, and that you will communicate it to masters Jewel, Sandys, and Pilkington; to all of whom, God willing, I will write at the next Frankfort fair. I have written this in the greatest haste, both in my own name and that of Gualter, and we send the letter to Basle to be forwarded from thence to Antwerp. We earnestly entreat you to let us know whether you have received it. Farewell, reverend sirs, and may the Lord bless both you and your labours! Zurich, May 3, 1566.

Yours,

BULLINGER.

[1 The original of this letter is printed in Strype, Annals, I. ii. p. 515.]

We pray you, reverend master Horn, to communicate this letter also to the illustrious personage, Edmund Grindal, bishop of London, whom, although he is not personally known to us, as you are, we love, and desire to be loved by him in return. Again and again, farewell.

LETTER V.

HENRY BULLINGER AND RODOLPH GUALTER TO BISHOPS GRINDAL AND HORN[2].

Dated at ZURICH, *Sept.* 6, 1566.

REVEREND fathers in Christ, honoured masters, and very dear brethren. It has been made known to us by a report, confirmed too by the letters of some of our brethren which have been brought to us from other quarters, that the letter of ours, which we wrote privately to our honoured brethren masters Humphrey and Sampson, and which, for certain reasons explained in our letter written to you, we communicated to you, our masters and very dear brethren, has been printed and published; and that by means of it encouragement has been given to those parties who have already deprived many pious and learned ministers of the churches, not indeed on account of the vestiarian question, about which that letter was written, but on account of many other points controverted among you.

Respecting these points we entered into no discussion at all in that our letter, and yet we are reported to have defended and approved every one of them against those who have been dismissed. It was indeed our endeavour not to increase the flame that had sprung up among you, but to extinguish it; and neither to declare our approval or disapproval of articles respecting which we had no information. It would therefore be doing us a manifest injustice, if our letter should be so misconstrued as to make us seem to

[2 For the reply to this letter, see above, p. 175. The original is printed in Burnet, Vol. IV. p. 584.]

approve of those articles, about which, when we wrote upon the vestiarian controversy, we were altogether ignorant. The sum of our judgment was this, that churches redeemed by the blood of Christ ought on no account to be deserted for the sake of caps and gowns, which are to be regarded as mere matters of indifference, since they are enjoined to be used, not with a view to any religious observance, but merely as a matter of civil concern, for the maintenance of proper decency. But we have now heard, though we hope the report is false, that it is required of ministers either to subscribe to some new articles, or to relinquish their office. And the articles are said to be of this kind; that the measured chanting[1] in churches is to be retained, and in a foreign language, together with the sound of organs; and that in cases of necessity women may and ought to baptize infants in private houses: that the minister also ought to ask the infant presented for baptism the questions that were formerly proposed to the catechumens: that the ministers too, who perform the office of baptism, must use breathings, exorcisms, the sign of the cross, oil, spittle, clay, lighted tapers, and other things of this kind: that ministers are to teach, that in the receiving of the Lord's supper kneeling is necessary, (which has an appearance of adoration,) and that the bread is not to be broken in common, but that a small morsel is to be placed by the minister in the mouth of every communicant; and that the mode of spiritual feeding, and of the presence of the body of Christ in the holy supper, is not to be explained, but to be left undetermined. It is stated moreover, that as formerly all things were to be had at Rome for money, so now there are the same things for sale in the court of the metropolitan; namely, pluralities of livings, licences for non-residence, for eating meat on days forbidden and during Lent, and the like, for which no permission is granted without being paid for: that the wives too of the clergy are removed apart from their husbands, (as if the living together of man and wife were a thing impure,) just as was formerly the practice among the priests of antichrist. They say moreover, that no one is allowed to speak against

[[1] See above, p. 178.]

any of these things either in public or private; and what is more, that ministers, if they wish to continue the exercise of their ministry in the churches, are under the necessity of remaining silent under these grievances: so that all the power of church government or authority rests solely with the bishops, and no pastor is allowed to deliver his opinion in ecclesiastical affairs of this kind.

If these things are true, they will indeed occasion exceeding grief not only to us, but to all godly persons. And we pray the Lord to efface these blemishes from the holy church of Christ which is in England, and to prevent any of the bishops from dismissing from his office any pastor who shall refuse either his assent to, or approval of, articles of this kind. And although we entertain the most entire persuasion concerning your piety and sincerity, that, if any of these things are now in use, (for we can scarcely believe that things so gross exist among you,) you are only tolerating and conniving at them until the opportune assembling of the great council of the realm, when fit and prudent measures may be taken for the abolishing of superstition; and if there be any who pervert that letter of ours for the purpose of confirming any abuses, yet you yourselves are not of the number of such persons; nevertheless we exhort your reverences by the Lord Jesus, that, if the case be as it is reported, you will consult with your episcopal brethren and other holy and prudent men touching the amendment and purification of these and similar superstitions, and faithfully vindicate us from the injustice inflicted upon us by others. For we have never approved those articles, as they have been reported to us. We moreover entreat you of your courtesy to receive in a spirit of kindness these remarks of ours, who are not only most anxious for your concord and for the purity of religion in the realm of England, but also most affectionately attached to you in Christ.

May the Lord Jesus bless, and preserve you from all evil! Salute, we pray you, in our name, the other right reverend fathers in Christ, our honoured masters and very dear brethren, the bishops of England. Commend us, too, always to her most serene majesty, to whom we desire long life, a happy reign, a firm and quiet and secure kingdom, and all other things which godly persons can wish for her.

Dated at Zurich, September 6, 1566.

Your reverences' most attached
HENRY BULLINGER,
RODOLPH GUALTER,
pastors and ministers of the church
of Zurich.

LETTER VI.

HENRY BULLINGER AND RODOLPH GUALTER TO LAURENCE HUMPHREY AND THOMAS SAMPSON[1].

Dated at Zurich, *Sept.* 10, 1566.

That letter[2] of yours, our honoured masters, and very dear brethren, in which you reply to that of mine which was written concerning the vestiarian controversy, we have received and read. The sum of it is this, that you are not yet satisfied by our letter. We foresaw, brethren, that this would be the case; and therefore, if you remember, soon after the beginning of my letter, I premised these words[3]: "If, therefore, you are disposed to listen to us, and desire our opinion respecting the vestiarian controversy, as you signified to me in your last letter, behold! you possess our opinion in this epistle. In which if you are unable to acquiesce, we are indeed most exceedingly grieved; and since we have no other advice to offer, we heartily and continually pray the Lord, who is under all circumstances and at all times to be looked up to, that by his grace and power he may provide a remedy for this afflictive state of things." To these remarks we are neither able nor inclined to make any addition. We might indeed answer your objections, but we are unwilling to give occasion to contention by a renewed

[1 The original is printed in Burnet, Vol. IV. p. 583.]
[2 See above, p. 157.]   [3 See above, p. 346.]

and interminable discussion. When Martyr, of blessed memory, was still residing in England, he often wrote upon the subject; but so many other questions have been suggested, and repeated from time to time, that I perceive it impossible, by any thing that I can say or write, to satisfy your minds. When we were applied to by you, we recommended you, with all brotherly love, to adopt such a conduct as appeared to us, in the presence of the Lord, to be for the advantage of the church. We stated that it seemed to us of far greater importance that you should comply with these habits for a time, and remain with the sheep committed to your charge, than that you should leave them, and at the same time desert the churches. We went no farther than this; nor did we approve of any popish filthiness or superstition, respecting which indeed we did not enter into any discussion, as we were entirely unacquainted with the matters controverted among you, and touching which you now write word, that the dispute has assumed a character of great importance, and that the question is no longer merely about a cap or a surplice, but that you have most grievous cause of complaint.

Though indeed that letter of ours, written privately to you respecting the vestiarian controversy, has been published by some parties without our knowledge; yet we hope that godly and prudent men will neither in convocation, nor out of convocation, so distort our letter, as if we seemed now to approve and desire the restoration of things that every pious person, who is acquainted with our writings, has long known us to disapprove of. We recommend you, as did also master Martyr, both before us and in conjunction with us, to act as seemed to us both honourably and usefully in the present emergency. Since we have hitherto failed to convince you, we commit the whole matter to God, and entreat you not to regard us with unkindness, but as friends, as heretofore, continuing to love us who love you in the Lord, whom we heartily pray, that he, who is the faithful guardian of his church, may compose this unhappy dissension that has arisen among you, and restore tranquillity to his church. Remember, brethren, we pray you by the Lord Jesus, that it is not only required of the ministers of the churches that they hold fast the faithful word, but that they be at the same time wise stewards of the house of God, having respect to his family, and to the times, and that they must with charity and patience endure many things, cherish true concord in the Lord, and lastly, by every possible means preserve peace in the church; and not by their too great vehemence, unreasonableness, and caprice, desiring indeed what is good, but not with prudence, throw an obstacle in the way of religion, and those who profess it.

May the Lord Jesus bestow upon you his holy Spirit, and direct you in his ways! Brethren, farewell. Dated at Zurich, Sept. 10, 1566.

HENRY BULLINGER,
in his own name, and in that of
his friend GUALTER.

LETTER VII.

RODOLPH GUALTER TO BISHOP COX[1].

Dated at ZURICH, *June* 9, 1572.

HEALTH. I have received, reverend father in Christ, your letter, in which you reply to the one which, six years ago, namely, in the year 1566, I had written to my old friend, master Parkhurst. And as I displayed some degree of vehemence in writing, so do you also with no less warmth refute my assertions. But you must know that I am so far from being offended by your freedom, that I rather regard your admonition, or, if you choose, your reproof, in the light of the greatest benefit. For I learn from it that I am loved by one, whom I was before wont to venerate, (though personally unknown to me,) for the erudition and piety of which Peter Martyr, of blessed memory, has often borne witness to me, and of which I now behold an evident proof in your letter. For I know it is the office of piety, to defend the common-

[1 The original of this letter is printed in Strype, Parker, III. 193. For bishop Cox's reply, see above, p. 279.]

weal against any adversaries; but free admonition is an evidence of love, by which is laid open the error of a brother imposed upon by others, to the end that he may learn to entertain a more correct opinion. And since you have exhibited both these qualities with no less erudition than truth, I duly venerate your piety, and hope that the disagreement which had arisen between us, will prove the occasion of an indissoluble friendship. For I promise myself thus much from your courtesy, that you will readily pardon this my fault, when you consider at what time, from what motives, and to whom I wrote what I did. That time abounded in sore contentions, and letters on both sides were sent to us almost every day, while that unhappy controversy about the habits was agitated among you. We then advised your adversaries not to stir up a contention in the church for a matter of no importance, and we thought that the whole affair had been laid at rest. But lo! contrary to all expectation, two Englishmen[2] arrive at Geneva, bringing with them a letter from master Beza, whose ears they had filled with calumnies and false accusations, in which he entreated us to do our endeavour to help the most afflicted state of England, and further exhorted me to make a journey to you for that purpose.

To this was added the account of those two men, who told us the same story that they had done at Geneva, and that with so much assurance and affectation of piety, that they set down in writing a great many errors and superstitious abuses, which, as they asserted, were now maintained in England; and that all such as would not consent thereunto were cast out of their ministry. They added, that their most grievous cause of complaint was this, namely, that most of the bishops had become the willing executors of those things which were daily coined at court by superstitious and ambitious courtiers.

Who would suspect that any persons could be so barefaced, as to dare to lie with such assurance on matters of such

[[2] One of these Strype suspects to be George Withers, whom he elsewhere states to be a man of good learning, preacher at Bury St Edmund's. Life of Parker, I. 374. The other was probably Perceval Wiburn. See above, letter LXXVIII.]

notoriety, and the truth of which could not long be concealed? The account given by these men certainly troubled us not a little; and I acknowledge, that on the impulse of the moment I composed and sent that letter to master Parkhurst, with whom I thought myself at liberty to act more freely on account of our ancient friendship, which commenced five and thirty years ago at Oxford, and was afterwards so confirmed by his being entertained for four years at my house, that I desire him to possess all influence with me, and I can promise myself in return the same from him.

Nothing was further from my thoughts than that he would publish my letter abroad. For I rather desired to hear his opinion, though indeed he had never written any thing upon the subject. The thing which moved me not a little was, that shortly after master Abel, a most worthy man, and a friend of us both, wrote to me concerning this matter, and acquitted all of you from any blame. I was not therefore at all anxious about that letter of mine, which I had written solely to my friend Parkhurst, of whose regard for me I neither can nor ought to doubt. But as I am at length given to understand that it has been published far and wide, this certainly distresses me exceedingly. And I own, my reverend father, that I am deeply indebted to your excellence for having made me acquainted with this circumstance, though after so long an interval. And as you tell me that you entertain no doubt of the candour and sincerity of my mind, I reverently ask your kindness to make my excuse also to others, into whose hands that letter happened to come. Since that time we have certainly had nothing to do with those vain brawlers, who neither at any time wrote to us, nor had it in their power to boast of any letters from us.

For not long after it appeared more evidently what were their designs, when, under the pretence of ecclesiastical discipline, (the principal part whereof they make to consist in excommunication,) they were the chief authors of those changes in the Palatinate, which have inflicted such a blow upon the churches in that quarter. I once more, therefore, entreat your excellence, reverend father in Christ, not to have any sinister suspicion of Gualter, who bears a singular affection to the English name. For I will take care, if the Lord will, that a public testimony[1] shall appear of my opinion of all of you who are the servants of Christ in that kingdom. And indeed, unless I had truly persuaded myself of our agreement, I should certainly never have sent my son[2], the only son of my departed Zuinglia, the remembrance of whom is so precious to me, into England. Whom if you are surprised that I have not hitherto commended to your excellence, you must suppose that I have omitted to do so for no other reason, than that there has heretofore been no intercourse between us by letter; and I should be ashamed to trouble a person of your station, and known to me only by name, with a letter of business on my private affairs. The reports that are rife among us you will learn from master Sandys, the bishop of London: I am unable to repeat them in this letter on account of the haste of the bearer, whom I have met with contrary to my expectation. May Christ Jesus preserve your excellence, and guide you by his Spirit! Amen. Zurich, June 9, 1572.

Your excellence's most devoted,

RODOLPH GUALTER.

[1 The *public testimony* which Gualter here promised to set forth, was his Epistle before his Homilies on the first Epistle to the Corinthians, in which his argument ran chiefly of the unity of the church; wherein he shewed that none ought rashly to depart from its society for the vices of any that lived in it. Strype, Life of Parker, II. 112, 113. See above, p. 279.]

[2 See above, p. 263.]

INDEX.

A.

ABEL, John, 8, 25, 207; his death, 211, 232.
Ackworth, George, public orator at Cambridge, answers Saunders' book, 281 *note*.
Acontius, 9, 58, 78.
Admonition to the Parliament; a book circulated by the Puritans against the Church of England, 284 *n*, 297 *n*.
Alexander, Peter, 79 *n*, 119.
Allen, Edmund, designed for bishop of Rochester, 40; his death, 46.
Altars, removed from churches, 63.
Alva, John, duke of, puts to death Counts Egmont and Horn, 204; defeated at Groningen, 205; his cruelty, 208 *n*; arrests the English at Antwerp, 209 *n*; recalled, 275.
Ambassador, Spanish, ordered to quit England, 266.
Ammian, 30.
Andreas, James, professor at Tubingen, head of the *Ubiquitarians* in Germany, 302.
Anjou, Francis, duke of, a suitor to queen Elizabeth, 250, 331 *n*.
Anthonius, one of the ministers in the Dutch church at Norwich, 256.
Apology for the Church of England, 101 *n*, 121, 339.
Aquila, bishop of, Spanish ambassador, 102; instigated a conspiracy against queen Elizabeth, *ib. n.*
Arau, 22 *n*.
Argyle, earl of, 197 *n*, 205 *n*.
Argyle, countess of, at the christening of James I. 183 *n*.
Armuyden, laid waste by the Walloon troops, 273.
Arran, James Hamilton, third earl of, escapes from France, 56 *n*; a suitor of queen Elizabeth, 68 *n*.

Arras, Anthony Perrenot, bishop of, and cardinal of Granvelle, 139.
Articles drawn up by the separatists, 280, 295.
Arundel, Henry Fitzalan, earl of, one of queen Elizabeth's privy council, 5 *n*; one of her suitors, 34 *n*.
Assembly, general, of Scotland, its proceedings, 197, 198, &c.
Athanasius, 62.
Augustine, an observation of, 64; referred to, 179.
Augustus, elector of Saxony, summons the convocation at Thorgau, 315 *n*.
Austria, Charles, archduke of, brother of the emperor Maximilian, and suitor to queen Elizabeth, 144.
Austria, Don John of, his death, 327 *n*.
Aylmer, John, successively archdeacon of Stow and Lincoln, and bishop of London, one of the disputants at the Westminster conference, 11.

B.

Bacon, sir Nicholas, lord keeper of the great seal, 5 *n*; president at the Westminster conference, 16 *n*.
Baden, Cecilia, margravine of, sister to the king of Sweden, much delighted queen Elizabeth, 257 *n*.
Baine, Ralph, bishop of Lichfield and Coventry, 10 *n*; one on the papist side at the Westminster conference, *ib.*; his death, 69.
Baldwin, Francis, a celebrated professor of law, 118 *n*.
Balkius, Isbrand, concerned in a dispute in the strangers' church at Norwich, 256 *n*; banished in consequence, 266.
Baltinglas, lord, raises a rebellion in Ireland, 332 *n*.

Baptism by women, not allowed in the church of England, 178.
Barlow, William, 302, 320.
Barlow, William, bishop of Chichester, 23, 40, 63.
Barwyk, Humphrey, condemned for treason, 129 n.
Basil, St, 301 n.
Bath, earl of, one of queen Mary's privy council, 5 n.
Bavarian inquisition, articles of, 110 n, 278.
Beaufort, Mr. de, a name assumed by the earl of Arran, 57 n.
Beaumont, Robert, archdeacon of Huntingdon, and master of Trinity College, Cambridge, 137 n; his death, 194.
Beddingfield, sir Henry, one of queen Mary's council, 5 n.
Bedford, Francis Russel, second earl of, one of queen Elizabeth's council, 5 n; ambassador in Scotland, 183; patron of Gualter's son, 289.
Belisarius, 18 n.
Bentham, Thomas, minister of a congregation in London in queen Mary's time, 7; bishop of Lichfield and Coventry, 63.
Bernardine, see Ochinus, 22, 26, 40, 58, 64.
Beti, Fr. 9.
Betta, 305.
Beza, Theodore, 312.
Bibliander, Theodore, a minister at Zurich, 30, 155 n; his commentary on Genesis and Exodus, 155, 355.
Bill, William, afterwards master of St John's and Trinity colleges, and dean of Westminster, preacher at St Paul's cross on the queen's accession, 4 n.
Birchet, Peter, 313.
Birkman, Arnold, 70, 78.
Birrus, description of the, 350 n.
Bishop, Thomas, executed at York, 225 n.
Bishops, some lands of, exchanged for parsonages impropriate, 20; authority of, in the church of England, 179.
Blaarer, 130.
Black, a Dominican friar, 166.
Blondus, 160.
Bonamy, 322.
Bonner, Edmund, bishop of London, complaint of Ridley's executors against him, 7; confined as prisoner to his house, 7, 10 n; deprived of his see, 23; sent to prison, 79, 82.
Bothwell, James Hepburn, earl of, suspected of the murder of lord Darnley, 192; marries the queen of Scots, ib.; made duke of Orkney, 193; death of, 195 n.
Bothwell, Adam, bishop of Orkney, 192.
Bowes, Richard, one of the royal visitors for the north, 73 n.
Boxal, John, dean of Peterborough, Norwich, and Windsor, one of queen Mary's council, 5 n; his death, 255.
Brentius, John, the patron of Ubiquitarianism, 108 n, 121; testament of, answered by Bullinger, 241, 243, 258.
Brill, the, taken by the lord of Lumey, 273.
Broadgate hall, now Pembroke college, 327 n.
Brooks, James, bishop of Gloucester, death of, 12; account of, ib. n.
Brown, sir John, one of queen Mary's council, 5 n.
Brown, George, one of the royal visitors for the north, 73 n.
Bruerne, Richard, deprived of his professorship, 12; provost of Eton, ib. n; has Peter Martyr's prebend, 66.
Bucer, Martin, his opinion respecting the habits, 161; and the book of common prayer, 234 n.
Buchanan, George, writes verses in praise of queen Elizabeth, 115; saying of the queen respecting him, 240 n; writes on behalf of the queen of Scots, 263.
Bull, of Pope Pius V, deposing queen Elizabeth, 221, 229; answered by Bullinger, 244; and Jewel, ib. n.
Bullinger, Henry, his treatise on two natures in Christ, 30; against the anabaptists, 87; his dispute with Brentius, 98 n; his sermons on the Apocalypse translated, 99; his discourses on Daniel, 144; his treatise on the Origin of error, 182; and on councils, 215; his homilies on the 130th and 133d psalms, 303; attacked by the plague, 142; last illness, 317;

his death, 318; eulogy on, 318; his decades ordered by convocation to be studied by the clergy, 308 n; children of, 30 n, 142 n, 171 n; letters of, 341, 345, 356, 357, 360.
Bullinger, Dorothea, 304, 305.
Bullinger, Henry, the younger, 105.
Bullinger, Rodolph, 29.
Burcher, John, 49, 70, 90, 105; divorced from his wife, 93.
Burghley, lord, see Cecil.
Butler, Henry, 244, 258, 263; patronised by bishop Parkhurst, 242.

C.

Caius, John, master and a founder of Caius college, some account of, 31 n.
Calais, restitution of, demanded, 24, 91 n.
Calvin, John, 119, 127 n.
Cartwright, Thomas, his admonition to the parliament, 297 n; escapes to Heidelberg, 312, 313 n; character of, 312 n.
Carrick, earl of, 183 n.
Carvil, Nicholas, death of, 194.
Cashel, archbishop of, retires to the continent, 309 n.
Casimir, John, duke, besieges Deventer, 325; visits England, 330 n.
Cassander, George, 118 n.
Cassilis, earl of, 205 n.
Cathedral churches, state of, 45.
Cave, sir Ambrose, one of queen Elizabeth's privy council, 5 n.
Cawood, a residence belonging to the see of York, 259 n.
Cecil, sir William, secretary of state, 5 n; favours the reformation, 55.
Cecilia, margravine of Baden, 257 n.
Chalcis, 335.
Chambers, Richard, 65, 141; notice of his death, 148.
Charlemagne, convokes a council at Frankfort, 156 n.
Charles Emanuel, duke of Savoy, 334 n.
Charles IX, king of France, 273.
Charles, archduke of Austria, suitor to queen Elizabeth, 24, 34, 46, 192.
Chatelherault, duke of, 197 n.
Châtillon, cardinal de, 209 n.
Chedsey, William, one of the disputants at the Westminster conference, 11 n.
Cheney, Richard, bishop of Gloucester, entertained Luther's opinions respecting the eucharist, 186.
Cheney, sir Thomas, one of queen Elizabeth's privy council, 5 n.
Christopherson, John, bishop of Chichester, preaches at Paul's cross, 4; committed to prison, 4; his death, 6.
Chrysostom, 160.
Clerk, Bartholomew, afterwards dean of the Arches, answered Sanders's book, *de visibili monarchiâ*, 281 n.
Cleve, the rectory of, held by Parkhurst, 48.
Clinton, Edward, lord, one of queen Elizabeth's privy council, 5 n; commands troops against the rebels in the north, 247 n.
Clough, sir Richard, his account of Embden, 140 n.
Coinage, base, called in by queen Elizabeth, 93.
Cole, Henry, warden of New college, and dean of St Paul's, a disputant at Westminster, 11, 14, 27.
Cole, Thomas, archdeacon of Essex and Colchester, death of, 256.
Cole, William, 256 n; death of, 242.
Coler, 30.
Coligni, Gasper, admiral of France, besieges Caen, 124; murdered in the massacre of Paris, 291.
Coligni, Odet de, archbishop of Toulouse, poisoned at Canterbury, 250.
Collin, 30.
Common prayer book established by act of parliament, 29, 84; Bucer's opinion respecting it, 234 n; puritan exceptions against, 283.
Compagni, Bartholomew, (factor to Edward VI.), 40, 58.
Condé, prince of, queen Elizabeth made a contract with him, 115 n.
Conders, Frederick, 273.
Confederate Scots lords, 193 n, 197 n; standard of, 195.
Confession of Helvetia, 304 n; eulogised by Bossuet, 169 n.
Cook, sir Antony, 5, 8, 21, 53, 59.
Copes, retained in churches, 74.
Cordell, sir William, one of queen Mary's privy council, 5 n.

24

370 INDEX.

Corinth, 335.
Cornicius, James, 23.
Cornwallis, sir Thomas, one of queen Mary's privy council, 5 n.
Corrichie, battle of, 129 n.
Cosyn, Edward, condemned for treason, 129 n.
Council of Frankfort, 156 n; in Trullo, 179 n.
Court of faculties, 164, 180.
Coventry, martyrs at, 86; queen of Scots removed to, 217.
Coverdale, Miles, bishop of Exeter, 131.
Cox, Richard, concerned in the disputation at Westminster, 11; designed for the bishoprick of Norwich, 23; bishop of Ely, 40, 63; objects to the crucifix in the queen's chapel, 66 n; writes to the queen upon this subject, ib.; one of the compilers of the liturgy, 234 n; required to surrender some property belonging to his see, 319 n; letters of, 26, 65, 112, 207, 220, 234, 243, 268, 279, 282, 284, 297, 306, 307, 314, 315, 316.
Cranmer, archbishop, 12.
Cranmer, (probably Thomas, son of the archbishop), 8.
Crawford, earl of, arms in defence of the queen of Scots, 205 n.
Crito, an assumed name of the earl of Arran, 56, 59, &c.
Crofts, sir James, one of the royal visitors for the north, 73 n.
Cross, sign of, used in the primitive church, 180.
Crucifix, retained in the queen's chapel, 55, 63, 129.
Crypto-calvinists, 315 n.
Cyprian, 160.
Cyprus, invaded by the Turks, 239 n.

D.

Dalmatic, the, a kind of dress, description of, 350 n.
Darnley, Henry Stewart, lord, 102 n; marries the queen of Scots, 144; attends mass, 150; murder of, 186, 196.
Daus, John, translates Bullinger's sermons on the Apocalypse, 99.

Demetrias, 335.
Denny, sir Henry, 230.
Derby, Henry Stanley, earl of, one of queen Elizabeth's privy council, 5 n; one of the commissioners for the north, 73 n.
Desmond, earl of, raises a rebellion in Ireland, 332 n.
Deventer, besieged by duke Casimir, 325.
Digby, Simon, executed at York, 225 n.
Disputation at Westminster, between eight papists and eight protestants, account of, 13 &c. 27.
Douglas, George, aids the queen of Scots in her escape from Lochleven, 202 n.
Douglas, lady Margaret, 102 n.
Drury, marshal of Berwick, 225 n.
Dudley, lord Robert, (afterwards earl of Leicester), one of queen Elizabeth's suitors, 34 n, 216 n.
Dumbarton, castle of, taken by the regent Lennox, 262.
Dutch church in London, dissensions in, 208; at Norwich, 256.

E.

Eaton, or Heton, Thomas, (a merchant of London who contributed to the afflicted professors of the gospel, and had been an exile at Strasburgh), 2, 80.
Ecebolus, 169 n.
Edinburgh, seized by the adherents of the queen of Scots, 262; castle of, taken by queen Elizabeth, 290, 292.
Eglinton, earl of, 205 n.
Egmont, count, put to death by the duke of Alva, 204; some account of, 204 n.
Eliperius, 78.
Elizabeth, queen, accession of, 3; reply to queen Mary's messengers, 3; list of her privy council, 5 n; retains the mass in her private chapel, 18; thinks of recalling Peter Martyr, 20, 53, 74; and of joining the league of Smalcold, 21; suitors of, 24; declines being called the head of the church, 24, 29, 33; reforms the currency, 93, 104; declines sending representatives to Trent, 101; meditates a progress to

York, 109; determines to assist the prince of Condè, 115; ill of the small pox, 124; succession of, debated in parliament, 185 n; proposed marriage with Charles of Austria, 192; her death attempted by the papists, 252; letter of, to the Swiss cantons, 333.

Embden, a mart for English merchants, 139 n; character of the place, 140 n.

England, church of, alleged blemishes therein, 163, &c.

Englefield, sir Francis, one of queen Mary's privy council, 5 n.

Epiphanius, 160 n.

Errol, earl of, 205 n.

Escot, Christopher, commissioner for a royal visitation in the north, 73 n.

Essex, earl of, 329; death and character of, 329 n.

Eusebius, 178.

Eustathius, 159, 348.

Evers, Thomas lord, in the commission for a royal visitation in the north, 73 n.

Exorcisms, form of, in the first book of Edward VI., 178 n.

F.

Fabricius, John Henry, son of the standard-bearer of Zurich, 108, 305; visits bishop Parkhurst, 111.

Faculties, court of, 164, 180.

Falconer, 69; death of, 79.

Feckenham, John, abbot of Westminster, one of the disputants there, 10 n; 11; speech of, in the house of lords, 20; sent to the tower, 79 n.

Felton, John, fixes the pope's bull against queen Elizabeth, on the bishop of London's palace gates, 221 n, 254.

Ferdinand, emperor of Germany, his son a suitor of queen Elizabeth, 46.

Feria, duke of, ambassador from Spain, 5 n, 10.

Field, John, one of the compilers of the admonition to parliament, 284 n.

Finland, John, duke of, see Sweden, prince of.

Fittich, Vespasian, 28.

Flanders, disorders in, 139 n; inundations there, 233.

Fleming, lord, 203.

Flushing, troops sent there, 273; pirates, 312.

Fortescue, Anthony, (comptroller to cardinal Pole) condemned for treason, 129 n.

Foxe, John, employed in collecting the history of the martyrs, 26; translates into Latin Cranmer's treatise on the Eucharist, 42 n; notice of his Acts and Monuments, 128; his letter to the duke of Norfolk, 216 n; Letters of, 22, 25, 35, 37, 41, 42.

France, peace concluded with, 24, 75 n, 139 n, 273; affairs of, 114; war declared against, 132.

France, king of, styles himself king of Scotland, 40; relinquishes the title, 89.

Frankfort, council of, 156 n.

French church in London, 93; collection for its benefit, 288 n.

Frensham, 22, 25, 36, 42, 58.

Frisius, 17, 97.

Froschover, Christopher, (a printer at Zurich, who received some of the English exiles,) 11 n, 30, 42 n, 224.

Fulthorp, J., executed for treason, 225 n.

Funckius, 30.

G.

Gangra, council of, 159, 350.

Gargrave, sir Thomas, one of the royal visitors for the north, 73 n.

Gates, sir Henry, one of the royal visitors for the north, 73 n.

Geneva besieged by the duke of Savoy, 334.

Gesner, Conrad, 17, 31 n; sends to England for MSS. of ancient ecclesiastical authors, 137 n; notice of his Bibliotheca, 305.

Gheast, Edmund, (afterwards bishop of Rochester and Salisbury) one of the disputants at Westminster, 11.

Goodman, Christopher, 21; tract by, 21 n; preaches in the Scots' camp, 60.

Goodman, Gabriel, (dean of Westminster) signs a warrant for the apprehension of Cartwright, 313 n.

Gordon, John and Adam, sons of lord Huntley, made prisoners at Corrichie, 129 n.

Grange, lord, see Kirkaldy.

24—2

Granvelle, cardinal, 139.
Grey, lady Catherine, (daughter of Henry, duke of Suffolk) marries the earl of Hertford, 103; committed to the Tower by queen Elizabeth, 103 n.
Grindal, Edmund, one of the disputants at Westminster, 11; made bishop of London, 23, 40, 63; translated to York, 224, 229, 233; illness of, 258; archbishop of Canterbury, 329, 332; sequestered by queen Elizabeth, 329 n; letters of, 168, 182, 191, 196, 201, 208, 215, 224, 258, 291, 293; (and jointly with Horn) 175.
Grinæus, 36.
Grisons, disturbances in the, 278.
Gualter, Rodolph, 17; publishes commentaries on St John's gospel, 141; and an exposition of the epistles to the Corinthians, 279 n, 286, 293; succeeds Bullinger as chief pastor of Zurich, 318; Letter of, 362.
Gualter, Rodolph, son of the preceding, 263, 264 n; maintained at Cambridge by bishop Parkhurst, 271 n, 289; goes to Oxford, 289 n; returns to Zurich, 304; death of, 324.
Guernsey, sir Thomas Leighton, governor of, 323.
Guise, Francis de Lorraine, duke of, 114, 118; death of, 124 n.
Guise, Henry de Lorraine, duke of, 325.
Guldebeckius, 110.
Gusman, don Diego, ambassador from Spain, 139 n.

H.

Habits, prescribed to the clergy, 84; objected to by many of the bishops, 84 n; controversy about, 148, 151, 153, 157, &c.; 168, 176, &c.; Bullinger's opinion concerning them, 345, &c.; Peter Martyr's judgment respecting them, 347.
Haddon, Walter, (successively public orator, and master of Trinity Hall, Cambridge, and president of Magdalene College, Oxford,) 111; death of, 240; saying of queen Elizabeth respecting him, 240 n.
Hales, John, 103 n.
Haller, 17, 30, 84.
Hamburgh, commerce of the English with, 140.

Hamilton, James, of Bothwellhaugh, assassin of the regent Murray, 218.
Hamilton, James, archbishop of St Andrew's, put to death at Dumbarton, 257 n.
Hamilton, duke of, leader of the popish party in Scotland, 228.
Harding, Thomas, 45 n; Jewel's controversy with, 139 n, 147.
Harpsfield, John, engaged on the popish side in the disputation at Westminster, 11.
Harvey, Henry, one of the royal visitors in the north, 73 n.
Hastings, Edward, lord, one of queen Mary's privy council, 5 n.
Hatton, Christopher, tries to get Ely house from bishop Cox, 319 n.
Havre de grace, plague at, 132.
Heath, Nicholas, archbishop of York, one of queen Mary's council, 5 n, 7, 10 n.
Helvetia, confession of, 169 n, 304 n.
Herbert, Henry, lord, (afterwards earl of Pembroke) divorced from his wife, 103 n.
Herman, 9, 13; visits bishop Jewel, 120.
Hertford, Edward Seymour, earl of, (son of the protector Somerset) committed to the Tower for his clandestine marriage with lady Catherine Grey, 103 n.
Heshusius, Tilman, 109 n.
Heton, Thomas, 2, 80. See Eaton.
Higham, sir Clement, one of queen Mary's council, 5 n.
Hilles, Richard, (a merchant, and contributor to the exiles in queen Mary's reign) 224. Letters of, 171, 211, 241, 270.
Hilles, Barnabas, 241, 270.
Hilles, Gerson, 271.
Hirter, 62.
Holland, Garland, a bookseller at Oxford, 328.
Holstein, Adolph., duke of, visits England, 89.
Hoper, Ann, wife of bishop, 36.
Horn, Robert, returns from exile, 6; disputes at Westminster, 11, 15, 27; bishop of Winchester, 93; his death, 332 n. Letters of, 134, 141, 245, 276, 320, 321, (and with Grindal) 175.

Horn, count of, executed at Brussels, 204; notice of, 204 n.
Hosius, cardinal, some account of, 113 n.
Howard of Effingham, Charles, lord, one of queen Elizabeth's privy council, 5 n.
Howard, Thomas, duke of Norfolk, proposes marriage to the queen of Scots, 216 n.; committed to the Tower in consequence, 216.
Huguenots, treaty with, 250; seek refuge in London, 291.
Huldrich, John, 324.
Humphrey, Laurence, (president of Magdalene College, Oxford) exile at Zurich, 11 n.; refuses to join the separatists, 202; writes the life of Jewel, 310 n. Letters of, 133, 151, 289, 310, 324, 326, (and with Sampson), 157.
Hunsdon, lord, 225; letter of, to lord Burghley, quoted, 219 n.
Huntley, earl of, his death, 129.
Hyperius, 131.

I.

Images removed from churches, 63; disputation respecting, 67, 73.
Innocent, 158.
Inundation in Norfolk and Suffolk, 233.
Ireland, state of, 140, 332.
Isbrandus, Balkius, minister in the Dutch church at Norwich, 256, 266 n.

J.

James VI. of Scotland, birth of, 167; baptism of, 183; crowned king of Scotland, 197.
Jernegam, (or Jerningham) Sir Henry, one of queen Mary's privy council, 5 n.
Jewel, John, returns from exile, 9; one of the disputants at Westminster, 11; a royal visitor for the north, 24, 39; bishop of Salisbury, 40, 50, 63; publishes his apology, 101 n, 121; his sermon at Paul's cross, 147 n; death of, 260; letters of, 6, 9, 13, 17, 19, 23, 32, 38, 44, 48, 50, 52, 54, 59, 67, 70, 77, 80, 88, 91, 96, 99, 104, 106, 114, 117, 120, 123, 125, 126, 138, 146, 155, 184, 226, 238.
John, don of Austria, 325, 326 n.
John de villa Garsya, a Spanish monk, 33 n.
Julius Santerentianus, a friend and attendant of Peter Martyr, 8, 51, 77, 224, 232.
Justinian, the emperor, 19.

K.

Killegrew, Sir Henry, (brother-in-law to Lord Burghley) sent ambassador into Sotland, 167, 290 n.
Kingsmill, Richard, one of the royal visitors for the north, 73 n.
Kirkaldy, Sir William, of Grange, 193, 198; governor of Edinburgh castle, 262; deserted to the queen's party, ib.; executed, ib. n.
Kitchen, Anthony, bishop of Llandaff, 10 n.
Knolles, Sir Francis, one of queen Elizabeth's privy council, 5 n.
Knox, John, 167; banished from Edinburgh, 24, 39, 170; preaches in the Scots' camp, 60; declaims against idolatry, 150; returns to his church at Edinburgh, 198.

L.

Lamoral, (see Egmont), 204.
Langdale, Alban, archdeacon of Chichester, one of the disputants at Westminster, 11 n.
Langside, battle of, 203 n.
Laodicea, council of, 159.
Lavater, Louis, (a minister at Zurich), 17.
Leicester, earl of, 216 n.
Leighton, Sir Thomas, governor of the isle of Guernsey, 323.
Leith, James, letter of, 230.
Leith, taken by the English, 82, 86, 88, 91; terms of capitulation, 89; levelled to the ground, 89; fortified by the king's party, 262.
Lennox, Matthew Stuart, earl of, committed to the Tower, 102; regent of Scotland, 226, 262; assassinated at Stirling, 262 n.
Lennox, Margaret Douglas, countess of, 102.

Lepanto, battle of, 270 n.
Lethington, lord Maitland of, 193 n.
Lever, Thomas, (master of St John's, Cambridge), 224; invited to be minister at Coventry, 86; minister at Arau, 88 n; refuses to join the separatists, 202; preaches at the funeral of Dr Turner, 206; letter of, 84.
Lewis, count, brother of the prince of Orange, occupies Valenciennes, 274.
Liberian, 62.
Lindsay, Lord, his behaviour to the queen of Scots, 197 n.
Linlithgow, the regent Murray murdered at, 218.
Liturgy of Edward VI, 234; Bucer's opinion of, 234 n.
London, plague at, 132 n.
Lord's supper, primitive mode of administering, 178 n.
Lovelace, William, in a commission for a royal visitation, 39 n.
Low countries, see Flanders.
Ludham, a residence of the bishop of Norwich, 98 n.
Lumey, William Vandermarke, lord of, takes the Brill, 273.
Luncher, 131.
Lutherans, called Martinists at Antwerp, 174.
Lycosthenes, Conrad, abridged Gesner's Bibliotheca, 305 n.

M.

Maclaine, Peter, a bookseller at Basle, 35, 41.
Magdalene college, 271 n, 289.
Maitland, lord, of Lethington, 193 n.
Mar, earl of, 193 n, 197; chosen regent, 262.
Marshal, Richard, notice of, 12 n.
Martinengo, abbot of, the Pope's nuncio, 102 n.
Martinists, Lutherans so called, 174.
Martyr, Peter, invited to return, 20 n, 45, 77 n, 81; sends a book to queen Elizabeth, 25; writes a commentary on Judges, 112; his book on vows, 46, 58; attends the conference at Poissy, 99 n; writes on the Ubiquitarian controversy, 100 n; death of, 123; his image, in silver, sent to Jewel, 126; his opinion of the Common Prayer book, 234, 235; wife of, 47 n; children of, 54 n; letter of, 339.
Mary, queen, message of, to Elizabeth, 3; death of, 3.
Mary, queen of Scots, 102; retains the mass, 104, 116, 124, 140, 169; seeks an interview with Elizabeth, 115; sends her presents, 120; marries lord Darnley, 144; marries the earl of Bothwell, 192; suspected of the murder of her husband, 193, 197 n; escapes to Dunbar, 193 n; confined in Lochleven castle, 196; resigns the crown to her son, 197; escapes from Lochleven, 202 n; flies to Castle Hamilton, 203; escapes to Carlisle after the battle of Langside, 203; association in defence of, 205 n; confined in Bolton, Tutbury, and Sheffield castles, 210 n; transferred to Coventry, 217; regulations respecting her imprisonment, 260 n; proposed marriage with the duke of Norfolk, 216 n; sought in marriage by the brother of the French king, 239.
Mason, Sir John, a privy councillor, 5 n; appointed to examine into a complaint against bishop Bonner, 7 n.
Mass, abolition of, 29; riots at Holyrood house occasioned by, 104.
Massacre of St Bartholomew's, 276, 291 n.
May, William, dean of St Paul's, and archbishop of York elect, death of, 93.
Meath, bishop of, 309 n.
Medina Celi, duke of, viceroy in Flanders, 275.
Melancthon, Philip, writes an answer to the articles of Bavaria, 110 n.
Merenda, Catherine, wife of Peter Martyr, 47 n.
Merrick, Rowland, bishop of Bangor, 63 n.
Meyer, 30.
Middleberg, invaded by the Walloons, 273.
Mont, Christopher, agent of queen Elizabeth, 173 n, 212.
Montague, viscount, one of queen Mary's privy council, 5 n.

Montmorenci, Francis, duke of, French ambassador in England, 34, 273.
Montmorenci, Philip, count Horn, 204 n.
Montrose, earl of, 205 n.
Moors, victory of, in Spain, 219.
Mordaunt, Sir John, one of queen Mary's privy council, 5 n.
Morley, Henry Parker, lord, a fugitive beyond sea, 309 n.
Morton, earl of, delivers the earl of Northumberland to the English, 217 n.
Muralt, 9.
Murderer discovered by a sheep, 109.
Murray, earl of, regent of Scotland, 197, 210; assassination of, 215, 218, 223.
Murray, lord, of Tullibardin, 193 n.
Musculus, Wolfgang, 84.

N.

Navarre, queen of, 250.
Netherlands, commerce of, interrupted, 209.
Newhaven, plague at, 132.
Nominalists, 53.
Norfolk, Thomas Howard, duke of, proposes marriage to the queen of Scots, 216; tried in Westminster hall, 261; peers present at the trial, 267 n; condemned, 267; executed, 269 n, 272.
Norfolk, Mary Fitz-Alan, duchess of, her funeral, 137 n.
Norfolk, rebellion in, 229, 248; late harvest and scarcity in, 301.
Norris, Sir Henry, ambassador in France, 231.
Norris, John, gallantry of, in Flanders, 325 n.
North, Roger, lord, obtains letters for the manor of Somersham, 319 n.
North, rebellion in the, 213, 247.
Northampton, William Par, marquis of, one of queen Elizabeth's privy council, 5 n; his death, 257 n.
Northumberland, Thomas Percy, earl of, one of the royal visitors for the north, 73 n; heads the rebellion of the papists in the north, 213, 217, 222, 227; his flight, and confinement in Lochleven, 214 n, 223; execution of, 217 n.
Norton, Richard, a rebel in the north, 214 n.
Norwich, cathedral of, injured by lightning, 132; Dutch church at, 256; disturbances in, ib.
Nowell, Alexander, dean of St Paul's, signs a warrant for the apprehension of Cartwright, 313 n.

O.

Occamists, 53.
Ochinus, Bernardinus, a learned Italian, invited by Abp. Cranmer into England, 22, 26, 40, 58, 64.
Œcolampadius, John, 110.
Oglethorp, Owen, bishop of Carlisle, 10 n; death of, 69.
Oil, use of abolished in the Church of England, 178.
O'Neale, John, rebels against queen Elizabeth, 186 n, 194; killed in an affray, 195.
Orange, William of Nassau, prince of, 273, 293.
Orenberg, count Von, killed at Groningen, 205.
Osiander, Andreas, 127 n.
Otho, constitutions of, 158.
Oxford, state of religion in, 33, 55, 77.

P.

Paget, William, lord, one of queen Mary's privy council, 5 n.
Pallium, description of the, 160.
Pamphilus, an assumed name of Thomas Randolph, 56, 59, &c.
Parker, Matthew, archbishop of Canterbury, 61, 63, 180 n; visitation of, in the isle of Wight, 323 n; death and character of, 317 n.
Parker, 253 n.
Parkhurst, John, exile at Zurich, 11 n; rector of Cleve, 48; 51 n, 61, 69; refuses a bishoprick, 61; writer of some epigrams, 49; made bishop of Norwich, 61 n, 76; interposes in the dissensions there, 256 n; embarrassed by the misconduct of his agent, 265; death of, 317; letters of, 29, 31, 49, 61, 90, 94, 97, 98, 107, 109, 110, 121,

128, 131, 136, 143, 165, 194, 205, 232, 255, 266, 277, 300, 302, 303, 304.
Parma, duchess of, 139 n.
Parry, Sir Thomas, one of queen Elizabeth's privy council, 5 n.
Parry, Henry, in a commission for religion, 39 n.
Pate, Richard, (bishop of Worcester) confined in the tower, 79.
Paullus, 80.
Paul's cross, 4, 71.
Peckham, Sir Edmund, one of queen Mary's privy council, 5 n.
Peckham, Sir Robert, one of queen Mary's privy council, 5 n.
Pellican, Conrad, (a minister at Zurich,) 62.
Pembroke, William Herbert, earl of, one of queen Elizabeth's privy council, 5 n; in a commission for religion, 39 n.
Peneman, Robert, executed for treason, 225 n.
Percy, Sir Henry, one of the royal visitors for the north, 73 n.
Perne, Peter, 41.
Petalum, description of the, 350 n.
Petre, Sir William, (secretary of state) one of queen Elizabeth's privy council, 5 n, 71, 80.
Peucer, Caspar, head of the university of Wittenberg, 302 n.
Philip II., king of Spain, proposes marriage to queen Elizabeth, 5 n.
Pickering, Sir William, one of queen Elizabeth's suitors, 24, 34.
Pilkington, James, (master of St John's, Cambridge,) bishop of Durham, 63 n; his property destroyed in the rebellion, 218; letter to Cecil quoted, 218 n; illness of, 260; his death, 321, 325; letters of, 222, 286.
Pius V., pope, his bull against queen Elizabeth, 221, 223, 238; answered by Bullinger, 244.
Plague, the, at London and Newhaven, 132; at Zurich, 141.
Plumtree, a priest, executed for treason, 225 n.
Pole, Reginald, cardinal, death of, 3.
Pole, Arthur, condemned for treason, 129 n.
Pole, Edmund, condemned for treason, 129 n.

Pontius, the deacon, 160 n, 350 n.
Port, Francis, Greek professor at Geneva, 231.
Possession, alleged demoniacal at Norwich, 303.
Prayers, in a foreign tongue, disallowed in the church of England, 178.
Preaching, prohibited by Queen Elizabeth at the beginning of her reign, 7.
Prestall, John, condemned for treason, 129 n.
Privy council, names of Queen Elizabeth's first, 5 n.
Puteo, James, cardinal, 12 n.

R.

Randau, count, plenipotentiary from Francis II., 89 n.
Randolph, Thomas, (queen Elizabeth's agent in Scotland,) 44; employed to convey the earl of Arran into Scotland, 44 n; designated by the name of Pamphilus, 56, 57 n.
Rebellion in the north, 213, 217, 222.
Reformation, how tolerated in France, 250 n.
Religion, commission for the establishment of, 24.
Renner, 62.
Ridley, Nicholas, bishop of London, executors of, complain against bishop Bonner, 7 n.
Rizzio, David, murder of, 166 n, 170.
Rogers, Sir Edward, (an exile for religion,) privy councillor to queen Elizabeth, 5 n.
Rohan, M. de, queen Elizabeth's contract with, 115 n.
Rotaker, Christopher, 62.
Rothes, Andrew Leslie, joined the association on behalf of the queen of Scots, 205 n.
Ruthven, Patrick, baron, took part in the murder of Rizzio, 166 n.
Russel, lord, 20, 34.
Ryche, lord, one of queen Mary's privy council, 5 n.

S.

Sackvil, Sir Richard, one of queen Elizabeth's privy council, 5 n.
Salisbury, cathedral of, injured by lightning, 78.

INDEX. 377

Sampson, Thomas, (dean of Christchurch), bishoprick of Norwich offered to, 75 n; preached at the funeral of the duchess of Norfolk, 137 n; Grindal's testimony to, 176; refuses to join the separatists, 202; letters of, 1, 62, 75, 130, 153.

Sandwich, dissensions among the Dutch there, 256.

Sandys, Edwin, returns from exile, 6; made bishop of Worcester, 63; one of the royal visitors for the north, 73 n; his second marriage, 74; translated to London, 229, 233; embarrassed in circumstances, 265; signs a warrant for the apprehension of Cartwright, 313 n; archbishop of York, 333. Letters of, 3, 72, 145, 264, 294, 311, 312, 331.

Saunders, Nicholas, 281.

Saxony, prince of, a suitor to queen Elizabeth, 24 n, 34.

Saxony, religious persecution in, 315.

Scambler, Edmund, a preacher in queen Mary's time; bishop of Lichfield and Coventry, 7 n.

Schneider, John, 105.

Scory, John, one of the disputants at Westminster, 11; some account of, 11 n; bishop of Hereford, 23, 40, 63 n.

Scot, Cuthbert, bishop of Chester, opposes the reformation, 10 n.

Scots, queen of, see Mary.

Scotland, religious disturbances in, 24, 39; reformation in, 46, 59; affairs of, 68, 193, 195, 225, 228.

Scroop, Henry, lord, invades Scotland, 225 n.

Separatists, statements respecting, 202, 237, 280, 283, 284, 298.

Shrewsbury, Francis Talbot, earl of, a privy councillor, 5 n; notice of, 15 n; president of the council in the north, 73 n.

Shrewsbury, George Talbot, earl of, high steward at the duke of Norfolk's trial, 261 n.

Sicilian vespers, 291.

Sidall, Henry, account of, 10 n, 45 n, 81.

Simler, Josiah, a minister at Zurich, 17; translates some of Bullinger's works, 96, 110; prepares an edition of Peter Martyr's works, 137; illness of, 120; death of, 125 n.

Sisinnius, 160, 350 n.

Sluys, sea-fight near, 274.

Smalcald, embassy from, 54.

Smith, Richard, account of, 12 n, 45, 81.

Smith, Sir Thomas, 290 n.

Soto, Peter, a Spanish friar, (nominated professor of divinity at Oxford), 33.

Southwell, Sir Richard, one of queen Mary's privy council, 5 n.

Spanish ships taken by the Dutch, 275.

Spencer, Thomas, archdeacon of Chichester, death of, 255.

Springham, Richard, notice of 9, 112 n.

Stancarus, notice of, 127 n; refuted by Simler, 127.

Staphilus, notice of, 339 n.

St Andrew's, archbishop of 60, 132; execution of, 257 n, 262.

St Antholin's, morning service at, 33.

St Bartholomew's, massacre of, 276, 291 n.

Stolberg, count, ambassador from the emperor, 192.

Story, John, sent to prison, 79; arrested, 111; escapes to Flanders, 253; reapprehended and executed, 254.

Stuart, James, see Murray.

Stuart, Matthew, see Lennox.

Stumphius, 62.

Superstition, instances of, 44, 259 n.

Sussex, Thomas Ratcliffe, earl of, sent against the rebels in the north, 214 n; invades Scotland, 225, 228.

Sutherland, earl of, one of the association in defence of the queen of Scots, 205 n.

Sweden, prince of, arrived in England, 46 n.

Sweden, Eric XIV., king of, a suitor of queen Elizabeth, 46, 83; expected in England, 90 n; dismissed, 102.

Sylverius, patriarch of Rome, 18 n.

T.

Tapers, use of, abolished in the church of England, 178.

Tertullian, 85 n, 158, 351.

Theodora, empress, 18 n.

Theophilus, administer of the strangers' church at Norwich, 256 n.

Thirlby, Thomas, bishop of Ely, one

of queen Mary's council, 5 n; commissioner about the restoration of Calais, 8 n.
Thorgau, convocation at, 315 n.
Throgmorton, sir Clement, 7 n.
Throgmorton, sir Nicholas, ambassador in France, 132 n.
Thymelthorp, George, his frauds on the bishop of Norwich, 265 n, 301.
Torquatus, an Italian astrologer, 47 n.
Tunstal, Cuthbert, bishop of Durham, death of, 69.
Turbervile, James, bishop of Exeter, 10 n.
Turner, Dr William, notice of, 206 n.
Turks, defeat of at Lepanto, 270.

U.

Ubiquitarian controversy, 92 n, 98, 135, 139, 302, 307.
Ulmis, John ab, 87.
Ulmius, Rodolph, son of the above, 324, 326.
Ulstat, Daniel, contracts for the reforming the debased currency, 93 n.

V.

Valence, bishop of, plenipotentiary from Francis II., 89 n.
Valenciennes, revolts from the duke of Alva, 274.
Vandermarke, William, lord of Lumey, takes the Brill, 273.
Venetians, war of with the Turks, 239.
Venlo, revolts from the duke of Alva, 274.
Vespers, Sicilian, 291.
Vigilius, patriarch of Rome, 18 n.

W.

Walsingham, sir Francis, ambassador to France, 230.
Warwick, earl of, sent against the rebels in the north, 247 n.
Watson, Thomas, bishop of Lincoln, 7; committed to the tower, 16, 79.
Weidner, Wolfgang, pastor at Worms, 26.
Wentworth, Thomas lord, one of queen Mary's privy council, 5 n; lord lieutenant of Suffolk, 99 n.
Westminster, disputation between protestants and papists at, 11, &c.

Westmoreland, Charles, earl of, heads the rebellion in the north, 213, 217, 222; his escape, 214 n, 223, 227.
Weston, Hugh, notice of, 12 n.
Westphaling, Herbert, bishop of Hereford, 328 n.
Wharton, sir Thomas, one of queen Mary's privy council, 5 n.
White, John, bishop of Winchester, preaches at queen Mary's funeral, 7; committed to the tower, 16; wrote against Peter Martyr, 71 n; death of, 69, 71.
Whitehead, David, death of, 242; notice of, 255 n.
Whitgift, Dr (afterwards archbishop of Canterbury) replies to Cartwright, 291 n, 297, 306 n; master of Trinity college, 294.
Wiburn, Perceval, 178; of St John's Cambridge, an exile for religion in the time of queen Mary, prebendary of Winchester and Rochester, but deprived for non-conformity, letter of, 187.
Wickius, 30, 305.
Wilcox Thomas, one of the compilers of the admonition to parliament, 284 n.
Wilford, Sir Thomas, 74 n.
Willoughby of Parham, William, lord, 214 n.
Winchester, William Paulet, marquis of, lord treasurer, 5 n, 7.
Witchcraft, an act against, 44 n.
Wolfius, John, a printer at Zurich, 17, 30.
Women, not allowed to baptize, 178.
Wonlychius, 62, 305.
Workington, queen of Scots lands at, 203 n.
Worms, congress at, 344.
Wotton, Nicholas, one of queen Mary's councillors, 5 n; commissioner in France, 8 n; plenipotentiary there, 89 n.
Wroth, Sir Thomas, 5, 53, 59.

Z.

Zanchius, Hieronymus, notice of, 8 n.
Zuinglius, Ulric, 36, 42.
Zuinglius, Rodolph, grandson of the preceding, 264 n, 267; death of, 269, 271.

EPISTOLÆ TIGURINÆ.

"Litteras has cum autographis collatas et accurate a verbo ad verbum transcriptas esse testor.

     Geroldus Meyer de Knonau,
        Archivarius Reipublicæ Turicensis.
Turici. xxi. Octobris,
 mdcccxxxx."

TABULA.

EPIST.		PAG.
I.	THOMAS SAMPSON ad Petrum Martyrem	1
II.	Edwinus Sandus ad Henricum Bullingerum.......................	2
III.	Johannes Juellus ad Petrum Martyrem............................	3
IV.	Idem ad eundem	5
V.	Idem ad eundem	7
VI.	Idem ad eundem	9
VII.	Idem ad eundem	11
VIII.	Johannes Foxus ad Henricum Bullingerum.......................	12
IX.	Johannes Juellus ad Petrum Martyrem............................	13
X.	Johannes Foxus ad Henricum Bullingerum.......................	14
XI.	Ricardus Coxus ad Wolfgangum Weidnerum....................	15
XII.	Johannes Parkhurstus ad Henricum Bullingerum	17
XIII.	Idem ad Conradum Gesnerum	18
XIV.	Johannes Juellus ad Henricum Bullingerum	19
XV.	Johannes Foxus ad eundem...	20
XVI.	Johannes Juellus ad Petrum Martyrem............................	22
XVII.	Johannes Foxus ad Henricum Bullingerum.......................	23
XVIII.	Idem ad eundem	24
XIX.	Johannes Juellus ad Petrum Martyrem............................	25
XX.	Idem ad Rodolphum Gualterum	27
XXI.	Johannes Parkhurstus ad Johannem Wolphium.................	28
XXII.	Johannes Juellus ad Josiam Simlerum	29
XXIII.	Idem ad Petrum Martyrem	30
XXIV.	Idem ad eundem	31
XXV.	Idem ad eundem	33
XXVI.	Johannes Parkhurstus ad Josiam Simlerum......................	34
XXVII.	Thomas Sampson ad Petrum Martyrem	35
XXVIII.	Ricardus Coxus ad eundem	38
XXIX.	Johannes Juellus ad eundem	39
XXX.	Idem ad eundem...	40
XXXI.	Edwinus Sandus ad eundem	42
XXXII.	Thomas Sampson ad eundem......................................	44
XXXIII.	Johannes Juellus ad eundem	45
XXXIV.	Idem ad eundem	47
XXXV.	Thomas Leverus ad Henricum Bullingerum	49
XXXVI.	Johannes Juellus ad Petrum Martyrem............................	52
XXXVII.	Johannes Parkhurstus ad Henricum Bullingerum	53

EPIST.		PAG.
XXXVIII.	Johannes Juellus ad Petrum Martyrem	54
XXXIX.	Johannes Parkhurstus ad Johannem Wolfium, &c.	55
XL.	Johannes Juellus ad Josiam Simlerum	56
XLI.	Johannes Parkhurstus ad Henricum Bullingerum	57
XLII.	Idem ad eundem	58
XLIII.	Johannes Juellus ad Petrum Martyrem	59
XLIV.	Idem ad Henricum Bullingerum	61
XLV.	Idem ad Josiam Simlerum...	62
XLVI.	Johannes Parkhurstus ad Henricum Bullingerum	63
XLVII.	Idem ad Josiam Simlerum et Ludovicum Lavaterum	64
XLVIII.	Idem ad Henricum Bullingerum..	65
XLIX.	Ricardus Coxus ad Petrum Martyrem	66
L.	Johannes Juellus ad Henricum Bullingerum	67
LI.	Idem ad Petrum Martyrem	69
LII.	Idem ad Josiam Simlerum...	71
LIII.	Johannes Parkhurstus ad Henricum Bullingerum	72
LIV.	Johannes Juellus ad eundem...	73
LV.	Idem ad Josiam Simlerum...	74
LVI.	Idem ad eundem	75
LVII.	Johannes Parkhurstus ad Henricum Bullingerum	76
LVIII.	Thomas Sampson ad eundem	77
LIX.	Johannes Parkhurstus ad eundem	78
LX.	Laurentius Humfredus ad eundem	79
LXI.	Robertus Hornus ad eundem...	80
LXII.	Johannes Parkhurstus ad Josiam Simlerum.......................	82
LXIII.	Johannes Juellus ad Henricum Bullingerum	82
LXIV.	Robertus Hornus ad Rodolphum Gualterum	84
LXV.	Johannes Parkhurstus ad Henricum Bullingerum	85
LXVI.	Edwinus Sandus ad eundem	86
LXVII.	Johannes Juellus ad eundem et Ludovicum Lavaterum	87
LXVIII.	Laurentius Humfredus ad Henricum Bullingerum................	90
LXIX.	Thomas Sampson ad eundem	91
LXX.	Johannes Juellus ad eundem...	93
LXXI.	Laurentius Humfredus et Thomas Sampson ad eundem.........	93
LXXII.	Johannes Parkhurstus ad eundem	98
LXXIII.	Edmundus Grindallus ad eundem	99
LXXIV.	Ricardus Hilles ad eundem	101
LXXV.	Edm. Grindallus et Rob. Hornus ad Hen. Bullingerum et Rod. Gualterum	104
LXXVI.	Edmundus Grindallus ad Henricum Bullingerum	108
LXXVII.	Johannes Juellus ad eundem...	109
LXXVIII.	Percevallus Wiburnus ad eundem	111
LXXIX.	Edmundus Grindallus ad eundem	114

Epist.		Pag.
LXXX.	Johannes Parkhurstus ad Henricum Bullingerum	115
LXXXI.	Edmundus Grindallus ad eundem	116
LXXXII.	Idem ad eundem	119
LXXXIII.	Johannes Parkhurstus ad Rodolphum Gualterum et Henricum Bullingerum	121
LXXXIV.	Ricardus Coxus ad Henricum Bullingerum	121
LXXXV.	Edmundus Grindallus ad eundem	122
LXXXVI.	Ricardus Hilles ad eundem	124
LXXXVII.	Edmundus Grindallus ad eundem	126
LXXXVIII.	Ricardus Coxus ad eundem	128
LXXXIX.	Jacobus Pilkingtonus ad eundem	129
XC.	Edmundus Grindallus ad eundem	131
XCI.	Johannes Juellus ad eundem	132
XCII.	Jacobus Letheus ad eundem	134
XCIII.	Johannes Parkhurstus ad eundem	136
XCIV.	Ricardus Coxus ad Rodolphum Gualterum	137
XCV.	Johannes Juellus ad Henricum Bullingerum	140
XCVI.	Ricardus Hilles ad eundem	141
XCVII.	Ricardus Coxus ad eundem	143
XCVIII.	Robertus Hornus ad eundem	144
XCIX.	Johannes Parkhurstus ad eundem	150
C.	Edmundus Grindallus ad eundem	151
CI.	Edwinus Sandus ad eundem	153
CII.	Johannes Parkhurstus ad eundem	155
CIII.	Ricardus Coxus ad eundem	156
CIV.	Ricardus Hilles ad eundem	157
CV.	Robertus Hornus ad eundem	160
CVI.	Johannes Parkhurstus ad eundem	162
CVII.	Ricardus Coxus ad Rodolphum Gualterum	162
CVIII.	Idem ad Henricum Bullingerum	164
CIX.	Idem ad Rodolphum Gualterum	166
CX.	Jacobus Pilkingtonus ad eundem	167
CXI.	Laurentius Humfredus ad eundem	169
CXII.	Edmundus Grindallus ad Henricum Bullingerum	170
CXIII.	Idem ad Rodolphum Gualterum	171
CXIV.	Edwinus Sandus ad Henricum Bullingerum	172
CXV.	Ricardus Coxus ad Rodolphum Gualterum	174
CXVI.	Johannes Parkhurstus ad Henricum Bullingerum	176
CXVII.	Idem ad Josiam Simlerum	177
CXVIII.	Idem ad Henricum Bullingerum	177
CXIX.	Idem ad Josiam Simlerum	179
CXX.	Ricardus Coxus ad Rodolphum Gualterum	179
CXXI.	Idem ad Henricum Bullingerum	181

Epist.		Pag.
CXXII.	Laurentius Humfredus ad Rodolphum Gualterum	182
CXXIII.	Edwinus Sandus ad Henricum Bullingerum	183
CXXIV.	Idem ad Rodolphum Gualterum	184
CXXV.	Ricardus Coxus ad Henricum Bullingerum	184
CXXVI.	Idem ad Rodolphum Gualterum	185
CXXVII.	Idem ad eundem	186
CXXVIII.	Idem ad eundem	187
CXXIX.	Robertus Hornus ad eundem	188
CXXX.	Idem ad [quosdam Fratres]	190
CXXXI.	Laurentius Humfredus ad Rodolphum Gualterum	191
CXXXII.	Idem ad eundem	192
CXXXIII.	Ricardus Coxus ad eundem	194
CXXXIV.	Edwinus Sandus ad eundem	195
CXXXV.	Elizabetha Regina ad Tresdecim Cantones Helvetiæ	196

EPISTOLA I.

THOMAS SAMPSON AD PETRUM MARTYREM.
Argentinæ. Raptim, 17 *Decembris.*

S. D. Ego te per Christum rogo, mi pater optime, ne graveris mihi quam citissime respondere ad hæc pauca. Quomodo nobis agendum sit in titulo illo vel concedendo, vel denegando, " supremum caput post Christum ecclesiæ Anglicanæ," &c. Universa scriptura videtur hoc soli Christo tribuere, ut caput ecclesiæ vocetur. Secundo, si regina me ad aliquod munus ecclesiasticum, dico ad ecclesiam aliquam regendam, vocaret; an salva conscientia recipere possem, quum hæc mihi videantur sufficere excusationis loco, ne in id consentirem: 1. Quod propter disciplinæ ecclesiasticæ defectum episcopus, vel pastor, non possit suo fungi officio. 2. Quod tot sint civilia gravamina episcopatui vel pastori imposita, ut puta primorum (ut dicimus) frugum, i. e. redituum primi anni, tum decimarum, ad hæc in episcopatibus tot et tanta insumenda sunt in equis alendis, in armis, in aulicis, quæ semper præsto debent esse, &c. ut tu nôsti, ut quam minima pars episcopatuum relinquatur ad necessaria episcopo munia obeunda, nempe ad doctos alendos, ad pauperes pascendos, aliaque facienda quæ illius ministerium reddant gratum. 3. Ut hoc ad episcopos præcipue referatur, quod nunc scribo, tanta est in eorum electione degeneratio a prima institutione, (neque cleri enim, neque populi consensus habetur,) tanta superstitiosi ornatus episcopalis vanitas, ne dicam indignitas, quanta vix puto bene ferri possit, si modo omnia nobis facienda ad id quod expedit.

Quod ad me attinet, non hæc scribo quasi talia sperarem; immo Deum precor ex animo, ne unquam talia mihi contingant onera; sed te fidissimo meo parente consilium peto, quo possim instructior esse, si talia mihi obtingant. Ego sic responderem, me quidem paratum esse in aliquo quocunque velit illa inservire concionandi munere; cæterum ecclesiam regendam me non posse suscipere, nisi ipsa prius, justa reformatione ecclesiasticorum munerum facta, ministris jus concedat omnia secundum verbum Dei administrandi, et quantum ad doctrinam, et quantum ad disciplinam, et quantum ad bona ecclesiastica. Si autem quæ sit illa reformatio, quam peto, interrogetur; ex prioribus tribus articulis poteris tu conjicere, quæ ego petenda putem.

Simpliciter, mi pater, apud te solum depono cordis mei secreta; teque per Christum rogo, ut mea secreta apud te solum teneas, et mihi quam citissime rescribas, quid mihi hic faciendum putes: adde etiam quæ addenda putas, ut urgeatur illa reformatio, et aliquid de ipsa reformatione.

Literas tuas ad Hetonum mitte : ille curabit ad me transferri. Cæterum te per Christum rogo, ut quanta poteris festinantia scribas. Ego brevi iturus sum versus Angliam. Habemus papistas, anabaptistas, et plurimos evangelicos adversarios et doctrinæ et piæ reformationi : contra hos ut tueatur gloriam Christi, promoveatque vexillum Christi, quis idoneus? O mi pater, pro me roga Deum incessanter.

Tuus totus,
TH. SAMPSON.

INSCRIPTIO.
Clarissimo viro, D. D.
Petro Martyri.
Tiguri.

EPISTOLA II.

EDWINUS SANDUS AD HENRICUM BULLINGERUM.

SALUTEM plurimam in Christo. Tardius quidem ad te scribo, vir colendissime ; sed jam primum occurrit certi aliquid quod scribam. Superiori die accepimus literas ex Anglia, quibus mors Mariæ, inauguratio Elisabethæ, et obitus cardinalis Poli confirmatur. Bonus ille cardinalis, ne turbas excitaret, aut cursum evangelii impediret, discessit e vita postridie quam Maria sua mortua est. Tantus enim fuit inter illos amor ac animorum consensus, ut ne ipsa quidem mors illos disjungere potuisset. Nihil ergo metuendum nobis est a Polo ; mortui quippe non mordent. Maria paullo ante mortem misit duos ex consiliariis suis ad sororem Elisabetham, quibus in mandatis dedit, primum ut significarent se velle dare illi coronam regiam et omnem illam dignitatem, quam jure hereditario illa tum possidebat. Et pro hoc tanto in illam collato beneficio tria ab illa petere : primum ut non mutaret consiliarios, secundum ut non mutaret religionem, tertium ut debita sua solveret et creditoribus satisfaceret. Respondet Elisabetha, et inquit : Vehementer quidem doleo, quod Regina vehementius ægrotat. Quod autem mihi diadema regni dare velit, non est cur gratias agam ; nam neque illa hoc mihi dare posset, neque hæc dignitas ullo jure a me auferri debeat, ut quæ mihi propria ac hereditaria est. Quod ad consiliarios spectat, æque liberum mihi esse puto, inquit, meos eligere, atque illi fuit eligere suos. De religione illud vero affirmo, me illam non mutaturam, modo ex verbo Dei, quod unicum fundamentum et regula religionis meæ erit, probari possit. Quod denique debita sua persolvenda petit, æquum petere mihi videtur : ego autem ut solvantur, quantum in me est, curabo. Et cum hac responsione dimissi sunt nuntii.

Regina Elisabetha proximo ab inauguratione sua Dominico fecit evanlium prædicari ad celebrem Divi Pauli crucem; quod quidem cum maximo populi applausu fiebat. At Dominico sequente episcopus Cicestrensis, nomine Christophersonus, (qui olim salutavit te in ædibus tuis in transcursu suo in Italiam, est enim egregius papista,) eundem locum occupabat, et in concione sua strenue et magna cum libertate (ut satis semper audaces sunt papistæ) refutabat omnia quæ prius dicebantur, clamans fortiter, Ne credatis huic novæ doctrinæ; non est evangelium, sed novorum hominum et hereticorum novum inventum, etc. Ad istum modum bonus ille papista sua confirmare et evangelii veritatem tollere contendebat. De qua re cum primum Regina audivisset, bonum illum episcopum ad se accersiri curavit, et de concione examinatum in carcerem conjici jussit.

Mutavit fere Regina omnes consiliarios suos, et pro papistis bonos Christianos sibi assumpsit. Et spes quidem magna est, quod totis viribus evangelium promovebit, et regnum Christi amplificabit. Quod ut faciat, ab omnibus piis rogandus est Deus. Philippus misit ad illam celebrem et magnificam legationem; quid autem sit, quod velit, ignoramus. At si cogitet id quod tua prudentia metuebat, operam perdet, nec hilum quidem proficiet. D. Wrottius, D. Cocus, et alii nobiles hodie primum ingressi sunt iter. Cras ego fausto Domino sequar. Cum in Angliam venero, quomodo res ibi gerantur, diligenter ad te perscribam. Interim roga tu Deum pro statu ecclesiæ Anglicanæ, et pro nobis miseris verbi ministris, quibus grave et difficile onus incumbit. Nos vicissim pro vestra ecclesia et pro vobis Deum vehementer precabimur. Jam media nox est, et cras mane mihi discedendum est. Tu igitur bene vale, vir colendissime. Turbulente. Argentorati Decembris 20, vel si mavis 21, 1558.

Tui studiosissimus,

EDWINUS SANDUS, *Anglus.*

INSCRIPTIO.
Colendissimo viro Domino Bullingero, Ecclesiæ Tigurinæ pastori vigilantissimo, Dno suo plurimum observando. Tiguri.

EPISTOLA III.

JOHANNES JUELLUS AD PETRUM MARTYREM.

S. D. De prima illa nostra profectione, et de novis omnibus, quæ tum ferebantur Basileæ, scripsi ad te per D. Simlerum nostrum. Quinto postridie vix pervenimus Argentinam; tantopere miseri coacti sumus hærere in luto. Hic omnes nostros invenimus incolumes et cupidissimos tui. Quid

Sandus, Hornus, aliique nostri fecerint in Anglia, nihil adhuc audivimus.
Neque id sane mirum. Profecti enim Argentina ad vicesimum primum
Decembris, vix vicesimo post die potuerunt pervenire Antverpiam, quod
Rhenus constrictus glacie illorum navigationem impediret. Hoc tantum
audimus, reditum illorum reginæ esse gratissimum; idque illam non obscure præ se ferre.

Si episcopi pergant porro ut cæperunt, erit brevi magna vilitas episcopatuum. Certum enim est, Christophersonum, rabulam illum Cicestrensem, esse mortuum; quod idem de Vatsono quoque Lincolniensi nunciatur: quod si ita est, vacant hoc tempore episcopatus quatuordecim. Whitus tuus in funere Mariæ, quemadmodum ad te scripsi cum essem Basileæ, habuit ad populum insanam et turbulentissimam concionem; omnia potius tentanda esse, quam ut quicquam de religione immutaretur; bonum factum, si quis exules reduces interfecerit. Accusatus est seditionis a marchione Vintoniensi thesaurario, et Hetho archiepiscopo Eboracensi. Londinensis jussus est reddere hæredibus D. Ridlæi quæcunque illis per vim et injuriam eripuerat. Vocabitur brevi ad causæ dictionem; interim jubetur se domi continere, tanquam in carcere. Regina edixit, ne quis habeat concionem ad populum, neve papista neve minister evangelii. Id alii factum putant, quod cum unus tantum esset minister verbi tum temporis Londini, Benthamus, tantus esset numerus papistarum: alii, quod audita una tantum Benthami publica concione, populus inter se cæperit litigare de ceremoniis; et alii Genevenses esse vellent, alii Francofordiani. Quicquid est, utinam ne nostri homines nimium prudenter et politice versari velint in causa Dei!

Multi putant D. Coquum fore magnum cancellarium; hominem bonum quidem, et pium, uti nosti, sed illi muneri, meo judicio, non aptissimum. Eliensis hæret adhuc apud Philippum, dum aliquid de ista præclara pace, si Deo placet, transigatur;[1] quæ qualis, aut quam firma et diuturna futura sit, θεῶν ἐν γούνασι κεῖται. D. Isabella, spero, vocabitur in Angliam. Video enim alios quoque nostros homines de ea re serio cogitare. D. Zanchius etiam scribet ad reginam: erat scripturus ad totum parliamentum, nisi ego dissuasissem; id enim mihi videbatur alienum. Cranmerus puer relictus est Argentinæ apud Abelum, ut meæ fidei committeretur: ego ab Abelo mutuo sumpsi coronatos pueri nomine. Oro Julium, ut sarcinam et pecuniam, quam reliquimus numeratam apud te, ad illum mittat Argentinam. Ille tibi curabit cautionem, eamque vel deponet apud D. Zanchium, vel, si mavis, ad te mittet. Bene vale, mi dulcissime pater, et plus quam animi dimidium mei. Nolo ad te omnia; oportuit enim me etiam ad D. Bullingerum aliqua scribere: cui ego viro, pro summa ejus erga me humanitate, debeo omnia. Sed ea, quæcunque sunt, non dubito tibi cum illo fore communia.

[1] Edit. Burn. *transfigatur.*

D. Hetonus, D. Abelus, D. Springhamus, D. Parkhurstus, te plurimum salutant, et cum tibi cupiant omnia, nihil tamen magis cupiunt hoc tempore quam Angliam. Saluta D. Muraltum, Hermannum, Julium, Juliam, et omnes tuos meosque, meo nomine. D. Fr. Beti et D. Acontius sunt nunc Argentinæ: uterque te plurimum salutant. Ego D. Beti reddidi literas D. Isabellæ: id obsecro ut illi significes.

Argentinæ, 26.
Januar.
     JOHANNES JUELLUS,
        ex animo, et semper, tuus.

INSCRIPTIO.
Ornatissimo viro, D. Petro Martyri, in ecclesia Tigurina professori S. Theologiæ, domino suo colendissimo.

EPISTOLA IV.

JOHANNES JUELLUS AD PETRUM MARTYREM.

Tandem tamen aliquando, quinquagesimo videlicet septimo post die quam solvissemus Tiguro, pervenimus in Angliam. Quid enim necesse est multa προοιμιάζειν, apud te præsertim, qui rem potius ipsam quæras, et longos istos logos non magni facias? Interea vero, Deum immortalem, quæ illa vita fuit, cum et aqua, et terra, et cœlum ipsum nobis indignaretur, et omnibus modis reditum nostrum impediret? Quid quæris? Omnia nobis toto illo tempore odiosissima et adversissima ceciderunt. Verum hæc antea ad te et ad D. Bullingerum fusius, cum adhuc hærerem Antwerpiæ. Nunc accipe cætera. Quanquam hic, ut vere dicam, arte opus est et myrothecio: non tam quidem, quod mihi nunc ornanda et polienda sint nova, quæ nescio an ulla sint hoc tempore, (scio tamen a te plurima exspectari,) quam quod recantanda sint vetera. Illa enim fere omnia, quæ ego ad te jam antea scripsi ex itinere, multo tum erant alia, et longe auditu jucundiora, quam quæ postea re ipsa inveni domi. Nondum enim ejectus erat Romanus pontifex: nondum pars ulla religionis restituta: eadem erat ubique missarum proluvies: eadem pompa atque insolentia episcoporum. Ista tamen omnia nunc tandem nutare incipiunt, et pene ruere.

Magno nobis impedimento sunt episcopi: qui cum sint, ut scis, in superiori conclavi inter primores et proceres, et nemo ibi sit nostrorum hominum, qui illorum fucos et mendacia possit coram dicendo refutare, inter homines literarum et rerum imperitos soli regnant, et paterculos nostros facile vel numero vel opinione doctrinæ circumscribunt. Regina interea, etsi aperte faveat nostræ causæ, tamen partim a suis, quorum consilio omnia geruntur, partim a legato Philippi comite *Ferio*, homine Hispano, ne quid patiatur innovari mirifice deterretur. Illa tamen quamvis lentius aliquanto quam nos velimus, tamen et prudenter et fortiter et pie persequitur institutum. Et quamvis hactenus principia paulo visa sunt duriora, tamen spes est aliquando recte fore. Interea, ne episcopi nostri queri possint se potentia tantum et lege esse victos, res revocata est ad disputationem, ut novem ex nostris, Scoræus, Coxus, Withedus, Sandus, Grindallus, Hornus, Elmerus, Ghestus quidam Cantabrigiensis, et ego, cum quinque episcopis, abbate Westmonasteriensi, Colo, Cheadsæo, Harpesfeldo, de his rebus coram senatu colloquamur. Prima nostra assertio est, in publicis precibus et administratione sacramentorum alia uti lingua, quam quæ a populo intelligatur, alienum esse a verbo Dei et a consuetudine primitivæ ecclesiæ. Altera est, quamvis ecclesiam provincialem, etiam injussu generalis concilii, posse vel instituere, vel mutare, vel abrogare ceremonias et ritus ecclesiasticos, sicubi id videatur facere ad ædificationem. Tertia, sacrificium illud propitiatorium, quod papistæ fingunt esse in missa, non posse probari ex sacris literis. Pridie calendarum Aprilis instituetur prima conflictatio. Episcopi interim, quasi parta victoria, jamdudum magnifice triumphant. Ubi Froschoverus ad nos venerit, scribam de his rebus omnia disertius. Regina te gerit in oculis. Literas tuas tanti fecit, ut eas iterum tertioque cupidissime relegerit. Librum tuum, ubi advenerit, non dubito multo fore gratiorem.

Oxonii a tuo discessu duæ præclaræ virtutes incredibiliter auctæ sunt, inscitia et contumacia: religio et spes omnis literarum atque ingeniorum funditus periit. Brochus episcopus Glocestriensis, bestia impurissimæ vitæ et multo impurioris conscientiæ, paulo antequam moreretur, miserabilem in modum exclamavit, sese jam se ipso judice esse damnatum. Faber tuus, præclarus scilicet patronus castitatis, deprehensus est in adulterio: et ea causa, quod alioqui vix solet fieri, cum Maria adhuc viveret, novo more, nullo exemplo jussus est cedere lectione theologica. Bruernus simili, sed longe flagitiosiori de scelere coactus est relinquere professionem linguæ Hebraicæ. De Martiali nihil scribo, ne chartas contaminem. De Westono audisti antea. Sed quid istos, inquies, commemoras? Ut intelligas, quibus judicibus oportuerit D. Cranmerum, D. Ridlæum, D. Latimerum condemnari. De Scotis, de pace, de bello nihil. Ternas ad te dedi literas ex itinere; quæ utrum[1] ad te pervenerint, nescio. Sed quoniam longe absumus, longius, O Deum immortalem! et diutius multo, quam vellem, literæ nostræ interdum ventis et fortunæ committendæ sunt.

Vale, mi pater, et domine in Christo colendissime. Saluta D. Bullingerum, D. Gualterum, D. Simlerum, D. Gesnerum, D. Lavaterum,

---

[1] Edit. Burn. *utrumq;*

Julium, Juliam, Martyrillum, D. Hermannum, et convictores tuos Tre
vicenses. Omnes nostri te salutant. Londini 20. Martii, 1559.

JO. JUELLUS, tuus.

P. S. Istæ sunt primæ, quas ad te scribo, ex quo redii in Angliam.
Ita posthac subscribam omnes, ut scire possis, si quæ forte
interciderint.

INSCRIPTIO.

Doctissimo viro D. Petro Martyri Vermilio,
professori sacræ theologiæ in ecclesia Ti-
gurina, domino suo colendissimo.

Tiguri.

EPISTOLA V.

JOHANNES JUELLUS AD PETRUM MARTYREM.

S. P. DE illis disputationibus inter nos et episcopos, quas proximis literis scripsi indictas fuisse in ante calendas Aprilis, quid factum sit, paucis accipe; sic enim visum est continuare orationem sine proœmio. Primum ergo, ut omnis causa jurgiorum et otiosæ contentionis tolleretur, senatus decrevit, ut omnia utrinque de scripto legerentur, et ita describerentur tempora, ut primo die assertiones tantum utrinque nudæ proponerentur; proximo autem conventu ut nos illis responderemus, et illi vicissim nobis. Pridie ergo cal. April. cum magna exspectatione, majori credo frequentia, convenissemus Westmonasterii; episcopi, pro sua fide, nec scripti nec picti quicquam attulerunt, quod dicerent, se non satis temporis habuisse ad res tantas cogitandas: cum tamen habuissent plus minus decem dies, et interea copias auxiliares Oxonio et Cantabrigia et undique ex omnibus angulis contraxissent. Tamen ne tot viri viderentur frustra convenisse, D. Colus subornatus ab aliis venit in medium, qui de prima quæstione, hoc est, de peregrina lingua, unus omnium nomine peroraret. Ille vero, cum omnibus nos contumeliis et convitiis indignissime excepisset, et omnium seditionum auctores et faces appellasset, et supplosione pedum, projectione brachiorum, inflexione laterum, crepitu digitorum, modo dejectione modo sublatione superciliorum, (nosti enim hominis vultum et modestiam,) sese omnes in partes et formas convertisset, huc postremo evasit, ut diceret, Angliam ante mille trecentos annos recepisse evangelium. Et quibus, inquit, literis, quibus annalibus, quibus monumentis constare potest, preces tum publicas in Anglia habitas fuisse Anglice? Postea cum in illo circulo sese satis jamdiu jactavisset, adjecit serio et vero vultu, atque etiam admonuit, ut omnes hoc tanquam quiddam de dictis melioribus diligenter attenderent atque annotarent, apostolos ab initio ita inter sese distribuisse operas, ut alii orientis ecclesias instituerent, alii occidentis. Itaque Petrum et Paulum in Romana ecclesia, quæ totam prope Europam contineret, omnia Romano sermone, hoc est, Latine docuisse: reliquos apostolos in oriente nullo unquam alio sermone usos fuisse, nisi Græco. Tu fortasse ista rides: atqui ego neminem audivi unquam, qui solennius et magistratius insaniret. Si adfuisset Julius noster, centies exclamasset, *Poh! horson knave.* Verum ille inter alia nihil veritus est mysteria ipsa et penetralia atque adyta prodere religionis suæ. Non enim dubitavit graviter et serio monere, etiamsi alia omnia maxime convenirent, tamen non expedire, ut populus, quid in sacris agatur, intelligat. Ignorantia enim, inquit, mater est veræ pietatis, quam ille appellavit devotionem. O mystica sacra atque opertanea bonæ deæ! Quid tu me putas interim de Cotta pontifice cogitasse? Hoc videlicet illud est, in spiritu et veritate adorare! Mitto alia. Cum ille jam calumniando, conviciando, mentiendo magnam partem illius temporis, quod nobis ad disputandum datum erat, exemisset; nos postremo nostra pronunciavimus de scripto ita modeste, ut rem tantum ipsam diceremus, nihil autem læderemus adversarium: postremo ita dimissa est disputatio, ut vix quisquam esset in toto illo conventu, ne comes quidem Salopiensis, quin victoriam illius diei adjudicaret nobis. Postea inita est ratio, ut proximo die lunæ de secunda quæstione eodem modo diceremus; utque die Mercurii nos illorum primi diei argumentis responderemus, et illi vicissim nostris.

Die lunæ, cum frequens multitudo ex omni nobilitate cupidissima audiendi convenisset, episcopi, nescio pudoreve superioris diei an desperatione victoriæ, primum tergiversari, habere se quod dicerent de prima quæstione, nec oportere rem sic abire. Responsum est a senatu, si quid haberent, id tertio post die, prout ab initio convenerat, audiri posse; nunc hoc potius agerent, neve turbarent ordinem. Dejecti de hoc gradu tamen huc evaserunt, si dicendum omnino sit, nolle se priores dicere; se enim in possessione constitisse; nos, si quid vellemus, priori loco experiremur: magnam enim se facturos injuriam causæ suæ, si paterentur nos posteriores discedere cum applausu populi, et aculeos orationis nostræ recentes in auditorum animis relinquere. Senatus contra, hanc ab initio institutam fuisse rationem, ut illi, quod dignitate priores essent, priori etiam loco dicerent; nec eam nunc mutari posse: mirari vero se, quid hoc sit mysterii, cum omnino necesse sit alterutros priores dicere; alioqui enim nihil posse dici: et præsertim, cum Colus in primis disputationibus etiam injussus, ultro prior ad dicendum prosiluerit. Postremo, cum altercationibus magna pars temporis extracta esset, nec episcopi ullo pacto concedere vellent de secundo loco, ad extremum sine disputatione discessum est. Ea vero res incredibile dictu est quantum imminuerit opinionem populi de episcopis: omnes enim cœperunt jam suspicari, quod nihil dicere voluissent, ne potuisse quidem illos quicquam dicere. Postero die Vitus Vintoniensis, amicus tuus, et Vatsonus Lincolniensis, de tam aperto contemptu et contumacia damnati sunt ad turrim: ibi nunc castrametantur, et ex infirmis præmissis concludunt fortiter. Reliqui jubentur quotidie præsto esse in aula, et expectare quid de illis senatus velit decernere. Habes ἔντευξιν ἀτελῆ et pene ἀνέντευκτον;[1] quam tamen, quo melius rem omnem intelligeres, descripsi pluribus fortasse quam oportuit.

Bene vale, mi pater, decus meum, atque etiam animi dimidium mei. Si quid est apud vos novarum rerum hoc tempore, id malo esse proximarum literarum argumentum. Saluta plurimum meo nomine venerandum illum virum, et mihi in Christo dominum colendissimum, D. Bullingerum, D. Gualterum, D. Simlerum, D. Lavaterum, D. Volphium, D. Gesnerum, D. Hallerum, D. Frisium, D. Hermannum, et Julium tuum meumque. Nostri omnes te salutant, et tibi omnia cupiunt. Londini, 6. April. 1559.

JO. JUELLUS, tuus.

Post-script'.
Istæ sunt secundæ, quas ad te scribo, ex quo redii in Angliam.

INSCRIPTIO.
D. Petro Martyri, professori sacræ theologiæ in ecclesia Tigurina, viro doctissimo,
et domino suo in Christo colendissimo.
Tiguri.

EPISTOLA VI.

JOHANNES JUELLUS AD PETRUM MARTYREM.

S. P. Magnam mihi fecit injuriam Sandus noster, qui, cum ego jam ad te scripsissem, et cum magnopere, ne id faceret, oravissem, tamen literas suas sine meis literis ad te miserit. Quanquam, nisi quod scio officium a te jamdudum requiri meum, nihil hactenus factum est quod te tantopere auditu juvare possit. O Maria et Mariana tempora! Quanto nunc mollius et remissius veritas propugnatur, quam pridem defendebantur mendacia! Adversarii nostri omnia præcipites, sine exemplo, sine jure ullo, sine lege: nos nihil nisi circumspecte, prudenter, considerate, callide; quasi sine nostris edictis et cautionibus Deus ipse vix possit auctoritatem suam retinere: ut multi nunc otiose ac scurriliter jocentur, "Christum antea ejectum ab hostibus, nunc excludi ab amicis." Ista

[1] Edit. Burn. ἀνεύτευκτον.

mora nonnihil nostrorum hominum animos emollivit; adversariorum autem furores et insanias incredibiliter confirmavit. Vix enim credas, quanto illi nunc sese confidentius gerant, quam unquam antea: populus tamen ubique, et in primis omnis passim nobilitas, et illorum odit triumphos et insolentiam, et mirifice sitit evangelium. Itaque factum est, ut multis jam in locis Missæ etiam invitis edictis sua sponte ceciderint. Quod si Regina ipsa eam abigeret e suo larario, res omnis facillime posset confici. Tanti sunt apud nos exempla principum: quod enim regis exemplo fit, id vulgus, ut scis, non dubitat recte fieri. Quanquam illa ita Missam illam suam, quam adhuc temporis tantum causa retinet, temperavit, ut, quamvis in ea multa gerantur quæ ferri vix possint, tamen non ita magno cum periculo audiri possint. Verum optima et veræ pietatis cupientissima fœmina, etsi omnia primo quoque tempore mutata cupiat, tamen induci non potest, ut quicquam velit immutare sine lege; ne res non tam sanorum hominum judicio, quam furentis impetu multitudinis administrari videantur. Interim in senatu multa de religione mutata sunt, etiam invitis et reclamantibus atque omnia turbantibus episcopis. Sed ea, quoniam adhuc in vulgus ignota sunt, et sæpe sub incudem redeunt, nolo scribere.

Sandus, Grindallus, Sampson, Scoræus (et quid istos dico?) omnes adhuc sumus Londini, integra omnes valetudine, eadem conditione, eodem loco, eadem gratia. Multi de te, ubi sis, quid vivas, quid doceas, an velis redire in Angliam, si revoceris, honorificentissime percontantur. Sidallus statim scripsit ad me, ne quid iniquis de se rumoribus velim credere. Memini te, cum Argentinæ doceres de potestate quam habent principes in episcopos, hoc etiam addidisse, Justinianum Imperatorem movisse loco Sylverium et Vigilium. Si quando huc scribes, quæso te, ut locum, ubi illa historia scripta sit, paucis indices. De Reginæ nuptiis, quas nos omnes maxime cupimus, hactenus nihil. Bene vale, mi pater, et Domine in Christo colendissime. Londini, 14. Aprilis, 1559.

JO. JUELLUS,

Tuus tuus.

P. S. Istæ sunt tertiæ. Adscribo numerum ut scire possis, an aliquæ, ut fit, perierint in itinere.

INSCRIPTIO.

D. Petro Martyri Vermilio professori sacræ theologiæ in ecclesia Tigurina, viro longe doctissimo et domino suo in Christo colendissimo.

Tiguri.

EPISTOLA VII.

JOHANNES JUELLUS AD PETRUM MARTYREM.

S. P. Accepi ternas a te literas, omnes eodem ferme tempore: quæ cum multis de causis mihi essent, ut certe debebant, jucundissimæ, vel quod essent a te, vel quod rerum tuarum statum significarent et amorem erga me tuum; tamen nulla alia causa mihi visæ sunt jucundiores, quam quod officium meum requirerent, meque vel oblivionis vel tarditatis blande ac tacite accusarent; quorum alterum magnitudo tuorum erga me meritorum, alterum negotia mea non sinunt. Scripsi quidem ego ad te ternas literas, ex quo redii in Angliam; quas tamen video, cum tu illas tuas scriberes, nondum ad te pervenisse. Et fieri potest, ut sæpe fit, ut aut hæreant uspiam, et ignavæ atque otiosæ imitentur religionem nostram, aut etiam pericrint in itinere. Sed quicquid est, nulla potest in ea re magna jactura fieri. Erant enim pene inanes, quod non multum adhuc esset, quod aut tu audire libenter velles, aut ego scribere. Nunc agitur causa pontificis, et agitur utrinque fortiter. Episcopi enim sudant, ne quid errasse videantur; atque ea causa moratur et impedit religionem. Difficile est enim cursum incitare, ut inquit ille, $\beta\rho\alpha\delta\upsilon\pi\acute{o}\delta\omega\nu$ ἵππων ἐνόντων. Fecnamus, abbas Westmonasteriensis, opinor, ut auctoritatem adderet professioni suæ, cum peroraret in senatu, Nazaræos, prophetas, Christum ipsum, et apostolos conjecit in numerum monachorum. Nemo causam nostram acrius oppugnat quam Eliensis. Is et locum suum in senatu, et ingenium retinet. Episcoporum prædia redacta sunt in fiscum: illis ex permutatione dabuntur sacerdotia, quæ antea erant attributa monasteriis. Interim de scholis, et cura literarum magnum ubique silentium. Hoc scilicet est δαίμονας ἐξελαύνειν, ἄλλον ἄλλῳ, ὥς φασι, δαίμονι.

Regina de te honorifice et loquitur et sentit. Dixit nuper D. Russelio, se velle te accersere in Angliam; id enim ille aliique urgent, quantum possunt. Sed nisi et serio, et cupide, et honorifice petaris, nunquam ero auctor ut venias. Nihil equidem magis aut miserius cupio, quam te videre, et dulcissimis illis sermonibus tuis frui, sive (quod O utinam aliquando contingat!) in Anglia, sive etiam Tiguri. Verum quantum video obstabit desiderio nostro inauspicata illa et saxis ac Saxonibus damnata παρουσία. Nostra enim nunc cogitat fœdus Smalcaldicum. Scribit autem ad illam quidam e Germania, illud fœdus non posse ullo pacto coire, si tu ad nos venias. Illum autem quendam si addo aliquando fuisse episcopum, si nunc esse exulem, si hominem Italum, si veteratorem, si aulicum, si Petrum, si Paulum, magis eum fortasse noris, quam ego. Sed quicquid est, nos articulos omnes religionis et doctrinæ nostræ exhibuimus Reginæ, et ne minimo quidem apice discessimus a confessione Tigurina: quanquam Ἀρχιμάγειρος amicus tuus inventum illud, nescio quod, suum tuetur mordicus, et nobis omnibus mirifice succenset. Adhuc nemini nostrum ne de obolo quidem prospectum est. Itaque ego nondum abjicio insignia illa, quæ mihi finxi Tiguri, librum et crucem. Goodmannum audio esse apud nos; sed ita, ut non ausit φαινοπροσωπεῖν et venire in publicum. Sed quanto satius fuisset sapuisse in tempore! Si velit agnoscere errorem, nihil erit periculi. Verum, ut homo est satis acer, et in eo, quod semel suscepit, nimium pertinax, non nihil vereor, ne nolit cedere.

Libri tui nondum venerunt: id ego tanto magis miror, quod tot Angli jam pridem redierint Francofordia. Munus tuum ubi advenerit, non dubito Reginæ fore gratissimum. Illud ego, quoniam tu ita jubes, quamvis alioqui sit per se ornatissimum, tamen si dabitur facultas, verbis ornabo meis. De illo autem libro, quem tu seorsim ad me misisti, equidem non invenio quibus verbis tibi agam gratias. Itaque malo et huic humanitati tuæ, et superiorum tuorum erga me meritorum magnitudini, ultro succumbere. Certe etsi te nunquam ex animo eram dimissurus, tamen hac commonefactione et mnemosyno excitatus, tanto acrius et reverentius colam, quoad vixero, nomen tuum. Alii tui libri jampridem allati sunt a bibliopolis, et emuntur cupidissime: omnes enim libenter videre cupiunt, quibus venabulis illa bestia confossa sit.

Bene vale, mi pater, et domine in Christo colendissime. Saluta D. Bullingerum, D. Bernardinum, D. Gualterum, D. Simlerum: dicerem et Frenchamum, nisi illum putarem jamdudum aut in balneo esse, aut in via: hoc enim anni tempore, cum auditur cuculus, vix solet esse apud se. Londini, 28. Apr. 1559.

Tui cupidissimus,
tuoque nomini deditissimus,

P. S. Istæ sunt quartæ.   JOHANNES JUELLUS.

INSCRIPTIO.

Doctissimo viro, D. Petro Martyri, professori S. theologiæ in ecclesia Tigurina, domino suo colendissimo.

Tiguri.

EPISTOLA VIII.

JOHANNES FOXUS AD HENRICUM BULLINGERUM.

SALUTEM in Christo. Mittimus isthuc Anglum cum birria; venturi et ipsi sumus, si audiamus eum vivere. Itaque quo celerius sciremus, placuit expeditum hunc internuncium præmittere cum equo conductitio; nam plures conducere non licuit. Quæso ut jubeas hunc iterum ad nos, si Frenchamus vivit, maturare. Aroviæ birria facilius et vicinius erit vobis parabilis, si opus fuerit. D. Jesus, omnis salutis fons, nos ad gloriam ipsius custodiat! Maii 6, 1559. postridie quam literæ huc vestræ perlatæ sunt. Basileæ.

Tuus in Christo,
J. FOXUS.

INSCRIPTIO.
Doctissimo viro, D. Henrico Bullingero.
Tiguri.

EPISTOLA IX.

JOHANNES JUELLUS AD PETRUM MARTYREM.

S P. Et quid tandem ego ad te scribam? nos enim adhuc omnes peregrini sumus domi nostræ. Redi ergo, inquies, Tigurum. Utinam, utinam, mi pater, id mihi aliquando liceat! Te enim, quantum video, nulla spes est venturum unquam in Angliam. O Tigurum, Tigurum! quanto ego nunc sæpius de te cogito, quam unquam de Anglia, cum essem Tiguri! Quamvis autem, ut dixi, in patria nostra simus hospites, excipimus tamen interdum quædam ἄφατα καὶ ἀδιήγητα. Verum πολλάκι τὸ κακὸν κατακείμενον ἔνδον ἄμεινον.

De religione transactum est, (utinam bonis auspiciis!) ut esset eo loco, quo fuit ultimis tuis temporibus sub Edouardo. Sed, quantum quidem ego adhuc videre possum, non est ea alacritas in nostris hominibus, quæ nuper in papistis fuit. Ita misere comparatum est, ut mendacium armatum sit, veritas autem non tantum inermis, verum etiam sæpe odiosa. Agitur nunc de sacro et scenico apparatu; quæque ego tecum aliquando ridens, ea nunc, a nescio quibus, (nos enim non advocamur in consilium,) serio et graviter cogitantur, quasi religio Christiana constare non possit sine pannis. Nos quidem non ita otiosi sumus ab animo, ut tanti possimus facere istas ineptias. Alii sectantur auream quandam, quæ mihi plumbea potius videtur, mediocritatem; et clamant, Dimidium plus toto.

Quidam ex nostris designati sunt episcopi, Parkerus Cantuariensis, Coxus Norvicensis, Barlovus Cicestrensis, Scoræus Herfordensis, Grindallus Londinensis, (nam Bonerus jussus est cedere:) qui quando adituri sint possessionem, nescio. Ego ex isto flore, quod tu de vino soles, facile divino quæ sit futura vindemia. Adversarii interim nostri καιροφυλακτοῦσι, et pollicentur sibi ista non fore perpetua. In Scotia, nescio quid audimus tumultuatum de religione: nobiles ejectis monachis occupasse monasteria; et aliquot milites præsidiarios Gallos in tumultu occidisse; Reginam iratam edixisse, ut Knoxus concionator inflato cornu, (est enim ille in Scotia mos solennis, si quem velint extorrem facere,) ex omnibus finibus ejiceretur. Quid de illo factum sit, nescio.

Nunc instituitur legatio in totam Angliam de formanda religione. Sandus ibit in Lancastriam; ego in Devoniam; alii alio. Regina non vult appellari caput ecclesiæ, quod mihi certe non displicet. Interim, quid *il cavetso della Chiesa* cogitet aut murmuret, aut quas turbas daturus sit, tu quoniam propius abes, facilius audire potes. Papistæ nostri odiosissime pugnant, neque alii ulli contumacius, quam qui a nobis discesserunt. Tanti est semel gustasse de missa! *Qui bibit inde, furit: procul hinc discedite, queis est Mentis cura bonæ: qui bibit inde, furit:* vident erepto illo palladio omnia ventura in periculum. Pax inter nos et Gallum ita convenit, ut Caletum octo post annos redeat in potestatem Anglorum. Quod ut Julius noster credat, opus est incredibili et robusta fide. Quicquid erit, tamen nos eo nomine exspectamus pignora e Gallia. De nuptiis Reginæ adhuc nihil. Tamen ambit hoc tempore Suecus, Saxo, Carolus Ferdinandi. Mitto Pikerinum hominem Anglum. Tamen, quid malim, scio. Et ista sunt ut scis μυστικώτερα: et apud nos proverbii loco dici solet, matrimonia esse fatalia.

Bene vale, mi pater, et domine in Christo colendissime. Saluta, quæso, optimum senem D. Bernardinum, D. Muraltum, D. Volphium meo nomine. Liber tuus, quem Reginæ misisti dono, redditus est a D. Cæcilio: ad meas manus, nescio quo casu, non pervenit. Ego tamen, quoties sum in aula, diligenter exquiro, numquid illa velit: et adhuc nihil audio. Sed quicquid erit, faciam ut intelligas. Londini.

Istæ sunt quintæ, tu vide an aliquæ perierint.

INSCRIPTIO.
Doctissimo viro D. Petro Martyri,
 professori sacræ theologiæ in
 ecclesia Tigurina, domino suo
 colendissimo. Tiguri.

EPISTOLA X.

JOHANNES FOXUS AD HENRICUM BULLINGERUM.

SALUTEM multam, doctissime simul et carissime in Christo Domino. Scripsit ad nos his diebus D. Abelus, mercator Anglus, ex Argentina; in quibus suis ad nos literis aliæ continebantur ad te, ad D. Simlerum, Gualterum, et Gesnerum literæ ex Anglia scriptæ. Quæ si ad vos pervenerint, cupio nostras literas in quibus illæ continebantur huc ad nos mitti. Si non pervenerint, nolebam id vos nescire tamen: id enim ex alteris jam Abeli literis ad nos scriptis intelleximus. Literæ illæ, quantum intelligo, mense Martio ad vos ex Anglia destinatæ sunt, ad nos mense Aprili mittebantur; jamque mense Maio de non redditis intelligimus. Scripseram præterea D. Frenshamo istic apud vos Aprilis 23; nec scio an redditæ sint illi literæ. Et de valetudine ejus valde scire cupio. Tua præstantia dignabitur eum hac de re admonere, simul et imbecillitatem illius sublevare, quoad poteris, si quid laboret.

In historiis Martyrum colligendis hic tumultuor pro viribus, ac ferme supra vires. Qua in re si quid poteris, nos adjuves velim. Poteris autem, si cum D. Bernardino istic cæterisque Italis agas, ut si quid habeant rerum hujusmodi ex Italia breviter annotatum velint; deinde si quid tua etiam memoria de rebus in vestro confinio gestis teneat, nomina saltem et oppida paucis consignare volueris. Nam etsi in Britannicis maxime laboramus, cæterarum tamen gentium sacras historias, si contingant, non præteriemus. D. Jesus salutem tuam, studia et labores, dirigat ad gloriam ipsius! Basileæ, pridie Pentecostes, 1559.

Tuus in Christo,
JOAN. FOXUS.

INSCRIPTIO.
Doctissimo ac integerrimo viro D. Henrico Bullingero, apud Tigurinos Ecclesiastæ. Tiguri.

EPISTOLA XI.

RICARDUS COXUS AD WOLFGANGUM WEIDNERUM.

Cum Wormatia discederem, reverende senex et frater in Christo plurimum observande, semper apud me decrevi ad te scribere, certioremque facere tandem aliquando de rerum nostrarum statu et conditione, quod te audire non ingratum esse existimavi propter ardentem sincerumque zelum, quo indies afficeris erga Christi Jesu evangelium. Coactus sum hactenus, fateor, invitus silere, ne parum tibi grata referrem. Sub sævo Mariæ imperio ita crevit invaluitque papismus ad quinquennium tantum, ut incredibile fuerit, quantopere pectora papistarum obduruerint; adeo ut non sine magna difficultate pientissima nostra Regina una cum suis, qui a veritate strenue steterunt, sinceræ Christi religioni locum obtinere potuerit. Restiterunt in summo nostro concilio (quod Parlamentum Gallico vocabulo appellamus) Pontifices, Scribæ et Pharisæi. Et quia eo loci paucos habebant, qui contra vel hiscere possent, vincere perpetuo videbantur. Interim nos, pusillus grex, qui apud vos in Germania hoc quinquennio Dei beneficio latuimus, in suggestis, maxime coram Regina nostra Elisabetha, contra intonamus, Pontificem Romanum vere Antichristum, et traditiones pro maxima sui parte meras esse blasphemias. Tandem paullatim resipiscere cœperunt ex nobilibus multi, ex plebe innumeri, ex clero prorsus nulli. Immotus enim stat clerus totus, *tanquam dura silex, aut stet Marpesia cautes*, ut poeta canit. Denique huc res est perducta, ut octo ex ipsorum antesignanis, seu episcopi, seu ex doctis selectissimi, cum octo nostrum, abjectorum scilicet atque profugorum, de quibusdam religionis capitibus dissererent. Et ut vitaretur verborum pugna, scriptis agi constitutum est. Statuta est dies. Adsumus omnes. Adsunt Reginæ consiliarii. Adest tota fere nobilitas. Decretum est ut ipsi primum de controversiis sententiam suam proponant. Unus quispiam, illorum nomine, tanquam Goliath contra Davidem, sua venditat, propugnat, et argumentis irrefragabilibus (ut videbatur) confirmat, sibique plaudit, tanquam jam victor evadens. Respondit nostrum unus veritate fretus, non ampullis verborum, in timore Domini, non in doctrinæ venditatione. Finita responsione incredibilis mox audientium applausus excitatus est, non sine magna adversariorum perturbatione atque confusione. Venit alter dies simili tractationi destinatus. Rogantur adversarii nostri a consultationis præside, ut eo ordine progrederentur, quo decretum antea fuerat; nimirum ut ipsi primum inciperent in altera controversia suam sententiam dicere, nosque sequeremur. Illi vero contra contendunt, territi scilicet primi diei successu parum prospero, clamitantque iniquum esse, ut ipsi primum dicere incipiant, cum ipsi jam tot annis perstiterint in possessione catholicæ ecclesiæ : si quid habeamus contra ipsos, proferamus[1] nos, ut ipsi pro sua auctoritate nos refutent, atque compescant tanquam filios degeneres, ut qui ab ecclesiæ unitate jamdiu exciderimus. Gratia Christo Domino nostro! Dum illi mandato obsistunt, merito coercentur, et sua causa cadunt. Itaque stabilitur apud nos per omnia regni loca sincera Christi religio, eadem prorsus ratione, qua sub Edvardo olim nostro beatissimæ memoriæ promulgata erat.

Hæc pauca, sed certa, visum est ad te scribere, quem scio nostra solide gaudere gaudia, ut nobiscum gratias Domino Deo nostro agas, qui nos in ista humiliatione et cruce vere paterna sua commiseratione respexit atque consolatus est. Det ipse ut tanta et incredibilia ejus beneficia e mentibus nostris nunquam elabantur! Gratam rem fecerit tua humanitas, si ista D. Jacobo Cornicio medico et Vespasiano Fittich, amicis meis summis, communicare dignetur. Jam jam aggredimur septa papistica disrumpere atque dissipare, et vineam Domini felicibus auspiciis restaurare. Jam sumus in opere. At messis multa, operarii pauci. Rogemus Dominum ut mittat operarios in messem. Hæc paucula habui tibi pro officio

---

[1] MS. *perferamus.*

in te meo impertiri.   D. Jesus te servet, pietatemque tuam servet auge-
atque ad ultimum usque spiritus halitum.   Londini in Anglia, 20 Maii,
1559.   Tui studiosiss.
              INSCRIPTIO.   RIC. COXUS.
Viro eximio, eruditione et pietate insignito,
  D. D. Wolfgango Weidnero Wormati-
  ensi, amico meo observandiss. Wormatiæ.

EPISTOLA XII.

JOHANNES PARKHURSTUS AD HENRICUM BULLINGERUM.

Humanissimas tuas literas Juellus et ego initio Aprilis accepimus; ex quibus perspexi, te ad tempus constitutum filium tuum Rodolphum, ob ingenii cultum capessendum, ad Academiam Oxoniensem missurum. Cujus, ut nunc sunt res, ego auctor tibi esse nolim. Nam adhuc spelunca est tenebrarum, tenebrionum, latronum. Pauci illic sunt evangelici, plurimi papistæ. Sed cum reformata fuerit, quod brevi futurum et speramus et optamus, tum demum veniat tuus Rodolphus. Quam gratus futurus sit mihi illius in Angliam adventus, jam nihil dicam. Malim animi mei in illum gratitudinem re quam verbis exprimere.

Liber communium precum, temporibus Edvardi regis usitatus, nunc iterum per totam Angliam in usu passim est, [et] ubique erit, renitentibus atque reclamantibus pseudoepiscopis. Regina caput ecclesiæ Anglicanæ dici non vult, tametsi hic titulus illi oblatus sit, sed gubernatricis titulum libenter recipit; qui in idem recidunt. Papa ex Anglia denuo est profligatus, mœrentibus episcopis et universa rasorum colluvie. Missæ sunt abrogatæ. Octavo Maii parliamentum est finitum. Comes Bedfordiensis tres coronatos nostro Wolphgango donavit. In hoc ille felicior multis aliis. Qui posthac fient episcopi, nullas habebunt arces, prædia, villas. Qui nunc sunt, iis quæ habent, donec vixerint, fruentur: digni, qui non solum ab officio, sed et capistro suspendantur. Sunt enim Davi, interturbantes omnia. Monasteria brevi dissolventur.

Plura jam scribere non possum. Nam intra quatriduum in solo natali cum pessimis bestiis Arianis et e pulpito et mutuis colloquiis est mihi conflictandum: in quem finem eruditissimum tuum librum de utraque in Christo natura diligenter evolvi. Spero me satis instructum in aciem venturum, atque adeo hostes Christi debellaturum. Vivit Christus, regnat et regnabit, invitis Arianis, Anabaptistis et papistis.

Vale, vir præstantissime atque animo meo carissime! Optimam tuam conjugem, filios, filias, et generosissimos tuos generos meo nomine salutationibus[2] (ut sic dixerim) adobruito. Gratissimam rem mihi fecit bonus

[2 MS. *salutabis.*]

Lavaterus, qui tam bonum libellum, eumque totum Tigurinum, ad me miserit. Salutabis mihi D. Bibliandrum, Collinum, Hallerum, Wolphium, Wickium, Frisium, Bernardinum, Ammianum, Meijerum, Sebastianum Colerum, Funckium, Pellicanum, Froschoverum et omnes. Uxor mea te, tuam, tuos, tuas, et omnes salutat. Sæpe erumpunt illi lacrymæ, cum de feminis Tigurinis fit mentio. Vestris magnificis magistratibus, urbi, atque adeo toti Tigurinæ ditioni omnia felicissima precor.

  Urbs Tigurina, vale: valeant male, prospera cuncta
   Qui tibi non optent. Urbs Tigurina, vale.
Raptim. Londini, 21 Maii, 1559.
      Tuissimus,
  INSCRIPTIO. JOHANNES PARKHURSTUS.
Præclarissimo Viro D. Henrico Bullingero.
   Tiguri.

EPISTOLA XIII.

JOHANNES PARKHURSTUS AD CONRADUM GESNERUM.

SALVE iterum atque iterum, clarissime atque animo meo carissime Gesnere. Cum primum venissem Londinum, Caium tuum quæsivi, ut illi tuas literas traderem; et cum non esset domi, ancillæ illius dedi: nam uxorem non habet, nec unquam habuit. Nulla præterit hebdomada, in qua bis terve illius ædes non adeam. Pulso fores: accedit puella, non patet tamen introitus; per rimam spectans rogat quid velim. Ego rursum rogo, ubi sit herus, an sit domi aliquando, an velit esse domi. Illa semper domi esse negat. Is nunquam et nusquam comparet. Et jam peregre agit. Quid igitur de illo scribam, nescio. Certe aliquid illi in faciem dicam, si quando forte fortuna obvium habuero. Sentiet, qui vir siem.

Papa ex Anglia denuo est ejectus. Sacrifices hoc male habet. Pseudo-episcopi piis Reginæ conatibus totis conatibus restitere, et ne multa finem a bonis optatum sortirentur effecere. At jam et Deo et hominibus sunt exosi, nec usquam nisi inviti prorepunt, ne forte fiat tumultus in populo. Multi coram eos vocant carnifices. Si qua alia sunt nova, in aliorum literis scripsi. Quando unum orbem tibi non satis esse credo, mittam plures, sed cum factus fuero pecuniosior: nunc enim sumus omnes vel ipso Iro pauperiores. Senties me non immemorem tui. Vale. Uxorem tuam, Frisium, Simlerum, et alios amicos omnes in meo nomine salutabis. Uxor mea vos omnes salutat. Raptim. Londini, 21 Maii, 1559.
      Tuus,
  INSCRIPTIO. JOANNES PARKHURSTUS.
Clarissimo viro D. Conrado Gesnero.
   Tiguri.

EPISTOLA XIV.

JOHANNES JUELLUS AD HENRICUM BULLINGERUM.

S. P. Gratissimæ erant mihi Parkhurstoque meo literæ tuæ, ornatissime vir, vel quod essent a te, cui quantum debeamus nunquam possumus oblivisci, vel quod suavitatis et humanitatis erga nos tuæ, quam toto nos tempore exilii nostri experti sumus maximam, altissima vestigia retinerent. Atque utinam possimus aliquando pietatis tuæ partem aliquam compensare! Quicquid erit, animus certe nobis nunquam deerit. Quod nos hortaris, ut strenue ac fortiter nos geramus, erat ille aculeus non tantum non ingratus nobis, sed etiam pene necessarius. Nobis enim in hoc tempore non tantum cum adversariis, sed etiam cum amicis nostris, (qui proximis istis annis a nobis defecerunt et cum hostibus conjurarunt, jamque acrius multo et contumacius resistunt quam ulli hostes,) quodque molestissimum est, cum reliquiis Hispanorum, hoc est, cum teterrimis vitiis, superbia, luxu, libidine, luctandum est. Facimus quidem nos, fecimusque, quod potuimus. Deus bene fortunet, et det incrementum! Sed ita hactenus vivimus, ut vix videamur restituti ab exilio. Ne dicam aliud, ne suum quidem adhuc restitutum est cuiquam nostrum: quanquam, etsi molesta nobis est ista tam diuturna expectatio, tamen non dubitamus brevi recte fore. Habemus enim reginam et prudentem et piam, et nobis faventem et propitiam. Religio restituta est in eum locum, quo sub Edvardo rege fuerat: ad eam rem non dubito tuas reipublicæque vestræ literas et exhortationes multum ponderis attulisse. Regina non vult appellari aut scribi caput ecclesiæ Anglicanæ: graviter enim respondit, illam dignitatem soli attributam esse Christo, nemini autem mortalium convenire; deinde illos titulos ita fœde contaminatos esse ab antichristo, ut jam non possint amplius satis pie a quoquam usurpari.

Academiæ nostræ ita afflictæ sunt et perditæ, ut Oxonii vix duo sint, qui nobiscum sentiant, et illi ipsi ita abjecti et fracti, ut nihil possint. Ita Soto fraterculus, et alius, nescio quis, Hispanus monachus, omnia ea, quæ D. Petrus Martyr pulcherrime plantaverat, everterunt a radicibus, et vineam Domini redegerunt in solitudinem. Vix credas tantam vastitatem afferri potuisse tam parvo tempore. Quare etsi magnam alioqui voluptatem capturus sim, si vel canem Tigurinum videre possem in Anglia, tamen non possum esse auctor hoc tempore, ut juvenes vestros aut literarum aut religionis causa ad nos mittatis, nisi eosdem remitti velitis ad vos impios et barbaros. Rogavit me nuper D. Russelius, qua maxime re posset tibi aliisque tuis fratribus et symmistis gratum facere. Hoc videlicet sensit, velle se humanitatis vestræ, quam semper prædicat, et hospitii causa aliquid ad vos dono mittere. Ego vero nihil tibi tuisque fore gratius, quam si religionem Christi studiose ac fortiter propagaret, et papistarum insolentiam imminueret. Quod ille et recepit se facturum, et certe facit, quantum potest.

Venerunt hodie Londinum legati regis Galliæ, qui gratulentur de pace: princeps legationis est juvenis Momorancius. De nuptiis Reginæ adhuc nihil. Ambit quidem filius Johannis Frederici, et frater secundus natu Maximiliani. Vulgi tamen suspicio inclinat in Pikerinum, hominem Anglum, virum et prudentem et pium, et regia corporis dignitate præditum. Deus bene vertat, quicquid erit!

Istæ primæ sunt, quas ad te seorsim scripsi, ex quo redii in Angliam: sed quoniam, quæ scripsi ad D. Martyrem, scio illum propter summam inter vos conjunctionem tecum habuisse communia, non dubito, quæcumque ad illum scripsi, eadem ad te quoque scripta dicere. Bene vale, mi pater, et domine in Christo colendissime. Saluta optimam illam mulierem, uxorem tuam; D. Gualterum, D. Simlerum, D. Zuinglium, D. Lavaterum. Si quid unquam erit, in quo possim aut tibi aut tuis esse voluptati aut usui, polliceor tibi non tantum operam, studium, diligentiam, sed etiam animum et corpus meum. Maii 22, Londini, 1559.

Tui studiosissimus,

INSCRIPTIO. JO. JUELLUS.

Viro longe doctissimo D. Henrico Bullingero,
pastori ecclesiæ Tigurinæ dignissimo, et
domino suo colendissimo. Tiguri.

EPISTOLA XV.

JOHANNES FOXUS AD HENRICUM BULLINGERUM.

SALUTEM in Domino. Nihil erat quod precibus mecum ageres, carissime Bullingere, si quid videres in quo opus esset officii mei ministerio. De literis illis, quarum facis mentionem, iterum adivi Petrum Maclinæum hic bibliopolam, cui tum literæ illæ ab Abelo, ut ad me scribit, destinabantur. Fuit pariter mecum et Laurentius noster, cui totum illum fasciculum literarum nostrarum inscripsit (ut scripsit ad me) Abelus. Petrus in hunc modum nobis respondit: Venisse ad se quemdam cum literis, qui auriga non esset, sed ab auriga conductus, vel qui ab auriga emisset literas illas, ut ipse postea majori quæstu revenderet. Unde Petrus iste, pretii importunitate offensus, et quia rem ad se nihil pertinere videt, sed ad Anglos, ut pecuniæ suæ consuleret, hominem misit ad diversorium ibi proximum hominis sylvestris, affirmans illic reperturum esse eum Anglos, qui literas ab eo acciperent: cum tamen nullos sciam Anglos qui id temporis in urbe essent præter nos; nec satis mirari possum, quid Petro in mentem veniret, ut hominem ad sylvestrem mitteret, quum satis sciret nos ubi in urbe essemus, ad quos hominem multo melius mittere potuisset. Itaque expostulanti mihi hoc nomine cum Petro, is ita respondet, putasse se atque audivisse Anglos apud sylvestrem tum fuisse, &c. Verum ita res habet: Petrus ille quia pecunias nolebat in avarum hominem exponere, nos literas perdidimus. Quod tamen non tam mihi dolet causa mea ac mearum literarum, quas in eodem fasciculo inclusas perdidi, quam tuarum potius, optime ac carissime D. Bullingere, quas tibi a veteri amico scriptas ex te intelligo. Atque utinam, ut Petro tum dixi, triplum illi dedissem, dummodo grammatophoro, vel potius grammatoclepto illi, quisquis is fuit, satisfecisset! Quo magis te sollicitum hac de re video in literis, hoc magis me quoque eadem res sollicitum habet, ut ingenue et simpliciter tibi fatear. Nec scio quid in hac re agam, aut unde quæram amplius.

Etsi literæ tuæ parum mihi bonam spem de Frenshamo pollicentur, tamen quia adhuc spirat, dumque spirat, non desinemus de illo sperare bene. Erat hic Anglus annorum 16 adolescentulus, qui hoc anno consimili ex tussi et phthisi non modo vicinus morti, sed mors ipsa videri poterat; et tamen stupentibus hic medicis revaluit, atque in Angliam cum parentibus profectus est. Sit Christo Domino laus! Utinam et Frenshamus noster simile aliquod in vestris quoque medicis ludat ludibrium aliquando, si ita Domino Christo Ἀρχιάτρῳ videatur! Sed fiat sancta ejus voluntas. Si quid habes de D. Grinæo, cujus facis in literis mentionem, rogo quamprimum huc transmittas, nobisque communices. Hoperus an istic apud vos an hic Basileæ uxorem duxerit, cupiam certior fieri. Dum ceteros colligimus Germanos martyres, nolim Zuinglium unum præteriri: de quo si quid habetis, aut si quid velitis nobis communicatum, si minus id commode per Germanos typographos fieri poterit, curabimus in Anglia illud, volente Domino, imprimendum.

Cupiam, si vitam dederit Dominus, te istic invisere et salutare ante meam in patriam profectionem, humanissime simul et doctissime Bullingere. Mone, precor, Frenshamum, si adhuc spirat, ne sic animo despondeat, bonasque omnes spes abjiciat, neve corporis morbo animi major videatur desperatio. Saluta, quæso, D. Petrum Martyrem meis verbis plurimum. D. Jesus labores tuos pariter cum incolumitate indies provehat ad ecclesiæ suæ emolumentum! Amen. Basileæ, Jun. 17, 1559.

Tuus in Christo,

INSCRIPTIO.   JO. FOXUS.

Doctissimo viro D. Henrico Bullingero.
    Tiguri.

P. S. Quæso has alteras literas D. Frenshamo, si vivit, impartias.

EPISTOLA XVI.

JOHANNES JUELLUS AD PETRUM MARTYREM.

HACTENUS minus frequenter ad te scripsi, mi pater, quod multa me negotia publica privataque impedirent. Nunc scribo, non quod plus nunc otii sit quam antea, sed quod minus posthac futurum sit multo quam nunc est. Alterum enim jam pedem in terra habeo, alterum pene sublatum in equum. Mox enim ingredior longinquam et difficilem legationem constituendæ religionis ergo per Redingum, Abindonam, Glocestriam, Bristolium, Thermas, Welliam, Exonium, Cornubiam, Dorcestriam, Sarisburiam. Ambitus itineris nostri erit plus minus septingentorum milliarium; vix ut quarto demum mense putem nos esse redituros. Quare ne me interea putares esse mortuum, etsi ante duodecim dies nescio quid ad te scripserim de rebus communibus, tamen non alienum fore duxi, si nunc quoque paucis te quasi in digressu salutarem. Res nostræ satis nunc sunt in proclivi: Regina optime animata: populus ubique sitiens religionis. Episcopi, potius quam ut relinquant papam, quem toties jam antea abjurarunt, malunt cedere rebus omnibus. Nec tamen id religionis causa faciunt, quam nullam habent, sed constantiæ, quam miseri nebulones vocari jam volunt conscientiam. Sacrifici jam tandem mutata religione passim abstinent a cœtu sacro, quasi piaculum summum sit cum populo Dei quicquam habere commune. Est autem tanta illorum nebulonum rabies, ut nihil supra. Omnino sperant, et prædicant, (est enim, ut scis, genus hominum prædictiosissimum, et valde deditum futuritionibus,) ista non fore diuturna. Sed quicquid futurum est, nos agimus Deo Optimo Maximo gratias, quod res nostræ eo jam tandem loco sint, quo sunt.

In Scotia fervent omnia. Knoxus, cinctus mille satellitibus, agit conventus per totum regnum. Regina vetula coacta est sese includere in præsidium. Nobilitas conjunctis animis et viribus restituit ubique religionem invitis omnibus. Monasteria passim omnia æquantur solo; vestes scenicæ, calices sacrilegi, idola, altaria comburuntur: ne vestigia quidem priscæ superstitionis et idololatriæ relinquuntur. Quid quæris? audisti sæpe, σκυθιστὶ πιεῖν: hoc vero est σκυθιστὶ ἐκκλησιάζειν. Rex Galliæ, qui nunc est, scribit se regem Scotiæ et hæredem Angliæ, si quid reginæ nostræ, (quod Deus avertat!) contingat humanitus. Id mirari non debes, si nostri homines moleste ferant: et quo res eruptura tandem sit, Θεοῦ ἐν γούνασι κεῖται. Fortasse, ut fit, communis hostis conciliabit nobis vicinum Scotum: quod si sit, etsi accedant etiam nuptiæ, — sed desino divinare.

D. Hetonus te salutat, idque non minus amice, quam si illi pater esses. Aliquot nostrum designamur episcopi: Coxus Eliensis, Scoræus Erfordiensis, Alanus Roffensis, Grindalus Londinensis, Barlovus Chichestrensis, et ego minimus apostolorum Sarisburiensis : quod ego onus prorsus decrevi excutere. Interea in academiis mera est ubique solitudo. Juvenes diffugiunt potius, quam ut velint in religionem consentire.

Sed comites jamdudum exspectant, et clamant ut veniam. Vale ergo, vale, mi pater et dulcissimum decus meum. Saluta venerandum virum, et mihi mille nominibus in Christo colendissimum, D. Bullingerum, ad quem etiam seorsim scriberem, si esset otium. Saluta D. Gualterum, D. Simlerum, D. Lavaterum, D. Hallerum, D. Gesnerum, D. Frisium, D. Hermannum. Habeo quinque pistolettos aureos a D. Barth. Compagno ad venerandum senem D. Bernardinum, et ab eodem ad eum literas. Scriberem ad eum de rebus omnibus, nisi excluderer angustia temporis : quanquam hoc, quæso te, ut illi significes, præter istos aureos nihil adhuc confectum esse. Res aulicæ, quantum video, ita sunt difficiles, ut nesciam an quicquam possit exprimi. Regina jam abest procul gentium in Cantio, ut agi nihil possit. Vale, mi pater, vale. Quantum ego tibi optare possum, tantum vale. Et Julium tuum, Annamque et Martyrillum meo nomine [saluta]. Londini, calendis Augusti, 1559.

JO. JUELLUS, tuus,

Tibi omnibus modis deditissimus.

INSCRIPTIO.
Viro longe doctissimo D. Petro Martyri Vermilio profitenti sacram theologiam in ecclesia Tigurina.

Tiguri.

EPISTOLA XVII.

JOHANNES FOXUS AD HENRICUM BULLINGERUM.

GRATIA et salus per Christum Dominum. Aut me fallunt omnes conjecturæ, Henrice humanissime, aut literas illas nostras jam repertas habemus, quæ tamdiu inveniri non potuerunt. Qua in re debemus nescio cui fortunæ magis quam industriæ. Occasio erat hujusmodi. Venit forte in domum mercatoriam Italus quidam, vir honestus, Petri Pernæ sororius, ob literas nescio quas. Cui tum præfectus et quæstor illius domus publicus obtulit illi literas, suspicans esse Italice scriptas, ut legeret: Italus, etsi nesciret Anglice, tamen quia videt nomen meum in inscriptione, recta via ad me venit cum literis, nuntians cupere præfectum illum ad se venirem. Veni illico, assumpto mecum Laurentio nostro, et hypodidascalo quodam Basiliensi qui interpres esset. Narrat præfectus literas illas jampridem rejectas in angulo nuper repertas fuisse a servulo ; repertas insuper et alias literas ad te et ad D. Gesnerum scriptas, quas Petro Maclinensi jam dedisset ad vos perferendas. Ego meas aperiens reperio easdem esse, quæ eodem tempore atque in eodem fasciculo cum vestris ab Abelo ad me mitterentur. Quæ res magnam mihi facit conjecturam et illas nostras esse quæ desideratæ sunt. Vos in resignando melius intelligetis; qua de re cupio me certiorem fieri per otium vestrum.

D. Frenshamus si vivit adhuc, precor ut diu vivat: jube ac mone ne quid diffidat sibi, multo minus divinæ gratiæ; quæ si videat sic expedire, facile possit omnem medicinam superare, et medicos etiam fallere. Quanquam nullum audivi medicum qui aperte et simpliciter de illo desperaret; et si desperarent, melius forsan de Germanis hominibus quam de Anglis judicare possent. Cupio si quid haberes περὶ τῶν μαρτυρικῶν, sive de Bartholomeo Grinæo, ut videbaris in literis significare, sive de toto illo negotio aut causa Zuingliana, in tempore admoneri. Res Zuinglianæ si hic non possent imprimi, possent tamen in Anglia, nusquam melius. Saluta inter ceteros D. Frenshamum in Christo, D. Petrum Martyrem. Memor sis mei in precibus tuis apud Dominum. Basileæ, Aug. 2, 1559.

Tuus in Christo,

J. FOXUS.

INSCRIPTIO.
Docto et observando viro D. Henrico Bullingero.   Tiguri.

EPISTOLA XVIII.

JOHANNES FOXUS AD HENRICUM BULLINGERUM.

Salutem multam. Etsi non erat animus nec consilium, doctissime Bullingere, libros Cantuar. a me versos de re eucharistica iis temporibus emittere, præsertim quum sententiarum et judiciorum non minus quam armorum tumultibus omnia exulcerata esse videam, tamen quia Christophorus hic vester ultro fidem et operam suam in hac re pollicetur tam candide, cœpi rursus negotio intermisso ac propemodum desperato animum adjicere. Nolim enim hic in me ullas hærere moras, si modo res aut illi aut vobis videbitur ejusmodi, in qua officium meum usus postulabit ecclesiæ. Atque de hac re jam ante superioribus ad te literis significavi. Nunc inito demum cum Froschovero consilio, visum est tum utrique nostrum, tum mihi vero imprimis necessarium, ne quid hujus negotii, nisi vobis prius consultis et approbantibus, incipiamus. Rogo itaque te, doctissime Bullingere, nobis in hac re cognoscenda adsit diligens censura tua. Statui enim propediem, Christo volente, juxta consilium Froschoveri aliquam partem ad te mittere; quod et nunc fecissem, sed opus est paulo accuratiore descriptione, quo facilius a vobis legatur. Hactenus enim sic tumultuor in Græcorum conciliis cum duplici commentario vertendis, tum in colligenda nostrorum martyrum historia aliisque, ut nihil fere supersit vacui temporis ad describendum. Quo minus mireris, si indiligentius has quoque literas ad te nunc scripserim. Opto te fauste valere, vir doctissime. Basileæ, 26 Septemb. 1559.

Tuus in Christo,

INSCRIPTIO.   J. FOXUS.
Ornatiss. et doctissimo
viro D. Henrico Bullingero,
    Tiguri.

EPISTOLA XIX.

JOHANNES JUELLUS AD PETRUM MARTYREM.

Tandem tamen aliquando Londinum redii, confecto molestissimo itinere, confecto corpore. Tu fortasse me, quod nihil scriberem, putabas esse mortuum. Ego vero interea tres totos menses longinqua et perdifficili legatione distinebar. Cum essem Bristolii, redditæ mihi sunt literæ tuæ, quas secum Randolphus noster adduxerat, ita amice scriptæ itaque suaves, ut mihi omnem illam molestiam itinerum atque occupationum prorsus eriperent ex animo: tanquam enim si præsens adfuisses, ita tum mihi videbar tecum colloqui. Randolphus, antequam ego redirem, abierat in Gallias: itaque ego miser privatus sum bona parte suavitatis tuæ, quam tu illi præsens præsenti verbis commendaveras. Literas meas in itinere intercidisse video: quas enim ego octavas dederam, eas video ad te vix quintas pervenisse.

Sed de legatione, inquies, illa vestra quid tandem factum est? Accipe ergo uno verbo, quod mihi exploratu perlongum fuit. Invenimus ubique animos multitudinis satis propensos ad religionem; ibi etiam, ubi omnia putabantur fore difficillima. Incredibile tamen dictu est, in illis tenebris Mariani temporis quanta ubique proruperit seges et sylva superstitionum. Invenimus passim votivas reliquias divorum, clavos, quibus fatui Christum confixum fuisse somniabant, et nescio quas portiunculas sacræ crucis. Magarum et veneficarum numerus ubique in immensum excreverat. Ecclesiæ cathedrales nihil aliud erant quam speluncæ latronum, aut si quid nequius aut fœdius dici potest. Si quid erat obstinatæ malitiæ, id totum erat in presbyteris, illis præsertim, qui aliquando stetissent a nostra sententia. Illi nunc, credo, ne parum considerate videantur mutasse voluntatem, turbant omnia. Sed turbent, quantum velint: nos tamen interim illos de gradu et de sacerdotiis exturbavimus.

Hardingus, homo constans, locum mutare maluit quam sententiam. Sidallus subscripsit quidem, sed constanter; hoc est, perinvitus. Smithæus autem tuus—quid ille? inquies. An potest a Nazareth quicquam proficisci boni? Mihi crede, ut veterem illam suam constantiam retineret, nunc tandem etiam quinto recantavit. Fatuus, cum videret religionem esse immutatam, mutata veste, statim fugam ornaverat in Scotiam: sed cum hæreret in finibus, captus est et retractus ex itinere. Ibi statim homo gravis, et columen atque antistes religionis, accessit ad nos, reliquit omnes suos, et repente factus est adversarius infestissimus papistarum. I nunc, et nega transubstantiationem! Papistarum acies pene sua sponte cecide-runt. O, nisi nobis deessent operæ, non male de religione sperari posset. Difficile enim est currum agere sine jumento, præsertim adverso monte.

Heri, ubi primum Londinum redii, audivi ex episcopo Cantuariensi te invitari ad nos, et tibi lectionem illam tuam veterem asservari. Quid sit, nescio: hoc tantum possum affirmare, neminem adhuc delectum esse, qui Oxonii doceat sacras literas. Equidem te, mi pater, videre percupio, et præsertim in Anglia. Quid enim ni cupiam, quem toties cupio etiam nunc videre Tiguri? Sed novi tuam prudentiam: nosti genium et ingenium insularum. Ea, quæ nunc videmus esse inchoata, utinam sint bene μόνιμα! Nihil est hodie illa schola desperatius. Putabis te, cum ibi esses, pene lusisse operam: ita in lætissima aliquando segete nunc *infelix lolium et steriles dominantur avenæ.*

Liber tuus de Votis, ut alia tua omnia, avidissime distrahitur. Omnes nunc exspectamus, quam mox editurus sis alias commentationes in librum Judicum et in duos libros Samuelis: omnes enim nunc nostri sciunt, te illos libros habere præ manibus, et velle edere. Suecus et Carolus Ferdinandi filius mirificissime ambiunt: sed Suecus impense; ille enim, modo impetret, montes argenteos pollicetur. Sed illa fortasse thalamos propiores cogitat. Alanus noster obiit diem suum, postquam designatus esset episcopus Roffensis. Ex Scotia hoc tempore nihil audimus, quod tibi possit videri novum. Docetur evangelium, ecclesiæ assidue colliguntur, et omnia priscæ superstitionis monumenta convelluntur. Galli tamen sperant se posse et regnum et religionem retinere. Quicquid futurum est, scribam ad te alias pluribus. Instat nunc annus sexagesimus, de quo mihi tu solebas aliquando ex Torquato quodam Italo nescio quæ mirifica prædicare. Faxit Deus, ut verum et solidum gaudium gaudeamus, ut aliquando orbi terrarum patefiat ὁ ἄνθρωπος τῆς ἀπωλείας, et in omnium oculos incurrat veritas evangelii Jesu Christi.

Vale, mi pater, et uxorem tuam meis verbis resaluta, mulierem mihi quidem ignotam, sed nunc ex tuis literis et Abeli nostri prædicatione notissimam. Gratulor et te illi, et illam tibi.

Saluta D. Bullingerum, D. Gualterum, D. Bernardinum, D. Hermannum, Julium, Juliam, Martyrillum. Frenshamum meum longum valere jubeo; puto enim illum jam solvisse a vobis, et esse cum Christo. Omnes nostri te salutant, tibique omnia precantur. Londini, 2 Novembr. 1559.

Tuus ex animo,

JO. JUELLUS.

D. Etonus instantissime rogavit, ut te suo nomine salutarem. Si posset ipse Latine scribere, non uteretur manu mea. Crede mihi, nemo de te aut sæpius aut honorificentius loquitur. Uxor etiam ejus salutem et tibi dicit et uxori tuæ.

INSCRIPTIO.
Doctissimo atque ornatissimo viro,
D. Petro Martyri, profitenti sa-
cras scripturas in ecclesia Tigu-
rina.

EPISTOLA XX.

JOHANNES JUELLUS AD RODOLPHUM GUALTERUM.

S. P. Quod novas istas curas et molestias non tam mihi, quam ecclesiæ nostræ, de qua jam tandem te non pessime sperare scribis, tam amice gratularis, ornatissime vir, ego tibi non mea sane causa, cui tam grave onus imponi video, sed ecclesiæ nostræ nomine, de qua video te tam sollicite cogitare, ago gratias. Nam quod ad me quidem attinet, tu optime nosti, quanti laboris sit, homini præsertim imperito rerum, et semper in otio atque in umbra educato, repente admoveri ad gubernaculum ecclesiæ; cumque res suas tueri vix possit, suscipere curam aliorum omnium. Tamen, quoniam Dei causa est, quanto minus possumus, tanto diligentius dabimus operam. Etsi enim desint alia, voluntas tamen, spero, non deerit. Vos interea, quoniam naves subduxistis in tutum, et consistitis in littore, orate Deum, ut navim nostram adhuc jactatam in fluctibus, et undique a piratis et prædonibus obsessam, educat aliquando in portum. Incredibilis enim est hoc tempore rabies nostrorum papistarum, qui potius quam ut errasse aliqua in re videantur, impotentissime ruunt et turbant omnia. Deus, cujus nos unius nomen et gloriam spectamus, juvet conatus nostros, et hostium suorum conjurationes et nefaria consilia dissipet!

Parkhurstus abiit Clevam ad suos: ibi nunc regnat, et omnes episcopos ex alto despicit. Si quid erat apud nos novarum rerum, quod certe nec valde certum nec ita multum erat, illud omne scripsi plenius ad D.

Bullingerum, et ad D. Martyrem. Si quid est, in quo ego tibi aut usui aut voluptati esse possim, memineris me, quocunque loco futurus sum, et esse et semper fore tuum. Bene vale, ornatissime vir atque optime. Saluta uxorem tuam, mulierem lectissimam, D. Bullingerum, D. Simlerum, D. Lavaterum, D. Zuinglium, D. Frisium, D. Gesnerum, D. Wolphium, aliosque vestros quos ego merito habeo carissimos, meo nomine. Etsi Parkhurstus abest hinc longe gentium, tamen ego tibi ejus nomine, uxorique tuæ, totique familiæ salutem dico. Nostri omnes te salutant, tuosque omnes. Iterum vale. Londini, secunda Novembr. 1559.

Tuus ex animo,
JOHANNES JUELLUS,

INSCRIPTIO.
Doctissimo viro D. Gualtero,
fideli ministro Evangelii
in Ecclesia Tigurina, ami-
co et fratri carissimo.
Tiguri.

EPISTOLA XXI.

JOHANNES PARKHURSTUS AD JOHANNEM WOLPHIUM.

LITERAS, quas nostro Burchero ad me dedisti, IX. Februarii accepi, humanissime Wolphi. Priores, quas ais te misisse, ad meas manus non pervenere. Hortaris ut edam epigrammata mea. Quid hujusmodi frivolas nugas ederem? Certe jam in aliquo nescio quo musæi angulo cum blattis et tineis rixantur. In fine tui epistolii rogas ut te amem. Mi Wolphi, non opus est ut hoc roges: non possum enim te non amare, tum propter tua in me beneficia, quæ nunquam dabo oblivioni, tum etiam propter raram eruditionem et varias animi dotes, quas in te ut summa Dei dona exosculor et veneror. Libri, quibus me donaras in discessu, in itinere periere. Male sit illis magnis furibus, qui me tanto thesauro spoliarunt! Cum tu sis magnus dominus magni hypocausti, magnas mihi dabis pœnas, si nomen meum e vestra tabula fuerit expunctum. Breve habes responsum ad breve epistolium. Cetera cognosces a nostro Gualtero. Saluta meo nomine tuam uxorem et amicos omnes. Mea vos salutat. Vale.

Tuus,
JOHANNES PARKHURSTUS,

INSCRIPTIO.
Humanissimo Viro,
D. Joan. Wolphio.
Tiguri.

EPISTOLA XXII.

JOHANNES JUELLUS AD JOSIAM SIMLERUM.

Gratularis tu quidem mihi pro tua humanitate, mi Josia; at egomet mihi ipsi non gratulor. Etsi enim nihil mihi adhuc aliud impositum sit quam nomen episcopi, rem autem ipsam et functionem nondum attigerim; tamen illud ipsum onus longe impar sentio esse meis viribus, et jam nunc tantum sub inani titulo incipio succumbere. Quid tu futurum censes, ubi ad rem ipsam ventum erit? Literæ tamen tuæ mihi multo jucundissime acciderunt. Vidi enim in illis et animum et amorem erga me tuum. Et certe quid potest a Josia, homine jucundissimo, proficisci non jucundum? Quare tibi et de literis tuis, et de illa gratulatione, etsi mihi res ipsa permolesta et ingrata videatur, quam possum gratissimas ago gratias.

Quod scribis, sperare te episcopos apud nos sine ullis superstitiosis et putidis ceremoniis inaugurari, hoc est, opinor, sine oleo, sine chrismate, sine novacula; nihil falleris. Frustra enim exhausta esset sentina, si istas reliquias pateremur in fundo residere. Unctos istos, et rasos, et personatos ventres Romam remisimus, unde illos primum accepimus. Nostros enim esse volumus pastores operosos[1], vigiles, episcopos. Quoque id commodius possit fieri, opes episcoporum imminuuntur, et ad mediocritatem quandam rediguntur; ut semoti ab illa regia pompa et strepitu aulico, possint tranquillius et attentius vacare gregi Christi. Quod autem Julium tuum meumque ita ambitiose commendas, etsi es Josias, tamen puto in ea re mihi a te injuriam fieri. Quid enim? An ego Julium meum, hospitem, amicum, fratrem meum non novi? An potest unquam ejus calvities, tanta præsertim, mihi excidere ex animo? Dii meliora! Quoties ego senem aliquem calvum, incurvum, obstipum, prementem alvum, et cacaturientem video, toties mihi in animum incurrit meus Julius. Certe quicquid erit, si vel consilio vel auxilio vel re vel etiam capistro opus erit, Julius apud Juellum semper erit Julius. Extra jocum, ubi Julius meus ad nos venerit, si quid Juello supererit, non egebit.

Bene vale, mi Josia, et uxorem tuam, optimam mulierem, et cultissimum atque humanissimum juvenem Hermannum saluta meo nomine. Parkhurstus rus abiit ad regnum suum. Oravit tamen me proficiscens, ut tibi suo nomine quam officiosissime salutem dicerem. Vale, mi Josia, vale. Utinam aliquando dicere possim tibi coram, Josia, salve! Londini, 2 Novembris, 1559.

Tuus ex animo,
JOHANNES JUELLUS.

INSCRIPTIO.

Doctissimo, atque humaniss.
  viro D. Josiæ Simlero,
    amico carissimo.
      Tiguri.

[1 MS. *operas.*]

EPISTOLA XXIII.

JOHANNES JUELLUS AD PETRUM MARTYREM.

S. PL. Biduo postquam ex longo et perdifficili itinere rediissem, et lassus de via atque anhelans, nescio quid ad te scripsissem, redditæ mihi sunt a te literæ ternæ eodem tempore: quarum suavissima lectione ita sum exhilaratus, ut omnem illam superiorum dierum molestiam prorsus abjecerim ex animo. Etsi enim quoties de te cogito, quod certo assidue et in singulas horas facio, et nisi facerem, ingratus essem, ipsa cogitatione et memoria tui nominis perfundor gaudio; tamen cum literas tuas ad me scriptas lego, videor mihi esse Tiguri, et te videre coram, et tecum amœnissime colloqui: quod equidem, mihi crede, pluris æstimo, quam omnes opes episcoporum.

De religione quod scribis, et veste scenica, O utinam id impetrari potuisset! Nos quidem tam bonæ causæ non defuimus. Sed illi quibus ista tantopere placuerunt, credo, sequuti sunt inscitiam presbyterorum: quos quoniam nihil aliud videbant esse, quam stipites, sine ingenio, sine doctrina, sine moribus, veste saltem comica volebant populo commendari. Nam ut alantur bonæ literæ, et surrogetur seges aliqua doctorum hominum, nulla, O Deus bone, nulla hoc tempore cura suscipitur. Itaque quoniam vera via non possunt, istis ludicris ineptiis tenere volunt oculos multitudinis. Sunt quidem istæ, ut tu optime scribis, reliquiæ Amorrhæorum. Quis enim id neget? Atque utinam aliquando ab imis radicibus auferri et extirpari possint! nostræ quidem nec vires ad eam rem nec voces deerunt.

Quod scribis esse quosdam qui nullam adhuc significationem dederint suæ erga te voluntatis, subolfacio equidem quos dicas. Sed, mihi crede, non sunt eo numero aut loco, quo tu fortasse putas, quoque omnis Israel illos sperabat fore: nam si essent—Non scripserunt hactenus ad te, non quod noluerint aut tui obliti fuerint, sed quod puduerit scribere. Nunc uterque gravissime laborat e quartana, sed ἀρχιμάγειρος, quoniam est natura tristiori, multo gravius.

Ingemuisti pro tua erga communem causam pietate, cum audires nihil prospectum esse cuiquam nostrum. Nunc ergo rursus ingeme; nam ne adhuc quidem quicquam. Tantum circumferimus inanes titulos episcoporum, et a Scoto et Thoma defecimus ad Occamistas et Nominales. Sed, ut scis, magna sunt momenta regnorum. Regina ipsa et causæ favet, et nobis cupit. Quamobrem, etsi satis dura sunt ista initia, tamen non abjicimus animos, nec desinimus sperare lætiora. Facile intereunt, quæ facile maturitatem assequuntur.

De libro tuo memini me, antequam discederem Londino, ad te scripsisse pluribus. Sed illæ literæ fortasse, ut fit, periere in itinere.

Hoc etiam adscripsi, Reginam ultro et cupide legisse epistolam, et opus ipsum, atque in universum doctrinam atque ingenium tuum mirifice prædicasse; librumque illum tuum ab omnibus bonis tanti fieri, quanti haud scio an aliud quicquam in hoc genere. Nihil autem tibi hactenus donatum esse, hei mihi, quid ego dicam? pudet me, nec scio quid respondeam. Tamen Regina sedulo sciscitata est nuntium, quid ageres, ubi viveres, qua valetudine, qua conditione esses, an posses per ætatem iter facere. Omnino velle se omnibus modis te invitari in Angliam, ut qui tua voce coluisses academiam, eandem nunc dissipatam et misere habitam eadem voce irrigares. Postea tamen, nescio quo pacto, deliberationes Saxonicæ et legationes Segulianæ ista consilia peremerunt. Tamen quidquid est, nihil est hoc tempore celebrius, quam Petrum Martyrem invitari, et propediem venturum esse in Angliam. O utinam res nostræ aliquando stabilitatem aliquam et robur assequantur! Cupio enim, mi pater, te videre, et suavissimis sermonibus et amicissimis consiliis tuis frui. Quem ego diem si videro, vel potius, uti spero, ubi videro, quas Samarobrivas aut Sarisburias non contemnam? Vale, dulce decus meum, atque *animi plusquam dimidium mei.* Saluta uxorem tuam, optimam mulierem, meo nomine. Deus faxit, ut feliciter pariat, et *pulchra faciat te prole parentem.* Saluta D. Bullingerum, D. Gualterum, D. Lavaterum, D. Simlerum, D. Gesnerum, D. Frisium, D. Hermanum, tuum meumque Julium, Juliam, et Martyrillum. Nostri omnes te salutant. Londini, 5 Novemb. 1559.

Tuus ex animo quantus quantus,

INSCRIPTIO.   JO. JUELLUS.
Doctissimo atque ornatissimo viro,
  D. Petro Martyri, profitenti sa-
  cras literas in schola Tigurina,
  domino suo colendissimo.
    Tiguri.

EPISTOLA XXIV.

JOHANNES JUELLUS AD PETRUM MARTYREM.

S. PL. Etsi ante non ita multos dies ad te scripserim, et hoc tempore nihil hic sit quod tu magnopere scire velis, tamen, quoniam te ita velle non dubito, illud ipsum nihil malo scribere, quam istum nuntium, quem forte audieram velle Coloniam proficisci, inanem a me dimittere.

Religio apud nos eo loco est, quo jam antea ad te scripsi sæpius. Omnia docentur ubique purissime. In ceremoniis et larvis passim plusculum ineptitur. Crucula illa argenteola male nata, male auspicata, adhuc stat in larario principis. Me miserum! res ea facile trahetur in exemplum. Spes erat aliquando tandem ereptum iri; idque ut fieret, nos omnes dedimus diligenter, et adhuc damus operam. Sed jam, quantum video, conclamatum est. Ita prorsus obfirmati sunt animi. Nimis prudenter ista mihi videntur geri, nimisque mystice. Et quo tandem res nostræ casuræ sint, Deus viderit. Ἵπποι βραδύποδες morantur currum. Cæcilius nostræ causæ impense favet. Episcopi adhuc designati tantum sunt: interim prædia pulchre augent fiscum. Academia utraque, et ea præsertim, quam tu non ita pridem doctissime atque optime coluisti, miserrime nunc disjecta jacet sine pietate, sine religione, sine doctore, sine spe ulla literarum. Multi de te cogitant primarii et tibi non ignoti viri, et te primo quoque tempore, vel invitis omnibus Seguleiis, accersitum cupiunt. Ego vero, qui tibi, si quis alius mortalium, ex animo atque unice cupio, auctor sum ut, si voceris, quod tamen inter ista arma futurum vix puto, tamen ne quid præcipites. Novi ego prudentiam tuam; et tu vicissim, spero, observantiam erga te meam. Equidem hoc possum vere affirmare, neminem esse hominem, cui conspectus tuus jucundior futurus sit, quam mihi. Tamen ut sunt res nostræ, fluxæ, incertæ, instabiles, utque uno verbo dicam, insulares, magis te salvum audire absentem cupio, quam præsentem videre cum periculo. Sed ista parum opportune: literas enim silere æquum est inter arma. Nos terra marique juvamus vicinum Scotum. Nosti enim, *tum tua res agitur paries cum proximus ardet.* Gallum adventurum aiunt cum omnibus copiis; et fortasse non minoribus excipietur.

Scripsit ad me nuper comes Critonis tui Pamphilus e Scotia, cum aliis de rebus, tum ut de Frenshamo nostro nescio quid, (neque enim id aperte scripsit,) ad te scriberem. Visus tamen mihi est de testamento Frenshami scribere aliquid voluisse: de quo quid actum sit, hactenus nescio. Oro tamen te, quoniam nemo isthic est alius, cui possim satis verecunde tantum negotium imponere, ut velis rem eam tibi Julioque tuo esse curæ. Frenshamo autem nostro, si adhuc vivit, cupio bene: sin autem, quod magis puto, quodque ad nos etiam scribitur, est mortuus, spero esse bene. Audio pervenisse Londinum fasciculum quendam librorum tuorum de Votis contra Smithum; et in illis unum esse quem tu ad me miseris nominatim. Equidem librum illum adhuc non vidi: sæpe enim absum Londino, et multum distineor laboribus. Nunc ubicunque est odorabor. Tibi vero interea pro eo ac debeo, proque eo ac humanitas tua postulat, ago immortales gratias. Nolo D. Bernardinus me sui oblitum putet. Fides quidem mea et industria non defuit; sed omnia quæruntur et conservantur hoc tempore alendo militi. Quinque coronatos Italicos, quos ejus nomine recepi a Barthol. Compagno, reddidi Acontio. Nunc agimus de ejus canonicatu: et bona spes est posse impetrari. Ego Julio meo, si ad nos venerit, omnia polliceor.

Moneo tamen, ut exspectet aliquantisper, ne cogamur una redire Tigurum. Bene vale, mi pater et domine in Christo colendissime. Saluta optimam illam mulierem, uxorem tuam; et filiolo tuo Isaaco, quem ego hucusque vagientem audire videor, basiolum dato meo nomine. Saluta D. Bullingerum, D. Bernardinum, D. Gualterum, D. Simlerum, D. Gesnerum, D. Lavaterum, D. Vickium, D. Hallerum, D. Volphium, hominem jucundissimum et in amplissima civitate natum, D. Frisium, D. Hermannum, tuum meumque Julium, Juliam, et moratissimum nunc puerum Martyrillum. Nostri nunc omnes pene sunt in dispersione gentium. Grindallus Londinensis, Sandus Vigorniensis, Coxus Eliensis, D. Coccus, D. Vrothus quartanenses te salutant. Iterum iterumque vale, mi pater. Londini, 16 Novembris, 1559.

JO. JUELLUS,
Totus tuus.

INSCRIPTIO.
Ornatissimo et longe doctiss. viro,
D. Petro Martyri, profitenti sacras scripturas in schola Tigurina, domino suo colendiss.
Tiguri.

EPISTOLA XXV.

JOHANNES JUELLUS AD PETRUM MARTYREM.

Allatæ sunt ad me hesterno die e Scotia literæ a Critonis nostri genio et comite Pamphilo de toto statu rerum Scoticarum ab illo usque tempore, quo primum cœptum est tumultuari. Quæ omnia oravit me ut ego diligenter atque ordine ad te perscriberem. Scripsisset ipse potius, si id vel temporis vel loci ratio ferre commode potuisset. Ego vero, quoniam te scio in primis brevitate delectari, scribam breviter.

Scoti ab initio edicta quædam proposuerunt publice: primum, se publico tantum studere bono: neminem sibi quicquam privatim quærere: deinde videri sibi esse ex usu reipublicæ, ut regina desisteret munire Letham, oppidum maritimum, et Gallis, si quid opus esset, valde opportunum. Id si illa facere recusaret, se facturos, quod deceret homines studiosos libertatis et amantes patriæ. Regina vero, ut est mulier ferox et sanguinis Gallici, repudiare conditiones: clamare indignum esse, legem imponi sibi a suis. Nec deerant Scoti complures, qui ejus fidem et auctoritatem sequerentur. Quid quæris? Venitur ad arma. Ibi episcopus D. Andreæ, homo militaris, dignus videlicet, qui inserviret mulierculæ, ante conflictum deseritur a suis omnibus. Duo tantum pueruli remanserunt, credo, ne solus atque incomitatus rediret ad dominam. Scoti habent in castris concionatores Knoxum et Goodmannum; et sese vocant cœtum Christi. Postea mittunt ad reginam, ut discedat Letha, nisi vi et malo extrudi malit. Et ab hoc tempore agi cœptum est de fœdere Anglico. Regina, virili mulier animo, quamvis in singulos dies relinqueretur a suis, tamen nihil perterrefieri, tenere præsidium, excursiones in hostem facere, omnia moliri, et suis oculis lustrare omnia. Scoti viribus valent et multitudine; et nisi imperiti essent obsidionis et artis bellicæ, jamdudum aliquid effecissent. Velitatum est leniter utrinque ad sextum Novembris. Postea Scoti sese receperunt in hiberna. Statim a reginalibus rumusculi dissipati sunt, Scotos fractis animis diffugisse. Verum illi adhuc et principes una retinent, et conferunt consilia, et augent numerum, et colligunt pecuniam, et, si quid opus erit, militem habent in procinctu.

Hæc volui breviter: plura posthac dabo, ubi plura resciero; multa enim exspectantur. Nos instruimus militem, et in hostem serio cogitamus. Vale, mi pater. Saluta uxorem tuam, D. Bullingerum, D. Bernardinum, D. Hermannum, Julium et Juliam. Londini primo Decembris, quo die nos primum audivimus Mariam esse mortuam, 1559.

Tuus,
JOHANNES JUELLUS.

INSCRIPTIO.
Doctiss. atque ornatiss. viro Domino Petro
Martyri profitenti sacras scripturas in
ecclesia Tigurina, domino suo colen-
dissimo.
Tiguri.

EPISTOLA XXVI.

JOHANNES PARKHURSTUS AD JOSIAM SIMLERUM.

VERBIS consequi non possum, Josia humanissime, quanta perfusus sum lætitia, cum ex tuis literis cognorim, te prospera uti valetudine: quod et antea mihi significavit noster Gualterus: cum tamen ego, non ad amussim illius pensitans literas, fatis concessisse existimarim. Tanta erat mea stupiditas, vel tantus potius amor, ut ex levi occasiuncula id suspicatus sim, quod minime erat verum, at certe quod animum meum vehementi dolore perculerit. *Res est sollciti plena timoris amor.*

Secundo Septembris restitutus sum meæ Clevæ, hoc est, post messem, cum omnia essent ablata, et nihil mihi reliquum. Quomodo ergo jam vivitur? inquis. Non ex rapto, sed mutuo. Una messis resarciet omnia. Habeant alii suos episcopatus: mihi satis erit mea Cleva. Multi ex episcopis perquam lubenter suam conditionem mecum mutarent: unus aut alter ambitiosulus fortassis recusaret. Et ne hoc nescias, ego in eorum numerum eram etiam asciscendus, sed obtestatus sum primarios quosdam viros, amicos meos summos, ut nomen meum ex illa schedula, quam habet Regina, expungeretur. Quod tametsi nullis precibus, nullis obtestationibus impetrare potuerim, tamen hactenus illorum opera collum ex illo capistro subduxi. Cum nuper essem Londini, unus ex consiliariis et D. Parkerus Cantuariensis nescio quam ἐπισκοπὴν mihi sunt minati. Sed *Dii meliora!* Ego enim non possum tantam ambire miseriam. Ego hic in mea parochia regno, et episcopum solus per duos annos ago. Glocestrensis toto hoc tempore hinc exulat: sed tertio quoque anno habet quod hic agat, quemadmodum et alibi.

Habes de meo statu, de quo certior fieri desiderabas. Pro institutionibus tuis astronomicis ago gratias ingentes. Collegisti præterea nescio quid ex Athanasio et aliis. Quando edes? Copiosissimam ad te epistolam scribere gestiebat animus, sed per varias occupationes non licet.

Salutabis diligenter meo nomine optimam tuam uxorem, et novam illam conjugem, tuam Annam. Vonlychio me officiosissime commendabis et castissimæ illius Susannæ. Quod tibi scribo illi scribo. Salutabis etiam meo nomine D. Martyrem, D. Bibliandrum, D. Bernardinum, Lavaterum, Zuinglium, Frisium, Pellicanum, Liberianum, Christopherum Rotakerum, Stumphium, Rennerum, Hirterum, vicinos, vicinas, et omnes. Uxor mea te et tuam et alios omnes salutat. Vale.

Von Bischoff Clouw in comitatu Glostrensi, 20 Decembris, 1559.

Tuus,

INSCRIPTIO.   JOHANNES PARKHURSTUS.
Humanissimo viro D.
Josiæ Simlero.
Tiguri.

EPISTOLA XXVII.

THOMAS SAMPSON AD PETRUM MARTYREM.

Quas scripsisti literas 4 Novembris, ego accepi 3 Januarii. Jam unum annum egi in Anglia, non ita quietum; vereor autem ne sequens hic annus plus molestiarum mihi pariat. Non tamen solus timeo mihi, sed omnes nobis timemus: nec tamen audeo scriptis mandare quæ imminere nobis videntur mala. Vos ergo, sanctissimi patres, teque imprimis, D. Petre, pater et præceptor carissime, per Jesum Christum obtestor, ut strenue Dominum deprecari velitis. Hoc, hoc, inquam, contendite, ne veritas evangelii vel obfuscetur vel evertatur apud Anglos. Gratias tibi ago, suavissime pater, quod tam sis diligens in scribendo. Satisfecisti tu, satisfecit et D. Bullingerus mihi in questionibus: utrisque immortalis Deus noster rependat. Consecratio episcoporum aliquorum jam habita est. D. Parkerus Cantuariensis, D. Cox Eliensis, D. Grindal Londiniensis, D. Sandus Vigorniensis, noti[1] tibi nomine. Unus alius Wallus etiam est episcopus, sed tibi ignotus. Sequentur brevi D. Pilkintonus Vintoniensis, D. Benthamus Coventrensis, et tuus Juellus Sarisburiensis. Brevi, inquam, ut audio, sunt isti consecrandi, (ut nostro utar vocabulo.) Ego in limine hæreo; neque enim vel egressus vel ingressus datur. O quam vellem egredi! Deus ipse novit quam hoc aveam. Episcopi fiant alii; ego vellem aut concionatoris solius, aut nullius ecclesiastici, munus subire. Domini fiat voluntas. O mi pater! quid ego sperem, cum exulet ex aula Christi ministerium, admittatur autem crucifixi imago cum accensis luminaribus? Altaria quidem sunt diremta et imagines per totum regnum: in sola aula crucifixi imago cum candelis retinetur; et miser popellus id non solum libenter audit, sed etiam sponte imitabitur. Quid ego sperem, ubi tres ex novitiis nostris episcopis, unus veluti sacer minister, secundus loco diaconi, tertius subdiaconi loco, mensæ domini astabunt, coram imagine crucifixi, vel certe non procul sito idolo, cum candelis, ornati aureis vestibus papisticis, sicque sacram Domini cœnam porrigent sine ulla concione? Quæ spes boni, cum a mutis istis idololatriæ reliquiis religionem nostri petere volunt, et non a viva Dei voce sonante? Quid sperem ego, cum concionaturis injungi debet ne vitia aspere tangantur, cum concionatores si quid dicant quod displiceat, non ferendi putantur? Sed quo me rapit æstus iste animi? Silendum est. Vix capita nostræ imminentis miseriæ tetigi. Deus æterne, nostri miserere per Christum Deum et Salvatorem nostrum.

Unicam hanc a vobis quæstionem proponam solvendam: mi pater, te volo uti mediatore apud D. Bullingerum et D. Bernardinum. Hæc est, num imago crucifixi cum candelis accensis in mensa Domini posita, num, inquam, sit inter adiaphora ponenda? Si non sit, sed pro re illicita et nefaria ducenda, tum hoc quæro: si princeps ita injungat omnibus episcopis et pastoribus, ut vel admittant in suas ecclesias imaginem cum candelis, vel ministerio Christi cedant, quid hic faciendum sit? An non potius deserendum ministerium verbi et sacramentorum[2] sit, quam ut hæ[3] reliquiæ Amorrheorum admittantur? Certe videntur nonnulli ex nostris aliquo modo huc inclinare, ut hæc pro adiaphoris accipi vellent. Ego omnino puto potius abdicandum ministerium, si modo id injungatur. Jam

[[1] MS. *notos*.   [2] MS. *sanctorum*.   [3] MS. *hæc*.]

te rogo, mi pater, tuas hic partes hac unica vice age, hoc est, ut quam diligentissime et citissime me certiorem facias, quid vestra pietas hic censet, quæque sit omnium vestrum sententia; tui, inquam, D. Bullingeri et D. Bernardini. Hujus auctoritas, ut audio, maxima est apud Reginam. Quod si vellet aliquando scribere hortatum illam ut strenue agat in Christi negotio; testor ex animo quod certo sciam, fidenter dico, quod vere filia Dei sit: opus tamen habet hujusmodi consiliariis, qualis ille est. Nam quod Augustinus Bonifacio dixit, id fere in omnibus principibus verum est, nempe quod plures habeant qui corpori, paucos qui animæ consulant. Quod autem ab illo contendo, vellem et a vobis petere, si auderem. Ego tamen hac in re vestræ me subjicio prudentiæ. Callet, ut nosti, linguam Italicam; Latine et Græce etiam bene docta est. In his linguis si quid scribatur a vobis vel a D. Bernardino, omnino puto rem gratissimam vos facturos regiæ majestati, et operam navaturos ecclesiæ Anglicanæ utilissimam. Deus vos Spiritu suo sancto ducat in perpetuum!

Bene vale, et rescribe unica hac vice quam poteris festinanter. Saluta meo nomine officiosissime D. Bullingerum, tuamque uxorem: saluta Julium. Quæ jam scripsi, tantum apud D. Bullingerum et D. Bernardinum promas: nollem enim ego rumores spargi meo nomine. Imo nec hoc vobis scriberem, nisi sperarem aliquid inde boni eventurum. Forsan vel scribetis (ut dixi), vel saltem bonum dabitis mihi consilium in proposita quæstione. Agite vos pro vestra pia prudentia. Iterum vale. Raptim, 6 Januarii.

Tuus ex animo,
THO. SAMPSON.

INSCRIPTIO.
Clariss. Theologo D. D. Petro
Martyri, sacrarum literarum
professori fidelissimo.
Tiguri.

P. S. Si quid scribatur regiæ majestati vel a te vel a D. Bernardino, vel a D. Bullingero, non quasi vos ab aliquo incitati fueritis scribendum, ut vos melius nostis. Salutat te ex animo noster Chamberus. Mea uxor quartana vexatur. Giana bene valet. Puto etiam Hetonum cum sua bene valere. Ruri ago inter rusticos Christum pro meo modulo tractans. Tu pro me Deum roga. Literas tuas Springamus vel Abelus ad me perferri curabit.

EPISTOLA XXVIII.

RICARDUS COXUS AD PETRUM MARTYREM.

Diu est, in Christo carissime Petre, quod literas tuas acceperim; librum autem, quem mihi humanissime dedicasti, nondum recepi. Contigit nuperrime amici cujusdam libellum inspectare, quem nomine meo evulgatum ipse intellexi. Plurimum tibi me debere agnosco vel in hoc, quod per te meæ obscuritati aliquid celebritatis accesserit. Etenim magni momenti res est a talibus viris, eruditione et pietate eximiis, commendari. Atque utinam tandem aliquando tuam benevolentiam aliquo officiolo demereri potuero! Mihi non deero: secundet vota Dominus! Novam uxorem tibi gratulor; speroque et novam prolem posse etiam gratulari. Julii tui causam hic sedulo agimus, atque in ea aliquid effecimus. Ricardus Bruernus, egregius Ebreus scilicet, tuam præbendam possidet. Si literas tuas procuratorias ad nos miseris, in recuperanda præbenda tua aliquid fortassis in rem tuam præstabimus.

Dum hæc scribebam, allatus est ad me liber tuus, qui auctor es meus, cui est dono datus. De rebus nostris quid scribam? Reddita sunt nobis Dei beneficio omnia illa religionis capita, quæ D. Edvardi tempore tenuimus. Tantum crucis crucifixique imaginem in templis tolerare cogimur, cum magno animorum nostrorum cruciatu. Rogandus est Dominus ut hoc demum scandalum auferatur. Galli perfidia et ambitio, instigante ecclesiæ antichristo, nobis negotium facessere meditatur. Sacerdotes papistici apud nos suo se ministerio passim abdicant, ne nostris, ut aiunt, hæresibus assentire cogantur. Adversarii sunt multi et potentes, sed omnibus potentior Dominus. Scoti, vicini nostri, evangelium pro maxima parte amplectuntur et profitentur, non sine gravi cruce, quam Galli injuria ferre adhuc coguntur. Nam Gallus eos in dies adoritur, internecionemque illis molitur, quibus nisi aliunde succurratur, et de illis et de evangelio apud illos brevi actum erit. Interim piorum precibus juvandi sunt. Salutabis meo nomine uxorem tuam, licet ignotam, et Julium. Dominus Jesus te diutissime nobis servet incolumem! Londini.

Tui studiosissimus et in Christo frater carissimus,

RICARDUS COXUS,

Eliensis Episcopus.

INSCRIPTIO.

Amico meo integerrimo D. Petro Martyri,
pietate ac doctrina præcellenti, sacræ
linguæ apud Tigurinos interpreti fide-
liss.

EPISTOLA XXIX.

JOHANNES JUELLUS AD PETRUM MARTYREM.

S. PL. O mi pater, quid ego ad te scribam? Rei non multum est, temporis vero multo minus. Sed quoniam te scio delectari brevitate, te auctore scribam brevius. Nunc ardet lis illa crucularia. Vix credas in re fatua quantum homines, qui aliquid sapere videbantur, insaniant. Ex illis, quos quidem tu noris, præter Coxum nullus est. Crastino die instituetur de ea re disputatio. Arbitri erunt ex senatu selecti quidam viri. Actores inde Cantuariensis et Coxus; hinc Grindallus Londinensis episcopus et ego. Eventus ἐν κριτῶν γούνασι κεῖται. Rideo tamen, cum cogito, quibus illi et quam gravibus et solidis rationibus defensuri sint suam crucularn. Sed quicquid erit, scribam posthac pluribus; nunc enim sub judice lis est: tamen, quantum auguror, non scribam posthac ad te episcopus. Eo enim jam res pervenit, ut aut cruces argenteæ et stanneæ, quas nos ubique confregimus, restituendæ sint, aut episcopatus relinquendi.

De Frenshamo nostro, quod illum ita humaniter tractaris, ago tibi, mi pater, quas debeo gratias. Mortuum ex tuis literis primum didici. De ejus pecunia, quam moriens reliquit Tiguri, quid scribam nescio. Neque enim ego testamentum ejus unquam vidi, et Randolphus noster, qui vidit, est nunc in Scotia. Tamen, si quid erit, ego omnibus modis consultum cupio meo Julio. Atque hoc, quæso, illi significa meo nomine, ut si quid est, quod Frenshamus non legarit nominatim, partim aliquid apud se retineat, et in ea re, κατ' Ἀλκόξονον tuum, utatur judicio suo.

E Scotia varia nunciantur, et omnia satis læta. Idque satis sit hoc tempore uno verbo significasse: adhuc enim de rebus singulis explorati nihil habeo. Nos magnas copias habemus in finibus; et terra marique Scotis auxilium ferimus. Crito hospes tuus, et ejus comes Pamphilus, non stertunt totas noctes. Venit ille Athenas insolens, et placuit Glycerio. Nosti? Sed quid ago? destituor tempore, et obruor negotiis, et invitus cogor finem facere. Tamen hoc scire debes, Vitum amicum tuum summum, et popularem episcopum Vintoniensem, et Oglethorpum Carleolensem, et Bainum Lichefildensem, et Tonstallum Saturnum Dunelmensem, ante aliquot dies esse mortuos. Samsonus rure agit longe gentium, Parkhurstus in regno suo. Itaque mirum videri non debet, si ad vos scribant infrequentius.

Saluta, quæso, reverendissimum patrem, D. Bullingerum, D. Bernardinum, D. Volphium, D. Hermannum, et Julium, ad quos ego omnes libenter scriberem hoc tempore, si esset otium. Saluta optimam illam mulierem, uxorem tuam, et Annam et Martyrillum tuum. Etonus, Etona, Abelus, Abela, Grindallus, Sandus, Scoræus, Falconerus, Elmerus te salutant; et cum tibi omnia cupiant, nihil tamen magis cupiunt, quam Angliam. Quanquam, ut adhuc sunt res nostræ, crede mihi, pulchrum est esse Tiguri. Bene vale, mi pater, bene vale. Londini, 4 Februarii, 1560.

Tibi deditissimus,

INSCRIPTIO.   JO. JUELLUS, tuus.

Doctiss. viro D. Petro Martyri Vermilio, profitenti sacras literas in schola Tigurina, domino suo colendissimo.

Tiguri.

EPISTOLA XXX.

JOHANNES JUELLUS AD PETRUM MARTYREM.

S. PL. in Christo. Negotia ista mea, etsi hoc efficiunt, ut ego minus ad te scribam, hoc tamen profecto non efficiunt, nec certe unquam effectura sunt, ut ego minus te diligam, aut de te minus cogitem. Qui enim minus possim, præsertim quem patris loco habere debeo? Scripsi ad te non ita pridem per Burcherum nostrum, a quo etiam literas recepi tuas, sed longo post tempore; scriptæ enim sub initium Octobris, redditæ mihi sunt Idibus, opinor, Januarii: tam diu ille hærere in itinere cogebatur. Idque puto in meas etiam ad te literas non raro accidere, et præsertim postquam Abelus noster discesserit Argentorato, nec Anglus ibi quisquam remanserit, qui res nostras curare possit. Si testamentum Frenshami nostri mittatur hoc tempore Francofordiam, negotium dedi Conrado, famulo Arnoldi Birkmanni, juveni probo et bonæ fidei, qui illud a Froschovero recipiat, et secum deferat, et apud se habeat. Ego enim, ubi ille redierit, non ero Londini: jamdudum enim cupio Sarisberiam; sed impedimur mille vinculis. Interim tamen, dum nos hic tenemur, nescio quis Pan curet oves! Verum ego de illo testamento et pecunia nihil scio; et sine Randolpho nihil possum. Nam si scirem aut possem, Julio tuo meoque summam aliquam et liberaliter et ultro deciderem. Randolphus autem abest adhuc longe gentium in Scotia. Itaque literas tuas et D. Bullingeri ad illum scriptas habeo adhuc apud me integras. Neque enim video, qua ratione ad illum tam procul satis tuto mitti possint.

Religio nunc aliquanto confirmatior est, quam fuit. Populus ubique ad meliorem partem valde proclivis. Magnum ad eam rem momentum attulit ecclesiastica et popularis musica. Postquam enim semel Londini cœptum est in una tantum ecclesiola cani publice, statim non tantum ecclesiæ aliæ finitimæ, sed etiam longe disjunctæ civitates, cœperunt idem institutum certatim expetere. Nunc ad crucem Pauli videas interdum sex hominum millia, finita concione, senes, pueros, mulierculas, una canere, et laudare Deum. Id sacrificos et diabolum ægre habet. Vident enim sacras conciones hoc pacto profundius descendere in hominum animos, et ad singulos pene numeros convelli et concuti regnum suum. Nihil tamen habent, quod jure ac merito queri possint. Missæ enim nostra memoria nunquam erant in majori pretio: singulæ enim nunc æstimantur, in singula spectatorum capita, non minoris quam ducentis coronatis. Vitus tuus, qui ita candide et amice in te scripsit, mortuus est, credo, ex rabie; et religio, quod mireris, habet nihilo deterius. Id hominem patientem male habuit, quod videret se suosque publice rideri a pueris.

Si Julius noster ad nos veniat, nihil illi a me neque ad victum, neque ad cultum, neque ad crumenam deerit. Cupio enim voloque meo Julio, non tantum tua causa, cui ego omnia debeo, sed etiam ipsius causa Julii. Tamen, ut adhuc sunt res nostræ, me auctore subsistat paullulum, dum istæ turbæ conquiescant. Interim ne putes, mi pater, neminem hic esse qui de te absente cogitet. Hucusque Oxonii asservatur lectio Theologica illa tua, non alii, spero, si tu ipse velis, quam tibi. Cæcilius tuus est: Gulielmus Petrus humanissime de te prædicat. Posthac si, re confecta, et religione reque publica constituta, et ultro et honorifice et Reginæ, quæ te gerit in oculis, et reipublicæ nomine revoceris, obsecro, ne pigeat redire. Redibis, spero, ad homines non ingratos, et tui memores bene.

Vale, mi pater, dulce decus meum, atque *animi plusquam dimidium mei.* Saluta uxorem tuam et filiolum suavissimum meo nomine. Saluta D. Bullingerum, D. Gualterum, D. Simlerum, D. Lavaterum, D. Gesnerum, D. Hallerum, D. Volphium, D. Frisium, et imprimis D. Bernardinum, (cujus res apud nos utinam irent paulo celerius!) juvenem cultissimum Hermannum, Julium, Juliam et Matyrillum. Vale, mi pater, vale: O quis mihi dabit, ut dicere aliquando possim, Mi pater, salve? Londini, 5 Martii, 1560.

Istæ sunt decimæ tertiæ, ni male memini. Tu vide an omnes ad te pervenerint. D. Lælium, si redierit in centrum suum, saluta, quæso, meo nomine.

Tui nominis observantissimus,

JO. JUELLUS, Sarisberiensis.

EPISTOLA XXXI.

EDWINUS WIGORNENSIS AD PETRUM MARTYREM.

Salutem in Christo. Quod nullas jam diu, vir reverende, literas ad te dederim, non officii quidem erga te mei oblitus, aut quid tua de me mereatur humanitas leviter perpendens, id feci; sed negotiorum multitudine obrutus, scribendi munus pro tempore invitus intermisi, quod, cum tabellarii jam sese offert opportunitas, diutius differendum non censeo. Sub Augusti initium cum literas ad te dedissem, in partes Angliæ boreales ad abusus ecclesiæ tollendos, et ritus pietati et veræ religioni consonantes eidem restituendos, tanquam inspector et visitator, ut vocant, cum principis mandato dimissus, et illic ad Novembris usque initium assidue in obeundo quod mihi creditum erat munere, non sine maximis cum corporis tum animi laboribus versatus, Londinum tandem redii; ubi novæ rursus curæ advenientem exceperunt, majorque negotiorum moles humeros premebat: opera enim mea in episcopatu Wigorniensi administrando a principe requirebatur, tandemque reluctanti episcopi munus imponitur. Volui quidem, ut antea Carleolensem, ad quem nominatus eram, hunc etiam episcopatum omnino recusare: at id non licuit, nisi et principis indignationem mihi procurare et Christi ecclesiam quodammodo deserere voluissem. Sub hæc literas tuas omni humanitate plenissimas Burcherus mihi tradidit; quibus per eundem, quum hinc discederet, respondere distuli, partim quod res Anglicæ tum temporis non ita mutatæ, sed in eodem quasi gradu consistentes, exiguam scribendi materiam suppeditabant; partim vero, quod novum illud onus (sic enim verius quam honos dici potest) novis curis et negotiis me mirum in modum distrahebat. En diuturni silentii mei causam habes, vir plurimum observande.

Eucharistiæ doctrina, hactenus Dei beneficio non impugnata, nobis salva et incolumis manet, mansuramque speramus; pro viribus enim et ipse et alii fratres coepiscopi illam, quoad vixerimus, Deo juvante tuebimur. De imaginibus jam pridem nonnihil erat controversiæ. Regia majestas non alienum esse a verbo Dei, imo in commodum ecclesiæ fore putabat, si imago Christi crucifixi una cum Maria et Johanne, ut solet, in celebriori ecclesiæ loco poneretur, ubi ab omni populo facillime conspiceretur. Quidam ex nobis longe aliter judicabant, præsertim cum omnes omnis generis imagines in proxima nostra visitatione, idque publica auctoritate, non solum sublatæ, verum etiam combustæ erant; cumque huic idolo præ ceteris ab ignara et superstitiosa plebe adoratio solet adhiberi. Ego quia vehementior eram in ista re, nec ullo modo consentire poteram, ut lapsus occasio ecclesiæ Christi daretur, non multum aberat quin et ab officio amoverer, et principis indignationem incurrerem: at Deus, in cujus manu corda sunt regum, pro tempestate tranquillitatem dedit, et ecclesiam Anglicanam ab hujusmodi offendiculis liberavit. Tantum manent in ecclesia nostra vestimenta illa papistica, (copas intellige,) quas diu non duraturas speramus.

Quantum ex eo quod te tuaque presentia jam destituitur Anglia, detrimenti capiat hic ecclesia et religionis negotium, diligenter et sæpissime apud eos, quibus reipublicæ cura imminet, commemorare soleo: nescio tamen quomodo, animis eorum in alias res gravissimas intentis, nihil hactenus de te accersendo statutum video. Semel, sat scio, Reginæ in animo fuit, ut te vocaret; quid vero impedivit, puto te facile ex te colligere posse: causa Christi multos semper habet adversarios, et qui optimi sunt, pessime semper audiunt: sacramentum illud unitatis magnas facit hodie divisiones. Novum tibi conjugium gratulor, atque precor ut felix faustumque sit; quemadmodum et mihi ipsi opto, qui eandem conjugii legem nuper subii. Mirus hic belli apparatus est, partim ad propulsandam Gallorum vim, si forte, dum Scotiam sibi subjugare conentur, nostros fines invaserint; partim ad auxilium Scotis contra Gallos ferendum, sicubi pacis fœdus nobiscum initum violaverint Galli. Det Deus ut omnia in nominis sui gloriam et evangelii propagationem cedant!

Hæc priusquam Wigorniam me recipiam, quo brevi profecturum me spero, literis tibi significanda duxi: fusius vero scripsissem, nisi quod sciam fratrem nostrum Juellum, episcopum Sarisberiensem, sæpe et diligenter de rebus nostris omnibus te certiorem facturum. Si qua in re tibi gratificari queam, crede mihi, mi honorande Petre, me semper uteris, quoad vixero, imo etiam post vitam, si fieri potest, pro arbitratu tuo.

Saluta, quæso, plurimum meo nomine clarissimum virum D. Bullingerum: debeo illi literas, imo omnia illi debeo, et tantum solvam quantum possim, si quando offerat sese occasio. Saluta uxorem tuam, Julium cum Julia, D. Hermannum, Paulum et Martyrillum meum, quibus omnibus omnia felicia precor. Vale, humanissime, doctissime, ac colendissime D. Petre. Londini festinanter, Aprilis primo, 1560.

Tuus ex animo,
EDWINUS WIGORN.

INSCRIPTIO.
Clarissimo ac doctissimo viro
D. Doctori Petro Martyri,
domino suo plurimum colendo.
Tiguri.

EPISTOLA XXXII.

THOMAS SAMPSON AD PETRUM MARTYREM.

Jam tandem per Dei gratiam solutus curis episcopalibus, liberius solito possum tecum agere, pater mi colendissime. Ne autem existimares me explicatum meo vitio, totam tibi narrarem historiam, nisi hoc temporis angustia impediret, tædium dissuaderet, et alia nonnulla vetare viderentur. Interim tamen hoc a te peto, ne cuivis referenti hæc facile credas: neque enim omnes norunt, quomodo res acta sit, qui libere de ea loqui volunt. Et aliqui etiam adhuc tui, quondam mei quoque, qui plus norunt ipsi quam nosse me vellent, forsan referent etiam minus vera, si quid referant. Non ego hæc scribo, vel meam sortem vel aliorum injuriam deflendo. Nil tale patior. Sed hoc volo: tuum judicium ne cito feratur, cum hoc audieris negotium, usque dum totum audieris, si tamen aliquando audire dabitur. Omnes, ni fallor, literas tuas accepi, et gratias tibi quam maximas ago, quod ita me ad rem instruxeras. Et omnino decreveram sano tuo et D. Bullingeri uti consilio. Sed res nunquam eo est perducta ut ad id adigerer. Nunc episcopatum illum Nordovicensem tenet noster Parkhurstus; et illi omnia felicia opto: optamus et omnes. Periculo ne malus aliquis eo potiretur episcopatu, probe est obviam itum. Deo optimo maximo sit laus! Una etiam, cum ita sit, meæ ineptitudini optime consultum. Quam ergo referam Domino Deo gratiam, vix scio. Tu autem, mi pater, Deum lauda, et pro me orare ne cesses.

Apud nos religio sicut ante viget; et ut magis floreat ad maturitatem, precor. Bellis implicari jam incipimus. Dignetur Dominus nos etiam explicare ad sui nominis gloriam! Mala quidem et multa timemus: nec immerito. At bonus ille pater misericordiarum nobis succurrat, et in suis miserationibus nostra medeatur mala. Paucis dico, nostras res plurimas omnium piorum petere orationes. Itaque habeas Angliam tuis orationibus commendatissimam.

Vale, optime pater et colendissime præceptor. Salutabis meo nomine quam officiosissime D. Bullingerum, tuam itidem uxorem cum prole, Julium tuosque omnes. Iterum vale. 13 Maii, 1560.

Tuus,

TH. SAMPSON.

INSCRIPTIO.
Clarissimo viro D.D. Petro Martyri,
 sacræ theologiæ professori fideliss.
  Tiguri.

EPISTOLA XXXIII.

JOHANNES JUELLUS AD PETRUM MARTYREM.

S. P. Si ex denis meis literis octo ad te, ut scribis, pervenerint, mi pater, et dulce decus meum, minus multo jacturæ factum est, quam putaram: ego enim sperare nunquam potui, vel tertiam literarum mearum partem ad te incolumem perventuram. Verum etsi illæ subsistant, ut fit, otiosæ, aut delitescunt uspiam, aut etiam pereant in itinere; tamen ego non desinam ea causa officium meum facere, neque unquam committam, ut tabellariorum perfidia videar velle liberare fidem meam. Crede enim mihi: nihil unquam facio libentius, quam cum aut ad te scribo, aut de te cogito. Itaque, O Deum immortalem, quoties ego me fingo esse Tiguri, et pro nostra inter nos amœnissima consuetudine modo te audire, modo tecum colloqui, ut interim, cum vera non liceat, saltem falsa atque umbratili voluntate possim perfrui! Confectis autem rebus nostris, et pace reque publica, quod brevi speramus fore, constituta, umbras istas et imagines missas faciemus, et te coram, spero, præsentem intuebimur. Id enim scire debes nobis bonisque omnibus esse curæ. Interim academiæ, et nostra illa imprimis Oxoniensis, miserum in modum deseruntur, sine bonis literis, sine lectionibus, sine studio ullo pietatis. Cœcum illud numen erit aliquando magis propitium. Verum adhuc tempora ista qualia sint vides: ὁ Ἄρης, ὁ Ἄρης ὁ βροτολοιγὸς fundum ipsum τοῦ πλούτου exhaurit. Ubi serenitas aliqua redierit, et istæ turbæ conquieverint, Eleazaro tuo Damasceno nec id, de quo[1] tu scribis, nec alia majora deerunt. Si ad nos venerit, vel potius ubi venerit, erit apud me eodem loco, quo si esset frater meus.

De Eliperio tuo non tribuo mihi tantum ut te consoler. Novi enim ego prudentiam tuam. Quod dies alioqui minueret, id scio te ratione solere antevertere. Utinam tamen puerum ita bellum, et ita tui similem, et hac potissimum ætate tua susceptum potuisses habere superstitem, non tantum qui tecum garriret aliquando, et te oblectaret domi, sed etiam qui ingenii, pietatis, virtutum tuarum omnium doctrinæque tuæ hæres esset! Sed quoniam Deus optimus maximus ita, ut est, esse voluit, melius quam est esse non potest.

De quinque illis coronatis Italicis scripsi ter ad Julium nostrum, bis ad D. Bernardinum. Tradidi autem eos ante septem menses D. Acontio Italo, qui nunc est apud comitem Bedfordiensem. Ille sese pollicitus

[[1] MS. *quod de.*]

est curaturum, ut quamprimum et quam optima fide redderentur Tiguri. Itaque D. Bernardinum toto hoc tempore nec pecuniam suam recepisse, nec vel a me vel ab Acontio quicquam audisse, miror. Redditum est mihi testamentum Frenshami nostri. Ducenti illi coronati sunt adhuc Antverpiæ, apud Arnoldum Birkmannum, non minus in tuto, quam si essent apud me. Pamphilus est in Scotia: ibi operam diligenter navat Critoni suo. In ejus reditum res manebit integra.

Nonis Maii summa turris ecclesiæ meæ Sarisberiensis ita non tacta, sed concussa est de cœlo, ut a fastigio ad quadraginta cubitos rima perpetua duceretur: tu vide, num quidnam in ea re sit divini ominis. Ego forte nondum eo veneram: quod si venissem, ut sunt hominum mentes superstitiosæ et fatuæ, omnis illa clades conjecta fuisset in adventum meum. Crastino tamen die proficiscor, et manum ad aratrum admoveo: Deus bene fortunet causam suam!

Petrus Alexander cum venisset ad nos calendis Maii, post aliquot dies restitutus est in præbendam suam in integrum. Agit nunc Londini apud D. Hetonum tuum, et concionatur in ecclesia Gallorum. Crito est in summa gratia. Si quos antea habebat adversarios, eos nunc tandem prudentia et pietate conciliavit sibi, et fecit suos. Id mihi inde usque literis significavit noster Pamphilus. Verum de illis rebus omnibus scribo plenius ad D. Bullingerum.

Falkonerus noster obiit diem suum. Parkhurstus factus est episcopus Norvicensis. Bonerus, Fecnamus monachus, Patus, Storæus jurisperitus, Vatsonus, quod animis obstinatis abstineant a sacro cœtu, et in omnibus angulis religionem istam, quam nos hodie profitemur, insectentur et lacerent, conjecti sunt in carcerem. Regina enim, femina prudentissima atque optima, virili prorsus animo et fortiter pollicita est, se non passuram, ut quisquam suorum possit impune ab hac religione dissidere.

Nos ubique scribimus militem, et omnia comparamus ad bellum. Gallus si advenerit, non opprimet, spero, imparatos. Quanquam, ut nunc sunt tempora, ille hostis non ita multum habet otii a re sua, ut possit curare aliena. Deus aliquando componat istas turbas, ut confectis rebus, possimus te revocare in Angliam! Crede enim mihi, nemo est mortalium, de quo nostri homines aut sæpius, aut amicius, aut reverentius loqui soleant. D. Cæcilius, quocum heri pransus sum in aula, D. Knollus, D. Wrothus orarunt, ut te plurimum suo nomine salutarem. Et, quod tu fortasse vix putes, D. Wilielmus Petrus cum audiret mentionem de te fieri, omnino oravit, ut suo etiam nomine idem facerem.

Salvere jubebis a me optimam illam mulierem, uxorem tuam, D. Bullingerum, D. Gualterum, D. Lavaterum, D. Gesnerum, D. Hallerum, D. Simlerum, D. Volphium, D. Frisium, D. Hermannum, D. Paulum, Julium meum, Juliam, et Martyrillum; quibus ego omnibus, totique ecclesiæ et reipublicæ Tigurinæ, omnia precor, omnia cupio. Vale, mi pater, mi pater, vale. Vale, mi domine in Christo colendissime. Ecclesiam causamque nostram commendo tuis precibus. Londini, 22 Maii, 1560.

JOHANNES JUELLUS,

ex animo, et vere tuus.

INSCRIPTIO.

Ornatissimo et longe doctissimo viro
D. Petro Martyri Vermilio, pro-
fitenti sacras literas in ecclesia
Tigurina, domino suo colendiss.
Tiguri.

EPISTOLA XXXIV.

JOHANNES JUELLUS AD PETRUM MARTYREM.

S. PLURIMAM in Christo. Scripsi ad e, mi pater, non ita pridem, biduo antequam discederem Londino. Eas dedi proficiscens Hetono nostro, ut ad te primo quoque tempore mitterentur. Nunc postquam ad meos veni Sarisberiam, etsi nihil detractum est de observantia erga te mea, imo etiam quamvis ea ex longo isto et mihi permolesto tui desiderio infinitis partibus aucta sit, et augeatur in dies, literarum tamen scribendarum opportunitas non eadem videtur nunc esse, quæ fuit antea. Longe enim nunc absum a turba et strepitu, minusque multo audio quid agatur. Et si quid volo, tabellarium tamen, qui isthuc eat, non invenio. Scribam tamen, quicquid erit, imo etiam quamvis nihil erit. Pereant istæ sane, si volunt, in itinere: meum erga te officium, obsequium, studium, non peribit. Erit, spero, aliquando tempus, cum propius nos mutuo salutabimus. Quam ego diem ubi videro, et in tuum complexum venero, satis me diu vixisse arbitrabor. Ea res nobis omnibus curæ est. Et quid impediat non videmus; nisi id forte est, quod suspicor, quodque ad te aliquando scripsi, Petrum et Paulum tibi reditum interclusisse. Sed Deus hujusmodi apostolis male velit! Lectio tamen tua adhuc vacat, nec scio, cui potius alii servetur, quam tibi. Interea tamen ibi omnia ruunt et pessum eunt: collegia enim nunc illa plena puerorum sunt, inanissima literarum.

Smithus abiit in Valliam: ibi enim aiunt duxisse uxorem, opinor ut omnia tua argumenta refutaret. Quicquid est, tamen jactat canos, et inane caput: habet nunc popinam, et vivit de taberna meritoria, contemtus a nostris, a suis, a notis, ab ignotis, a senibus, a pueris, a se ipso, ab omnibus. Sidallus noster Harpocratem colit, et tegit sententiam:

itaque nunc nec inter aves nec inter quadrupedes numeratur. Bonus quidem vir, uti nosti, utque ego sat scio, observans atque amans tui. Et fortasse, ubi copias nostras videbit esse auctas, ultro accedet, et ponet istam simulationem, et aperte se geret. Nam in lustrando exercitu oportet aliquem esse ultimum.

Episcopi aliquot Mariani sunt in turri: Londinensis in veteri hospitio suo, ubi antea fuerat sub Edvardo rege. Quo cum abductus esset, et in medium jam carcerem pervenisset, et, ut est homo perurbanus, et non tantum animo, sed etiam facie, ut scis, liberali, vinctos, quos ibi reperit, officiose salutasset, et amicos ac socios appellasset, reclamavit statim quidam e numero: " Et egone," inquit, " bestia, videor tibi socius esse tuus? Abi, quo dignus es, ad inferos; ibi invenies socios. Ego unum tantum hominem, eumque inductus aliqua causa, occidi: tu magnum numerum bonorum virorum, martyres Christi, testes atque assertores veritatis, sine causa occidisti: et me quidem facti pœnitet; tu vero ita obduruisti, ut nesciam an possis duci pœnitudine." Hoc scribo, ut scias, quo ille loco sit, quem etiam scelerati homines et malefici repudient et fugiant, nec ferant socium.

Constans rumor est, isque jam sermone multorum et literis confirmatus, militem nostrum post longam oppugnationem tandem deditione cepisse Letam, et Gallos præsidiarios cum singulis vestimentis emisisse De conditionibus multa sparguntur: sed adhuc nihil certi. Summa est nunc necessitudo inter Anglos et Scotos, non solum humana societate, sed etiam cœlesti fœdere sancita. Quod si illud etiam accedat, quod speramus, quodque cupimus, de Critone et Glycerio recte erit. Atque utinam ne illi id impediant, qui nec nobis nec illis bene volunt. Verum ista adhuc inchoata tantum sunt, et cruda quodammodo; post audiemus omnia clariora. Pamphilus nondum rediit, datus est Critoni comes a Glycerio. Ille, ut potest, scribit interdum ad me, et sperat fore ut volumus. Quicquid est, Crito non erit in mora. Suecus exspectatur cum numerosa classe, princeps potens, et dives argenti, et in faciendo sumptu perliberalis. Sed habitat longe gentium; et per hyemem maria omnia coguntur frigore, ut neve accedere ad nos possit, neve ad se redire.

Gallicis istis tumultibus Deus aliquando imponat finem optabilem, et Guisanos furores et consceleratam nequitiam reprimat. Dei beneficio apud nos omnia tranquilla sunt, non tantum de religione, sed etiam de republica. Messis copiosa est; messores tantum desunt. Tamen, quia Gallus dicitur armare classem, et nescio quas irruptiones minitari, ne quid nobis periculi, ut fit, creetur ex improviso, delectus facimus passim, et militem, si quid opus erit, habemus in procinctu. Ego tamen, ut nunc sunt tempora, vix puto illi tantum esse otii a re sua, ut nostra curare possit. Habes nostra. De Julio meo tuoque desino polliceri. Tantum veniat: novit viam: nihil illi a me deerit. Imo quid ego illum jubeo venire solum? Exspectet potius paullulum, et tecum veniat. Imo quid exspectare jubeo? Jamdudum venisse oportuit. Vale, mi pater, vale. Dicam tibi, spero, aliquando coram et in os, Mi pater, salve. Saluta meo nomine optimam illam mulierem, uxorem tuam, D. Bullingerum, D. Gualterum, D. Lavaterum, D. Frisium, D. Simlerum, D. Gesnerum, D. Hallerum, D. Wickium, D. Hermannum, si est adhuc apud te, Julium, Juliam, et Martyrillum. Nos omnes dissipati jam sumus in dispersionem gentium, ut quid alii fratres nostri faciant, nihil possim certo scribere: esse tamen pie occupatos in promovendo evangelio, et tui vestrique omnium memores, nihil dubito. Iterum, mi pater, vale, et ora Deum, ut hanc lucem velit nobis esse perpetuam. Sarisberiæ, Calendis Junii, 1560.

Tui nominis observantissimus,

JO. JUELLUS, Anglus.

INSCRIPTIO.
Doctissimo et ornatissimo viro, D. Petro Martyri Vermilio, docenti sacras literas in schola Tigurina, domino suo colendiss.

Tiguri.

EPISTOLA XXXV.

THOMAS LEVERUS AD HENRICUM BULLINGERUM.

SAL. PL. in Christo Jesu. Binas a dominatione tua accepi literas, ex quo in Angliam redii: et semel ad te scripsi de religione, et de me ipso quædam, quæ ex prioribus tuis ad me literis ad manus tuas pervenisse intellexi. In posterioribus tuis 20 Martii a Tiguro, et tamen mihi traditis non ante 22 Junii in Anglia, scribis apud vos de rebus nostris varios incertosque rumores spargi, vos autem a nobis ipsis exspectare certiora. Ecce ergo, vera certaque sunt quæ nunc scribo, ut et cetera quæ anno superiori ad te et Bernates scripsi, nimirum ad D. Johannem Hallerum et D. Musculum. Doctrina vera sinceraque libere prædicatur per Angliam ab illis, qui cognoscuntur posse et velle id præstare, per literas commendatitias a Regina vel ab episcopo aliquo ignotos admittendi in ecclesiis ut concionatores: ceteris enim omnibus interdicitur in ecclesiis concionandi munus. Nulla adhuc disciplina ulla auctoritate publica hic constituitur. Sed liturgia pro publicis precibus et ceteris in ecclesia ritibus eadem, quæ fuit sub Edouardo sexto, nunc auctoritate Reginæ et parliamenti, (sic enim summum vocatur concilium,) apud nos restituitur. Verum enimvero in injunctionibus a Regina editis post parliamentum præscribuntur ministris ecclesiasticis ornatus aliqui, quales sacrificuli olim habuerunt et adhuc habent. Plurimi ministri, qui omnes tales deposuissent antea, nunc tamen obedientiæ, ut aiunt, causa iterum similes resumunt et induunt. Pauci sane sumus, qui tales vestes perinde abhorremus atque miles ille Christianus coronam, de qua scripsit Tertullianus. Non enim ignoramus, quam inde occasionem papistæ captant ad offensionem infirmorum. Nam in cathedralibus ecclesiis præbendarii, et in ceteris ecclesiis rurales sacrificuli, externas vestes et internos animos ex papismo retinentes, ita fascinant aures et oculos multorum, ut non possunt non credere papisticam quoque doctrinam adhuc retentam esse, aut saltem brevi restituendam fore. Multæ parœciæ apud nos nullum habent ecclesiasticum ministrum, et aliquot diœceses destituuntur episcopis. Atque ex illis valde paucis, qui per magnam hanc regionem sacramenta administrant, ne centesimus quisquam verbum Dei prædicare potest et vult; sed tantum legere, quod in libris præscribitur, omnes coguntur. Sic sane apud nos jam messis Domini copiosissima, et operarii paucissimi sunt. Qui fuere quondam episcopi, et ceteri archipapistæ apud nos, præponentes primatum papæ auctoritati Reginæ, privantur omnibus honoribus et stipendiis in Anglia. Quidam etiam ex illis nuper custodiis et carceribus committuntur; et quo tandem evasuri sint, adhuc ignoratur.

In Scotia non publico consensu ab omnibus, sed tamen magno cum zelo et sinceritate a quam plurimis, evangelium recipitur. Et Scoti jam diu Gallos omnes e Scotia expellere tentant; unde apud nos videre est magnos bellorum apparatus, et plurimi milites in subsidium Scotorum adversus Gallos mittuntur. Est portus in Scotia, qui nostro idiomate vocatur *Leith:* illum fossis, aggeribus, tormentis et armis munitum Galli tenent, Angli oppugnant. Multi certe utrinque interficiuntur, et captivi vivi, ut aiunt, nulli servantur. Audivi, quod verum esse suspicor, nunc dierum talia esse mundanæ pacis fœdera, ut penitus dissolvantur, si vel unus ab alterutra parte captivus detineatur vivus; possint tamen eadem firmissima perseverare, si interficiantur vel utrinque plurimi. Atque id inde conjicio, quod adhuc inter Gallos et Anglos nullum bellum sit publice indictum, sed potius talis pax, ut mercatores libere negotiantur Angli in Gallia et Galli in Anglia, cum interim milites utriusque misere et hostiliter confligendo pereunt in Scotia.

De me ipso, si placeat audire, intelligas velim, quod statim post reditum meum in Angliam lustravi magnam ejus partem evangelii annunciandi causa. Estque civitas in medio Angliæ sita, quæ vocatur Coventria. In ea semper, ex quo semel emersit evangelium, fuere plurimi zelosi evangelicæ veritatis; adeo ut in ultima ista persecutione sub Maria comburebantur aliqui, exulabant una nobiscum alii, reliqui in magnis miseriis et difficultatibus diu jactati, tandem restituta sincera religione, alios prædicatores et me potissimum solicitarunt, apud illos Coventriæ evangelium annunciare. Ego posteaquam per aliquot ebdomadas expertus essem, hic copiosissimam multitudinem frequentare solere publicas conciones evangelicas, consensi illis, qui me rogabant, ut uxorem et familiam meam apud eos in Coventria locarem; et sic nunc fere per integrum annum ego libere sermones habui, et illi liberaliter me et meos in hac civitate aluerunt. Nam non astringimur neque ego illis, neque illi cives mihi, ulla vel lege vel pactione, sed tantum libera benevolentia et caritate. Uxor mea nuper mihi peperit filiam, quæ vivit et valet cum tribus aliis liberis parvis, quos ex priori marito defuncto ad me attulerat. Nos igitur te cum tuis salutamus, et omnia fausta atque felicia in Christo vobis precamur. Nam cum ex literis tuis intelligerem, uxorem tuam, liberos tuos et generos cum eorum liberis bene valere, perinde mihi gratum fuit, ac si essem natura, quemadmodum ex animo sum, unus ipse ex tuis illis, quos oro Deum in Christo tibi benedicere et beare perpetuo.

Libros contra anabaptistarum sectas te scripsisse libenter audio: et capitis tui dolores ingravescente jam ætate majores et frequentiores esse non miror, sed doleo annos et labores tuos cogitans, Deumque oro ut te diu alvum et sanum nobis et ecclesiæ suæ servare velit.

Qui pariter viximus unis in ædibus Tiguri Angli multi jam, necessitate ita urgente, longe ab invicem per Angliam distrahimur. Sed fieri non potest, quin omnes perseveremus memores præclaræ hospitalitatis [et] beneficentiæ, quam Tigurum vestro patrocinio nobis præstitit, valde commode, pie et amanter. Itaque solus et seorsim a ceteris scribens te tamen rogo, simul omnium nostrorum nominibus gratias agere magistratibus reipublicæ et ministris ecclesiæ, atque reliquis bonis viris Tiguri, pro tam opportuno, grato et necessario hospitio nobis exulibus ibi Christi causa exhibito; et matronæ illi Elizabethæ, quæ nobis inservivit, dicas quæso a nobis omnibus salutem in Domino.

Obsecro etiam, ut meo nomine salutare digneris pientissimos simul et doctissimos dominos, Petrum Martyrem, Bernardum Ochinum, R. Gualterum, Theodorum Bibliandrum, generos tuos mihi carissimos, Lavaterum, Zuinglium, et Simlerum, præterea Johannem ab Ulmis, qui vixit olim in Anglia, et Johannem Burcherum Anglum, cum reliquis piis apud vos mihi notis in Domino. Gratum quoque esset, si aliquando in literis tuis ad Bernates vel Arovienses mentionem nostri cum gratiarum actione feceris. Ego pro mea tenuitate ad utriusque ecclesiæ ministros et archigrammateos scripsi, et rescribam Deo volente brevi. Faxit Deus ut simus semper memores et ad omnem occasionem parati ad referendas debitas gratias vobis in Christo. Vale. Coventriæ, 10 Julii, 1560.

Tuus fideliter in Christo,

INSCRIPTIO. TH. LEVERUS.

Illustrissimo viro Domino Henrico Bullingero pientiss. et vigilantissimo patri atque pastori in ecclesia.

Tiguri.

EPISTOLA XXXVI.

JOHANNES JUELLUS AD PETRUM MARTYREM.

S. PL. in Christo. Scripsi ad te ante non ita multos dies, si satis me memini, calendis Junii, de universo statu nostrarum rerum qui vel tum erat, cum scriberem, vel certe esse dicebatur. Nunc accipe ea, quæ et passim jactantur in vulgus, et hodierno die ad me ex aula perferuntur.

De Scotia res confecta est. Galli præsidiarii, quos noster miles longa lentaque obsidione et quasi per ludum oppugnaverat, postremo vi maloque coacti, sese nostris dediderunt. Habita a nostris ratio imprimis est, ne quid per insolentiam et rabiem militum nimium crudeliter factum videretur. Itaque præterquam quod velitationes illæ, quæ subinde, ut fit, utrinque factæ sunt, non potuerunt esse incruentæ, quam minimum alioqui haustum est humani sanguinis.

Gallus, cum pacem aliquam suis rebus quæreret, pollicitus est, se imposterum relicturum esse titulos et insignia regum Angliæ, quæ propter uxorem Scotam, proneptim Henrici VIII., jam antea cum suis titulis et insignibus miscere cœperat, seque posthac veteribus tantum liliis et avitis titulis contentum fore: regnum Scotiæ per duodecim viros, homines Scotos, administratum iri: si quid posthac vocetur in quæstionem, vel de religione vel de republica, ejus rei judicium fore penes totius regni parlamentum: centum tantum et viginti milites Gallos relictum iri in tota Scotia, non qui illi regno creent periculum, sed qui acceptæ cladis et dedecoris testes esse possint, si quis in posterum ea de re forte dubitet; eos velle duodecim virorum senatui, si quid imperent, dicto audientes esse. His conditionibus utrinque discessum est. Letha præsidium solo æquata est a nostro milite. Galli impositi sunt in classem, ut abducerentur domum, mœsti et afflicti vix cum singulis vestimentis. Ista ego, mi pater, omnia non dubito ad vos jam antea vel nunciis vel rumoribus perlata esse. Tamen ea non dubito tibi etiam nunc, cum a me narrantur, nec injucunda nec ingrata fore.

Dux Holsatiæ abiit domum magnifice acceptus a nostris, egregie donatus a Regina, cooptatus in ordinem garterium, ornatus aurea et gemmata periscelide. Succus semper venire dicitur, atque etiam nunc esse in itinere, et velle propediem appellere: tamen ille, quod sciam, pedem unum non promovet. Hic nunc omnes pacem, nescio quam, fore praedicant; et de constituenda religione exspectari concilium orbis terrarum publicum. At ego nec pacem his temporibus convenire posse arbitror, nec coire concilium.

Habes, mi pater, quae nunc apud nos dicuntur nova. Bene vale, et te cura! Curabis *animi dimidium mei*. Saluta optimam illam mulierem, uxorem tuam, D. Bullingerum, D. Gualterum, D. Simlerum, D. Lavaterum, D. Volphium, D. Hallerum, D. Gesnerum, D. Frisium, D. Hermannum, D. Julium, Juliam, Martyrillum. Salisberiae, 17 Julii, 1560. Raptim.

JOHANNES JUELLUS,
ex animo tuus.

INSCRIPTIO.

Ornatissimo viro Do. Petro Martyri Vermilio, profitenti sacras literas in schola Tigurina, domino suo colendissimo.

Tiguri.

EPISTOLA XXXVII.

JOHANNES PARKHURSTUS AD HENRICUM BULLINGERUM.

TANTIS negotiorum undis adobruor, mi Bullingere, ut cogar brevior esse quam vellem. Breviter ergo tuis respondeo, idque ordine. Burchero perquam lubenter benefaciam, tum illius tum tui etiam causa. Utinam Burcheri moribus Burchera responderet! sed hoc tibi soli. Gualterus meam fefellit exspectationem, nihil ad me jam scribens. Fui in aedibus Abeli, cum fascis literarum adferretur: tum tamen temporis praeter tuas et Julii literas nullas accepi; quod valde sum miratus.

De statu regni in religione sic habeto. Multis piis omnia placent, mihi paucula adhuc displicent: sed spero meliora. Plus paucis mensibus Scoti in vera religione profecerunt, quam nos multis annis. Inter Scotos, Gallos et nos, (dedito oppido Leith) coaluit pax: conditiones ad te perscripsit Abelus. Caletum non est a nobis recuperatum; imo nihil tale tentatum.

Saluta meo nomine optimam tuam conjugem, filios, filias, generos, et omnes viros doctos et amicos meos. Opto omnia prosperrima vestrae civitati, atque adeo universae Tigurinorum ditioni. Uxor mea vobis omnibus multam jussit adscribi salutem. Vale. Raptim. Londini, 23 Augusti 1560.

Tuus,
JOHANNES PARKHURSTUS.

INSCRIPTIO.

Clarissimo viro D. Henrico Bullingero.

Tiguri.

EPISTOLA XXXVIII.

JOHANNES JUELLUS AD PETRUM MARTYREM.

S. PL. in Christo. Quid ego ad te hoc tempore scribam, mi pater, nescio. Nam et rerum novarum parum est, et temporis ad scribendum multo minus; nunc enim accingor ad agendos conventus et obeundam provinciam: ille labor erit bimestris. Eram scripturus, nescio quid, ad te ante mensem; et jam non nihil etiam scripseram. Sed cum rumor hic de te parum secundus, nostris omnibus molestus, mihi autem imprimis audiendum peracerbus, passim spargeretur; isque non tantum populari fama, sed etiam de literis D. Grindalli et archiepiscopi Cantuariensis confirmaretur; præ mœrore, mihi crede, atque animi ægritudine coactus sum desistere, atque abrumpere inchoata. Nunc autem, postquam fratres nostri Genevenses, qui ad nos nuper admodum redierunt, nuntiant apud vos omnia ista esse ut volumus, non possum mihi imperare quin scribam aliquid ad te, etsi hercle nihil sit hoc tempore quod scribam.

Ecclesia nostra nunc Dei beneficio tranquilla est. Nec mirum. Nunc enim illi venti, qui antea fluctus concitabant, ne quid turbare possint, egregie ab Æolo conclusi sunt. Concionatores tantum nobis desunt: illorum est enim magna et miserabilis inopia; et scholæ desertæ prorsus sunt, ut, nisi Deus nos respiciat, nulla in posterum supplementa sperari possint. Concionatores tamen illi qui sunt, qui pauci sunt, præsertim qui aliquid possunt, a populo secundis auribus atque animis audiuntur. Invenimus primis temporibus Elizabethæ magnam et inauspicatam segetem Arianorum, anabaptistarum, et aliarum pestium, qui, nescio quo pacto, ut fungi noctu et in tenebris, ita illi in illa caligine et infausta nocte Mariani temporis excreverunt. Eos nunc audio, spero quidem certe, ad lucem melioris doctrinæ, tanquam noctuas ad aspectum solis, oblituisse, et prorsus jam nullos esse: aut si qui sunt, tamen ecclesiis nostris molesti non sunt.

Volatica illa doctrina Ubiquitaria non potest apud nos consistere ullo modo: etsi non deerant ab initio, quibus ea res magnopere curæ fuerit. In Gallorum ecclesia, quam habent nunc Londini, audio esse quosdam importunos homines et turbulentos, qui aperte incipiant Ἀῤῥιανίζειν. Deus nobis aliquando auferat ista lolia!

Regina, pacatis rebus, pollicetur se daturam nobis argentum purum putumque; itaque jam incipit omnem superiorum temporum adulterinam monetam revocare. E Scotia nihil præterquam quod superioribus literis ad te scripsi, de expugnato præsidio et rebus confectis ex sententia. Crito quid agat, nescio. Pamphilus nondum rediit. De Glycerio utinam— sed ταῦτα ἐν τοῦ Θεοῦ γούνασι κεῖται. Maius decanus Paulinus, designatus archiepiscopus Eboracensis, mortuus est. D. Hornus erit episcopus

Vintoniensis. Cetera sunt eo loco quo scripsi antea Parkhurstum, Sandum, Samsonum, Leverum, ceterosque nostros, minus pene nunc video quam tu: ita prorsus disjecti sumus, non in dispersionem, sed, spero, ad collectionem gentium. Audio literas et alia quædam ad me advecta esse e Germania; sed unde, aut a quibus, nescio: suspicor tamen a te. Idcirco omnia nunc mihi longa sunt, dum rescisco quid sit. Ego, nisi quod tu ita procul abes, ceteroqui recte valeo.

Mi pater, vale. Vale, potior pars cordis mei. Scriberem hoc tempore ad ornatissimum virum, D. Bullingerum, nisi excluderer negotiis. Ignoscat mihi in præsentia; posthac scribam prolixius, quicquid erit. Saluta, quæso, illum, D. Gualterum, D. Simlerum, D. Gesnerum, D. Hallerum, D. Vickium, D. Lavaterum, D. Zuinglium, D. Volphium, D. Frisium, quam potes officiossisime meo nomine. Ego illos omnes illorumque omnia amo in Domino. Julium nostrum nec scribere ad me, nec ad vos venire, miror. Illi ego non minus cupio voloque quam fratri meo. Si quid de fide mea dubitat, faciat periculum. Tamen illi quoque, et Juliæ, et inprimis, vel potius ante omnes primos primasque, optimæ illi mulieri, uxori tuæ, et Martyrillo et D. Hermanno salutem dicito. Iterum, mi pater, vale. Salisberiæ, 6 Novembris, 1560.

Tui nominis observantissimus,

JOHANNES JUELLUS, Anglus.

INSCRIPTIO.

Ornatiss. et longe doctissimo viro, D. Petro Martyri Vermilio Florentino, profitenti sacras literas in schola Tigurina, domino suo observandiss.

Tiguri.

EPISTOLA XXXIX.

JOHANNES PARKHURSTUS AD JOHANNEM WOLPHIUM, JOSIAM SIMLERUM, ET LUDOVICUM LAVATERUM.

Quum una vos civitas, eadem studiorum societas, mutuaque amicitia conjungat pariter; denique eadem adhuc arctius professio communisque religionis amor contineat, dulcissimi sodales carissimaque capita; dabitis hanc mihi veniam, vel negotiis imputabitis, quibus in præsentia distineor, si, quos simul connectunt philtra, eadem quoque vos ipsos conjungat epistola. Etenim si qua veteri parœmiæ fides, qua amicus alter ipse dicitur, sitque ea amicitiæ vis ut ex pluribus, quamlibet natura diversis, unum veluti hominem conciliet constituatque, perinde igitur facturus videbor ad triumviratum hunc junctissimorum amicorum unica scribens epistola, ac si eosdem diversis compellarem literis. Itaque ut tribus simul vestris ad me disertissimis epistolis una velut manu respondeam, habeo vobis pro tam candida gratulatione vestra gratias: quas neque ideo a vobis velim minoris fieri, quod singulatim inter vos minus distribuantur. Amor nihil magis propterea distrahitur, etiamsi contrahitur paullulum scribendi officium. Vos interim pro facilitate vestra communem inter vos epistolam, ceu pignus et monumentum[1] gratissimi erga vos studii, perinde partietis, ac si pro justa officii ratione singulis seorsim accurateque respondissem. Posthac a negotiis ubi plus concedetur otii, volente Domino, experiar si quo modo declarare queam, quanti Tigurinos amicos, hoc est veteranos meos hospites, faciam, haudquaquam commissurus, ut in hoc officiorum genere, quæ ad amicitiam quidem attinent, cuiquam vestrum cedere videar, licet ceteris in rebus vobis cessurus libenter. Atque hæc hactenus, præ turba occupationum mearum, ad vos scripsisse sufficiat, tametsi molestum est sermonem cum jucundissimis sodalibus abrumpere. Vos, quæso, æqui bonique consulite. Humanissimam pietatem vestram in dies magis ac magis florere faustissimeque valere in Domino exopto plurimum. Valete. Raptim. Nordovici, 9 Martii, 1561.

Mi Josia, ago gratias pro libro Bullingeri, quem latinitate donasti et ad me misisti. Mea vos omnes.

Vester,
JOHANNES PARKHURSTUS,
Nordovicensis.

INSCRIPTIO.
Eximiis viris D. Josiæ Simlero,
   D. Johanni Wolphio, et D.
    Ludovico Lavatero.
     Tiguri.

EPISTOLA XL.

JOHANNES JUELLUS AD JOSIAM SIMLERUM.

S. Pl. O mi Josia, quas ego nunc agam gratias? Libellus ille tuus, primum ita pie et docte scriptus, deinde a te ita eleganter et commode redditus, erat mihi utroque nomine gratissimus. Felices vos, quibus et facultas istiusmodi, et ingenium, et otium obtigit. Nos vero, qui ista non possumus, facere tamen id æquum est, quod putamus. Perge, mi Josia, hunc animum ita instructum, ita ornatum, quod facis et jamdudum magna cum laude, dicare templo Dei.

[1] MS. *momentum.*

De Julio nostro nihil erat opus ut ita serio ad me scriberes: ego enim illum novi, et ille me. Laudo tamen animum et pietatem tuam, qui homini amico ita ex animo consultum cupias. Illi ego non dubito a vobis prospectum iri. Silentium meum, fateor, mi Josia, longius erat quam oportuit, quamque ego voluissem. Verum magnitudo negotiorum, quibus urgeor assidue, sæpe mihi calamum excutit de manibus. Etsi enim alia habeo omnia, vitam, vires, valetudinem, otium tamen ad scribendum vix unquam habeo. Vel hoc ipso tempore quam sim occupatus, Julius ipse nisi vellet esse testis, utinam esset sine testibus! Jamjam proficiscor Londino domum. Jamdudum equus me exspectat. Quare nova nostra omnia et statum universarum nostrarum rerum committo Julio. Quicquid dicet, quamvis nonnihil affingat de suo, ut solent qui peregre redeunt, tamen tu pro tua humanitate putare debes, illum esse virum bonum. Quod si ille ita se geret, non errabis.

Vale, mi Josia. Et uxorem tuam, et D. Hermannum, Frisium optimum et cultissimum juvenem, saluta meo nomine, et hoc manusculum boni consule. Vale. Londini, 4 Maii, 1561. Raptim.

Tuus ex animo,
JOHANNES JUELLUS, Anglus.

INSCRIPTIO.
Doctissimo et amicissimo viro,
D. Josiæ Simlero, profitenti
sacras literas in ecclesia Ti-
gurina, amico veteri et sin-
gulari.

EPISTOLA XLI.

JOHANNES PARKHURSTUS AD HENRICUM BULLINGERUM.

OPPORTUNUS nuncius si non esset, carissime Bullingere, nihil rescripsissem hoc tempore; nunc enim minus vacat, quam unquam alias. Explorando, extirpando errores et vitia totos dies sum occupatus. De Scotia nihil certi habeo; sed quod audio, narrabit Julius. Ipse erit pro fasce literarum vobis omnibus. Salutat te uxor mea. Vale. 23 Maii, ex itinere, Thetfordiæ.

Ais te scripsisse de conciliis et misisse ad me duos libros, quos nondum vidi: sed spero tamen ad meas manus perventuros. Si tuus Christophorus venerit in Angliam, ei gratificabor quacunque in re possum. Julius fuit mecum, in cujus gratiam scripsi Oxonium. Signiferi vestri filium audio esse apud Bedfordiensem. Cum venero Londinum, eum ad me arcessam, et Tigurinum Tigurino more tractabo. Tigurinis omnibus omnia faustissima precor. Mea vos omnes. Iterum vale. Scripsi ad te mense Martio.

Tuus,
JOHANNES PARKHURSTUS,
Nordovicensis.

INSCRIPTIO.
D. Henrico Bullingero,
Tiguri.

EPISTOLA XLII.

JOHANNES PARKHURSTUS AD HENRICUM BULLINGERUM.

HUMANISSIMAS tuas literas 23 Junii scriptas accepi ultimo Augusti, doctissime Bullingere. Quæ quantum mihi animum addidere, quantum inflammarint, ut in functione mea alacris sim et fortis in Domino, haud facile dixero : tu hujusmodi calcaribus subinde me instiges oro. Equo tardigrado admovenda calcaria. Dominus convertat aut conterat quinque Palæstinorum satrapias, quæ piis molestias exhibere non desinunt! Quod Burcherus a putido illo scorto, facto divortio, sit avulsus, gaudeo; quod aliam duxerit, felix illi faustumque sit. De Burchero Burcheriqe rebus ad Burcherum nunc scribo. Ab illo cetera disces. Ubiquitistis meliorem mentem opto, si modo mentem habeant, cum sint et amentes et dementes; quos facile debellabitis tu et dominus Martyr. Sed novi gloriosorum ingenium. Victi non cedent; at nisi resipuerint, vincet eos Christus, vinciet et Satanas. Dominus Palatinum Rheni et Hessum suo Spiritu corroberet, et incolumes diu servet! Cetera narrabit tibi Julius, qui fuit multorum non tantum auritus, sed et oculatus testis. Resaluta nostro nomine optimam tuam uxorem, filios, filias, generos, D. Martyrem, D. Gesnerum, Wolfium et omnes. Mea vos omnes. Raptim, Ludhamiæ, 1 Septembris, 1561.

Tuus,
JOHANNES PARKHURSTUS,
Nordovicensis.

Omnibus verbi ministris per totam Suffolciam et Norfolciam in mandatis dedi, ut tuas conciones in Apocalypsin sibi comparent vel Latine vel Anglice. In nostram enim vernaculam linguam transtulit Johannes Daus, vir bonus et doctus, ludimoderator in urbe Ypsvico. Iterum vale, et valeant Tigurini.

INSCRIPTIO.
Clarissimo viro D.
Henrico Bullingero,
Tiguri.

EPISTOLA XLIII.

JOHANNES JUELLUS AD PETRUM MARTYREM.

SALUTEM plurimam in Christo. Gratissimæ mihi fuerunt literæ tuæ, mi pater, non solum quod essent a te, cujus omnia mihi debent esse, ut sunt, gratissima, verum etiam quod omnem statum renascentis in Gallia religionis luculentissime describerent; quodque ego me, cum eas legerem, et te ita prope abesse scirem, propius etiam aliquanto te audire, et propius tecum colloqui arbitrarer. Nam quamvis res Gallicæ ad nos rumoribus, ut fit, et nuntiis adferebantur; tamen et certiores, et multo etiam jucundiores visæ sunt, quod a te scriberentur, ab illo præsertim, quem ego scirem partem illarum fuisse maximam. Quod scribis, illos, qui rerum potiuntur, omnino velle mutationem in religione aliquam fieri, non tam studio et amore pietatis, quam quod papistarum ineptias videant nimis esse ridiculas, quodque non putent populum aliter posse in officio contineri; quicquid est, quacunque causa ista fiant, modo prædicatur Christus, εἴτε προφάσει, εἴτε ἀληθείᾳ, καὶ ἐν τούτῳ χαίρω, ἀλλὰ καὶ χαρήσομαι. Tamen fieri non potest, quin disputatio illa vestra multum et evangelium promoverit, et adversarios adflixerit. Quod autem scribis, *interim* quoddam a quibusdam et farraginem religionis quæri, Deus id avertat! Scio omnes in republica magnas mutationes odiosas et graves esse, et multa sæpe a principibus temporis causa tolerari; atque illud fortasse ab initio non fuit incommodum: nunc vero, postquam erupit lux omnis evangelii, quantum quidem fieri potest, vestigia ipsa erroris una cum ruderibus, utque aiunt, cum pulvisculo auferenda sunt. Quod utinam nos in ista λινοστολίᾳ obtinere potuissemus! nam in dogmatis prorsus omnia ad vivum resecavimus, et ne unguem quidem latum absumus a doctrina vestra. De ubiquitate enim nihil est hic periculi. Ibi tantum audiri ista possunt, ubi saxa sapiunt.

De Orothete autem tuo an ego me tibi dicam agere gratias? Equidem non dubito, quin ipse ille quem notas, si sapit, se multum tibi debere putet. Sed fortasse colliget animos, et patrocinabitur suo Pantacho, et sese parabit ad respondendum, et teque tuumque Palæmonem repudiabit. Laudes illas, quas tu mihi ita cumulate tribuis, non agnosco. Eas tuas potius esse scio, et tibi uni proprie convenire. Tamen, ut ait ille, jucundum est abs te laudari, mi pater, laudato viro. Erat illud non tam judicii testimonium, quam amoris erga me tui; cui ego, etsi non aliis rebus, tamen amore certe respondebo.

Apud nos de religione omnia sunt pacata. Episcopi Mariani servant turrim, et antiquum obtinent. Quod si leges æque nunc vigerent, atque olim sub Henrico, facile succumberent. Est genus hominum contumax et indomitum: ferro tamen et metu vincitur. Edidimus nuper apologiam de mutata religione et discessione ab ecclesia Romana. Eum ego librum, etsi dignus non est qui mittatur tam procul, tamen ad te mitto. Est multis in locis vitiosus, qualia sunt ea fere omnia, quæ apud nos excuduntur; tanta est typographorum nostrorum negligentia.

Regina nostra prorsus decrevit, nolle mittere ad concilium: quod an ullum aut uspiam sit, nos nescimus. Certe si uspiam aut ullum est, perarcanum et valde obscurum est. Nos nunc cogitamus publicare causas, quibus inducti ad concilium non veniamus. Ego quidem sic statuo et sentio, istis congressionibus et colloquiis nihil posse promoveri hoc tempore, nec Deum velle uti istis mediis ad propagandum evangelium.

Regina nostra, magno nostro cum dolore, innupta manet; neque adhuc quid velit sciri potest: tametsi, quo suspiciones nostræ inclinent, satis te jamdudum scire arbitror. Suecus, diuturnus procus et valde assiduus, nuper admodum dimissus est. Ille, accepta repulsa, minatur, quantum audio, in Scotiam; ut, cum apud nos hærere non possit, saltem possit in vicinia.

Est mulier quædam nobilis, domina Margareta, neptis Henrici octavi, mulier supra modum infensa religioni, supra etiam rabiem Marianam. Ad ejus filium, juvenem plus minus octodecim annos natum, summa rerum judicatur spectare, si quid Elizabethæ, quod nolimus, quodque Deus avertat, accidat. Ejus mulieris maritus, Leonesius Scotus, proximis istis diebus conjectus est in turrim. Filium aiunt vel ablegatum esse a matre, vel profugisse in Scotiam. De eo, ut solet fieri, sermo est multiplex. Regina Scotiæ, ut scis, innupta est: potest inter illos convenire aliquid de nuptiis. Quicquid est, credibile est, papistas aliquid moliri: sperant enim adhuc nescio quid, non minus quam Judæi Messiam suum. Nuntius pontificis hæret adhuc in Flandria: nondum enim impetrare potest fidem publicam, ut tuto veniat in Angliam. Episcopus Aquilanus, legatus Philippi, astutus et callidus veterator, et factus ad insidias, satagit, quantum potest, ejus causa; saltem, ut audiatur; ne tam procul frustra venerit: sperat enim uno colloquio aliquid, nescio quid, posse fieri.

Est puella quædam nobilis, domina Catherina, ducis Suffolciensis filia, ex sanguine regio, eoque nominatim scripta ab Henrico octavo in testamento, ut si quid accidisset, quarto loco succederet. Ex ea comes Herfordiensis, juvenis, ducis Somersetensis filius, suscepit filium, ut multi putant, ex stupro, sed ut ipsi dicunt, ex legitimis nuptiis: se enim clam inter se contraxisse, et advocato sacrificulo, et paucis quibusdam arbitris, junxisse nuptias. Ea res turbavit animos multorum: nam si sunt veræ nuptiæ, puer, qui susceptus est, alitur ad spem regni. O nos miseros, qui non possumus scire, sub quo domino victuri simus! Deus nobis Elizabetham, spero, diu vivam et incolumem conservabit. Id nobis erit satis. Tu, mi pater, ora Deum, ut rempublicam nostram et ecclesiam conservet. Vale, mi pater, vale. Vale, dulce decus meum.

Saluta meo nomine uxorem tuam, D. Bullingerum, D. Gualterum, D. Lavaterum, D. Zuinglium, D. Hallerum, D. Wickium, D. Gesnerum, D. Frisium, D. Wolphium, Julium, Juliam, et Martyrillum. Salisberiæ, 7 Febr. 1562, ex Anglia.

Tui nominis studiosissimus,

JO. JUELLUS, Anglus.

P. S. Regina Elisabetha omnem nostram monetam auream argenteamque ad pristinam probitatem restituit, et puram putamque reddidit; opus plane regium, quodque tu mireris tam brevi tempore potuisse fieri.

INSCRIPTIO.
Viro longe doctissimo, D. Petro Martyri Vermilio, professori sacræ theologiæ in schola Tigurina, domino suo colendissimo. Tiguri.

EPISTOLA XLIV.

JOHANNES JUELLUS AD HENRICUM BULLINGERUM.

S. Pl. Vix quicquam nunc superest, clarissime vir et domine in Christo colendissime, quod ad te scribam: omnia enim, quæ opus erant, quæque scribenti occurrebant, perscripsi diligenter ad D. Petrum Martyrem. Tamen quicquid est, pro observantia et amore erga te meo, non possum te insalutatum dimittere, saltem ut intelligas me vivere, et pro tuis maximis erga me plurimisque meritis memorem esse tui. Parkhurstum, Sandum, Leverum, Elmerum, Samsonem biennium jam totum non vidi, nec illi me. Tamen nihil dubitio, illos omnes erga te, tuosque, vestrosque adeo omnes, ea esse voluntate, qua debent.

Ex Scotia nihil ad nos adfertur novi: nisi religionem ibi et secundis animis recipi, et constanter defendi, et in singulos dies latius propagari. Reginam tamen Scotiæ missam suam adhuc aiunt retinere. Deus illi, spero, aliquando aperiet oculos: est enim alioqui, uti dicitur, mulier non mala. Utinam prorsus exuerit omnes spiritus atque animos Lotharingicos!

Apud nos omnia sunt pacata. Episcopi quidam pauci, qui superioribus istis temporibus Marianis insani erant, non possunt adhuc tam brevi tempore satis verecunde redire ad sanitatem. Itaque asservantur in turri, ne contagione sua inficiant alios. Papa clam palamque molitur quantum potest. Ante quatuordecim menses ad Reginam Elizabetham misit nuncium: is quoniam nondum etiam recipi potest in Angliam, hæret adhuc in Flandria. Sperant adhuc aliquid posse effici; nondum omnes ineptiarum suarum radices evulsas esse; esse adhuc aliquos, quos non dubitent esse suarum partium. Sed quid ego ista? ea enim omnia ad D. Petrum, ut dixi, scripsi fusius. D. Johannem Schneider, juvenem illum vestrum Tigurinum, ex quo Julius noster discessit ex Anglia, nunquam vidi. Nec mirum; longe enim gentium absumus. Tamen illum ante aliquot menses audivi satis commode agere: quod si quid opus erit, et ego ejus rationes scire potero, dabo diligenter operam, ne quid illi a me desit. Id ego et humanitati tuæ et Tigurinæ civitati debeo, et me debere profiteor. Nonnihil miror, Burcherum nostrum ad nos ante hoc tempus non venisse: scripsit enim se venturum; et ex literis videbatur esse in itinere. Ego illi valde cupio, et tuæ dominationi ejus nomine ago gratias.

Deus vos omnes, et te, mi pater, imprimis, et ecclesiam rempublicamque vestram conservet incolumem: et si quis est, qui vobis male velit, det illi breve vivere et parum posse. Scriberem plura, si occurrerent plura digna quæ tam procul scriberentur. Saluta optimam illam feminam, uxorem tuam, D. Gualterum, D. Josiam Simlerum, D. Lavaterum, D. Zuinglium, D. Hallerum, D. Gesnerum, D. Volphium, D. Vickium, D. Frisium, D. Henricum Bullingerum, filium tuum, optimum juvenem. Etsi nullus nostrum est mecum, tamen ego te non dubito omnium illorum nomine salutari; scio enim illos de tua dominatione, uti debent, quam honorificentissime cogitare. Vale, mi pater, et domine colendissime: et si quid ego aut sum aut possum, id omne puta esse tuum. Sarisberiæ, 9 Februar. an. 1562.

Tuæ dominationi deditissimus,
JOHANNES JUELLUS, Anglus.

EPISTOLA XLV.

JOHANNES JUELLUS AD JOSIAM SIMLERUM.

S. PL. in Christo. Quid ego nunc ad te scribam, mi Josia? nova enim omnia quæ erant, imo etiam fortasse quæ non erant, jam antea conjeci in eas literas quas scripsi ad D. Bullingerum et ad D. Petrum Martyrem. Crambe autem, uti scis, bis posita mors est. Putidum autem esset vetera et obsoleta scribere. Nihil ergo ego ad te? Johannes ad Josiam? Juellus ad Simlerum? Amicissimus ad amicissimum? Scribam certe, saltem ut intelligas me vivere, et te tuosque omnes in oculis gerere, et nec spatia locorum nec intervalla temporum mihi ex animo eximere potuisse εἴδωλα illa multo jucundissima Josietatis tuæ. Quod mihi de Julio tuo meoque agis gratias, ego tibi vicissim ejus ipsius causa ago gratias. Ego quidem Julio meo cupio et volo, quantumque possum pro mea exiguitate polliceor me illi velle commodare; idque me illi et sua et multo maxime D. Petri causa debere ingenue profiteor. Tibi vero, mi suavissime Josia, de omni tua humanitate quantum debeam, nihil dico. Hoc solum te scire velim, ex quo tempore te primum novi, me et fuisse semper, et esse, et semper fore tuum.

Vale, mi carissime Josia atque optime, vale. Saluta uxorem tuam, ejusque sorores, et matrem, D. Bullingerum, D. Gualterum, D. Lavaterum, D. Lupum, D. Zuinglium, D. Hallerum, D. Vickium, D. Frisium. Iterum, mi Josia, vale. Sarisberiæ, 10 Februarii, 1562.

Tuus in Domino,

JOHANNES JUELLUS, Anglus.

INSCRIPTIO.

Viro doctissimo D. Josiæ Simlero, profitenti sacras literas in schola Tigurina, amico suo carissimo.

Tiguri.

EPISTOLA XLVI.

JOHANNES PARKHURSTUS AD HENRICUM BULLINGERUM.

SALVUS sis in Christo, clarissime Bullingere! Objicis meis conterraneis Anglis ingratitudinem, quod nihil ad vos dent literarum. Et vereor ne idem crimen mihi impingas, quia superioribus nundinis nihil ad te scripserim. Mi Bullingere, quidvis potius mihi impingas, quam ingratitudinem. Mihi crede, malim non esse quam esse ingratus. Quod non scripserim, morbo, eique valde periculoso, imputes, non mihi. Egone Tigurinorum meorum oblivisci possum? Non possum, *dum memor ipse mei, dum spiritus hos reget artus.* Et ne vestri oblitum crederetis, (quia per valetudinem scribere non potui,) misi aliquid ad vos. Si unquam primitias persolvero, et ex ære alieno me extricavero, sentietis, quis et qualis sit vester Parkhurstus. Fratres meos episcopos, et alios quos ingratitudinis accusas, nec immerito, satis acerbe satisque imperiose (tametsi illi dixerint satis pro imperio,) coram tractabo. Nec interea temporis cessabunt ad illos meæ literæ: amanuensem enim habeo, qui

Anglice scribat, et non Latine. Tu interim, optime Bullingere, de conterraneis meis dicas bene, tametsi mereantur audire male.

Ago gratias pro libro, quem ais te misisse ad me elucubratum hac hyeme contra Brentium. At nondum recepi: brevi recepturus spero. Dominus Brentii et Lutheranorum omnium oculos aperiat, ne in tanta luce caligine opprimantur! Fabritii signiferi vestri filium nondum vidi. Intra triduum arcessam etiam Nordovicum; nam ultro ad me venire fortassis recusat. Gratissimus adveniet, nec omnino indonatus abibit. Si canis Tigurinus ad me commearet, (nullum tamen novi præter Gualteri Wartlœum,) plurimi facerem, nec canino more tractarem.

Hæc breviter ad binas tuas literas. Religio apud nos in eo statu est, quo antea, statu inquam non omnino contemnendo. Sed ego spero aliqua meliora in proximis comitiis. Sunt in Anglia multi boni viri et spiritu ferventes; sunt multi nimium frigidi; sunt et tepidi non pauci, quos Dominus ex ore suo evomet. Sed ut nihil apud te dissimulem, metuo ne multa mala nostris capitibus impendeant. Omnes enim fere avaritiæ student, omnes diligunt munera. Nulla veritas, nulla beneficentia, nulla Dei cognitio. Maledicere et mentiri et occidere et furari et mœchari perruperunt. Et quod Empedocles de suis Agrigentinis dixit, hoc ego dicam de meis Anglis: Angli sic indulgent voluptatibus, quasi postridie morituri; sic ædificant, quasi semper victuri. At faxit Deus, ut ex animo pœnitentiam agamus!

Bene vale, suavissime Bullingere. Saluta meo nomine optimam tuam conjugem, filios, filias, generos omnes doctos, magistratus, et amicos meos omnes. Pro vestra republica fundo ad Deum preces nocte dieque. Iterum vale. Mea vos omnes. Raptim. Ludhamiæ, 28 Aprilis, 1562.

Tuus ex animo,
JOHANNES PARKHURSTUS,
Nordovicensis.

INSCRIPTIO.
Clarissimo viro D.
Henrico Bullingero.
Tiguri.

EPISTOLA XLVII.

JOHANNES PARKHURSTUS AD JOSIAM SIMLERUM ET LUDOVICUM LAVATERUM.

QUARE ad vos proximis nundinis non scripserim, ex D. Gualtero discetis. Religio in Anglia et Scotia satis feliciter procedit. Paucissima sunt, quæ ego improbare ausim. Meliora speramus in proximis comitiis. Tantum mihi displicet vita Anglorum evangelio non consona. Nunquam prædicatum est apud nos evangelium aut sincerius aut diligentius. Dominus donet nobis suum Spiritum, ut quæ Spiritus sunt, sectemur, facta autem carnis mortificemus!

Regina nostra brevi Eboracum profectura est, quo etiam sese recipiet Scotiæ regina. Ovis in Essexia non ita pridem prodidit homicidam, quemadmodum corvi in Helvetia. Unde nobis prodit Tilmannus ille Hellhusius? Fortassis e domo infernali, unde nomen sortitus videtur. Laudo populum Rheticum, quod antichristum non agnoscunt suum patrem. De operibus Œcolampadii scribam ad Froschoverum. Vestrum erit quæ Germanica sunt Latinitate donare; quemadmodum tu, mi Josia, superiori anno fecisti, qui libros Bullingeri contra anabaptistas et articulos Bavaricos Latinos reddidisti in magnum studiosorum omnium commodum.

Salutate meo nomine vestras uxores, feminas honestissimas, Zuinglium, Wolphium, Hallerum, Wickium, Frisium, Pellicanum, Guldebeckium, omnes Bullingeros cum uxoribus omnium, denique omnes meos amicos Tigurinos. Valete, amici integerrimi, et me, quod facitis, amare pergite. Nihil ad te, Lavatere, adhuc misi, missurus proxima hyeme, si non hac æstate, Deo volente. Valete. Raptim. Ludhamiæ, 29 Aprilis, 1562. Dominus omnes Tigurinos servet! Mea vos omnes.

Vester quantuscunque est,

JOHANNES PARKHURSTUS,
Nordovicensis.

INSCRIPTIO.
Humanissimis viris Josiæ Simlero,
et L. Lavatero.
Tiguri.

EPISTOLA XLVIII.

JOHANNES PARKHURSTUS AD HENRICUM BULLINGERUM.

SALVE, humanissime Bullingere. Librum tuum contra Brentium recepi 16 Maii: quem nondum legi; dedi enim bibliopolæ compingendum. Sed legam intra pauculos hosce dies, quamprimum remiserit bibliopola Nordovicensis. Pro eo ago gratias ingentes. Obsecro, ut ad me semper mittas doctissimas tuas lucubrationes: nihil mihi gratius facere poteris. Storæus, homo leguleius et papista impudentissimus, in partibus Angliæ occidentalibus, more aulico vestitus, est captus, ut audio: nihil enim præter auditum habeo. Fabritius 15 Maii ad me venit, quem ut Tigurinum et ut meipsum tracto. Doleo illum diutius mecum non mansurum. Malim cum aliquot menses, imo aliquot annos mecum detinere, quam aliquot dies. Loquor cum eo Latine, Anglice et (quod tu mireris) Germanice: miratur et ille, me tam bene posse Germanizare.

Vertigo capitis adhuc me non reliquit, sed mitius aliquantulo sese habet. Cetera ex Gualtero. Scripsi circa finem Aprilis literas ad te, ad D. Martyrem, D. Gesnerum, D. Gualterum, Lavaterum, Simlerum, Julium et Froschoverum, quas spero vos accepisse. D. Gualterus Haddonus ante triduum mecum pransus est, homo doctus et pius. Salutem tibi jussit adscribi, et D. Martyri et aliis. Saluta meo nomine tuos omnes. Omnia prospera opto Tigurinis omnibus. Vale, carissime Bullingere, et me, quod facis, ama, et Deum pro me ora. Raptim. Ludhamiæ, 25 Maii, 1562. Mea vos omnes. Obsignavi has literas ultimo Maii, 1562.

Tuus,
JOHANNES PARKHURSTUS,
Nordovicensis.

INSCRIPTIO.
Clarissimo viro D. Henrico
Bullingero.
Tiguri.

EPISTOLA XLIX.

RICARDUS COXUS AD PETRUM MARTYREM.

VIDETUR mihi nimis longum intercessisse temporis intervallum, quod mutuis literis nos salutaverimus: quanquam fateri cogor, me a te accepisse literas, ex quo ad te quicquam scripserim. Interim tamen ex te una cum aliis voluptatem magnam capio, quod adeo strenue indefesseque operaris in vinea Domini ad propagationem atque ædificationem ecclesiæ Dei in hoc seculo nequam. Laboris tui gustum suavissimum subinde accipio non sine delectatione et fructu. Haud ita pridem in tuo Judicum libro versatus sum, quem tu humanissime ad me misisti; exspectoque commentaria, quæ in libros Regum es pollicitus, ut sæpius cum meo Petro versari possim, dum in ejus scriptis libere expatiari queam. Pensare tuam erga me benevolentiam non est penes me. Interim tamen misi ad te per D. Springamum viginti coronatos vel aliquam grati animi significationem. Scio te æqui boni consulturum.

Si de nostra conditione quicquam novisse juvat, cum hominum ingenia et inconstantiam perpendimus cum verbi vel contemptum vel piæ vitæ neglectum spectamus; vix verbi in hisce regionibus diuturnitatem sperare audemus. Ingens est ubique papistarum numerus, larvatus tamen pro aliqua parte, quietus etiam hactenus, nisi quod clanculariis conciliabulis suos fovent errores, et ad verbi auditionem aures libenter obstruunt. Cum vero Dei immensam bonitatem consideramus, quæ nos ad sedes patrias revocavit, et verbi cursum fecit liberum, ejusque ministerium nobis credidit, animos erigimus, et spem alimus firmam, non nos iterum desertum iri a tam pio Patre. Proinde pergamus animo forti atque robusto illi inservire, curam omnem et rerum successum in illum conjicientes.

Capita cleri nostri papistici adhuc in carcere clauduntur. Humaniter quidem tractantur, sed de papismo nihil remittunt. Alii libere degunt sparsi in variis regni partibus, at sine functione tamen, nisi clanculum fortassis suæ impietatis semina jaciant. Scoti vicini nostri evangelium (gratia sit Deo!) feliciter provehunt. Mirifice animos erigunt papistæ ex tumultu in Gallia. Deus pro solita sua bonitate diligentibus ipsum omnia vertat in bonum, defendat suos, hostiumque ferociam brevi contundat! Amen. Quid vero agatur in istis vestris regionibus, maxime quod ad Christi regnum attinet, avide cupimus cognoscere. Dominus Jesus te nobis diutissime servet incolumem! Salutabis meo nomine D. Henricum Bullingerum, virum omni observantia dignissimum. Salutamus te tuamque ego meaque. Londini, 5 Augusti, 1562.

Tuus in Christo frater,

RICARDUS COXUS,

Episcopus Eliensis.

Adhuc nemo retundit ferocientem Hosium.

INSCRIPTIO.

Amico meo plurimum observando
D. D. Petro Martyri, divinarum
literarum professori in schola
Tigurina.

EPISTOLA L.

JOHANNES JUELLUS AD HENRICUM BULLINGERUM.

SALUTEM plurimam in Christo. Redditæ mihi sunt non ita pridem literæ tuæ, scriptæ Tiguri ad quintum diem Martii: quæ quamvis essent ὑπομεμψίμοιροι et querulæ, tamen mihi perjucundæ videbantur; non tantum quod a te essent, cujus omnia scripta dictaque mihi semper visa sunt honorifica, sed etiam quod officium meum ita obnixe requirerent, et meam in scribendo negligentiam et socordiam excitarent. Ego vero, mi pater, et domine colendissime, etsi minus fortasse ad te sæpe scribo quam velim, tamen quoties occasio aliqua offertur, ne hoc quidem officium intermitto. Binas enim dedi nuper ad te literas, alteras Francofordiam ad nundinas Martias, alteras statim a paschate. Quæ si adhuc, ut fit, subsistant forte in itinere, tamen expedient se aliquando, et postremo, uti spero, ad te pervenient. Ego interim de te cogitare, et honorifice, ut debeo, de te loqui nunquam desino.

De Gallicis rebus ad te scribere hoc tempore, esset fortasse putidum: omnia enim ad vos etiam sine ventis et navibus afferuntur. Sanctissimus nihil relinquet intentatum. *Flectere si nequeat superos, Acheronta movebit:* videt enim jam non agi de reduviis, sed de vita et sanguine. Utinam ne nostri sese patiantur circumveniri! Dux Guisanus, ut, nescio qua spe moderandæ religionis et recipiendæ Confessionis Augustanæ, moratus est principes Germaniæ, ne se admiscerent huic bello; ita omnibus modis persuadere conatus est reginæ nostræ, non agi nunc in Gallia negotium religionis; esse manifestam conjurationem, causam esse regis, cui illam, cum regium locum teneat, non oporteat adversari. Interea id egit, ut neptis sua, regina Scotiæ, ambiret gratiam atque amicitiam reginæ nostræ, et munuscula mitteret, et nescio quas fides daret: velle se hac æstate honoris causa venire in Angliam; et æternum amicitiæ fœdus, quod nunquam postea convelli possit, velle sancire. Misit ea adamantem maximi pretii, gemmam pulcherrimam, undique vestitam auro, et commendatam pulchro et eleganti carmine. Quid quæris? Putabant festivis colloquiis, et venationibus, et blanditiis, animos nostros abduci facile posse a strepitu bellico, et consopiri. Interea regina nostra, cum subodorata esset rem omnem, et quid ageretur intelligeret, (neque enim id erat adeo difficile,) mutare consilium de profectione, a Guisanis paulatim alienari, et ad principem Condensem non obscure inclinare. Tulit id Guisanus indigne, consilia sua non procedere; accepit contumeliose legatum nostrum, proposuit edicta publice, reginam Angliæ insidias facere regno Galliarum, et solam istos tumultus concitasse. Ista regina nostra patienter ferre non potuit, nec sane debuit. Statim aperte agere, legatum, uti audio, revocare, militem scribere, navibus omnibus, undecunque atque ubicunque essent, et suis et alienis vela tollere, ne quis exire posset, et quid ageretur nuntiare. O si ea id antea facere voluisset, aut si nunc principes Germaniæ hoc exemplum sequi vellent! Facilius et minori jactura sanguinis christiani tota res posset transigi. Et Regina quidem misit hoc tempore in Germaniam ad principes; et nunc in aula legatus a Guisano, cum novis, ut opinor, blanditiis, ut nos moretur et impediat. Sed non ita erit facile, spero, imponere videntibus.

Res Scotiæ de religione satis sunt pacatæ. Regina sola missam suam retinet invitis omnibus. Incredibilis fuit hoc anno toto apud nos cœli atque aëris intemperies. Nec sol, nec luna, nec hyems, nec ver, nec æstas, nec autumnus, satisfecit officium suum. Ita affatim et pene sine intermissione pluit, quasi facere jam aliud cœlum non queat. Ex hac contagione nata sunt monstra: infantes fœdum in modum deformatis corporibus, alii prorsus sine capitibus, alii capitibus alienis; alii trunci sine brachiis, sine tibiis, sine cruribus; alii ossibus solis cohærentes, prorsus sine ullis carnibus, quales fere imagines mortis pingi solent. Similia alia complura nata sunt e porcis, ex equabus, e vaccis, e gallinis. Messis hoc tempore apud nos angustius quidem provenit, ita tamen ut non possimus multum conqueri. Sarisberiæ, 14 Augusti, 1562.

Tuus in Christo,
JO. JUELLUS, Anglus.

INSCRIPTIO.
Ornatissimo viro, domino Henrico Bullingero, summo pastori ecclesiæ Tigurinæ, domino suo colendissimo. Tiguri.

EPISTOLA LI.

JOHANNES JUELLUS AD PETRUM MARTYREM.

S. PL. in Christo. Scripsi ad te et seorsim ad D. Bullingerum statim a paschate. Eas spero jam pridem esse redditas. Nam de superioribus, quas misi Francofordiam ad nundinas Martias, et curavi reddendas Froschovero juniori, quin ad te aliosque pervenerint, nihil dubito. Tamen D. Bullingerus videtur mihi in literis suis nescio quid de negligentia nostra conqueri. Ex eo tempore allatæ sunt a te ad me literæ datæ Tiguri ad quartum diem Martii, quæ quam mihi gratæ et jucundæ fuerint, tu potes facile pro mea erga te observantia et amore perpetuo judicare. Etsi enim ea quæ scribebas essent jam satis vetera et pene obsoleta, (literæ enim illæ tuæ vix ad me pervenire potuerunt ante 27 diem Junii, anhelantes jam et lassæ de via,) tamen in illis videbar mihi te agnoscere, et audire vocem tuam, et suavissime tecum colloqui. Te incolumem atque alacrem rediisse e Galliis, et integram corporis firmitatem et valetudinem retinere, pro eo ac debeo valde gaudeo.

Quod ad me scribebas, cum jam tum esses in Galliis, non tibi videri spectare ad arma, neque alia ratione posse transigi, id nunc nimium vere re ipsa videmus accidisse. Dominus Deus Sabaoth exsurgat aliquando, et pessundet ac dissipet hostes suos; nostris autem fratribus, qui illum sancte colunt, addat animos! Dux Guisanus, hostis potens, et jam ætate atque usu rerum callidus, nihil tam ambire videtur, quam opinionem de se bonam. Itaque ante aliquot dies nuntii et literæ passim volitabant; addebantur munuscula quædam honoraria; et omnibus modis gratia et bonæ existimationis usura quærebatur. Sic scilicet sperabat fucum hominibus simplicibus posse fieri. Quicquid est, apud nos non successit. Nos enim jam conscripsimus militem, armavimus classem, stamus in procinctu, ut si quid opus erit, eamus subsidio. Adversarii omnes, quicunque sunt apud nos egregii aut alicujus notæ, jussi sunt conqueri et asservari, ne quid noceant.

Utinam vestri etiam principes et respublicæ aliquando expergefiant, et cogitent causam esse communem; se quoque involvi posse, nisi caveant ne nimium diu otiose spectare velint quid agant alii. Res eo loco nunc est, ut cunctando nec restitui possit nec retineri. Sed Dii illi vestri selecti Tridentini quid? an repente obmutuerunt? O sanctos patres et magna mundi lumina! Tanto tempore, septendecim jam totis mensibus, ne verbum quidem? Atqui sanctissimus jamdudum exspectarat $\dot{\alpha}\pi o\theta\acute{\epsilon}\omega\sigma\iota\nu$, et fortasse ab illis putat sibi injuriam fieri. D. Balduinus scribit ad me magnopere probari sibi nostram in mutanda religione moderationem, seque daturum operam, (putat enim se posse aliquid,) ut similis ratio obtineat in regno Galliæ; $\dot{\alpha}\kappa\rho\acute{\iota}\beta\epsilon\iota\alpha\nu$ autem illam sibi vestram et Genevensium non placere. Est in ea re, ut mihi quidem videtur, iniquior D. Calvino, nimium fortasse memor veteris simultatis. Petrus Alexander laborat Londini e podagra, bonus vir et jam senio non nihil debilitatus. Hermannus tuus est nunc apud me: transmisit ad nos e Galliis, quod ibi videret istis tumultibus, quibus antea non assueverat, studia sua impediri. O quoties nos inter nos de te, de D. Bullingero, de uxore tua, de tota familia, deque universo Tiguro, quam suaviter et quanta cum voluptate colloquimur! Est mihi illius convictus jucundissimus: est enim, ut scis, juvenis bonus et perhumanus, et literarum bonarum admodum studiosus.

Res nostræ de religione recte habent. Papistæ obstinatiores nunc sunt quam unquam antea. Pendent scilicet ab eventu rerum Gallicarum. Nos viginti jam dies e Gallia nihil audimus.

Sunt alia quædam pauca: sed ea scribo prolixius ad D. Bullingerum, quem video literas nostras avidissime legere, et de illarum intermissione nullo meo merito mecum conqueri. Mitto ad te decem coronatos Gallicos, quos tuo et D. Bullingeri arbitratu insumi cupio in coenam in vestro hypocausto publicam, ad quam de more ministri ecclesiarum, et juvenes studiosi, aliique quos videbitur, convocentur. Mitto ad Julium meum coronatos Gallicos viginti, quos cum esset proxime in Anglia pollicitus illi sum in annos singulos: alios etiam octo coronatos, et nescio quos præterea baziones, hoc est solidos Anglicos quinquaginta, quos vix tamen expressi ab Annæ socero.

Vale, mi pater et domine in Christo colendissime. Saluta quæso optimam illam mulierem, uxorem tuam, D. Bullingerum, D. Gualterum, D. Lavaterum, D. Simlerum, D. Volphium, D. Zuinglium, D. Gesnerum, D. Vickium, D. Hallerum, D. Frisium, D. Franciscum, et suavissimum puerum Martyrillum, meo nomine. Sarisberiæ, 14 die Augusti, 1562.

Tuo nomini deditissimus,

JOHANNES JUELLUS, Anglus.

INSCRIPTIO.

Viro longe doctissimo D. Petro Martyri Vermilio, profitenti sacras literas in schola Tigurina, domino suo colendissimo.

EPISTOLA LII.

JOHANNES JUELLUS AD JOSIAM SIMLERUM.

S. PL. in Christo. Hermannus tuus nunc tandem, mi Josia, factus est meus, prorsus, inquam, et κτήσει et χρήσει meus. Quo pacto? inquies. Dicam. Alluvione: appulit enim Sarisberiam ad octavum diem Julii, cum se e tumultibus Gallicis vix eripuisset. O quoties nos inter nos de toto statu reipublicæ Tigurinæ, imprimis vero de Josia nostro, colloquimur! Prorsus nunc fruor illis dulcissimis sermonibus, quos, ut verum fateor, tibi antea subinvidebam. Quod si tu esses una, nihil posset esse dulcius, animo quidem meo nihil optabilius, modo ut podagram illam tuam relinquas domi. Crede mihi, mi Josia, etsi nobis dolori sunt esseque debent dolores tui, tamen videmus interdum, cum de te cogitamus, teque ante oculos nostros ita constituimus, hominem senem, vietum, incurvum, obstipo corpore, nitentem scipionibus, trahentem alterum pedem, et molliter, ac delicate prementem terram. Miramur etiam nonnihil, quomodo te podagra capere potuerit, cum tu semper ita fueris juvenis impiger atque alacer, illa autem vetula ita ignava et deses.

Regina Scotiæ, neptis ducis Guisani, proximis istis diebus, cum ambiret gratiam atque amicitiam reginæ nostræ, misit ad eam adamantem, gemmam pulcherrimam et summi pretii, inclusam et fixam in aurea lamina, et commendatam blando et eleganti carmine. Illud ego carmen ad te mitto, ut intelligas verum esse, quod olim dicere solebat Ludovicus, si bene memini, undecimus: Qui nescit simulare, nescit regnare. Vale, mi Josia, vale. Saluta uxorem tuam, feminam lectissimam, D. Gualterum, D. Volfium, D. Zuinglium, D. Hallerum, D. Vickium, D. Frisium,

D. Guldebeckum, quam potes diligentissime, meo nomine. D. Hermannus te salutat. Sarisberiæ, 18 Augusti, 1562.

Tuus in Christo,
JOHANNES JUELLUS, Anglus.

INSCRIPTIO.

D. Josiæ Simlero, profitenti sacras literas in schola Tigurina, viro doctissimo et amico suo longe carissimo.

EPISTOLA LIII.

JOHANNES PARKHURSTUS AD HENRICUM BULLINGERUM.

LITERAS tuas scriptas 22 Junii recepi sub initium Augusti. Editus est apud nos libellus, cui titulus Apologia ecclesiæ Anglicanæ; in quo ostenditur, cur discesserimus a papa ad Christum, et cur recusemus concilium Tridentinum. Potest fieri quod duo editi sunt libelli, sed ego tantum unum hunc vidi. Dedi in mandatis meo famulo, ut Londini quærat vel unum vel utrumque, (si modo duo sint,) et tradat Birkmanno ad Froschoverum hisce nundinis perferendum. Qui habitant Londini, videntur sui officii obliti, qui tales libros ad vos non mittant. Nisi episcopus Cantuariensis ad me unum misisset, nullum adhuc vidissem.

Est in Norfolcia mea venerandus quidem senex, concionator optimus, et antiquus antichristi inimicus: in ejus manus pervenit sententia Brentiana, quam ubi perlegit, ambabus manibus est amplexus, imo etiam contra aliquos pios et doctos strenue et mordicus defendit. Quod ubi ad meas aures perlatum esset, misi ad eum tuam responsionem, quam mihi dono dedisti; quam ubi diligenter perlegisset, ad me remisit, agens gratias primum tibi, qui tale scriptum evulgaveris, deinde mihi, quod ad aliquos dies ei mutuo dederim: jam enim valedixit sententiæ Brentianæ, veritatem te auctore amplexus. Credo eum esse fere nonagenarium; quem nunquam vidi, nam procul a me abest: equitare minime potest, imo vix incedere. In ecclesia cui præest assidue concionatur. Si conciones tuas Hieremianas in unum volumen redegeris, recte meo judicio feceris.

De classe Reginæ et militibus Anglis scripsi ad nostrum Gualterum; item de literis quas ad me scripsit miser Burcherus. Ante quatuor dies recepi literas a clarissimo Cantuariensi. Summa earum hæc est, ut diligenter omnibus quibus possim rationibus, iis tamen clanculariis, disquiram, qui et quot sint in mea diœcesi, qui puræ religioni non faveant, (puto eos suæ perfidiæ daturos pœnas.) Quod et sedulo faciam, et quamprimum eos de Christi inimicis certiores reddam. Hoc mi perplacet; ex hoc enim colligo clarissimum Cantuariensem veræ religioni constanter velle adhærescere. Faxit Dominus!

Saluta meo nomine optimam tuam uxorem, filios, filias, nurus, generos, affines; Hallerum, Wolfium, Frisium, Collinum, Wickium, Pellicanum, Mejerum, Froschoveros, etc. Mea vos omnes.

Cum hæc scripsissem, ecce evangelium ad me adfertur, crucem scilicet et candelabra in capella Reginæ esse comminuta, et, ut quidam retulit, in cinerem redacta. Abeat crux in malam crucem! Nimium diu illic perstitit, piis id maximopere deplorantibus, papistis nescio quam spem inde concipientibus. Præterea pseudoepiscopi, qui sunt in turri Londinensi, propediem reddent rationem suæ perfidiæ: sic enim audio. Vale, optime Bullingere. Raptim. Ludhamiæ, 20 Augusti, 1562.

Tuus,

JOHANNES PARKHURSTUS,
Nordovicensis.

INSCRIPTIO.
Clarissimo viro D. Henrico
Bullingero. Tiguri.

EPISTOLA LIV.

JOHANNES JUELLUS AD HENRICUM BULLINGERUM.

S. PL. De D. Petro Martyre etsi dolere nihil prodest, tamen nescio quo pacto dolor ipse jucundus est. Hei mihi! dignus quidem ille fuit, illa ingenii magnitudine, illa literarum multitudine, illa pietate, illis moribus, illa vita, qui nunquam e vita tolleretur. Sed hoc ego jam antea fore divinabam, ubi primum audissem, hominem id ætatis animum adjecisse ad nuptias. Deus Opt. Max. benigne respiciat ecclesiam suam, et illi demortuo suscipiat alios. Pauci estis, mi pater, pauci estis, quibus nunc rerum summa nititur; nam te semper numeravi inter primos. O utinam semper existant aliqui, quibus possitis hanc lampadem committere! Sed missa ista facio. Hercules vester Tubingensis, monstrorum fabricator, non domitor, otiose jam triumphat. In toto illo suo regno Ubiquitario tam amplis spatiis et regionibus miror si possit consistere. Si quid moliri velit in hominem mortuum, et ejus scripta possint ad nos perferri, nisi quis vestrum mihi velit antevertere, ego mearum partium esse puto, quantum negotia mea patientur, ut illi respondeam; si nihil aliud, saltem ut intelligi possit, Angliam et Helvetiam contra istos Ubiquitarios convenire.

Interitus Guisani Pharaonis, quem hodierno die pro explorato et certo accipimus, crede mihi, intimum mihi animum et pectus perculit. Ita erat repentinus, ita opportunus, ita faustus, ita omnem spem atque exspectationem nostram superabat. Quid nunc animi putemus esse fratribus nostris; quos illa bestia jam cinxerat obsidione, quosque spe et cogitatione prope jam cruentis faucibus devorarat? Sit nomen Domini benedictum. Chattilio nunc oppugnat arcem Canensem, et crescit in dies; et spes bona est adversarios venturos ad conditiones nostras, et omnia ita futura ut volumus. Regina nostra colligit militem e Germania, et dat stipendium, et nihil parcit sumptibus. Nos hoc tempore conventus agimus totius regni, et de religione secundis animis tractamus, deque republica, et de nervis bellorum, hoc est, de pecunia.

E Scotia nunciantur recte omnia. Regina pene sola et pertinaciam animi Guisianam et missam suam retinet, invitis omnibus. Nostra regina superiori autumno laboravit e variolis, satis cum periculo. Impatiens æstus et tædii se ipsam pene perdiderat. Sed agimus Deo gratias, qui et illam periculo liberavit et nos metu. Quid paterculi illi vestri Tridentini et papa hydropicus parturiant, nihil audimus. Fortasse Spiritus sanctus adesse non vult, aut fari non potest. Quicquid est, tanto in conventu, tanta exspectatione, nihil agi mirum est.

Ego post superioris æstatis atque hujus hyemis intemperiem, et aliquot dierum spasmos et catarrhos, jam tandem incipio convalescere. Scripta D. P. Martyris ne intercant, non dubito tibi curæ fore: magno illi viro constiterunt, et digna sunt, ut scis, quæ magni fiant.

Vale, vir ornatissime, et frater ac domine in Christo colendissime. Saluta optimam illam mulierem, uxorem tuam, filios, nurus, D. Gualterum, D. Simlerum, D. Lavaterum, D. Zuinglium, D. Wickium, D. Wolphium, D. Hallerum, D. Gesnerum, D. Frisium, meo nomine. Dominus te nobis diu servet salvum et incolumem! 5 Martii, 1563.

Tuus in Christo frater et
tuo nomini deditissimus,
JO. JUELLUS.

EPISTOLA LV.

JOHANNES JUELLUS AD JOSIAM SIMLERUM.

SCRIBEREM ad te quoque, mi Josia, nisi me occupationes meæ impedirent. Verum nos, ut scias, hoc tempore conventus agimus, et de religione, de republica, de pace belloque deliberamus. Ego vero inter istos æstus etsi mei ipsius meminisse vix possum, tamen Josiæ mei oblivisci non possum; quem etsi commentantem, scribentem, legentem multis maximis de causis admiror et veneror, et in oculis gero, tamen cum illum cogito senili gibbo, nitentem scipionibus, trahentem alterum aut utrumque pedem, diligenter circumspectantem vias ne quid incurrat in digitos, molliter ac delicate prementem terram, et Chremetis in modum ægre et seniliter tussientem, crede mihi, risum tenere vix possum. Dic dum enim mihi, mi Josia, quod istud est senium? vel quæ potius ista est dissimulatio? Tantamne mutationem factam esse tam brevi tempore? Sed quicquid est, ego te puto hominem esse bonum, nec aliud in vultu, aliud in pede gerere. Hermannus meus tuusque mecum est. Utinam tu adesses una! Facile et podagras et fascias et baculos abjiceres. Vale, mi Josia. Londini, 7 Martii, 1563.

Tuus in Christo,
JOHANNES JUELLUS.

INSCRIPTIO.
Doctiss. viro D. Josiæ Simlero, profitenti sacras literas in schola Tigurina, amico suo longe carissimo. Tiguri.

EPISTOLA LVI.

JOHANNES JUELLUS AD JOSIAM SIMLERUM.

Semper amavi, doctissime Josia, humanitatem, suavitatem, amorem tuum. Quis enim non amet hominem hoc ingenio, hac comitate, istis literis, ita veteris amici memorem, ita denique amabilem? Verum cum ad amorem erga te meum nihil videretur addi posse, tu tamen tuo merito facis ut quotidie videar videre, ut si amor maximus major esse posset, magis amem.

Recepi a te eiconam argenteam, et vitam atque obitum optimi illius senis, Petri Martyris. In eicone quidem etsi multa egregie conveniant, tamen erat etiam aliquid nescio quid, in quo artificis solertiam requirerem. Et quid mirum in illius hominis similitudine erratum esse, cujus equidem cum omnia circumspicio, vix quicquam puto fuisse simile? Libellum autem tuum avidissime et summa cum voluptate perlegi. Videre enim mihi videbar illum ipsum senem, quocum antea suavissime vixeram, eum nescio quo pacto propius etiam et penitius videre, quam cum una cum illo viverem. Stancarum autem obscurum et insolentem scurram, quem ego nunquam natum audieram, et argute, et pererudite, neque, uti spero, sine magno ecclesiæ commodo confutasti. Parcius ad te ista, mi Josia, de te præsertim: auribus enim tuis dare non est nec amicitiæ nostræ nec pudoris mei. Equidem libenter illa legi, ut soleo tua omnia; erant enim scripta de rebus jejunis plenissime, de obscuris splendidissime. De omni ista tua humanitate agnosco et fateor, atque etiam profiteor, me esse in ære tuo.

Ecclesia nostra Dei beneficio immunis est ab istis monstris. Tantum res nobis est cum satellitibus quibusdam pontificiis. Illi turbant quantum possunt in angulis, atque etiam hoc tempore impediunt quo minus ea possim pertexere contra ubiquitarios quæ cogitaveram: sed de ea re ad D. Bullingerum scripsi plenius. Si scripta D. Martyris edideris, et ecclesiæ consulueris, et multorum bonorum exspectationi, qui ea cupiunt, satisfeceris. Commentaria autem in Genesin, quoniam de illis quærere videris judicium meum, equidem ea, mi Josia, nunquam legi: tamen non dubito esse ejusmodi, ut si edantur, videri possint Petri Martyris.

Nova ea quæ erant, conjeci in literas ad D. Bullingerum. Nisi Rhenus vester nobis ita esset adversus, et scriberem ad te et mitterem sæpius. Sed iter longum est, et præterea ad istas nundinas vix unum aliquem invenire possum qui isthuc eat. Nunc autem etiam de nundinis dubito. Quicquid autem de literis istis meis fiet, ego tuus, mi Josia, totus sum, sive scribo sive taceo. Saluta, &c.

INSCRIPTIO.
Ad D. Josiam Simlerum, apud Tigurinos sacræ Theologiæ professorem, Juelli episcopi Sarisburiensis literæ.

EPISTOLA LVII.

JOHANNES PARKHURSTUS AD HENRICUM BULLINGERUM.

Cum essem Londini, objurgavi meos conterraneos qui Tiguri fuerunt, quod vestri immemores nihil unquam ad vos scripserint: quosdam pudebat, quosdam pœnitebat etiam alti silentii. Sed spero, eos jam scripsisse, et postea diligentius scripturos. Foxus ingens volumen scripsit de martyribus Anglis, idque Anglice: prodiit typis excusum quatriduo ante pascha. Ipsi papistæ jam incipiunt archipapistarum sævitiam exosam habere. Sex vel septem circa initium quadragesimæ condemnati sunt, rei læsæ majestatis; sed clementia Reginæ adhuc eos patitur vivere in turri Londinensi. Duo ex illis vocabantur Poli, nimirum cardinalis Poli consanguinei. Comes Huntlæus unus ex præcipuis Scotiæ proceribus et papista insignis, consilio Guisii motus, in Scotia piorum sanguinem fundere meditabatur, ut Guisius in Gallia, et magna erat multorum seditiosorum conspiratio; et haud dubie iidem tumultus et sanguinolenti quidem fuissent in Scotia, qui et in Gallia, nisi Dei beneficio in tempore detecti fuissent illorum conatus. Quidam in prælio occisi, inter quos unus erat ex filiis Huntlæi, alter filius capite plexus cum aliis quibusdam. Ipse Huntlæus ad carcerem ducebatur; at in itinere retrorsum ab equo decidit, et fracto collo exspiravit. Incertum est an casu hoc sit factum, an de industria.

Scripsi ad te, crucem, cereos, candelabra e Reginæ capella abducta; sed paullo post sunt reducta, magno piorum mœrore. Cerei antea quotidie incendebantur, nunc minime. Tepiditas in quibusdam multum remoratur evangelii cursum. Ex animo bene cupio omnibus Tigurinis quos meo nomine salvere jubeas, et præcipue uxorem tuam optimam, filios, filias, &c. Mea vos omnes. Raptim. Ludhamiæ, 26 Aprilis, 1563.

Tuus,
JOHANNES PARKHURSTUS,
Nordovicensis.

INSCRIPTIO.
Clarissimo viro D.
Henrico Bullingero,
Tiguri.

EPISTOLA LVIII.

THOMAS SAMPSON AD HENRICUM BULLINGERUM.

SANCTE Bullingere, salutem æternam in Christo nostro Servatore opto tibi. Miraris forsan, quod ego te meis audeam interpellare literis. Parce, paucis scribam. Non ita pridem habui Tiguri, cujus possem omnia mea in sinum effundere. Ejusdem apud vos exuvias habetis. Tigurum ergo sæpius mihi venit in mentem. Sed ad quid ego effutirem ea quæ tum cogito? Vivit Martyr; valeat et feliciter vivat Tigurum. Et ne una cum Martyre intereat etiam Tigurinæ apud me benignitatis memoria, te nunc compello. Tuguriolum aliquando dabatur mihi Tiguri. Si meis votis nunc Deus annueret, id obnixe repeterem. Me forsan quæro, dum talia opto: non diffiteor. At cum Christi Domini nostri gloria unice sit quærenda, meas desero petitiones, quatenus me spectant. Hac in re, (in quærendo hospitiolo,) nolo tibi iterum esse molestus. O si aliquando daretur attingere mansiones a Christo Domino nobis paratas in cœlis! Interim, sanctissime pater, Angliam nostram et me quoque tuis precibus commendo. Angliæ res male se habent. Pejora vereor, ne dicam pessima. At Christo Domino interim inserviendum est. Felix ille est, quem Christus noster in famulitium adsciscit. Angliam ergo tibi commendatissimam habe in precibus; necnon et mei sis memor. In perpetuum amoris erga te mei signum mitto chirothecas Oxonienses per D. Blaarerum vestratem: illæ inveterascent, nunquam tamen apud te Angliæ meique inveterascat amor. Vale, et in Domino vive felicissime, carissime pater. Oxonii, die 26 Julii, 1563.

THO. SAMPSON.

Saluta, quæso, meo nomine et meæ uxoris Julium Terentianum.

INSCRIPTIO.
Eximio viro D. Henrico
Bullingero, verbi divini
concionatori fideliss.
Tiguri.

EPISTOLA LIX.

JOHANNES PARKHURSTUS AD HENRICUM BULLINGERUM.

SALVUS sis in Christo, doctissime Bullingere! 26 Aprilis dedi ad te literas, quas spero te accepisse. Tuæ autem 6 Martii scriptæ, mihi traditæ sunt 23 Maii; exemplum autem tuæ responsionis secundæ datæ Brentio non accepi, uti scribis. Quid imprecor hujusmodi hominibus, qui tantum mihi surripuere thesaurum? Si cum literis Gualteri Lavateri et Simleri ligasses, tuto ad manus meas pervenisset. Ego nihil adhuc vidi, quod scripsit Brentius adversum te vel D. Martyrem, nec multum hujusmodi scripta vel nænias moror. Literas tuas scriptas 16 Octobris, 1562, 27 tandem die Junii accepi. Hyperius misit Lunckero, Lunckerus mihi, quem diu non vidi. Sed pecunias ad eum misi 4 Julii: ejus ad me literas habes hic inclusas, ex quibus cognoscere possis, quam duros et inexorabiles habeat collegii præfectos, a quibus veniam abeundi impetrare non possit.

Ante pauculos hosce dies venit ad me juvenis quidam Scotus, concionator optimus, commendatus mihi literis Grindalli episcopi Londinensis et Coverdali quondam Exoniensis. Is in mea diœcesi jam agit, nimirum oppido maritimo quod vocatur *Lynn*. Nova hæc mihi nuntiavit e Scotia: Archiepiscopus S. Andreæ, quia audivit missam, condemnatus est ad mortem; duo vel tres proceres ob eandem causam conjecti in carcerem. In Parliamento decreverunt, ut adulterium morte puniatur. Regina Scotiæ hæc tria postulabat in domo parliamentari, 1. ut missas ei audire liceret, 2. ut contra Anglos bellum movere posset, 3. ut Germani (videlicet papistici) satellites in aula essent, quibus committeretur sui corporis custodia. At in his tribus postulatis passa est repulsam. Hæc ille mihi.

Magnum fuit apud nos tonitru circa initium Julii. Pinnaculum templi cathedralis in civitate Nordovicensi vehementer est quassatum, sed non dejectum, paulo post vero reparatum. Pestis grassatur Londini, et in novo Portu, et in exercitu Gallorum, ut fama est. Cetera ex literis Gualteri. 20 Julii misi literas ad consiliarios per unum ex præcipuis meis famulis. Is mihi 26 ejusdem mensis attulit responsum, et post quatriduum peste obiit. Dominus misereatur nostri! Circa initium Augusti bellum publice denuntiatum contra Galliam.

Saluta meo nomine honestissimam matronam, tuam uxorem, item filios et filias, amicos doctos et humanissimos cives, quos mihi noveris esse notos. Raptim. Ludhamiæ, 13 Augusti, 1563. Mea vos omnes; et tibi agit gratias pro literis. Quia nullus adest Germanus, non potest rescribere; quod illi ex animo dolet.

Tuus,

JOHANNES PARKHURSTUS,

Nordovicensis.

Audio pacem inter Gallos et nos initam. Faxit Deus! Scio pro certo inducias factas ad aliquod tempus. Uxor mea mittit ad te duo paria caligarum, quibus uti possis quando asper ab Aare ruit Boreas, frigus, gelu et nives pariens.

INSCRIPTIO.
Clarissimo viro D.
Henrico Bullingero,
   Tiguri.

EPISTOLA LX.

LAURENTIUS HUMFREDUS AD HENRICUM BULLINGERUM.

SALUTEM in Christo et pacem sempiternam! Bellorum tumultus sedatos esse etiam atque etiam gaudeo et gratulor, religionis autem negotium parum processisse dolendum. Dabit Jesus aliquando dies halcyonios et lætiora evangelia; et habebit, spero, ecclesia suos filios, et evangelium suum cursum, omnibus inferorum potestatibus invitis et obnitentibus. Vincet enim veritas, et divinæ voluntati ac manui nulla hominum vel potentia resistere vel astutia poterit. Tibi autem et tuis, nostris patribus et fratribus, optamus longam vitam, ne suis parentibus et patronis ac tutoribus orba sit christiana respublica.

De re vestiaria iterum quæso ad me perscribas sententiam tuam, vel pluribus vel paucis, vel uno verbo: primo, videaturne tibi ἀδιάφορον, quod tam longo tempore inveteravit tanta cum superstitione, quodque animos simplicium tamdiu splendore suo fascinavit, et religionis ac sanctitatis cujusdam opinione imbuit. Secundo, An mandatu principis, papæ jurisdictione profligata, et ordinis causa, non cultus, ejusmodi vestes ecclesiæ a piis hominibus licite et pie salva conscientia gestari possint. Loquor autem de pileo illo sphærico et superpellicio papistico, quæ nunc non papæ illicita tyrannide, sed reginæ justa ac legitima auctoritate mandantur. An nunc omnia hæc mundis hominibus munda esse possint et libera? Rogo dominationem tuam strictim, quæ tua mens sit, ad me scribas.

Sampsonus suas literas alio miserat: is te ac D. Gualterum aliosque etiam atque etiam salutat. Dominus conservet ecclesiam vestram ac suam! Oxoniæ, 16 Augusti, 1563.

Tuus,

INSCRIPTIO.   LAURENTIUS HUMFREDUS.

Eximio et doctiss. viro D. Henrico Bullingero, patri ac fratri in Christo dilectiss. Tiguri.

EPISTOLA LXI.

ROBERTUS HORNUS AD HENRICUM BULLINGERUM.

ACCEPI tuas tres jam epistolas, carissime Bullingere, unam ad 10 Octobris, alteram ad 10 Martii, 1563, datas, mihi quidem serius pridie calendas Junii ultimi redditas; tertiam Augusti 29 scriptam, mense Octobri satis in tempore mihi traditam. Ex quibus animadverti vim amoris tui uberem et vehementem, qui suavissimis se verbis expressit, et literis tantummodo meis sive munusculis contentus esse poterat. A me autem ideo missa sunt, ut intelligeretis non modo ipsum me sed et res meas ac fortunas ad vestrum commodum esse paratas. Et quod de panno gratias agis, et repensurum te ais, agnosco singularem humanitatem tuam, qui mihi, cum ipse multum tibi debeam, debere te et obligatum esse fateris. Quod vero in argenteo poculo assiduam mei recolitis memoriam, id ita accipio, ut cum benevolentia et humanitate vestra nihil mihi sit gratius, tum in frequenti esse memoria, et quasi in oculis vestris ac conspectu versari, sit mihi longe gratissimum. Et quia perexiguum est tam modici æris poculum, misi vobis alios quatuordecim coronatos et insignia mea, quæ cupitis, ut majus inde poculum et pleno aptum convivio fabricari curetis.

De insidiis et furoribus adversariorum, quibus periclitamini, angor equidem ut vos, et rursus erigor ea consolatione, quam tu proponis per eum qui vicit mundum, cujus qui sunt a mundo vinci aut superari non possunt. Et ex pontificiis injuriis non tam nos affligimur, quam illustratur gloria Dei, et amplificatur evangelium. Nos per totam Angliam eandem habemus ecclesiasticam doctrinam quam vos, in ritibus et ceremoniis mi[1] ...... illis quidem, nec, ut docetur populus, in magna æstimatione harum paululum dissentimus. Nunquam autem desivimus, ut hortaris, quæ recta et sequenda sunt ex sacris scripturis docere, commonefacere, et instare, ne nostro vitio grex nobis commissus dissipetur per inveteratos errores, qui adhuc a pontificiis clam sparguntur.

E libris, quos in secundis commemoras literis, accepi tres ejusdem argumenti contra Brentii Ubiquitatem: quam materiam suscepit, ut tu cupis, Anglus quidam, eandemque ope divina acriter ac diserte tractabit, ut omnibus innotescat, idem Anglos cum Tigurinis in ea re sentire. De clarissimi viri Petri Martyris morte ante tuarum literarum adventum accepi. De successore a se moriente designato gaudeo. Tridentinum conciliabulum adversus Christum institutum, cum ad summum perductum fuerit, dissipabit, qui sedens in cœlis irridet eos, quemadmodum vana hominum consilia irrita semper fecit, et ad nihilum redegit.

Reliquum est, mi Bullingere, ut meo et uxoris meæ nomine salutem ascribam tibi plurimam, et optimis matronis, uxori tuæ et Froschoveri: generis item tuis, Simlero, Losio, Lavatero atque Zuinglio; tum fratribus in Christo dilectis D. Gualtero, Bibliandro, Wolphio et Hallero, hospitique meo, et viduæ pauperculæ, quæ nobis in Froschoveri domo communiter agentibus ministravit, cui duos coronatos misi. Vestram a Domino opto salutem. Deinceps curabo ut meis non careas literis, quod ut tu vicissim facias etiam atque etiam rogo. Vale. Dominus Jesus te suæ ecclesiæ diu servet incolumem! Wintoniæ, 13 Decembris, 1563.

Tuus in Christo,

quantus quantus sim,

ROBERTUS WINTON.

INSCRIPTIO.
*Ornatiss. viro et fratri in Christo
cariss. D. Henrico Bullingero.*

[1 Deest aliquid.]

EPISTOLA LXII.

JOHANNES PARKHURSTUS AD JOSIAM SIMLERUM.

Mitto ad te, uti petis, duas epistolas, quas ad me scripsit D. Martyr: si plures invenero, plures mittam. Scripsi ad te 26 Aprilis, item 14 Augusti. Pro argenteo Martyre misimus auream Elizabetham. Bene facis quod paras editionem operum Martyris: sic enim bene mereberis de omnibus piis, et rem utilissimam præstabis ecclesiæ Christi. Dominus tuis cœptis faveat, et ad felicem exitum perducat! Uxor ducis Norfolciæ 10 Januarii obiit puerpera, et 24 ejusdem mensis est sepulta Nordovici. Ego concionem habui funebrem. In funere nulla erant funeralia, cerei nec lucernæ. Præter solem nihil lucebat; quod male habuit papistas. Nec tale quid unquam visum est in Anglia, præsertim in funere herois aut heroissæ. Cetera ex aliorum literis. Vale, mi Simlere. Ludhamiæ, 17 Februarii, 1564. Saluta meo nomine omnes meos amicos, et præsertim optimam tuam uxorem. Mea teque tuamque omnesque salutat.

Tuus,
JOHANNES PARKHURSTUS,
Nordovicensis.

Trade hunc catalogum D. Gesnero.

INSCRIPTIO.
D. Josiæ Simlero. *Tiguri.*

EPISTOLA LXIII.

JOHANNES JUELLUS AD HENRICUM BULLINGERUM.

Salutem plurimam in Christo Jesu. Quid ego dicam, doctissime vir et clarissime pater? Et pudet et dolet: pudet primum non scripsisse sæpius; deinde dolet, eas ipsas quas scripsi non potuisse ad vos pervenire. Obsecro tamen te, ne putes mihi aut scholam Tigurinam, aut rempublicam, aut illam vestram humanitatem tantam tam cito ex animo elabi potuisse. Equidem vos omnes in oculis et in sinu gero, et te imprimis, mi pater, lumen jam unicum ætatis nostræ. Quod autem ad literas attinet, equidem, præterquam anno illo superiori, cum peste et lue omnia ubique clausa essent, ceteroqui nunquam intermisi scribere ad te, ad

Lavaterum, ad Simlerum, et ad Julium. Quod nisi facerem, videri vix possem, non dico officii, sed ne humanitatis quidem rationem ullam retinere. Et de aliis quidem meis literis superioribus quid factum sit, nescio; proximas autem audio in navali conflictu exceptas fuisse a Gallis, atque ablatas Caletum. Sed missa ista facio.

Nunc accipito de rebus nostris, quas tibi pro tua pietate magis cordi esse sat scio. Primum, de religione omnia domi Dei optimi maximi beneficio pacata sunt. Papistæ exules turbant et impediunt quantum possunt; et evulgatis libris, nescio quo meo, fatone, dicam, an merito? me petunt unum, idque terni maximis clamoribus uno tempore. Illis omnibus dum unus respondeo, tu me ne putes esse otiosum. Offertur mihi inter alia causa illa ubiquitaria, quam ego in senis illius nostri Tubingensis gratiam, ut potui, utque res tulit, de industria ornavi pluribus: sed nostra lingua, utpote hominibus nostris. Si quidem otium erit, partem aliquam transferam, et ad vos mittam. De illo autem sene, equidem non video quid debeam statuere: ita mihi videtur in singulos dies magis magisque delirare. Legi enim novum Menandri phasma, quod nunc nuper dedit: et tibi et de illo libro, et de omnibus literis tuis, et de omni tua humanitate, ago gratias.

Respublica domi forisque, terra marique tranquilla est. Pacem habemus cum Gallis constitutam: Flandrica etiam illa turba jam tandem consiluit. Mercatores utrinque commeant, Flandri ad nos, et nostri vicissim ad illos. Granvelanus, cujus unius nequitia hæc omnia cœpta sunt, id egit ut, turbatis atque impeditis emporiis, cum neque invehi quicquam neque exportari posset, attonitis mercatoribus, et oppidano vulgo, quod vere e lanificio victum quærit, ad otium atque inopiam redacto, popularis aliquis motus et seditio domestica sequeretur. Ita enim sperabat religionem una posse concuti. Sed Deus ista consilia convertit potius in auctorem: nostri enim in officio, uti par erat, remanserunt; Flandricum autem vulgus, digressis nostris mercatoribus, et emporio Embdæ constituto, eam rem indigne ferre, atque etiam tantum non tumultuari.

Hiberni, uti te audisse scio, nobis parent, et nostris utuntur legibus. In illam insulam papa ante aliquot admodum dies immisit hominem sceleratum et callidum cum mandatis, qui huc illuc concursaret. Erat enim Hibernus, qui gentem feram et silvestrem contra nos religionis causa commoveret. Quid quæris? Nebulo statim primo appulsu comprehenditur, et excussus et vinctus ad nos mittitur. Ita sacerrimus pater prorsus decrevit, cum flectere non possit superos, Acheronta movere! In Scotia......ita est ut volumus. Regina sola missam illam suam retinet, invitis omnibus.

Parkhurstus, Hoperus, Sampson, Sandus, Leverus, Chamberus valent, et officium faciunt. Biennium jam est, quod ego illorum quenquam viderim. Vale, mi pater. Dominus Jesus te quam diutissime servet superstitem et incolumem! Saluta D. Gualterum, D. Lavaterum, D. Simlerum, D. Lupum, D. Hallerum, D. Gesnerum, D. Frisium, D. Zuinglium, D. Wickium; ad quos singulos darem literas si esset otium, vel potius nisi prorsus obruerer negotiis. Sarisberiæ, in Anglia, calend. Martiis, 1565.

Tui nominis studiosissimus,

tibique deditissimus,

JO. JUELLUS, Anglus.

EPISTOLA LXIV.

ROBERTUS HORNUS AD RODOLPHUM GUALTERUM.

LITERAS tuas, mi Gualtere, primas quam amanter et jucunde acceperim, vel hinc existimare debes, quod de Tigurinæ reipublicæ statu, in cujus fide ac liberalitate exul collocatus fueram, tum de tui reliquorumque amicissimorum et de me optime meritorum valetudine cognoscebam. Accedebat tua in Johannis evangelium lucubratio. Scribendi, ut tu ais, occasio, quam ita probo, ut ad veram scripturarum scientiam et pietatem conferre multum judicem, et non solum a tironibus, quibus tu potissimum studes, sed ab ipsis professoribus legendam existimem.

In fœdere Gallico et Helvetico perspicaciam Tigurinam probo, quæ astutias Gallicas religionis prætextu adumbratas olfecit et patefecit. Bernenses etiam vicinos vestros spero suasu vestro ab inhonesto fœdere assensum cohibituros. De peste, quæ regionem Tigurinam invasit, opinionem habeo, quod impiorum causa etiam ipsi pii affliguntur. Qua perculsus pater Bullingerus quod periculum evasit, debemus putare, eum qui duriora tempora sustulit, felicioribus esse a Domino reservatum. Tuam domum ab ea contagione tutam, divinæ clementiæ, quæ laboribus tuis noluit otium, ascribo.

Res nostræ ita se habent, quod, ut vos vicinas Gallicas, sic nos intestinas papisticas timemus insidias. Primates papistici in publicis custodiis, reliqui exilium affectantes, scriptis quibusdam in vulgus disseminatis, sese in gratiam, nos in odium vocant, ansam minutam sane et ejusmodi nacti. Controversia nuper de quadratis pileis et superpelliciis inter nos orta, exclamarunt papistæ, non esse quam profitemur unanimem in religione fidem, sed variis nos opinionibus duci, nec in una sententia stare posse. Auxit hanc calumniam publicum senatus nostri decretum de profliganda papistica potestate ante nostram restitutionem sancitum, quo, sublata reliqua fæce, usus pileorum quadratorum et superpelliciorum ministris remanebat; ita tamen ut superstitionis opinione careret, quod disertis decreti verbis cavetur. Tolli hoc decretum non potest, nisi omnium regni ordinum, quorum consensu constitutum fuit, conspiratione atque consensu. Nobis, penes quos tunc non fuit sanciendi vel abrogandi auctoritas, pileis et superpelliciis uti, vel aliis locum dare, injunctum est. Usi his sumus, ne munera christiana, per nos deserta, occuparent adversarii. Sed cum jam hæc res in magnam contentionem inter nostros devenerit, ut noster grex pusillus etiam in duas abierit partes, quarum altera ob illud decretum deserendum ministerium, altera non deserendum putet, peto abs te, mi Gualtere, quid de hac controversia, quæ nos una vexat, senseris, ut quam primo tempore scribas. Speramus certe, proximis comitiis illam decreti partem abrogaturos. Sed si id obtineri non poterit, quoniam magna ope clam nituntur papistæ, ministerio nihilominus divino adhærendum esse judico, ne, deserto eo ac a nobis ea conditione repudiato, papistæ sese insinuarent. Qua de re sententiam, mi Gualtere, exspecto tuam, an hæc, quæ sic facimus, salva conscientia facere possumus. De vestra etiam ecclesia ita sum solicitus, ut, quoniam multos fideles ministros ex peste interiisse suspicer, per tuas literas scire vellem eorum nomina qui jam supersint. Dominus Jesus, magnus gregis sui custos, vos et universam suam ecclesiam custodiat! In eodem vale.

Datum e Fernamiæ castro, 16 cal. Augusti, 1565.

Tuus in Christo,

INSCRIPTIO.
Ornatiss°. theologo, domino Gualtero, Tigurinæ ecclesiæ ministro digniss°.

ROB. WINTON.

EPISTOLA LXV.

JOHANNES PARKHURSTUS AD HENRICUM BULLINGERUM.

Dolui supra modum, gavisus sum supra modum, quod ægrotaveris, quod et convalueris. Scribis te in meis literas D. Juello inscriptas inclusisse, et petis ut earum exemplum ad hoc usque signum (†) describi curem et mittam D. Horno. Certe, mi Bullingere, ego Juelli literas non vidi; quare nec tibi nec Horni exspectationi satisfacere potui. Sed Abelus meis apertis illas Juello Londini tradidit. Promisit is Abelo, se exemplum quam primum ad me missurum. *Pollicitis dives quilibet esse potest.* Pollicitus est, at nihil præterea. Sic et te et me et Hornum defraudavit. At ego hoc imputo infinitis negotiis, quibus ille distringitur. Veniam petis, quod hoc oneris mihi imposueris : ego non onus sed honorem æstimo, si quacumque occasione Bullingero inservire possim. Cum Germanica tua meæ uxori legerem, mentione facta obitus uxoris et filiæ tuæ statim in acerbissimas erupit lacrymas : ita coactus sum aliquamdiu a legendo desistere, cum illa auscultando aures non præberet.

Regina Scotiæ 1mo Augusti nupsit Henrico domino Darnley, primogenito comitis Lenox. Huic novo conjugio minime favent proceres aliquot in Scotia. Quis erit exitus, dubitamus adhuc. Certe evangelium illic radices egit firmissimas. Fama erat non ita pridem nostram reginam duci Austriæ nupturam. Quid futurum sit, equidem ignoro : cum cognovero, te certiorem reddam. Exspecto doctissimas tuas Homilias in Danielem. Bene vale, optime Bullingere, cum tuis omnibus, quos salvos esse cupio. Dominus Tigurinos omnes servet a malo! Amen. Raptim. Ludhamiæ, 18 Augusti, 1565. Mea teque tuosque salutat.

Tuus ex animo,
JOHANNES PARKHURSTUS,
Nordovicensis.

INSCRIPTIO.
D. Henrico Bullingero, viro clarissimo. Tiguri.

EPISTOLA LXVI.

EDWINUS SANDUS AD HENRICUM BULLINGERUM.

HUMANISSIMAS literas tuas, vir clarissime, una cum doctissimo commentario tuo in Danielem prophetam, Abelus noster superioribus hisce diebus mihi tradendas curavit. Ex quibus et quanti me facias, recte animadverto; et quantum ipse tibi vicissim debeam, facile intelligo. Quod tam amanter ac fraterne ad me scribere voluisti, multum quidem est et multas habeo gratias : quod vero eximium hoc opus tuum omni eruditione plenum ad me transmittere, et etiam, quod summi beneficii loco repono, meo nomine in publicum exire dignatus es, revera mihi fecisti rem longe gratissimam. Mirabilis quidem est ista humanitas tua erga omnes, qua quoscunque, qui te norunt, tibi devinctissimos reddere soleas; sed erga me rara est et singularis : qui non solum me exulantem et quasi incertis sedibus vagantem, olim cum Tigurum venerim, perbenigne acceperis, et omnibus benevolentiæ officiis prosequutus sis; quinetiam divina providentia patriæ jam restitutum non solum non desinis amare, verum omnibus quibus poteris rationibus insignire ornareque contendis. Pro qua quidem summa benevolentia tua quam gratiam referam, dum mecum diligenter cogito, his tantis beneficiis tuis dignum quod rependam, nihil omnino invenio. Cum igitur majora sunt beneficia in me tua, quam ut ipse parem gratiam referre queam, (nam tu dando, ego accipiendo beneficia collocamus,) libenter agnoscam me debitorem esse tuum; et cum ipse non sum solvendo, rogabo ut ipse solvat qui pro omnibus debitis nostris ad plenum satisfecit. Interim mei erga te amoris qualecunque pignus Abelo nostro tradendum curavi, qui id ipsum tuto ut tuæ humanitati mittatur, in se recipit. Rogo te multum, ut grato animo accipias, et non munusculi exiguitatem, sed mittentis propensum animum pro tua humanitate spectare velis.

Quæ hic geruntur, et quo in statu res nostræ collocatæ sunt, ex aliorum literis cognosces. Quod maximum est dicam. Vera Christi religio apud nos locum habet: evangelium non est ligatum, sed libere ac pure prædicatum. De ceteris autem rebus non est quod multum curemus. Contenditur aliquantulum de vestibus papisticis utendis vel non utendis: *dabit Deus his quoque finem.* Vale, colendissime vir, et me, quod facis, ama, meique precibus tuis ad Deum memor esto. Saluta, quæso, meo nomine D. Gualterum, D. Simlerum, filium tuum Henricum, ceterosque dominos ac fratres mihi in Christo carissimos. Wigorniæ, tertio Januarii, 1566.

Frater tuus tui amantissimus,

EDWINUS WIGORN.

INSCRIPTIO.
*Ornatissimo clarissimoque viro, domino
Henrico Bullingero, Tigurinæ ecclesiæ
pastori vigilantissimo, domino ac fratri meo carissimo.*
Tiguri.

EPISTOLA LXVII.

JOHANNES JUELLUS AD HENRICUM BULLINGERUM ET LUDOVICUM LAVATERUM.

S. PL. in Christo Jesu. Rarius multo ad vos scribo, reverendissime pater, tuque optime Ludovice, quam aut ego velim, aut vos exspectatis. Idque quam vos in partem accipiatis, nescio: cupio equidem, ne in malam. Quanto enim magis ego me vestræ omnium pietati obstrictum esse sentio, quantoque pluris judicium de me vestrum semper feci, tanto minus velim me a vobis aut oblivionis aut negligentiæ condemnari. Jam vero occupationibus meis tam longa silentia tribuere putidum fortasse videatur: tametsi, si me nossetis et curas meas, nihil excusatione alia opus esset. Nam præter alias assiduas, meas, alienas, domesticas, publicas, civiles, ecclesiasticas molestias, (sine quibus in hoc munere his temporibus vivi non potest,) cogor pene solus cum hostibus (externisne dicam, an domesticis?) conflictari. Nostri quidem sunt, sed hostili animo, hostili etiam in solo. Profugi enim nostri Lovanienses cœperunt sese magno numero, anno superiori, commoveri; et in nos omnes acerbissime scribere, et me unum nominatim petere. Cur ita? inquies. Nescio, nisi me unum omnium ἀμαχώτατον et ad resistendum infirmissimum esse scirent. Tamen ante sex annos cum in aula coram regia majestate haberem concionem, et de nostræ papisticæ religionis antiquitate dicerem, hoc memini dixisse me inter alia, adversarios nostros, cum nostram causam arguant novitatis, et nobis injuriam et populo fraudem facere: illos enim et pro veteribus probare nova, et ea damnare pro novis, quæ sunt vetustissima. *Missas* enim *privatas* et *truncatas communiones*, et *naturales* et *reales præsentias*, et *transubstantiationes*, &c. (quibus rebus omnis istorum religio continetur) nullam habere certum et expressum testimonium aut sacrarum scripturarum, aut veterum conciliorum, aut priscorum patrum, aut ullius omnino antiquitatis.

Id illi indigne ferre: latrare in angulis, hominem impudentem, confidentem, insolentem, insanum dicere. Quarto postremo anno prodiit ex insperato Hardingus quidam, non ita pridem auditor atque assectator D. Petri Martyris, et acerrimus evangelii præco, nunc vilis apostata et nostro Julio probe notus; qui me ex Amphilochiis, Abdiis, Hippolytis, Clementibus, Victoribus, Athanasiis supposititiis, Leontiis, Cletis, Anacletis, epistolis decretalibus, somniis, fabulis, refutaret. Illi ego pro mea tenuitate respondi anno superiori, ut potui. Sed O Deum immortalem! Quæ hæc vita est! Ὡς ἔρις ἔκ τε θεῶν ἔκ τ' ἀνθρώπων ἀπόλοιτο. Vixdum absolveram, evolat exemplo Apologiæ nostræ Confutatio; opus ingens, elaboratum, et convitiis, contumeliis, mendaciis, sycophantiis refertissimum. Hic ego rursum petor. Quid quæris? Respondendum est. Vides, reverende pater, quam non simus otiosi; ego præsertim, cui (nescio quo meo fato) semper cum istis monstris dimicandum est. Dominus addat vires atque animum, et proterat Satanam sub pedibus nostris! Hæc idcirco visum est scribere prolixius, ut si posthac literæ isthuc a me infrequentius venerint, quam aut vos exspectatis aut ego velim, id cuivis potius rei, quam aut oblivioni vestri aut ingratitudini, tribuatis.

Respublica nostra et ab armis et de religione pacata est. Lovanienses quidem isti nostri turbant, quantum possunt; verum populus est in officio, et futurum spero. Domina regina recte valet, et abhorret a nuptiis. Hyems superior ita misere afflixit nascentem segetem, ut nunc ubique per Angliam magna frumenti difficultate laboretur. Hoc anno, Dei beneficio, omnia lætissime provenerunt. Ego D. Parkhurstum, episcopum Norvicensem, D. Sandum, episcopum Vigorniensem, D. Pilkingtonum, episcopum

Dunelmensem, triennium jam totum non vidi: ita procul disjecti sumus. Vivimus tamen omnes incolumes et vestri memores. Solus Richardus Chamberus obiit diem suum; sed pie in Domino.

Contentio illa de ecclesiastica veste linea, de qua vos vel ab Abele nostro vel a D. Parkhursto audiisse non dubito, nondum etiam conquievit. Ea res nonnihil commovet infirmos animos. Atque utinam omnia etiam tenuissima vestigia papatus et e templis, et multo maxime ex animis omnium, auferri possent! Sed Regina ferre mutationem in religione hoc tempore nullam potest.

Res Scoticæ nondum etiam satis pacatæ sunt: nobiles aliquot primi nominis apud nos exulant: alii domi remanserunt, et sese, si vis fiat, ad resistendum parant: et ex arcibus suis excursiones interdum faciunt, et ex papistarum agris agunt feruntque, quantum possunt. Regina ipsa, etsi animo sit ad papismum obfirmato, tamen vix satis exploratum habet, quo se vertat. Nam de religione adversariam habet magnam partem et nobilitatis et populi: et quantum quidem nos possumus intelligere, numerus indies crescit. Submiserat proximis istis mensibus Philippus rex abbatem quendam Italum cum auro Hispanico, hominem vafrum, et factum atque instructum ad fraudes, qui et Regem Reginamque juvaret veteratorio consilio, et impleret omnia tumultibus. Rex novus, qui semper hactenus abstinuisset a missis, et ultro accessisset ad conciones, ut se populo daret, cum audiret navim illam appulsuram postridie, factus repente confidentior, sumptis animis, noluit longius dissimulare. Accedit ad templum: jubet sibi de more dici missam. Eodem ipso tempore D. Knoxus, concionator in eodem oppido, et in proximo templo, maxima frequentia clamare in idolomanias, et in universum regnum pontificium, nunquam fortius. Interea navis illa Philippica, jactata tempestatibus et ventis, fluctibusque concussa et fracta, convulso malo, ruptis lateribus, amissis gubernatoribus, vectoribus et rebus omnibus inanis, et lacera, et aquæ plena, defertur in Angliam. Hæc vero non dubito divinitus contigisse, ut rex fatuus intelligat, quam sit auspicatum audire missas.

E Galliis multa turbulenta nunciantur. Domus illa Guisiana non potest acquiescere sine aliquo magno malo. Verum ista vobis multo propiora sunt, quam nobis. Danus et Suecus cruentissime inter se conflixerunt, et adhuc dicuntur esse in armis. Uterque affectus est maximis incommodis; nec adhuc uter sit superior dici potest.

Libri vestri, tuus, reverende pater, in Danielem, et tuus, doctissime Ludovice, in Josuam, incolumes ad me delati sunt. Ego et Deo optimo maximo de vobis, et vobis de istis laboribus et studiis deque omni vestra humanitate, ago gratias. Misi hoc tempore ad Julium nostrum in annuum stipendium viginti coronatos, et alteros totidem ad vos duos; ut eos vel in cœnam publicam more vestro, vel in quemvis alium usum pro vestro arbitrio, consumatis. Deus vos, ecclesiam, rempublicam, scholamque vestram conservet incolumes! Salutate D. Gualterum, D. Simlerum, D. Zuinglium, D. Gesnerum, D. Wickium, D. Hallerum, D.D. Hen. et Rod. Bullingeros, meo nomine. Sarisberiæ, 8 Februar. 1566.

Vestri amans et
studiosus in Domino,

INSCRIPTIO.   JO. JUELLUS, Anglus.

Clarissimo viro D. Bullingero, pastori ecclesiæ Tigurinæ, domino suo colendissimo.   *Tiguri.*

EPISTOLA LXVIII.

LAURENTIUS HUMFREDUS AD HENRICUM BULLINGERUM.

CONVALUISSE te et ex morbo diuturno, quo afflictabaris, recreatum et relevatum esse, Dei beneficio, pater in Christo reverende, tibi, nobis, ecclesiæ gratulor; et ut magis ac magis confirmeris, etiam atque etiam precor.

Lucubrationes tuas in Danielem una cum præfatione, et honorifica mei fratrumque exulum mentione, vidi et legi libenter, ac tuæ humanitati gratiam habeo. Quod in Jesaiam te commentaturum promittis, equidem gaudeo; et ut Domino juvante perficias, extremamque manum cœpto operi imponas, vehementer rogo. Liber est totus evangelicus, densus ac infertus mysteriis, alicubi propter concisas sententias, et historias interpositas, ac crebros schematismos et nonnullas interruptiones obscurior. Quare licet optimi et doctissimi homines magnam lucem attulerint, et præclaram operam navaverint; tamen laboris tui accessio pia erit et perutilis. In tertio capite, ubi de ornamentis muliebrique mundo propheta disserit, si quædam de re vestiaria interserueris, meo judicio operæ pretium feceris. Quid hactenus scripseris, non ignoro; tamen et breviter nimis et perspicue non satis videris protulisse sententiam. Itaque ut paucis respondeas quæstiunculis hisce meis, pietatem tuam iterum atque iterum oro: 1. An ecclesiasticis viris leges vestiariæ præscribi debeant, sic ut forma, colore, etc. a laicis distinguantur? 2. An ceremonialis cultus Levitici sacerdotii sit in ecclesiam Christi revocandus? 3. An vestitu et externo ritu cum papistis communicare liceat? et an ceremonias ab ulla ecclesia adulterina et adversaria Christianos mutuari oporteat? 4. An vestitus sacerdotalis ac peculiaris tanquam civilis habitus gestandus sit? annon monachismum, papismum, Judaismum redoleat? 5. An qui hactenus in libertate sua acquieverunt, vi regii edicti hac servitute implicare se et ecclesiam salva conscientia possint? 6. An clericalis habitus papisticus dici queat res indifferens? 7. An sumendus vestitus potius quam deserenda statio? Miseram ad D. Bezam itemque ad pietatem tuam alias quæstiones : nescio an acceperis. Rogo, ut quam primum digneris paulo fusius judicium tuum et opinionem explicare, et rationes, cur id sentias, attingere seu notare. Vides Lernæam hydram esse vel caudam papalem. Vides quid pepererint reliquiæ Amorrhæorum. Vides importunitatem nostram. Quæso ut de re tota conferas cum D. Gualtero et symmystis, et ad me vel D. Sampsonum perscribas sententiam. Oxonii, Febr. 9, A⁰ 1565, juxta computationem Anglicam. Christus te bene valentem et florentem diu servet ecclesiæ suæ!

Tui observantissimus,
LAURENT. HUMFREDUS.

INSCRIPTIO.
Reverendo in Christo patri ac domino
D. Bullingero, ecc. Tigurinæ pas-
tori fideliss⁰.

EPISTOLA LXIX.

THOMAS SAMPSON AD HENRICUM BULLINGERUM.

REVERENDE in Christo pater, scripsi sex abhinc mensibus literas ad te, multorum fratrum votis satisfacturus, si modo responsum a tua dignitate retulissem, prout enixe tum orabam. Sed cum vel meæ tibi non sunt redditæ, vel tuæ (si quas scripseris) interceptæ videntur esse, id ipsum, quod ante, nunc denuo scribere cogor. Ea est nostræ ecclesiæ conditio, quæ ad vos jamdudum perlata est : jam enim post expletum in evangelii professione septennium recruduit certamen de re vestiaria, in quo olim velitabant Cranmerus, Rydleius et Hoperus, sanctissimi Christi martyres. Status tamen quæstionis non per omnia idem est, at potentium placita magis implacabilia. Quod quidem admodum placet adversariis nostris Lovaniensibus; hæc enim illi in cœlum laudibus evehunt.

At quo facilius rem controversam plane perspicias, volui illam in quæstiones quasdam redigere. Hæ sic habent:

I. An vestitus peculiaris, a laicis distinctus, ministris evangelii melioribus temporibus unquam fuerit constitutus, et an hodie constitui debeat in reformata ecclesia?

II. An ejusmodi vestium præscriptio cum libertate ecclesiastica et christiana consentiat?

III. An rerum indifferentium natura admittat coactionem, et an conscientiis multorum nondum persuasis ulla vis inferenda sit?

IV. An ullæ ceremoniæ novæ præter expressum verbi præscriptum institui aut cumulari possint?

V. An ceremonias Judæorum de amictu sacerdotali per Christum antiquatas renovare liceat?

VI. An ritus ab idololatris aut hæreticis petere, et illorum sectæ ac religioni proprie dicatos, ad ecclesiæ reformatæ usus transferre oporteat?

VII. An conformatio et convenientia in ejusmodi ceremoniis necessario sit exigenda?

VIII. An ceremoniæ cum aperto scandalo conjunctæ retineri possint?

IX. An ullæ constitutiones ecclesiæ ferendæ, quæ impietate natura quidem sua carent, ad ædificationem tamen non faciunt?

X. An quicquam ecclesiis a principe præscribendum in ceremoniis, sine voluntate et libero consensu ecclesiasticorum?

XI. An consultius ecclesiæ sic inservire, an propterea ecclesiastico ministerio ejici, si nullum sit tertium?

XII. An boni pastores, qui doctrinæ et vitæ inculpatæ sunt, propter hujusmodi ceremonias neglectas jure a ministerio moveri possint?

En! habes, domine colendissime, nostras difficultates. Hic hærent multi et pii viri. In quorum gratiam jam secundo a te peto, ut re cum D. Gualtero, reliquisque symmystis, pro vestra pietate bene perpensa, quid tandem vobis videatur, velis aperte significare, et responsiones ad unamquamque quæstionem scriptis consignare. Multis sane, mihi vero imprimis, rem longe gratissimam facies; ecclesiæ etiam nostræ optimam navabis operam.

Est etiam aliud de quo te certiorem facere volui. Decedente nostro Chambero mihi concredita erant quædam scripta, quæ D. Hopero aliquando erant, ut videtur, carissima. Inter alia reperi D. Theodori Bibliandri commentarium, amplum quidem et manuscriptum, in Genesin et Exodum. Equidem cum (quod sciam) non sit usquam impressus hic liber, nollem tali beneficio ecclesiam Christi diutius privari. Si tua dignitas velit hæredes D. Bibliandri certiores facere, hoc scriptum apud me esse, illique velint evulgare, significa cui sim librum traditurus, aut quo modo ad vos tuto perferri poterit, et me senties paratissimum voluntatis tuæ executorem. Hæc sunt, de quibus tuam in dies exspectabo responsionem; in quæstionibus præcipue quid sentias tu, quidque fratres sentiant, ego multorum nomine ut indices submisse peto. Deus optimus maximus te ecclesiæ suæ valentem et viventem diutissime conservet! Londini, 16 Febr. 1566.

Tuæ dignitatis observantissimus,

THOMAS SAMPSON.

INSCRIPTIO.

Reverendo in Christo patri ac do-
  mino D. Henrico Bullingero,
  ecclesiæ Tigurinæ pastori fide-
  lissimo.

EPISTOLA LXX.

JOHANNES JUELLUS AD HENRICUM BULLINGERUM.

S. PL. in Christo. Etsi proximis his diebus ad te prolixe scripserim, reverendissime pater, tamen cum occurrerent quædam, in quibus magnopere mihi opus est judicio tuo, non alienum me facturum arbitrabar, si iterum scriberem. Sunt autem res ejusmodi, quas non dubitem te, pro tua multiplici rerum omnium cognitione, facile posse expedire.

Primum, scire velim, ecquid Christiani illi qui hodie sparsim habitant in Græcia, Asia, Syria, Armenia, &c. utantur privatis istis missis, quæ nunc receptæ ubique sunt in papismo; quoque genere missarum, privatone an publico, Græci hodie Venetiis uti soleant?

Deinde, cum citetur interdum quidam Camotensis, qui in paparum vitam et insolentiam scripserit acerbius, quis ille Camotensis, et cujus ordinis, et quorum temporum hominumque fuerit?

Postremo, quid tibi videatur de concilio Germanico, quod aiunt olim celebratum sub Carolo Magno contra concilium Nicenum secundum de imaginibus? Sunt enim qui confidenter negent unquam hujusmodi concilium ullum extitisse.

Peto a te per pietatem tuam, ne me insolenter putes facere, qui ista ex te quæram, tam procul præsertim : tu enim solus jam superes unicum prope oraculum ecclesiarum. Si ad proximas nundinas rescripseris, satis erit: id autem ut facias magnopere a te peto. Iterum, iterumque vale, reverendissime pater, et domine in Christo colendissime. Sarisberiæ, 10 Martii, 1566.

Tuus in Christo,

JOHANNES JUELLUS, Anglus.

EPISTOLA LXXI.

LAURENTIUS HUMFREDUS ET THOMAS SAMPSON AD HENRICUM BULLINGERUM.

CUM diligentia tua, clarissime vir, in scribendo nobis probatur; tum vero ex literis illis quidem humanissimis incredibilis tuus erga nos amor, et ecclesiæ nostræ singularis cura, et concordiæ ardentissimum studium apparent. Quæstiones aliquot misimus pietati tuæ, in quibus vis et quasi cardo totius controversiæ sita esse videbatur: quibus est a pietate tua accurate responsum; nobis tamen, quod bona cum venia tua dicimus, non est plene satisfactum.

Primo respondet pietas tua, ministris præscribi posse leges vestiarias, ut iis colore et forma a laicis distinguantur; esse enim civilem observationem, et apostolum velle episcopum esse κόσμιον. Cum hæc quæstio de ecclesiasticis hominibus proposita sit, et ad ecclesiasticam politiam spectet, quomodo habitus ministrorum singularis et clericalis civilem rationem habere possit, non videmus. Ut episcopum κόσμιον esse debere fatemur; sic ad ornatum mentis, non ad cultum corporis, cum Ambrosio referimus. Et ut in vestitu honestatem, dignitatem, gravitatem requirimus; sic decorum ab hostibus religionis nostræ peti negamus.

Secundo respondes hypothetice: si pileus et vestis non indecora ministro, et quæ superstitione carent, jubeantur usurpari a ministris, Judaismum propterea vere non revocari. At qui esse potest vestis simplici ministerio Christi conveniens, quæ theatro et pompæ sacerdotii papistici serviebat? Neque enim (quomodo nostri pietati tuæ persuadent) pileus quadrus et externus vestitus solummodo exiguntur, sed etiam sacræ vestes in templo adhibentur, superpellicium, seu alba chori vestis, et capa revocantur, quæ Judaismi μιμήματα quædam esse et simulacra non modo papistæ ipsi in suis libris clamitant, sed pietas tua non semel ex Innocentio docuit. D. Martyris, præceptoris nostri colendissimi, testimonio libenter subscribimus. Sed quæ ille affert exempla, ad decorum et ordinem pertinent: hæc ecclesiam deformant, εὐταξίαν perturbant, condecentiam omnem evertunt. Illa lumini naturæ congruunt; hæc prodigiosa et monstrosa sunt. Illa, juxta Tertulliani regulam, meras necessitates et utilitates habebant; hæc inepta prorsus et supervacanea et inutilia sunt, nec ædificationi nec ulli bono usui conducentia: sed verius, (ut ejusdem Martyris nostri verbis utamur,) cultui, quem hodie quotquot pii sunt execrantur, splendide inservierunt. Vestium ecclesiasticarum discrimen hodie receptum papisticum esse inventum, ipsi papicolæ gloriantur, Othonis constitutiones loquuntur, liber pontificalis ostendit, oculi et ora omnium comprobant. Usus et templorum, stipendii, baptismi, symboli, etc. ante papam natum divino instituto inolevit: et cum Augustino, quicquid in aliqua hæresi divinum ac legitimum reperimus, id approbamus, retinemus, non inficiamur. Hoc autem quia erroris illius ac dissensionis proprium est, veraciter cum eodem arguimus et sanamus.

Quod addis, rem vestiariam ab initio reformationis non fuisse abolitam, in ea rursus nostri minime vera retulerunt. Multis enim in locis, serenissimi regis Edvardi VI. temporibus, absque superpellicio cœna Domini pure celebrabatur: et capa, quæ tum lege abrogata est, nunc publico decreto restituta est. Hoc non est papismum extirpare, sed denuo plantare; non in pietate proficere, sed deficere. Vestitum sacerdotalem civilem esse ais: monachismum, papismum, Judaismum redolere negas. De superpellicio quid blaterent papistæ, habitus clericorum apud eos quanti fiat, et quomodo religioni dicatus sit; prudentiam tuam ex libris eorum intelligere non dubitamus. Deinde, monachatum ac papismum sapit illa ambitiosa et pharisaica peculiaris vestitus præscriptio, cui illi hodie non minus quam olim suæ cucullæ monachi tribuunt. Neque vero simul ac semel irrupit sanctitatis et meriti opinio, sed paulatim et sensim irrepsit. Quod ne hic quoque fiat, quia veremur, idcirco non abs re cunctamur, et principiis obstare conamur. Cum Eustathio non facimus, qui in veste religionem collocabat; imo his, qui religiosas et singulares vestes sui sacerdotii indices superstitiose requirunt, adversamur. Idem etiam de canone concilii Gangrensis et Laodicei et synodi sexti dicendum. A libertate, in qua hactenus stetimus, discedere servitutis auctoramentum quoddam esse judicamus. Neque hic nos rixati sumus, non odiose contendimus, acerbas contentiones semper fugimus, amicas consultationes quærimus; lupis non cedimus, sed coacti et pulsi loco inviti et gementes discedimus. Fratres et episcopos Domino suo stare et cadere permittimus: eandem erga nos æquitatem submississime, at frustra, petimus. In ritibus nihil est liberum: nec ad hoc a nobis regia majestas irritata est, sed aliorum suasu inducta est: ut nunc demum non, quod ecclesiæ expedit, sed quod aliquo modo licet, constituatur; et quod omnino impium non est, id sanum et salubre, id sacrosanctum, id ratum habeatur.

Ceremonias et vestes sacerdotum, cum religionis testes et professionis notæ sunt, non civiles esse; et ab hostibus omnium consensu mutuo corrogatæ, non decoræ haberi; et anathemate divino notatæ, et piis omnibus invisæ, et malis ac infirmis admirabiles, sine quibus nec nos ministros esse nec sacramenta rite administrari credunt; in rebus indifferentibus numerari nec possunt nec debent. Habebant patres antiqui suas vestes, sed nec episcoporum omnium proprias, nec a laicis distinctas. Exempla D. Joannis et Cypriani singularia sunt. Sisinius hæreticus erat, nec aut laudatus aut nobis imitandus proponitur. Pallium erat omnium Christianorum commune, ut Tertullianus in illo libro refert, et paternitas tua alibi notavit. Chrysostomus candidæ vestis meminit, sed obiter; nec commendat, nec reprehendit; et fueritne sacerdotum an aliorum Græcorum, linea aut lanea, alba an munda, nondum constat. Certe ad populum Antiochenum ab eodem et ab Hieronymo opponitur sordidæ, et apud Blondum de pallio laneo fit mentio. Quare ex ambiguo nihil concludi potest.

Vestium præscriptionem non congruere cum christiana libertate, Bucerus est testis, qui discrimina vestium propter præsentem abusum in ecclesiis Anglicanis, propter pleniorem declarationem detestationis antichristi, propter pleniorem professionem libertatis christianæ, propter tol· lendas inter fratres dissensiones, omnino tollenda esse censuit: his enim verbis ille usus est in epistola ad D. a Lasco, qui totus noster fuit. Itaque hinc grave scandalum oriri, et ædificationem impediri, manifestum est. Cedendum quidem est tempori, sed ad tempus: sic ut progrediamur semper, regrediamur nunquam. Absit, ut nos vel schismata in ecclesia altercando odiosius seramus, vel fratribus nos hostiliter opponendo Camerinam moveamus. Absit, optime Bullingere, ut res natura indifferentes impietatis damnemus: absit, ut sub scandalo nostras affectiones contegamus, vel ex φιλονεικίᾳ conscientiam faciamus. Hæc fæx et fermentum papisticum, nobis crede, omnis dissensionis est seminarium: illud tolli et sempiterna oblivione obrui ac sepeliri cupimus, ne ulla extent antichristianæ superstitionis vestigia. In papatu primatus et supercilium semper nobis displicuerunt: et tyrannis in ecclesia libera placebit? Libera synodus apud Christianos controversiarum nodos hactenus solvit: cur nunc ad unius aut alterius arbitrium referrentur omnia? Ubi hæc votorum et vocum regnat libertas, ibi valet et viget veritas.

Breviter sic habeto, reverende pater, hæc nobis potissimum fidem facere, auctoritatem scripturarum, simplicitatem ministerii Christi, puritatem ecclesiarum primarum et optimarum, quæ brevitatis studio commemorare supersedemus. Ex altera vero parte, legem nullam, nullum decretum generale vel Dei optimi maximi, vel repurgatæ alicujus ecclesiæ, vel universalis concilii (quæ Augustini regula est,) legere nobis hactenus contigit vel audire. Præterea illud comperimus, hæc quæ adducta sunt hactenus exempla particularia esse, et universalia non confirmare.

Ad hæc statuimus, non quicquid est licitum ullo modo, obtrudendum; sed quod ecclesiam ædificat omni modo, esse introducendum, nec quod alicui licet, statim licere omnibus. Doctrinam castam et incorruptam (Deo sit laus!) habemus; in cultu, religionis parte non infima, cur claudicabimus? cur mancum Christum potius, quam totum, quam purum ac perfectum, recepimus? Cur a papistis hostibus, et non a vobis fratribus, reformationis exempla petimus? Eadem est nostrarum ecclesiarum confessio; eadem doctrinæ et fidei ratio: cur in ritibus et ceremoniis tanta dissimilitudo, tanta diversitas? Signatum idem: cur signa adeo variant, ut dissimilia vestris, similia papisticis existant? Idem dux et imperator Christus: cur in ecclesiis nostris vexilla hostilia eriguntur? quæ si homines Dei, si ullo zelo præditi essemus, jamdudum detestati et demoliti fuissemus. Nos de episcopis semper optime sensimus: illorum fastum candide interpretati sumus: cur nos, olim crucem cum ipsis exosculantes, et nunc eundem Christum prædicantes, idem jugum suavissimum una ferentes, ferre non possunt? cur in carceres conjiciunt? cur propter vestem persequuntur? cur victu ac bonis spoliant? cur libris publice traducunt? cur causam malam posteritati edito scripto commendant? Verterunt etiam in idioma nostrum schedulas aliquot D. Buceri, P. Martyris, et nunc tuas privatas ad nos literas nobis invitis et insciis in publicum emiserunt. Unde dum suam causam agunt, suum honorem vindicant, nec ecclesiæ nostræ, nec fratribus suis, nec dignitati tuæ, nec seculo alteri consulunt.

Quo autem paternitas tua intelligat, non levem aut ludicram, sed magni ponderis esse controversiam; nec de pileo solum aut superpellicio certari, sed de re gravissima nos conqueri; stipulas aliquot te quisquilias papisticæ religionis mittimus, ex quibus facile, quæ est tua prudentia, reliqua conjicias; et remedium aliquod, quæ est tua pietas, primo quoque tempore excogites. Oramus autem Dominum nostrum Jesum Christum, ut hos tumultus et turbas consopiat, gloriam suam asserat, operarios in vineam extrudat, quo messis læta et uberrima proveniat. Teque oramus, ut consilio paterno, scripto publico, literis privatis agas, satagas, facias, efficias, ut vel hæc mala tollantur, vel boni viri, nondum persuasi, tolerentur; ne quos doctrinæ firmissimum vinculum copulavit, ceremonia Romana disjungat.

Salutem dicas Gualtero, Simlero, Lavatero, Wolphio, dominis colendis, quibuscum si contuleris, et nobis et ecclesiæ universæ gratissimum feceris. Dominus Jesus suo tugurio, vestro Tiguro, benedicat! Julii, anno 1566.

Hæc paucis et raptim, et non tam respondendi quam admonendi causa: quæ in hanc sententiam dici possent, infinita sunt. Tu nunc non quid fiat aut fieri possit, sed quid fieri debeat, pronuncia.

Tuæ paternitatis studiosissimi,
LAURENTIUS HUMFREDUS,
THO. SAMPSON.

Aliquot maculæ, quæ in ecclesia Anglicana adhuc hærent:
1. In precibus publicis etsi nihil impurum, est tamen species aliqua superstitionis papisticæ. Quod non modo in matutinis et vespertinis, sed in sacra etiam cœna, videre est.
2. Præter musicæ sonos fractos et exquisitissimos, organorum usus in templis invalescit.
3. In administratione baptismi, minister infantem alloquitur: ejus nomine sponsores, parente absente, de fide, de mundo, carne, diabolo deserendo respondent: baptizatus cruce signatur.
4. Mulierculis etiam domi baptizandi potestas facta est.
5. In cœna Dominica sacræ vestes, nempe copa et surperpellicium, adhibentur: communicantibus genuflexio injungitur: pro pane communi placentula azyma substituitur.
6. Extra templum, et ministris in universum singulis, vestes papisticæ præscribuntur: et episcopi suum lineum, (rochetum vocant,) gestant; et utrique pileos quadros, liripippia, togas longas, a papistis mutuo sumptas, circumferunt.

7. De nervo autem religionis, disciplina, quid dicemus? Nulla est, nec habet suam virgam ecclesia nostra; nulla censura exercetur.

8. Conjugium ministris ecclesiæ publicis regni legibus concessum et sancitum non est; sed eorum liberi a nonnullis pro spuriis habentur.

9. Solemnis desponsatio fit more rituque papistico per annulum.

10. Mulieres adhuc cum velo purificantur.

11. In regimine ecclesiastico multa antichristianæ ecclesiæ vestigia servantur. Ut enim olim Romæ in foro papæ omnia fuerunt venalia: sic in metropolitani curia eadem fere omnia prostant; pluralitates sacerdotiorum; licentia pro non residendo, pro non initiando sacris, pro esu carnium diebus interdictis, et in quadragesima, quo etiam tempore, nisi dispensetur et numeretur, nuptias celebrare piaculum est.

12. Ministris Christi libera prædicandi potestas adempta est: qui jam concionari volunt, hi rituum innovationem suadere non debent; sed manus subscriptione ceremonias omnes approbare coguntur.

13. Postremo, articulus de spirituali manducatione, qui disertis verbis oppugnabat et tollebat realem præsentiam in eucharistia, et manifestissimam continebat veritatis explanationem, Edvardi VI. temporibus excusus, nunc apud nos evulgatur mutilatus et truncatus.

INSCRIPTIO.
D. Henrico Bullingero, ecclesiæ Tigurinæ ministro fidelissimo et doctissimo, D⁰ in Christo nobis colendo.

EPISTOLA LXXII.

JOHANNES PARKHURSTUS AD HENRICUM BULLINGERUM.

Salvus sis in Christo, optime Bullingere. Secundo Februarii scripsi ad te, et una cum literis misi viginti coronatos, vel decem coronatos et pannum pro toga: nam hoc Abeli arbitrio permisi.

Tuas accepi 23 Maii. Paulo post Londinensis episcopus exemplar responsionis tuæ ad literas Laurentii Humphredi et Thomæ Sampsonis ad me misit. Quæ scripsisti, typis apud nos excuduntur et Latine et Anglice. Accepi præterea 12 Julii confessionem fidei orthodoxæ, sane pulcherrimum libellum.

Mense Martio Italus quidam (vocatur senior David, necromanticæ artis peritus), in magna gratia apud Reginam Scotiæ, e Reginæ cubiculo, illa præsente, vi extractus, et aliquot pugionibus confossus, misere periit. Abbas quidam, ibidem vulneratus, evasit ægre, sed paulo post ex vulnere est mortuus. Fraterculus quidam, nomine Blacke (niger, Swartz,) papistarum antesignanus, eodem tempore in aula occiditur.

> Sic niger hic nebulo, nigra quoque morte peremptus,
> Invitus nigrum subito descendit in orcum.

Consiliarii, qui tum simul in unum cubiculum erant congregati, ut de rebus quibusdam arduis consultarent, audientes has cædes (nam prius nihil tale sunt suspicati), alii hac, alii illac, alii e fenestris sese proturbantes certatim aufugerunt. Atque ita cum vitæ periculo vitæ consulebant suæ. Regina Scotiæ principem peperit; et cum antea maritum (nescio quas ob causas) non tanti faceret, jam plurimi facit. D. Jacobum, suum ex patre fratrem, quem antea exosum habuit, nunc in gratiam recepit; nec solum illum, sed omnes (utinam verum esset!) proceres evangelicos, ut audio. Evangelium, quod ad tempus sopiebatur, denuo caput exerit.

Cum hæc scriberem, ecce Scotus quidam e patria profugiens, vir bonus et doctus, narravit mihi, Reginam ante decem hebdomadas puerum peperisse, necdum esse baptizatum. Rogo causam. Respondet, Reginam velle filium in summo templo Edenburgi cum multarum missarum celebratione tingi. At Edenburgenses id omnino non permittent; nam mori potius malunt, quam pati, ut abominandæ missæ in suas ecclesias iterum irrepant. Metuunt Edenburgenses, ne illa e Gallia auxiliares vocet copias, ut facilius evangelicos opprimat. Oremus Dominum pro piis fratribus. In mandatis dedit cuidam pio comiti, ut Knoxum apud se manentem ex ædibus ejiciat. Dominus illam convertat, vel confundat! Plura scribere non possum. Diu ægrotavi, necdum plene convalui. Est hæc scribendo debilitata manus. Vale, carissime mi Bullingere. Salutem, quæso, adscribas omnibus tuis, atque adeo omnibus piis, meo nomine. Dominus sua dextra protegat ditionem Tigurinorum! Raptim. Ludhamiæ, 21 Aug. 1566.

Tuus,
JOHANNES PARKHURSTUS, N.

INSCRIPTIO.
D. Henrico Bullingero.

EPISTOLA LXXIII.

EDMUNDUS GRINDALLUS AD HENRICUM BULLINGERUM.

SAL. in Christo, clarissime D. Bullingere, ac frater in Christo carissime. D. Johannes Abelus tradidit mihi literas tuas D. Wintoniensi, Norwicensi, et mihi communiter inscriptas, una cum scripto vestro de re vestiaria; quorum ego exemplaria ad D. Wintoniensem et Norwicensem statim transmisi. Quod ad me attinet, ago tibi maximas gratias, tum quod nostrarum ecclesiarum tantam curam geris, tum quod me, hominem tibi ignotum, participem facis eorum, quæ ad nostros de rebus controversis scribuntur.

Vix credibile est, quantum hæc controversia de rebus nihili ecclesias nostras perturbarit, et adhuc aliqua ex parte perturbat. Multi ex ministris doctioribus videbantur ministerium deserturi; multi etiam ex plebe contulerunt consilia de secessione a nobis facienda, et occultis cœtibus cogendis. Sed tamen Domini benignitate maxima pars ad saniorem mentem rediit. Ad eam rem literæ vestræ, plenæ pietatis ac prudentiæ, plurimum momenti attulerunt; nam eas Latine atque Anglice typis evulgandas curavi. Nonnulli ex ministris, vestro judicio atque auctoritate permoti, abjecerunt priora consilia de deserendo ministerio. Sed et ex plebe quam plurimi mitius sentire cœperunt, postquam intellexerunt nostros ritus a vobis, qui iisdem non utimini, nequaquam damnari impietatis, quod ante publicatas vestras literas nemo illis persuasisset. Sunt tamen, qui adhuc manent in priore sententia, et in his D. Humfredus et Sampsonus, etc. Nihil vero esset facilius, quam regiæ majestati eos reconciliare, si ipsi ab instituto discedere vellent. Sed quum hoc non faciunt, nos apud serenissimam reginam, ista contentione irritatam, nihil possumus. Nos qui nunc episcopi sumus, (eos dico qui in Germania et ceteris locis exulaverant) in primo nostro reditu, priusquam ad ministerium accessimus, diu multumque contendebamus, ut ista, de quibus nunc controvertitur, prorsus amoverentur. Sed cum illud a Regina et statibus in comitiis regni impetrare non potuimus, communicatis consiliis, optimum judicavimus non deserere ecclesias propter ritus non adeo multos, eosque per se non impios, præsertim quum pura evangelii doctrina nobis integra ac libera maneret, in qua ad hunc usque diem (utcunque multi multa in contrarium moliti sunt) cum vestris ecclesiis vestraque confessione nuper edita plenissime consentimus. Sed neque adhuc pœnitet nos nostri consilii. Nam interea, Domino dante incrementum, auctæ et confirmatæ sunt ecclesiæ, quæ alioqui Eceboliis, Lutheranis, et Semipapistis prædæ fuissent expositæ. Istæ vero istorum intempestivæ contentiones de adiaphoris (si quid ego judicare possum) non ædificant, sed scindunt ecclesias et discordiam seminant inter fratres.

Sed de nostris rebus hactenus. In Scotia non sunt res tam bene constitutæ quam esset optandum. Retinent quidem adhuc ecclesiæ puram evangelii confessionem; sed tamen videtur Scotiæ Regina omnibus modis laborare, ut eam tandem extirpet. Nuper enim effecit, ut sex aut septem missæ papisticæ singulis diebus in aula sua publice fierent, omnibus qui accedere volunt admissis; quum antea unica, eaque privatim habita, nullo Scoto ad eam admisso, esset contenta. Præterea, quum primum inita est reformatio, cautum fuit, ut ex bonis monasteriorum, quæ fisco adjudicata sunt, stipendia evangelii ministris persolverentur: at ipsa jam integro biennio nihil solvit. Johannem Knoxum Regina urbe Edinburgo, ubi hactenus primarius fuit minister, non ita pridem ejecit, neque exorari potest, ut redeundi facultatem concedat. Publice tamen extra aulam nihil hactenus est innovatum; et proceres regni, nobiles item ac cives, multo maxima ex parte evangelio nomen dederunt, ac multa magnaque constantiæ indicia ostendunt. In his præcipuus est D. Jacobus Stuardus, Murraiæ comes, Reginæ frater nothus, vir pius ac magnæ apud suos auctoritatis. Perscribitur etiam ad me ex Scotia, Reginæ cum rege marito pessime convenire. Causa hæc est: fuit Italus quidam, nomine David, a cardinale Lotharingo Reginæ Scotiæ commendatus. Is quum Reginæ a secretis atque intimis esset consiliis, fere solus omnia administrabat, non consulto Rege, qui admodum juvenis et levis est. Hoc male habebat Regem. Itaque facta conspiratione cum nobilibus quibusdam et aulicis suis, Italum illum, Reginæ opem frustra implorantem, ex ipsius conspectu abripi, et statim, indicta causa, multis pugionum ictibus perfodi atque interfici curavit. Hujus tam immanis facti memoriam Regina, tametsi nuper filium Regi pepererit, ex animo deponere non potest.

Hæc paulo verbosius de Scotia, ex qua fortassis raro ad vos scribitur. Oro, ut D. Gualterum ac reliquos collegas tuos meo nomine salutes. Dominus te nobis et ecclesiæ suæ quam diutissime conservet! Londini, 27 Augusti, 1566.

Deditissimus tibi in Domino,
EDMUNDUS GRINDALLUS,
Episc. Lond.

INSCRIPTIO.
Reverendo in Christo, D. Henrico Bullingero, Tigurinæ ecclesiæ ministro fideliss°. ac fratri in Domino carissimo.
Tiguri.

EPISTOLA LXXIV.

RICARDUS HILLES AD HENRICUM BULLINGERUM.

Dominus Jesus confortet te in omni re, teque nunc in senium declinantem sustentet, ac tibi maxime in senectute tua nunquam deficiat!

Tam diu a literis ad te scribendis abstinui, vir doctissime, præcipue autem propter meum in Latine scribendo stilum durum atque barbarum, minusque congruum, ut jam fere ad tuas literas mihi gratissimas, die 28 Augusti proxime elapsi Tiguri scriptas, pudet fere pigetque respondere. Una cum iis literis Helveticarum ecclesiarum confessionem colligatam et Germanica lingua scriptam a Domino Abelo fratre carissimo accepi. Tuo libello (sicuti etiam facies) veterem nostram amicitiam renovare cupis; atque pro eo magnas habeo gratias. Latinam antea Londini habui per eundem Dominum Abelum, idque, si bene memini, proximis nundinis Francofordiæ tentis quadragesimalibus prius a te receptis. Liber ipse mihi bene placet, sicut etiam deberet; doctrina namque pia et sincera ubique in eo traditur.

Dominus Abelus mihi etiam retulit, tres tuas filias maritatas peste extinctas. Non dubito autem eas in Domino esse mortuas: beatæ autem sunt ideo, quia nunc non solummodo a laboribus suis cessant, sed etiam absque omni dubio una cum Christo Servatore nostro perenni fruuntur vita, sicuti etiam earum mater, uxor tua pia. Postquam autem sis per divinam providentiam viduus, nec juvenis, non dubito quin divi Pauli apostoli sequutus fueris consilium, ubi dicit, " Nam velim omnes homines esse ut ipse sum. Sed unusquisque proprium donum habet a Deo, alius quidem sic, alius autem sic. Dico autem inconjugatis et viduis, Bonum eis est, si manserint ut et ego, etc." Et iterum: "Alligatus es uxori? ne quæras divortium: solutus es ab uxore? ne quæras uxorem."

Laudandus Deus, quod 190 homilias in Isaiam prophetam absolveris. Postquam excusæ fuerint, mihi earum volumen unum, si vixero, volente Domino comparabo. Non enim dubito quin multo cum fructu prodibunt in lucem. Doleo quod sentis sensim vires tuas deficere: spero tamen certe Deum optimum maximum te in senectute tua non derelicturum; oraboque pro te illum, sicuti ipse cupis. Faxit Deus ut exaudiat, qui dixit, " Quodcunque petieritis Patrem in nomine meo, dabit vobis."

Uxorem meam nomine tuo salvere jubebo. Scio eam gavisuram multum, quam cito de tua bona precatione audiat: valde enim te diligit profecto. Recreabit eam etiam, cum per me resciet, te quidem adhuc valere utcunque, ut dicis, per Dei gratiam. Graviter laborat conjunx mea subinde de calculo in renibus, imo ad mortem fere aliquando. Tu pro ea Dominum orare digneris, precor. Vereor ne hic morbus illam conficiet tandem. Dominus Abelus, postquam ex ejus vesica extractus fuit ingens calculus, non adeo bene habuit. Metuo autem mihi, ne non diu nobis supersit. Vir est pius, amicus fidelis, et verus Israelita. Uxorem habet, ut audivisti procul dubio vel nosti, piam et honestissimam. Illa bene valet, sed claudicat pedibus semper, postquam Argentinam reliquit, sicuti illic etiam per biennium antequam eo discessit. " Quem diligit Dominus castigat, corrigit autem omnem filium quem recipit." Et " permultæ sunt tribulationes justorum: ab iis omnibus autem liberabit eos Deus."

Volo aliquando aliquid ecclesiarum Helveticarum confessionis uxori meæ interpretari. Ipsa etiam subinde leget in ea; intelligit enim linguam vestratem utcunque, et in eadem meditatur nonnunquam.

Tuas alteras literas, imo binas, domine, domi habeo, quas mihi post mortem Mariæ Reginæ nostræ nuper misisti: oblitus autem sum certe, quibus die et anno fuerant Tiguri datæ. Habeo tibi pro eis gratias magnas; plenæ sunt enim adhortationis piæ et consolationis optimæ. Reddat tibi vicissim Dominus noster Jesus Christus consolationem uberem in die illo, quo dissolvetur corpus ab anima tua, et etiam cum iterum adjungetur et restauretur!

Ita mihi per totum fere triennium deficiunt vires, et animus tam pusillus, ut miror subinde me tot annis adhuc supervixisse. Voluntas tamen Domini fiat semper. Cupio autem dissolvi et esse cum Christo. Interim enim, dum hic maneam, ita innumeris quandoque crucior curis et solicitudinibus inanibus (propter conditionis mercaturæ scilicet vocationem), ut multo plus mallem, si ita Dominus voluerit, tantillis voluptatibus et gaudiis istius mundi vanis, et adeo cruciatibus et animi perturbationibus permixtis, imo potius nimis conditis, carere, quam talibus frui. Sed Domini fiat voluntas!

Fui hic Antverpiæ per integros fere tres menses cum dimidio. Interim dominum Christopherum Montium, amicum nostrum communem, per literas meas quandoque certiorem feci de statu rerum Brabanticarum, maxime autem Antverpiensium; quantum ad religionis mutationem et evangelicæ prædicationis tolerationem spectat. Neque dubito, quin de iis rebus ab Argentinensibus concionatoribus satis novorum acceperis, sive per aliorum fratrum scripta. Idcirco non puto nunc mihi opus esse de iisdem rescribere.

Jam autem undique dicunt, qui literas ab Hispaniis, Italia, Gallia, et Anglia sæpius recipiunt, Regem Philippum ex Hispania in proximo vere huc in Brabantiam et omnem Germaniam inferiorem venturum, vel ad totius patriæ celebranda comitia (ad cujus præscriptum omnis religionis controversia reformetur sive transformetur) vel pontificiam superstitionem, idololatriam et sævitiam restituendam et stabiliendam. Deus autem, in cujus manu sunt corda omnium principum, auferat ab rege isto et principibus istius regionis corda saxea, detque carnea, ut ad Christum vere ex animo conversi de anteactis suis peccatis et criminibus valde doleant, et eos peniteat, quo veniam et misericordiam a Domino consequantur, et postea ejus gloriam totis viribus suis promoveant!

Dolendum est, quod Lutherani quidam, uti scribis, licet pacem offerentes, vexare vos non desinunt. Hic autem Martinisti (ut cupiunt plerumque nominari Lutherani, potius quam Lutherani) aperte orthodoxos symmystas (quos etiam Calvinistas denominant) taxare et improbare in concionibus suis publicis non desinunt, sed maxime audent.

Habent autem Martinisti pauciores ecclesias quam orthodoxi; ipsi enim solummodo duas, (quarum unam in magno convocant horreo,) illi autem, quos vocant Calvinistas, tres habent vel quatuor. Adhuc autem utraque pars (præterquam quendam qui in horreo illo concionatur) sub dio, et non sub tectis, prædicant. Sed jam ante menses fere duos templa ædificare cœperunt, et illa exstruere magna festinatione pergunt. Attamen adhuc parietes (qui ex lateribus et lapidibus constructi sunt) eminent tantum, et manent intecta templa.

Vale in Christo Jesu, domine colendissime, qui semper te servet! Amen. Antverpiæ, 23 Decembris, Anno 1566.

Tuus,

RICARDUS HILLES.

INSCRIPTIO.
Doctissimo viro domino Henrico
Bullingero, amico suo carissimo.
Tiguri.

EPISTOLA LXXV.

EDMUNDUS GRINDALLUS ET ROBERTUS HORNUS AD HENRICUM BULLINGERUM ET RODOLPHUM GUALTERUM.

ERUDITAS vestras literas ad Humfredum et Sampsonem, et commodissimas cum ad nostras de vestibus animorum dissensiones tum verborum altercationes atque pugnas sedandas, quam libentissime accepimus: acceptas non sine certo consilio, parcentes tamen fratrum nominibus, typis excudi atque publicari curavimus: indeque fructum quidem amplissimum, quemadmodum speramus, percepimus. Nam sanis quidem viris, universum evangelicorum institutum et finem spectantibus, multum profuere: ministros certo nonnullos, qui de deserendo ministerio propter rem vestiariam, quæ jam sola controversa ac causa dissensionis inter nos fuerat, cogitarunt, persuasos ne ecclesias fraudari sua opera sinerent propter rem tantillam, confirmatosque reddidere et in vestram sententiam retraxere: plebem autem, quæ per importunos quorundam clamores concitata in varias partes distrahebatur, piosque ministros contumelia afficiebat, quasi concordia quadam illos placavere ac leniere temperantia: morosis vero, et nihil præterquam quod ipsi statuerant perferre valentibus, etsi non satisfecere, eo tamen eis profuere, ut pios conviciis minus proscindere pacemque ecclesiæ salutarem sermonibus suis morologis non adeo audacter fœdare velint aut possint: ex hiis quosdam esse exauctoratos, etsi sua ipsorum culpa, ut graviora in illos non dicamus, fatemur et dolemus. Verum illud æquiori animo ferendum putamus, quod non sint multi sed pauci, et utut pii, certe non adeo docti. Nam solus Sampsonus inter eos, qui exauctorati sunt, et pius pariter ac doctus est habendus: Humfredus vero ac doctiores omnes in sua hactenus statione manent. Quod si vestra epistola typis excusa ac publicata fuisset, ut qui exauctorarunt confirmarentur; si qui exauctorati sunt, propter alios articulos apud nos controversos, et non ob rem solam vestiariam, de gradu fuissent dejecti suo; si denique illa epistola, quæ verbis adeo exquisitis ac perspicuis solam controversiam vestiariam pertractat, ut alio transferri non possit, ad approbandos articulos nobis ignotos, necdum apud nos Dei gratia controversos, (nam nulli nobis cum fratribus articuli in contentionem hactenus venere, nisi hic solus vestiarius,) raperetur; luculenta profecto vobis, quos amamus, colimus, et in Domino honoramus, facta fuisset injuria: sicut nobis manifesta adhibita est calumnia ab hiis, qui auctores fuerunt vanissimi rumoris, quo apud nos perlatum fuit, a ministris ecclesiæ requiri novis quibusdam subscribant articulis, aut statione sua cedant.

Summa controversiæ nostræ hæc est: nos tenemus ministros ecclesiæ Anglicanæ sine impietate uti posse vestium discrimine, publica auctoritate jam præscripto, tum in administratione sacra tum in usu externo; præsertim cum ut res indifferentes proponantur, tantum propter ordinem et debitam legibus obedientiam usurpari jubeantur, et omnis superstitionis, cultus, ac necessitatis, quod ad conscientias attinet, opinio legum ipsarum præscripto et sincerioris doctrinæ prædicatione assidua, quantum fieri potest, amoveatur, rejiciatur, ac omnino condemnetur. Illi contra clamitant, vestes has in numerum τῶν ἀδιαφόρων jam haudquaquam ascribendas, impias esse, papisticas ac idololatricas; et propterea omnibus piis uno consensu ministerio cedendum potius, quam cum istis panniculariis papisticis, (sic enim loquuntur,) ecclesiæ inservire; licet doctrinam sincerissimam prædicandi, nec non omnimodos errores seu abusus sive in ritibus sive in doctrina sive in sacramentis sive in moribus per sanam doctrinam subaccusandi, exagitandi, condemnandi summam habeamus libertatem. Isthuc istorum immaturum consilium accipere non possumus; quomodo nec impetuosas eorum adhortationes, quibus pacem ecclesiæ continenter pro suggestu disturbant, religionemque nostram universam in periculum trahunt, ferre debemus. Nam istiusmodi suis celeusmatibus serenissimæ Reginæ animum, alioqui ad optime merendum de religione propensum, irritari, (proh dolor!) nimium experti sumus; et procerum quorundam animos, ut de aliis taceamus, ægros, imbecilles, vacillantes, hiis vulnerari, debilitari, abalienari, certo certius scimus. Ecquis dubitare possit, quin papistæ, hujusmodi occasionem nacti, virus suum pestilentissimum eructabunt, evoment in evangelium Jesu Christi ejusque professores omnes, in spem erecti, jam oportunitatem se habere, suam sibi ereptam Helenam recuperandi? Quod si inconsulto nostrorum consilio acquiesceremus, ut omnes junctis viribus impetum in vestes legibus constabilitas contra legem faciamus, perimamus, ac deleamus omnino, aut simul omnes munia exuamus; papisticum profecto, vel saltem Lutherano-papisticum, haberemus ministerium, aut omnino nullum. Illud autem Deum optimum maximum testamur, fratres in Christo honorandi, neque culpa evenisse dissidium hoc nostra, nec per nos stare quo minus istiusmodi vestes e medio tollerentur; imo sanctissime licet juremus, laborasse nos hactenus quanto potuimus studio, fide, diligentia, ut id effectum daremus, quod fratres postulant et nos optamus. Verum in tantas adductis angustias quid faciendum, (multa vobis, qui prudentes et ad pericula ecclesiis impendentia perspicienda estis sagaces, conjicienda relinquimus,) nisi ut cum non possumus quod velimus, velimus in Domino id quod possumus?

Hactenus rem controversam et plenam dissensionis inter nos, ut se habet, exposuimus. Nunc vero quod reliquum est, accipite. Falsissimus omnino est ille rumor, si tamen rumor dicendus sit, (novimus enim prudentiam vestram ac modestiam, et laudamus,) de receptione, subscriptione et approbatione novorum istorum articulorum quos recensetis; nec magis sunt veraces, qui sive scriptis suis epistolis sive verbis coram hoc prætextu vobis fucum facere, nobis autem calumniam inurere, sunt conati. Plerique enim omnes isti articuli falso nobis objiciuntur: perpauci recipiuntur: horum omnino nulli fratribus sua subscriptione approbandi obtruduntur. Cantum in templis figuratum una cum strepitu organorum retinendum nos non affirmamus, imo, prout decet, insectamur. Peregrinam linguam, exufflationes, exorcismos, oleum, sputum, lutum, accensos cereos, et ejus generis alia, ex legum præscripto nunquam revocanda, penitus amisit ecclesia Anglicana. Mulieres posse aut debere baptizare infantulos, nullo modo prorsus assentimur. In cœnæ Dominicæ perceptione panem communiter frangere cuilibet communicaturo, non ori inserere sed in manus tradere, modum spiritualis manducationis et præsentiæ corporis Christi in sacra cœna explicare, leges jubent, usus confirmat, oblatratores nostri Anglo-Lovanienses nefariis suis scriptis testantur. Uxores ministrorum non arcentur a suis maritis; cohabitant, et eorum conjugium apud omnes (semper papistas excipimus) habetur honorabile. Denique non minus falsum est quod oblatrant, penes solos episcopos omnem esse ecclesiasticæ gubernationis potestatem, etsi primas illis dari non negamus. Nam in rebus hujusmodi ecclesiasticis in synodo deliberari solet: synodus autem indicitur edicto regio eo tempore quo habetur totius regni parliamentum, ut vocatur. Adsunt episcopi, adsunt etiam totius provinciæ pastorum doctiores quiqui, qui triplo plures sunt quam episcopi. Hii seorsum ab episcopis de rebus ecclesiasticis deliberant, et nihil in synodo statuitur aut definitur sine communi eorum ac episcoporum aut majoris saltem illorum partis consensu et approbatione: tantum abest ut pastoribus non permittatur in hujusmodi rebus ecclesiasticis suam dicere sententiam. Recipimus quidem, seu potius toleranter ferimus, donec meliora Dominus dederit, interrogationes infantium, et crucis characterem in baptismo, in cœnæ perceptione genuflexionem, et regiam facultatum curiam, quam metropolitani vocant. Quæstiones istiusmodi non adeo accommode infantibus proponi, etsi ex Augustino videantur emendicatæ, publice profitemur ac sedulo docemus.

Crucis charactere frontem jam baptizati infantis notare, etsi minister palam conceptis verbis profiteatur signatum esse cruce infantulum solummodo in signum, quod in posterum illum non pudebit fidei Christi crucifixi, idque ex vetustiori ecclesia videatur transsumptum, tamen non defendimus. Genuflexionem in sacræ cœnæ perceptione, quoniam ita lege constitutum est, permittimus; ea tamen expositione seu potius cautione, quam ipsi genuflexionis auctores, viri sanctissimi ac martyres Jesu Christi constantissimi, adhibuerunt, diligentissime populo declarata, promulgata, inculcata. Quæ sic ad verbum habet: "Etsi in libro precum statutum sit, ut communicantes genuflectendo sacram accipiant communionem, id tamen eo trahi non debere declaramus, quasi ulla adoratio fiat aut fieri debeat, sive sacramentali pani ac vino, sive ulli reali et essentiali præsentiæ ibi existenti naturalis carnis ac sanguinis Christi. Nam sacramentalis panis et vinum permanent in ipsis suis naturalibus substantiis, et propterea non sunt adoranda. Id enim idololatria horrenda esset, omnibus Christianis detestanda; et quantum ad corpus naturale ac sanguinem servatoris nostri Christi attinet, in cœlo sunt, et non sunt hic, quandoquidem contra veritatem veri naturalis corporis Christi est, pluribus quam uno inesse locis uno atque eodem tempore."

Facultatum curia, undecunque est allata, regia est, non metropolitani. Is enim prudens pater, doctus et ad sincerissimam religionem propagandam optime affectus, omnimodas Romanas fæces prorsus eluere peroptat, conatur, satagit. Et licet omnes hujus fiscalis curiæ, sicut etiam alios nonnullos, abusus e medio tollere non possumus, eos tamen carpere, contumeliis insequi, ad tartara usque, unde prorepserunt, detrudere non desistimus. Nobis credite, fratres venerandi, unicuique licet ministro omnibus istiusmodi articulis cum modestia et sobrietate et privatim et publice contradicere: pastores vero articulos istos, nobis falso impositos, recipere aut approbare nolentes, statione sua haudquaquam dejicimus.

Pergite ergo nos amare, admonere, juvare, ut incendium inter nos exortum solummodo pro re vestiaria extinguatur. Nosque operam dabimus, quantum fieri possit, quemadmodum in proximis comitiis fecimus, etsi nihil obtinere potuimus, ut omnes errores et abusus ad amussim verbi Dei corrigantur, emendentur, expurgentur. Commendamus vos, fratres, gratiæ Domini nostri Jesu Christi, quem oramus, ut vos incolumes vestrasque ecclesias in pace quam diutissime conservet. Salutate nostro nomine fratres at symmystas Tigurinos omnes.

Londini, 6 Febr., Anno Domini 1567.

Vestrum omnium amantiss.

EDM. LONDON.
ROB. WINTON.

P. S. Obsecro et ego vos, fratres mihi plurimum observandi, ignoscatis mihi quod literis vestris, ad me privatim scriptis, hactenus non responderim, nec pro doctissimis vestris commentariis ad me transmissis ullas hactenus gratias retulerim. Neque mihi illud ipsum vitio vertant Wolvius et Lavaterus, quos, quæso, meo nomine plurimum salutate, et me apud illos excusate. Scio enim officii mei rationem hoc ipsum efflagitasse; et vos illosque meas literas desiderasse non dubito. Efficiam posthac, scribendo vos omnes expleam, et officio non desim meo. Salutem etiam a me dicite, oro, D. Simlero, Zuinglio, Hallero. Vivite omnes ac valete in Christo.

Totus vester,

ROBERTUS WINTON

INSCRIPTIO.
Ornatiss. viris D. Henrico Bullingero et D. Rod. Gualtero, Tigurinæ ecclesiæ pastoribus fideliss.

EPISTOLA LXXVI.

EDMUNDUS GRINDALLUS AD HENRICUM BULLINGERUM.

Salus in Christo, clarissime D. Bullingere, ac frater in Christo carissime! Quod præter communes illas literas privatim etiam ad me scripsisti, gratias ago. Sed non est, cur tu mihi gratias ageres tam diligenter, quod sæpius, idque non illibenter, honorificam tui mentionem faciam. Facio enim hoc merito tuo, quum non sim nescius quantum et ministerio et scriptis ecclesiæ profueris, et adhuc prodesse non desinis. Hoc etiam privatim tibi debeo, quod ante annos plus minus viginti lectione libri tui de Origine erroris primum excitatus sum ad veram de cœna Domini sententiam amplectendam, quum antea Luthero fuissem addictus. Æquum est igitur, ut illum colam, per quem profeci.

Hæc volui paucis ad literas tuas respondere, quæ mihi erant gratissimæ. In Scotia ecclesiæ aliquanto meliore in conditione sunt, quam quum proxime ad te scribebam; sed ipsa Scotiæ Regina non mutat sententiam. Decembri elapso baptizatus fuit filius illius primogenitus, more papistico, per quendam mitratum pseudo-episcopum; sed ex universa illius regni nobilitate tantum duo reperti sunt, qui baptismo interesse dignati sunt: ceteri euntem et redeuntem infantem tantum ad valvas usque sacelli comitati sunt. Quid in Brabantia et Flandria geratur, scio vos non ignorare. Spero illis cœleste auxilium non defuturum, postquam magna ex parte humanis præsidiis destituti videantur, præsertim si Hispaniarum Rex cum exercitu, quod timemus, ad illos opprimendos veniat. Oro ut D. Gualterum et ceteros tuos collegas meo nomine salutes. Dominus vos conservet! Londini, 8 Febr. 1567.

Deditissimus tibi in Domino,

EDMUNDUS GRINDALLUS,

Episc. London.

INSCRIPTIO.
Reverendo in Christo, D. Henrico Bullingero, Tigurinæ ecclesiæ ministro fidelissimo, ac fratri in Domino carissimo.
Tiguri.

EPISTOLA LXXVII.

JOHANNES JUELLUS AD HENRICUM BULLINGERUM.

S. P. IN Christo. Proximæ literæ meæ, ornatissime vir, cum Londinum tardiuscule venissent, et Francofordiam ad nundinas proficisci non possent, re infecta, domum ad me reversæ sunt: quod nonnihil vereor, ne nunc quoque in istas accidat.

De prolixis et pereruditis illis tuis ad me literis proximis, prolixe tibi ago gratias. Nunc mihi de synodo illa Francofordiensi, ut de re obscura et controversa, egregie satisfactum esse et fateor et gaudeo. Res nostræ ecclesiasticæ, publicæ privatæque, eo loco nunc sunt, quo fuerunt. Lovanienses nostri clamant, et turbant, quantum possunt: et habent fautores, etsi non ita multos, plures tamen multo quam velim. Et quamvis complures sint, et in universum in omnes scribant, tamen, nescio quo meo fato, omnes in me feruntur unum. Itaque dum illis respondeo, ne me esse otiosum putes.

Habuimus proximis istis mensibus comitia totius regni: illis ego per valetudinem interesse non potui. Scriptæ sunt leges de religione, quibus papistarum obstinata malitia atque insolentia in officio contineatur. Actum etiam est de successione; hoc est, cui familiæ jus regni debeatur, si quid Elizabethæ Reginæ humanitus acciderit, quod nolimus. Ea contentio mensem unum atque alterum omnium animos occupavit; cum Regina ea de re agi nollet, reliqui omnes vehementer cuperent, et utrinque magnis viribus et studiis pugnaretur. Quid quæris? Effici postremo nihil potuit: Regina enim, ut est femina imprimis prudens et provida, hærede semel designato, suspicatur aliquid sibi creari posse periculi. Nosti enim illud, Plures orientem solem adorant, quam occidentem.

De religione, causa illa vestiaria magnos hoc tempore motus concitavit. Reginæ certum est nolle flecti: fratres autem nostri quidam ita ea de re pugnant, ac si in ea una omnis nostra religio versaretur. Itaque functiones abjicere et ecclesias inanes relinquere malunt, quam tantillum de sententia decedere. Neque aut tuis aut D. Gualteri doctissimis scriptis, aut aliorum piorum virorum monitis, moveri volunt. Agimus tamen Deo gratias, qui non patitur nos inter nos hoc tempore gravioribus quæstionibus exerceri. Unus tamen quispiam e nostro numero, episcopus Glocestrensis, in comitiis aperte et fidenter dixit, probari sibi Lutheri sententiam de eucharistia; sed ea seges non erit, spero, diuturna.

In Hibernia nonnihil hoc tempore tumultuatur. Insula ea, uti scis, paret nostris regibus. Johannes quidam Onelus, spurius, conscripsit nuper militem, et nostros insolenter provocavit. Sed plus in ea re moræ est, quam periculi: is enim longe abdit sese in paludes et solitudines; quo noster miles consequi facile non possit.

E Scotia vero (quid ego dicam? aut tu quid credas?) horrenda atque atrocia nuntiantur. Ea quamvis ejusmodi sint, ut credi vix possint, et ex aula usque ad me scribuntur, et passim jactantur, et creduntur ab omnibus. Regem juvenem aiunt proximis hisce admodum diebus, una cum uno famulo, quem habuit a cubiculis, interfectum esse domi suæ, et exportatum foras, et relictum sub dio. Crede mihi, horret animus ista commemorare. Si ista vera sint, (ne sint! tamen si sint,) quid causæ fuerit, aut quibus ille insidiis petitus sit, faciam te posthac, ubi omnia rescivero, de rebus omnibus certiorem. In præsentia nec ea, quæ ita constanter jactarentur, reticere potui, nec ea, quæ comperta non haberem, nimium fidenter affirmare.

Julium nostrum audio Tiguri esse mortuum: mitto tamen ad illum viginti coronatos Gallicos, si vivit, ut illi cedant; sin autem, quod nolim, est mortuus, ut in epulum scholasticum insumantur. Si esset otium, scriberem ad D. Lavaterum, ad D. Simlerum, ad D. Wolphium, ad D. Hallerum, et alios; imprimis vero ad D. Gualterum; ad quem hactenus, homo ingratus, nunquam scripsi. Quæso ut hosce omnes, atque etiam in primis D. Rodolphum et D. Henricum tuos, meo nomine plurimum valere jubeas.

Vale, mi pater, et domine in Christo colendissime. Sarisberiæ in Anglia. Feb. 24, 1567.

Tuus in Christo,
JOHANNES JUELLUS, Anglus.

INSCRIPTIO.

D. *Henrico Bullingero, ministro ecclesiæ Tigurinæ fidelissimo, viro longe doctissimo, et domino suo colendissimo. Tiguri.*

EPISTOLA LXXVIII.

PERCEVALLUS WIBURNUS AD HENRICUM BULLINGERUM.

S. Cum Tiguri apud vos essem superiori æstate, reverende vir, quod me, hominem obscurum nulloque publico testimonio tibi commendatum, tam habueris gratum, ut etiam mensa tua communicaveris, id sane singularis cujusdam humanitatis tuæ ac φιλοξενίας fuit, quo equidem nomine me tibi plurimum debere agnosco. Quod autem per valetudinem tuam impeditus sum, quominus de rebus nostris, ecclesiæ hic statu ac conditione, libere ac fuse tecum agerem, sicuti cupiebam; id quidem etsi cum in urbe adhuc vestra manerem me habuit male, utpote qui hac ratione itineris mei fructu carebam non minimo, postea tamen non sine divini numinis consilio ac providentia ita optime accidisse animadverti.

Meministi, ni fallor, gravissime vir, quo die me ex hospitio per filium vocares, ac quæ volebam in medium proferre juberes, præsente tum etiam D. Gualtero, me de hujus ecclesiæ nostræ calamitate ac miseria multis conquestum non fuisse, partim quoniam tu jam antea satis superque rerum nostrarum intelligere tibi videbaris, partim etiam quoniam fratrum quorundam literis, nominatim vero tunc temporis D. Bezæ, ita certior de omnibus hic rebus factus es, ut istis aliquid adjicere nihil fuerit necesse. Traditis ergo duabus schedulis, quarum in D. Bezæ ad te literis mentio fiebat, sic a vobis ad hospitium dimissus sum, ut interim de certo aliquo religionis capite verbum nullum fecerim. Postea etiam per biduum illud, quo literas vestras exspectabam, me nihil vel tecum vel cum aliis egisse satis constat, nisi quod quæstiones aliquot de vestitu ac ceremoniis in genere uni ac alteri ex cœtu vestro proposuerim. Ecce tamen, doctissime pater, cum domum ad meos redeo, quasi ad maledicendum ac aliis detrahendum, quod minime decebat, destinate ad vos venissem, aut de industria falsa fictaque de hac ecclesia comminisci studuissem, sic mihi detractionis ac calumniæ crimen objicitur. Dum vero hujus rei causam fontemque exquiro studiosius, omne hoc malum ex literis tuis ad episcopos oriri deprehendo, quas ut receperam clausas, eorum ignarus plane quæ continebant, ita jam antea diligenter in illorum manus tradi curaveram. Quid multa? Innocentiæ hac in parte meæ bene conscius, D. Vintoniensem, qui tum Londini aderat, statim adeo, cum illo serio (ut par erat) hac ipsa de re ago: proferuntur tandem literæ tua ipsius manu scriptæ, quæ rumores ad vos usque perlatos ostendunt de lingua peregrina, luto, sputo, cereis, et nescio quibus aliis rebus in sacris hic adhibitis: nam unam aut alteram tantum sententiam inspiciendi mihi tum copia facta est: hujusce autem rumoris auctorem me esse volunt. Quanquam autem futile prorsus hoc commentum sit, ipsaque conjectura sua pereat vanitate; quoniam tamen, sive diaboli ipsius instinctu, sive odio quodam hominum ac malevolentia, sive credulitate quorundam nimia, robur sibi fidemque ita acquisivit, ut ego interea gravi suspicione laborem apud eos, quos per aliquot jam annos tamquam amicos fratresque in Christo complexus sum, quibuscum etiam deinceps, quantum in me est, pacifice vivere cupio; propterea ad fidem tuam hoc tempore confugere cogor, ut, qua es pietate ac sanctimonia præditus, testimonio tuo innocentiam meam a maledicentia vindices. Oblivisci facile non potes, venerande vir, de quibus ego capitibus in articulis questus sim; ut minime opus fuerit linguam peregrinam, lutum, sputum, cereos, aliaque πάρεργα ad augendum hoc malum corradere. Utinam ab aliis oneribus ac maculis tam esset hæc ecclesia libera, quam Dei gratia ab his malis est aliena! non tam justa tum quidem certe esset piorum querimonia, quam est hodie, eheu! justissima.

Meam in hac petitione libertatem æqui boni consules, si consideres primum, meum de me ipso hac in re testimonium (utcunque simplex et verum) non facile probari; deinde, eousque esse quorundam temeritate ac incogitantia progressum, ut quibusdam ex summis hujus regni magistratibus res sit patefacta; causam denique ministrorum, bonam alias et sanctam, hoc prætextu apud multos male audire; quo fit, ut abusus hodie hæreant ac retineantur pertinacius, omnisque reformationis spes pene præjudicatur[1]. Nam (præterquam quod avitæ superstitiones ac reliquiæ papisticæ quam plurimis hic nimium placent, ex nostris quoque reperiuntur illarum patroni, qui doctissimorum virorum scripta, tuaque imprimis, huc detorquent,) si falsarii semel deprehendantur reliqui ministri, quantum studio postea ac labore proficient suo etiam in rebus optimis, tibi non est difficile conjicere. Et meum ergo periculum privatum et ipsa causa communis, quæ hominum certe non est sed Jesu Christi, opem ac auxilium tuum in primis flagitant. De te ergo, quin manum tuam prompte ac alacriter porrecturus sis in causa tam honesta ac necessaria, nihil est quod dubitem. Equidem ut alios perstringas aut vellices, (id quod tamen ex usu fortassis foret, etsi mihi non ita tutum, nisi in genere id fiat et prudenter,) id, inquam, minime peto · ut me periclitantem justa defensione tuearis ac defendas, hoc unice quæro; idque privatis tuis ad me, si placet, literis, ne major hinc

[¹ MS. *prædicatur.*]

oriatur turba, si hoc quibusdam innotescat : quod si quiescant, aliud non quæro ; sin minus, aliquid penes te habere cupio, quod illis pro me respondeat. Et quamvis citius hoc, quicquid est, a me suscipi potuit, ac forte etiam debuit, hactenus tamen a scribendo abstinui, ut tibi et seni et valetudinario, et in hac ipsa causa jam plus satis interpellato, parcerem; ac utinam etiamnum id licuisset et omnino! Ceterum cum non ita pridem primus hujus regni consiliariis privatim et amice me ad se accersitum submonuerit de hac re, ac suaserit ut duo saltem aut tria verba a te parata pro me haberem, si opus fuerit ; tandem tua, clarissime vir, æquitate fretus aliquid (ut vides) ausus sum : qua in re ne repulsam a te patiar, obnixe precor et obtestor ; simulque ne hac occasione illos contra me provoces, quos jam satis habeo duros et adversos. Quod si quæ scribes Genevam mittere placebit vel ad D. Bezam vel D. Raymundum, quo postea Gallicanæ ecclesiæ Londini ministro ab illis mittantur, (id quod frequenter faciunt et sæpe tutissime,) hac ratione ad manus meas pervenient literæ tuæ, si inscriptio ad me nominatim dirigatur.

Ex his colligere tibi promptum est, mi pater, quod responsum a te jam non tam ardenter expetam et serio, quam anxius et solicitus etiam exspectem. Interim me, ut potero, conscientiæ testimonio solabor ac sustinebo. Dominus Jesus te ecclesiæ suæ diu incolumem servet, ac favore suo magis magisque assidue prosequatur!

Salutem, quæso, a me dicas eximio Jesu Christi servo, D. Rodolpho Gualtero, cum uxore, quibus si etiam mea causa gratias agas vel meo potius nomine, pergratum mihi feceris : quæso etiam, saluta reliquos symmystas tuos mihi notos, D. Simlerum, D. Wolphium, utrumque filium tuum, præcipue autem juniorem, cui plurimum debeo propter humanitatis officia quæ mihi Tiguri præstitit.

Vale in Christo plurimum, reverende pater, hujusque ecclesiæ nutantis in precibus, quæso, apud Deum memineris. Iterum vale. Londini, 5º Calend. Mart. 1567.

       Tuæ paternitatis studiosissimus,

        PERCEVALLUS WIBURNUS.

INSCRIPTIO.
Ornatissimo viro D. Henrico Bullingero,
 Tigurinæ ecclesiæ pastori dignissimo,
 patri sibi plurimum observando.
   Tiguri.

EPISTOLA LXXIX.

EDMUNDUS GRINDALLUS AD HENRICUM BULLINGERUM.

Sal. in Christo, clarissime D. Bullingere, ac frater in Domino carissime! Ago tibi gratias ex animo, quod literas meas tam grato animo accepisti; similiter etiam pro homiliis tuis in Esaiam, quas accepi per D. Johannem Abelum. Ad literas vestras mense Septembri per Wiburnum missas, sed ab alio traditas, respondimus D. Wintoniensis atque ego superioribus nundinis Francfordianis; et illas literas spero vos jamdudum accepisse.

Quod ad publicationem epistolæ de re vestiaria attinet, sciebam quidem vos eam non in hoc scripsisse ut ederetur; sed quia ex publicatione magnam ecclesiarum nostrarum utilitatem consequuturam certo providebam, vos hoc æquo animo laturos esse mihi persuadebam.

Res nostræ eodem fere in statu sunt, quo hactenus fuere. Habemus jam apud nos comitem a Stolberg, Germanum, legatum a Cæsare Maximiliano. Petit (ut audio) annuum subsidium pecuniarum ad bellum Turcicum. Sed non videtur hic aliquid impetraturus, nisi cetera regna ac provinciæ in commune conferant. Est etiam aliquis sermo de matrimonio inter Reginam nostram et Carolum Austriacum; sed in omni tractatione semper cavetur de religione. Itaque nisi Carolus papismo renuntiare velit, non habet hic, quod speret. Scotia jam in novos motus incidit. Henricus, nuper Scotiæ rex, uti te audivisse existimo, decimo Februarii elapsi in horto quodam hospitio suo, quod extra aulam habebat, adjacente inventus est mortuus. De genere mortis nondum convenit apud omnes. Alii dicunt, incensis vasis aliquot pulveris tormentarii, quæ sub cubiculo, in quo dormiebat, ex industria reposita fuerant, ædes eversas atque ipsum in hortum proximum projectum fuisse. Alii vero, intempesta nocte vi extractum e cubiculo, et postea strangulatum, ac tum demum incenso pulvere ædes disjectas fuisse, affirmant. Hujus cædis apud omnes suspectus fuit comes quidam nomine Bothwellius. Huic comiti, postquam uxorem legitimam interveniente auctoritate archiepiscopi S. Andreæ repudiasset, 15 Maii nupsit Scotiæ Regina, atque eundem ex comite Orchadum ducem creavit. Paulo ante hoc matrimonium omnes fere regni proceres, quum nullam in cædem Regis inquisitionem institui viderent, discesserunt ex aula, et seorsum apud Sterlynum oppidum conventum habuerunt. In hoc conventu certis indiciis nefandam hanc cædem a Bothwellio perpetratam fuisse compertum est. Itaque collecto exercitu ipsum comprehendere satagunt: Bothwellius vero dat se in fugam; sed quo profugerit, adhuc nescitur. Reginam alii aiunt obsideri in arce quadam; alii vero in arce Edinburgensi, tamquam necis mariti consciam, captivam detineri asserunt. Quomodocunque sit, infames illæ nuptiæ non possunt non in aliquam diram tragœdiam desinere. Sed de his omnibus exspectamus in dies certiora, de quibus efficiam brevi ut cognoscas.

De persecutionibus Flandriæ nihil scribo, quod eas vos non latere existimem. Multa apud nos jactata sunt de obsessa Geneva, sed spero vana esse. Dominus Jesus pietatem tuam nobis et ecclesiæ incolumem conservet! Londini, 21 Junii, 1567.

Deditissimus tibi in Domino,
EDMUNDUS GRINDALLUS,
Episcop. London.

INSCRIPTIO.
Reverendo in Christo D. Henrico
Bullingero, Tigurinæ ecclesiæ
ministro fidelissimo, et fratri
in Christo carissimo.
Tiguri.

EPISTOLA LXXX.

JOHANNES PARKHURSTUS AD HENRICUM BULLINGERUM.

17 Octobris abs te literas accepi, item 16 Maii; pro quibus et pro doctissimis tuis in Esaiam homiliis ago gratias quam possum maximas. Superiore æstate obiit Nicolaus Carvilius, initio hujus mensis Robertus Beamundus, Collegii S. Trinitatis in academia Cantabrigiensi præses. Illi præivere; nos, cum Domino visum fuerit, sequemur.

Johannes Neale princeps, et maximæ auctoritatis apud barbaros et inurbanos Hybernos, non obstante jurejurando, contra nostram Reginam seditionem movit. Toto hoc anno ab armis non quievit. Nuper in conflictu occisus est. Jam spes est, rudes illos et inhumanos et spoliis solum viventes humaniores et urbaniores futuros.

Occiso Henrico Scotiæ Rege, Regina nupsit comiti Bothwelliæ, qui non ita pridem creatus est dux Orchadum. Uxor ejus adhuc vivit, femina nobilissima et optima, ut audio. Divortium, interveniente papæ auctoritate, factum est. Proceres Reginam in ordinem coegerunt, et tamen humanissime tractant, non obliti (ut decet) debitæ obedientiæ. Dux nescio quo aufugit, invisus fere omnibus, eo quod suum regem tam crudeliter occiderit: quibus consentientibus id fecerit, non scribam; sed fama mira et horrenda divulgat:

Fama, malum quo non aliud velocius ullum,
Tam ficti pravique tenax, quam nuntia veri.

Principes Scotiæ aliquot habent cohortes, et in omnibus vexillis sive insigniis hanc habent pictam imaginem. Pingitur viridis et perpulchra arbor, sub qua jacet vir procerus et nudus, et fune strangulatus: prope hunc nudus juvenis multis confossus vulneribus. Deinde pingitur puerulus corona aurea redimitus, genibus flexis, manibus in altum sublatis, et hæc verba 'scripta ab ejus ore promanantia, "Domine, miserere mei, et patris mei sanguinem vindica!" Per hæc designantur rex, famulus, filius. Non possum plura. Urgent negotia. Festinat tabellio. Cetera tibi Rodolphus Gualterus.

Scripsissem Wolphio, Lavatero, Simlero, Wonlichio, Froschovero, Julio; at non licet: utinam liceret! Illi in bonam partem interpretentur. Alias scribam. Vale. Saluta amicos meos omnes. Raptim. Ludhamiæ, 31 Julii, 1567.

Tuus,

JOHANNES PARKHURSTUS,

Nor.

INSCRIPTIO.
Cl. viro D. Henrico Bullingero.
Tiguri.

EPISTOLA LXXXI.

EDMUNDUS GRINDALLUS AD HENRICUM BULLINGERUM.

SALUTEM in Christo Servatore. Res Scotiæ, de quibus superioribus meis literis promisi me plenius scripturum, sic se nunc habent. Proceres regni, offensi matrimonio Reginæ Scotiæ cum Bothwellio illo regicida, circa finem Junii elapsi exercitum satis numerosum collegerunt. Bothwellius, qui etiam milites collegerat, quum se imparem videret, cum quatuor aut quinque navibus fugit ad Orchades insulas. Regina dedidit se suis proceribus, qui illam ad arcem quandam munitissimam in medio lacu (qui Levinus dicitur) sitam, ubi adhuc custoditur, deduxere: post aliquot dies Regina solenni publico instrumento dignitatem suam regiam principi filio resignavit. Circa finem Julii sequentis princeps coronatus est Rex Scotiæ: non multo post habitus est conventus statuum, in quo hæc quinque sunt decreta: I. D. Jacobum Steuartum, Murriæ seu Moraviæ comitem, de cujus pietate credo me antehac ad te scripsisse, Regis et regni gubernatorem declararunt. II. Omnia papisticæ religionis exercitia sub gravi pœna interdixerunt. III. Universalis ecclesiarum reformatio instituta. IV. Ministrorum stipendia constabilita sunt atque aucta. V. Postremo cædis regiæ auctores et ministros conquirendos et suppliciis afficiendos fore decreverunt. Regina adhuc sub arctissima custodia asservatur, et sunt qui putant eam custodiam futuram perpetuam. Fama est, in scriniis Bothwellii inventas fuisse literas ipsiusmet Reginæ manu scriptas, in quibus Bothwellium ad necem regis mariti accelerandam hortata est. Quam hoc sit verum, nescio. Nuper missus fuit baro quidam (Grangius nomine) cum quatuor armatis navibus ad Bothwellium persequendum. Jam enim satis constat, illum suis manibus regem strangulasse, et postea supposito atque incenso pulvere tormentario evertisse ædes, ut res videretur fortuita. Ex his facile colligere potes, quanti quamque horribiles motus in illo regno nuper extitere. Interim tamen optima spe ducimur, hæc omnia in maximam evangelicæ doctrinæ propagationem cessura. Johannes Knoxius ad ecclesiam suam Edenburgensem, a qua antea prorsus exulabat, cum magna populi gratulatione nuper rediit.

Hactenus de rebus Scoticis. Res nostræ fere eodem statu sunt, quo fuere, cum D. Wintoniensis atque ego proxime ad te scripsimus. Nondum conquievere omnium animi, sed speramus in dies meliora. Contra Bernates et Genevenses nihil attentatum fuisse superiori æstate, multum gavisi sumus: verebamur enim, ne Sabaudus, adjutus ab Hispanis, aliquid magni contra ipsos moliretur. Salutabis ex me D. Gualterum ac ceteros tuos collegas. Dominus benedicat vobis ac vestris laboribus, tuamque pietatem ecclesiæ suæ quam diutissime incolumem conservet! Londini, 29 Augusti, anno 1567.

Deditissimus tibi in Domino,
EDMUNDUS GRINDALLUS,
Episcop. London.

Quod attinet ad senatus consulta publicis regni comitiis lata, volui etiam brevibus summam eorum ad te scribere, quibus sincera Christi religio stabilitur, et impia papistarum superstitio abrogatur. Ea autem prætermittam, quæ ad civilem regni politiam pertinent, siquidem infinitum esset singula commemorare; imo non necessarium, tibi præsertim, quem eadem omnia satis scire mihi persuasum habeo.

Primo autem non solum omnes impiæ papistarum traditiones et ceremoniæ tolluntur, sed ea etiam tyrannis, quam papa ipse multis his seculis in ecclesia exercuit, prorsus abrogatur; cautumque est, ut omnes illum pro ipso antichristo et perditionis filio, de quo Paulus loquitur, in posterum agnoscant.

II. Missa tanquam execranda abominatio et diabolica cœnæ Dominicæ prophanatio abrogatur; ac interdicitur, ne quis in toto Scotiæ regno eam vel celebret vel audiat: quod si quis secus fecerit, prima vice omnia ejus bona, tam mobilia, ut appellant, quam immobilia, in fiscum referuntur, et ipsi legis violatores dant pœnas arbitrio magistratus, in cujus jurisdictione deprehensi fuerint. Secunda vice exilio multantur, tertia capite puniuntur.

III. Omnia illa senatus consulta, quibus auctoritas papæ anteactis tenebrarum temporibus vel constituebatur, vel constituta confirmabatur, rescinduntur.

IV. Coronatio Regis confirmatur, propterea quod Regina, mater ejus, sponte sua imperium deposuerat, eumque in regem creari literis suis mandaverat.

V. D. Jacobus, Moraviæ comes, in regni (ut loquuntur) regentem eligitur, et illi potestas conceditur, ut nomine Regis rempublicam administret, imperetque donec Rex ipse ad 17 ætatis annum pervenerit: id quod etiam jubente Regina et annorum numerum præscribente factum est.

VI. Formula jurisjurandi præscribitur, quod in posterum reges omnes præstabunt, eo quo creantur tempore. Promittent enim et sancte jurabunt, se pro viribus operam daturos, ut christiana religio, quæ hodie per totum regnum prædicatur, sincere retineatur, neve ullis papistarum ceterorumque hæreticorum traditionibus, quæ ipsius puritati repugnant, contaminetur.

VII. Continetur ratio concedendorum beneficiorum his, qui ministerii officio fungi debent. Illi enim, ad quos patronatus jus hæreditario jure pertinet, aliquem ecclesiæ repræsentabunt, quem si ecclesia diligenti facta examinatione dignum deprehenderit, admittet: sin minus, rejiciet, et alium illo digniorem ad illud officium deliget.

VIII. In judices, scribas, notarios, publicos apparitores, et lictores nulli eliguntur, qui non prius religionem christianam professi fuerint.

IX. Tertiæ decimarum solis verbi Dei ministris solvuntur tantisper dum, morientibus veteribus beneficiorum possessoribus, beneficiis ipsis in solidum frui possint.

X. Ad instituendam juventutem in bonis literis et moribus nemo prius admittitur, quam religioni subscripserit.

XI. Ministris potestas conceditur, ut verbum Dei sincere prædicent, sacramenta administrent legitime, et vitia ac corruptos populi mores acriter vituperent.

XII. Patroni eorum beneficiorum, quibus prius sacrificuli in collegiis fruebantur, possunt eadem nunc convertere ad eos alendos, quos vulgato nomine Bursarios dicimus, in quorum numerum eligi solent juvenes, qui, amicis et facultatibus destituti, operam literis aliter dare non possunt.

XIII. Pœna in fornicatores statuitur. Nam prima vice 80 libras solvunt, aut 8 dierum spatio carceribus mandantur, ubi solo pane et cervisia tenuissima pascuntur. Postea, quum publice habentur nundinæ, in loco eminentiore constituuntur, ut ab omnibus facile conspici possint. Hic manent ab hora decima in duodecimam, detectis capitibus, ferreis circulis religati. Secunda vice 130 libras solvunt, aut 16 dies carceri mancipantur; panis et aqua pro cibo. Postea in publicis nundinis, ut prius, spectandi populo proponuntur, ita tamen ut rasa sint eorum capita. Tertia autem solvunt 200 libras, aut triplicato dierum spatio incarcerantur. Eo autem tempore absoluto, in aquam profundam ter demersi, urbe vel parœcia perpetuo exulant. His pœnis subjicitur tum vir, tum femina, quoties peccare eos contigerit.

XIV. Incestus capitalis pœna constituitur. De adulterio autem nihil in comitiis constitutum est; sed ejus rei ratio in proxima comitia dilata est.

XV. Justæ declarantur nuptiæ inter personas in secundo gradu contractæ, cujusmodi sunt duorum fratrum aut sororum.

INSCRIPTIO.
Reverendo in Christo, D. Henrico Bullingero, Tigurinæ ecclesiæ ministro fidelissimo, et fratri in Christo carissimo.
Tiguri.

EPISTOLA LXXXII.

EDMUNDUS GRINDALLUS AD HENRICUM BULLINGERUM.

SALUS in Christo. Credo me omnes pietatis tuæ literas accepisse, pro quibus tibi maximas gratias ago. Superioribus nundinis Francfordianis non respondi, quia initio quadragesimæ tertiana febre laborabam, cui successit ocularis morbus; at nunc gratia Domini bene convalui.

Gratulor vobis et Genevensibus tam quietum rerum statum; quod plane miraculi instar esse potest. Habetis enim ex omni parte adversarios infensissimos.

Nostra controversia vestiaria, de qua scribis, ad tempus deferbuerat; sed hyeme elapsa recruduit, idque opera quorundam qui magis fervidi sunt, quam aut docti aut pia prudentia præditi. Cives Londinenses nonnulli infimi ordinis, adjunctis quatuor aut quinque ministris, qui neque judicio neque eruditione pollebant, apertam defectionem a nobis fecerunt, atque aliquando in domibus privatis, aliquando in agris, nonnunquam etiam et in navibus, suos habuerunt conventus, et sacramenta administrarunt. Sed et ministros seniores et diaconos suo more ordinarunt; quosdam etiam, qui ab eorum ecclesia defecerant, excommunicarunt. D. Laurentium Humfredum, Sampsonem, Leverum et alios, qui multa passi sunt pro libertate circa res adiaphoras obtinenda, quia sese cum illis non conjungunt, pro semipapistis jam habent, neque illorum conciones audire suis permittunt. Qui hujus sunt factionis numero sunt fere ducenti; sed feminarum quam virorum major est numerus. Consiliarii regii præcipua hujus factionis capita nuper carceribus mandarunt, et hoc agunt, ut hæc secta tempestive coerceatur.

De rebus Gallicis et Belgicis scio vos subinde certiores fieri. In Scotia novæ turbæ nuper exortæ sunt. Secundo Maii elapsi Regina, quæ in arce sita in lacu Levino captiva detinebatur, corruptis custodibus evasit ex carcere, et ad arcem Hamiltoniam confugit, atque ibi milites collegit. 13 Maii regni gubernator (regentem vocant), collecto exercitu, cum iis qui a Regina stabant levi prœlio conflixit. Fugatus est exercitus Reginæ. Desiderati sunt circiter centum: ceteris fugientibus, qui ad unum deleri potuerant, parcitum est. Ipsa vero, paucis comitata, confugit ad mare, et conscensa parva navicula angustum fretum, quod est ad Solvei fluminis ostia, trajecit, et ad civitatem Carliolensem, quæ est in nostro regno, pervenit. In arce illius urbis adhuc manet, sed tamen sub honorifica custodia. Regina Scotiæ petit a nobis auxilia, ut restituatur in regnum, quod metu (ut ait) coacta filio resignavit; aut saltem ut in Gallias tuto mittatur, ut ibi amicorum fidem exploret. E contra proceres Scotiæ petunt per legatos, ut ipsis denuo ad custodiam tradatur, indignum asserentes, ut iterum regnet, quæ et regis mariti necem procuravit, et postea cum ipso regicida Bothwellio, cui adhuc uxor in vivis erat, adulterinis nuptiis sese conjunxit. Quid de istis statuetur, adhuc nescimus. Dominus omnia in bonum vertat! Quidquid erit, si Dominus vitam dederit, efficiam ut cognoscas. D. Gualterum et ceteros fratres oro ut meo nomine salutes. Dominus te conservet, vir vere in Domino reverende, et frater carissime! Londini, 9 Junii, 1568.

Deditissimus tibi in Domino,

EDM. GRINDALLUS,
Episcop. London.

Quum istas essem obsignaturus, renunciatum est mihi, ducem Albanum Bruxellis 5 hujus mensis comitem Egmondanum et Hornum ac circiter viginti alios nobiles capitali supplicio affecisse. Apparet hominem natura satis ferocem, prœlio illo cum Ludovico Nassoviensi prope Groningam infeliciter commisso, irritatum eo crudelitatis descendisse. Amisit autem in eo prœlio Albanus Hispanorum (ut fertur) duo millia, et Wallonum (ut vocant) tria. Occubuerant etiam ibi comes ab Orenburg, et Hispani duces insignes nonnulli. Egmondanus monachum confessorem admisit, et crucem in ipso supplicii loco adoravit. Comes ab Horn hæc omnia respuit, et in vera confessione mortuus est.

INSCRIPTIO.

Reverendo in Christo, D. Henrico
  Bullingero, ecclesiæ Tigurinæ
  ministro fidelissimo et fratri
  carissimo.

EPISTOLA LXXXIII.

JOHANNES PARKHURSTUS AD RODOLPHUM GUALTERUM ET HENRICUM BULLINGERUM.

Scripsi literas ad vos in finem Februarii: spero esse redditas. 11 Maii Bullingeri et Lavateri literas accepi, tuas vero, Gualtere, 18 ejusdem mensis. Regina Scotiæ e carcere evasit circa idem tempus. Cruentum subito commissum est prœlium inter papistas Reginæ amicos, et protestantes regis fautores. Illa, cum bellum ferveret, in colle celeri equo insidens omnia oculis lustrabat. Sed cum tandem videret victoriam cessisse D. Jacobo et suis, aufugit cum paucis in Angliam. Maluit enim se Anglis committere, quam suis Scotis: et credo tutius fuisse. Agit jam Carleoli, in loco satis munito, brevi in medio Angliæ commoratura, ut audio.

13 Julii D. Gulielmus Turnerus, medicus bonus et vir optimus, Londini obiit. Leverus in ejus funere est concionatus. Scripsi unicas has ad vos literas, et breves quidem; dubito enim, utrum hæ in tantis rerum tumultibus ad vestras manus sint perventuræ. Quare plures in præsentia scribere nolui.

Salutate meo nomine amicos meos omnes, et præcipue D. Simlerum, Lavaterum, Wolphium, Hallerum, Wickium, Wonlichium, Zuinglium, etc. Bene valete. Raptim. Ludhamiæ, 4 Augusti, 1568.

Vester quantus quantus est,

JOHANNES PARKHURSTUS, Nor.

INSCRIPTIO.
*Doctissimis viris et integerrimis
amicis, D. Rod. Gualtero et
D. Henrico Bullingero.
Tiguri.*

EPISTOLA LXXXIV.

RICARDUS COXUS AD HENRICUM BULLINGERUM.

Salve in Christo Jesu, mi Bullingere, frater carissime et in ecclesia Dei jubar fulgidissimum. Habeo apud me ternas literas præterito anno scriptas: datæ fuere primæ quidem 6 Januarii 1568; alteræ 20 Martii 1568; tertiæ 24 Augusti 1568. Ad hæc libri tui de Origine erroris penes me sunt ex tuo dono. Quod literis tuis suavissimis et pietatem spirantibus hactenus non responderim, malo nullas causas in medium afferre, quam eas quidem tenues et inanes. Omissis igitur causationibus, magnas ago Henrico meo gratias, tum quod me suis literis tam frequenter invisere sit dignatus, tum quod tam piis donis me beare perpetuo pergit. Imo ex animo Deo opt. max. gratiam habeo maximam, qui te veritatis suæ propagandæ columnam solidissimam statuerit. Longævum precor te faciat D. Deus noster ad gloriam ipsius et ecclesiæ commodum, quæ jam in arctum cogitur, et undique premitur; de qua etiam adversarii triumphum meditantur et exspectant avidissime. Sed "quare fremuerunt gentes, etc.?" Confidentissime sperandum, quod Deus non deseret suos in finem. Dissipet Dominus consilia illorum Helvetiorum, qui tantis animis a vobis discesserunt ad Gallos! Assyrii terribiliter minati fuerunt Hierosolymitis, sed cum magno suo malo. Si Deus pro nobis, quis contra nos? Res nostræ (sit Deo gratia!) satis adhuc sunt pacatæ, nisi quod Cananei inter nos incredibiliter densantur, exspectantes in dies quando loquetur asinus.

Vivit adhuc noster Abelus, optimus vir, sed suo calculo gravissime vexatus. Magna est seges piorum adolescentium in academiis nostris. Dominus, speramus, augebit operarios, qui mittantur in messem suam; quod singulare nostrum esse debet solatium, qui brevi exspectamus solutionem nostram, ut animæ cœlo reddantur, et corpora terræ tradantur.

Vale, carissime frater, mutuisque apud Deum precibus nos juvemus. Resalutabis meum Julium, virum mihi non incognitum. 1568.

Tui studiosissimus,

RICARDUS COX, Eliensis.

INSCRIPTIO.

Carissimo in Christo fratri, D. Henrico Bullingero, ecclesiæ Tigurinæ pastori dignissimo.

EPISTOLA LXXXV.

EDMUNDUS GRINDALLUS AD HENRICUM BULLINGERUM.

SALUS in Christo. Quod rarius ad pietatem tuam scribo, carissime D. Bullingere, imputabis præteritis bellis et interrupto commercio Belgico. Libros tuos de Origine errorum et Conciliis superiori anno accepi, pro quibus etiam magnas gratias ago.

Dissidia illa in ecclesia nostra Londino-belgica, de quibus ad me scripsisti, per Dei gratiam consopita sunt. Vestrarum ecclesiarum judicia plurimum nobis profuerunt.

In vicino nostro Belgio Albanus plane Phalarismum exercet. Locupletiores omnes, cujuscunque sunt religionis, summo vivunt in discrimine: rapiuntur enim homines in dies ad supplicia, ditiores præsertim, nulla observata juris forma. De rebus Gallicis vos omnia melius nostis. Nos Dei benignitate in magna tranquillitate sumus, utut nobis minetur Albanus. Commercium Belgicum hac ratione interruptum fuit. Superiore hyeme naves Hispaniæ, quæ Albano a papa, mediantibus Genevensibus mercatoribus, pecuniam advehebant, vi tempestatum in nostros portus, quos habemus plurimos et tutissimos, adactæ sunt. Summa erat, credo, 300 millia coronatorum. Hanc summam, quasi divinitus missam, omnibus circumcirca regionibus bello ardentibus, Regina nostra, ut in omnem eventum pecuniam in promtu haberet, voluit ab ipsis mercatoribus mutuo accipere, data cautione sufficienti de sorte et de fœnore suo tempore restituendis: quod apud ceteros principes sæpe in usu fuit. Albanus, hoc audito, fecit omnes nostros mercatores una cum suis navibus et mercibus in Belgio arrestari. Nostri idem fecerunt Hispanis et Belgis. Itaque nunc nostri coguntur Hamburgi, loco non tam commodo, sua commercia exercere, idque non sine damno totius Belgii.

In Scotia nobis vicina omnia, ut prius, geruntur auspiciis pueri regis. Administratio est penes eximium virum, D. Jacobum Stuartum, Moraviæ comitem, avunculum ipsius regis, cui jam ceteri proceres, qui ante repugnabant, sese submiserunt. De religionis negotio apud illos quæstio non fuit; nam utraque pars doctrinam evangelii, tum quum maxime dissidebant, profitebatur, et adhuc profitetur. Scotiæ Regina, quæ adhuc sub satis honorifica et libera custodia apud nos detinetur, hanc Scotiæ gubernationem ratam non habet, et sibi injuriam fieri putat. Sollicitat igitur suos, quantum potest: sed nisi externis auxiliis juvetur, non poterit facile regnum recuperare.

Hæc sunt, quæ de nostris et vicinorum nostrorum rebus hoc tempore scribere volui. D. Hornus, Parkhurstus, Juellus, Coxus, Sandus, Pilkingtonus, omnes recte valent, et me ipsorum nomine, si quando rescriberem, ut tuam pietatem resalutarem rogarunt. Salutato, quæso, ex me D. Rodolphum Gualterum et ceteros tuos symmystas. Commendate nos precibus vestris Domino. Dominus Jesus te nobis et ecclesiæ suæ diu incolumem conservet, frater in Domino colendissime et carissime! Fulhamiæ ad ripam Thamesis, 13 Augusti, 1569.

Tuæ pietati deditissimus in Domino,
EDM. GRINDALLUS,
Episcopus Londinensis.

Frater noster Johannes Abelus ante aliquot menses post longos ex calculo cruciatus hanc vitam cum meliore commutavit.

INSCRIPTIO.

Reverendo in Christo domino, Henrico
Bullingero seniori, ecclesiæ Tigu-
rinæ ministro fidelissimo, et fratri
in Christo carissimo.
       Tiguri.
            Tradantur typographis Tigurinis
                Francofurti ad Mænum.

EPISTOLA LXXXVI.

RICARDUS HILLES AD HENRICUM BULLINGERUM.

Hæc mea sunt, vir eruditissime, quibus mortuo nostro Johanne Abelo tuas ad me 14 Martii proximi præteriti literas pervenisse, unaque cum illis epistolam a D. Rod. Waltero 17 ejusdem mensis unam, ambabus ad me in absentia Johannis Abeli prædicti conscriptis, ad meas manus allatas intelligas. Quam ego ob causam illas et aperui et perlegi literas, literasque cum libris, de quibus in eisdem mentionem feceris, ad quos direxeris dedi. Julii præterea literas 16 Martii anno 1569, quædamque opera separatim obligata ad D. episcopum Sarisberiensem, episcopum Eliensem, episcopumque Wigorniensem, et ad dominum Antonium Cokum consignata, nec nonnullos ad eorum quemque libellos, (quos cum codicibus tradi curavi præfatis hominibus,) accepi. De quibus omnibus te cupio certiorem facere. Tua etiam epistola, 24 Augusti data, est mihi reddita : cumque mihi in eadem et de literis a te ad alios tradendis, ab iisque ad te alias transmittendis, videris agere, ut Abeli amici nostri, qui in Domino mortuus sit, ideoque jam beatus laboribusque liberatus, quos in hoc seculo vivens passus sit, (haud dubito,) vice utar; ego eadem quam potero optime lubenti animo faciam. Quod ad scripta illa, quæ meis prædictis alligata significas, ipsa ego quam primum ad manus meas allata erant ad reverendos episcopos aliosque viros eruditos, ad quos consignaveras, detuli. Dolebat autem certo, cum ex tuis perspexissem, quæ ad Johannem Abelum miseras, te, quamvis in vesica nullis cruciabaris calculis (sicuti ille), perturbatum tamen eodem morbo in renibus, ita ut a die Sti Martini ad 14 Martii 60, quorum aliqui majusculi fuerint, calculos evacuaveris. Gaudeo tamen tibi, quamvis ægerrime illo ægritudinis genere laboraveris, tantam patientiam a divina providentia fore impertitam, quam in finem remansuram a Deo imprecor.

Duos ante annos literas unas ad te misi, quarum materiam ex epistola per quendam ad D. Christoferum Montium Argentinensem scriptam verbatim extraxerim, qua certior fiebat de inferioris Germaniæ, præcipueque de Antverpiæ, statu parum ante ducis de Alva adventum. Quarum literarum secundas ad nundinas quadrigesimales in anno 1568, in literis meis ad te inclusas, (ut ea alicui bibliopolæ Tigurino traderentur quo ad te transferrentur,) misi. Quas quidem literas ad D. Christoferum Montium, quia in tuis 24 Augusti, anno 1569, ne verbum quidem de illis feceris, amissas potius quam ad te apportatas suspicor, ideoque earum secundas in ista mea includo epistola. Cum vero scribis literas istinc ad te, si mea opera ad D. Christoferum Montium adducentur, ad te absque dubio adventuras, reverendum illum Londinensem episcopum Edmundum G. si ejus utar auxilio, multum in illis ad prædictum dominum Christoferum

Montium convehendis posse, raro mihi in istiusmodi rebus posse prodesse. Ego etenim sæpissime, quo tum ad doctorem Christoferum Montium, cum ad te, eorum scripta transferrentur, illis, quamdiu licebat literas per inferiorem transmittere Germaniam, auxilio fore solebam. Nunc tamen per integrum totum annum ne literas quidem ullas ad viros aliquos doctos per inferiorem Germaniam, quæ in superiorem Germaniam Helvetiamve importarentur, ne ibidem aperirentur, misimus; ita ut, necessitate coacti, ut literæ Hamburgum convehentur curamus. Quapropter, donec hæc inter Reginam serenissimam nostram Hispaniæque Regem jamdudum exorta controversia cessaverit, et te et prædictum D. Christoferum Montium perpaucas istinc, præterquam a nundinis Francfordiensibus, literas accepturos opinor.

Gratias tibi ago quod mihi nova, quæ et apud vos in Helvetia et in finibus Galliæ ad Helvetiam spectantibus erant, designaveris. Hic vero nulla jam existunt nova, de quibus certo scribam, præterquam quod duo comites, videlicet Northumbriæ et Westmartiæ, (ut abhinc aliquot ante dies audisse te existimo,) quos regia majestas mense Decembris proximi præteriti coram honorabilibus suis consiliariis sistere jussit, ut seipsos suspectione conspirationis ab illis præconsultatæ adversus religionem et fidem per sacras scripturas probatam, et ex auctoritate Reginæ nostræ serenissimæ 10 abhinc annos ad minimum editam, purgarent, bellum suscitaverunt, ipsique cum aliquot Reginæ subditis episcopatum Dunelmensem, cui Pilkington episcopus præfuit, incolentibus, quos una ad prœlium incitassent, quam impie arma ceperunt. Reliqui tamen subditi in aliis regionis partibus insigni Dei gratia, ut decebat, in officio manebant; pacem coluerunt, et in eadem sub Dei et Reginæ imperio pie vixerunt. Illique qui prope episcopatum Dunelmensem habitaverunt, nobilibus illis viris, quos Regina miserat, in supprimendo isto tumultu officium præstabant. Ac ita comites illos duos totumque eorum exercitum prosequuti sunt, ut comites ipsi equitesque nonnulli qui illos comitabantur in Scotiam fugam ceperunt, ubi a domino Jacobo gubernatore et a nobili quodam de Humeis nuncupato vi capti sunt; ita ut brevi in Angliam adducentur, spero; condigna etiam ibi pœna, quæ eorum facta postulant, plectentur, non dubito. Dum dicti in armis erant impium conatum defendentes, communionum non solum mensas dejiciebant, sacra biblia dilacerabant, libros pios dilaniabant, et homilias impressas pedibus conculcaverunt; sed impiam etiam missam, ut pro viventibus et mortuis sacrificium, rursus erigerunt. Et quo melius fictam suam pietatem tegerent, cruces insigniaque quædam quorundam sanctorum, quos patronos suos et defensores esse crediderunt aut commentiti sunt fore, inter arma extendi fecerunt.

Quod ad amicum nostrum D. R. Walterum, cum Joh. Abelum orabat, ut sibi quantum pannus Anglice cariseus in Anglia valeat, quotque ulnas

Germanicas contineat, istis meis oro intelligas, cariseos nostros diversorum pretiorum diversæque longitudinis existere; communes autem et crassiores 28 vel 30 ulnarum Francfordiensium vel Argentinensium sunt, valetque eorum quisque circa 8 vel 10 coronatos Gallicos: et uniuscujusque dicti panni carisei nuncupati infectio sive tinctio in glasto duos coronatos Gallicos cum dimidio sive 3 constabunt.

Priusquam has literas sigillassem, allata sunt nobis pro certo nova, prædictum dominum Jacobum, Scotiæ gubernatorem, a nobili quodam de familia Hamiltonorum tormento quodam (Germanice *byxe* vocato) percussum et occisum.

Vale in Christo Jesu, mi domine colendissime, qui semper te servet! Amen. Londini, sexto die Februarii, anno 1569, secundum computationem ecclesiæ Anglicanæ. (1570.)

Tuus,
R. H[illes.]

INSCRIPTIO.
Doctissimo viro, domino Henrico
Bullingero, amico mihi caris-
simo, dentur literæ. Tiguri.

EPISTOLA LXXXVII.

EDMUNDUS GRINDALLUS AD HENRICUM BULLINGERUM.

Carissime domine Bullingere, frater honorande, accepi literas tuas 24 Augusti scriptas. Acceperam etiam superiori anno librum tuum de Origine erroris et de Conciliis, quemadmodum in literis meis ad Francofurtenses nundinas autumnales missis fusius scripsi, quas spero te ante aliquot menses accepisse. Jam non possumus literas nostras nisi in utrisque nundinis Francofurtensibus per Hamburgum transmittere, propter occlusa per Albanum itinera. Alioqui nihil mihi dulcius esset, quam tecum sæpius per literas colloqui.

Gratulor tibi ex animo convalescentiam ab infirmitate æstiva, et multum cupio audire de valetudine tua bene confirmata. Si ista æstate post morbum vires tolerabiles recuperare poteris, videtur nobis spem facere, quod te adhuc diutius frui poterimus. Morbus enim sæpenumero est instar pharmaci, seu potius remedii.

Res nostræ jam per Dei gratiam sunt satis pacatæ, sed nuper fuerunt turbatissimæ. Superiore æstate tentatum fuit, ut Thomas Houardus, Norfolciæ dux, Reginæ Scotiæ matrimonio jungeretur; sed Regina nostra, hoc conatu offensa, dictum ducem 11 Septembris in arcem Londinensem conjecit, ubi adhuc captivus detinetur. Initio Novembris duo comites,

Northumbrius scilicet et Westmorlandius, seditionem excitarunt, collecto exercitu, in agro Eboracensi et Dunelmensi, ut falso nominatam catholicam religionem restituerent. Habebant in exercitu 1200 equites et quatuor millia peditum. Putabant ad nomen missæ infinitam multitudinem statim ad se venturam, et exspectabant auxilia ab Albano: statuerant etiam Reginam Scotiæ ex custodia liberare; sed omni ex parte de spe sua deciderunt. Nam Regina Scotiæ in Coventriensem civitatem, quæ est in meditullio regni, recomperta, statim abducta fuit. Domestica auxilia partim hyemis asperitate, partim angustiarum præoccupatione, interclusa fuere. Emissæ etiam naves armatæ, quæ auxilia externa prohiberent. Postea Regina exercitum viginti quatuor millium, equitum et peditum, collegit, cujus aspectum rebellis exercitus sustinere ausus non est. Itaque 16 Decembris rebelles peditem dimiserunt; equites vero ad Scotiæ limites fugerunt, ubi maxima pars sese dedidit, ceteri sibi fuga consuluere. Duo isti comites fugerunt in Scotiam cum centum ex selectioribus. Sed Northumbrius per Scotiæ regentem captus fuit, et adhuc ibi manet captivus. Westmorlandius vero, qui juvenis est et moribus Catilinariis, in locis Scotiæ desertis inter latrones vivit. Ita sine sanguine fuit hæc seditio intra quadraginta dies suppressa, nisi quod quingenti ex illa rebellium factione capitali supplicio postea affecti sunt, et multi adhuc in carceribus detinentur, pari supplicio afficiendi. Rebellis iste exercitus in vexillis suis habebat quinque vulnera (ut vocant), et crucis effigiem cum hac inscriptione, *In hoc signo vinces*. In omnibus templis missas suas faciebant. Biblia vero in nostram linguam versa, quæ in omnibus nostris templis reperiuntur, discerpebant aut comburebant. Episcopi Dunelmensis et omnium pastorum ac ministrorum bona diripiebant: neminem tamen interfecere. D. Pilkingtonus, episcopus Dunelmensis, (Deo ita disponente,) tum temporis Londini valetudinis recuperandæ causa versabatur: alioqui sine dubio in summo vitæ discrimine fuisset. Sed statim post nostros tumultus sedatos tristissima nova ex Scotia accepimus de morte optimi et pientissimi principis Jacobi Stuarti, Scotiæ regentis. Is etenim 23 die Januarii pila tormenti manuarii per imum ventrem transverberatus, post biduum exspiravit. Cum regens eo die (sic enim commissa fuit cædes) in platea oppidi Lithgow nobilibus suis ex more stipatus equitaret, proditor quidam ex familia Hamiltonorum, tormento ex fenestra quadam contra illum librato, illum percussit. Parricida celeri equo conscenso, quem ad posticum domus paratum habebat, effugit, et in arcem quandam se recepit. Metuendum quidem est, ne magnæ mutationes hujus tanti viri mortem sequantur; sed tamen audimus proceres et consiliarios Scotiæ, qui evangelio nomen dedere, magno consensu et constantia religionis et reipublicæ defensionem in se suscipere. Exspectamus in dies certiora. Ex Hispania nuper audivimus, Mauros sive Marranos illos regium exercitum, castris exutum, magna clade affecisse. Albanus classem paratam habet, sed nescitur quid moliatur. Sunt qui putant, illum missurum auxilia in Hispaniam; alii suspicantur, trajecturum exercitum in Scotiam; neque desunt, qui illum in nos aliquid moliri existiment. Nos igitur in omnem eventum classem optime instructam emittimus, ut quo cursum dirigat observetur.

Hæc de rebus nostris et vicinorum nostrorum paullo fusius scribo, ut diuturnum silentium aliqua ex parte compensem. Domini Wintoniensis, Norvicensis, Dunelmensis et Sarisburiensis, omnes recte valent; similiter etiam et Humfredus, Sampsonus et Foxus. Sampsono et Foxo literas tuas superiore die communicavi, qui te officiose resalutant. Salutabis ex me collegium vestrum. Oro ut me meumque ministerium in precibus vestris Domino commendetis. Precor Patrem nostrum cœlestem, ut vobis omnibus, laboribusque vestris, quos quotidie sustinetis, quam amplissime benedicat. Dominus Jesus pietatem tuam nobis et ecclesiæ suæ diu incolumem conservet!

Londini, 11 Februarii, 1569.

Deditissimus tibi in Domino,
EDM. LONDON.

INSCRIPTIO.
Domino Henrico Bullingero seniori, ecclesiæ Tigurinæ ministro fidelissimo, et fratri in Christo carissimo.
Tiguri.

EPISTOLA LXXXVIII.

RICARDUS COXUS AD HENRICUM BULLINGERUM.

Resaluto te ex animo, frater in Christo dilectissime. Literæ tuæ datæ secundo Martii, qui proxime præteriit, non prius ad manus nostras venerunt, quam advenisset 22 mensis Junii: id quod accidere solet vel tanto locorum intervallo vel tabellariorum negligentia. Acceptas tandem studiose et cum gaudio perlegi, quod mihi significarunt te commoda frui valetudine, licet senem, et multis laboribus defatigatum, ægritudinibusque debilitatum. Libros tuos et in Danielem et in Esaiam (in quibus subinde non sine pia delectatione versor) libenti animo suscepi; pro quibus tibi magnam habeo gratiam, nec minus omnes pietatis studiosi pro istis ipsis tibi plurimum debere agnoscunt. Germanicas tuas conciones, cum ad manus meas pervenerint, vel meo vel alieno Marte intelligere conabor. Jam vero, mi Henrice, cum hactenus per tot annos usus te sit Deus optimus maximus pro suo instrumento ad magnam ecclesiæ suæ utilitatem, perseverandum est tibi in ecclesiæ Christi propugnatione ad finem vitæ, quantum per ætatem licet. Multa restant adhuc antichristi capita exscindenda, quæ subinde negotium nobis facessunt; in quibus exscindendis utinam operam tuam serio collocares! Contendit antichristus, nixus suæ ecclesiæ et suorum conciliorum auctoritate, fidem non esse servandam hæreticis; nimirum quos ille hæreticos esse judicat. Deinde auctoritatem sibi arrogat, subditos a fide et obedientia suorum principum et magistratuum revocandi et retrahendi atque absolvendi; aliisque principibus mandat, ut pios magistratus invadant, devastent, spolient, omnique dominandi jure exuant: uti etiam superiori mense constitit ex bulla papistica in nostram Angliam clam submissa. Denique sunt apud nos non infimæ sortis papistæ, qui nervis omnibus contendunt, ut sibi suisque conscientiis vivere permittantur, utque nulla ratio suæ religionis a quoquam exigatur. Clam interim multa cadunt nefaria, et exemplo pessimo piis sunt offendiculo. In his tribus capitibus si operam tuam posueris, et Christo et ecclesiæ rem feceris gratissimam. Crescit adhuc (non sine dolore narro) schisma de vestibus sacerdotum inter purioris notæ homines. Deus tandem det, ut idem sentiamus omnes!

Dominus Jesus te servet cum tuis vestraque inclyta civitate! In Domino gaudeamus, mutuisque precibus juvemus.

E Tusculo meo Eliensi, 10 Julii, 1570.

Tuus in Christo frater,

RICARDUS COX, Elien.

INSCRIPTIO.
Fratri meo in Christo cariss.
domino Henrico Bullingero,
ecclesiæ Tigurinæ pastori
dignissimo.

EPISTOLA LXXXIX.

JACOBUS PILKINGTONUS AD HENRICUM BULLINGERUM.

JESUS! Objurgatrices tuas literas, datas 2 Martii, quod tam diu ad te non scripserim, reverende in Christo mi pater, recepi 29 Junii. Perge porro quod cœpisti; instiga, stimula, et tandem vi saltem aliquid extorquebis. Meliora sunt vulnera diligentis, etc. Tardus et rarus ad scribendum accedo, sed pudorem omnem non abjeci; nec adeo memoria vestri apud me refriguit, quin recte quod Psalmista de Jerusalem, id ego de felici vestro Tiguro canam: "Si non meminero tui, Jerusalem, in principio lætitiæ meæ, oblivioni detur dextera mea."

Audivit prudentia tua, licet sero, sicut scribis, de turbis nostris, quæ aspere et subito in nos irruere; et etiam, quam bene sunt consopitæ; sed utinam extinctæ liceret dicere!

In proximis meis ad te literis, Reginam Scotorum ad nos confugisse narravi, et statum nostrum cum populo Lais contuli. Verebar ne vobis eveniret, quod illis contigit; et quod verebar, evenit. Comites Northumb. et Westmor. inter quos medius ego habito, rebellionem parantes, e somno nos concitarunt; et quamdiu poterant, summa cum vi persequebantur. Religioni et ministris singulis vim omnem intentabant. Dominus tamen nos omnes ex ore leonum eripuit, illæsos quidem corpore, etsi fortunis omnibus exutos et bonis spoliatos. Miraris forte, unde hoc evenit: mundus non patitur duos soles, nedum regnum duas reginas aut religiones. Lovanienses nostri bullas papales impetrarunt, ut populum ab obedientia regiæ majestati debita absolverent: qui ad ecclesias et preces nostras non amplius convenirent, illorum synagogæ reconciliarentur; et peccatorum omnium veniam etiam neglecto purgatorio consequerentur, qui istis se submitterent. Multorum animis hæ impietates sic insident, ut an unquam eradicari poterunt, dubitem. Nonnulli his de rebus in carcere detinentur: multi fugerunt, sed maxima pars latitat, occasionem novorum tumultuum exspectans avide. Ex nobilioribus aliqui se his conjunxerunt: sed bonus noster Dominus eos omnes spe sua frustratus est, et Elizabetham nostram nobis conservavit, et conservabit diu, quod omnes boni tum sperant, tum optant. Northumbrius, in Scotiam fugiens, in carcere illic detinetur, cum nonnullis aliis ejusdem factionis. Westmor. exul ibidem vagatur cum aliquot sui similibus. In Flandria alii confugiunt, opem petituri, qui sibi sunt conscii. Sed Dominus non deerit suis. Jacobus, Regis Scotorum tutor et in regno secundus, insidiis cujusdam Scoti, quem morti condemnatum servavit, interemtus est; quod multos bonos male habet: nam erat vir bonus in omnes et Deum timens. Melior Scotorum pars Reginæ nostræ favent: ceteros ferro et flamma persequimur.

Nos gregi nostro sumus restituti Dei beneficio; et quamvis omnium animi non sint tam pacati, quam optarem, est tamen et hic et in Scotia, cum legibus exercendis, tum religioni locus libere relictus. Vestris precibus Dominus dabit meliora. Londinensis episcopus jam factus est archiepiscopus Eboracensis, mihi proximus; quod quidem ego serio gaudeo.

Thomas Leverus quam primum Londinum venerit, aliquam collectionem in subsidium bonæ nostræ matrisfamilias faciet et transmittet. Ego jam mitterem, si quo modo perferri poterit, intelligerem. Mortuo jam diu bono Abelo nostro, communi nuncio, quomodo hæ ad te devenient, ignoro. Vale, mi Domine, cum omnibus symmystis tuis. Felix sit Tigurum! 9 Julii, 1570.

Tuus in Christo,
JACOBUS PILKINGTONUS.

INSCRIPTIO.
Reverendo in Christo et doctiss.
  viro, D. Henrico Bullingero,
  Tigurinorum pastori digniss.

EPISTOLA XC.

EDMUNDUS GRINDALLUS AD HENRICUM BULLINGERUM.

SALUTEM in Christo. Accepi homilias tuas Germanicas, pro quibus gratias ago. Ego adhuc Germanice scripta satis intelligo; nam multum laboravi in lingua vestra addiscenda; sed loquendi usum amisi.

Julii Santerentiani pensionem ante mensem tradidi Ricardo Hilles, ut ad proximas nundinas Francfordienses Froschovero persolvendam curaret. Literas meas, quas ad vernas nundinas misi, spero te accepisse. Interea temporis visum est serenissimæ Reginæ nostræ, me ab hac urbe ad Eboracensem sedem, ubi res non adeo bene constitutæ sunt, transferre. In agro Eboracensi et Dunelmensi (ut nuper scripsi) orta est illa superiori hyeme nobilium et rusticorum seditio ad papatum restituendum. Fuerunt quidem ibi multi extremo supplicio affecti: nihilominus audio vulgi animos valde esse exulceratos, et novis motibus inhiare. Quid me igitur ibi maneat, ignoro. Sed si novæ turbæ ibi oriantur, fieri non potest, quin ego cum carissimo fratre D. Pilkingtono, Dunelmensi episcopo, in summo periculo versabimur. Verum hæc nihil me movent: voluntas Domini fiat! Hæc tamen eo commemoro, ut nos et ministerium nostrum tanto ardentius in precibus tuis Domino commendes.

Ego quum hæc scriberem, ad iter Eboracum versus capessendum pene eram accinctus: non potui igitur fusius hoc tempore ad te scribere. Sunt res nostræ, Dei beneficio, satis tranquillæ. Initio superioris Maii exercitus noster Scotiam ingressus est duce comite Sussexiæ, ut rebelles nostros et eorum in Scotia receptatores persequeretur. Nostri intra paucos dies arces in Scotia 50 supposito pulvere tormentario everterunt, et pagos 300 nemine resistente exusserunt. Scotia jam satis est pacata; sed hoc fortassis ideo fit, quia Regina nostra ad Scotiæ fines exercitum alit: nam alioqui qui stant a partibus Reginæ Scotiæ, quæ adhuc apud nos est in custodia, videntur res novas molituri. Nunc prævalent regii, et comitem de Lenox, avum pueri regis, in regem elegerunt: qui religionis et Regis defensionem in se suscepit. Distat Eboracum ab hac urbe 160 milliaria nostratia: non potero igitur tam commode literas ad te mittere, quam solebam. Scribam tamen subinde, etiamsi tardius ad te perferentur, et tuas avidissime exspectabo. Dominus Jesus pietatem tuam nobis et ecclesiæ suæ incolumem conservet, frater vere in Domino venerande et carissime! Londini, ultimo Julii, 1570.

Tuus in Christo,

EDMUNDUS EBORACENSIS.

Oro, ut collegas tuos meo nomine salutes, et nominatim D. Rodolphum Gualterum.

INSCRIPTIO.
Reverendo in Christo D. Henrico Bullingero seniori, Tigurinæ ecclesiæ ministro fideliss. et fratri carissimo. Tiguri.

EPISTOLA XCI.

JOHANNES JUELLUS AD HENRICUM BULLINGERUM.

S. Pl. in Christo. Pergratæ visæ mihi sunt literæ tuæ, mi pater et domine in Christo colendissime, vel quod a te essent, cui ego uni omnia tribuo, vel quod submorosæ et querulæ viderentur, et officium meum requirerent. Equidem agnosco culpam et peto veniam: sic enim agere satius est, quam summo jure experiri; tametsi non dubitem esse quo me defendam, quamvis apud severissimum judicem ageretur. Primum enim procul absum Londino: deinde Jo. Abelus, communis rerum nostrarum procurator, excessit e vita: postremo turbæ istæ Belgicæ aliquot jam annos ita impediunt itinera, ut neque nostri mercatores Antverpiam commeare possint, neque Antverpiani ad nos. Literæ autem nostræ sæpe in itinere relinquuntur, sæpe auferuntur alio, sæpe redeunt, sæpe pereunt: et quid in has ipsas quas nunc scribo casurum sit, Deus viderit. Hæc certe causa facit, ut et infrequentius quam velim et parcius et cautius ad te scribam.

Quicquid est, gaudeo res vestras eo esse loco, quo scribis. Deus vobis mittat auxilium de sancto, et vos de Sione tueatur! Vobis enim inhiant hostes hoc tempore, nec minus feroces, nec minus multi quam nobis. Videtur enim jam antichristus prorsus omnem jecisse aleam, et orbem terrarum seditionibus, tumultibus, bellis, furoribus, ignibus, incendiis miscuisse. Videt jam conclamatum esse, et sibi suisque exitium atque interitum imminere. Itaque id nunc agit miser, ut ne ignobiliter aut obscure pereat. Pereat ergo sane memoria eorum cum sonitu.

Quod vulgo apud vos obscuris rumoribus ferebatur de mutatione status nostri, nihil erat. Nam et Regina nostra Dei opt. max. beneficio imperium tenet, et religio eo loco est, quo fuit, quoque volumus. Pontificii tamen nostri, suasore atque impulsore papa Pio, omnia sibi sumere proposuerant. Sed benedictus sit Deus noster, pater Domini nostri Jesu Christi, quod dum quærunt alios perdere ipsi pereunt! Duo quidem comites nostrates, et juvenes, et fatui, et obærati, et perditi, quibus alea magis quam religio curæ esset, sub extremum autumnum in ultimis Angliæ finibus aliquot millia rusticorum conscripserunt. Ea freti multitudine, edicta etiam ausi sunt publicare homines levissimi, velle se, nescio quos, (neque enim quenquam nominabant,) e sacro Reginæ senatu submovere et avitam religionem restituere. Quid quæris? Non mora. Eriguntur in castris altaria, comburuntur sacra biblia: dicuntur missæ. Post aliquot hebdomadas mittitur in illos comes Sussexius, vir bonus et strenuus et magni consilii, cum exigua manu. Illi se paulatim recipere et retrocedere. Sussexius insequi prudenter atque acriter, et urgere cedentes. Ad extremum miseri, cum hostes infestis signis sibi viderent imminere, homines imperiti rerum, qui hostem nunquam prius viderant, non ausi experiri fortunam belli, perculsi conscientia sceleris, amentes et cœci, destituunt exercitum sine duce, et relictis castris, clam noctu cum paucis profugiunt in Scotiam. Habes historiam nostrarum rerum, quarum vel meminisse non possum sine rubore: pudet enim fuisse unquam in Anglia nostra vel tam ignavos vel tam fatuos. Regina nostra per suum oratorem repetit e Scotia perduelles. Sunt hoc tempore in Scotia factiones duæ. Alii enim puram religionem et evangelium colunt, et pendent a nobis; alii abhorrent a pietate, et papismo potius student, et inclinant ad Gallum. Horum princeps est dux Hameltonius, vir, uti aiunt, nomine magis multo pollens, quam consilio. Cogitur senatus; cœptum est deliberari: nostri reddendos censent, Hameltonii negant. Vincunt postremo Hameltonii. Nostri impatientes injuriæ armant militem, et in mediam usque progressi Scotiam, nemine repugnante, arces oppidaque ducis Hameltonii hostili more populantur. Nostri vero illi, quos dixi, egregii bellatores, cum se in Scotia tenere amplius non possent, profugerunt in Flandriam. Ibi nunc hærent apud ducem Albanum, et tumultuantur quantum possunt.

Omnes istas turbas nobis dedit sanctissimus pater. Is enim pro sua sanctitate et sapientia submiserat in Angliam ad suos bullam (aureamne dicam an plumbeam?) magni ponderis. Ea menses aliquot inter paucos obscure ferebatur. Significabat videlicet bonus pater, Elizabetham reginam Angliæ non esse; sibi enim illius instituta non placere: itaque mandare se, ne quis illam agnoscat principem, neve illi obtemperet imperanti; qui secus fecerit, illum se omnibus diris devovere atque exitio dedere. O sanctam sedem! Sic, scilicet, Petrus olim factitabat. Erant alioqui quibus ista sacrosancta videbantur : ceteri non ita flexibiles erant ad omnes nutus pontificis, nec ita didicerant evangelium. Mitto ad te exemplar illius putidissimæ atque inanissimæ bullæ, ut intelligas, quam illa bestia solemniter hoc tempore atque impudenter insaniat. Proximis istis diebus novæ turbæ cœptæ sunt in Norfolchia: sed auctores statim primo quoque tempore capti sunt et conjecti in carceres.

Regina Scotiæ et patriæ profuga asservatur, uti scis, apud nos; satis illa quidem honorifice, sed ita tamen, ut turbas ciere non possit. Hæc ea est cui papa Pius non tantum Scotiam, sed etiam Angliam despondet: sperat enim feminam catholicam, mariti carnificem, atque adulteram, ad restituendum papismum magnum pondus allaturam. Nos armamus classem, et militem habemus in procinctu. Ecclesia nostra ceteroqui, Dei beneficio, tranquilla est. D. Grindallus factus est archiepiscopus Eboracensis; D. Sandus, qui ante fuerat Vigorniensis, nunc factus est episcopus Londinensis. Parkhurstus Norvicensis vivit et valet: illum ego sexennium jam totum nunquam vidi. Deus te quam diutissime conservet incolumem ad usum evangelii atque ecclesiæ suæ!

Saluta meo nomine D. Gualterum, D. Simlerum, D. Lavaterum, D. Zuinglium, D. Vickium, D. Hallerum, et Bullingeros tuos, quos ego amo in Domino. Ex itinere: nunc enim obeo provinciam meam, 7 Augusti, 1570.

Tuus in Christo,
JO. JUELLUS,
Episcopus Sarisburiensis.

INSCRIPTIO.
Doctissimo clarissimoque viro, D. Henrico Bullingero, pastori ecclesiæ Tigurinæ dignissimo, tradantur hæ. Tiguri.

EPISTOLA XCII.

JACOBUS LETHEUS AD HENRICUM BULLINGERUM.

Quod nihil hactenus literarum, vir doctissime, dominus meus D. Henricus Denneius ad te dederit, qui 13 kal. Junii, dum Tiguri suavissima tua consuetudine frueretur, tibi ultro pollicitus est se, si quid novi, quod scriptione dignum videretur, Genevæ intellexerit, tecum illud communicaturum; scito eum, quo minus promissi munus confecerit, præpropero hinc suo discessu fuisse impeditum. Nam cum Geneva Lugdunum ante tres menses esset profectus, necessariis quibusdam suis occupationibus impulsus, nihil interim minus quam de non revertendo cogitans, ecce! ea nec opinata illic accepit, quæ omni exempta mora ejus recta in Angliam profectionem postulabant. Verum cum jam Caleto, magnis itineribus contendens, prope admoveretur, nec ad summum a portu medium diei iter abesset; opportune sane ornatissimum virum, quasi cœlitus objectum, habuit obvium in via D. Franciscum Walsinghamum, cognatum suum germanum, qui et tum a serenissima nostra principe Elizabetha ad Carolum regem, novam pacem gratulandi causa, missus est legatus, et nunc datus D. Norrisio successor, continua legatione apud Gallos fungitur. Ab eo rerum omnium statum domi forisque melius edoctus, atque ita magnis animi angustiis et molestiis liberatus, una cum illo Lutetiam Parisiorum reversus est, ubi apud eundem ejusdem ædibus hyemem (favente Deo) ducere constituit. Lutetia igitur superioribus hisce diebus ad me scribit, inter cetera mandans, ut cum primum commode possem, liberandæ suæ fidei causa hæc tibi significarem per literas suo nomine; simulque suæ in te benevolentiæ summæ summam constantiam declararem, re magis quam verbis ad omnia tua causa, si quid poterit, si quid voles, paratæ; in primis vero, ut pro maxima illa tua, qua erga illum usus es humanitate, pares, id est maximas, tibi gratias agerem. Et adscribit, ut si qua in re mea opera (qui in collegio Genevensi apud D. Portum, Græcarum literarum professorem, demoror) tibi usui esse queat, eam et literis tibi offeram, et de quibuscunque tuis negotiis, quæ mihi accuranda dederis, parem ac de suis cogitationem curamque suscipiam. Ego vero facio, ac lubens: non solum domini mei, cui debeo, causa, quem ita velle video; sed tua etiam ipsius gratia, quem ob insignes illas Dei dotes et illustria ornamenta, quibus quasi stella quædam primæ magnitudinis (ut ἀστρονομικῶς loquar) splendes in ecclesia Dei, te veneror et colo. Jube igitur, manda, impera; invenies in me ad nutum omnia: quæ si ut efficiam, prudentia, industria, opera consequi non potero; illis tamen præstandis officio, diligentia, fide non deero. Nihil igitur jam restat, nisi ut quid velis exspectem, exspectato satisfaciam, tametsi fortasse non exspectationi.

Sed pene oblitas eram te domini mei nomine salutare, quod utique jusserat; sed modum non audeo subjicere. Nam si, te ut diligenter salutarem, jussisse dicerem, illud *diligenter* mihi præjudicium parere possit, utpote de cujus in rebus hic tuis gerendis diligentia in dubium tibi venire queam, qui me tam negligentem gesserim in te salute modo impertienda, eam, quæ primo quoque tempore fieri oportebat, in calcem epistolæ rejiciendo. Quid quod etiam mihi majorem in modum rogandus es, ut de me salutem dicas D. Julio Martyritio (nam quod aliud ei sit nomen nescio), qui operam suam ponit corrigendis typis Froschoveranis. Vide nunc aliam ex alia impudentiam, qua ita apud summum virum agam infimus homuncio, ut et tibi aliquid oneris audeam imponere, et prius quidem imponere, quam ab eodem aliquid faciundum acceperim, qui mihi præscribendi et imperandi jus habes. Sed novi D. Bullingeri humanitatem, cui me commendo, illum Christo.

Vale, vir sanctissime. Genevæ, 13 kal. Decembr. (1558).

Tuus vere ex animo,

INSCRIPTIO. JACOBUS LETHEUS, Anglus.

Optimo viro ac doctissimo theologo,
D. Henrico Bullingero, ministro
verbi Dei Tiguri, tradantur hæ
literæ.

EPISTOLA XCIII.

JOHANNES PARKHURSTUS AD HENRICUM BULLINGERUM.

SALVE, mi Bullingere. Quod rarius ad te scripserim, mors Abeli in causa fuit, cui soli meas literas et alia quæcunque committere solitus sum: erat enim fidissimus amicus: et ubi alium Abelum invenire possim, plane dubito. Sed Dominus, uti spero, suscitabit mihi similem, qui ejus munere in posterum fungatur. Nordovicum fere 100 milliaribus distat ab urbe Londinensi, quo ego non soleo equitare, nisi ad parlamentum vocatus, quod proxima hyeme futurum est. Ibi quærendus est fidus aliquis, qui mea ad vos tuto curet deferenda. Nostri mercatores nec Flandriam nec Hispaniam libenter adeunt: metuunt enim sibi ab Hispanica inquisitione plus quam diabolica, quæ nec suis nec exteris parcit.

Grindallus, nuper Londinensis episcopus, factus est archiepiscopus Eboracensis; Sandus Wigorniensis, Londinensis. Circa initium Novembris magnæ maris inundationes multum damni diversis Angliæ partibus attulere; nec immunes sunt mea Norfolcia et Suffolcia. Flandria præ aliis omnibus est adflicta. Solum apud nos altis nivibus (quales ego nunquam vidi) aliquot septimanis adopertum et fuit et est. Nihil viride usquam apparet. Lues pecorum propter inopiam cibi metuitur.

Uxor mea ab initio Novembris ad hunc usque diem ægrotavit, nondum convaluit. Quod si scivero has meas ad vos tuto delatas, sæpius scribere conabor. Nam mors Abeli, tumultus Belgici, et exploratores undique, conatum hactenus aliqua ex parte retardarunt meum.

Opta omnia felicissima vestris consulibus, senatoribus, verbi ministris, civibus et toti ditioni Tigurinæ. Bene valete omnes in Domino. Et iterum jubeo te valere, suavissime Bullingere. Mea valetudinaria vos omnes. Raptim. Nordovici, 16 Januarii, 1571.

Tuus ex animo,
JOHANNES PARKHURSTUS, N.

INSCRIPTIO.
D. Henrico Bullingero,
Tiguri.

EPISTOLA XCIV.

RICARDUS COXUS AD RODOLPHUM GUALTERUM.

Tardius ad me, nimirum mense Septembri anno 1571, delatum fuit epistolæ tuæ exemplum, Gualtere doctissime et frater in Christo carissime, ad Norwicensem episcopum scriptæ. Quæ cursim tractat de quibusdam religionis in Anglia ceremoniis, et de quibusdam fratribus nostris eas non approbantibus. Persuasum habemus te virum esse, qui pium ac sincerum affectum geris erga nos et erga sinceram Christi, quam profitemur, religionem. Utinam tu quidem paucis ex fratribus nostris, nonnihil factiosis, tam faciles non admovisses aures! Optandum etiam, ut pro pietate tua non tam libere pronuntiasses, antequam intellexisses plene ortum et progressum nostrum in restauranda apud Anglos religione. Editus fuit olim jussu Edouardi regis piæ memoriæ libellus de publicis precibus et sacramentis in ecclesia Anglicana usurpandis, nec sine consilio et judicio optimorum virorum D. Buceri et D. Petri Martyris, tunc in Anglia degentium. Jam vero, quamprimum inclyta nostra Regina Elizabetha regno inaugurabatur, non sine summa totius regni auctoritate sacrum illum libellum ecclesiæ Anglicanæ restituit. Quo quidem tempore nobis, qui jam ecclesiis præficimur, nullus adhuc locus aut religionis cura demandata erat. Cum vero ad ecclesiarum ministerium vocabamur, obviis ulnis amplectebamur libellum illum, non sine gratiarum actione Deo, qui eum thesaurum nobis servavit et restauravit incolumem: scimus enim libellum nihil contra Dei verbum statuere.

Nec abs re fuerit meminisse, quod scripsit olim ad nos Francofordiæ exulantes piæ memoriæ D. P. Martyr: "Nihil," inquit (libellum notans), "in eo libro invenio impium. Scimus homines aliquot contentiosos spargere cavilla et calumnias struere. Meminisse potius deberent, Dominum nostrum Deum esse non contentionis sed pacis." Hæc si tibi innotuissent, D. Gualtere, non adeo fuisses territus, (uti scribis,) ne post impositas vestes majus aliquod malum daretur. Vanissima sunt sane, quæ a contentiosis tuis auribus insusurrantur, nimirum præter vestes multa alia obtrudi ecclesiis, et esse qui Reginæ nomine abutantur: præterea, ministros ejici ab ecclesiis, qui decretis quorundam subscribere nolunt. Quasi vero quidam sint in Anglia, qui privata auctoritate decreta condere audeant, et fratribus observanda proponere. Illud autem ut falsum, ita etiam injurium est et Reginæ et verbi ministris, nimirum quod indulgeamus regiæ celsitudini, audacioremque reddimus, ut quidvis ex suo arbitrio statuat. Absit hoc, ut quisquam tale suspicetur de tam pia et religiosa heroina, cui summa semper religio est a præscriptis legibus vel tantillum quidem deflectere. Imo conciones acres et satis mordaces animo patientissimo solet audire. Iterum absit longissime, ut verbi ministri in turpem adulationem fœde degenerare judicentur. Nos equidem neminem hactenus novimus vel tua, Gualtere, vel quorumcunque piorum patrum auctoritate, abusum ad comprobandas papisticas fæces, quas una cum illis rejicimus serio et condemnamus. Neque verum est, nos quicquam fratribus obtrudere ex papæ culina profectum. Vestis candida longe ante papismum in ecclesia Christi usurpata fuit. A nobis autem proponuntur ista legibus ante sancita, non uti papistæ fuerunt abusi ad superstitionem, sed tantum ad distinctionem, ut ordo et decorum servetur in ministerio verbi et sacramentorum. Neque pastores boni, neque homines pii istis offenduntur.

Ægre ferre videris, quod episcopi istarum rerum executores constituebantur. Imo insinuare videris, ex Christi parabola, nos esse perfidos, ebriosos, et conservorum cæsores, et quasi aulicorum superstitiosorum figmenta probemus, etiam quasi ministros pios inhumaniter tractemus, et temeritatis ministros nos præbeamus. Putabas nos talium ministrorum causas esse defensuros.

Dura sunt admodum ista et a veritate alienissima. Annon semper ab exordio ecclesiæ bene constitutæ, rituum ecclesiasticorum cura et conservatio fuit præcipue penes episcopos? Annon rituum contemptores et violatores ab episcopis reprehensi fuerunt, et in ordinem redacti? Legatur sanctæ ecclesiæ praxis, et liquido constabit hoc verum esse. Jam vero, qui hoc munus obeunt, iniquissimum fuerit ut inter perfidos aut ebriosos computentur. Ingenue vereque fateris, domine Gualtere, esse ex fratribus istis quosdam morosulos, imo dicere potuisses, obstreperos, contentiosos, et ecclesiæ non male constitutæ unitatem scindentes, et divini cultus formam ex suis capitibus confictam passim populo tradentes, eo interim libello, a piis patribus composito et justa auctoritate promulgato, jam penitus spreto et conculcato. Ad hæc, concionibus suis nimium popularibus contra sordes papisticas et portentosas vestes invehuntur, quas clamant impietatis et damnationis æternæ ministras. Nihil illos movet vel regni, vel ecclesiæ nostræ, vel serenissimæ Reginæ, vel fraternæ commonitionis, vel piæ exhortationis auctoritas. Neque quicquam pensi habent infirmorum fratrum nostrorum, instar lini adhuc fumigantium, sed animos illorum periculose exulcerare nituntur. Hi nostri fratres prudentiam Paulinam nos imitari non sinunt, qui omnibus omnia factus fuit, ut omnes lucrifaceret. Consilium vestrum, maxime vero venerandorum patrum, Martini Buceri, Petri Martyris et Henrici Bullingeri, apud hos homines nullum habere potest locum. Immerito non præstiti officii nobis nota inuritur, quod illorum causam non defendimus, quos habemus pacis et religionis turbatores, quique concionum suarum impetu ita miseram plebeculam dementarunt, eoque vesaniæ nonnullos adegerunt, ut jam templa nostra ingredi obstinate recusent, aut ad baptizandum suos parvulos, vel ad sacram cœnam manducandum, vel ad conciones audiendum. Segregantur penitus et a nobis et ab illis bonis fratribus nostris; diverticula quærunt; privatam religionem instituunt, privatasque domus frequentant, ibique sua sacra peragunt; uti olim Donatistæ, uti hodie Anabaptistæ, uti etiam papistæ nostri, qui civitates circumeunt, ut alicubi missas clanculum audiant. Illud denique nimis odiosum, Reginam nostram cum papa copulare. Facessat papa quo dignus est. Reginæ nostræ, summo magistratui, non iniqua præcipienti, functionis nostræ reddenda ratio, etiam coram Deo.

Hæc pauca habui notanda in tua epistola, dilectissime frater, ut posthac fidem non habeas cuivis spiritui, utque quandoquidem tanta te Deus eruditione et pietate imbuerit, nominis tui rationem habere cures. Hæc ab animo candido profecta æqui boni consulturum te non diffido. In Christo vale.

Ex Insula Eliensi in Anglia, 12 Februarii, 1571.

Tuus in Christo frater,

RICARDUS COXUS,

Episcopus Eliensis.

INSCRIPTIO.

Pientissimo atque eruditissimo fratri meo in Christo, dilectissimo D. Rodolpho Gualtero, ecclesiæ Tigurinæ ministro fidelissimo.

EPISTOLA XCV.

JOHANNES JUELLUS AD HENRICUM BULLINGERUM.

S. PL. in Christo. Scripsi ad te, ornatissime vir et pater in Christo colendissime, sub initium Septembris satis prolixe de omni statu nostrarum rerum. De illis literis quid factum sit, adhuc nescio. Fit enim sæpe turbulentis istis temporibus, ut literæ aut concidantur innocentes, aut extinguantur in itinere. Si eas intellexero ad te incolumes pervenisse, ero alacrior ad scribendum.

Ecclesiæ nostræ hoc tempore Dei opt. max. beneficio tranquillæ sunt. Sanctissimus conatus est, quantum potuit, omnibus modis miscere omnia. Summiserat ad nos inanissimas bullas, quibus et Elizabethæ Reginæ gubernacula reipublicæ et Christo regnum suum abjudicaret. Illarum ego ad te superioribus nundinis exemplar misi, ut intelligeres, quam ille senex et fatuus solemniter insaniat. Omnia illius consiliorum mysteria ita ab illis, qui regni nostri clavum tenent, prudenter patefacta et dextre appositeque refutata sunt, ut nunc a pueris rideantur. Perduelles illi miseri et fatui, qui jam ante menses octodecim cœperant in agro Dunelmensi tumultuari, nunc exulant in Flandria eversi rebus omnibus. Lovanienses nostri unum jam atque alterum annum nihil scribunt. Regina Scotiæ asservatur, uti scis, apud nos liberali custodia, honorifice et apparatu prope regio: tamen asservatur. Id illa impatienter et indigne fert, et sibi injuriam fieri clamitat: nosti enim spiritus atque animos Guisianos. Aiunt fratrem Regis Galliæ illam ambire conjugem. Interim res Scoticæ in illorum sunt potestate, qui profitentur evangelium. Societas illa, quæ nobis aliquando fuit cum Antverpiensibus, ante aliquot annos illorum injuriis et perfidia violata, non potest adhuc coalescere. In Hispaniis Mauri numero, viribus, et victoriis crescunt; Philippus in singulos dies imminuitur. De Cypro vero et Venetis rebus quid ego tibi? Turcam nunc aiunt imminere Italiæ. Ille saltem frænabit antichristi ferociam: nam Christiani principes toties admoniti nihil audiunt. Elizabetha Regina nostra convocavit proceres, et indixit parlamentum in secundum diem Aprilis; quod felix faustumque sit et ecclesiæ et reipublicæ! Ibi demum, spero, videbo Parkhurstum tuum meumque, quem septennium jam totum nunquam vidi.

Gualterus Haddonus, vir pius et facundus, obiit diem suum. D. Grindallus Eboracensis, Sandus Londinensis, Hornus Vintoniensis, absunt a me longe gentium, quisque in sua specula. Omnes tamen tibi cupiunt et te salutant.

Ego Julio meo debeo xl. Gallicos coronatos, videlicet duorum annorum proximorum pensionem. Scripsi ad illum semel jam atque iterum, ut significaret, cui me velit numerare. Pecunia præsto est, modo sit qui accipiat. Si nihil scribet, non est quod accuset fidem meam: ipse sibi facit injuriam.

Vale, mi pater, et domine in Christo colendissime. Dominus Jesus te ecclesiæ suæ quam diutissime servet incolumem! Sarisburiæ, secunda Martii, 1571.

Tuus in Christo,
JO. JUELLUS,
Episcopus Sarisburien.

INSCRIPTIO.
Ornatiss. viro, D. Henrico Bullingero, pastori ecclesiæ Tigurinæ, domino suo colendissimo, tradantur hæ. Tiguri.

EPISTOLA XCVI.

RICARDUS HILLES AD HENRICUM BULLINGERUM.

SALUTEM plurimam in Domino. Octavo die Martii scripsi ad te, domine colendissime, quas Barnabas filius meus, ut mihi postea scripsit, superioribus nundinis Francofordianis, per D. Christophorum Froschoverum ad te transmisit. Easdem spero ante hunc diem te accepisse: per eas humanitatem tuam certiorem feci, superiores literas tuas, quas in præterito anno mense Augusto copiose ad me scripsisti, dudum mihi esse redditas. Hodie autem primum tuas mihi gratissimas literas, Tiguri, 25 Februarii, anno 1571 præsenti, ad me datas accepi, una cum tribus literis tuis reverendis episcopis, Eboracensi, Eliensi, et Sarisburiensi inscriptis, ac etiam tribus tuis manuscriptis exemplaribus, de quibus in prædictis literis tuis mentionem facis; quæ omnia episcopis, quibus consignasti ea, fideliter jam reddi curabo. Miror certe multum, ubinam tamdiu in itinere hæserint: gaudeo tamen me ea vel nunc tandem recepisse; habeoque tibi gratias pro libro uno Germanico impresso, quem mihi dono dedisti sic titulo inscripto: Auf Herrn Jahn Brentzen testament, etc. Qualium librorum duos, præterea et Latine impressos quinque libros, et tres literas, videlicet ad episcopum nostrum Londinensem unas, ad episcopum Dunelmensem alteras, atque ad Henricum Butlerum alias hic recepi, cum tribus exemplaribus manuscriptis prædictis; quas literas etiam ac omnes præfatos libros septem impressos, quibus per literas tuas dari cupiebas, reddi curabo quam cito possim.

Quantum autem ad pannum, quem vocant *caresex*, attinet, duas virgas Anglicanas et $\frac{3}{4}$ tenuioris generis, quo nostrates ut plurimum utuntur solummodo in subcaligariis suis, sive, ut vestrates (puto) loquuntur, in irer nieder hosen, hic tradidi in mense Junio proxime elapso domino Christophoro Montio pro tua humanitate; et in mandatis dedi famulo cuidam meo, cui est nomen Simon Tailor, ut pro illis duabus virgis, cum $\frac{3}{4}$ Francofordi in autumnalibus nundinis proxime futuris, duos coronatos Gallicos et 7 batzios, videlicet tres florenos et batzios decem a prædicto domino Froschovero peteret et reciperet: quia tu, domine, in proximis sive novissimis tuis literis volebas me indicare pretium, ut Francoforti persolveret præfatus pro te Froschoverus. Dedi hic prædicto domino Christophoro Montio virgam unam Anglicanam et $\frac{3}{4}$ crassioris generis, (quo nostrates quam plurimum in suis superioribus femoralibus, sive, ut Germani (puto) solent dicere, In die brouch oder niedergwand des menschens hosen) quam virgam, cum tribus quartis crassioris sed durabilioris caresex, dono do tuæ humanitati, precorque Deum optimum maximum ut quam diutissime fruaris, quamvis haud sit valde verisimile ut hoc facias. Verissime enim ait Hieronymus, philosophum sive poetam citans: "Juvenis cito mori potest, senex autem diu vivere non potest."

Proculdubio labor ille tuus, de quo mentionem facis, in respondendo ad totam illam papisticam bullam impudentem, quam evomuit antichristus Romanus contra serenissimam nostram Reginam, maxime probabitur tribus prædictis episcopis, quibus illa tria exemplaria tua misisti; et vulgabunt illa etiam, siquidem illis videbitur e re fore regni et ex voluntate serenissimæ Reginæ nostræ. Doleo certe, quod ita suppliciter me oras, ut tuam scriptionem ad me nunc boni consulam, ac tibi condonem, quod mea opera sic utaris familiariter; poteris enim semper mea uti opera quam familiarissime, quamdiu vixero.

Per Dei gratiam fuit hic, antequam absolutum sive finitum erat parliamentum Westmonasterio tentum, Henricus prænominatus Butlerus cum domino suo Parkhursto, Nordovicensi episcopo, anxie exspectans literas a matre sua, quia adhuc ab ea, postquam Angliam appulit, nullas accepit, sicuti tum mihi ipse retulit. Dominus tamen doctor Montius hic illi in meis ædibus retulit, fuisse propter eum Argentinæ in ipsius doctoris domo sarcinulam literarum relictam, in qua putabat fuisse aliquas illi Henrico inscriptas.

In mense Junio prope præterito doctissimus theologus, dominus David Witheade, (qui tempore regni Reginæ Mariæ propter professionem orthodoxæ doctrinæ exulabat,) feliciter ad Dominum migravit. Viduus vixit etiam per septennium plus minus, sicuti ipsemet nunc de tua conditione scripsisti. Ante medium tamen annum nuperrime juvenem duxit viduam, ipse octogesimum fere agens annum. Dominus quoque Colus, qui tum temporis in Germania etiam exul erat propter evangelii prædicationem, eodem fere tempore angina laborans secundo, postquam ægrotare cœperat, die obiit. Archidiaconus Essexiæ diœcesis Londinensis comitatus, is ipse ante mensem unum aut duos priusquam mortuus erat ad Decanatum Sarisburiensis ecclesiæ cathedralis prælatus, migravit hic Londini, eodem, uti fertur, die aut pridie, quo decrevit Londino Sarisburiam versus ad inductionem recipiendam multis comitatus famulis et amicis proficisci. Sic

"Omnia sunt hominum tenui pendentia filo,
Et subito casu, quæ valuere, ruunt."

Antequam has literas totas perfeceram, omnia prædicta exemplaria manuscripta, et reliquos libros omnes præfatos impressos, reverendissimis episcopis, quibus inscripti erant, tradidi ac jam reddi certo curavi: speroque eos brevi ad tuam humanitatem rescripturos. Londini, 27 Julii, anno 1571. Vale, mi domine colendissime, in Christo Servatore nostro.

Tuus ex animo, quem nosti, Anglus,

(RICARDUS HILLES.)

(P. S.) 31 Julii. Obsignata jam epistola mea, vidi et perlegi epistolam tuam ad reverendissimos tres episcopos (Eboracensem scilicet, Eliensem et Sarisburiensem) jam impressam, atque prædicti laboris tui (de manuscripto illo tuo exemplari, quod domino Eliensi episcopo misisti, intelligo) priorem partem jam impressam. Et certior factus sum, nonnulla etiam alia jam impressa esse folia ejusdem operis: adeo ut quam citissime impressum erit totum illud exemplar tuum manuscriptum, atque in publicum prodibit.

EPISTOLA XCVII.

RICARDUS COXUS AD HENRICUM BULLINGERUM.

VEHEMENTER me delectarunt tuæ literæ, frater in Christo carissime: eas vero recepi non ante mensem Junii fere expletum. Recepi etiam una duos libellos, alterum contra Johannis Brentii testamentum, hominis multiplici errore dementati: huic ejus errori subinde serpenti viam tempestive obstruxisti. Alter est defensio munitissima contra terrificam illam bullam, quavis bulla vaniorem: in qua ita auctorem jugulasti, ut nullus supersit libere spirandi halitus. Multum tibi debemus omnes, quod nostra omnium causa adeo sit tibi cordi. Ego de hoc argumento jejune atque dilute ad te scripsi; at alter ex fratribus meis plenius et copiosius egit, qui et ipsius bullæ copiam tibi fecit. Extorsit a tua pietate hanc bullæ impugnationem et nostri amor, et rei indignatio, et veritatis zelus ardentissimus. Hactenus vixisti in sanctissimis sacratissimisque divini verbi studiis, ut illud modis omnibus coleres et promoveres. Huc ab ineunte ætate vocatus fuisti; hanc tuam vocationem strenue ornasti, in eaque usque ad terminum vitæ dabit Dominus ut perseveres, ad conscientiæ tranquillationem et piorum omnium exspectationem avidissimam. Hinc est quod occasionem captes undicunque de religione christiana bene merendi, et in pietatis hostes acriter animadvertendi. Hinc est quod tum tempestive Brentii morbo mederis, et bullæ furorem compescis. Equidem diligentissime curabo ut Regina nostra, et Latine et Græce doctissima, intelligat tuum erga ipsam studium et benevolentiam, efficiamque ut libelli tui gustum capiat suavissimum. Quod autem nobis commendas rationem tractandi libellum tuum, cogitamus ut quam primum typis excudatur, et sub Henrici Bullingeri nomine in publicum prodeat; mittamque ad te, quam primum potero, aliquot exemplaria.

Henricus ille Butlerius, quo de scribis, nondum me invisit. Dabo operam ut, cum ad me accesserit, mea opera non indiguerit. Servet te Deus optimus maximus, frater in Christo dilectissime, idque multos annos, ad ecclesiæ utilitatem; precamurque ut precibus tuis nos Domino commendes, maxime qui in ipsius vinea laboramus. Nova nulla tibi impertio; nam frater meus dominus Hornus id se præstaturum esse promisit.

Tuus in Domino frater carissimus,

RICARDUS,

Episcopus Elien.

INSCRIPTIO.

Colendissimo in Christo fratri mihique dilectissimo, D. Henrico Bullingero, ecclesiæ Tigurinæ ministro meritissimo.

EPISTOLA XCVIII.

ROBERTUS HORNUS AD HENRICUM BULLINGERUM.

ETSI, carissime Bullingere, ingratitudinis suspicionem amor non admittit, neque judicii temeritatem permittit prudentia; tamen et officii debiti exspectationem ardentem lædit tarditas, et prætermissi excusationem seriam postulat negligentia. Verum accusationem causa non patitur; non est enim mihi culpæ conscientia: nec excusationem sane efflagitat natura tua, quia non est suspicax aut iracunda. Attamen vel quia dubitare potes de causa, instruendus es, ne vacillet opinio; vel quia scire fortasse cupis, satisfaciendum est voto, ne vulneretur. Neque enim aut officii mei contemtu temere, aut humanitatis tuæ oblivione negligenter, aut ulla ratione factum putes inhumaniter, quod literis tuis jamdudum missis jamdiu non responderim. Sed quia cum et domi nostræ turbatum sit nonnihil, et foris undique vehementer sit tumultuatum, sic ut ipsa etiam ad vos usque maria quotidianis bellorum flammis exarserint: nec data est certe ulla scribendi opportunitas, nec oblata est hactenus, ex quo e medio sublatus est noster Abelus, mittendi ratio; neque si scribere libuisset, aut licuisset mittere, explorata tamen fuisset tradendi certitudo. Nunc vero et opportunitatem nactus et nuntium, nec argumentum deesse debuit amantissimis tuis literis jamdiu provocato, et salutationibus amicissimis in epistola bullæ papali præfixa nuperrime factis instigato; nec voluntas abesse potuit, jam pridem ante multumque cupienti. Facio tamen, quod solent ii, qui cum ære alieno vehementer obstricti sunt, sic ut multis multa debeant, omnibus tamen plene solvendo non sint; quod habent, id totum tradunt uni aut alteri creditorum, qui ex æquo aliis partiatur, sicque singulis pro posse suo satisfaciunt. Ita, quando non tibi modo, sed etiam Gualtero meo, Simlero, Zuinglio, Lavatero, Wolfio, ceterisque fratribus Tigurinis in Christo mihi dilectissimis, hoc nomine multa debeam; quod habeo, id totum tibi in manus trado, ut inde tibi et illis creditoribus isthic meis satisfiat. Æqualiter igitur partire atque communica cum illis, quidquid novarum mercium vobis extrudo ex Anglia, Scotia, Gallia, Flandria. Mercimonia vero Romana vobis non offero; vilescunt enim apud vos, sat scio; quod cum multis modis constet, tum maxime ex doctissima bullæ papalis refutatione, quam ad nos jam pridem transmisisti, quæ etiam modo omnibus promulganda, sub prelo est, manifestissime apparet.

Respublica nostra jam fere per integrum triennium periculose quidem et horribiliter agitari cœpta est, dum et foris perfidis hostium insultibus conquassata, et intus domesticis perduellionum vulneribus confossa et conturbata est. Utrumque pestis genus, ut fieri solet, exitialis illa et execrabilis totius orbis Erinnys, papismi stirps et propago, genuit. Sed nobilis illa nostra et excellens virgo, domi suæ secure conquiescens, utrasque una vires fregit, et illos sine sudore et istos sine sanguine profligavit. Ita omnia, quasi ex insperato, cœlitus obvenerunt, ut non immerito de cœlo suo exercituum et virtutis Dominus evangelii sui causam suscepisse, suisque quasi manibus propugnasse, videretur. Illorum arma, thesauros, classes nobis de cœlo venti, spontaneis quasi flatibus, invexerunt; istorum apparatus, munitiones, milites, ipse regalis exercitus advenientis rumor perterrefecit ac dissipavit. Ita illi, priusquam devicti, invicti sunt; isti, antequam provecti quoquam, plane devicti sunt. Duo tantum nobiles, iique nullius auctoritatis aut nominis, homines, ut levissime dicam, levissimi, veteris quidem farinæ, seu, (ut ipsis loqui placet,) antiquæ religionis, certe honestatis prorsus antiquatæ, fuere. Qui et clam postea transfretantes, adhuc in transmarinis partibus exules delitescunt, et, ut fama est, quasi Caini maledicti ac profugi, vagantur misere. Quæ fax aliis regni nostri partibus postea scintillas seditionum quasdam exhalavit; sed procerum prudentia, seu divina potius providentia, non difficulter extincta est et evanuit. Ita nunc, (immortali Deo sit gratia!) alcyonios plane dies consecuta Anglia tota conquiescit.

Atque utinam, si Deo opt. max. sic visum esset, idem liceret vere aut fere saltem de ecclesia dicere! Ecclesia enim nostra nondum e vestiariis illis offensionum scopulis enatavit, quibus primum impegit. Clavum, ut scis, tenet, et adhuc qua vult vertit, princeps optima. Nos vero, quod solum licet, divini flatum spiritus exspectamus, et quotidie omnes invocamus serio ac vehementer, ut tandem alio vela torqueat. Interim tamen, qui alteriore in loco stamus, non id agimus, quod vulgus importunis urget clamoribus, (id enim esset valde periculosum,) ut invitam, quo nondum pervenire placet, pertrahamus, quasi clavum e manibus extorquentes. Verum id enitimur, ut, licet male vestiti, bene certe cordati in opere Domini conficiundo simus: nec tam de panno nostro nobis gestando pulchre cura est, quam de pane Domini secando recte: nec denique tanti facimus, si tunica nostra futilis appareat, quam id curamus ne tunica Domini inconsutilis distrahatur. Non desunt tamen inferioris loci atque ordinis homines, sine sale quidem aut sensu, et ignari et ignoti penitus, qui, quoniam ecclesiam suis votis aut potius vanitatibus nondum quadrare conspiciunt, necdum satis suis ineptiis respondere, sed ventum prorsus contrarium esse, idcirco alii stationes suas deserunt ac otiosi delitescunt; alii, scaphas sibi suas fabricantes, conventicula convocant, episcopos suos sibi eligunt, ac inter se synodos celebrantes, suas sibi leges comminiscuntur et fingunt. Conciones respuunt, communionem aspernantur, templa diruta volunt omnia, utpote papismo olim consecrata; nec ministros modo nostros habent pro ludibrio, sed ipsum etiam ministerium ne pili quidem faciunt. Atque ita, quantum in illis est, miserabile naufragium ecclesiæ nostræ temere nimis ac præcipitanter arcessunt: certe non parum liberum evangelii cursum remorantur. Ipsi interea, nescio quibus errorum fluctibus mire jactati, et variis vanitatum flatibus nescio quo misere prætervecti, in absurdissima opinionum deliria devolvuntur. Ideoque abscindunt sese a nobis, ut aiunt, seu potius, quasi Theudas, cum suis abscedunt; ac perinde faciunt ac ii, qui cum auram sibi adversam aliquantulum sentiant, nec possunt statim quo volunt pervenire, ad meliorem sese ventum reservare nolunt, sed exilientes e navi in pelagus se præcipitant ac submergunt. Hic autem religionis nostræ adversarii mirum est quam idoneam, ut sibi videntur, evangelii deformandi ansam arripiant: regiæ majestatis auribus insusurrant, hunc esse evangelii nostri fructum maturescentem, hanc solam doctrinæ nostræ messem exspectandam; ita ut, nisi sacrosanctum cor illud veritatis esset amore prorsus inflammatum, jamdudum istorum aspersionibus refrixisset. En! Bullingere optime, effeci, quanta potui brevitate, ut uno quasi obtuitu rerum nostrarum rationem universam, et reipublicæ faciem, et ecclesiæ formam integram, intueare.

Gallia, longo jam tempore suis ipsius vulneribus sauciata, et quasi lassata bellis, nunc tandem aliquantulum respiravit: evangelium quidem admittit, sed quasi pestem; sic ut civitates nullas invisat, nisi paucas easque perpusillas, aut si majores, sic ut extra mœnia commoretur. Curiæ vero curiose admodum cavetur, ne Christum admittat aliquando vel hospitem; ideoque ad quædam milliaria, sub gravi pœna, jubetur exulare. Cardinalis et nobilis cum primis et pius vir, religionis causa hic apud nos exulans, dum Cantuariæ nostræ ad dies aliquot commoraretur, ventum exspectans ad reditum secundum ac salutarem, lethali veneno pontificiorum, ut aiunt, et sane credibile est, flagitio ac scelere confectus contabuit. Sed quid ego ex Gallia Tigurum quicquam exporto? Nihil enim ex Gallia convehi solet, quod Tigurinis non sit vulgare, quo etiam non abundatis. Hoc unum tamen arbitror vos non accepisse, vel saltem rarius apud vos esse: Dux Andegaviensis, Galliæ regis frater, vehementer Reginæ nostræ factus est procus. Quem successum habitura res est, nondum constat. Ut plane approbari nondum audio; ita quicquam adhuc improbari prorsus non video. Si quæras, quid ipse sentiam; difficile est profecto in principum rebus esse judicem. Id tantum dicam: quas credunt fore, has arbitror non futuras vere nuptias. Multa sunt, quæ faciunt ut metuam; non pauca sunt etiam, quæ adducunt ut optem. Ceterum ista, ut nostra omnia, divino judicio prudenter et bonitati probe disponenda relinquo. Quod si tam ad evangelii fructum propagandum et nominis Christi gloriam illustrandam faciet, quam et ad res privatas singulorum utile, et ad publicas omnium futurum videtur prima facie salutare, abunde satis et vitæ et voto nostro fuerit satisfactum.

Atque ut hic nonnulla de vicina nostra Scotia intertexam. Ea quidem fœdissimis nuper homicidiis labefactata, et nobilissimorum hominum cruentata sanguine, et regis sui, juvenis ex Anglia præclarissimi, et post eum Jacobi regentis optimi, quos duos horribili et luctuosa cæde sustulerunt, adhuc mutuis istarum rerum odiis incandescit. Regina dum ob mariti necem suspecta, ab ejus regni proceribus sive ad purgationem sive ad pœnam perquisita est, ut proximis significavi, clam huc fugit in Angliam, ubi adhuc captiva retinetur. Illa fugam, alii furtum, sæpe sunt machinati; hactenus tamen tentatum est frustra: diligenter enim admodum et serio custoditur: quo consilio, pauci norunt; quo eventu, nondum constat; qua spe, aut potius quo metu, dolet dicere. Qui eam huc coegit, et facile valet, quia potens est, si videbitur; et non difficulter volet, quia misericors est, si orabitur, omnia pro voluntate sua etiam ad voluntatem nostram dispensare. Hic vero, quam mire hæc omnia, præter spem omnem, bonitatis ille omnis Deus ac gloriæ Dominus integra conservarit, 'experientia certum cum sit, dictum sane fuerit verum : etsi quia eventu rarum est, auditu prope fuerit incredibile. Nam et Gallico tumultu illo, et Scotica ista contentione, etiamque simultate Hispanica, quæ omnia exili apparatu aut exiguo labore confici nunquam potuerunt, Elizabetha nostra, unica quasi negotiorum illorum nutrix, evangelii solius causa partes piorum illæsas conservavit, quæ alioqui haud dubie jam olim defecissent. Sed vide antiquum sane pontificiorum et commodissimum quasique præcipuum stratagema, quod jam et quotidiana consuetudine familiare factum est, illis et longo usu ac possessione plane proprium. Nobilissimæ virginis Elizabethæ corpusculum tenue infinitis prope conatibus obsident, et quam studiosissime jam ad mortem conquirunt, et veneno et violentia et fascinatione et proditione, ceterisque ejus generis, quæ cogitari unquam potuerunt, modis omnibus, quod profecto horribile est vel recordari. Hactenus tamen ut eam evangelio suo Deus fidelem et industriam habuit Deboram; ita sane Juditham fecit triumphantem: annosam quoque faciat Annam comprecamur.

Habes quidem Scoticas merces, non modo sordidas atque improbas, sed vere tenebrosas. Nunc ergo Flandricas accipe, perpaucas quidem illas, quas tamen haud dubie dixeris elegantes. Fuit apud nos nuper homo quidam, non ineruditus doctor legis, cujusmodi, opinor, Christo inter Judæos olim mortem intentarunt, cognomento Story, vir quasi ad crudelitatem natus, Marianis temporibus sævissimus persecutor, cui sanctos occidere pro lucro, sanguinem effundere pro ludo erat: is igitur, postquam felix ille dies nobis illuxit, quo Deus Elizabetham nostram ad Anglicani culmen imperii evexit, pro læsæ majestatis aperto scelere captus continuo et incarceratus est. Paullo post, quum esset custos justo negligentior, carcerem perfregit, ac profugit in Flandriam, atque Albæ duci, capitali regni nostri adversario, in illis locis degenti, fit servus. Hic ille, quasi ex inferis furia quædam prolapsa, seu ut verius, tanquam sceleratus quidam Davus, mirum est continuo quam interturbat omnia : mercatores in iis locis appulsos, impetrata ducis licentia, spoliat, affligit, incarcerat: populum Anglicanum ad seditiones sollicitat: strenue ac vehementer agit cum Albano, ut milites ac apparatum tam sancto negotio munifice largiatur: denique manibus pedibusque obnixe agit omnia, ut nobilissimæ Reginæ, principi suæ, et regno præclarissimo, patriæ suæ, immaturam et luctuosam cædem inaudita quadam crudelitate arcesseret. Hic vero mercatores, qui Davi istius crudelissimis verberibus quotidie vapulati pleniorem istarum rerum sensum, majore cum dolore suo, sine ulla remedii spe haurirent, commune consilium quoddam ineunt, et una quasi voce tollendum clamitant; id quod egregia astutia hac perfecerunt. Venit ad eum quidam familiaris ejus a mercatoribus subornatus, cujus fidem minime suspectam habuit, clam ei in aurem insusurrans, navem modo ex Anglia appulisse, nescio quos thesauri montes aureos continentem. Evolat ille continuo prædæ amore inflammatus, aurum sibi, cædem mercatoribus certam vovens. Qui postquam navem conscendisset, ea in omnes ejus angulos proreperet, jamque in ipsa navis penetralia prorupisset, illi clausis subito repagulis ac sublatis velis, secundo ac salutari vento in Angliam devehuntur. Hic vero illi, si ad omnes Turcici imperii naves thesauris onustas, vel universam Venetiarum classem cum suis divitiis, obvias etiamque oblatas in itinere habuissent, exiguam hanc naviculæ suæ mercem ac vile onus omnibus illis gazis, sat scio, non permutassent. Atque ita demum, magna populi reditum ei suum gratulantis exspectatione Londinum advectus, paulloque post læsæ majestatis crimine condemnatus, suspensus et dilaniatus, secundus a Feltono, (is enim erat, qui bullas papales episcopi Londinensis valvis affixerat,) ecclesiæ Anglico-Romanæ factus est martyr putidus, pontificio sanctorum gregi connumerandus.

Transmisi vobis præterea, Bullingere mi, per tabellionem hunc decem coronatos, non tam munus honorabile, aut certe honorarium, quam benevolentiæ erga vos meæ qualecunque testimonium: quos omnes in hypocausto vestro communi convivio in memoriam nostri sacro, sine tamen sacrificio, dicari volo.

Vos valete una omnes ac felices vivite: itaque vobis de me persuaderi cupio atque de eo soletis, qui vestri causa libenter velit, quicquid aut consilio effingere, aut auxilio efficere, aut cogitatione complecti, aut facultate denique expedire possit. Christus Jesus ecclesiam suam, quam pretioso sanguine suo expiavit, servet, adversariorum omnium consilia fallat, conatus frustret, viresque frangat! Vale, amantissime Bullingere, et vive in auctore vitæ. Londini, 8 Augusti, 1571.

Totus tuus,
ROBERTUS WINTON.

INSCRIPTIO.
Præstantissimo viro D. Henr.
Bullingero seniori.
Tiguri.

EPISTOLA XCIX.

JOHANNES PARKHURSTUS AD HENRICUM BULLINGERUM.

SALVUS sis, suavissime Bullingere. Quarto Martii insignis papista Boxalus, Reginæ Mariæ secretarius, Lambethæ obiit. Quo quidem loco ante illum unus ex ejus consiliariis, Thirlbæus episcopus Eliensis etiam mortuus est. Circa finem Junii David Whithedus octogenarius, vir omni literarum genere excultus, ex hac vita Londini migravit. Thomas Spenserus, doctor S. theologiæ et archidiaconus Cicestriæ, 8 Julii diem clausit supremum. Is diligentissimus in mea Suffolcia munus obiit concionandi. Fuit is nobiscum Tiguri. D. Colus, non ille qui fuit Tiguri, sed quem tantopere amabat D. Wolphgangus Weidnerus, archidiaconus Essexiæ, eodem tempore ad superos concessit. Fuit uterque in concionando mirus artifex.

Hoc fere biennio fuit hic Nordovici inter extraneos implacabilis contentio, necdum est consopita; sed aliqua jam spes affulget, omnia in meliori et pacatiori statu futura. Quantos ego toto hoc tempore insumpserim labores (de sumptibus nihil dico), vix credideris: et tamen refractarii homines nihil de suo jure cedere volunt. Ego semper mitissime et humanissime cum illis egi, at nuper duriuscule, mea renitente natura. Sed quid facias? Cum hac res non succedat, alia aggrediundum est via. Tres eorum concionatores, ambitiosi quidem illi et gloriolæ cupidi, has turbas dederunt et continuarunt. Parum abfuit, quin tota congregatio dissolveretur. Numerus eorum circa quatuor millia. Turbulenti fuerunt Angli in Germania, fateor; at si ad hos conferas, erant quietissimi. Nihil profecto fingo. Magna fuerunt inter horum conterraneos dissidia, Sandwici in Cantio, sic etiam Londini, quæ nondum sunt sepulta, ut audio. In ecclesia Gallica apud nos omnia sunt valde pacata. Sunt hi in numero fere quadringenti.

In Scotia vera religio floret. Sed proceres inter se nonnunquam prœliantur, non pro religione (cui omnes fere favent), sed pro custodia Regis, cui inter hos præcipui inhiant. Regina Scotiæ in Anglia adhuc detinetur. Archiepiscopus Sancti Andreæ, multarum auctor turbarum in Scotia, mense Maio ad furcas et ex hac vita est sublatus.

Marchio Northamptonensis, frater reginæ Catherinæ, ultimæ Henrici VIII. conjugis et dominæ meæ clementissimæ, (cui ego in munere concionandi ante viginti tres annos inservivi,) circa initium Augusti fatis concessit. Cum ego essem Londini, duxit pulcherrimam puellam Germanam, quæ post discessum Marchionis Badensis et Ceciliæ ejus uxoris ex Anglia in Reginæ aula remansit. Fuit noster marchio annos natus sexaginta et, credo, multo plures. Tuus filius Henricus Butlerus valet.

Opto omnia felicissima vestris consulibus, senatoribus, concionatoribus, civibus, et toti ditioni Tigurinæ.

Saluta meo nomine tuos filios, Henricum, Rodolphum, et tertium, cujus nomen dedi oblivioni, tuas filias Veritatem et Dorotheam, Simlerum, Lavaterum, Zuinglium, tuos generos, Wolphium, Hallerum, Wickium, Froschoverum, Julium, Johannem Henricum Fabricium, et ceteros omnes. Mea valetudinaria te, tuos, tuas, et omnes salutat. Raptim. Ludhamiæ, 10 Augusti, 1571. Cetera omnia ex literis Gualteri disces.

Tuus,
JO. PARKHURSTUS, N.

INSCRIPTIO.
Clarissimo viro D. Henrico Bullingero,
Tiguri.

EPISTOLA C.

EDMUNDUS GRINDALLUS AD HENRICUM BULLINGERUM.

SALUTEM in Christo. Literas tuas 25 Febr. datas anno 1571, non accepi ante 25 Augusti proxime elapsi. Accepi etiam una refutationem bullæ papalis manuscriptam et responsionem ad testamentum Brentii. Miror Brentium tam virulentum testamentum post se relinquere voluisse. Vestra sane responsio et modesta est et pia. Bullæ refutatio Anglice et Latine impressa est; cujus etiam aliquot exemplaria impressa credo te antehac accepisse.

Agimus vero tuæ pietati gratias, quod nostrarum ecclesiarum tam solicitam curam geris. Quisnam vero fuerit post meam huc commigrationem rerum mearum status, paucis accipe. Primo Augusti 1570 Londino discessi: biduo post in ipso itinere ex lassitudine (quia equitando, dum essem Londini, non assueveram) in febrim tertianam incidi, et ea de causa per decem dies in medio itinere decumbere coactus fui. Tandem 17 Augusti veni Cawodam, ubi ædes habeo ad ripam Ousæ fluminis, septimo ab urbe lapide, febri, ut postea eventus docuit, non satis bene curata. Nam secundo Septembris insequentis in aliam gravissimam et acutissimam febrim incidi, quæ me supra modum debilitavit, ita ut non solum medici et amici de vita mea desperaverint, sed et ipse etiam sententiam mortis in memetipso acceperim. Sed Dominus, qui mortificat et vivificat, (vi morbi paullatim decrescente, sed tamen ita, ut per totam hyemem cubiculo non fuerim egressus,) tandem post sextum mensem pristinæ me sanitati restituit. Ex eo tempore in visitanda mea diœcesi ac provincia, et superstitionum reliquiis abolendis, quæ his in partibus, majore doctorum et piorum ministrorum penuria laborantibus, tenacius hærebant, pro virili laboravi, atque adhuc laboro. Jam post suppressam seditionem plebem, quoad externam obedientiam, obsequentiorem invenio quam putabam: fuerunt enim his malis, quæ bella civilia comitari solent, satis afflicti, atque idcirco humiliores. Utinam illos tam bene in vera religione institutos invenissem, quam meos Londinenses et Essexenses successori meo reliqui! Sed tamen spero, Domino dante incrementum, cum tempore etiam hic multum confici posse. Dominus Dunelmensis, qui perpetuo est valetudinarius, nuper graviter laboravit; sed jam Domini benignitate revaluit.

Bonum Juellum, Sarisburiensem (ecclesiæ nostræ juxta nomen suum gemmam et unicum ornamentum) circa initium Octobris elapsi amisimus, vel potius præmisimus.

Scio te nulla curiositate, sed ex aliis causis, uti scribis, justissimis, velle de rebus nostris aliquando certior fieri, quemadmodum et nos de vestris, qualescunque illæ sunt, audire cupimus: sumus enim ejusdem corporis membra. Spero igitur me posthac, compositis jam rebus, singulis annis bis ad minimum, more solito, ad nundinas scilicet utrasque Francofordianas, ad tuam pietatem scripturum. Res nostræ ad præsens, summa Dei benignitate, satis sunt tranquillæ; quum tamen in fine superioris æstatis, nihil tale suspicantes, in maximo discrimine fuerimus, ut ex scripto quodam istis incluso, et sub epistolæ forma, non sine publica tamen auctoritate, nostra lingua evulgato et in Latinum verso, facile[1] conjicere poteris. Guisiaca proles, quæ se Scotiæ reginam vocat, jam arctiori custodiæ deputatur. Thomas dux Norfolciæ 16 hujus mensis ad judicum subsellia adtractus fuit, et ob crimen læsæ majestatis capitali sententia condemnatus. Sed an sit brevi de eo extremum supplicium sumendum, nos, qui ab aula procul absumus, adhuc ignoramus. Alii ejusdem conspirationis socii in vinculis sunt, similem aleam subituri.

Scotia propter intestina dissidia toto hoc anno miserrime afflicta fuit. Nam post mortem Jacobi regentis surrogatus fuit avus pueri regis. Is fere ante annum arcem Dunbartonensem munitissimam, ad Cludæ fluminis ostia positam, nocte admotis scalis et interfectis excubitoribus, ex improviso occupavit, atque archiepiscopum S. Andreæ in eadem inventum, qui fuit ducis Hamiltonii frater nothus, suspendio vitam finire coegit. In hujus suspendii ultionem circa initium Maii elapsi, Hamiltonii cum 300 equitibus nocte Sterlingum oppidum intrarunt, atque ibi novum regem in hospitio suo apprehensum statim interfecerunt. Huic suffectus est per regios comes de Mar, vir bonus, sed non admodum potens. Grassantur igitur Scoti inter se cædibus mutuis, in plurimas factiones tum publicas tum privatas divisi. Qui pro Regina stant, Edinburgum et arcem ejusdem occuparunt. Regii Lytam, portum propinquum, muniverunt et præsidio firmarunt. Arcem Edinburgensem Jacobus regens Kirkcaldio cuidam,

[1 MS. *facere*.]

tanquam sibi fidissimo et Reginæ infensissimo, commiserat. Is paullo post, vivente adhuc Jacobo, corruptus fortassis auro Gallico, ad Reginam defecit. Illa defectio istorum malorum omnium causa fuit: nam alioqui reginales nunquam tutam belli sedem invenissent. Sed tamen speramus Reginam nostram brevi his malis finem impositram. Nam si colloquio et tractatu de pace, quod nunc agitur, res componi non possunt, dubium non est, quin Regina nostra illi parti, quæ æquas conditiones oblatas repudiavit, hostis sit futura; cui altera pars cedere necessario cogetur.

Scripsi ad Ricardum Hilles, ut Julio mittat aliquot coronatos. Butlerum commendatum habebo. Is si linguam nostram addiscat, poterit posthac nostræ ecclesiæ inservire. Mitto etiam tibi una cum istis historiam de virtutibus Reginæ Scotiæ, nuper a Georgio Buchanano Scoto publicatam. Dominus Jesus pietatem tuam quam diutissime conservet! Bischopsthorpiæ in suburbiis Eboraci, 24 Januarii, 1572.

Pietati tuæ deditissimus in Domino,
EDMUNDUS EBORACENSIS.

Cum istas essem obsignaturus, accepi tuas et D. Gualteri literas, quibus tu nepotem, ille filium commendat. Procul absum ab academiis nostris: sed tamen scribam ad amicos, ut ipsos commendatos habeant. Audio D. Londinensem illos Cantabrigiam misisse et viatico instruxisse. Ego etiam, quod solum possum, pecunia aliquando illos juvabo. Saluta, quæso, nomine meo D. Gualterum, cui nunc rescribere non vacabat. Libellum illum anonymum, quem mihi misisti, suspicor scriptum fuisse a nostro piæ memoriæ Sarisburiensi: sed præter conjecturam ex stylo et methodo nihil habeo. Iterum in Christo vale, frater carissime et colende.

EDMUNDUS EBORACENSIS.

INSCRIPTIO.
Domino Henrico Bullingero seniori,
ecclesiæ Tigurinæ ministro fide-
lissimo et fratri carissimo.
Tiguri.

EPISTOLA CI.

EDWINUS SANDUS AD HENRICUM BULLINGERUM.

SALUTEM in Christo. Carissime frater et colendissime domine, quod tuis crebris literis nihil quicquam responderim, id non tam ingratitudini meæ, quam gravissimis variarum rerum impedimentis, tribuas velim. Nam ut alia multa omittam, quæ hoc iter amoris erga te mei et scribendi consuetudinem impediverunt, prima et gravissima causa hæc est, recentis cujusdam mei morbi summa vis et magnitudo, qua ita misere et ad diuturnum tempus Dominus me exercuit, ut istarum rerum cogitationem penitus abjecissem. Huc etiam accedit quotidiana quædam negotiorum moles, quæ mihi indies locus ille facessit, in quo jam positus sum; quibus ita propemodum opprimor, ut nulla mihi opportunitas, vel ad me ipsum relaxandum, vel ad alios scribendum concedatur. Postremo, etiamsi temporis et otii satis daretur, hæc tamen hujus tempestatis ratio est, ut nihil a nobis transmitti ad vos poterit, præsertim cum omnia terra marique ita interclusa sint, ut literas mittere non sit tutum.

Literas vero tuas proxime scriptas accepi ultimo Decembri, quibus perlectis, ut tuæ petitioni satisfacerem, quanta poteram cura providebam. Quod nepotem illum tuum et ceteros illos vestros episcopo Nordovicensi commendaveras, incidisti in eum virum, cui voluntas fortasse summa tibi gratificandi fuit, facultas certe ne minima quidem adfuit. Nam dum nuper suarum rerum procurationem perfidis hominibus nimis confidenter imposuit, eorum opera perfectum est, ut grandi ære alieno opprimeretur: ita fit, ut nec se ex istis miseriis expediat, nedum aliis subsidio esse possit. Ego vero, partim tuæ benevolentiæ recordatione permotus, partim quod et Deo et tibi imprimis gratum me facturum intelligebam, illos mihi suscepi adjuvandos. Itaque illos ad academiam Cantabrigiensem celeriter curavi ablegandos; et ut facilior via esset, cum ad nostram, tum ad alias linguas perdiscendas, in diversis collocandos collegiis censui, ne assidua illorum coitio alienas linguas discendi studium retardaret. Tametsi vero ego ipse mearum rationum et sumtuum difficultate magnopere perturbor, illorum tamen singulis viginti coronatos de meo impertivi, ut vivendi molestia in peregrinis locis minueretur. Ceteris in rebus omnibus, quantum meæ ipsius rationes patientur, me non defuturum illis polliceor, ut liberius possint in his suis studiis excurrere, quæ aliquando Christi ecclesiæ sunt profutura. Præclarum enim esse semper duxi, beneficium serere, quod suo postea tempore Christi oves metere possunt. Meæ erga illos etsi non summæ liberalitatis, at rectæ tamen voluntatis et amoris testes, ipsorum literas ad te misi; ut ego quid fecerim, plenius ex ipsorum quam ex meis literis intelligas. Amico meo et fratri in Christo carissimo, D. Rodolpho Gualtero, ut salutem ex me dicas plurimam, te etiam atque etiam rogo. D. Jesus Christus te et tuos labores, quos in Christi evangelio amplificando sustines, promoveat!

Dat. Londini in Anglia, 17 Febr. 1572.

Tuus in Christo frater carissimus,

EDWINUS SANDUS,

London. episcopus.

INSCRIPTIO.
Venerando patri et fratri in Christo carissimo, D. Henrico Bullingero, Tigurinæ ecclesiæ in Helvetia ministro dignissimo.

EPISTOLA CII.

JOHANNES PARKHURSTUS AD HENRICUM BULLINGERUM.

DOCTISSIMA tua refutatio bullæ papisticæ per omnium manus volitat: loquitur enim Anglice, et excusus est Londini. Bene a vobis factum est, quod tam diligenter responderitis insulso et furioso Brentii testamento.

Tribus illis litigiosis in ecclesia Belgio-Germanica concionatoribus impositum est silentium, et duo alii in eorum locum surrogati: 17 ex eadem ecclesia calendis Novembr. propter fœdum ebrietatis vitium e nostra civitate sunt expulsi. Circa medium Decembris Legatus Hispanicus jussus est intra triduum (sub pœna capitis amputandi) ex Anglia discedere: sic enim quidam ad me scripsit Londino; sed id an verum sit, nescio. Certe abiit, excessit, evasit.

Dux Northumbriæ, 16 Jan. a septima in aurora ad septimam sub noctem in aula Westmonasteriensi suam causam egit. Multa sunt illi læsæ majestatis crimina objecta, quæ ille, ut potuit, diluit. Tota illius causæ cognitio et judicatio ad novem comites, unum vice-comitem, et quindecim barones devoluta est. Isti omnes unanimi consensu eum reum pronunciarunt; atque ita tandem morti adjudicatus est. Vivit tamen adhuc in turri Londinensi inter spem metumque.

Superiori anno nives circa initium Februarii sunt liquefactæ. Hoc anno tum demum cœperunt, et circa initium Martii liquescebant.

Bene convenit inter nos et Gallos: at Hispani frontem corrugant. Ago ingentes gratias pro elegantissimo illo libello de auctoritate scripturæ et ecclesiæ: quisquis composuit, certe vir doctus est et pius. Si Zuinglio tuo opus erit nostra opera, illa minime frustrabitur. Hoc tibi et illi persuasissimum esse velim. Certe vestram de me opinionem nunquam fallam. Non possum plura; nam multis iisdem seriis negotiis adobruor. Vale, mi Bullingere. Saluta omnes amicos. Mea vos omnes. Raptim. Ludhamiæ, 10 Martii, 1572.

Tuus,
JOHANNES PARKHURSTUS,
Nordovicensis

INSCRIPTIO.
Eximio viro D. Henrico
Bullingero. Tiguri.

EPISTOLA CIII.

RICARDUS COXUS AD HENRICUM BULLINGERUM.

Salve plurimum in Christo, frater. Literas tuas multis nominibus mihi gratissimas, quas 12 Martii scriptas fuisse significas, ad finem mensis Maii accepi; ex quibus intelligo nullos hactenus te accepisse libellos hic typis excusos, quos contra bullam papisticam doctissime et pientissime scripseras. Misi equidem ad nundinas Francfordianas autumnales et literas, et libros quatuor, et pauxillum pecuniæ in usum tuum et Julii nostri. Pecuniam traditam fuisse intelligo, sed literas et libros adhuc hærere in via significatum est. Iterum igitur mitto pauca exemplaria, quibus, si alia non receperis, uti liceat.

Quæ autem scribis nova, Deus optimus maximus vertat omnia in commodum nostrum et in nominis sui gloriam! Volupe nobis est, quod ecclesiæ vestræ pacatæ sunt, non sine accessione aliarum ecclesiarum ad sinceram christianæ religionis professionem. Cum dabitur regiam majestatem convenire, non ero immemor ipsi declarare, quanto illam studio et benevolentia prosequaris. Vehementer illi placuit tuus ille libellus contra bullatas nugas, quem avidissime perlegit, quemadmodum superioribus literis, nondum tibi traditis, significavi.

De bello Turcico hoc tantum dico:

> Tunc tua res agitur, paries cum proximus ardet.

Hactenus antichristus extitit papa: quod si alterum, nempe Turcam, excitare voluerit Dominus, id merentur peccata nostra. Res nostræ sic habent. Dux (Norfolciæ), qui Reginæ nostræ insidias nequissime molitus fuerat, merito supplicio affectus est. Maria, Scotorum nuper regina, hostis regni nostræ et Reginæ publice declaratur, et carcere diligenter asservatur: quæ quidem et nostri regni demolitionem et reginæ nostræ internecionem et religionis nostræ subversionem modis omnibus meditabatur.

De nepote tuo Zuinglio malo pauca dicere, quam cum dolore multa. Res mortalium non nostro arbitrio, sed divina providentia, reguntur. Conditio Rodolphi longe felicissima, quamquam carnis affectus illi insulse adversetur. Denique ferendum est, non culpandum, quod vitari non potest. Dominus Jesus Christus te diutissime nobis servet incolumem, frater observande! Londini ex ædibus meis Holburnensibus, 6 Junii, 1572.

Tui studiosissimus,

RICARDUS COXUS, Eliensis episcopus.

Statui libellos ad te mittere; sed hic noster tabellio literas, non sarcinas, libenter portat. Alias mittendi sunt libri ad nundinas Francfordianas proximas, si fieri potest.

INSCRIPTIO.

Observandissimo in Christo fratri, D. Henrico Bul-
 lingero, ecclesiæ Tigurinæ pastori vigilantissimo.

EPISTOLA CIV.

RICARDUS HILLES AD HENRICUM BULLINGERUM.

SALUTEM plurimam. Superiore mense Martio literas meas, datas 18 die Februarii proxime elapsi, misi ad filium meum Barnabam, ut Francforti D. Christofero Froschovero in vernis nundinis pro te traderentur, quas literas spero itidem te ab eodem Froschovero accepisse. Ab eodem tempore amicissimas binas a te literas accepi, et peramplas quidem; priores ad vigesimum Decembris, posteriores ad duodecimum Martii proxime elapsi scriptas; et in eis inclusam aliam chartulam, in qua ad me perscribis ea quæ Venetiis acceperas de Turcarum cæde, quæque de statu Germaniæ et persecutione consopita commemoras, etc. De quibus et literis et novis summas tibi gratias habeo.

Ab earundem nundinarum tempore accepi a te alias etiam literas ad quosdam episcopos nostrates, quas pari cum fide et diligentia tradidi Rodulpho Gualtero et Henrico Butlero, ut, quia et ipsis alia erant de suo cum episcopis transigenda, (qui jam publico conventui, quem parlamentum Anglice nominamus, intersunt,) eas ad singulos deferrent; prout se detulisse mihi significarunt, præter eas quas ad D. Juellum Sarisburiensem conscripsisti, qui quia mortuus est, e voluntate tua illas D. Parkhursto Nordovicensi episcopo tradidi. Sed audin'? Unde factum sit, nescio: atqui neque tum neque ab eo tempore accepi de adhortatione inscriptos, quos dicis, neque Latinos nec Germanicos libros; ita ut modo quid de hac re respondeam præterea nescio. Interim tamen habeo tibi gratiam de duobus illis Germanicis et uno Latino exemplaribus, quæ tu decrevisti huc ad me transferri. Quin iidem Rodolphus et Henricus nihil etiam certi habent de illis libris. At vero quos emisit Rodulphi pater alias Latine editos cum illis libris accepi, quos iidem illis viris distribuerunt, quibus distributos voluit Rodulphi pater; cui meo nomine gratias, quæso, agas propter eum librum quem ad me misit, et amicissimas literas quas ad me decimo Martii mensis ultimi dedit.

Quod ad triginta duos, de quibus ad me scribis, aureos attinet: sedecim in postremis hibernis nundinis Francforti habitis solvit filius meus Gerso D. Christofero Froschovero pro illis decem verendissimi episcopi Vintoniensis coronatis, de quibus facis mentionem. Sedecim alii erant pro aliis decem coronatis, quos episcopus Eliensis numeravit hic prædicto Gersoni, ut tibi eos renumeraret: adjecit præterea filius meus, se eodem tempore eidem Froschovero persolvisse decem aureos pro Julio Sancterentiano, quos eidem Julio solvendos reverendissimus Eliensis episcopus ipsi prius hic dissolverat. Quod vero scribis ad me his verbis, ("pari errore aut dubio factum est vernis nundinis, ut viginti septem dalleri allati sint huc per Froschoverum, dati ipsi Francfordiæ˙et allati ex Anglia,") in ea re nescio quomodo tibi satisfaciam, quia nihil ad me scribis, num filius meus Barnabas, qui eisdem etiam nundinis Francforti fuerat, eos viginti septem dalleros Froschovero numerarit.

Nepos tuus Zuinglius die Junii... proxime elapsi hic Londini ex hoc corruptissimo seculo migravit ad Deum, et cœtui sanctorum adjunctus est, in quo laudes Deo Liberatori concinit. Sed Rodolphus Gualterus una cum Henrico Butlero reversi jam sunt Cantabrigiam, unde huc sub initium parlamenti venerunt cum episcopo Nordovicensi, quem audio singularem esse patronum Henrico Butlero; cujus vel matri vel amicis apud vos quæso significes, dicere illum nullam se ab illis pecuniam accepisse, ex quo in Angliam venit. Ego ideo illi, cum ægrotaret Cantabrigiæ, et paulo ante, mutuas dedi duas libras et decem solidos monetæ Angliæ, quæ valent in moneta Germanica tredecem florenos et quinque batzios: quos oro recipias ab ea, et eorundem tibi serva duodecim florenos et duodecim batzios, pro octo coronatis Gallicis quos mihi misit reverendus episcopus Nordovicensis una cum schedula illa quam in his inclusi literis. Et alios octo batzios velim ut pauperi aliquo studenti des. Æquum autem est (ut ante ad te scripsi) eos qui filios suos in Angliam mittunt, prius Francforti suam pecuniam dependere præ manu, quam petere ut alii pro illis hic in Anglia prius dependant, et Francforti postea exigant. Henrici Butleri mater, ut ipse mihi retulit, Lindaviæ habitat.

Secundo hujus mensis dux Norfolcius, cum læsæ majestatis damnatus multo ante fuisset, merito suo Londini securi percussus est. Gaudeo quod scribis in iisdem literis vos satis pacifice Dei gratia vivere et valere. Interim vero doleo, vos annonæ et omnium rerum caritate premi. Spero tamen fore ut post illam vestram publice institutam supplicationem Deus velit pro misericordia sua vos respicere, et correctionem illam paternam, qui sibi maxime solet dilectos sæpius punire, rursum avertere. Illud etiam doleo, te tam gravi catarro laborasse ad tertiam hebdomadam, priusquam has ad me literas conscriberes. Sed pro tua prudentia nosti Deum ipsum illos sæpius invisere quos vult; quem precor tibi patientiam concedere, et, ut ipse scribis, concedat tibi misericorditer quæ sunt ipsius bonæ voluntatis. Uxor mea te plurimum salutat, oratque ut se Deo in precibus tuis commendas, quod musculorum et nervorum contractione, quam spasmum vocamus, et calculorum in renibus dolore multum prematur.

Hoc anno initum est fœdus inter serenissimam nostram Angliæ, Franciæ, et Hyberniæ reginam et regem Galliæ, solemniter ex utrisque præstito juramento die dominico, qui fuit quindecimus dies Junii proxime elapsi, in cathedrali ecclesia S. Petri apud Westmonasterium.

Vicesimo quinto Junii recepi primum literas tuas Tiguri prima Octobris, anno 1571, datas, et missas per Dominum Friderichum Conders, nobilem quem mihi commendasti. Et si possum illum qua in re juvare citra meum incommodum aut molestiam, ut petis, lubentissime faciam. Præterea hæc adjicio, ut tibi significem, quid novarum rerum accepi e Germania inferiore, quæ est sub ditione regis Philippi: nempe, quomodo in fine Martii proxime præteriti nobilis quidam Belgius, nomine Monsieur Lumell, invasit urbem quandam maritimam in Hollandia dictum *Brill*, et vi ademit ab obedientia Philippi regis. Deinde etiam mille Hispanos et Wallos (subditos regis Philippi intelligo) qui Gallicam loquuntur linguam, in urbem dictam Middelburg intrasse accepimus, eosque in via depopulatos fuisse pagum quendam Zelandiæ dictum Armne. Est quoque e Gallia et Anglia et ex aliis regionibus finitimis magna militum turba collecta in Flusshinga; at nihil adhuc magni audio gestum esse ab Hispanis adversus illos qui sunt in prædicta Brilla aut Flusshinga, nisi quod posterius dicetur: sed perbrevis quidem exhortatio allata nuper huc erat e Flandria, impressa tam Gallica quam Belgica lingua, in qua princeps Orangiæ usus est iisdem titulis dignitatis et auctoritatis, quibus usus est in inferiore Germania ante suum exilium; suadetque Belgicos, qui jam obstiterunt Hispanis, aut nunc aut nunquam viros se præbere contra tyrannidem et injustas exactiones Hispanorum, et contra episcopos ejus regionis et clericos consocios istorum; hortaturque, si se viros præstare velint, facile removere posse grave jugum servitutis, quod dux Albæ cum præfatis Hispanis et episcopis iniquissime superimposuit illis, non solum contra rempublicam vel communem ejusdem regionis salutem, verum etiam contra honorem et fidem regis Philippi. Præterea proximo mense Maio præterito urbs Valentia in comitatu Hannoniæ in Gallia Belgica defecit ab imperio præfati ducis Alvæ, ejecitque Hispanos et primarios omnes qui ibidem præfuerunt, et passa est comitem Lodovicum, fratrem principis Orangiæ, cum octoginta vel mille armatis militibus (quorum maxima pars sunt Galli) intrare et munire urbem ad usum regis Philippi, uti simulabant, auctoritatem tamen ducis Albæ vel consociorum non suscipiunt. Sed ex eo tempore, quia dicti milites non expugnaverunt arcem Valentiæ, coacti sunt inde iterum aufugere, et relinquere urbem duci et militibus suis, qui nuperrime multo agmine venerunt.

Deinde pro certo accepimus urbem quandam dictam Phenlo, quæ est minutissima urbs in Geldria, remisisse quoque nuntium duci Alvæ; et sicut Brilla et Flushinga, sic multas alias urbes in inferiore Germania defecisse, et ducem Alvæ deliquisse ob tyrannidem qua usus est ibidem his proximis annis. Præterea, ut mihi pro certo nunciatum est, hic in Thamisi nostro appulerunt naviculæ duæ profectæ a Flusshinga, in quibus allatæ sunt literæ, significantes quibusdam Belgicis hic manentibus, magnum fuisse navale prœlium ultima hebdomada in oris inferioris Germaniæ non procul a Sluce. Flusshingæ cives, quorum vis nunc et potentia in advenis consistere videtur, tum ibidem medio inter Flandriam et Flusshingam apprehenderunt 15 aut 16 naves oneratas aromatibus et opulentis mercibus, et quoque nummis; quæ naves venerunt ab Hispania et Lusitania, et erant profecturæ Antverpiam una cum aliis triginta aut quadraginta navibus bellicis, et onerariis quæ vexerunt ducem Medinæ Cœli cum mille et ducentis militibus Hispanis, qui comitati sunt ducem, et appulerunt in inferiore Germania. Philippus enim rex præfecit vice sua hunc ducem Medinæ Cœli inferiori Germaniæ, quia prefatus rex Philippus, ut fertur, constituit ducem Alvæ rediturum inde domum in Hispaniam.

Deinde etiam, ut fama est, et ea pro certo, iidem cives Flushingæ impulerunt in vada duas aut tres naves alias earum navium quas apprehenderunt, ibique naufragium facere coegerunt, incendebantque præterea duas aut tres alias naves, et igne consumebant. Sed, ut multi hic dicunt, hæ duæ aut tres naves proximæ prædictæ, quæ combustæ erant, oneratæ sunt lana Hispanensi, profecturæque Brugam, erantque de numero earum 30 aut 40 navium, quæ venerunt ab Hispania sub præsidio et conductu præfati ducis Medinæ Cœli, non de numero 15 aut 16 navium quæ erant profecturæ Antverpiam, et captæ in conspectu Flushing et Middelburg. Mihi vero videtur lamentabile, mercatores Antverpienses (qui procul dubio impium illum et crudelem Albæ ducem non plus diligunt, quam eum diligunt qui nunc Brillæ et Flushingæ agunt) et mercatores Hispanienses et Lusitaniæ deberent ita spoliari bonis et mercibus suis, et fortassis major pars nautarum suorum interfecti, submersi, aut suspensi: ita et nunc metuendum est, ne in regionibus dicti regis Philippi tam parva sit imposterum per annos aliquot negotiatio, (seu mercatura, ut dici solet, trafica), et tanta ac tam magna sint ibi tandem civilia bella, quanta ante paucos annos fuerunt in Gallia, nisi optimo maximo Deo placuerit indignationem suam ab inferiori avertere Germania, sicuti pro sua misericordia orandus est ne faciat. Vale: Deusque optimus maximus te ad gloriam suam promovendam atque ad ecclesiæ suæ ædificationem quam diutissime conservet! Londini, 10 die Julii, anno 1572.

Tuus,
RICARDUS HILLES.

EPISTOLA CV.

ROBERTUS HORNUS AD HENRICUM BULLINGERUM.

GRATIAM et pacem in Christo. Etsi multis magnisque negotiis, cum privatis tum publicis, et reip. et ecclesiæ, distringi me plerumque vere scribis, Bullingere mi, in Christo dilectissime; tuis tamen et perlegendis et respondendis literis, utcunque occupatus, semper vaco. Cujus mihi ut præsentis sermo delectabilis semper fuit, ita et absentis literæ suaves nunc sunt et perjucundæ: quibus solis, cum hic sim, audire eum mihi videor, magno meo quidem et incredibili solatio, quem, cum isthic essem, non sine summa et singulari quadam voluptate intuebar. Verum ut ad eam literarum tuarum partem deveniam, quæ et maximi est momenti, et quod tu a me expressis verbis valde petis, ut quis nunc sit religionis ac reipublicæ status in his nostris partibus ac vicinis, intelligas.

De Gallia primum, quam miserabiles ac calamitosæ in illis locis sint ecclesiæ, quemadmodum horribili et cruenta strage infelix illa regio quasi adhuc madida, sanctorum sanguine tincta squalleat, haud dubie non sine summo dolore vestro jam dudum accepistis. In quo nos id solum, et tamen certum, habemus solatium, quod ut sanguis christianorum est semen evangelii, ita quo illi abundantius semen sparserint, eo nos pleniorem messem exspectamus.

De rebus Belgicis nihil fere est, quod scribam. Princeps toto hoc hyberno tempore in Hollandia conquiescens nihil plane, quod scimus, fecit memorabile. Ineunte vere quid acturus sit, nondum constat. Verum amisso nunc in Galliis subsidio, veremur ne in deterius omnia prolabantur.

Scotia, ut nunc res sunt, tranquilla quidem est et pacem colit: plerique enim in Regis partes transierunt, qui et omnium fere suffragio dominatur. Quem exitum tamen ea pax habitura sit, tam incerta rerum omnium conditione, affirmare non possumus: speramus quidem, prout et optamus, optima.

Anglia nostra domi tranquillitatem, foris pacem consequuta, plenis quasi velis ac secundo vento navigat. Ecclesia vero non tam papistarum obstaculis, qui severis quotidie legibus cohibentur, quam falsorum fratrum offendiculis, qui in anabaptismum videntur prolapsuri, vehementer ac periculose fluctuat. Dominus Jesus adventu tandem de cœlis suo omnes orbis tumultuantis flammas extinguat, et ecclesiæ militantis dolores tollat, ut omnes ab oculis nostris lacrymæ abstergantur, ac una omnes in ævum cum eo in cœlesti illa et nova Jerusalem triumphemus!

Vale in Christo Jesu. Ex arce mea Fernhamiæ, 10 Januarii, 1572.

Tuus totus in Christo,

ROBERTUS VINTON.

INSCRIPTIO.
Cariss⁰. in Christo fratri, D. Henrico Bullingero seniori. Tiguri.

EPISTOLA CVI.

JOHANNES PARKHURSTUS AD HENRICUM BULLINGERUM.

PULCHERRIMAM piissimamque tuam adhortationem, una cum literis ad me Juellumque scriptis, 23 Maii accepi. Juelli literas, quia is prius fatis concesserat, apud me retinui.

Regina Scotiæ adhuc apud nos manet. Superioribus comitiis multum sibi metuebat; nec immerito quidem: nam nisi Reginæ nostræ maxima clementia obstitisset, actum de ea fuisset. Quid de illa fiet proximis comitiis, adhuc incertus sum. Certe paucissimos apud nos habet amicos. Et quid mirum? cum nostro inhiarit regno, et cum tot tantisque flagitiis. sit conspurcata et quasi cooperta.

Tribus litigiosis concionatoribus hinc exclusis, summa quies et concordia in ecclesia Belgio-Germanica viget. Responsio tua ad articulos Bavaricos in Anglicam linguam conversa est, et omnium manibus teritur. Alias literas abs te accepi 10 Decembris, in quibus scribis, ingentem tumultum in Rhetia excitatum. Antiquum obtinet papa, qui hujus et omnium aliorum scelerum est auctor. Sed bene est, quod rursum sit sedatus morte papisticissimi nebulonis, qui papismum reducere conatus sit. Calendis Aprilis celeberrima nostra comitia initium habebunt. Hisce octo hebdomadibus gelu et nives continuarunt, et raro admodum toto hoc tempore se intermiserunt: sed jam evanuerunt. Laus Deo optimo maximo!

Vale, optime Bullingere. Saluta meo nomine tuos tuasque omnes, et omnes amicos meos Tigurinos. Uxor mea jam podagrica te, vos quoque omnes salutat. Raptim. Ludhamiæ, 20 Januarii, 1573.

Tuus ex animo,

JOHANNES PARKHURSTUS, N.

INSCRIPTIO.
Clarissimo viro, D. Henrico Bullingero. Tiguri.

EPISTOLA CVII.

RICARDUS COXUS AD RODOLPHUM GUALTERUM.

ALLATÆ sunt ad me superiori æstate binæ tuæ literæ, Rodolphe in Christo dilectissime, quas non sine magno animi gaudio accepi. Priores vero ingentem pii pectoris candorem declararunt; raro enim invenias, qui ea animi sinceritate præditi sunt, ut amici monita æqui boni consulant.

Sed ea te illustravit divini Spiritus gratia, eaque perfudit caritate, ut omnia speres, et omnia credas, et omnia in optimam interpreteris partem. Posteriores vero affectum vere fraternum erga nostram ecclesiam et erga me et aliquot fratres meos episcopos planissime indicarunt, quod videlicet eo nos honore afficere fueris dignatus, ut epistolarum illarum divi Pauli ad Corinthios enarrationem nobis dedicares. Quæ quidem enarratio adeo docta, pia, et dilucida est, ut nostra, quæ minima est, auctoritate non egeat. Quod autem admonitionem ad fraternam unitatem subtexueris, manifeste significas, te nostræ ecclesiæ cura maxima tangi, optareque ut Domino Deo nostro serviamus sine impedimento et animorum distractione. Hac enim via gloria Dei et evangelium Domini nostri Jesu Christi felicissime propagandum est: quanquam interim oporteat hæreses esse, ut probentur electi. Multis equidem persuasionibus, efficacissimis quidem illis, in præfatione uteris: verum quanti ponderis apud nostros novatores habituræ sint, pronuntiare non audeo. Interim tamen nolo diffidere, quin verbum Domini suo tempore fructum suum allaturum sit.

Magnas ago tibi gratias ob missum ad me librum. Quod si humanitati tuæ plene respondere non potuero, interim tamen optimæ spei filio tuo, quamdiu apud nos versabitur, prospicere atque consulere non desistam. Et quod ad illum attinet, jubemus te in utramque dormire aurem; ingratissimos enim merito nos judicare possis, si non tantillam tibi gratiam præstiterimus. Cum autem præfationem tuam plene percurissem, dolui vehementer eam adhuc editam fuisse, antequam nostrorum hominum vanitates plene intellexisses. Nuper enim totius ecclesiæ nostræ ordinis scriptis contumeliosis repagula ruperunt. Ut autem quid moliantur partim intelligas, mitto ad te quædam capita seu articulos, quos typis promulgarunt, quosque defendendos susceperunt. Optarem te cum fratre meo in Christo carissimo, D. Bullingero, de his dispicere et dijudicare, vestramque sententiam de his ferre, si vobis molestum nimis non fuerit.

Articuli quorundam Anglorum statum ecclesiæ Anglicæ hodie perturbantium:

I. Archiepiscoporum et episcoporum atque aliorum officiariorum nomina et officia penitus tollenda.

II. Electio ministrorum verbi et sacramentorum ad plebem revocanda est, quippe quæ ad episcopos non pertineat.

III. Præscriptis precibus nemo alligandus est.

IV. Nullum sacramentum administrari debet, nisi præcesserit concio sacra pronuntiata, non lecta.

V. Solus pater filium suum in baptismo suscipere debet, non alii susceptores.

VI. Omnes ecclesiæ ministri æquales esse debent, non alter altero superior.

VII. Damnant ordinem confirmationis, quo episcopi catechismum recitantibus pueris manum imponunt, Dominumque precantur ut verbi notitiam et pietatem in illis augere dignetur.

VIII. Conciones, quæ habentur dum mortui sepeliuntur, non ferunt.

IX. Lectionem scripturarum sacrarum in ecclesia non ferunt.

Alia præterea sunt nimis sane inepta, quibus nolo te diutius detinere et tædio nimis importuno fatigare. Invidet nobis Sathan beatam felicitatem. Non satis est papistas habere adversarios, nisi excitentur suæ sententiæ homines, qui ἀλλαξίαν in ecclesiam inducere satagant. Unum pene omiseram. Prodiit superiori æstate monstrosum volumen cujusdam Nicolai Sanderi nostratis, ut jactant, cui titulum fecit, "Monarchia ecclesiæ." Apparet esse mercenarius a quibusdam cardinalibus conductus, et aliorum opera adjutus, et ornatus tanquam Æsopia cornicula. Tempestas valida, et nostra omnia uno flatu prosternere videri vult. Omne in religione judicium christianis magistratibus eximit, papæ, summo in ecclesia monarchæ, et suis totum vendicat. Mortuus est noster Juellus: paucos apud nos reliquit sibi pares. Vestri proinde atque nostri interest, hujus hydræ capita resecare. Habeo libellum tuum de papa antichristo, quem ille strenue refutat. Non sines, spero, illum triumphare. Faciat te Deus optimus maximus in multos annos superstitem ad ecclesiæ suæ incolumitatem!

Apud insulam Eliensem in Anglia, 4 Februarii, 1572, juxta computationem Anglorum.

Mitto ad te mnemosynon, licet nimis exiguum, quinque coronatorum Anglicorum.

Tui studiosissimus in Christo frater,

RICARDUS ELIENSIS,

Episcopus in Anglia.

INSCRIPTIO.
Viro doctissimo et verbi Dei professori eximio, et fratri meo in Christo carissimo, D. Rodolpho Gualtero, Tigurino.

EPISTOLA CVIII.

RICARDUS COXUS AD HENRICUM BULLINGERUM.

Non possunt non esse mihi jucundissimæ tuæ literæ, frater in Christo reverende, tantam nimirum spirantes pietatem et humanitatem. Gratulor tibi ex animo eas, quas prædicas, corporis vires, quæ tibi per Dei gratiam sufficiunt ad munus tuum obeundum. Multis annis has tibi ministret benignus Dominus ad gloriam nominis sui et ecclesiæ ædificationem!

Ego una tecum in Domino glorior, quod sua munificentia annum agens septuagesimum quartum viribus non destituor, quo minus Spartam, quam nactus sum, utcunque exornem, nisi quod manuum tremor usum scribendi nonnihil remoratur. Tantum a Domino meo contendo, ne in functione mea languescam, sed usque ad extremum fabulæ actum ardentior evadam. Doleo te copia librorum tuorum destitui. Misi ad typographum nostrum, ut ad te transmittat aliquid; quod fideliter ipsum præstaturum esse recipio, nisi omnes libri fuerint distracti.

Quod de Turcis et Turcizantibus scribis, fateri oportet nos in seculo nequam vivere, et incidisse in tempora longe periculosissima. Atque hæc res cum subit animos piorum, inscrutabilia judicia Dei ad stuporem usque admirantur, quid de piis futurum sit: tot Christianorum regna a Turca occupata atque vastata, et jam ipsum capitibus nostris imminere; Christianorum religionem in angulum detrusam, et infinitis dissidiis et contentionibus dissectam et dilaceratam; denique persecutionibus crudelissimis papistarum passim exagitatam et vexatam. *Super tribus sceleribus et quatuor non convertet Dominus.* Timeo etiam vehementer, quem exitum habituræ sint pertinacissimæ nostræ contentiones et improborum hominum spiritus a dilectione alienissimi. Utinam sano libelli tui consilio, quem de concordia ministrorum nuper edidisti, parerent! Sed optandum id quidem magis quam sperandum. De hisce dissidiis poteris nonnihil a D. Gualtero, optimo viro, cognoscere. Pergunt nostri adhuc nova cudere. Reprehendunt orationem illam, qua Deum oramus, ut ab omnibus adversitatibus liberemur. Utimur in precibus cantico divæ virginis, Joannis Baptistæ et senis Simonis: id illi non ferunt. Utimur in fine singulorum psalmorum, cum præsente populo recitantur, "Gloria Patri et Filio et Spiritui Sancto:" id battalogiam vocant. Sed cesso istis vanitatibus te ulterius interturbare. Medelam istis a Deo postulamus. Interim tamen hujusmodi malis occurrere non cessamus, quatenus Dominus vires suppeditare dignatur.

Librum tuum de persecutionibus ecclesiæ nondum accepi. Opto te, mi frater in Christo observande, multos annos incolumem vivere, et ad finem usque ecclesiæ Dei restaurandæ operam dare. Misi ad Julium nostrum sex coronatos nostrates.

Tui studiosissimus in Christo frater,
Eliensis ecclesiæ episcopus et servus,
RICARDUS COXUS, Episcopus Eliensis.

INSCRIPTIO.

Venerando patri et carissimo in
  Christo fratri, D. Henrico
  Bullingero, ecclesiæ Tigurinæ
  pastori fidelissimo.

EPISTOLA CIX.

RICARDUS COXUS AD RODOLPHUM GUALTERUM.

Accepi literas tuas mense Junio, 1573, Gualtere, frater in Christo dilectissime. Equidem miror literas meas ad te non esse delatas, quas initio superioris veris scripsi et ad te, et ad venerandum patrem et fratrem meum D. Bullingerum. Longe mihi gratius et optandum magis, ut ex literis meis didicisses, quas tum temporis scribebam, quanta cum gratulatione acceptæ fuerint tuæ homiliæ, una cum epistola prudenter, docte, et pie de rebus aliquot controversis disserente. Didicisses præterea ex illis meis literis, quantas turbas excitarint in ecclesia nostra non male constituta homines factiosi et capitosi; qui scriptis et concionibus atque privatis colloquiis universam ecclesiæ nostræ œconomiam refutant et convellunt, episcoposque omnes et ceteros verbi ministros apud plebem et apud magistratus et nobiles in odium vocant incredibile. Imo hunc ordinem tanquam Christi ecclesiæ inutilem rejiciunt, et ut prorsus aboleatur, modis omnibus contendunt. Sed sanctissimam nostram Reginam et ex summis magistratibus aliquot ea imbuit Dominus Deus noster prudentia et pietate, ut frustra homines illi contendant, uti speramus. Antiquum illud in primæva ecclesia presbyterium revocare conantur, et ministrorum omnium æqualitatem ita constituere, ut vel ab ipsa contemnantur et conculcentur; adeo ut timendum sit, ne paullatim Christus ipse exulet.

Quod autem ad eum, quem scribis, modum filius literas dedit, equidem ingenue probi adolescentis functus est officio. Si frequentius me inviseret vel literis salutaret, tantilli officii ipsum non pœniteret. Non ægre ferendum tibi est, mi Gualtere, quod homines sectarii sententiæ tuæ justissimæ mali atque improbi interpretes evadunt. Aliter enim fieri non potest, quin zizania crescant in agro Dominico, eaque numero non mediocri. Hujus farinæ sunt anabaptistæ, Donatistæ, Arriani, papistæ, et universa sectariorum gens nequissima. Sed solidum est a Christo solatium nostrum: "Beati estis cum maledixerint vobis homines mentientes propter me." Quæ autem de moderatione in rebus externis servanda scribis, modo veritas Christi et fides illæsa retineatur, a sincera pietate et solidissimo judicio proficiscuntur. Quod ad existimationem nominis tui attinet, contemnendi quidem sunt, qui bonorum omnium famam corrodere non cessant; interim neque tuam neque nostram famam suis maledictis labefactare valent: non enim illis, sed Domino nostro, cadimus et stamus.

Spero te priores meas literas ad D. Bullingerum et ad te missas antehac recepisse. Curavi illas cum 25 *gulden*, ut vocant, per Ricardum

Hilles, mercatorem nostratem, Froschovero vestro tradi, ut ad vos deferrentur. Dominus Jesus te nobis diutissime servet incolumem ad ecclesiæ suæ commodum maximum! Salutabis meo nomine ecclesiæ Christi columnam, D. Henricum Bullingerum. Ex ædibus meis in Insula Eliensi in Anglia constitutis, die 12 Junii, 1573.

Tui in Christo amantissimus,
RICARDUS COXUS,
Eliensis Episcopus.

INSCRIPTIO.
Carissimo in Christo fratri, D. Rodolpho Gualtero, ecclesiæ Tigurinæ præconi fidelissimo.

EPISTOLA CX.

JACOBUS PILKINGTONUS AD RODOLPHUM GUALTERUM.

Jesus! S. P. Si quantum tibi datur temporis et virium ad scribendum tantillum mihi daretur otii et valetudinis ad legendum, quæ tu indefessis laboribus tuis prelo commisisti; bene, mihi crede, mecum agi putarem: sed quum crebris infirmitatibus impedior ne possim, præterque quotidianas ecclesiarum curas et publica negotia perpetuo cum morbis et morte colluctor, ecclesiæ Dei gratulor, cui tu tantus et talis contigisti operarius; (senescente jam mundo et ingravescente ætate mea mihi doleo, cui tam suaves fructus tuos degustare vix licet;) et tibi Nestoreos annos exopto, ut quæ tam feliciter cœpisti, felicius exædificare queas. Quam multi multis doctissimis tuis commentariis multum delectantur, præcipueque postremis tuis in utramque ad Corinthios epistolam (propter quos ego quoque ingentes ago tibi gratias seorsum), nolo nunc tibi commemorando narrare, nec quam[1] magnifice ego de illis sentiam, explicare, ne vanus fortassis adulator potius, quam verus in os laudator tibi fore videar. Tu perge porro, quod cœpisti. Dominum Deum scriptis tuis prædicato: ecclesiam illius mysteriis aperiendis ædificato: indoctos instrue, doctiores ad labores provocato: singulos hortare, mone, increpa; et Dominum communem omnium habebis inspectorem, laudatorem, et remuneratorem amplissimum laborum tuorum in illius vinea repurganda positorum.

Sed hic, quæso, paulisper mecum consiste, et ecclesiam hanc nostram, nunc miserrime scissam, ne dicam penitus dilaceratam, deplora; Domino Deo tuo commenda, et ut nostri misertus quam cito piam quandam medelam provideat, ut hæc ulcera sanentur, ne prorsus corruat, exora. Audivit, sat scio, prudentia tua, idque sæpius ad nauseam, de infelici illa inter quosdam e nostris contentione de re vestiaria et habitu ministrorum,

[1 MS. *quaquam.*]

quantas tragœdias concitarit: at ea nunc sic recruduit, imo se ipsam nunc totam palam explicuit, quæ prius dissimulando delituit, ut jam non solum vestis, sed quicquid habemus politiæ ecclesiasticæ, disciplinæ, patrimonii episcopalis, rituum aut precum publicarum, liturgiæ, vocationis ministrorum, aut sacramentorum ministerii, id omne jam publicis libellis convellatur, et non ferendum in Christi ecclesia acerrime contendatur. Solam doctrinam nobis integram relinquunt: quicquid aliud sit, quocunque nomine appellaris, rejiciendum clamitant. Dolent pii, papistæ rident, quod nos invicem jam mordemus, qui illos conjunctis copiis prius expugnare solebamus: infirmi, quid aut cui credendum sit, ignorant; ἄθεοι suaviter in utramvis aurem dormiunt: ἱεροφάνται prædæ inhiant, et ut majus incendium crescat, velut folles sedulo inflant. Miserum spectaculum et horrendum auditu, hæc inter ejusdem religionis professores fieri: et tamen tota culpa in episcopos transfertur, quasi illi soli, si vellent, omnia hæc mala eradicare queant. Multa, fateor, toleramus inviti gemendo, quæ tollere, si maxime velimus, nequimus orando. Sub imperio vivimus, et nihil sine principe innovare, aut abrogare sine legum auctoritate possumus; et num hæc ferenda, vel potius ecclesiæ pax abrumpenda, sola nunc datur optio. Quam sanum sit consilium tuum in præfatione tua ad Corinthios epistolæ de varietate rituum et disciplinarum in singulis ecclesiis, utinam omnes intelligerent, et sequerentur! At isti nihil tolerandum in ritibus ecclesiæ præter tempora apostolica, et omnem disciplinam illinc derivari debere, idque sub animæ et salutis æternæ dispendio, vociferando crepant.

In bonam partem cape, quæso, pauculos hos coronatos, pignus amoris mei erga te et sanam doctrinam tuam. Plures dedissem, nisi quod collectionem quandam instituimus in pauperes Gallos, qui, patria ejecti et bonis spoliati, partim Genevam, partim huc confugerunt.

Quid nuper factum sit in Scotia, ex his versibus totum perdisces. Symmystas tuos omnes in Domino valere jubeo, præcipueque venerandum D. Bullingerum cui excusatum; diligenter me vellem, quod non privatim ad eum scripserim; precorque ut cum unus sitis, unis his literis contenti sitis. Has illi, si libet, communica, ut nostris miseriis compati et condolere queat. Dominus Jesus diu servet felix Tigurum in antiqua sua pace et Dei timore! Vale in Domino, frater in Christo carissime. 20 Julii, 1573.

Doctrinæ et pietatis tuæ studiosissimus,

JACOBUS PILKINTONUS,

Dunelmensis.

INSCRIPTIO.
Doctissimo viro, D. Rodolpho
Gualtero, Tigurino pastori
fidelissimo.

EPISTOLA CXI.

LAURENTIUS HUMFREDUS AD RODOLPHUM GUALTERUM.

IMMANUEL! Venit ad me Oxoniam literis tuis comitatus Gualterus filius tuus, imago tui et vere Zuinglianus, et vivit apud Magdalenenses, jucundus mihi et acceptus meis et gratus academiæ. Commendarunt eum D. comes Bedfordius et Parkhurstus, amicus tuus et episcopus noster, mihi multis nominibus observandus. Itaque et tua causa et illorum honoratissimorum rogatu eum in meam fidem et in collegium recepi, mihi gratulans talem me habere hospitem. D. Parkhurstus amplissime pollicetur, se omnia necessaria suppeditaturum; et ego meam opem et operam ultro offero, si quo modo tanti adolescentis utilitatibus inservire potero. Nam et ingenuos hominis mores ac liberale ingenium amo; et patri tali, qui tot dies ac noctes in gignendis evangelii filiis et in propagando christianæ ecclesiæ seminario consumit, omnia me debere fateor. Perge porro in illud divinum studium incumbere, ut dum licet, etiam libeat religionis puritatem tueri, et veritatem hactenus in caliginoso specu Romanistarum vel inscitia vel malitia abstrusam illustrare. Pulcherrimum enim est usque ad canos canere, et seniles atque adeo cygneæ commentationes sunt dulcissimæ et gravissimæ. Hinc vobis talentum magis a Domino concessum, hinc pax et otium et secessus dantur, hinc typographiæ præstantissima commoditas, ut in hac affluentia rerum omnium, in summa opportunitate prositis nobis Britannis, toto orbe divisis, qui omnibus fere his adminiculis indigemus. Quamquam Dei beneficio omnia sunt apud nos pacata, licet proximus paries ardeat. Nondum enim faces civilium bellorum in Gallia et Flandria penitus extinctæ sunt, tametsi de honestis quibusdam conditionibus pacis colloquium instituatur.

In Scotia illa virginalis arx Edinburgensis, (sic enim Scoti vocarunt,) quantumvis hactenus invicta, nunc demum prostituta est et capta; quam Regina nostra non sibi sed puero regi subegit. Itaque, Regina ipsorum apud nos asservata, et conjuratis omnibus vel se dedentibus vel deletis, et amicitia inter eos mutua coalescit, et una religio summo omnium consensu recepta in eo regno efflorescit. Dominus Jesus te et tuos, D. Bullingerum, Simlerum, Lavaterum, ac totam ecclesiam vestram conservet, et omni benedictione cumulet! Raptim, in mediis comitiis Magdalenensibus. Oxoniæ, 28 Julii, 1573.

Tuæ pietatis observantissimus,
LAURENTIUS HUMFREDUS.

INSCRIPTIO.
Carissimo viro, D°. et fratri
 colendissimo, D. Rodolpho
 Gualtero. Tiguri.

EPISTOLA CXII.

EDMUNDUS GRINDALLUS AD HENRICUM BULLINGERUM.

SALUTEM in Christo! Sub finem Decembris elapsi accepi literas tuas, carissime D. Bullingere, 24 Augusti scriptas, quo die immani et inaudita crudelitate trucidati sunt Parisius admiralius cum aliis nobilibus et maxima fidelium multitudine. Hos nobis protulit fructus egregium illud fœdus Gallicum, de quo tanta bona sperabamus. Fuerunt quidem antea infames vesperæ Siculæ; sed istæ, ut ita dicam, matutinæ Gallicæ illas quam longissimo intervallo post se relinquunt. Videt hæc Dominus et requiret. Multi exules ex Galliis Londinum confluxere, et inter hos multi ecclesiarum ministri, qui satis benigne ibidem hospitio excipiuntur, et piorum eleemosynis sublevantur.

Res nostræ post sopitam illam controversiam de ritibus aliquandiu valde erant tranquillæ; quum in medium provolarunt quidam libelli satis virulenti, furtim contra leges impressi, in quibus universa fere ecclesiæ nostræ externa politia oppugnabatur. Archiepiscopos enim et episcopos prorsus in ordinem cogendos esse censent; ministros ecclesiæ a plebe tantum eligendos; inter ministros æqualitatem esse constituendam; in singulis urbibus, oppidis, parochiis sive pagis, erigendum esse consistorium, ex pastore et senioribus illius loci constitutum, qui soli de omnibus ecclesiasticis negotiis judicent: ecclesiam Anglicanam christianæ ecclesiæ vix faciem aliquam habere; precum ecclesiasticarum non debere aliquam certam formam præscribi, sed in cœtibus sacris unicuique ministro orandum, prout Spiritus Sanctus dictaverit: pertinacium papistarum infantes quoad usum baptismi (utor enim illorum verbis) immundos esse, nec tamen idcirco a divina electione excludendos: multa alia prætereo, quæ recensere nimis longum esset. Sed nuper promulgatum fuit edictum regium, quo cavetur, ne hujusmodi libelli famosi posthac publicentur; quod istorum conatus, uti spero, retardabit. Juvenes sunt, qui ista spargunt, et habent suos suffragatores, præsertim ex his qui bonis ecclesiasticis inhiant: sed tamen gaudeo, Humfredum et Sampsonum ac ceteros nonnullos, qui antea de ritibus quæstiones movebant, ab hac factione prorsus esse alienos.

Arx Edinburgensis in Scotia, de qua antea scripsi, Anglicis nostris tormentis per viginti dies continuos quassata, tandem 28 Maii elapsi ad deditionem coacta est: de primariis supplicium sumptum. Est igitur jam Scotia universa ad pueri regis obedientiam redacta; a Gallis propter disparitatem religionis et crudelitatem erga fideles superiore anno exercitam prorsus aliena; nostræ vero Reginæ, quæ toties Scotos in libertatem vindicavit, deditissima; quod ex versibus inclusis, Edinburgi impressis, facile conspicere potes.

Res Gallicæ sunt vobis satis notæ. In Hollandia et Selandia princeps Auriacus classe superior est; terra dubio semper eventu certatur. Dominus misereatur ecclesiæ suæ, et his malis tandem aliquando finem imponat, ut ipsum uno ore glorificemus; qui tuam pietatem ecclesiæ suæ quam diutissime incolumem conservet! Eboraci, ultimo Julii, 1573.

Deditissimus tibi in Domino,
EDM. EBORACENSIS.

P. S. Statui (volente Domino) ad nundinas vernas aliquid nostri μνημόσυνον ad te mittere: quod nunc artificis negligentia paratum non erat.

INSCRIPTIO.
Domino Henrico Bullingero seniori, ecclesiæ Tigurinæ ministro fidelissimo, fratri ac symmystæ in Domino carissimo.

EPISTOLA CXIII.

EDMUNDUS GRINDALLUS AD RODOLPHUM GUALTERUM.

SALUTEM in Christo, carissime D. Gualtere! Quod homilias tuas in 1 ad Corinthios nuper editas sub meo ac aliorum quorundam carissimorum fratrum et collegarum meorum nomine apparere voluisti, gratissimum fuit; atque eo nomine, quod ad me attinet, (spero autem ceteros idem facturos,) gratias pietati tuæ ago quam maximas. Duo exemplaria ligata misit ad me filius tuus, quorum alterum misi ad D. Dunelmensem, cui etiam, uti scribit, gratum fuit munus; alterum apud me retineo. Non est cur audaciam tuam in scribendo ad me tam diligenter excuses: es enim mihi, etsi non ex facie, ex scriptis tamen tuis, singulari eruditione et doctrina refertissimis, satis notus; et propter eximiam pietatem, quam ubique spirant tua scripta, addo etiam, propter arctissimam in vera Christi doctrina consensionem, carissimus.

Filium tuum, quia ipse a Cantabrigia procul absum, D. Johanni Whitegifto, optimo viro, et collegii, in quo degit filius, præfecto, serio commendavi; quem etiam oravi, ut morum quoque se censorem satis severum, si opus esset, præberet: sed non erit opus, uti spero; audio enim filium tuum admodum studiosum esse ac modestum, et ab omni levitate alienum.

De rebus nostris pauca scripsi ad D. Bullingerum, quæ ipse, non dubito, communicabit. Scripsi etiam ad Ricardum Hilles, mercatorem Londinensem, ut quinquaginta coronatos Gallicos tibi ad sequentes nundinas

Francfordianas transmittendos curaret; 30 scilicet ex me, reliquos mittit D. Dunelmensis, cujus etiam literas una cum istis recipies. Hoc tenue munusculum oramus ut bonam in partem accipias. Vale in Christo quam optime, frater in Domino carissime. Eboraci, ultimo Julii, 1573.

Tuus in Christo,
EDMUNDUS EBORACENSIS.

INSCRIPTIO.

Domino Rodolpho Gualtero, ecclesiæ Tigurinæ ministro, fratri carissimo.

EPISTOLA CXIV.

EDWINUS SANDUS AD HENRICUM BULLINGERUM.

MULTIS modis multum tibi debeo, vir colendissime; et quod me semper summa benevolentia ac caritate complexus es, et quod tam diligenter atque etiam frequenter ad me perscribere non es dedignatus. Pro quibus omnibus cum ipse parem gratiam referre nequeam, agam tamen gratias quam maximas, et me tibi propter istam singularem humanitatem tuam multo devinctissimum esse libenter et perpetuo agnoscam.

Quod rarius ego ad te scribo, id haud negligentiæ meæ adscribas velim, sed quod rarius (his præsertim turbulentissimis temporibus, cum omnia bello, tumultibus, et cædibus flagrant) reperiuntur tabellarii qui ad vos proficiscuntur. Nemo enim est homo, cui libentius scriberem, quam domino Bullingero, quem ut propter summam humanitatem suam plurimum semper amavi, sic propter singularem eruditionem et raram pietatem, ceterasque virtutes eximias, multum veneratus sum. Cum enim in animo revolvo, (id quod sæpissime facio,) quanto cum favore et gratia a vobis exceptus eram, quam fraterne et humaniter me exulantem tractastis, et in quanta felicitate mihi apud vos visus sum vivere; nihil magis mihi in votis est, quam ut liberatus istis curis et solicitudinibus, quibus jam obruor, quod reliquum est temporis, Tiguri tamquam peregrinus et privatus consumerem. Hujusmodi cogitationes mihi quotidie occurrunt, nec quicquam est quod potius exoptarem. Sed video hoc fieri non posse. Non mihi sum natus: ecclesia nostra, quæ pessimis his temporibus pessime agitatur, et infeliciter turbata est, meam operam vehementer efflagitat; sponsam Christi periclitantem non audeo deserere; reclamaret etenim conscientia, et proditionis me argueret. Oriuntur ex nobis novi oratores, stulti adolescentes, qui cum auctoritatem contemnant, nec superiores patiantur, totum ecclesiæ nostræ statum, pie constitutum et summo optimorum consensu confirmatum et stabilitum, funditus sublatum ac eradicatum esse volunt; et nescio quam novam ecclesiæ formam nobis fabricare contendunt. Et non putares, quanto cum applausu hæc nova facies rerum cum a populo tum a nobilitate amplexa sit. Populus mutationes amat, et libertatem quærit; nobilitas vero utilitatem. Isti boni viri utrumque dant, idque largiter. Verum ut rem omnem melius cognoscas, summam controversiæ in capita quædam redacta accipies:

I. Civilis magistratus nullum jus habet in res ecclesiasticas. Est tantum membrum ecclesiæ, cujus gubernatio penes ecclesiasticos viros esse debet.

II. Ecclesia Christi non admittit aliam gubernationem, quam illam solum, quæ fit per presbyterium: scilicet per ministrum, seniores et diaconum.

III. Nomina et auctoritas archiepiscoporum, archidiaconorum, decanorum, cancellariorum, commissariorum, cum hujusmodi titulis et dignitatibus, ab ecclesia Christi omnino submoveantur.

IV. Habeat unaquæque parochia suum proprium presbyterium.

V. Electio ministrorum necessario spectat ad plebem.

VI. Bona, possessiones, terræ, proventus, tituli, honores, auctoritates, et alia quæcunque spectantia vel ad episcopos, vel ad ecclesias cathedrales, et quæ illis jam jure debentur, prorsus auferantur et in perpetuum tollantur.

VII. Nemo debet concionari, nisi qui est pastor alicujus gregis; et apud suum tantum gregem, non alibi, concionem habeat.

VIII. Infantes papistarum non sunt baptizandi.

IX. Judicialia Mosis spectant ad christianos principes, nec ab illis unguem latum discedere debent.

Multa sunt alia ejusdem generis, non minus absurda, quæ non commemorabo; quæ omnia, si quid ego judico, non faciunt ad bonum et pacem ecclesiæ, sed ad ruinam et confusionem. Tolle auctoritatem, ruit populus in omne flagitium. Tolle patrimonium ecclesiæ, et eadem opera non solum bonas literas, sed et ipsam religionem auferes. Sed jam videor rem præjudicare. Percupio, doctissime vir, tuam et D. Gualteri, D. Simleri, reliquorumque fratrum audire de istis rebus sententiam, quam ut sanam et verbo Dei consentaneam libenter ipse sequar. Si enim vestrum de tota controversia interponeretur judicium, dubio procul multum faceret ad pacem ecclesiæ nostræ. Clamitant isti boni viri, quod habeant omnes ecclesias reformatas stantes ex partibus suis.

De statu reipublicæ nostræ nihil dicam: hactenus omnia sunt pacata; sed verendum ne intestinæ istæ dissensiones tandem in perniciem patriæ evadant.

Mitto ad tuam dominationem tantum panni Anglici, quantum sufficit ad conficiendam tibi togam. Utere, quæso, et pro tua humanitate boni consule. Bene vale, vir colendissime, et precibus tuis Deo me habeas commendatum, quæso. Raptim. Londini in Anglia, 15 Augusti, 1573.

Tuus in Christo frater,
EDWINUS SANDUS,
Episcopus Londinensis.

INSCRIPTIO.

Viro colendissimo et fratri suo carissimo, domino Henrico Bullingero, ecclesiæ Tigurinæ pastori vigilantissimo.

In Helvetia.

EPISTOLA CXV.

RICARDUS COXUS AD RODOLPHUM GUALTERUM.

Quod literis tuis longe humanissimis mense Decembri mihi traditis me inviseris, Gualtere in Christo carissime, gratias ago tibi quam possum maximas; quibus plane significas te ecclesiæ Christi vel procul dissitæ solicitudine affici: quæ quidem omnium in ecclesia pastorum cura non postrema debet esse, inprimis vero eorum, qui præ aliis eruditionis et judicii atque pietatis munere pollent. D. Whitgiftus, schismaticorum hostis acerrimus et præcipuus in ecclesia nostra malleus, cum animadvertisset effrænes homines repagula legum religionisque bene quieteque constitutæ suo temerario impetu rupisse, libellosque famosos clam prelo commissos palam sparsisse, et ex tuis ad Parkhurstum nostrum literis, quas multis communicarant, jam ansam arripuisse ad suos errores confirmandos; ad veritatis defensionem magnopere interesse putabat, si literæ ad me tuæ publicarentur. Priores tuæ literæ per falsos accusatores a te extortæ fuerunt; posteriores vero simplex veritas in lucem protulit. Neque enim est, quod istarum publicatione movearis, quæ laudem tibi decusque pepererunt, eo quod veritati suffragantur, cujus neminem pudere debet.

Nonnullos nostrorum hominum errores quæstionibus ad te meis patefeci: in quibus quod animi tui sensum tam candide et sincere explicuisti, rem nobis gratissimam fecisti. Non enim levis momenti est in ecclesia nostra D. Bullingeri et D. Gualteri judicium. Sed rixatores nostri ita tergiversantur, atque ita suo sensu abundant, ut nemini cedant qui suis sententiis adversetur, vestraque omnia scripta in suas partes, tanquam obtorto collo, trahere nituntur. Utque aliquod specimen illorum candoris tibi depingam; universum ecclesiæ nostræ Anglicanæ ordinem invertere sedulo conantur. Noctes et dies et plebeios et nobiles solicitant, incitantque ad odium eorum, qui jam, abdicato papismo, ministerio fideliter funguntur, fidemque eorum apud omnes infirmare atque elevare satagunt. In qua re ut gratiores et plausibiliores fiant, harpyiis nostris, quæ prædis et rapinis nostris avide inhiant, ecclesiarum cathedralium proventus ac reditus in alios nescio quos usus transferendos esse clamitant. Nec alios episcopos contendunt esse præficiendos, nisi in singulis parœciis singulos pastores, quorum summam volunt esse auctoritatem cum suo presbyterio regendi ceteros parochianos. Atque hac ratione suam erigunt atque stabiliunt æqualitatem. Præter hanc nullam omnino agnoscere volunt ecclesiæ gubernationem. Præterea fundos et ædes episcoporum verti volunt in pios usus. At, talpis cæciores, non vident a voracibus lupis mox esse devorandos. Sunt apud nos 23 episcopatus, quorum alii satis tenues habent posessiones, alii mediocres, alii pinguiores: sed omnes intra mediocritatem. Hi omnes præter verbi et sacramentorum administrationem nullis negotiis se immiscent, nisi ad legis præscriptum aut ad summi magistratus mandatum. Neque in his, quod sciam, duriter cum fratribus agunt; sed quæ dura sunt, mira lenitate temperant: id quod dolenter conquererentur, si nostra jurisdictio ad laicos, ut vocant, transferretur. Facile sentirent aurea æneis esse commutata. Quam vera autem sint, quæ auribus piorum contra nos insusurrarunt, dies declarabit. Et *nostra gloriatio est testimonium conscientiæ*[1]. Utinam acquiescerent sano et prudenti tuo consilio, nimirum ut tolerarent, quæ non sine ingenti periculo corrigi possunt! Aggressi primum fuerunt parva; jam vero parva et magna sursum et deorsum miscent et confundunt omnia, ecclesiamque in grave discrimen conjicerent, si Regina nostra pientissima non summa fide sibi constaret, vanitatemque et hominum levium inconstantiam exhorresceret atque compesceret. Ut autem isti tumultuantes fratres frænentur, si quid magistratus mandat, ejus mandati executores esse non detrectamus, hinc nimia severitas, ne dicam crudelitas, nobis injustissime imputatur. Sed illud unicum habemus solatium, Christi religionem comitem habere crucem, quam libenter ferre juvabit nos Spiritu suo.

Filius tuus, optimæ spei adolescens, hoc solum habet peccatum, quod rarius me invisit. Sed modo cogor illi ignoscere, quod in altera nostra academia, Oxoniensi scilicet, longe a me distanti, degit. Sed spero illum me salutaturum esse in discessu. Prudenter a te factum, quod filio tuo tam provide consulis, ut instar Ulyssis multorum mores et urbes videat, et, tanquam apis sedula, pietatem sugat ex omnibus ecclesiis. Deus illum reducem faciat ad benedictionem patris! Christus Jesus te nobis diutissime servet incolumem!

[[1] MS. *constantiæ*.]

Ex insula Eliensi in Anglia, tertio Februarii, 1573, juxta computationem Anglicam.

Tui in Christo amantissimus,
· RICARDUS COXUS,
ecclesiæ Eliensis pastor et servus,
RICARDUS ELIENSIS.

INSCRIPTIO.
Amico meo carissimo et verbi Dei ministro fidelissimo, D. Rodolpho Gualtero, Tigurino.

EPISTOLA CXVI.

JOHANNES PARKHURSTUS AD HENRICUM BULLINGERUM.

SALVE, suavissime D. Bullingere. Literas tuas scriptas 26 Augusti accepi 21 Novembris, quo quidem tempore nova et severa edicta publicata sunt contra eos, qui vel nostras ceremonias contemnunt, vel observare nolunt. Deus bene vertat, et omnium Christi ecclesiarum misereatur! Faxit Deus ne lateat anguis in herba! Gratias ago ingentes pro libro tuo doctissimo, scripto de persecutionibus ecclesiæ, a Simlero nostro Latine reddito, quem non ita pridem accepi. Germanicus nunquam ad meas pervenit manus.

Scribis te septuagenarium esse: utinam tandem fias centenarius vel ipsius ecclesiæ caussa! Ego certe annum sexagesimum tertium, annum scilicet mihi climactericum, fere absolvi. Uxor mea est puella sexaginta septem annorum et ultra, ut ipsa refert. Quod omnia pacifica sunt in Helvetia, gaudeo. Quod cum militibus mercenariis tam infeliciter sit actum, non doleo. Ante festum Bartholomæi non cœpta est apud nos in Norfolcia messis; quæ valde fuit humida et pluviosa: vix fuit in tota messe serena dies, ita ut non parva pars frugum nobis perierit; at indefessa operariorum diligentia pars maxima servata est. Non solum frumenti, sed omnium rerum, caritas apud nos est maxima. Unde ista caritas, quæris? Quia frigescit apud nos caritas. Ante festum purificationis nullas hic vidimus nives, nullum penc sensimus gelu: nunc utrisque abundamus.

Salutes, quæso, meo nomine omnes amicos meos, et ipsum Julium, inter amicos non postremum. Male sit Thimelthorpo, collectori longe omnium pessimo, qui me aliquid pro amicis colligere non patitur. Sed spero meliora. Deus servet te et omnes meos Tigurinos! Amen. Raptim. Ludhamiæ, 6 Februarii, 1574. Mea teque tuosque salutat. Vale.

Tuus,
JOHANNES PARKHURSTUS, N.

INSCRIPTIO.
Clarissimo viro D. Henrico
Bullingero.
Tiguri.

EPISTOLA CXVII.

JOHANNES PARKHURSTUS AD JOSIAM SIMLERUM.

LITERAS tuas scriptas 22 Februarii, 1573, accepi 20 Augusti. Juvenis ille Gulielmus Barlous, cui dedisti, nunquam mihi (quod sciam) est cognitus vel visus. Ubiquitarius ille Jacobus Andreæ, qui minatur se scripturum contra Vitebergenses et meos Tigurinos, laterem lavabit, et suam omnibus prodet stultitiam. Nos Angli neque Ubiquitatem neque alia opinionum portenta ferre possumus; tantum abest, ut talia defensemus. Tantum pro ceremoniis, vestibus, et rebus nihili digladiamur. Utinam tandem aliquando hæ velitationes et lites sopiantur et sepeliantur! Certe papistæ in spem, nescio quam, eriguntur; at spero, vanam. Dominus det istis rebus finem, et papistis funem! Spero nostram Magdalenam ante multos menses quartana liberatam.

Et Dominus te et meam uxorem liberet podagra! Amen. Raptim. Ludhamiæ, 8 Februarii, 1574. Saluta tuam et omnes meos amicos. Mea vos omnes.

Tuus,
JOHANNES PARKHURSTUS,
Nordovicensis.

INSCRIPTIO.
Eximio viro D. Josiæ Simlero.
Tiguri.

EPISTOLA CXVIII.

JOHANNES PARKHURSTUS AD HENRICUM BULLINGERUM.

SALVUS sis in Christo, carissime Bullingere!

In prioribus meis literis, quas 6 Februarii ad te misi, ingentes egi gratias pro doctissimo libello, quem de persecutionibus ecclesiæ ad me miseris, et nunc etiam ago. Latinum accepi, Germanicum ne adhuc quidem vidi. Literas tuas 10 Martii datas 26 Junii accepi; in quibus scribis, te responsum quoddam ad Brentianos nunc ad me misisse, et præterea duas homilias in psalmum 130 et 133: at ego nihil horum accepi. Male sit illis, per quos tanti thesauri mihi subtrahuntur!

Puella quædam Belgio-Germanica septendecim vel octodecim annorum toto integro anno Nordovici a Sathana miserrime est vexata, et hæc illius ecclesiæ concionatori servivit. Quæ quidem puella omnibus tentationibus et dilacerationibus in fide firma perstitit, et adversario plus quam viriliter restitit. Tandem Dei auxilio victus diabolus illam reliquit, et eodem quasi momento filium cujusdam senatoris invasit, quem etiam ad aliquot septimanas incredibiliter adflixit. Fiebant me jubente in civitate publicæ preces, indicto etiam jejunio usque ad vesperam. Dominus misertus est etiam pueri, et hostem profligavit. Puer erat tredecim vel ad summum quatuordecim annorum, in sacris literis pro pueritia diligenter versatus, quas fide immotus fortiter contra hostem est ejaculatus. Vivit Dominus, per quem pueri et puellæ imbecillis alioqui naturæ tantum et tam immanem adversarium vincere possunt. Deo sit laus!

Confessio illa veræ religionis, quam 1566 edidistis, loquitur Anglice, et omnium manibus teritur. Adhuc durat apud nos omnium rerum caritas. Revertitur ad vos Rodolphus Gualterus, nostri Gualteri filius, juvenis valde eruditus, ingenio acri, moribus piis. Pater illi est offensus, quod parcius non vixerit. In hoc si peccavit, juvenili ætati est condonandum. Tu illius patrem exora, ut filium non aliter amplectatur reducem, quam optimus ille pater, Luc. 15.

Saluta, quæso, meo nomine omnes meos amicos, tuos filios et filias, præsertim Dorotheam, quam utinam Deus velit nostro Rodolpho in matrimonio adjungere! Certe ego id serio opto. Quod si evenerit tuo nostri Gualteri consensu, ego mirum in modum gaudebo, et vos merito, uti spero, gaudebitis, et Dominus illorum nuptiis benedicet. Vale, mi Bullingere, et me, quod facis, ama. Mea vos omnes. Raptim. Ludhamiæ, penultimo Junii, 1574.

Tuus,

JOHANNES PARKHURSTUS, N.

INSCRIPTIO.

Eximio viro D. Henrico
Bullingero.
Tiguri.

EPISTOLA CXIX.

JOHANNES PARKHURSTUS AD JOSIAM SIMLERUM.

SALVE, mi Simlere. Non est quod tantas mihi agas gratias pro nostro Rodolpho: dignus est in quem multo plura beneficia expendi debeant. Vocatus a patre per literas mihi missas, et tuo consilio persuasus, jam properat domum. Ego constitueram eum diutius in Anglia detinere, et in academia Oxoniensi alere, idque absque patris impensis. Sed cum ita vultis, discedat me non renitente, sed bona cum venia. Ego illi beneficiam vel absenti.

Mirum est quod vacca cervum pepererit: sed minus mirum, quod ita sit factum non procul a monstrosis monachis et sodomiticis bestiis.

Ego nec libellum tuum contra Brentianos, nec bibliothecam abs te auctam, accepi. Fortassis oblivioni dedit Froschoverus. Quicquid sit, ego tibi pro tua benevolentia gratias ago. Optarim ut de uxore Rodolpho prospicias. Si meum consilium aspernari nolueritis, erit illa Dorothea D. Bullingeri filia. Est illa pia, et piis parentibus genita. Ita etiam noster. Quare bene feceritis, si pio conjugio per vos copulentur.

Bene vale, carissime Josia. Nostram Magdalenam, Annam, Nobilitatulam, una cum maritis, meo nomine salvere jubebis. Salutibus etiam adobrues Hallerum, Lavaterum, Wonlichium, Wickium, Julium, Froschoverum, Johannem Henricum Fabricium, Michaelem, si vivit, Mejeros, Cellarios, Thaddeum, Bettam, et omnes alios. Mea vos omnes. Iterum vale. Raptim.

Ludhamiæ, 30 Junii, 1574.

Tuus,

JOHANNES PARKHURSTUS, N.

INSCRIPTIO.
Præclaro viro D. Josiæ Simlero.
Tiguri.

EPISTOLA CXX.

RICARDUS COXUS AD RODOLPHUM GUALTERUM.

LITERÆ tuæ, quas 16 Martii scripsisti, 1574, frater in Christo carissime, accepi sequente mense Junio; quæ quidem me magnopere delectarunt, et quod a viro amicissimo profectæ, et quod commonefecerint omnes veritatis hostes jam passim conspirare et sese expedire ad internecionem omnium, qui Christi religionem profitentur. Equidem expedit piis omnibus hæc scire, ut arment se tempestive tota armatura Dei. Et quanquam adhuc securi esse videamur, videmus tamen periculosa papistarum molimina undique nos cingentia. Imo ex nobis ipsis subinde, quasi e suis cavernis, prodeunt aculeati serpentes, aculeos venenatos exercentes, quos hactenus per Dei gratiam vitavimus. Verum cum animum adverto ad scelera, quæ passim exundant, et ad divini verbi cum neglectum, tum contemptum, horrore concutior, et cogitando pertimesco, quid Deus de nobis statuturus sit. Si unquam, jam locum habet psalmus: *Dixit insipiens in corde suo*, etc. si unquam, jam: *Exsurgat Deus, et dissipentur inimici ejus*, etc.

Justo judicio de nostrorum hominum presbyterio judicas, doctissime Gualtere, tibique astipulantur saniores Anglicæ ecclesiæ ministri; et nullum fere jam tumultuosi homines nobis negotium facessunt, nisi quod instar lamiarum in tenebris nostros ritus rodere pergunt. Severiori castigatione jampridem compescuntur, et doctissima refutatione convincuntur. Cum tot undique sanguinarios adversarios habemus præter Turcas, papistas nimirum, dolendum quidem certe tot dissidia in ecclesiis reformatis existere, ut suo ipsorum gladio sese conficere videantur. His malis tandem medeatur Dominus Jesus Christus, unicus noster Medicus! Non dubito quin ea in te vigeat veritatis vis, ut cum patrocinio eguerit vel apud nos vel apud vos, vel quocunque tandem loco, te Christi athletam præstiteris. Disciplinam morum, de qua mentionem facis in tuis literis, utcunque retinemus: sed si qui nostros magnates cogant ei colla submittere, perinde facient atque si quis barbam leonis raderet.

Ubiquitariorum insaniam jam olim Petrus Martyr, modo vero vester Josias Simlerus, doctissime et fortissime contuderunt. Sed *veniens veniet et non tardabit*, qui præfractos omnes suo malleo contundet et conteret.

Filius tuus, optimæ indolis adolescens, jam discessurus humaniter me salutavit. Precor Deum ut redeat ad te incolumis, et ut longævus pater fruaris pio filio. Vale. Ex insula Eliensi in Anglia, 12 Julii, 1574.

Tui in Christo frater amantissimus,

RICARDUS COXUS.

EPISTOLA CXXI.

RICARDUS COXUS AD HENRICUM BULLINGERUM.

Ex literis, quas superiore vere scriptas mense Junio accepi, meas, quas anno 1573 ad te dederam, tibi non fuisse traditas intellexi. Quæ res tibi suspicandi causam subministrare potuit, me scribere neglexisse. Certe ea negligentia, frater in Christo dilectissime, crimine non vacaret, si passus fuissem eam ingratitudinis notam mihi inuri, ut amicorum literas et pias et doctas et humanissime scriptas negligerem, iisque officiose respondere detrectarem. Scripsi equidem ad te literas (spero non ingratas) anno 1573, quas cum munusculo, licet exiguo, tradendas curavi cuidam Ricardo Hill, ut ejus opera ad vos deferrentur. Quod si factum non est, non cessabo indagare cujus culpa ea res non successit.

Ex literis tuis intelligo, te non adeo defecta senecta laborare, quin munus tibi creditum satis commode possis obire : id quod meo judicio consecutus es partim usu, rerum omnium magistro, partim pio affectu, quo vehementer excitatus nunquam cessasti evangelii et pietatis negotia incessanter propagare; maxime vero, quod Christi Spiritu inflammatus nunquam ejus motibus defuisti. Utcunque est, tibi et ecclesiæ Christi ex animo gratulor, post tot labores ad gloriam Dei exantlatos te ad vegetam senectutem feliciter pervenisse, quæ non cessat pro omnibus ecclesiis curam gerere. Atque hoc quidem constat ex scriptis, quibus doces, mones, consolaris, non solum Tigurinam, sed etiam ecclesiam Christi vere catholicam. Libellus tuus de persecutionibus hisce ultimis temporibus nequam et periculosis apprime utilis est ad confirmandos pios in patientia Christi et religionis sinceritate.

Falleris, si putas me Germanica intelligere : jam quindecim plus minus anni sunt, quod eam linguam vel summis labris degustaverim. Attamen Helveticas tuas conciones curabo Latinas fieri, ut cum majori delectatione et fructu legam. Doleo ecclesias vestras infelicibus controversiis exagitari; ut vere dixerit Christus, *Inimicus homo superseminat zizania*. O tandem reddamur omnes bona terra! Puri nostri fratres partim ferula nostræ Reginæ territi delitescunt, partim docti cujusdam libello doctissimo refutati silent. Interim quid monstri secreto alant, nescitur.

Nobiles quidam nostrates, Romani pontificis alumni, suæ felicitatis pertæsi, aut tam diuturnum evangelii cursum non ferentes, transfugerunt, hi in Galliam, illi in Hispaniam, alii alio, ut aliquid mali moliantur contra pietatis professores. Tantæ molis est ecclesiam Christi contra Satanæ ministros sartam tectam servare. Sed defendit nos hactenus Domini robur et turris ejus fortissima ; et usque ad finem proteget suos Dominus, ringentibus et grassantibus duobus illis antichristis. Interim noctes et dies orandus Dominus, ut exsurgat et dissipentur inimici ejus, etc.

Dominus Jesus senium tuum ecclesiæ faciat esse diuturnum! Ego vero, annum jam agens 75, per Dei gratiam valeo, nisi quod manuum tremor scribendi officium remoratur. Vale, in Christo Jesu frater carissime. Ex Eliensi insula in Anglia, 20 Julii, 1574.

Tui studiosissimus in Christo frater,
RICARDUS,
Eliensis ecclesiæ primus minister.

INSCRIPTIO.
Eximiæ pietatis atque eruditionis viro, D. Henrico Bullingero, ecclesiæ Tigurinæ pastori vigilantissimo, et fratri in Christo dilectissimo.

EPISTOLA CXXII.

LAURENTIUS HUMFREDUS AD RODOLPHUM GUALTERUM.

IMMANUEL! S. in Christo Jesu, observandissime Gualtere. Redit ad te filius tuus, non, ut tu scribis, prodigus, sed et doctrina et moribus ornatior. Quid enim de illo sentiam, imo quid judicet tota academia, locupletissimo universitatis testimonio facile apparebit. Sic apud nos vixit, ut omnes modestiam, candorem, multas et magnas virtutes ejus uno ore prædicent, et te beatum æstiment, cui Dominus talem Gualterum et nominis et pietatis hæredem dederit. Salutabit te suis literis episcopus Norvicensis: de quo homine nihil dicam; nam et tibi satis notus est, et filius tuus testis idoneus esse potest, qui nunquam ipsius erga se munificentiam clausam esse senserit. Quoniam vero ille et causam reditus et alia generis ejusdem per literas exponet, non est necesse ut idem frustra repetam.

Significavit mihi D. Parkhurstus tibi hoc placere, et intellexi ex aliis Tigurinorum literis amicos petere, ut nunc hac ætate et de matrimonio et de ministerio cogitet; et ut ei omnia et auspicatissima et faustissima accidant, iterum atque iterum precor.

Exemplar tuum de Christi præsentia in terris accepi. Quid autem reddam aut reponam, non habeo, nisi forte Juellum meum, imo potius tuum, videre cupias, quem per G. nostrum mitto, et rogo, ut et corrigas et boni consulas levidense munusculum.

Nos hic Dei beneficio et pacem et evangelicam margaritam possidemus; et ut diu fruamur, optamus. Vicinus paries ardet, et valde timemus, ne aliqua illius incendii scintilla nos sit conceptura. Ita securi et soluti sumus, ut quotidie divinæ iræ flammas accendere videamur. Avertat Dominus Jesus omne malum, misericordiæ suæ, non nostrorum meritorum, memor; ecclesiam vestram conservet, patres et fratres nostros D. Bullingerum, Simlerum, Lavaterum et alios, teque cum tua familia! Raptim. Oxoniæ, secunda Augusti, 1574.

Tuus,
LAURENTIUS HUMFREDUS.

INSCRIPTIO.
Reverendo in Christo patri et fratri
D. Rod. Gualtero. Tiguri.

EPISTOLA CXXIII.

EDWINUS SANDUS AD HENRICUM BULLINGERUM.

SALUTEM plurimam in Christo, colendissime vir et venerande pater!

Quod tam diligenter tamque amanter ad me scribere voluisti, quam maximas habeo tibi gratias. Gratius quippe nihil mihi esse potuisset, quam tuam de nostris controversiis intelligere sententiam. Quid autem ipse sentis de toto negotio, plenissime scribis; video et amplector. Ego autem spero, novum hoc ædificium novæ disciplinæ brevi sua mole ruiturum, quando constat multos nostratium jamdudum ejus pertæsos esse, qui prius illud admirabantur; et qui vehementissimi esse videbantur ad stabiliendam hanc novam fabricationem, jam quasi mutata sententia cœperunt mirum in modum frigescere. Dominus det ut, sublatis omnibus dissidiis et contentionibus, idem omnes loquamur et sentiamus secundum Jesum Christum, et ut unanimiter uno ore glorificemus Deum et Patrem Domini nostri Jesu Christi!

De rebus Anglicanis nolo ad te scribere, quia pius et doctus hic adolescens, qui has ad te perfert literas, de omnibus certiorem te reddet. Primum pannum, quem ad te misi, piratæ Flussingenses interceperunt; secundum mittendum curavi, quem audio ad tuas pervenisse manus. Bene vale, vir colendissime, et ut precibus tuis me Deo commendatum habeas, plurimum rogo. Raptim.

Fulhamiæ in Anglia, 9 Augusti, 1574.

Tuus in Christo frater, et tui amantissimus,
EDWINUS SANDUS,
Episcopus London.

INSCRIPTIO.
Viro colendissimo et fratri suo carissimo,
 domino Henrico Bullingero, ecclesiæ
 Tigurinæ pastori vigilantissimo in
 Helvetia.

EPISTOLA CXXIV.

EDWINUS SANDUS AD RODOLPHUM GUALTERUM.

Salve, doctissime vir et carissime frater. Non opus est ut ad te scribam: en! accipe filium tuum. Is erit mihi apud te pro literis, utpote qui quo in statu res nostræ Anglicanæ collocantur, optime tibi narrare possit. Innovatores nostri, qui novam ecclesiæ formam nobis cudere contenderunt, non multum efficiunt; nec tam feliciter progreditur hoc novum ædificium, uti putabant. Sentiunt tandem nobiles, in quem finem hæc insolita tendit fabricatio. Auctor istarum novarum rerum, et post Bezam primus inventor, est adolescens Anglicanus nomine Thomas Cartwrightus, quem aiunt jam hærere Heidelbergæ. Inde jampridem scripsit librum Latine in defensionem novæ istius disciplinæ, quam nobis obtrudere voluit. Non vidi hactenus librum, sed audio impressum et ad nos allatum esse: quamprimum venerit ad manus meas, curabo ut ad te mittatur. De ceteris rebus, quæ hic aguntur, filius tuus te certiorem faciet. Ipse festinat ad iter; ego vero ad publica ecclesiæ negotia, quibus opprimor.

Primus quem ad te misi pannus erat a prædatoribus subreptus. Rursus misi, et mercator dicit mihi te accepisse illum. Bene est, si ita sit. Bene vale, vir colendissime, et perge, ut facis, me amare. Raptim. Fulhamiæ in Anglia, 9 Augusti, 1574.

Tuus in Christo frater et amicus,
EDWINUS SANDUS,
Episcopus London.

INSCRIPTIO.
Doctissimo viro et fratri suo carissimo,
D. Rodolpho Gualtero, in ecclesia Tigurina verbi Dei ministro, in Helvetia.

EPISTOLA CXXV.

RICARDUS COXUS AD HENRICUM BULLINGERUM.

Salve in Christo. Plurimum tibi me debere fateor, frater carissime, quod me literis tuis, licet brevibus, humaniter inviseris. Ægrotare te subinde non est mirum, cum senectus ipsa sit morbi genus. Si a scribendo supersedeas, in his interim acquiescemus, quæ hactenus per Dei gratiam utiliter scripsisti ad ejus gloriam et suæ ecclesiæ ædificationem. Deus autem tibi vires suppeditet ad ea præstanda, quæ animo pio præsumis!

Quod in concordiam apud vos ventum sit, plurimum lætor. Apud nos nostrorum factio utcunque remittitur formidine pœnæ; nam magistratus nostri subolescunt pericula nasci ex futilibus et inutilibus innovationibus. Eademque formidine compescunt papistarum furores. Atque illos in Gallia, qui papæ militant, ultima tentare audimus. Dominus Jesus suis adesse dignetur! Utinam dirumperet cœlos Dominus et descenderet, et ora papistarum, Turcarum, schismaticorumque frœnaret! Sed peccata nostra non sinunt. Faxit Deus ut ad eam unitatem connitamur omnes, ad quam tu ecclesiastas omnes multis solidisque rationibus pulchre adhortaris.

Ut fert occasio, saluto fratres meos tuo nomine. Mitto animi mei testimoniolum tibi et Julio communicandum, meque tuis precibus commendo. Servet te Deus optimus maximus cum sanctissima vestra civitate!

Ex insula Eliensi in Anglia, 25 Januarii, a. 1574, juxta nostram computationem.

Tui studiosissimus et frater
in Christo carissimus,
RICARDUS, Eliensis Episcopus.

INSCRIPTIO.
D. Henrico Bullingero, fratri meo carissimo, et ecclesiæ Tigurinæ pastori fidelissimo.

EPISTOLA CXXVI.

RICARDUS COXUS AD RODOLPHUM GUALTERUM.

Salve in Christo. Septimo Novembris, anno a Christo nato 1574, recepi literas tuas datas 26 Augusti, anno 1574. Ex quibus intelligo æquissimum tuum judicium de hominibus suæ sententiæ et veritati cedere nesciis, nec a concepta opinione discedere volentibus. Queruntur duriter nos illos tractare. Interim acerrimis conviciis publice et clam nos incessunt; concionibus, et scriptis typis excusis, calumniisque nos passim adoriuntur. A nostris modeste satis refutantur. Interim optima nostra Regina, veritatis et pacis amantissima, legibus latis contra illos venit: unde nonnihil terrentur, paulatimque dilabuntur, nisi quod clam contentionis virus subinde evomunt. Nec tamen diffitemur, piis et eruditis tuis scriptis nos nonnihil fuisse adjutos, quanquam nostri adversarii non tanti momenti ea æstimarunt. Spero item venerandi senis, D. Henrici Bullingeri, libellum, quo ministros ecclesiarum ad concordiam invitat atque incitat, plurimum in hoc regno profuturum. Utinam perinde in tota Germania! De persecutionibus in

Saxonia nuper natis vehementer doleo. Est admodum ferox illud Lutheranorum genus. Dominus adesse dignetur causam ipsius sincere agentibus! O hominum inimicum, qui seminato bono semine zizania superseminare non cessat! Interim per Dei gratiam agendum pro virili : cetera Domino Deo nostro permittenda. Hactenus nos Dominus sua gratia conservat in pace. Submurmurant papistæ, et nescio quid monstri alunt; sed Deus ipse malos male perdat, teque ecclesiæ suæ diutissime servet incolumem, et me in tuis precibus Deo commenda. Ex insula Eliensi in Anglia.

Tuus in Christo frater carissimus,
RICARDUS COXUS,
Eliensis Episcopus.

INSCRIPTIO.
D. Rodolpho Gualtero, amico meo carissimo, et veritatis propugnatori fortissimo.

EPISTOLA CXXVII.

RICARDUS COXUS AD RODOLPHUM GUALTERUM.

LITERAS tuas, doctissime Gualtere et frater in Domino carissime, 8 Martii a. 1575 datas, quæ mihi eodem anno mense Maio tradebantur, non sine magna voluptate perlegi. Sunt enim gratitudinis officiis plenæ, majoraque de me prædicant quam ego vero agnoscere possum. Non sine admiratione de divina providentia cogitare possumus, quæ nunc afflictionis igne suos probat, nunc vero respirandi spatium concedit, paceque gratissima frui sinit. Etsi peccata plagas gravissimas mereantur, confidimus tamen Dominum nostrum Jesum Christum habere suam pusillam gregem, cujus pietate et precibus flecti sistique solet justissima Dei vindicta. Sed misserrima est hypocritarum conditio, quos Dominus justissimo suo judicio propter exundantia scelera tradere solet in manus diripientium, quales sunt hodie Turca, papa, et schismaticorum furibunda turba. Atque hæc quidem turba apud nos plausibili sua doctrina magnates in rete suum facile alliciunt, dum magno spiritus boatu subvertunt credula pectora miserorum, eorum maxime, quæ possessionibus ecclesiarum cathedralium, collegiorum et episcoporum inhiant, uti lupi corvique famelici. Ita Satan omnes machinas movet ad evangelium obruendum. Vehementer doleo, Saxonem illum ita incensum esse contra pios. Nec minus ingemisco ex tristi illo nuntio, quo ad nos defertur ecclesiæ solidissimam columnam, D. Henricum Bullingerum, morbo laborare gravissimo. Misereatur ecclesiæ suæ benignus Dominus, et suum Henricum pristinæ valetudini restituat! Sin divinæ clementiæ visum fuerit illum in cœlesti suo tabernaculo collocare, orandus est Pater Domini nostri Jesu Christi, ut illius alterius Eliæ Spiritum infundat in multos Elizæos, qui jam singulari Dei gratia adhuc restent in Tigurina civitate sanctissima.

Ablati sunt a nobis nuper, sed meliorem cum Christo conditionem sortiti, Parkhurstus Norwicensis episcopus, et Mattheus Parkerus, Cantuariensis archiepiscopus, Angliæ nostræ primas, vir *teres atque rotundus*, et sinceræ religionis assertor vehemens. Rogandus est Dominus, ut operarios non minus idoneos mittere dignetur in messem suam, quæ multa est. Dominus Jesus te ecclesiæ suæ diutissime servet incolumem!

Ex insula Eliensi in Anglia, ultimo Julii, 1575.

Tuus in Christo frater carissimus,

RICARDUS, Eliensis Episcopus.

EPISTOLA CXXVIII.

RICARDUS COXUS AD RODOLPHUM GUALTERUM.

Posteriores literas tuas idibus Februarii recepi, doctissime Rodolphe. Verum priores illæ multo magis me affecerunt, cum dolore vehementi, tum gaudio non mediocri. Dolor erat vehemens ex morte Henrici Bullingeri, quem per literas, per erudita scripta et pia, multos annos jam noveram, et quasi familiariter pernoveram, etsi a facie mihi hactenus fuerit ignotus. Tali tantoque viro summoque amico orbari, quis non anxius redderetur? Ne dicam, quod tota Christi ecclesia ingenti mœrore concussa est, cum stella adeo lucida in terra diutius lucere prohibita est. Johannes inauspicatas stellas de cœlo cecidisse scribit: at nostram stellam in cœlum ascendisse et cœlo fixam esse, et ut in terra lucebat, ita magis jam in cœlo clarescere, persuasum habemus. Qualis autem fuerit in terra, pia fama non tacet, pia vita loquitur, doctissima scripta abunde testantur: qualis vero jam sit in cœlo, Deus novit, angeli gaudent, et animæ piorum exultant. Atque hoc talem virum desiderantium non leve est lenimen. Adde et aliud, unde merito lætitiam accipimus, quod ecclesia illa Tigurina, illi valedicente Bullingero, non sit destituta pastore: nam qui nunquam deserit gregem suum, clementissimus Dominus, te in locum Bullingeri substituit, non minori zelo in pascendo grege, nec minori fortitudine ad propulsandos gregis hostes. Benedictus es tu, qui spontanea voluntate hoc onus in te suscipis, ut Dei gloriæ inservias, et ipsius religionem fideliter procures.

Quod autem ad ecclesiarum turbas et hæreses attinet, scimus oportere hæreses esse, ut probentur electi, et per multas tribulationes regnum Dei acquirendum esse, et in patientia nostra possidendæ sint animæ nostræ. Dolendum id quidem certe, quod Saxo adeo hostiliter sæviat. Det Deus aliquando piam reconciliationem! Nullam videmus spem pacis in Gallia: tyrannide ibi aguntur omnia: Rex cum fratre et matre decreverunt, omnes evangelicos aut in exilium mittere, aut ad internecionem adigere. In Belgico quid agatur, nondum satis constat, nisi quod nostra Regina lites componere satagat. Nostri autem singularitatis homines formidine pœnæ quiescunt, nisi quod clam nescio quid monstri alant. Et qui curas et res hujus mundi sectantur, negotium nobis facessunt, ut quæ nostra sunt, nescio quibus artibus et dolis, nobis auferre, et nos ad mendicitatem pertrahere nitantur, ut ad conditionem primitivæ ecclesiæ et apostolorum paupertatem nos revocent. Misereatur Deus afflictæ ecclesiæ suæ, et a mundi malignitate tueatur, et vobis omnibus, qui Christum Jesum profitemini, benedicat!

Misi ad te exiguam animi mei significationem, cujus partem velim te Julio Terentiano impertire.

Tuus in Christo Jesu frater,
RICARDUS COX, Eliensis.

INSCRIPTIO.
Eruditione et pietate ornatissimo
D. Rodolpho Gualtero, ecclesiæ
Tigurinæ ministro fidelissimo.

EPISTOLA CXXIX.

ROBERTUS HORNUS AD RODOLPHUM GUALTERUM.

GRATIA et pax in Christo! Etsi sermo multus fereque quotidianus, Gualtere in Christo carissime, quem habeo cum Barloö meo de fratribus Tigurinis, multum me oblectat, carusque valde mihi est; isto tamen colloquio, quantumvis jucundo, animus contentus non est, neque tranquillus esse vult, nisi cum Gualtero meo, quem intime amo, et per illum cum ceteris ministris Tigurinis plurimum mihi dilectis, per literas saltem colloquar. Literæ autem eo erunt breviores, quod materia scribendi mihi uberior in præsentia non suppetat.

Nova apud nos prope nulla sunt, quæ scribam. Eodem in statu, (sit laus Deo!) belle satis persistunt omnia. Contentiosi autem illi, aut si mavis ambitiosi, imo plane malitiosi, qui apud nos importunis suis discordiarum inurgiis liberum evangelii cursum remorabantur, plebemque ineptiis suis dementatam per varias nuper opinionum vanitates, aut potius errorum insanias, in nescio quas puritates distrahebant, obticescunt, delitescunt, vilescunt. Quantum tamen istis tu, Gualtere, ceterique istic fratres nostri, qui cum illis non senserint, debeant, ex libri illius, quem de ecclesiæ Anglicæ a vera disciplina aberratione inscripserunt, pagina 46, si evolveris, facile recognosces.

Cetera quidem apud nos, ut primum, constituta permanent, præcipue vero et pax et pietas. Floret evangelium, cursumque habet liberrimum. Ecclesia alioqui satis sana est, nisi quod cum antiquo illo morbo conflictetur, quo semper hactenus etiam ab incunabulis laboravit: a papismo enim ante supremum Medici illius magni Jesu Christi adventum penitus non convalescet. Respublica tranquilla est. Regina vivit, valetque: valeat autem in multos annos, Deum opt. max. precor, vivatque in æternum! Maximus omnium statuum conventus, quem nos vocamus parliamentum, ineunte vere agebat Londini: Regina vero vestro Helvetiorum more mutationes non admittet, quæ in eam tamen curam incumbit tota, ut plenis velis, cum apud suos tum apud exteros, evangelii veritas provehatur[1]. Ut a parvula papismum semper est abominata, ita etiam Lutheranismum, qui multum interturbat Christianismum, nunquam est admissura.

Scotia illius auspiciis in pura evangelii confessione constans permanet. Rex optimis pietatis veræ præceptis imbuitur. Regis mater salva, ut prius, apud nos custodia detinetur. Quo in loco sint res Gallicæ, scitis: Belgicis felicem exitum optamus: de utrisque multum dubitamus. Pilkingtonus noster, nuper episcopus Dunelmiæ vigilantissimus, diem obiit supremum, et paulo ante dimidium mei alterum, uxor mea.

A me dicas, quæso, salutem multam fratribus meis Tigurinis omnibus mihi in Christo dilectissimis, ac nominatim D. Simlero, Lavatero, Hallero, Rod. Gualtero juniori, et Henrico Bullingero jam seniori. Dominus Jesus Christus vos omnes ad ecclesiæ suæ instaurationem quam diutissime conservet incolumes! Valete. Ex ædibus meis Walthamiæ, 10 Augusti, 1576.

Tui omniumque Tigurinorum amantissimus,

ROBERTUS WINTON.

INSCRIPTIO.
Carissimo in Christo fratri D.
Rodolpho Gualtero seniori,
Tigurinæ ecclesiæ pastori dignissimo.

[1 MS. *provehat.*]

EPISTOLA CXXX.

ROBERTUS HORNUS AD [QUOSDAM FRATRES.]

GRATIA et pax in Christo! Doleo profecto, fratres in Christo carissimi, tam inanem cuiquam inesse vecordiam, ut cum sancta pace gaudere possit, male tamen, licet ex multorum incommodis, suam sibi, ut vult videri, comparare tranquillitatem: quando revera, dum cæcam, temerariam, impiam cupiditatem satagit explere suam, non aliis adeo incommodat, atque se ipsum in summum præcipitem dat discrimen. Verum Satanæ τὰ νοήματα haud ignoramus: quam prompta sit scelerata illius voluntas ad ecclesiæ tranquillitatem interturbandam; quam sit nefandum ejus consilium ad horrenda facinora aptum; quam paratos suos habeat satellites, qui astute et accurate illius imperium exequantur, non opus est ut disseram. Quis enim ignorat, qui vel a limine salutare Christi evangelium salutaverit? Certe, certo scio, vos, fratres, non dico vestro malo, sed summo vestro et totius ecclesiæ incommodo, edoctos didicisse, quot et quantos excitaverit hactenus, et quotidie excitat, Satan Davos, qui omnia interturbent, et maxime ecclesiæ pacem labefactent. Immanis illa bestia, quanta potest ferocitate, invadit ovile Christi: gregem Dominicum dissipare, imo dilaniare, infestissimus lupus cogitat: violenta frendentis leonis vi raptatur misella ovicula. Quid facias? Obfirmata fide bestiæ est resistendum, assiduis precibus implorando defensionem a summo Pastore, Jesu Christo: patefactis et detectis lupi machinationibus, abigendus est baculo pastorum et latratu canum: stolidum pecus ex unguibus, antequam leonis dentibus dilanietur, eripiendum est, et, si fieri potest, ad caulas reducendum. Atqui hic (quantum ex vestris literis intelligo) nihil reliquistis intentatum: omnem curam et diligentiam ad haud bonum illum Bonamy conservandum adhibuistis: quod est fidissimorum officium pastorum, istius insolentiam, superbiam, contumaciam quibuscunque licebat rationibus emollire, supprimere, retundere, strenuam navastis operam; et cum quod velitis efficere non possitis, me adjutorem dari postulatis. Ne dubitetis, fratres, quin plures habituri sitis adjutores; et me ipsum, quantum possum, ad hanc rem adjutorem fore profiteor paratissimum. Spero me eam rationem initurum, qua sentiet falsus ille frater (si tamen frater sit dicendus) quid sit summum animarum Pastorem Christum Jesum provocare, ecclesiam Dei contemnere, et sacrosanctam disciplinam ludificare, imo proculcare.

Consilii autem mei rationem exposui communi utriusque nostrum amico et fratri in Christo, mihi summopere dilecto, D. Leighton, insulæ præfecto. Quod reliquum est, fratres, rogo vos συναγωνίσασθαί μοι vestris pro me apud Deum precationibus. Ego vero, nisi mei ipsius oblitus, vestri immemor haud sum futurus. Salutate, quæso, ex me συνεργούς omnes et totam ecclesiam. Valete. Ex meis ædibus, Waltamiæ, 16 Januarii, 1576.

Vester in Christo frater

carissimus et symmysta,

ROBERTUS HORNUS, Winton.

EPISTOLA CXXXI.

LAURENTIUS HUMFREDUS AD RODOLPHUM GUALTERUM.

Immanuel! Agnosco in literis tuis, doctissime Gualtere, expressa signa solitæ tuæ humanitatis et prudentiæ. Nam quod me jamdiu plane mutum et pene ingratum salutare volueris, id ego summæ humanitatis, singulari cum humilitate conjunctæ, argumentum esse interpretor. Quanquam vero rarius scripsi, tamen nec ingratitudini nec oblivioni tribuas velim; utpote qui vestra beneficia in me et Anglos sæpe et largiter collata animo subinde repeto, et quamdiu vixero, Deo dante, sempiterna memoria recolam. Nunc vero provocatus quamcunque occasionem et opportunitatem arripiam; nec unquam committam, ut sine literulis meis vacuus ad vos nuncius abeat. Malim nempe omnino rudis et αὐτοσχέδιος videri, quam dissolutus et immemor.

Quod autem de tuorum Helvetiorum, Ulmii et comitis, profectu tam sis sollicitus, prudenter facis; præstat nempe prudenter timere, quam nimis sperare: tamen id vero affirmare possum, utrumque hic apud nos et graviter studere et honeste se gerere, quod ipsos revera et tibi et senatui comprobaturos non diffido. Itaque, quia exitum hoc vobis declaraturum confido, non potui non optimæ spei juvenes vobis commendare. Scripsi ad D. Episcopum Wintoniensem, qui aliquid jam contulit, et deinceps quoque se rationem ipsorum habiturum pollicetur. Quod de morte P. M. et aliorum patrum, et tui filii, olim mei alumni, scribis, est sane luctuosum et acerbum, privatim nostra causa, qui illos merito coluimus et amavimus, publice ecclesiæ nomine, quam quotidie ubicunque locorum tot præclara sua lumina amittere dolendum et funestum est. Tu vero, gravissime pater, instar multorum es; ideoque eruditis et piis lucubrationibus porro perge christianam rempublicam juvare, ut istæ tuæ seniles meditationes, quasi cygneæ cantationes, iterum atque iterum nos delectent. Quanta sit hæc virorum optimorum jactura, suo malo jamdiu sensit nostra Anglia, nec unquam, credo, oblivisci potest: certe non sine dolore recordari debet recentia tot martyrum busta, tot optimorum, Juelli, Parkhursti, Pilkingtoni, aliorumque funera Sed hæc sunt ultimæ periodi seculorum, et novissima et nequissima temporum prognostica, in quæ hæc nostra (proh dolor!) incidit. Satan quasi leo rugit, mundus insanit, antichristus extrema quæque tentat, ut oviculas Christi lupina rapacitate devoret: mare piratis refertum est, terra Flandrica madet sanguine Christianorum, in Gallia dicitur Guisianus nova laniena in protestantes sævire. Anglia tuta adhuc est Dei gratia; sed hominum malitia secura esse quî potest? Parietis nempe proximi ad nos perveniat incendium valde pertimescendum, Tridentinis patribus suum illud sanguinarium decretum urgentibus, et nostris sceleribus quotidianis id merentibus.

Nova in Flandria hæc nunc circumferuntur, Cassimirum hærere in Geldria et Daventriam obsidere, statuere brevi cum ordinibus copias conjungere; Austriacum se fossis et vallis ac mœnibus intra civitates munire; 1º die Augusti suos velites contra Anglos, Gallos, Scotos emisisse; utrinque acriter ab hora octava ad quintam vespertinam dimicatum; ex nostris ducentos quinquaginta, ex hostibus octingentos, desideratos fuisse; nostros ἀριστεῖον tulisse; D. Norrhesium, Anglum, quatuor equos subter se cæsos amisisse, et tum evasisse, non sine laude sua et strage Hispanorum, quos fugarunt aut prostrarunt. Quis sit hujus belli futurus eventus, novit omnipotens Dominus; cui ego ecclesiam universam, et vestram ac nostram particularem, et tua studia, omnesque patres et fratres, nominatim D. Lavaterum, et Ulmium et Christ. Froschoverum, ac totum Tigurum, Anglorum quondam hospitium, iterum atque iterum commendo. Vale, clarissime vir. D. Colus valet: nunc rusticatur. Oxoniæ, Augusti 11, (1578).

Tui observantiss.
LAURENTIUS HUMFREDUS.

INSCRIPTIO.
Clarissimo viro D. Rodolpho Gualtero, ecclesiæ Tigurinæ pastori digniss. domino suo plurimum observando.

Tiguri.

EPISTOLA CXXXII.

LAURENTIUS HUMFREDUS AD RODOLPHUM GUALTERUM.

S. IN Christo Jesu. De rebus privatis et statu Rodolphi Ulmii et Johannis Huldrichi ut aliquid hoc tempore scribam, movit me partim observantia interna ac in eos animi propensio et benevolentia, partim ipsorum etiam meritum et necessitas. Equidem ingenue fateor, non esse illis hic prospectum, quomodo tu optas et ego cupio, quod ipsi academici, qui aliis deberent suppeditare, ipsi egeant et ex aliorum liberalitate pendeant. Scripsi ad D. episcopum Wintoniensem, qui aliquid Rodolpho dedit, et ad D. comitem Bedfordium, qui mearum et tuarum imprimis literarum eam, quam decuit et oportuit, rationem habuit. Rediit nempe ex Devonia, ubi nunc degit D. comes, ad nos, non quidem onustus pecuniis, sed aliquantum onustus et donatus stipendio. Ego utrumque collocavi in aula Lateportensi, ut vocamus, non procul a collegio Christi, ubi D. Johannis pater optime et amicissime exceptus fuerat Regis Edouardi tempore. Si quid potero nummorum concedere, libenter impertiam. Sed quia friget caritas in hac mundi senecta, et Galli multi subinde ad nos convolant cum familiis, et nostri homines putant Helvetios spectandi causa peregrinari voluntarie, non autem religionis ergo exulare necessario, idcirco hactenus pejus et malignius illis contributum est. Itaque te rogo, ut patrocinio tuo illos adjuves, et diligenter causam ipsorum agas, quo salarium promissum primo quoque tempore perferendum curetur. Boni sane et studiosi mihi videntur; et licet adhuc nostris ignoti sint propter Rodolphi cum D. comite morantis absentiam, tamen ubi innotuerint, magis ac magis se insinuabunt, et hominum studia ac voluntates conciliabunt.

Nos ut quimus, [ut] aiunt. Domi pacata omnia: non aperto Marte, sed cuniculis, papa nos oppugnat, bullis, libellis famosis, clandestinis machinationibus. Gallus quiescit, nec ulla belli scintilla erumpit: quin et in Flandria flammæ illæ omnes restinctæ sunt, consopito Johanne Austriaco, vel potius peste sublato. Periculum vero est, ne ipsi inter se commissi, et bello sive dissidio intestino distracti, in sua viscera irruant. Quid enim non efficiet factionum fæcula? D. Jesus malignitatem istorum temporum novissimorum bonitate sua temperet!

Salutat te et D. Christoph. Froschoverum Garbrandus Hollandus, bibliopola Oxoniensis. D. Colus hodie abest. D. Westphalingus jussit me D. Julio dicere salutem, quod et ego quoque meo nomine facio, vobis omnibus omnia faustissima comprecans. Spero D. Lavaterum optime valere. Pergite vestris conatibus piis rem literariam et negotium religionis promovere, ut hoc cœco seculo per vos homines magis ac magis illustrati, divinæ veritatis lucem aspiciant Dei beneficio ac multi,[1] quem iterum atque iterum oro tuam pietatem una cum tuis omnibus et ecclesia Tigurina, Anglorum quondam hospitio, diu tibi ac nobis florentem conservare. Raptim. Oxoniæ, Decembr. 17, 1578. Vale, vir doctissime.

Tui observantissimus,

LAUR. HUMFREDUS.

[1 Sic MS.]

EPISTOLA CXXXIII.

RICARDUS COXUS AD RODOLPHUM GUALTERUM.

Ut exhilaratus eram tuis literis et libro ad me misso post superiores nundinas Francfordianas, ita vehementer doleo, mi Gualtere, turbatam esse aliquam Germaniæ partem nonnullorum importunis dissensionibus, quarum auctor Deus non est, sed malignus ille, qui ministris suis periculose abutitur ad viros principes erroribus involvendum, et ad ecclesiam perturbandam, atque pietatis hostes ad iniquitatem animandum.

De Cantuariensi bene speramus. Nonnihil offensa fuit in Cantuariensi Regina nostra alioqui clementissima. Serio animadvertit ipsa in papistas et contentiosos. Vult omnia secundum ordinem et decorum fieri. Consilarios habet doctos et prudentes et pietatis studiosos. Non tamen admittuntur hactenus in sacrum illum coetum verbi ministri.

De Hibernia quod scribis, (qua quidem abuti solet antichristus Romanus, sed frustra,) si quid tumultus exoritur, aut per milites nostros, ibi perpetuo manentes, aut (si quando res ita postulat) per justum exercitum facile reprimitur. Nuper vero vir et nobilissimus et sanctæ religionis studio deditus, et Hibernorum malleus gravissimus, non sine multorum dolore, comes scilicet Essexiensis, morbo extinctus est.

Ingenti perfundor gaudio, quod Deus incredibili sua providentia Genevenses ab hostibus Satanæ liberavit. Hoc est Domino turri fortissimæ confidere; hoc est Dei gloriæ sollicite adhærere, atque pro ea animam ponere. Hæc fides et pia unanimitas hostes licet acerrimos superat et profligat. Ecce quam bonum et quam jucundum habitare fratres in unum! Adest apud nos jam nunc dux Cassimerus, magnæ fortitudinis et fidei vir: adest, inquam, non sine magni exspectatione boni. Dominus Jesus te cum sanctissimo tuo grege protegat et a papisticis hostibus, et ab his qui exierunt a nobis, cum tamen non essent ex nobis!

Sed Julii nostri non omnino ero immemor. Mitto ad te quinque nostratis nummi libras. Tres partes tibi sume, duas vero a te recipiat Julius. (28 Febr. 1579.)

Tuæ pietatis et tuæ sanctæ functionis studiosissimus,

RICARDUS COXUS,

Eliensis episcopus.

INSCRIPTIO.

Eximio ecclesiæ Tigurinæ pastori,
Rodolpho Gualtero, amico meo
spectatissimo.

EPISTOLA CXXXIV.

EDWINUS SANDUS AD RODOLPHUM GUALTERUM.

Uno ac eodem fere temporis articulo duas a te, doctissime vir multisque nominibus honorande, literas accepi, easque biennio pene postquam mitterentur, inscriptionis credo errore. Nam cum Londinensem episcopum illa peteret, tres jam anni sunt elapsi a mea in archiepiscopatum Eboracensem commigratione: quærentes ergo me Londini, serius ad regni boreales plagas literæ tuæ pervenerunt. Nunc autem scriptis cum cupiam respondere tuis, hæc sunt potissimum, quorum te velim certiorem fieri, me et memorem esse tui in me amoris, et amicum tibi fratremque fidelem constanter permanere.

Non me fugit devenisse nos in eam temporum conditionem, quæ res novas in dies parturiat; quarum aliquas tua cognitione dignas mandarem literis, nisi hujus ætatis infortunio multa viderem scripta sobrie, cogitata pie, partim amissa, partim intercepta, grande periculum suis auctoribus creare: ne autem nihil referam, hæc habeas. Nuptiarum fœdus, quo majestas regia cum fratre Galli copuletur, agitatur. Quid tandem aliquando fiet, quemque res nostræ finem sortientur, vix est qui intelligat. Deum optimum maximum precamur, nobis ut perstare dignetur propitius. Religionis christianæ floret ac viget apud nos puritas, nec ullis Satanæ machinis vel everti vel contaminari potest. Licet enim novos, quos appellamus, puritanos auctoritatem omnem conculcantes, veteranos pontificios clanculum in angulis suis mysteria celebrantes, profanos diagonistas cultum verum divinum irridentes, penitus ab ecclesia non valemus depellere, quominus et mentium et nominum insignis appareat varietas; is tamen est vere fidelium et numerus et dignitas, quæ et multitudine et splendore longe multumque reliquos omnes antecellat; spesque nos alit optima, eum qui cœpit in nobis bonum opus, illud ipsum perfecturum in diem Domini Jesu. Archiepiscopus Cantuariensis, Edmundus Grindallus, qui et Londinensem et Eboracensem ante me regebat ecclesias, regiæ voluntati non ab omni parte respondens, ædium tantum suarum, e quibus egredi non debet, fruitur libertate; eam autem brevi plene restitutum iri et speramus et credimus. D. Horn, episcopus Wintoniensis, vitam cum morte commutavit, necdum est ullus sedis illius antistes renunciatus.

Hibernia seditiosis rebellium vexatur tumultibus. Duces autem ad eos compescendos et designati sunt, et conscripti milites. Res bene se habent protestantium Flandrorum; nuperrime enim damnum maximum passi sunt male contenti papistæ, qui illorum et vitis et fortunis insidiantur, nec procul ab extrema rerum suarum in illis regionibus omnium abesse putantur amissione.

In testimonium et signum mentis meæ tibi, carissime, nonnihil vehementer cupivi mercium nostrarum mittere, eas modo vellet mercator exportare quispiam. Cum vero neminem repererim, qui illo sit ausus fungi munere (sic undique hæc tempora cincta sunt periculis), has meas nudas literas æqui bonique te consulturum spero. Atque ita non minorem tibi, quam mihi ipsi, precatus felicitatem, jam agens Londini, et parliamentum Januarii 20 incipiendum exspectans, te tuosque omnes in Christo valere jubeo.

Londini in Anglia, 9 die mensis Decembr. 1579.

Tuus in Christo frater et tui amantissimus,

EDWINUS SANDUS,

Eboracensis.

INSCRIPTIO.
Doctissimo viro, et fratri in Christo carissimo, Rodolpho Gualtero, ecclesiæ Tigurinæ pastori vigilantissimo. Tiguri.

EPISTOLA CXXXV.

ELIZABETHA REGINA AD TRESDECIM CANTONES HELVETIÆ.

ELIZABETHA Dei gratia Angliæ, Franciæ et Hiberniæ Regina, fidei defensor, etc. Magnificis viris et spectabilibus dominis, consulibus ac proconsulibus, dynastis, syndicis, regulis ac gubernationibus tresdecim cantonum præclaræ gentis Helveticæ, amicis nostris carissimis, salutem.

Magnifici domini et spectabiles viri, sociæ vestræ urbis Genevæ afflictæ res, permultos jam annos diuturna prope obsidione pressæ a potentissimis duobus hostibus, Hispaniarum rege et ejus genero, duce Sabaudiæ, quam opem quodque auxilium desiderant, vos, quia socii et vicini estis, non potestis ignorare: extraque dubium sumus, V. P. pro fide fœderum inter vos junctorum, proque dignitate gentis, eam rationem habituras esse communis vestræ in hac causa defensionis, ut deseri eam exponique novorum hominum libidini, quantum in vobis erit, non sitis passuri: ad quam certe rem, si necesse esset, vos hortaremur; intenti autem qui sua sponte satis sunt in salutem publicam, quoniam monitore non habent opus, ab hoc genere orationis libenter abstinemus: unum hoc V. P. rogantes, pro antiqua benevolentia et amicitia, quæ regibus

Angliæ, majoribus nostris, cum spectabili gente vestra intercessit, ne salutis privatæ vestræ negligentes sitis.

Sic enim P. V. existimare convenit, in obsidione Genevensium peti obsidionem vestrarum cujusque civitatum; in excidio illius urbis verti internecionem omnium vestrum. Periculum faciatis licet ex iis, quæ in nosmet regnaque nostra, quæque jam nunc in florentissimum Galliæ regnum idem rex molitur, præter impotentem dominandi libidinem; cum nihil subsit aut subesse queat, quod ab armis movendis et consociandis, per omnes fere orbis nostri occidentalis partes, nullam ipsi requiem neque diurnam neque nocturnam impartiat. Quæ tamen arma frustra inter nos consociabit, atque in nos frustra movebit, si junctis animis, pro fide inter vos data acceptaque, non dissui vestras amicitias et conjunctiones patiamini. In hoc enim uno posita sunt tum quorumcunque hostium maxima præsidia armorumque momenta, tum justarum quarumcunque defensionum fortissima propugnacula munimentaque. Ac in utramque partem tantarum virium cum sit hoc unum caput, omnesque ingenii sui nervos huc intendant, qui vinci se cupidine regnandi patiuntur; cautis vos animis esse oportet, qui istius beneficio multos jam annos in libertate vivitis, in quam majores vestri sua virtute vindicarunt vos, quam vobis supra modum invident superbi dominatores. Ea si in perpetuum frui, posterisque vestris tanquam hæreditariam transmittere mavultis, quam servorum more in illiberali servitute vivere, cavendus est vobis hic primus impetus, nec aures accommodandæ captiosis illecebris, memores, multo plures vulpeculæ fraude deceptos quam armis devinctos concidisse. Certumque habetote, ut antiquorum fœderum fucus, diuturnæ amicitiæ simulacrum, officiorum in speciem oblatus usus obtendi queat; nullas tamen esse pejores et magis capitales inimicitias, quam quæ latent in simulatione officii.

Ac si licet in opinione hominum modica res et minoris momenti civitas Genevensium, uti Corinthus quondam apud Achæos, et Chalcis apud Eubœos, et Demetrias apud Thessalos; tamen, ut illæ totius Græciæ, sic Genevenses ab Hispano Sabaudo subacti, verendum est, ne universæ fœderatæ gentis vestræ compedes futuri sint. Naturam loci, spiritus et animos hostis, ipsius potentiam magnitudine sua laborantem, cum angustis vestris rebus comparate. Qui S. R. F. majestati invidet, qui contra Belgarum supra viginti jam annos dimicat libertates, qui Galliæ regno insidiatur, qui diadematis nostri siti conficitur, eum credibile est non eversis antiquis juribus vestris, legibus, libertate quieturum? Quod quo vobis funestius et nobis tristius spectaculum foret, eo vos etiam atque etiam monemus rogamusque, sitis in eam rem ne eveniat providi intentique, ut de dignitate vestra pristina libertateque conservata vobis invicem gratulantes, amicis vestris solatio, vicinis præsidio, posteris æterno emolumento esse queatis. In hanc arenam ipsæ, fæmina licet sumus, priores descendimus, otium, dignitatem, regias opes, quicquid denique carum vel habemus vel habere possumus, libertati vicinarum gentium sartis tectisque conservandis, aliorum justis imperiis postponentes, ad hoc positæ et institutæ a Deo, ut quantum in nobis est, nullis inferamus, ab omnibus propulsemus, injurias; non ignaræ, qui alterum non juvat, cum potest, tam esse in vitio, ac si ipse occidisset.

Sed vos ista pro vestra prudentia satis edocti estis, et pro optima vestra in vos invicem voluntate, studio, pietateque prompti satis ad afflictis succurrendum vestræque saluti providendum: proptereaque desinimus, recrementum obsidione pressorum vobis vestræque fidei, pro ea quam geritis erga Deum hominesque pietate, commendantes: et vos in æternum Deus ille salutis fortunet beetque!

Datæ e regia nostra Grenvici, 18 die mensis Julii, anno Domini post millesimum quingentesimum nonagesimo, regni vero nostri tricesimo secundo.

ELIZABETHA, R.

www.ingramcontent.com/pod-product-compliance
Lightning Source LLC
Chambersburg PA
CBHW071216290426
44108CB00013B/1194